MEDIEVAL LANDSCAPES OF SOUTHERN ETRURIA

MediTo | ARCHAEOLOGICAL AND HISTORICAL LANDSCAPES
OF MEDITERRANEAN CENTRAL ITALY

VOLUME 2

GENERAL EDITORS
Alessandro Sebastiani – *University at Buffalo – SUNY*
Carolina Megale – *Università degli Studi di Firenze*
Riccardo Rao – *Università degli Studi di Bergamo*

EDITORIAL BOARD
Giorgio Baratti – *Università Cattolica del Sacro Cuore, Milan*
Emeri Farinetti – *Università Roma Tre*
Todd Fenton – *Michigan State University*
Michelle Hobart – *The Cooper Union University, New York*
Richard Hodges – *American University of Rome*
Daniele Manacorda – *Università Roma Tre*
Marco Paperini – *Centro Studi Città e Territorio, Follonica*
Anna Maria Stagno – *Università di Genova*
Emanuele Vaccaro – *Università di Trento*

Submissions should be sent to:
Alessandro Sebastiani – as424@buffalo.edu
Carolina Megale – carolina@archeodig.net
Riccardo Rao – riccardo.rao@unibg.it

Medieval Landscapes of Southern Etruria

The Excavations at Capalbiaccio Tricosto (1976–2010)

Edited by

MICHELLE HOBART

BREPOLS

British Library Cataloguing in Publication Data
A catalogue record for this book is available from the British Library.

© 2023, Brepols Publishers n.v., Turnhout, Belgium.

All rights reserved. No part of this publication may be reproduced, stored in a retrieval system, or transmitted, in any form or by any means, electronic, mechanical, photocopying, recording, or otherwise without the prior permission of the publisher.

D/2023/0095/21
ISBN: 978-2-503-59775-1
e-ISBN: 978-2-503-59776-8

DOI: 10.1484/M.MEDITO-EB.5.126588

Printed in the EU on acid-free paper.

Table of Contents

List of Illustrations — 7
Acknowledgements — 17

Part I
Genesis of the Project

Michelle Hobart
1. The Archaeology of Coastal Southern Tuscany — 23

Stephen L. Dyson
2. Capalbiaccio: The Initial Archaeological Campaigns (1976–1980) — 33

Part II
Recent Research and Non-Invasive Archaeology

Nicoletta Barocca
3. Geo-Archaeology of Coastal Southern Tuscany — 43

Laura Cerri and Emanuele Mariotti
4. Geophysical Prospecting, Topography, Thermal Camera and DEM — 57

Irene Corti
5. Medieval Wall Reading: The Archaeology of Architecture — 69

Part III
Material Culture and Survey of Post Medieval Southern Tuscany

Michelle Hobart
6. Analysis of the Material Culture — 87

Valeria Acconcia
7. Pre-Etruscan, Etruscan, and Roman Pottery — 93

Emanuele Vaccaro
8. Capalbiaccio and Medieval Pottery in Southern Tuscany (900–1000) — 119

Chiara Valdambrini
9. A Comparative Study of Pottery from Southern Tuscany
and Latium (1000–1200)　　　　　　　　　　　　　　　　　　163

Michelle Hobart
10. Medieval Pottery (1200–1400)　　　　　　　　　　　　　171

Elisa Rubegni
11. Small Finds　　　　　　　　　　　　　　　　　　　　　203

Alessia Rovelli
12. Coins　　　　　　　　　　　　　　　　　　　　　　　223

Diana C. Crader
13. Archaeozoological Remains　　　　　　　　　　　　　231

Hermann Salvadori
14. Field Survey of the Post-Medieval Settlement Patterns in Southern Tuscany　　247

Part IV

Historical Reconstructions and Conclusions

Michelle Hobart
15. Reassessing the Etruscan Valle d'Oro　　　　　　　　　273

Michelle Hobart
16. Builders of Landscapes: The Aldobrandeschi and the Castle of Tricosto　　289

Michelle Hobart
17. Concluding Remarks and Open Questions　　　　　　309

Appendix — Stephen L. Dyson
Castle and Countryside: Capalbiaccio and the
Changing Settlement History of the Ager Cosanus　　　313

Works Cited　　　　　　　　　　　　　　　　　　　　　321

Author Biographies　　　　　　　　　　　　　　　　　　358

Index　　　　　　　　　　　　　　　　　　　　　　　　359

List of Illustrations

1. The Archaeology of Coastal, Southern Tuscany — *Michelle Hobart*

Figure 1.1.	The Tyrrenic coast of central Italy, with sites mentioned in the text.	24
Figure 1.2.	Aerial view of the hilltop of Capalbiaccio in the 1970s.	25
Figure 1.3.	Drone view of the hilltop of Capalbiaccio 2021.	29
Figure 1.4.	View from Tricosto, Capalbiaccio towards the Valle d'Oro, the promontory of Cosa and the Argentario Peninsula.	30

2. Capalbiaccio: The Initial Archaeological Campaigns (1976–1980) — *Stephen L. Dyson*

Figure 2.1.	View from Capalbiacio of the Valle d'Oro looking north-west towards the promontory of Cosa and the Argentario Peninsula facing the Tyrrhenian Sea.	35
Figure 2.2.	View of the Capalbiaccio Hilltop from the Roman villa of Giardino looking north-east at the partition wall inside the fortification.	35
Figure 2.3.	Interior elevation of the eastern fortification wall.	36
Figure 2.4.	Partition wall dividing the fortified village.	36
Figure 2.5.	Part of the gate of a possible entrance into the northern fortified area.	36
Figure 2.6.	Building J. Compare the different state of the building: a) 1978. b) 2010.	37
Figure 2.7.	Church A during excavation, with the partition wall abutting it.	38
Figure 2.8.	Diagnostic pottery found in 1978.	38

3. Geo-Archaeology of Coastal Southern Tuscany — *Nicoletta Barocca*

Figure 3.1.	Geological map of southern Tuscany.	44
Figure 3.2.	*Map of the vicinity of Orbetello* with an indication of the work carried out by the *Real amministrazione del bonificamento* [Royal Administration of Redevelopment], 1864.	47
Figure 3.3.	Ancient Pleistocene lagoons.	48
Figure 3.4.	The port of Cosa (late 2–1 century BCE) with its industrial complex for the production of and commerce in conserved fish (*garum*) and wine.	49
Figure 3.5.	Detail of the 1864 *Map of the vicinity of Orbetello* with reclamation canals. The dotted circle indicates the 'ruined stronghold of Capalbiaccio'.	50
Figure 3.6.	Detail of Ieronimo Bellermato's *Chorographia Tusciae*, 1536.	51
Figure 3.7.	a. Historical fluctuations of the borders of Lake San Floriano. b. Survey of Lake Scuro.	52
Figure 3.8.	Detail of Giuseppe Rosaccio's *Geografia della Toscana*, 1662.	52
Figure 3.9.	Detail of the *Map of the Vicinity of Orbetello*, cit., 1864, tracing the hydraulic works used to reclaim the lagoon of Orbetello.	54
Figure 3.10.	a. Site distribution during the Classical period, with the main roads and hypothetical reconstruction of the ancient lake basins. b. Detailed map of the Valle d'Oro in the Classical period.	55

4. Geophysical Prospecting, Topography, Thermal Camera and DEM — *Laura Cerri and Emanuele Mariotti*

Figure 4.1.	Map of Capalbiaccio with the magnetic anomalies.	58
Figure 4.2.	Interpretation of the anomalies.	58
Figure 4.3.	Final master plan with Dyson's original excavated structures and the newly identified structures.	61
Figure 4.4.	a. DEM (Digital elevation model) and cross section of the hilltop of Capalbiaccio showing the roads leading up to the fortified village and the springs surrounding the hilltop. b. Cross Section of the Capalbiaccio hill.	62
Figure 4.5.	Oval Structure outside of Area E (as visible in 2009).	63
Figure 4.6.	Photo taken in 2010 of the overgrown mound or tomb.	64
Figure 4.7.	Photo of the wall elevation of the dry stone structure.	64
Figure 4.8.	Drawing of a segment of the elevation of the dry stone structure.	64
Figure 4.9.	Overlap between aerial photo by UAV (2021), the general plan of the site and geophysical anomalies.	66
Figure 4.10.	Overlap between aerial photo captured in 1970 showing the general plan of the site and geophysical anomalies.	66
Figure 4.11.	Thermal photo of the east side of the site.	67
Figure 4.12.	Overlap between the general plan of the site, geophysical anomalies and the thermal photo.	67

5. Medieval Wall Reading — *Irene Corti*

Figure 5.1.	Map of places mentioned in the text.	70
Figure 5.2.	Plan of the first buildings, the tower and the church and hypothetical structures. Twelfth century.	71
Figure 5.3.	Plan of the second medieval phase of buildings; circuit wall, palace, houses, second church and hypothetical structures. Thirteenth century.	71
Figure 5.4.	a, b. Building technique with decorative elements in the style *spina di pesce* found in the cloister of the monastery of Sant'Angelo Rovinato and same style *spina di pesce* in the defensive walls of the fortified site, Torre Argentiera.	72
Figure 5.5.	Plan of the third medieval phase of buildings; the division wall inside the castle and Building J and hypothetical structures. Fourteenth century.	73
Figure 5.6.	A: Technique 1, Buildings 1=D and 5=E (twelfth century). B: Detail of the wall pile for Technique 1.	77
Figure 5.7.	A: Technique 2, Buildings 19, 20, and 21 (thirteenth century). B. Detail of the wall pile for Technique 2.	77
Figure 5.8.	A: Technique 2, variant A, in Buildings 2 and 17=K (thirteenth century). Sample 1 × 1 m. B: Detail of the wall pile for Technique 2, variant A.	77
Figure 5.9.	A: Technique 3, Building 18=P (thirteenth century). B: detail of the wall pile for Technique 3.	78

Figure 5.10.	A: Technique 4, in the city walls and Building 21 (thirteenth century). Sample 1.5 × 1.5 m. B: Detail of the wall pile for Technique 4.	78
Figure 5.11.	Technique 4, variant A, in the city walls and Buildings 7, 8, 9, 10, 11, and 12. Sample 1.5 × 1.5 m.	79
Figure 5.12.	A: Technique 5, in the city walls. Technical sample, 1.5 × 1.5 m. B: Detail of wall pile for Technique 5.	80
Figure 5.13.	A: Technique 6 in Building 3=J and the dividing wall. Sample 1.5 × 1.5 m. B: detail of the wall pile for Technique 6.	80
Figure 5.14.	The large collapsed tower, Building 19. Photo by Hermann Salvadori.	80
Figure 5.15.	Photographic straightening and stratigraphic reading of a section of the wall from the east side of the defensive bailey (city walls).	82
Figure 5.16.	Photographic straightening and stratigraphic reading of the façade of building 3=J.	83
Figure 5.17.	Section of the dividing wall of Capalbiaccio stronghold.	84

6. Analysis of the Material Culture — *Michelle Hobart*

Figure 6.1.	Original plan compiled during the three years of excavation.	88
Figure 6.2.	Building J, Pit 1. Cross section with Levels I–IV.	88
Figure 6.3.	Quantitative material culture.	88
Table 6.1.	List of buildings and areas excavated by Dyson's during the three campaigns at Tricosto, Capalbiaccio.	89
Table 6.2.	In *italics*, are notes from Dyson's field books; in capital letters are our interpretations of Dyson's levels, based on the pottery found inside.	89
Table 6.3.	Quantification of material culture from the three campaigns, 1976–1980.	91

7. Pre-Etruscan, Etruscan, and Roman Pottery — *Valeria Acconcia*

Figure 7.1.	Map of Southern Etruria with Proto-historic and Etruscan places.	94
Figure 7.2.	Seventh-century BCE places mentioned in the text.	95
Figure 7.3.	Sixth-century BCE places mentioned in the text.	96
Figure 7.4.	Fifth-century BCE places mentioned in the text.	97
Figure 7.5.	Quantification of all classical pottery from Capalbiaccio.	100
Plate 7.1.	Late Bronze Age and Iron Age pottery (Fabric A).	102
Plate 7.2.	Pottery from the seventh to the first half of the third century BCE (Etruscan Period).	105
Plate 7.3.	Coarse ware: Jars.	107
Plate 7.4.	Coarse ware: Pithoi, braziers, basins.	109
Plate 7.5.	Coarse ware: bowls. Amphorae.	111

Plate 7.6.	Coarse creamware. Black-glaze pottery.	113
Plate 7.7.	Roman pottery: coarse ware.	114
Plate 7.8.	Roman pottery: coarse ware.	116

8. Capalbiaccio and Medieval Pottery in Southern Tuscany (900–1000) — *Emanuele Vaccaro*

Figure 8.1.	Digital Terrain Model of Tuscany with the study area corresponding to the modern Province of Grosseto.	119
Figure 8.2.	Map of the study area and the sites mentioned in the text.	120
Figure 8.3.	Capalbiaccio, Level 5 of Building J (tenth century): ceramic classes and MNI.	122
Figure 8.4.	Aerial picture of the church, the cistern, the tower and the wall circuit at Poggio Cavolo during excavation in 2005.	130
Figure 8.5.	Poggio Cavolo, contexts 1522=1593 (second half of the tenth century): ceramic classes, fragments and MNI.	131
Figure 8.6.	Poggio Cavolo, contexts 1522=1593 (second half of the tenth century CE): ceramic classes, forms and MNI.	131
Figure 8.7.	Poggio Cavolo, contexts 1522=1593 (second half of the tenth century CE): presence of the grey core in the *acroma depurata* and *acroma selezionata* wares.	143
Figure 8.8.	Poggio Cavolo, contexts 1506 and 1534 (late tenth/early eleventh century CE): ceramic classes, fragments and MNI.	143
Figure 8.9.	Poggio Cavolo, contexts 1506 and 1534 (late tenth/early eleventh century CE): presence of the grey core in the *acroma depurata* and *acroma selezionata* wares and in the kitchen ware.	144
Figure 8.10.	Poggio Cavolo, contexts 1506 and 1534 (late tenth/early eleventh century CE): ceramic classes, forms and MNI.	144
Figure 8.11.	Distribution of the class of red-painted/*colature rosse* ware in southern Tuscany between the eighth/ninth and early eleventh century CE.	151
Figure 8.12.	Distribution of the classes of *vetrina pesante*/Forum ware and Sparse Glazed ware in southern Tuscany between the ninth and early eleventh century CE.	153
Plate 8.1.	Capalbiaccio, Level 5 of Building J (tenth century). *Acroma depurata* and *acroma selezionata* wares: 1–8. Small amphorae.	123
Plate 8.2.	Capalbiaccio, Level 5 of Building J (tenth century). *Acroma depurata* and *acroma selezionata* wares; Red-painted/*colature rosse* ware: Kitchen ware;. *Testi*.	124
Plate 8.3.	Capalbiaccio, Level 5 of Building J (tenth century). Kitchen ware. Cooking pots from Rome or Latium: 4. Type 1; 5. Type 1 *bis*; 6. Type 2; 10. Type 6; 11. Type 6 *bis*; 14. Type 9; 17. Type 12. Local or sub-regional cooking pots: 7. Type 3; 8. Type 4; 9. Type 5; 12. Type 7; 13. Type 8; 14. Type 9; 15. Type 10; 16. Type 11. Local or sub-regional lids: 1–3.	128

Plate 8.4.	Poggio Cavolo, contexts 1522=1593 (second half of the tenth century CE). *Acroma depurata* and *acroma selezionata* wares: 1. *Olla acquaria*-water amphora; 2–3. Table jugs; 4–6. Bases of table jugs.	133
Plate 8.5.	Poggio Cavolo, contexts 1522=1593 (second half of the tenth century CE). Kitchen ware: 1–12. Cooking pots; 13–14. Bases of cooking pots (or other closed forms).	136
Plate 8.6.	Poggio Cavolo, contexts 1522=1593 (second half of the tenth century CE). Kitchen ware: 1–2. Bases of cooking pots (or other closed forms); 3. Table jug; 4. Table or storage jug; 5. Small amphora (?); 6–8. *Testi*; 9. Bowl-lid.	137
Plate 8.7.	Miscellaneous pottery from context 1600 of Poggio Cavolo (second half of the tenth century) and surface sites.	140
Plate 8.8.	Poggio Cavolo, contexts 1506 and 1534 (late tenth/early eleventh century CE).	145
Table 8.1.	In-phase and residual pottery from Level 5 of Building J at Capalbiaccio.	121
Table 8.2.	Medieval small amphorae at Capalbiaccio (tenth century CE): types, fabrics, and MNI.	122
Table 8.3.	Cooking pots at Capalbiaccio (tenth century CE): fabrics, types, and MNI.	126
Table 8.4.	Kitchen ware open forms at Capalbiaccio (tenth century CE): fabrics, forms, and MNI.	128
Table 8.5.	Number, function, location, and date of the contexts from the church at Poggio Cavolo yielding the ceramic assemblages discussed in this chapter.	131
Table 8.6.	Poggio Cavolo, contexts 1522=1593 (second half of the tenth century CE): fabrics and MNI in the *acroma depurata* and *acroma selezionata* wares.	132
Table 8.7.	Poggio Cavolo, contexts 1522 = 1593 (second half of the tenth century CE): fabrics and MNI in the kitchen ware.	134
Table 8.8.	Poggio Cavolo, contexts 1506 and 1534 (late tenth/early eleventh century CE): fabrics and MNI in the *acroma depurata* and *acroma selezionata* wares.	146
Table 8.9.	Poggio Cavolo, contexts 1506 and 1534 (late tenth/early eleventh century CE): fabrics and MNI in the kitchen ware.	148
Table 8.10.	Summary of the incidences of the grey core in the ceramic classes from Capalbiaccio and Poggio Cavolo.	148
Table 8.11.	Frequencies of vessels in *acroma depurata* ware and red-painted/*colature rosse* ware manufactured with fabric AD2=AD36=DR 1 attributable to a source in (northern?) Latium.	148

9. A Comparative Study of Pottery from Southern Tuscany and Latium (1000–1200) — *Chiara Valdambrini*

Figure 9.1.	Comparative provenance from Latium and Tuscany.	164
Plate 9.1.	Capalbiaccio castle. Pottery from the eleventh and twelfth centuries.	167

10. Medieval Pottery (1200–1400) — *Michelle Hobart*

Figure 10.1.	Map of Tuscany and Latium kitchen coarse-ware open shape.	172
Figure 10.2.	Map of Tuscany and Latium kitchen coarse ware closed shape.	173
Figure 10.3.	Map of Tuscany and Latium Archaic majolica drawings.	174
Figure 10.4.	Latium Archaic majolica from Viterbo.	175
Figure 10.5.	Spain lustreware from Manises and Paterna.	175
Figure 10.6.	Map of Tuscany and Latium Depurated closed vessels.	175
Figure 10.7.	Tuscany Archaic majolica handles.	175
Figure 10.8.	Viterbo *zaffera a rilievo*.	176
Plate 10.1.	Testi – Fabric 1.	178
Plate 10.2.	Testi – Fabric 1.	179
Plate 10.3.	Lids and closed shapes – Fabric 2.	181
Plate 10.4.	Testi – Fabric 2.	183
Plate 10.5.	Lids and closed shapes – Fabric 3.	184
Plate 10.6.	Closed shapes: *Olle* – Fabric 4.	185
Plate 10.7.	Lids and closed shapes – Fabric 6.	187
Plate 10.8.	Fine wares or Depurated Fabrics.	188
Plate 10.9.	Painted under glaze or *dipinta sotto vetrina*.	189
Plate 10.10.	Lead glazed pottery.	190
Plate 10.11.	White Archaic majolica or Monochrome and rays.	192
Plate 10.12.	Archaic majolica from Pisa.	193
Plate 10.13.	Ceramics from Siena 'Famiglia Verde'.	194
Plate 10.14.	Ceramics from Orvieto and Viterbo.	197
Plate 10.15.	Ceramics from Latium and Orvieto.	198
Plate 10.16.	Graffita arcaica tirrenica.	199
Plate 10.17.	Imported pottery from Spain and North Africa; Cobalt and Manganese.	200

11. Small Finds — *Elisa Rubegni*

Figure 11.1.	Percentage of small finds recovered at Capalbiaccio according to their raw material.	203
Figure 11.2.	Quantity of functional objects from Capalbiaccio.	204
Figure 11.3.	Quantity of glass.	204
Figure 11.4.	Spatial distribution of the small finds discovered at Capalbiaccio.	205
Figure 11.5.	Distribution of nails from excavated areas.	221

Plate 11.1.	1. Glass bead. 2. Bronze bead. 3. Stone bead. 4. Bronze button. 5. Bronze button. 6. Clay spindle. 7. Clay spindle. 8. Clay spindle. 9. Clay spindle. 10. Clay spindle. 11. Clay spindle. 12. Clay spindle. 13. Clay spindle. 14. Clay spindle.	206
Plate 11.2.	1. Bronze thimble. 2. Iron knife handle. 3. Iron knife blade. 4. Iron knife blade. 5. Iron knife blade. 6. Iron knife handle. 7. Bronze piece of a knife handle.	210
Plate 11.3.	1. Iron hammerhead. 2. Iron nail. 3. Iron nail. 4. Iron nail. 5. Iron horseshoe. 6. Iron nail. 7. Iron buckle. 8. Bronze stud.	212
Plate 11.4.	1. Iron ring. 2. Iron ring. 3. Iron ring. 4. Iron ring. 5. Iron key. 6. Iron key. 7. Iron key.	214
Plate 11.5.	1. Iron lock plate. 2. Iron arrowhead. 3. Bronze bell.	216
Plate 11.6.	1. Iron plate of armour. 2. Iron plate of armour. 3. Iron plate of armour. 4. Iron plate of armour. 5. Iron plate of armour. 6. Lead missile. 7 Unidentified lead object.	218
Plate 11.7.	Photograph of chess piece, 7.6 cm tall, 4.2 cm diameter of base.	220
Plate 11.8.	Photograph of end of clay smoking pipe.	220

12. Coins — *Alessia Rovelli*

Figure 12.1.	Geographical Map charting the origins of the coinage found during the excavations at Capalbiaccio 1976–1980.	224

13. Archaeozoological Remains — *Diana C. Crader*

Figure 13.1.	DEM of Tuscany and the sites mentioned in the chapter.	232
Table 13.1.	Summary of faunal remains from Building J and Area M by NISP.	244
Table 13.2.	Faunal remains from Areas C, F, I, R, and T by NISP.	245
Table 13.3.	Faunal remains from the Etruscan levels at Building J by NISP.	246

14. Field Survey of the Post-Medieval Settlement Patterns in Southern Tuscany — *Hermann Salvadori*

Figure 14.1.	Map of the modern Grosseto Province with sites mentioned in the text.	251
Figure 14.2.	Map of 128 castles identified in the Grosseto province (ASFAT) and their approximate date of their decline.	253
Figure 14.3.	The seven castles surveyed inside two buffer zones (one with a radius of 1.5 km and the other a radius of 5 km).	254
Figure 14.4.	Farmhouses in the Catasto Leopoldino present in the territory of Tricosto.	256
Figure 14.5.	Distribution map of the farmhouses investigated in the Tricosto area.	257
Figure 14.6.	View from the west coast of the hilltop of Capalbiaccio with the Spanish Tower under restoration (scaffolding) and the modern farmhouse called 'Torre/Casale di Tricosto'. The castle place name has shifted below during the Spanish occupation.	258

Figure 14.7.	Pottery concentration near the Salaiolo quarry.	258
Figure 14.8.	Areas that have been surveyed inside the buffer-zone of the Tricosto castle: Casale Tricosto, il Salaiolo, La Sicilia, Casa Marotti.	259
Figure 14.9.	Detail of the Catasto Leopoldino with Tricosto and three farmhouses (casolari) inside the smaller buffer zone.	260
Figure 14.10.	Map of the castles and farmhouses identified during the field survey in the buffer zone of the Tricosto castle dated between the end of thirteenth and the sixteenth century.	260
Figure 14.11.	Two examples of the transformation of the landscape resulting from human activity: an abandoned farmhouse is contrasted with the removal of earlier settlements for agricultural purposes.	261
Figure 14.12.	Detail of the IGM map showing different visibility established by the field survey in the Megarozzo area.	263
Figure 14.13.	Detail of the Catasto Leopoldino with the newly identified sites of Salaiolo, Le Fornaci and Cicilia in the vicinity of Tricosto.	263
Figure 14.14.	Detail of the Tricosto farmhouse with Capalbiaccio Castle in the background.	265
Figure 14.15.	Map indicating all castles and farmhouses within the buffer zone of the Montepescali castle between the end of thirteenth and the sixteenth century.	266
Figure 14.16.	Map indicating all castles and farmhouses within the buffer zone of the Sassoforte castle between the thirteenth and the sixteenth century.	267
Figure 14.17.	Map indicating all castles and farmhouses within the buffer zone of the Castel di Pietra castle between the end of the thirteenth and sixteenth century.	268
Figure 14.18.	Abandoned sites in the Grosseto Province.	269
Table 14.1.	The seven sites examined in this chapter and the data available from texts before fieldwork began.	252
Table 14.2.	Summary of the Farm houses and the traces found in the survey inside the buffer zones around the Tricosto castle.	256
Table 14.3.	Evidence collected between the thirteenth and sixteenth century during the field survey.	262

15. Reassessing the Etruscan Valle d'Oro — *Michelle Hobart*

Figure 15.1.	Map of Etruscan settlements around Capalbiaccio.	274
Figure 15.2.	Aerial photograph and IGM map of the Valle d'Oro area between Cosa and Capalbiaccio. Photo reproduced from Carandini 1985.	275
Figure 15.3.	Archaic burials around Capalbiaccio and its surroundings. Adapted from Celuzza and Regoli 1982, 36. Map adapted from Celuzza and Regoli 1982, 36.	275
Figure 15.4.	Geophysical survey of Capalbiaccio hilltop and castle. Image by Laura Cerri and Emanuele Mariotti.	276
Figure 15.5.	Sketch of oval structure and walls outside the castle of Tricosto.	279

Figure 15.6.	Well within the city walls and reused since the pre-Roman period.	280
Figure 15.7.	Comparison between the settlement plans of Lago dell'Accesa.	282
Figure 15.8.	Etruscan and Roman Settlements in the Valle d'Oro.	283
Figure 15.9.	Photograph showing how Cosa's *decumanus maximus* was connected to the valle d'Oro through still visible alignments part of the centuriation land redistribution.	286
Figure 15.10.	Centuriation of the Valley d'Oro at the foot of the Capalbiaccio hill.	287
Table 15.1.	Timeline of settlement in southern Etruria.	277

16. Builders of Landscapes — *Michelle Hobart*

Figure 16.1.	View of *Ager Cosanus* facing the Argentario Mountain.	291
Figure 16.2.	Post hole inside Building J Pit 1 and cross section of Dyson's levels.	291
Figure 16.3.	Tower 1: Exterior.	291
Figure 16.4.	Tower 1: Interior.	291
Figure 16.5.	Church 1: Overview.	291
Figure 16.6.	Church 1: East End Apse.	291
Figure 16.7.	Church 1: Plan. Note the intersection of the church predating the division that cut the castle in half.	292
Figure 16.8.	a: Reconstruction: Castle of Tricosto. b: DEM Reconstruction: Castle of Tricosto. c: Castle of Tricosto.	292
Figure 16.9.	Exterior face of Church B.	294
Figure 16.10.	Long side of Church B.	294
Figure 16.11.	Residential palace.	294
Figure 16.12.	Residential palace: slit window.	294
Figure 16.13.	Residential palace: corner.	294
Figure 16.14.	a, b, c. Tower: collapsed.	295
Figure 16.15.	Scarp supporting the tower butting against the western circuit wall, to the right of Building J.	296
Figure 16.16.	Plan of Building H.	296
Figure 16.17.	House.	296
Figure 16.18.	House wall: interior.	296
Figure 16.19.	Building H: Pit 3.	296
Figure 16.20.	Building H: Pit 5.	296
Figure 16.21.	Main Gate: northern side.	297
Figure 16.22.	Scarp of northern circuit wall: exterior.	297

Figure 16.23. View of the promontory of Cosa. 297

Figure 16.24. Smaller southern service gate. 297

Figure 16.25. a. Long wall. b. Long wall showing horizontal length. 298

Figure 16.26. Fortification wall: East interior. 299

Figure 16.27. Division wall with post holes for stairs. 299

Figure 16.28. Division wall: Detail. 299

Figure 16.29. Building J. 299

Figure 16.30. Building J: From the interior looking east towards Structure K. 299

Figure 16.31. Building J: Interior – niche with sink against the northern wall. 299

Figure 16.32. Building J: Exterior – drainage system. 300

Figure 16.33. Area K: Water collector – drainage system (cistern). 300

Figure 16.34. Area K: Wall facing Building J with opening into the rounded drainage system. 300

Figure 16.35. Area K: Open trench revealing axial alignments below the walls. 300

Figure 16.36. Castle of Tricosto, Capalbiaccio — Reconstruction as it would have appeared in the fourteenth century. 305

17. Concluding Remarks and Open Questions — *Michelle Hobart*

Figure 17.1. Photo of Capalbiaccio, with a view of Cosa and the Argentario. 310

Appendix: Castle and Countryside — *Stephen L. Dyson*

Figure A.1. Cosa and Italy. 313

Figure A.2. Archaeological Sites in the *Ager Cosanus*. 314

Figure A.3. [Original legend is unclear]. 316

Figure A.4. Variation in Villa Size in the *Ager Cosanus*. 316

Figure A.5. The Plan of Capalbiaccio. 318

Figure A.6. Capalbiaccio Church. 318

Figure A.7. View of Capalbiaccio Church. 319

Figure A.8. The Keep Tower at Capalbiaccio. 319

Acknowledgements

The Capalbiaccio journey has been a very *longue durée* project. Darby and Ann Scott led me to Steve Dyson, whose preliminary report of the 1970s excavations set the stage for this undertaking. The contents of that report are herein republished (see Appendix 1) with the permission of the author and Western Michigan University.

Of all those associated with this research, gratitude goes firstly to the late Antonia Arnoldus Huyzendveld, who brought the past alive with her incomparable descriptions of landscapes that were transformed by man and nature. Emanuele Papi has been a constant source of encouragement and a critical interlocutor from the inception, contributing his intellectual rigour most generously. Philip Perkins offered many ways of seeing Etruria, stimulating debate and bold thinking about the region he knows so well. I am especially grateful for all the long conversations with Maria Grazia Celuzza, who willingly shared her encyclopedic knowledge of this region. Other colleagues and friends made innumerable contributions from their own fields, among them Marco Giamello, Giancarlo Pagani, Marco Firmati, Fabio Gabrielli, Giovanna Bianchi, Carlo Citter, Vittorio Fronza, Maria Ange Causarano, Andrea Zifferero, and Chiara Valdambrini. I am also grateful to Alessandro Sebastiani, my co-director on the Monteverdi Paganico project.

I am most appreciative of the hospitality and of the anecdotes that were shared with me about the site, the Castle of Tricosto, and the hill of Capalbiaccio by its stewards, Giuliano Teodoli and Paolo Bertolini. Members of the local Soprintendenza, responsible for protecting Italy's historical patrimony, are also to be thanked for their gracious cooperation, not least among them Gabriella Poggesi, Maria Turchetti, Paola Gambogi, Paola Rendini, and the late Giuliana Agricoli.

Two non-invasive field campaigns were conducted at the site with several students, who are now colleagues from the University of Siena. Most of them are contributors to this book, while the others certainly enabled its publication. In particular, I mention Laura Cerri, Irene Corti, Giuseppe Fichera, Luca Passalaqua Leoonardo Bigi, Davide Caruso, and Gioia Gaianigo. Special thanks go to Hermann Salvadori and Emanuel Mariotti for helping us to identify the road and the springs around the hill, and for letting us publish his spectacular images. Emanuele Mariotti's work in the final phases of geographical documentation is particularly worthy of praise. The Cosa Museum stored the pottery excavated at Capalbiaccio and acted as our home base thanks to the superb staff who guarded the archaeological park. Graziano Bonino, Gianni, Emilia, Patrizia, Luigina, and Lucia are among many wonderful colleagues there who took care of our frequent requests with invariable good humour. Thanks are due, too, to the Instituto Nazionale di Geofisica e Vulcanologia of Pisa for donating the DEM of the three regions of Tuscany, Umbria, and Lazio. I am further indebted to Barbara and Michele Melega, who graciously housed me one winter while I was studying the pottery, and to Marella Caracciolo Chia, who kindly turned her home into headquarters for the geophysics survey team. I also thank Viviana Calvisi at Garavicchio for inviting Antonio Zandomenichi to testify that WWII bombs destroyed the tall towers at Capabiaccio, which was turned into a refuge for the Germans between 1943 and 1944, at which time Porto Santo Stefano on the Argentario promontory was also destroyed.

Maintaining coherence in a multi-authored text full of technical data requires a good team and I was fortunate to have one. Tracy Scott ably re-drafted the original maps by Dyson with the help of Miranda Richardson and Paul Henderson, who contributed vital topographical mapping and renderings. Rossella Pansini patiently gave the book visual form and organization. Matthew Teti deserves deep recognition, not only for his impeccable editing and rigorous attention to detail, but for helping to resolve unexpected challenges. At Brepols, Rosie Bonté, Maria Whelan, Maria Tryfinopoulou, and Martine Maguire-Weltecke all followed the post production and assembled these pages with care and kindness. The two peer reviewers provided ample and insightful comments that improved this text. Any mistakes are my responsibility.

I would like to think that the late Riccardo Francovich, my mentor and a 'place-maker' who created a field for the medieval archaeological world, would have been pleased to see this project completed in this form. Among his many ambitions was his desire to create an archaeological park in Southern Maremma; this would have included medieval Cosa (Ansedonia) as well as the fortified site of Tricosto, including Roman and Etruscan sites such as Settefinestre and other villas. I am fortunate to have had the guidance of Richard Hodges, who recruited me to excavate an early medieval monastery near Siena. It was this good work that led me to Capalbiaccio.

Anna Serena Zambon has been my model and muse. I am likewise grateful for the constant support of Peter John, Masha, Julia, and Eddy Hobart. Spending time with Charlotte and Altea at the end of each day was its own best reward. Justin has anchored, edited, and conferred with me throughout the project, always with an eye to the present and to the long view.

Finally, this book would not exist if it were not for Steve Dyson's confidence in me to dig inside the previous excavation at Capalbiaccio. When, in the mid-1970s, he first started digging a medieval town and an invisible Etruscan site, monumental Roman buildings were all the fashion. So the Capalbiaccio site became the forerunner of forty years of medieval and Etruscan excavations, interpretations, and publications. I am therefore immensely grateful to Steve and Pauline Dyson, and will never forget their kind nurturing in their welcoming Buffalo home and library. They have materially and intellectually sustained this enterprise. It is to them that I dedicate this book.

MH

Emanuele Mariotti and Giuliano Teodoli at Capalbiacci in 2009.

Part I

Genesis of the Project

MICHELLE HOBART

1. The Archaeology of Coastal Southern Tuscany

ABSTRACT This chapter introduces the entire scope of the Capalbiaccio project and the work that continued after the early excavations at the site in the late 1970s and early 1980s. It begins with a brief historiographical reconstruction of the archaeological excavations, field surveys, pottery analysis, and aerial photography that were carried out in the southern region of Tuscany over the course of the last century. Amongst this data set, one site in particular plays a key role in our understanding of Capalbiaccio — that of the nearby Roman colony of Cosa. The foundational efforts of Stephen J. Dyson and his team from Wesleyan University are here introduced, along with a summary of the more recent, non-invasive campaigns directed by the author and starting some thirty years subsequent to the original field work. Here, our research goals are set forth and a synopsis of the finds are laid out, with chapter-by-chapter breakdowns.

It is perhaps not an exaggeration to state that southern Tuscany has been among the most progressive archaeological laboratories in the Mediterranean. Its proximity to Rome and the origin of colonial settlements during the republic's first territorial expansion has produced a vast literature that sets the foundations for many of the quintessential debates in the prehistoric, classical, and medieval fields. Archaeological data, combined with a vast number of surviving documents, has allowed generations of scholars to trace the major historical occurrences from the Holocene to the late Bronze Age, from Villanovan huts to large Etruscan cities, scattered fortifications, expansive agro-towns, sanctuaries, and 'hypothetical' borders. Topics deriving from sites excavated in the Maremma include the controversial process of 'Romanization', the colonial Roman subdivision of land (centuriation), as well as the presence of slavery in Roman villas. Many pioneering archaeological studies have borne out important economic indicators like organized manufacturing, standardization of products, such as amphorae, and construction materials.

L'archeologo esplora con attenzione la superficie del territorio e tutto ciò che è stato costruito; registra tutte le informazioni fisiche, scritte e trasmesse oralmente; effettuerà i rilievi geofisici e le analisi archeometriche e solo quando avrà un quadro generale sufficientemente accettabile deciderà per lo scavo minimo necessario per completare la storia di quel territorio.

Tiziano Mannoni[1]

Furthermore, the crafting of local pottery and the development of kilns has been contrasted with coexisting imports from all over the Mediterranean. Another first for the region was the excavation of the 'colonial' Roman harbour outside Cosa and its aquacultures, fisheries, baths, and docks. The post-Roman period in southern Tuscany is equally rich in novel archaeological subject matter, including the study of early forms of medieval villages, mining communities, the rise of the seigniorial system, and territorial reorganization. As far as architectural advancements are concerned, the shift from perishable building materials to stone constructions that morphed into walled cities with towers, contributed to the *incastellamento* that is emblematic of the medieval Tuscan landscape. However, natural resources, which have drawn people to the region since time immemorial, are the real protagonists of the local history, in that they attracted cyclical waves of exploitation by outsiders. Trade and exchange that connected the coast to the hinterland gave rise to new cities, such as Massa Marittima, Siena, and Grosseto. Facilitating such connectivity were the extensive network of roads that were rebuilt over pre-existing Roman ones, as well as smaller routes that bridged hilltop castles.

---

1 'The archaeologist explores carefully the surface of the territory and all that has been built; records all of the physical information, written and orally transmitted; will undertake the geophysical surveys and archaeometric analysis and only when she has a sufficiently acceptable general picture will decide for the minimal necessary excavation to complete the history of that territory.' Tiziano Mannoni, together with Riccardo Francovich, is among the founders of medieval Italian archaeology. For an overview of Mannoni's work, see Blake 2011; and of Francovich see Hodges 2014.

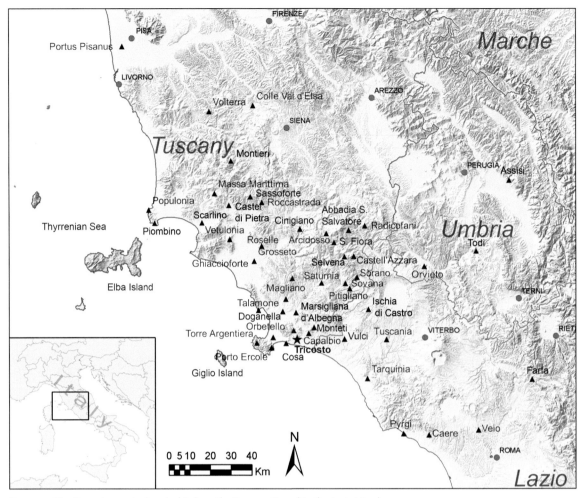

Figure 1.1. The Tyrrenic coast of central Italy, with sites mentioned in the text. Map by Rossella Pansini. Basemap/DTM reproduced with the permission of CTR Regione Toscana.

This phenomenal economic growth, with some interruptions, started to slow down in the second half of the thirteenth century and when Black Plague struck in 1348, the productivity of southern Tuscany never fully recovered. The demographic decline of the countryside resulted in sparse agricultural settlements in the fifteenth century, whereupon farmers worked small patches of land in the rich Albegna Valley, which once fed the city of Rome. However, most of this coast reverted to swampy marshes, probably unsafe and increasingly abandoned, stopping time so that archaeologists today have found hardly anything. The hilltop of Capalbiaccio sits in this extremely fertile countryside, overlooking flat lands and springs of fresh water that are crossed by the coastal Aurelian way and other roads reaching into the inner region, making it an ideal research site. These, among other reasons, are why in 1976 Steve Dyson chose this location for one his first archaeological excavations. To return to this project more than thirty years later was a mixed pleasure and a challenge, as continuous excavations in the region, discoveries, and publications kept enlarging the scope of our understanding (Fig. 1.1).

The Archaeology of Coastal, Southern Tuscany: Cosa and Capalbiaccio

The hilltop of Capalbiaccio[2] was a significant place in the making of ancient Cosa and its hinterland — the Ager Cosanus — which overlooks Roman slave-run villas, such as Settefinestre, in Tuscany. The hilltop later had a second life, no less important, as a liminal point in the long-running struggle between the powerful Aldobrandeschi, communal towns, and the papal state to the east and the immediate south.

---

2 Throughout the book the two terms are used as equivalent. The name 'Tricosto', originally used for the fortified village on top of the Capalbiaccio hill, was later used by the Spanish for the Tricosto tower below the hill when they settled over the ruins of a Roma bath and a casolari also called Tricosto.

This struggle was largely transacted over the tenth to the fifteenth centuries before the fortification was effectively destroyed by the communal city state of Siena, which was expanding its *contado*. Here, in a nutshell, the context of the site is provided, but it will be useful to first give insight into how the project came into being.

Archaeologists came together to work on the first Roman colony of Cosa in southern Tuscany right after World War II. In the summer of 1948, the American Academy in Rome excavation began in a region where world conflict had depleted the local community. Within the beautiful cyclopic walls of Cosa, they found residual structures from the war — barracks and a watchtower abandoned years before by the allies — while much of the rest of the Roman colony was well preserved. Together with Lawrence Richardson and later with Russell Scott and others, Frank Brown directed the project and worked at Cosa for decades. Brown's publications, including *Cosa: The Making of a Roman Town* (1980), summarized the results of the excavations and his interpretation of the site's history. Central to Brown's argument was the idea that two very early Roman colonies (Paestum and Cosa), both founded in 273 BCE, were built as idealized models of what a perfect Roman colony should be.[3] Digging a site such as Cosa helped to understand the process of Roman republican and imperial expansion, while setting the foundation for generations of debates and fostering new questions. The rare opportunity of excavating an abandoned archaeological site in Italy is what led Brown and his team to focus on the three pillars of communal living: the sacred, the public arena, and the domestic sphere. The urban arrangements of Cosa set the stage for future generations to explore how a Roman colony was conceived and reproduced, and thus the shaping of Rome's provinces in the Mediterranean.

During World War II and in its wake, the entire region of southern Tuscany was documented by aerial photography, and archaeologists soon recognized the potential to integrate those images with landscape archaeology (Fig. 1.2). In 1956, Ferdinando Castagnoli used aerial photographs to survey the area around Capalbiaccio — more precisely Cosa, the Valle d'Oro, and the Albegna Valley — and published his seminal article on the *centuriazione*, the colonial Roman subdivision of land. Castagnoli's work not only supported the project underway at Cosa, but provided important information on the organization of the landscape, which could be applied

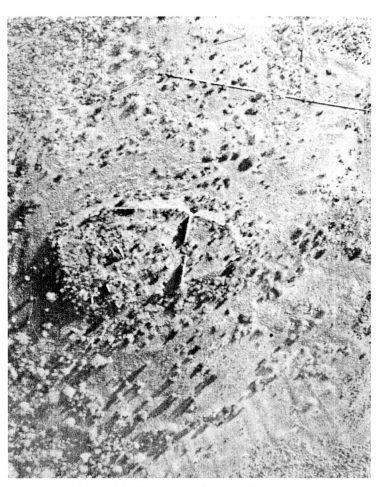

Figure 1.2. Aerial view of the hilltop of Capalbiaccio in the 1970s. Photo by Dyson's Team, reproduced with permission.

to other Roman colonies in Europe.[4] In the early 1970s, another team, under the direction of Anna Marguerite McCann, worked just below the hilltop at Cosa at the Portus Cosanus and connected activities around the colony's countryside and the coast. Agricultural goods, including grains and wine, were transported through the port in locally produced amphorae, and were subsequently found in every Roman harbour in the provinces. While most of the Roman settlers were scattered in the *ager* outside of the city, the excavators of Cosa were mostly focused on the monumental ruins on the hilltop. It was another later generation that would focus their attention on the neighbouring countryside.

Inspired by the results of the British School excavations in southern Etruria,[5] Steve Dyson, who was then teaching at Wesleyan University, undertook a

---

3 For Cosa, see the volumes of the MAAR, Memoirs of the American Academy in Rome.

4 Castagnoli 1956. For a further discussion of *centuriazione* and the Etruscan Albegna Valley, see *infra* Hobart 'Reassessing the Etruscan Valle d'Oro'.

5 For the British School at Rome, see Hodges 2000; Bignamini and Hornsby 2010.

series of surveys in the area neighbouring Cosa.[6] His field research aimed to relate the evolution of settlement in the countryside to the reconstructed history of the town of Cosa itself and the developing debate on the evolution of the Roman countryside.[7] Dyson's intent coincided with an expanding interest in Italian rural archaeology, best represented by the projects of the Universities of Siena and Rome in the region. Central to much of this research was the wider debate on the evolution of rural Roman Italy, stimulated in part by the earlier publication in 1965 of Arnold Toynbee's influential history, *Hannibal's Legacy*.

British survey archaeology in the post-war period arose in part from financial constraints, which precluded the type of 'big site' excavations done by the American Academy at Cosa during the era of Italian reconstruction. It also reflected new directions in social and economic history that stemmed from Lucien Febvre and the French *École des Annales*, and which gave life to generations of systematic micro-histories. The Annales School's more focused specializations were followed by Marxist interpretations of the past, which emphasized research on the social and economic bases of society. These new impulses increasingly underpinned the theoretical and methodological approaches of archaeologists working in Italy after World War II.

In the post-war era, the British School at Rome was directed by a series of outstanding archaeologists — John Ward Perkins, David Whitehouse, Graeme Barker, and Richard Hodges — who combined the methodological rigour of British archaeology with a far-reaching perspective, which contemplated a *longue durée* approach, not only to prehistory and the Classical period, but also the Middle Ages and modern times. They mostly applied new methods to landscape research, which were important undertakings for the emerging field of medieval archaeology that investigated the continuity between the Middle Ages and earlier periods, mostly in rural environments.

Beginning in the late 1970s and 1980s, other subfields were developing as archaeologists laid the groundwork for specialized disciplines that focused on cataloguing and dating previously unknown types of pottery, creating settlement paradigms for the landscape, and refining chronological sequences. These combined efforts helped interpret the early and later medieval topography of central Italy and set new models, based on material culture, which would stimulate a reworking of traditional histories.

New stratigraphic methods were imported to Italy in the late 1970s and employed at the large-scale Italo-British excavation at the Roman villa of Settefinestre, which is also located in the Ager Cosanus.[8] Italian and American archaeologists, although not in collaboration, covered aspects that complement one another. On the survey front, Andrea Carandini's team expanded the work started at Cosa by Brown, McCann, and Dyson, who had investigated the coastal portion of Etruria (the Roman *regio* VII), including the Valle d'Oro and the Albegna Valley.[9]

At the same time, the discipline of medieval archaeology was developing, especially in central Italy, led by Riccardo Francovich. With an excavation along the city walls of Grosseto and a number of medieval Tuscan castles, Francovich used archaeological evidence to challenge the French historian Pierre Toubert's reconstruction of landscape development in the area surrounding medieval Roman hilltops. Toubert placed emphasis on the process of *incastellamento* based on the construction of eleventh- and twelfth-century towers and castles in the countryside, largely as a result of landowner initiative and a form of economic and territorial control.[10] Francovich did not agree, believing that the *incastellamento* process started much earlier in Tuscany, with small villages inhabited by a 'golden age peasantry' formed around a *curtes*, or the common areas of manorial residences; a process whose beginnings he saw in the eighth or ninth century.[11] The significance is that Toubert's arguments were derived from documents while Francovich and his school, utilizing information from excavations at a number of castles and villages in southern Tuscany, initiated a new season of information derived from material culture. Research conducted by the University of Siena revealed that there were other narratives to be created by combining history with archaeology. In over thirty years of excavating rural settlements, Francovich and his colleagues formulated new mod-

---

6 Dyson 1978b; 1979; 1981a; 1981b; Potter 1979; Cascino, Di Giuseppe, and Patterson 2012.
7 Dyson 1992; and more recently, Dyson 2003; Dyson 2005.
8 Carandini 1985a.
9 The survey project of the University of Siena covered an area of about 249 km² (17.5 per cent of the total surface area of Etruria) and produced a number of preliminary articles, and a partially updated final report, which appeared in 2002: Dyson 1978b; Manacorda 1978; Manacorda 1980; Celuzza, Regoli 1982; Celuzza and Regoli 1985; Celuzza 1985; Celuzza and Zona 2002; Carandini and others 2002.
10 Toubert 1973; Hubert 2000.
11 For responses to Toubert, see Francovich 1973; Francovich and Noyé 1994, Wickham 1995; Wickham 1996.

els that continue to be re-evaluated in relation to the region's diverse micro-histories.[12]

Before Siena set the foundations for rewriting medieval history under the lens of archaeology (two years after the first volume of *Archeologia Medievale* and three years after Toubert's *Les structures du Latium medieval* appeared) Tricosto at Capalbiaccio was, in 1976, the first medieval castle to be excavated in Tuscany. Dyson's attention focused on the impressive medieval fortified compound at Capalbiaccio, located some 20 km inland from Cosa and about 130 km north of Rome. While much of the site was buried in the massive rubble of collapsed towers and fortification walls, sufficient open areas existed for small soundings within the city walls. Even with a modest budget, the excavations would hopefully produce useful information.[13]

The first archaeological campaign at Capalbiaccio took place in 1976. Dyson, primarily a classicist who had worked with Frank Brown at Cosa and excavated the nearby Roman villa of Le Colonne, had little exposure to later medieval layers, as both villas were soon abandoned after Roman occupation.[14] Dyson and his team conducted three archaeological campaigns at Capalbiaccio, but by the end of the third season in 1980, the excavators felt that, with the limited resources available, further work at Capalbiaccio was not justified. The results of the research were summarized by Dyson in a single article published by the Medieval Institute at Western Michigan University.[15] It was a paper written for an audience of medievalists, few of whom had much archaeological background. It presented, for the first time, the results of an Italian medieval archaeological excavation in a concise manner, and tied it to the contextual history available through local historiography.

In 1990 it was the American Academy in Rome's continuing excavations at Cosa that eventually connected this author to Capalbiaccio and Dyson's work there. While the monumental remains at Cosa seemed to be exclusively of Roman manufacture, a medieval community reused, in large part, the infrastructure of Cosa and resettled parts within the city walls, where an abundant quantity of medieval pottery was recovered. While studying the post-Roman pottery of Cosa, I learned that similar medieval material excavated from the nearby Capalbiaccio in the 1970s was stored in the same warehouse of the small local museum.[16] This was what led to my collaboration with Steve Dyson and the State University of New York at Buffalo.

Return to the Site of Capalbiaccio

In 2009, the principal aim of the new project was to address, with new insight and a better understanding of medieval archaeology, some of the questions that had emerged from the excavations of medieval Cosa and Dyson's research and report on Capalbiaccio. The long pause of more than thirty years between the original excavation and our return to Capalbiaccio had seen major developments in Italian medieval archaeology, particularly in Tuscany. It allowed us to rethink some of the questions posited by Dyson's work, utilizing more updated mapping techniques and surveying new areas with the help of information and methodologies that were not previously available. There has been no further excavation since Dyson's, yet it was possible to elucidate several findings:

- First of all, the confirmation of the presence of an Etruscan settlement occupying large areas of the hilltop.
- The pre-medieval pottery analysis confirmed that there were two habitations of the site prior to the Middle Ages:
  - The earliest settlement is dated during the Late Bronze Age.
  - An Etruscan (minor?) centre was established during the sixth to circa the third century BCE.
  - Abandonment in Roman times, with the possible exception of a farm, outside the fortification walls.
- The magnetometry, Thermal Camera and DEM surveys determined that the pre-medieval physical parameter was larger than the area covered by the fortified medieval hilltop.
- An early medieval village preceded the construction of the twelfth-century community, laying the foundations for the growth of a for-

---

12 Francovich and Hodges 2003; Francovich, Ginatempo, and Augenti 2000; Wickham 2005. For more recent updates on the *incastellamento* debate, see *Archeologia Medievale* 2010.

13 The hilltop is currently owned by the 'Communion of Capalbiaccio', established by the Maremma Authority on the land previously belonging to the *Società Anonima Capalbio Redenta Agricola* (SACRA). The land was redistributed to local farmers and the growing co-ownership was turned into a natural reserve open to seasonal hunting activities.

14 On Le Colonne, see Dyson 2002; and on the villa di Giardino, see Celuzza 1985.

15 Dyson 1984, presented his work at Kalamazoo, the largest medieval conference in the USA, and here re-published in the Appendix of this volume.

16 Hobart 1991; Fentress and others 1991; Hobart 1992; Cirelli and Hobart 2003.

- tified village that peaked in the thirteenth and fourteenth centuries.
- Post-medieval farmhouses scattered midway up the Capalbiaccio hill showed the continuation of life after the decline of the town.

The long period of complete abandonment of the site (over ten centuries), despite the hilltop's protected location and abundant supply of water, was similar to what occurred in other sites in central Italy and the Italian peninsula.[17] In the post-Roman period, communities shrank and became self-sustainable, mostly in the plains, trading within a small radial zone.[18] Similarly, this early medieval settlement pattern can be detected once again for the late medieval and modern periods, when abandoned castles were substituted with mid-hill farms, or *casolari*, above the insalubrious coastal marshes of the Maremma, where farming families welcomed the transhumant, seasonal herds of animals. Capalbiaccio's history mirrors the larger Tuscan narrative of settlement patterns flourishing during the Etruscan, Roman, and medieval eras, but with interruptions, up to the present. The lack of urban development, which gave rise to the theory of the Maremma as a place of 'failed cities' in the large rural area of southern Tuscany, will be a question present throughout this book.[19] Seen in its context, the castle of Tricosto retains a vital, if somewhat peripheral, status during much of this time period, even though for only one century — the thirteenth — it could have potentially become a successful city, similar to the nearby Capalbio, or, on a wider scale, Campiglia Marittima.[20]

Much of our research at the site of Capalbiaccio concentrated on non-invasive techniques. The recent phase involved re-analysing the material recovered during Dyson's excavations, the reading and dating of the wall construction techniques, identification of the extension of the site, and finally the discovery of two, an Etruscan and an early medieval, communities. Relatively little new pottery was added, besides that which was discovered during the survey and is discussed in the post-medieval chapter (*infra* Salvadori). The recent campaigns would not have been possible without the collaboration of an excellent team from the University of Siena.

Methodologies and Outline of the Text

In her chapter on the geomorphological traits of Capalbiaccio and the surrounding area, Nicoletta Barocca discusses the hilltop in the context of changes to southwestern coastal Tuscany, at the intersection of the Maremma Grossetana and the Maremma Laziale. Key to the significance of Capalbiaccio is its location between two ample river valleys that contain fertile soil, pasture, and access to wood on and around the hillside. Limestone for building is also plentiful. Unlike Roman Cosa on the coast, Etruscan and medieval Capalbiaccio had fresh water drinking wells (drilled through soft rock), as discovered by Dyson's team. Cosa, by comparison, did not have any wells, and therefore depended more on rainfall. Barocca indicates that Capalbiaccio is also metalliferous — rich in manganese, quartz, and cinnabar (mercury) — which is typical for this part of Tuscany. Our 2010 fieldwork confirmed some of Barocca's findings, as we located Etruscan, Roman, and medieval quarries surrounding the hilltop. The wealth of raw materials and the crucial role played by water in the territory surrounding Capalbiaccio set the stage for the intermittent occupation and abandonment of the site since prehistoric times. Water, which often signed the frontiers among the local communities, was a mixed blessing; while allowing production and growth for one of the richest agricultural valleys in central Italy, when it was too plentiful, it provoked abandonment via malaria, as seen at Cosa (Ansedonia). Much attention is given here to this essential element.

Several more recent mapping and recording techniques have proved very applicable to sites like Capalbiaccio.[21] The geophysical survey adopted magnetometry, which is a type of ground-penetrating radar that detects built structures and other anomalous materials buried up to five meters. Geomagnetic survey is particularly successful at sites that have been abandoned, and do not share complicated, subsequent building phases near or on the surface. Other examples of its usage can be found in different areas of the Mediterranean.[22] The University of Siena has been a pioneer in this field and has continued to make wide use of geophysical survey in projects

---

17 Francovich and Hodges 2003.
18 Vaccaro 2011; Vaccaro 2018.
19 Farinelli 2007.
20 Bianchi 2003c.

21 In the 2010s, magnetometry and other geophysical explorations were starting to be used in Tuscany, in particular electrical resistance survey and sub-surface laser scanning. See Campana, and Piro 2009 for an introduction and the UNISi links for archaeological activities; and Hobart and others 2012.
22 For example, at Ostia Antica ground-penetrating radar exposed the outline of most of the old roman port; see Heinzelmann and others 1997.

in Tuscany at Pava (Montalcino),[23] Buonconvento (Siena),[24] and San Pietro d'Asso (Montalcino).[25]

During the month of January 2009 and the following June 2010, two geophysical surveys took place covering a total of 5100 m² of the hilltop of Tricosto. Quadrants were set both inside and outside the fortified area. The anomalies that emerged from the geophysical survey revealed a whole other chapter in the medieval life of Capalbiaccio. Before the medieval phase a larger, pre-existing settlement was found to cover most of the hilltop. The structures uncovered via the use of ground-penetrating radar face northeast to southwest and northwest to southwest, and thus are at variance of about 45 degrees from the medieval layer. Now, in tandem with a more precise dating of the pottery, the evidence shown from the magnetometry suggests that there was a substantial Etruscan community occupying Capalbiaccio between the sixth and the fifth century BCE.

While drafting a new map of the site, it became increasingly clear that the erosion of the hilltop during the last thirty-five years brought to the surface what seems to be a much larger medieval community within the castle than what had been identified during Dyson's excavations. Further, new alignments of houses were plotted on the map together with the discovery of a second church. Outside of the fortified area, snaking around the hilltop, traces of the ancient road that led to the top to the castle's entrance touched five springs that still provide good drinking water today. This wide road and the *fontanile*, which have both been integrated in the DEM (digital elevation model), followed the natural inclination of the hill and were carved out of the limestone, something which is visible from the magnetometry readings taken outside the main gate of the castle.

With a site of this nature, characterized by a thick layer of wall, collapsed in many parts, within the fortification walls, it is essential to keep in mind that certain contexts remain invisible to the geophysical surveys and their cautious use prevents mistakes due to overly speculative interpretation. One cannot ignore the limited visibility of non-invasive techniques and the time constraints that limit the success of such a method of data collection. In fact, the direct correlation between the intensity of research and the queues of data collected is tied to the amount of time invested on a particular site,

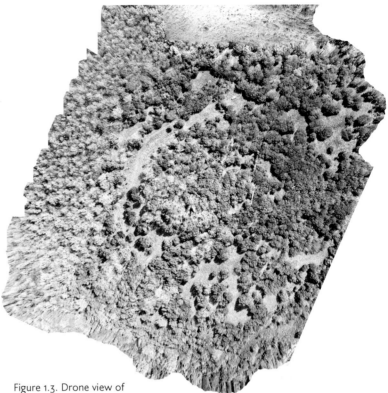

Figure 1.3. Drone view of the hilltop of Capalbiaccio 2021. Photo by Emanuele Mariotti.

which will directly shape the quantity of information gathered.[26] Furthermore, some non-invasive methods, such as aerial photography, drones, and certain forms of geophysical archaeology, yield different results over time, as a result of seasonal environmental factors (Fig. 1.3). Therefore, what we capture in each instance not only allows us to reconstruct the whole history of the landscape under investigation, but rather fragmented capsules of time. These aspects of visibility and variability always need to be taken into account within any form of archaeological investigation.

The geophysical survey was complemented by analysing the masonry techniques employed to construct walls: the detailed study of structural or building archaeology. This other non-invasive technique has particularly been used on medieval walls, because many of them survive above ground. It was during the late 1980s that this new field expanded, with the increased number of medieval castles excavated and studied in Tuscany. Most walls have a story to tell, in much the same way that stratigraphic layers do. It is particularly useful to understand the radical changes in building materials and techniques that

---

23 Campana and others 2005; Campana and others 2008; Campana and others 2009; Campana, Felichi, and Marasco 2005.
24 See the University of Siena report on Santa Cristina (Buonconvento), online at http://archeologiamedievale.unisi.it/santa-cristina/indagine-di-superficie (accessed 22 July 2020).
25 Hobart and others 2012.

26 Cambi and Terrenato 1994; Terrenato 2000; Campana 2009a.

Figure 1.4. View from Tricosto, Capalbiaccio towards the Valle d'Oro, the promontory of Cosa and the Argentario Peninsula. Photo by Hermann Salvadori.

started in the eleventh century, when stone architecture progressively replaced constructions, in wood and other perishable materials, making the archaeology of architecture a key translator for understanding the history of building in the medieval period, without the need for archaeological intervention.

Deriving from the latter, structural archaeology has developed a number of sub-specialties, such as the measurement of building materials, the analysis of wall elevations, the investigation of masonry techniques, and the reading of the different mortars. In addition to these methods, laser scanning, another new tool of geophysical archaeology, can be used to model standing structures. Thus the archaeology of architecture allows us to develop chronological sequencing of manufactured materials, such as bricks and stones, and provide for relative and absolute chronologies. These interpretive readings, further, contribute to reconstructing the social, cultural, and economic factors that are the basis of transformation at a given site.[27] With its wealth of extant medieval villages, castles, and communal urban centres, such as Lucca, Pisa, Siena, and Florence, Tuscany has proven to be, once again, fertile ground for the use of building archaeology.[28]

In her chapter, Irene Corti identifies seven groups of major masonry techniques used at Tricosto, including variations within each type, and dates them. While Dyson's preliminary report discusses two major moments of building — the city wall and the later addition dividing the village in half — correctly indicating the thirteenth century as the high point of the community's life, Corti was able to identify three other major phases (and their variation of sub-categories), which are associated with different workshops operating on site between the twelfth and the fourteenth centuries. All the standing buildings are located on the northern part of the fortification. Since building archaeology has been carried out in southern Maremma, this research provides a further data to compare to the many other Aldobrandeschi castles in the area analysed, and it invites new questions about architectural construction in a wider context that includes not only Tuscany and the neighbouring northern Latium, but also Rome.

Capalbiaccio presented an ideal situation, where data from past excavations could be compared to edited *comparanda*. Our ability to understand the sequence of the site has been greatly augmented as a result of utilizing the two approaches together. The non-invasive research produced excellent results, without undue strain, on our limited human and financial resources. At Capalbiaccio, we discovered structures and made conclusions about building history that were inconceivable in Dyson's era, fortu-

---

27 For a brief history of the evolution of the method, see Gelichi 1997a, 89–109.

28 The scientific journal for the field is *Archeologia dell'Architettura*, which was founded in 1996. See also, Parenti 1986; Bianchi 1996; Quirós Castillo 1999; Bruttini 2013.

nate as we were to have his good records and that of ongoing activities in the region.

The detailed building analyses also raised important issues of structural conservation and site preservation. There is great need for a program of site management at Tricosto because it has already suffered great irreversible damage from earthquakes and bombing during World War II, and continues to deteriorate. Another aim of this book is to raise awareness about these conditions, so as to attract the attention of those who have the resources to protect this site. Ideally, a larger initiative such as an archaeological park would be developed to preserve the historical heritage of the region.[29]

A combination of old and new approaches has also been applied to the study of the different categories of material culture found at Capalbiaccio.[30] Our knowledge of Etruscan and medieval pottery has advanced greatly since the days of the initial Capalbiaccio excavations. Both types and production centres are now much better known. They have also provided information on the distribution of different ratios of ceramic types within medieval settlement patterns. Other categories of material culture were also investigated, such as a small, but illustrative series, of coins (*infra* Rovelli). Finally, in a decision unusual for the 1970s, excavators saved animal bones from all parts of the site. Their analysis provides insight into continuity and change in the use of animal resources (*infra* Crader).

This book seeks to demonstrate how the application of these different tools and strategies can deepen our knowledge of a site and its surroundings (Fig. 1.4). It also endeavours to encourage a return to excavations undertaken by others, and to dispel the fear of challenges that inevitably accompany an already excavated context. It is our hope that the full publication of the site report on the campaigns at Tricosto, Capalbiaccio will prove the merits of the methods we espouse, ignite new debates, and contribute further understanding of Etruscan and medieval settlements in southern Tuscany.

---

29 The project of unifying local archaeological sites in one archaeological park has been an idea proposed by many, starting with Carandini in the 1980s at Orbetello on the occasion of the opening of five Etruscan exhibitions in, later discussed by Francovich and Dyson, and more recently by a team under Maria Grazia Celuzza, when she was director of the Archaeological Museum of Grosseto. The project was also presented at Capalbio, to no avail; see Celuzza and Luzzetti 2013.
30 Fentress, Perkins 1988; Fentress and others 2004.

STEPHEN L. DYSON

2. Capalbiaccio: The Initial Archaeological Campaigns (1976–1980)

ABSTRACT In this contribution, Stephen L. Dyson describes the impetus behind, and motivations for, carrying out the three initial archaeological campaigns at Capalbiaccio, situating the work that he directed in the context of the time and place in which the work was undertaken. He outlines the survey work carried out by teams from Wesleyan University in the surrounding *Ager Cosanus* and explains how it led to the first excavation of a medieval castle in Tuscany and to the origin of medieval archaeology in Italy. Dyson provides his own overview of the site and what attracted him to it, as well as a summary of his team's findings, which can also be found in the primary article he authored, which is reproduced in Appendix 4 of this volume.

In 1976 a team of surveyors and excavators, mainly from Wesleyan University, started topographical work, building analysis, and selected excavations at the site of Capalbiaccio in the *Ager Cosanus*. It was continued in the summer of 1978 and 1980. The season of 1978, supported by a grant from the National Endowment for the Humanities, was the most extensive. At the end of the 1980 season, I felt that our immediate questions had been answered. Since we did not have the resources to undertake the massive interdisciplinary studies that the complex site clearly required, I decided to suspend excavations. These have been resumed and considerably expanded by Dr Michelle Hobart and a team from the University of Siena. The results of their research comprise the bulk of this volume. However, it seems appropriate that in a volume that publishes the results of their research some description be provided of the background, motivation, methods, and preliminary results of those earlier excavations.

My initial involvement with the Cosa/Ansedonia area came with my research on the utilitarian pottery, which had been unearthed during the many years of excavation at the urban site. Not only did it provide me with an interesting research project on collection of material then little studied, but also allowed me to observe the intellectual framework, methodology, results, and sociology of the excavations. The Cosa excavations as conducted for most of their history by Professor Frank E. Brown were superb exercises in the then standard conceptualization and execution of Roman urban archaeology. Stratigraphy, structural analysis, and architectural reconstruction were superbly handled. Systematic studies of the major categories of material culture were undertaken. As one would expect given the era and the emphases of classical archaeology, there had been little interest in environmental archaeology, faunal and floral studies, or in the investigation of the post-classical remains.

The sociology of the excavations assigned long-term roles to the various staff members. It was assumed that an 'artefacts specialist' remained in a certain area of material culture study and made it a lifetime pursuit. An amphora person was always an amphora person, and the pursuit of black glaze required a lifetime of dedication. There was little opportunity at the central site of Cosa for a utilitarian pottery expert like myself to pursue wider horizons. For that reason, with the completion and publication of my study on the Cosan utilitarian pottery, I turned my research interests elsewhere.

Several seasons of villa/rural homestead excavation in the late 1960s and early 1970s at Buccino (SA) under the initial guidance of Professor R. Ross Holloway of Brown University introduced me to the world of Roman rural history and rural archaeology. While the history and structures of the Roman countryside was already a subject of considerable research and controversy among ancient historians, especially those interested by Marxism, systematic rural archaeological studies were still very limited. Roman rural archaeology continued to be largely 'villa archaeology'. The significance of more wide ranging studies, such as the British School at Rome South Etruria rural surveys and excavations was only beginning to be appreciated.

During those same years American classical archaeology operated in a disciplinary world largely separate from that of North American anthropological archaeology. That was a period of ferment associated with the 'New Archaeology' or 'Processual Archaeology'. The orientation toward a more 'scientific approach', the emphasis on more refined method and the experimental use of theory was not much appreciated in Classical Archaeology. Nor was the interest in extensive survey, settlement studies, and diachronic reconstructions of society development based largely on archaeological data.

In North American classical archaeology such extensive survey research was largely limited to the pre-classical time periods. The most successful project of that era was William MacDonald's extensive survey research and diachronic settlement reconstruction in the Western Peloponnese. However, in an era where North American classical archaeology was dominated by large scale excavations, the significance of MacDonald's survey research was not widely appreciated.

The situation was different for British archaeologists, especially for those working in Italy in Italy. Shortly after World War II archaeologists associated with the British School at Rome had begun systematic survey work around Etruscan Veii. John Ward Perkins, long director of the British School, guided that project. While classical archaeology in Italy was still dominated by large, fixed site excavations, certain archaeologists like myself came to appreciate the potential of survey in providing new research tools for reconstructing the Roman, pre-Roman, and post-Roman countryside. It was also a research approach that required fewer resources than a 'big site' excavation, and could be conducted beyond the limits of sometimes rigid national permit systems.

The *Ager Cosanus* seemed like an ideal candidate for such research. However, during all of the years of the American excavations at Cosa, little attention had been paid to the extensive countryside, the *Ager Cosanus*, where most of the colonial settlers lived. That was especially regrettable, since the zone around Cosa had seen extensive land redistribution after World War II. That had meant the resettlement of the countryside with small farms and the introduction of mechanized agriculture. Extensive deep ploughing made the area ideal for survey archaeology. However, until the start of the Wesleyan University surveys no systematic rural research had been undertaken.

During the summers 1972–1976 teams from Wesleyan University conducted surveys in different parts of the ancient *Ager Cosanus*. From that research we were able to make the first settlement reconstructions of the Cosan countryside. Our rural research overlapped with the start of Professor Andrea Carandini's own surveys in the *Ager Cosanus*, which grew out of his Sette Finestre project. As a result of both the American and the British-Italian projects the *Ager Cosanus* went from being a little explored archaeological territory to one of the best known archaeological landscapes in Italy.

One of the most important and innovative aspects of the *Ager Veiantanus* surveys had been their emphasis on the study and reconstruction of settlement history and landscape use over long periods of time. Their reconstruction of that regional history started with the earliest prehistoric evidence and continued through the Middle Ages. It fitted in with the emphasis on the *longue durée*, which had been emphasized by historians working in the *Annales* tradition. The creation of long term, diachronic histories had also been the aim of many 'processual' archaeological studies in the New World. The *Ager Veiantanus* project represented one of the first in Italy, and influenced how we approached our research in the countryside of Cosa. It was especially important in directing us to undertake research in medieval archaeology.

Interest in a 'scientific' Italian medieval archaeology was just beginning when we started our research at Capalbiaccio. More British medieval archaeologists had begun working in Italy. They brought to Italy lessons and approaches drawn from a discipline of medieval archaeology that had a long, if variegated, history in the United Kingdom. North American archaeologists seeking to do Medieval Archaeology in the Mediterranean had very few precedents. There had developed an important tradition of medieval architectural studies, which involved some archaeology, but those scholars had mainly worked north of the Alps. Some Byzantine archaeology had been undertaken by Americans working at Corinth and the Athenian Agora, but it was a small, marginal sub-discipline.

Even among the Italians a medieval archaeology, which was a 'real archaeology' and not research based essentially on art and architectural analysis had seen only limited development. Indicative of that is the fact that the journal *Archeologia Medievale*, designed to give the emerging discipline a new level of professionalism, started publishing only in 1974.

The excavation history at Cosa reflected that limited interest in post-Roman archaeology. While the site at Cosa had yielded considerable evidence for medieval occupation, the archaeologists of the Frank Brown era, focused on the history of the Roman colony, had paid relatively little attention to those remains. Some material was saved for study by later investigators. A considerable amount was displaced.

When the Wesleyan team started at Capalbiaccio the medieval archaeological excavations conducted by Elizabeth Fentress and Michelle Hobart were still in the future.

Several factors led me as director of the Wesleyan Archaeological Program in the *Ager Cosanus* to expand our research into the medieval period and to complement the survey approach with excavation. The Archaeology Program at Wesleyan was an interdisciplinary one with participation by colleagues from Classics, Anthropology, and Art History. Diana Crader, who researched the animal bone analysis for this volume, was a member of the group. Among scholars in Art History and History there was strong interest in the medieval period.

There was at that moment in North America a developing interest in expanding the range of research in medieval studies and that included a developing interest in archaeology. Scholars working on the Early Middle Ages, especially in England and France, had long drawn on the expertise of their archaeological colleagues. The *Annales* School, which was having increased influence in many areas of North American Medieval Studies, encouraged approaches which drew on archaeological evidence.

Still there were almost no established American medieval field projects in Europe. The major exception was the field programme that Carole Crumley was launching in Burgundy. Crumley was an Iron Age specialist with a strong background in both anthropology and classical studies. She established a truly *longue durée* research agenda, whose chronological range extended from prehistory to the present and embraced specialized studies from settlement archaeology to folklore and historic landscapes.

That state of development of medieval archaeology in the United States in the late 1970s and early 1980s is captured in the collection of papers *Archaeological Approaches to Medieval Europe*, edited by Kathleen Biddick. They were first presented at the Kalamazoo Medieval Conference in 1978 and published in 1981. The majority of papers were British/North European in focus and rural in subject matter. Only two dealt with the Mediterranean, one being my own report on Capalbiaccio. Clearly in taking the *Ager Cosanus* into the medieval period, we as North Americans were entering into relatively unexplored territory (Fig. 2.1).

The next question was how to focus a research programme on the medieval *Ager Cosanus*. Our field surveys had indicated that the rural data from the medieval era would be very thin on the ground, and the type of reconstructions which we did for the Roman period would be difficult, if not impossible. While the urban site of Cosa had already yielded con-

Figure 2.1. View from Capalbiacio of the Valle d'Oro looking north-west towards the promontory of Cosa and the Argentario Peninsula facing the Tyrrhenian Sea. This fertile portion of land had traces of the centuriazion and remains of first-century Roman villas. Photo by Dyson's Team, reproduced with permission.

Figure 2.2. View of the Capalbiaccio Hilltop from the Roman villa of Giardino looking north-east at the partition wall inside the fortification. Photo by Dyson's Team, reproduced with permission.

siderable quantities of medieval material, the excavators working there were focused on the Roman period. Some combination of a village and fortification site seemed most feasible. Within the territory of the *Ager Cosanus* the hilltop fortified settlement of Capalbiaccio appeared to be our best option.

A focus on a fortified settlement like Capalbiaccio would also contribute to emerging research agendas both in medieval history and in medieval archaeology. In 1973 the French scholar Pierre Toubert had published his *Les structures du Latium medieval* with its emphasis on the role that castle/communities played in shaping the human landscape of medieval Latium. It encouraged not only historical research, but also archaeological investigations focused on castle sites. There the seminal investigations of David Andrew proved useful.

It was clear from the beginning that the fortified community at Tricosto/Capalbiaccio would be the ideal site for our investigations. Both the written and the visual documentation on the post-Roman *Ager Cosanus* indicated that it had been a centre of considerable importance in region during the later Middle Ages. It was in some respects the medieval successor to Cosa as the dominant settlement in the area (Fig. 2.2).

Figure 2.3. Interior elevation of the eastern fortification wall. Photo by Hermann Salvadori.

Figure 2.4. Partition wall dividing the fortified village. Photo by Hermann Salvadori.

Figure 2.5. Part of the gate of a possible entrance into the northern fortified area. Photo by Dyson's Team, reproduced with permission.

The defining feature of the site was the oval boundary wall, which enclosed a settlement of considerable area. The wall was unevenly preserved (Fig. 2.3). Some sections remained intact up to the sentry walkways, while others showed little more than the foundations. Interpreting the meaning of those differentiations in preservation was then and remains one of the key questions in the archaeology of Capalbiaccio

The area enclosed by the oval boundary wall was divided into two sectors by a division wall, which had been completed up to the walkways (Fig. 2.4). The southern sector, which consisted of about 1/3 of the settlement area had only thin scatters of rubble visible on the surface. There were no structure walls or other habitation features within that sector. The soil was very thin and survey yielded few artefacts. However, detailed study of the perimeter and transect walls in that area showed two features worthy of investigation. At the south end of the west wall there was a slight indentation visible on the surface. It seemed likely that it represented one of the gates that provided entrance into the complex.

The other distinctive feature stood at the centre of the transverse wall (Fig. 2.5). The two halves of the wall ran toward each other, but ended in a slight offset. That created a gap between them as though some type of gate between the north and the south sections had been contemplated, but never completed (Fig. 2.6).

The northern sector, which enclosed two-thirds of the area within the wall was very different. The remains of a number of buildings were scattered over much of the surface. Preservation ranged from foundations only to some walls, which were intact up to the original roof line. Several of the structures in the central area of the North Sector were similar in plan and seemed to form the core of a village. In the northwest part near the perimeter wall was an especially well preserved rectangular structure (Fig. 2.7a–b, Building J).

Some remains were defensive more than residential. Near Building J were the collapsed fragments of a heavily fortified structure, which we designated the 'keep tower'. Fragments from that tower were scattered around, as if impacted by some heavy force. The geologist with the project suggested that the collapse might have been caused by an earthquake. Much of this part of the site was covered by vegetation including a number of trees and bushes. Obviously that posed a challenge to our work, but also indicated the presence of deep soils, which might have recoverable stratigraphy.

Capalbiaccio was clearly a large and complicated site. The resources we had to execute the project were limited, so we had to design our research strategies carefully, and focus on activities that would yield the most results with the least expenditure of limited resources. We had a small dig crew, and the site did not lend itself to the use of mechanical equipment.

The first objective was to undertake a preliminary survey of the site that would provide us with a map of the standing remains. That was before the days of total stations, satellite imaging, and GPS. All we had was the high-altitude photographs from World War II and the information on the 1:25,000 IGM maps. Our survey was executed using a theodolite and tapes. Sight lines had to be cut through often thick vegetation. The more recent mapping surveys used in other sections of this study have obviously improved on our first, primitive results. However, that initial survey, whatever its limitations, provided a working plan of the site which we could use, as we worked to recover the architectural development of the site designed our excavation strategies.

Time and resources limited the number of actual excavations, which had to be selected carefully. We decided to clear the open area at the end of the two transverse wall sections. We assumed that we would find there the foundations of the gate structure, which controlled access to the two parts of the castle. The results were unexpected. What we actually unearthed were the foundations and lower walls of a small chapel. It had clearly preceded the construction of the transverse wall, and later had largely been demolished with the lower remains incorporated into the wall structure (Fig. 2.8). The chapel had a single entrance and a small apse. The soil within the chapel walls was sterile with no burials and almost nothing in the way of artefacts. Our hypothesis about its history was that the chapel represented an early phase of medieval occupation at the site. The building may have preceded any wall construction and certainly the building of the transverse wall.

Rubble and thick vegetation that covered much of the 'village' area made surface survey difficult and on the whole unprofitable. Our decision about where to dig could not be guided by concentrations of surface artefacts. We decided to concentrate on excavations within several of the extant building areas. The results were mixed. Soundings in the buildings in the core 'village' area showed very shallow fill, but produced a certain number of artefacts including pottery and coinage. They included a chess piece, which was our only indicator of refined leisure activities at Capalbiaccio. The ceramic and numismatic evidence placed our occupation in the later medieval phase of the use of the site.

The excavations at Building J in the northwest sector of the site produced very different results

Figure 2.6. Building J. Compare the different state of the building: a) 1978. Photo by Dyson's Team, reproduced with permission. b) 2010.

and proved key for our understanding of the site. The structure itself was impressively intact. Its rear was built right up to the exterior fortification wall, while the entrance faced inward toward the village. The entrance portal was largely intact. The north wall was preserved up to the second storey, which had a row of intact niches.

The stratigraphy of the interior of the building proved to be very different from that of the other buildings that we sounded. There was a thick medieval occupation layer, filled with artefacts, faunal material, and seeds. It ended in a hard packed *terra*

Figure 2.7. Church A during excavation, with the partition wall abutting it. Photo by Dyson's Team, reproduced with permission.

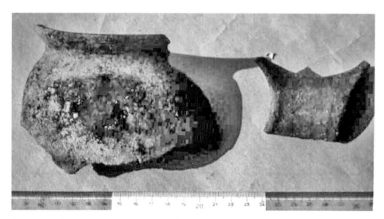

Figure 2.8. Diagnostic pottery found in 1978. Photo by Dyson's Team, reproduced with permission.

rossa layer, very different from the bedrock found in our excavation of the houses in the 'village'.

That compact *terra rossa* suggested that we had reached the end of the occupation fill. However, we decided to take one test pit down deep into the *terra rossa*. The upper sections proved to be sterile, but we decided to take at least one survey down to bedrock. However, we found that it ended not at bedrock, but at the top of another thick layer of occupation debris, the richest discovered at the site. Artefacts were mixed with thick deposits of seeds and animal bones. However, there were no coins, glass, glazed pottery sherds, or other distinctively medieval artefacts. Most of the pottery that was unearthed was undecorated cooking ware. The thick layer of *terra rossa* clearly indicated a break in occupation of considerable length. The important question was how long?

Again it is worth remembering how little was known about Italian medieval artefacts including ceramics. The refined typologies, fabric studies, and dating which are evident in other parts of this book did not exist at that time. Pioneering studies like that of David Whitehouse and Otto Mazzucato on Forum Ware were just being studied. Our initial inclination was to label lower level as early medieval (Fig. 2.9). However, the identification of a few decorated sherds suggested that we were dealing with Etruscan or even earlier levels. Occupation at Capalbiaccio clearly ended in the later Middle Ages. It began centuries earlier in the Iron Age.

Limitations of resources and shifting research agendas within the excavation leadership forced us to end our project with the third season (second full excavation season). We felt that we had determined the parameters of the occupation history. We suggested that the initial occupation came in the Iron Age-Etruscan period. The first medieval occupation was a village with houses, a small keep, and a church. The main fortification circuit came later. Its construction development was uneven. The foundations of the full circuit were completed. However, only certain sectors were completed up to the walkway. We do not know the reasons for this discontinuity. It was probably related to the last occupation history of the site and the events that determined its abandonment.

In contrast the transverse wall was largely completed up to its walkways. Only the area where the foundations of the church were found was left open. Very probably, that gap was to be plugged by a gate structure that was never built. The thick mound of earth that covered the church remains may have represented the remnants of an earth bank designed to defend the site at that weak point. The impressive transverse wall would have been visible from the sea and have discouraged maritime raiders from climbing up to a castle, which they would have found poorly defended.

This essay is designed to present the excavation strategies and results, as they emerged in the seasons of the initial excavations. Such a presentation is important. Much of the material presented in this book represents new research strategies and new information deriving in large part from 'museum archaeology', that is taking material from an old excavation, documented by old and often inadequate records, and relating it to interpretations developed decades later. These pages document that archaeological baseline from which all of the later research began. This is a pioneering project that has benefitted from the serendipitous conditions and unique collaboration of two different generations operating in the same space. Without Dr Michelle Hobart's leadership, perseverance, and rigorous investigation of both the material and records of our campaigns, this project would have been relegated to the long list of unpublished excavations.

PART II

Recent Research and Non-Invasive Archaeology

NICOLETTA BAROCCA

3. Geo-Archaeology of Coastal Southern Tuscany

ABSTRACT Geographically, the key factor in the reversal of fortunes of settlements in coastal Maremma has been the extent to which their inhabitants have been able to contain the spread of marshes. Land reclamations completed during the Roman era, the Renaissance, and the early twentieth century have enabled the area to flourish agriculturally. But when the marshes were left untamed, mosquito-borne malaria caused significant depopulation and stagnation: a backwater. In subsequent chapters, we will discuss the conditions that led political actors to concentrate resources in concerted efforts to reclaim lands.

After World War II, Ferdinando Castagnoli surveyed the Albegna Valley and published his results, prior to Stephen L. Dyson's surveys and excavation in the late 1970s. Both had a focus on the Roman occupation and the exploitation of the Etruscan region. Since then, several extensive surveys have taken place, allowing for territorial reconstruction of changes in settlements and land use over a long period of time. Nicoletta Barocca, in this chapter, uses such an approach by also analysing a bounty of historical cartography. She discusses Capalbiaccio (Tricosto) in context of changes of southwestern coastal Tuscany, at the intersection of the Maremma Grossetana and the Maremma Laziale.

The hilltop site (or *poggio*) of Capalbiaccio is located between two ample river valleys that contain fertile soil, pasture, and access to wood in and around the hillside. Limestone for building is also plentiful. Unlike Roman Cosa on the coast, Etruscan and medieval Capalbiaccio had fresh water drinking wells (drilled through soft rock). Cosa, by comparison did not have any wells, and therefore depended more on rainfall. As mentioned, the soil composition is excellent for farming on both the north and south sides of the hill. Barocca indicates that Capalbiaccio is also metalliferous — rich in manganese, quartz and cinnabar (mercury) — which is typical for this part of Tuscany. Our 2010 fieldwork confirmed some of Barocca's findings, as we located Etruscan, Roman, and medieval quarries surrounding the hilltop.

In sum, the geomorphological traits on and around Capalbiaccio facilitated its reoccupation in the medieval period, following the shift from highland to lowland dwelling in classical times, when the Etruscans merged with Romans in cities like Cosa and in the villas that flourished in the Albegna Valley. The wealth of raw materials and the crucial role played by water in the Capalbiaccio territory set the premises for intermittent occupation and abandonment from prehistoric times. Water, which often signed the frontiers among the local communities, was a mixed blessing; while allowing production and growth for one of the richest agricultural valleys in central Italy, it provoked abandonment via malaria when overabundant, as seen at Cosa (Ansedonia). Much attention is given here to this essential element.

Barocca's study adds the following new insights to understanding Capalbiaccio, upon which Dyson could only speculate in the 1970s. They are:

1. A picture of the geophysical nature of the Capalbiaccio region
2. Mineral and water resources
3. A description of the swamps and coast lagoons (notable waters)
4. Navigable rivers in antiquity
5. Reclamation projects for the use of water in modern and more recent times
6. Hypothetical reconstruction of the coastal water basin of the *Ager Cosanus* [MH]

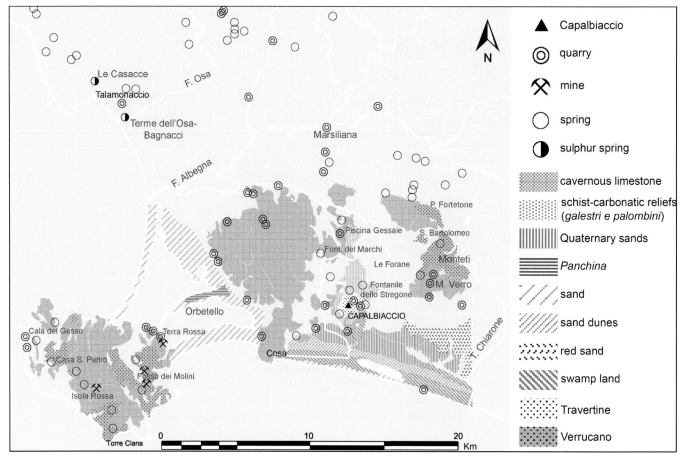

Figure 3.1. Geological map of southern Tuscany. Map by author.

Overview of Geological Features (Fig. 3.1)

The area under consideration is the stretch of the Tyrrhenian coast extending from the mouth of the Chiarone to the hilltop of Uccellina Park, with particular focus on the zone closest to Poggio Capalbiaccio.

Preliminary analysis of the geological map reveals that in addition to alluvial sediments, this area consists mostly of sedimentary rock (cavernous limestone and calcitic dolomites) and acidic metamorphic rock (quartz and quartzite).[1]

Uccellina Park and the Monte Argentario — essentially an island connected to the coast by only two sandy littoral belts (the tombolo of Giannella and the tombolo of Feniglia) on either side of the lagoon of Orbetello — are the two principal hilly ranges in this region, which correspond to a basin created by a tectonic depression.[2]

The most ancient terrains to surface in Tuscany — those made up of Verrucano[3] — emerge in three elevated groups in this area: the mountains of Capalbio (Monteti and Poggio Fortetone), Uccellina, and Monte Argentario.[4] Tuscan Verrucano is currently identified as belonging to the Upper Triassic.[5] The other formation attributable to the Upper Triassic is cavernous limestone, a deposit of calcareous breccia created largely from limestone and dolomites, with a structure consisting of 'cellules'.[6] These types of terrains flourished extensively in the mountainous band of southern Tuscany, including the mounds east of Orbetello, which are constituted entirely of cav-

---

1 Cocozza and others 1968; Signorini 1967; Carandini and others 2002, 30–31; Calastri 2007, 45–46.
2 Signorini 1967, 10; Mazzini and others 1999, 290–91; Boschian and others 2006, 164–67.
3 Verrucano is named after Monte Verruca in Tuscany. It denotes a rocky formation that consists of a quartzose conglomerate characteristic of the continental coastal environment, varying in colour from a purplish red to a greyish green, very strong (c. 1000 m), and widespread in Tuscany. See Manzoni 1968, ad voc. 'Verrucano'.
4 Signorini 1967, 10–11.
5 The first period of the Mesozoic era, which is deemed to have lasted for 30 to 40 million years, depending on the author. In absolute dates, it fell between 182 and 152 million years ago. The Triassic is subdivided into early, middle, and late.
6 McCann and others 1987, 18.

ernous limestone, and the mountains of Capalbio, which abound in all the deposits typical of the 'reduced series' of metalliferous Tuscany: Verrucano, Cavernoso, and the limestone/slate group[7] (Marl and Palombini),[8] which rests directly on cavernous limestone.[9] In addition to Marl and Palombini, the north slope of Poggio Capalbiaccio also contains travertine, a rather soft limestone when cut, but one that hardens rapidly and feeds various stone caves.[10] To the south, the seaside, dunes, lagoons, and marshes of the coastal terrain date to the Quaternary period[11] and extend between the mountainous strip and the sea.[12]

The landscape inland from the coast, which is low and sandy up to the promontory of Ansedonia, undulates frequently. In Antiquity, the most typical feature of this stretch of the Tyrrhenian coast must have been the lagoon that extended from Ansedonia to Pescia Romana and occupied the depression between the line of the older inner dunes and that of the more recent ones along the sea.[13] The older dunes are coastal ridges composed of brown sand, more or less hardened into a type of conchitic limestone (*panchina*), which likewise crops up on the coast to the north and east of Lake Burano.[14]

Mineral and Water Resources

Various forms of mineralization have occurred as a result of the tension faults (*faglie di distensione*) that characterize the area's tectonics. In the area around Capalbio, there are many spots with abundant lode quartz (magmatic rock that crystallizes at great depths).[15] At Monte Argentario, the most important areas of mineralization occur on the eastern slopes: pyrites and chalcopyrites can be found in the vicinity of Fosso dei Molini; another deposit has been identified beneath the manganese mine at the site of Terra Rossa; and small quantities of cinnabar have been found in the area of Olmo-Casa San Pietro.[16] Furthermore, a lens particularly rich in magnetite, still being used in the 1960s, was found on the sandy coast near Lake Burano.[17]

Gypsum, a material associated with cavernous limestone, can be found on the west coast of Argentario (at the site of Cala del Gesso), in the Uccellina, and near Capalbio (Piscina Gessaie, Monte Verro, and the slopes of Poggio Capalbiaccio).[18] In the cavernous areas, there are also frequent pits of rubble, one of which lies on the northeast side of Monte Argentario. Travertine quarries at Capalbiaccio and Marsiliana also contain substantial gravel pits.[19]

The valleys of Albegna and Oro, the geological structures of which belong to the Quatenary era, are constituted, for the most part, of clay-rich soil created by the weathering of local limestone.[20] At certain points, springs can well up (at least five have been identified in the Valle d'Oro alone)[21] thanks to the existence of clay lenses. Large parts of the valleys are covered by alluvial deposits of more or less recent origin, which owe their existence to the overflow of watercourses.[22] If irrigated, these deep grounds are extremely fertile for differentiated crops; if neglected or abandoned, they quickly turn into bogs.[23]

In the thalwegs (the lowest elevation line within the valley), soil fairly rich in nutrients predominates, while along separate stretches of the slopes, there is some coarse and rocky terrains, as well as *terra rossa* (red clay soil), created by the disintegration of cavernous limestone (*calcare cavernoso*), which have all been used for the cultivation of olives and vineyards.[24] This formation is characterized by a heightened permeability that results in the inevitable lack of springs and watercourses. It also produces karstic

---

7   Slate is a metamorphic rock derived from the transformation of argillaceous rocks; metamorphic agents (temperature and pressure) cause recrystallization and a new mechanical orientation of clay minerals, which leads to marked schistosity (*galetstri* e *palombini*) in the final product. For this reason, slate is easily split along its parallel surfaces. This property makes it suitable for covering houses, as is evident in slate roofs. See Manzoni 1968, *ad voc*. 'Argilloscisti'.

8   Marls are slates that are either more or less rich in silica; Palombini is a siliceous limestone. See Manzoni 1968, *ad voc*. 'galestri;' 'palombini'.

9   Signorini 1967, 10–12; Mazzanti 1983, 542; Boschian and others 2006, 167.

10 Signorini 1967, 19.

11 Quaternary (or Neozoic) indicates the most recent geological era (the one in which we live), which began in the late Pliocene, c. 2588 million years ago. See Manzoni 1968, *ad voc*. 'Quaternario'; Mazzini and others 1999.

12 Signorini 1967, 10; Mazzanti 1983, 542–43; Boschian and others 2006, 162–63.

13 Signorini 1967, 19–20; McCann and others 1987, 18–19; Boschian and others 2006, 159–60.

14 Signorini 1967, 19; Mazzanti 1983, 542; Boschian and others 2006, 162–63.

---

15 Signorini 1967, 23.

16 Signorini 1967, 23.

17 Signorini 1967, 20–23.

18 Signorini 1967, 24.

19 Signorini 1967, 24.

20 Signorini 1967, 19–20; Mazzini and others 1999, 290–91; Calastri 2007, 45–46.

21 Signorini 1967, 19–20; which ones they are is not specifically indicated.

22 Mazzanti 1983, 540; Boschian and others 2006, 159.

23 Carandini and others 2002, 30.

24 Lotti 1891, 19–21; Mori 1932, 121; Signorini 1967, 20; McCann and others 1987, 18; Carandini and others 2002, 30–31; Boschian and others 2006, 159; Calastri 2007, 45–46.

phenomena (dolinas),[25] which can be found particularly in the mounds of Orbetello.[26]

The main springs are found in the oldest terrains, where there is contact between Verrucano and cavernous limestone; at Monte Argentario, springs can be found in Fosso dei Molini to the west of Porto Ercole, at Ciana, and at Casa San Pietro above Porto Santo Stefano.[27] The valleys of Capalbio and the Radicata channel are rich in surface waters, including the spring known as Fontanile dello Stregone, north of Capabiaccio. The karstic nature of the soil turns it into a natural reservoir for rainwater and a collector of the subterranean veins of the thalweg that flow out from the subsoil in tiny troughs along the edges of the mounds.[28]

In the Roman era, the problem of water purveyance in the *Ager Cosanus* was resolved with the construction of public and private cisterns, even in villas.[29] Aqueducts too existed in the territory, such as the one running from Orbetello to Monte Argentario along the present road that links the two and cuts across the lagoon (the so-called *Diga*). When this road was built in 1841, the remains of the ancient structure were still visible.[30]

The remains of an aqueduct inside the Le Forane landholding, in the district of Monte Nebbiello, attest to the fact that the springs of the region were active and exploited in the Roman period.[31] Recent examinations conducted at Le Colonnine, where Doro Levi located the aqueduct in 1927, have succeeded in distinguishing not only the remains of the aqueduct described by Levi, but also other traces attributable to a second structure, hitherto unknown, but one that was probably part of the same water system.[32]

The aforementioned remains are located in the vicinity of the present Fosso delle Colonette, approximately 800 m to the east of the Giardino road, and are composed of a series of quadrangular masonry bases (presently eleven are visible) that rise approximately 24 cm from the ground level and follow a linear course for about 93 m.[33] The structures of the second water complex have been identified at the site of Fontanile Secco, to the southeast of the Colonette aqueduct, and pertain to an underground conduit.[34] Here there are remains of a barrel-vaulted cement cistern faced with *opus incertum* and composed of calcareous rock, into which two water conduits flow.[35] On the exterior, it is possible to follow the course of the subterranean conduit, which is distinguishable along the road excavated towards the east. Around 60 m further, towards the mountain, in the vicinity of the abandoned water trough after which the site is named, there is a fissure, through which it is possible to see the conduit's interior. Most likely, the fount, possibly of medieval origin, received the ancient water structure's man-made water conduit.[36]

The area around Capalbio, on the other hand, must have been more arid. We learn from a sixteenth-century document that its inhabitants travelled more than 2 miles to obtain water from the spring of San Bartolomeo on the slope of the mound of Monteti.[37]

Some shallow lakes lie in the area, but, having been exploited for irrigation, they are less extensive than they formerly would have been. These include: Lake San Floriano at the mouth of the valley of Capalbio, Lake Acquato, Lake Scuro, and the Cutignolo (by this point dried out), as well as some artificially created ones, most notably Lake Uccellina, and water basins known as *piscine* (fishponds), such as Piscina Gessaie.[38] The water from these lakes is excellent for the cultivation of crops, as its temperature approaches that of the atmosphere, thus making it warmer than the water from the springs.[39]

One of the reasons for the success of the port at the Roman colony of Cosa (Portus Cosanus) was, in fact, the availability of freshwater resources.[40] While the city of Cosa (founded in 273 BCE) and the neighbouring Portus Herculis (present-day Porto Ercole) on the Argentario must have relied on rainwater, the port of Cosa had numerous springs that provided abundant drinking water for ships, sailors, and various industries, such as the production of amphoras, wine, and farmed fish, as well as providing for a facility to salt-cure fish (Fig. 3.2).[41]

Finally, there are two thermal springs in the area of Talamone: one at the site of Bagnacci, near

---

25 A dolina is a depression of a circular form that often occurs in calcareous terrain and is caused by karstic corrosion or the subsidence of subterranean cavities. See Zingarelli, Dogliotti, and Rosiello 1997, *ad voc.* 'dolina'.
26 Lotti 1891, 19–21; Venerosi Pesciolini 1925, 53–59; Signorini 1967, 24–25; Calastri 2007, 45–46.
27 Signorini 1967, 24.
28 Calastri 2007, 46.
29 Brown 1951, 84.
30 Raveggi 1933, 55.
31 Levi 1927; Carandini and others 2002, 30–33; Calastri 2007, 45–55.
32 Calastri 2007, 45–55.
33 Calastri 2007, 45–51.
34 Calastri 2007, 51.
35 Calastri 2007, 51–53.
36 Calastri 2007, 53.
37 Venerosi Pesciolini 1925, 53–59.
38 Calastri 2007, 54–55.
39 Carandini and others 2002, 31; Mori 1932, 6.
40 McCann 1979, 393.
41 McCann 1979, 391–94.

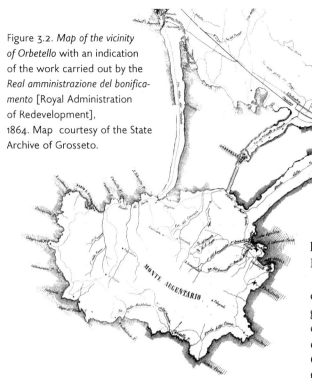

Figure 3.2. *Map of the vicinity of Orbetello* with an indication of the work carried out by the *Real amministrazione del bonificamento* [Royal Administration of Redevelopment], 1864. Map courtesy of the State Archive of Grosseto.

the mound of Talamonaccio and the mouth of the still-extant Osa River (alongside the Via Aurelia); the other gushes out by the slope of the Uccellina, at the site of Casacce on the estate of San Giuseppe, in the area created by the early twentieth-century land reclamation.[42]

Swamps and Coastal Lagoons

The Maremma coast can be defined as a 'barrier coast', that is, as characterized by coastal lagoons that came into being after the sea's action caused the littoral belts to surface.[43] On the strip of coast south of Cosa, there are two such belts.[44] The one closer to shore contains ancient dunes that date to the Pleistocene era. Behind them, a vast lagoon has taken shape,[45] the expanse of which is made up of peaty and detrital lands that are 10 m below sea level, and which likewise contain Lake San Floriano and the Bassa swamp.[46] Still visible in late nineteenth-century maps, these are the remains of the lagoon that must have already disappeared in the Prehistoric era (Fig. 3.2).[47]

The sand and gravel deposits have a breadth of 2 km, maximum, and testify to the historic progression of the coastline.[48] Running parallel to this coast, there is a second belt composed of more recent dunes that can be dated to the final ice age of the Quaternary period. The depression between the two belts was filled with another lagoon, which ran from the promontory of Cosa to the mouth of the Tafone, and of which only Lake Burano remains today (Fig. 3.3).[49]

The lagoons have been an important resource in the area since Antiquity. On the coast of the Vulci, the range of settlements since the Neolithic era seems to have privileged the shore on the lee side of the littoral belt, which is separated from it by a system of coastal lagoons and near watercourses.[50]

The peak exploitation of these water resources occurred in the Roman period, with the establishment of farms for the intensive breeding of fish for salt curing and the production of garum. It is not by accident that the principal types of fish (mullet, in particular) still present today are the very same mentioned by ancient authors (Varro, Columella).[51]

Portus Cosanus lies on the western slope of the promontory of Cosa (Ansedonia) (formed of cavernous limestone), while the adjacent fish pools are connected to the lagoon.[52] The port area was in con-

---

42 Lotti 1891, 26–28.
43 Perkins 1999, 30; Mazzini and others 1999, 289–91.
44 McCann and others 1987, 48; Mazzanti 1983, 540; Boschian and others 2006, 162–63.
45 The Pleistocene is the period of the Quaternary which lasted from about 1,800,000 to 10,000 years ago. On the ancient dunes, see *supra*, note 13; Mori 1932, 40; Signorini 1967, 19; Mazzanti 1983; Casi 2000, 301.
46 Mori 1932, 41.

47 *Pianta del circondario di Orbetello* 1864; Mori 1932, 42; Merciai 1929, 355–56.
48 Cardarelli 1924–1925, 207–09; Mori 1932, 20–52; Mazzanti 1983, 540–43; Mazzini and others 1999, 289–91; Boschian and others 2006, 162–63.
49 McCann and others 1987, 18, 48; Cardarelli 1924–1925, 205–24; Casi 2000, 301–03; Boschian and others 2006, 162–63.
50 Casi 2000, 301–14.
51 Columella, *De Re Rustica* 12, 16–17; Varro, *Rerum Rusticarum* 3, 17.2–10; McCann 1979, 393.
52 McCann and others 1987, 18, 49; Ciampoltrini and Rendini 2004, 131–35.

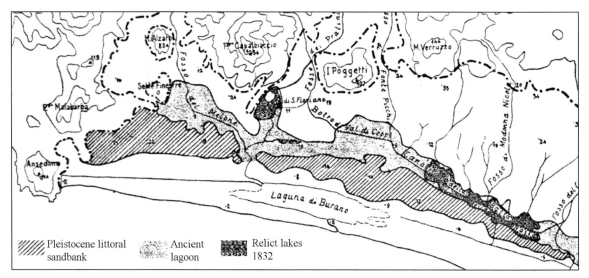

Figure 3.3. Ancient Pleistocene lagoons. Map reproduced from Mori 1932.

tinuous use from the third century BCE to the fifth century CE.[53] Three nearly parallel canals cut the western coast of the promontory facing the port. The longest of these (c. 260 m) is the Spacco di Regina, originally a natural karstic fracture.[54]

Around 30 m to the southeast of this lay the 140 m-long Piccolo Spacco della Regina, which, at its north end, crosses the third canal, the Tagliata. This entirely artificial break was probably created because the other two canals had become obstructed after a cave-in.[55] The canals must have served as a crossover between the fresh- and saltwater of the lagoon and the sea, and also as a means of passage for fish.[56] In the winter, when rainfall caused the level of the lake to rise vis-à-vis the sea, the canals helped drain the lagoon, as still occurs today, thanks to a man-made canal that connects Lake Burano with the sea. The lagoon was also given an outlet to the sea, consisting of a jetty of cemented tufa and pozzolana, which enables the port's activities.[57]

The preparation of the first port facilities at Cosa was tied to the construction of the fortifications on the promontory. A portion of the polygonal blocks that were used in the construction were, in fact, quarried from the man-made Tagliata Canal on whose western wall traces of the removed material are still visible.[58] The construction of the breakwaters also dates to this first period and was essential not only for protecting ships, but also for the earliest regularization of the Spacco della Regina.[59]

The structure of the port was comprised of five docks and a breakwater, and it might have had a lighthouse. Anna Marguerite McCann's hypothesis dates the construction of the lighthouse, which would have been located at the far end of the breakwater and corresponded to the final pillar, to c. 75 BCE.[60] The utilization of the lagoon for fish breeding probably began in the first half of the second century (Fig. 3.4).[61]

The feature that most characterizes the coast is definitely the lagoon of Orbetello, with the tombolos of Orbetello, Feniglia, and Giannella, which enclose and connect it to Monte Argentario and the mainland. The lagoon of Orbetello has survived thanks to the meagre and turbid flow of the rivers in the region.[62] The tombolo from which Orbetello rises is the oldest of the three and it is constituted of cemented fossiliferous sea sand (known as *panchina*), the formation of which can be dated to the mid-high Pleistocene era, when the sands of the vast coastal planes were sedimented and later formed after the lowering of the sea level.[63] The other two tombolos are still in formation.[64] Until the last century, it was completely unknown whether or not the tombolo of

---

53 Carandini and others 2002, 245; Ciampoltrini and Rendini 2004b.
54 Carandini and others 2002, 135–36; McCann and others 1987, 85; Mori 1932, 169; McCann 1979, 397.
55 McCann 1979, 397; Celuzza 2002 [1993], 235–41; Merciai 1929, 355–56.
56 McCann 1979, 398.
57 Ciampoltrini and Rendini 2004b, 135.

58 McCann and others 1987, 322.
59 Carandini and others 2002, 135–36.
60 McCann and others 1987, 329.
61 McCann and others 1987, 323.
62 Mazzanti 1983, 541.
63 On the Pleistocene, see *supra*, note 33; Signorini 1967, 19; Mazzini and others 1999, 290–91; Boschian and others 2006, 164–67; Pallecchi 2009, 65.
64 Signorini 1967, 19; Mazzanti 1983, 541; Mazzini and others 1999, 291–92; Boschian and others 2006, 164–67.

Giannella, which is more recent than Feniglia, was already open in the Etruscan era.[65] Romualdo Cardarelli claims that in that era, the lagoon was closed and that the Nassa canal, which connected it to the sea from the northwest, was man-made, possibly built by the Romans.[66]

Monte Argentario closes the lagoon on the west and stands as a geomorphic unit in itself, constituted, as noted earlier, of a complex series of lithological types, with intense tectonic phenomena. It is nearly an island, in contrast to the low and uniform appearance of the shoreline discussed thus far.[67]

The littoral of the tombolo of Gianella, as far as the Talamone, consists of dunes similar to those of the southern coast.[68] These enclose the plain of Camporegio, a strip of alluvial terrain that stretches between the Albegna and Osa Rivers, parallel to the coastline.[69] The fluvial terraces of the Albegna begin immediately inland of the plain of Camporegio.[70] The ancient alluvial formations were composed of pebbly and sandy terrain, sedimented by the Albegna and left on the terraced borders at a height of 20–30 m above the level of the present alluvion of the channel.[71] In this area, the valley is fairly ample and forms a plane that extends up to the Marsiliana hill, which is the point at which the low valley of Albegna ends and is replaced by a hilly landscape.

Looking towards the upper valley of the river, one notes the mound of Ghiaccioforte, which, at a height of 264 m, anticipates a landscape that grows gradually more rugged and predominantly forested. An Etruscan fortified stronghold occupied the summit of the hill, in a strategic position on the ford of the Albegna, north of the river and heading towards Marsiliana; incredibly, it was possible to see all the way to the sea.[72] It is necessary to pass Marsiliana in order to reach the upper valley of the Albegna, where the river ceased to be navigable in Antiquity; a ford was

---

65 Merciai 1929, 355–56.
66 Cardarelli 1924–1925, 211–13; Antonelli 1870, 5–6.
67 Signorini 1967, 7–10; Carandini and others 2002, 30–33; Boschian and others 2006, 164–67.
68 Cardarelli 1924–1925, 211; Carandini and others 2002, 30–33; Mazzanti 1983, 540.
69 Boschian and others 2006, 157–59; Mazzini and others 1999, 291–92.
70 Mazzini and others 1999, 291–92.
71 Signorini 1967, 19; Mazzini and others 1999; Boschian and others 2006, 157–61.
72 Rendini and Firmati 2008.

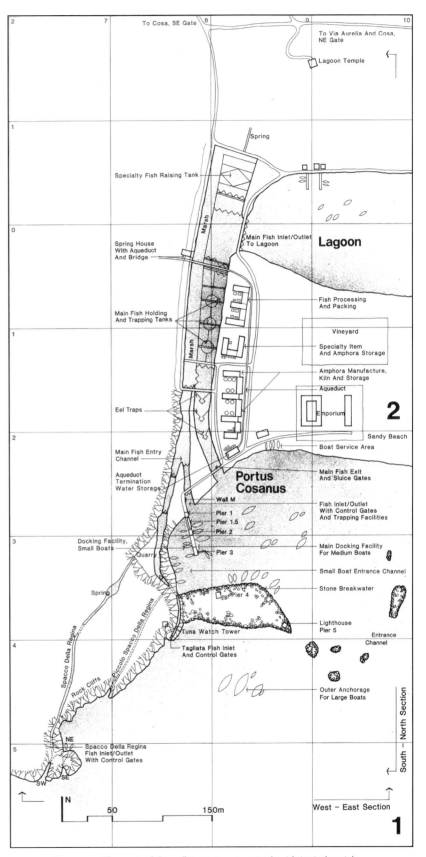

Figure 3.4. The port of Cosa (late 2–1 century BCE) with its industrial complex for the production of and commerce in conserved fish (*garum*) and wine. Map reproduced from McCann 1987, Fig. VII–10.

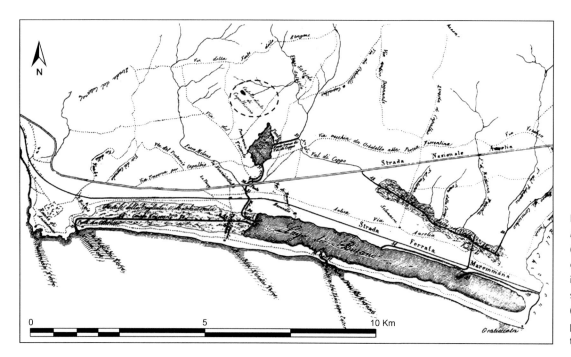

Figure 3.5. Detail of the 1864 *Map of the vicinity of Orbetello* (Fig. 3.2) with reclamation canals. The dotted circle indicates the 'ruined stronghold of Capalbiaccio' (geo-referenced with GIS platform). Map courtesy of the State Archive of Grosseto.

still in use as recently as the early 1980s.[73] A bit closer to the mountain, the Albegna receives the Elsa brook from the east. Following the Albegna towards the northeast, the hilliness of the landscape increases, reaching heights of over 200, and in some cases, 300 m.

Returning to the coast and following the direction of the Via Aurelia, at the height of the mound of Talamonaccio, the level of the terrain rises and the alluvial plane of Talamone once again opens after Fonteblanda.[74] In this area, the swampy lands are quite extensive[75] and constituted of silty sediments, sometimes peaty, deposited in the lagoons of the older dunes that precede those closer to the coastal dunes (as in the case of Talamone, Burano, and Camporegio) or at the borders of internal lacustrine basins (the lakes of San Floriano, Acquato, Cutignolo).[76] We know that, until early in the last century, this terrain became dangerous (particularly for livestock) at certain points, known as *pollini*, where the land appeared dry and solid, but, in reality, was composed of a superficial crust that rested on a muddy semi-liquid mass that created a type of quicksand.[77]

Reclamation Projects

The earliest attempts at reclamation in the Maremma Grossetana occurred in the sixteenth century through the efforts of the Medici family. However, they were not fully carried out and were limited to the swamps of Castiglion della Pescaia, because, at this time, the territory between Talamone and Lake Burano belonged to the State of the Presìdi.[78]

The situation did not change until the nineteenth century, when, at the end of the Napoleonic era, the regime of Lorena was instituted over a territory significantly expanded by the annexation of the State of the Presìdi and the Principate of Piombino.[79] A project for a land registry was initiated in 1817 and completed in 1825–1826.[80] In 1828, under Leopold II of Lorraine (1824–1859), reclamation was resumed on a grand scale with the establishment of the 'Deputazione di bonificamento'.[81] The hydraulic works carried out until 1864 are recorded in the *Pianta del circondario di Orbetello con le indicazioni delle opere eseguite dalla Reale Amministrazione del bonificamento* (*Map of the surroundings of Orbetello with indications of the works executed by the Royal Administration of Reclamation*).[82]

---

73 Carandini and others 2002, 30–33.
74 Carandini and others 2002, 30–33.
75 Mazzanti 1983, 539–40; Boschian and others 2006, 156–57.
76 Signorini 1967, 20.
77 Vivarelli Colonna 1937, 112; Lotti 1891, 26–28; Vacano 1985, 342–49.

78 Barsanti 1980, 39–64; Rombai, Pinzani, and Squarzanti 1997, 86–99; 101–03.
79 Detti 1998, 147.
80 Detti 1998, 168; Barsanti and Rombai 1986, 111–35.
81 Rombai, Pinzani, and Squarzanti 1997, 107–10; 126–30.
82 *Pianta del circondario di Orbetello* 1864, 242–43.

Notable Water Features

Lake Burano and the Lakes of the Interior

In Antiquity, Lake Burano must have been regarded with favour, considering the proximity of settlements of the Roman era, such as the villas of the Colonna,[83] Settefinestre,[84] and Tagliata,[85] which could have used it for breeding fish (Fig. 3.5).[86]

Upon the foundation of Cosa, much of the territory was restructured and centuriated.[87] The construction of a network of canals that followed the slope of the leads bordering on the Albegna would have ameliorated the problems of the coastal plane's drainage.[88] The borders of the colony's territory were the Albegna, the Elsa, the Tafone brook, and the sea. We owe the reconstruction of these boundaries to the 1924–1925 research of Romualdo Cardarelli, who pieced them together from the area's dioceses and medieval boundaries.[89] In this territory, eternally plagued by hydraulic concerns, troughs must have played an important role, even though no definite traces of them have been preserved.[90]

Palaeoecological excavations of the ancient landscape, conducted in the zone around the villa of Settefinestre, have made it possible to identify vegetal species typical of Mediterranean forests, predominantly oaks among the wild species and wheat, grapes, and olives among cultivated ones.[91] The villa itself was abandoned in the second century CE, perhaps following an epidemic. Traces of plants linked to the habitat of the swamp can be found for the first time in the archaeological strata of the late second-early third century. One can suppose that, following the drop in population in rural areas, the maintenance of drainage troughs and canals linked to the network of the centuriation was abandoned and that this led to the formation of a swamp, which endured for centuries.[92] With the abandonment of the villas and their sophisticated forms of agriculture, the entire area fell victim to dramatic patterns of erosion. These, added to alluvial phenomena, which were accentuated by the decline in artificial drainage facilities, must have hastened the deterioration of the region.

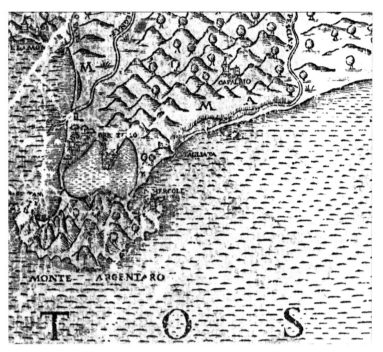

Figure 3.6. Detail of Ieronimo Bellermato's *Chorographia Tusciae*, 1536. Map reproduced from Rombai, Ciampi, and De Vita 1979.

As we have seen, in ancient times the Spacco della Regina — a karstic fissure regularized in the Roman era and later replaced by the Tagliata, possibly after an obstruction caused by a landslide — helped prevent the Burano lagoon from reverting to a swamp.[93] These apertures fell into disuse in late antiquity.[94] The drainage problem in the area was resolved only in the 1800s when the ancient inlet extending across the marsh of Macchiatonda between Lake Burano and Lake Tagliata was restored.[95] This canal was among the drainage works carried out between 1861 and 1864 (Fig. 3.5). During the reclamation, two diversions emptied the waters of Lake San Floriano and the Bassa swamp into Lake Burano. Another two streams connect Lake Burano to the Chiarone and the sea: one functions as a feeder of river waters in the southern stretch of the lake; the other is excavated from the central part of the tombolo, from which rises the tower of Buranaccio. The latter first appears in historical cartography in the mid-sixteenth century (Fig. 3.6).[96]

It has already been emphasized that Lake San Floriano and the Bassa swamp were the remnants of

---

83 Dyson 2002.
84 Carandini 1985a; Celuzza 2002 [1993], 236.
85 Carandini and others 2002, 201–02; Carandini 1985b, 151–52.
86 Celuzza 2002 [1993], 235.
87 Carandini and others 2002, 121.
88 Celuzza 2002 [1993], 235.
89 Cardarelli 1924–1925; Carandini and others 2002, 121.
90 Carandini and others 2002, 122.
91 Carandini 1985a, 90–91.
92 Celuzza 2002 [1993], 236; Carandini 1985a, 180.

---

93 Celuzza 2002 [1993], 235–41; McCann 1979, 391–411; Merciai 1929, 355–56.
94 Del Rosso 1898, 20–22.
95 Cardarelli 1924–1925, 218.
96 Rombai, Ciampi and De Vita 1979; Ieronimo Bellarmato, *Chorographia Tusciae* [1536].

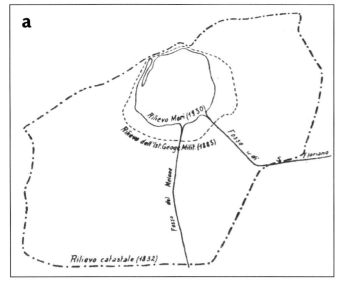
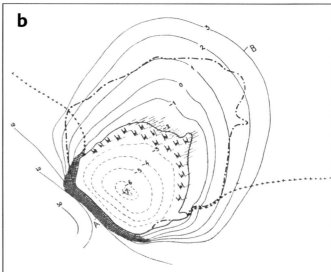

Figure 3.7. a. Historical fluctuations of the borders of Lake San Floriano. The outermost line indicates the cadastral survey of 1832; the interrupted line traces the survey of the Geographic Military Institute (IGM), done in 1883. It is not possible to provide geo-references as the pinned point from the survey is missing. b. Survey of Lake Scuro. No geo-references points as above. Maps reproduced from Mori 1932, 43, 49.

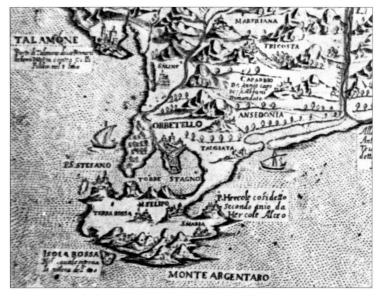

Figure 3.8. Detail of Giuseppe Rosaccio's *Geografia della Toscana*, 1662. Map reproduced from Rombai, Ciampi, and De Vita 1979.

the oldest lagoon.[97] From what Attilio Mori claims, on the basis of his study of a cadastral survey of 1832, another even smaller lake lay to the southeast of Lake San Floriano. From both of these lakes flowed two streams that were later joined in a single channel, which in turn gushed into Lake Burano.[98] In the 1864 map, the tiny lake appears completely silted up and the surface of Lake San Floriano is nearly identical to what it had been in 1832. San Floriano was a lake of karstic origin: the collapse of a subterranean cavity carved out the aquifer from the cavernous limestone that constitutes the base of Poggio Capalbiaccio. At this point, less than 10 m below sea level, we are close to the base levels of the region's subterranean hydrography, into which the aquifers empty out.[99] For the same reason there are six springs at the base of this mound, one of which is only approximately 10 m from the Lake itself.[100] By the time of Mori's 1930 survey, the Lake was reduced to less than one tenth of what it had been a century earlier (Fig. 3.7a). The drainage of Lake San Floriano was related to the opening of a feeder canal that drained it all the way to the Fosso dei Pratini. On the basis of this indicator, the ditch can be identified as the one which the 1864 map designates 'Nuovo tronco di Val di Ceppo' (Fig. 3.5).[101]

The lakes on the interior are Lake Acquato, the Cutignolo, and Lake Scuro. Lake Acquato, which is karstic, is the largest and has its own basin, which is fed by a subaquatic source and a watershed. Until the 1920s, it too was exploited for its fish, but gradually dried out after the reclamation projects of the early 1900s.[102] Emanuele Repetti reinserted the Cutignolo among the 'mini-lakes of Capalbio' and claimed that it did not deserve the designation of 'lake' because it was merely 'a lagoon of stagnant waters'.[103] Mori tells us that it actually fills the bottom of a depres-

---

97 Mori 1932, 1–52; Merciai 1929, 355–56.
98 Mori 1932, 43.

99 Mori 1932, 45.
100 Mori 1932, 45.
101 Mori 1932, 44.
102 Mori 1932, 7–22.
103 Repetti 1833–1845, *ad voc.* 'Lagaccioli di Capalbio'.

sion on an alluvial tract that descends towards the Radicata brook and its span thus depends on the amount of precipitation (it practically dries up in the summer).[104] Two canals have been dug out in order to drain the zone: a feeder that channels the rainwater from the overhanging ridge, and an outflowing stream on the north side, which conveys the excess waters towards the Radicata.[105]

Lake Scuro is located to the southwest of the Radicata. It occupies the base of a vast cavity and is around 2.5 m beneath sea level.[106] At the time of Mori's survey, the Lake had neither feeders nor outlets. Moreover, having a very small basin, it did not suffer from variations in rainfall and maintained nearly the same level during every season. Noteworthy, on the other hand, are the historical variations of Lake Scuro. The cadastral survey of 1832 reveals that its area was nearly double that of a hundred years later, albeit maintaining the same form (Fig. 3.7b).[107] This lake too is of a karstic nature, meaning that its origins lay in the dissolution and collapse of the cavity that it occupies. This phenomenon can thus be explained by progressive adjustments of the terrain.[108]

The Lagoon of Orbetello

The conditions of the lagoon of Orbetello — always subject to the problems of river depositions (silt) and the elevation of the seabed — were apparently rather good until the sixteenth century, so much so that it was called *parvum mare* (little sea).[109] The 'Golden Book (*Libro d'Oro*)', or 'Ancient Statutes of Orbetello', describes a situation that was unusual in the territory of the Maremma: a flourishing fish industry.[110] In the sixteenth century the waters could still be sailed by military craft.[111]

Things deteriorated in the eighteenth century, when the waters became 'insalubrious', a problem attributed to masses of decomposing aquatic vegetation.[112] All the same, there was no lack of communication with the sea. In 1550 Leandro Alberti noted the existence of various deltas.[113] It appears that the canals of Pertuso and Ansedonia, on the flanks of the Feniglia tombolo, have likewise been there since the Roman era.[114]

In the late nineteenth century, the gradual silting up caused, above all, by the overrun of the sands of Feniglia, was advancing annually by around 7 m.[115] The fishponds of Nassa and Fibbia, at the sides of the Giannella, already existed in 1544 and were most likely a good source of revenue for the Republic of Siena, which owned them. In 1544, Siena gave them to Orbetello as reparation for the damage in the area, which was caused by the Saracen raids, and as compensation for Orbetello's demonstrated loyalty.[116]

The creation of the canal and fishpond of Nassa, near Santa Liberata, has been attributed to the Romans and, although there is no proof, it could have been a work annexed to the villa belonging to the Ahenobarbi.[117] The fishpond of Fibbia, which appears in two seventeenth-century maps, fed the waters of the Albegna into the lagoon (Fig. 3.8).[118] It was for this very reason that the fishpond was ordered to be shut in 1860, so as to prevent freshwater from mixing with seawater.[119] At the time, such a mixture was believed to be the cause of malaria. Various attempts were made to improve the hygienic conditions of the lagoon. Among the works carried out the canal of Ansedonia proved to be a failure. With the sand missing and no protection from docks, it was obstructed almost immediately by algae and sand.[120]

By 1898, the problems with the lake of Orbetello do not seem to have been resolved. The foundations of the bridge over the Albegna were in such a ruinous condition that floodwaters burst into the lagoon, even when the cataracts were closed. The Ansedonia canal appears again to have silted over and the new bridges built over the dyke in order to facilitate the flow of water had their apertures blocked by the clay structures that had served for their construction 12 years earlier (Fig. 3.9).[121]

---

104 Mori 1932.
105 Mori 1932, 47.
106 Mori 1932, 49.
107 Mori 1932, 51.
108 Mori 1932, 52.
109 Del Rosso 1898, 7.
110 *Libro d'Oro*.
111 Ademollo 1881, 36–38.
112 Ademollo 1881, 32.
113 Del Rosso 1898, 7.

114 Del Rosso 1898; Ademollo 1881, 36; McCann 1979, 391–411.
115 Del Rosso 1898, 7, 13; Antonelli 1870, 6–8.
116 Ademollo 1881, 36–38.
117 Raveggi 1933, 78.
118 Rombai, Ciampi, and De Vita 1979; Giuseppe Rosaccio, *Geografia della Toscana* [1662]; Giacomo Filippo Ameti, *Parte Seconda Maritima del Patrimonio di S. Pietro* [1696].
119 Del Rosso 1898, 8.
120 Del Rosso 1898, 8; 12–13; 20.
121 Del Rosso 1898, 16–17.

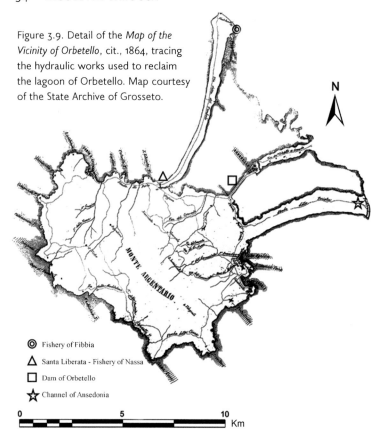

Figure 3.9. Detail of the *Map of the Vicinity of Orbetello*, cit., 1864, tracing the hydraulic works used to reclaim the lagoon of Orbetello. Map courtesy of the State Archive of Grosseto.

A Hypothetical Reconstruction of the Coastal Water Basins of the Ager Cosanus
(Fig. 3.10a and detail 3.10b)

In light of the data emerging from the study of the mentioned sources and the local morphology, and with the location of sites, it is possible to outline certain hypothetical conclusions. It can be affirmed that the extensiveness of lacustrine basins on the interior of the Maremma coast did not undergo important changes over the course of centuries, until the modern era, with the onset of reclamation efforts and agrarian reform.[122]

The internal lakes of the Capalbiese region (Lake Scuro, Lake Acquato, and Lake San Floriano) shrunk notably after the drainage works in the early twentieth century.[123] From historical cartography, we can deduce what could have been the original surface area of Lake Burano, which must have extended to the north until it nearly met the promontory of Cosa; it extended to the Chiarone River in the south.[124] The ultimate confirmation of this comes from the villa of the Tagliata, with its complex of fishponds, as well as the Tagliata canal itself.[125] It is not known when the extremities of the Lake began to turn into marshes, but this might have occurred relatively recently. Until the seventeenth century, Lake Burano was cartographically represented with a well-defined perimeter, without swampy contours, and connected to the Chiarone. Only in the next century did the swampy areas of the Paglieti and Bassa marshes begin to appear. Lake Burano and these swampy areas have been interpreted as relics of ancient lagoons. However, it is possible to retro-date the swamp, which appears on seventeenth-century maps, to the moment that the sites of the Roman and Etruscan era took shape along the strip between Lake Burano and the Bassa, along which runs the Via Aurelia.[126]

The lagoon of Orbetello must have remained largely unchanged, if we exclude possible shrinkage during the Etrusco-Roman period, due to a sea level that was lower than the present one.[127] In fact, the lagoon is at sea level and the remains that exist along the tombolo of Feniglia lie at a height of between 0.01 and 1.53 m above sea level, while others are immersed around 40–50 cm from the seashore. All the same, it is clear that the sea level had to be lower by at least 1 m.[128]

In light of studies and the traces of habitations discovered by R. C. Bronson and G. Uggeri, which have been dated to the Prehistoric and Etruscan eras, we know that the tombolos of Feniglia and Giannella were already formed in the historical era.[129] However, as has been noted, we do not have information on the formation and ancient characteristics of the canals that connected the lagoon to the sea. Certainly the canal at the site of Santa Liberata (the fishpond of Nassa) was navigable, at least for smaller craft, in the time of the State of the Presìdi.[130] The Roman fishpond at Santa Liberata also offers proof that the ancient level of the sea was lower than it is today.[131]

---

122 Ente 1960; Detti 1998, 263–89.
123 Mori 1932, 7–22.
124 Rombai, Ciampi, and De Vita 1979; Anonymous, *Costa Tirrenica dall'Argentario a Corneto nel Lazio*; Agostino De Greys, *Paesaggio Agrario e Forestrale nello Stato dei Presìdi*; *Carta Topografica della Provincia Inferiore Senese*.
125 Celuzza 2002 [1993], 234–36.
126 Rombai, Ciampi, and De Vita 1979; Anonymous, *Costa Tirrenica dall'Argentario a Corneto nel Lazio*; Agostino De Greys, *Paesaggio Agrario e Forestrale nello Stato dei Presìdi*; *Carta Topografica della Provincia Inferiore Senese*.
127 Mazzanti 1983, 541; Schmiedt 1972; Mazzini and others 1999, 307–09; Boschian and others 2006, 167–69.
128 Mazzanti 1983, 542–43; Schmiedt 1972, 230; Mazzini and others 1999, 307–09; Boschian and others 2006, 167–69.
129 Bronson and Uggeri 1970, sites 69, 70, 71/72, 77; Signorini 1967, 19; Mazzanti 1983, 541; Mazzini and others 1999, 291–92; Boschian and others 2006, 164–67.
130 Ademollo 1881, 36–38.
131 Schmiedt 1972, 232.

3. GEO-ARCHAEOLOGY OF COASTAL SOUTHERN TUSCANY 55

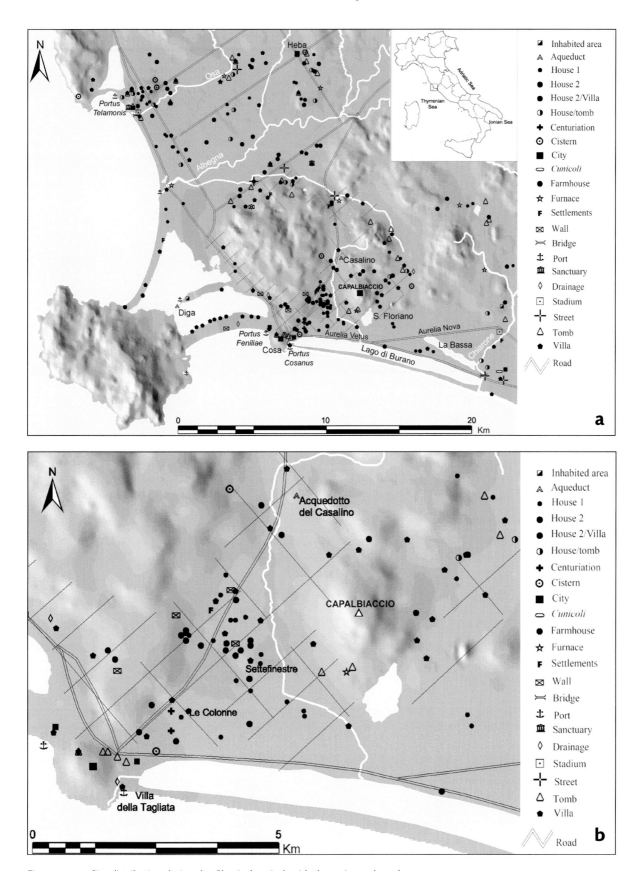

Figure 3.10. a. Site distribution during the Classical period, with the main roads and hypothetical reconstruction of the ancient lake basins. b. Detailed map of the Valle d'Oro in the Classical period. Maps courtesy of the State Archive of Grosseto.

LAURA CERRI AND EMANUELE MARIOTTI

4. Geophysical Prospecting, Topography, Thermal Camera and DEM

ABSTRACT During the month of January 2009 and the following June 2010 two geophysical surveys took place covering a total of 5100 m² of the hilltop of Tricosto. Quadrants were set both inside and outside the fortified area. The anomalies that emerged from the geophysical survey revealed a whole other chapter in the medieval life of Capalbiaccio. Before the medieval phase, a pre-existing larger settlement covered most of the hilltop. The surface collection of material and the aerial photography do not reveal much of the nature of the site as it is mostly covered by olive trees and local flora with the addition of thick blocks of collapsed medieval layers. The pottery that predated the medieval settlement, found during Dyson's excavations and recently re-analysed by Valeria Acconcia (*infra*) is what prompted the questions that are herein analysed in the magnetometry. The small quantity of Etruscan and little Roman pottery identified and dated confirmed that some form of earlier occupation of the hilltop indeed existed. The reason for adding three campaigns was to better understand the nature of the settlement underneath the ruins of the Tricosto Castle and its immediate suburbia and compare it within the other regional sites that have been studied since the 1970s.

The geophysical survey indeed confirmed a much wider pre-exiting settlement below and beyond the castle with a different orientation from the medieval village. The dwellings face northeast to southwest and northwest to southwest are at variance of about 45 degrees clockwise from the medieval layer. Now, with a more precise dating of the pottery and the evidence shown from the magnetometry, we can suggest there was an Etruscan community between the sixth and the fifth century BCE. It's still not clear if the oval structure facing the sea and about 50 m from the city walls is an Etruscan burial or something else. The tumulus has never been excavated nor noticed before (see Chapter 15, Fig. 15.5).

While drafting a new map of the site, it became increasingly clear that the erosion of the hilltop during the last thirty-five years brought to the surface what seems to be a much denser medieval community within the castle than had been identified during Dyson's seasons. Further, new alignments of houses were plotted on the map together with the discovery of a second church. Outside of the fortified area and around the hilltop there are traces of the ancient road that led to the top to the castle's gate and touched five springs that provide good drinking water still today. These wide roads, which have both been integrated in the DEM (digital elevation model), followed the natural inclination of the hill and were carved out of the limestone, which is visible from the magnetometry outside the main gate of the castle. They were likely reused in pre-medieval times. Two nearby quarries of travertine — one to the northeast of the fortified village and one, of cavernous limestone, to the southwest at the bottom of the hill, near the later Torre del Tricosto — have been used through time. A final confirmation of our findings was obtained in 2021 with the use of a Thermal camera to compare and contrast the anomalies identified, showing the different information each approach provides staged on both aerial and drone views of the 1970s and 2021. [MH]

The Geophysical Prospecting: Magnetometry, the Project Goals, the Methodology and the Areas Investigated

The geophysical prospecting conducted at the stronghold of Capalbiaccio was done with the magnetic method and executed in two stages during the course of 2009 and 2010.[1] The first campaign focused on the internal area of the stronghold's bailey and the second examined the external area right outside the wall.

---

1 Coordinates of the Capalbiaccio hilltop: 42.4385, 11.3546.

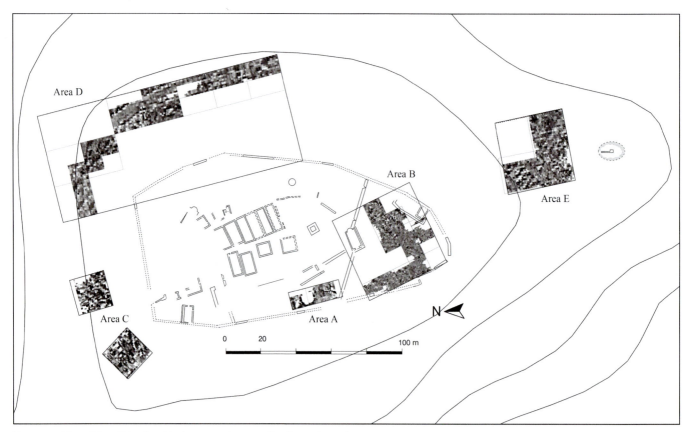

Figure 4.1. Map of Capalbiaccio with the magnetic anomalies. Image by authors.

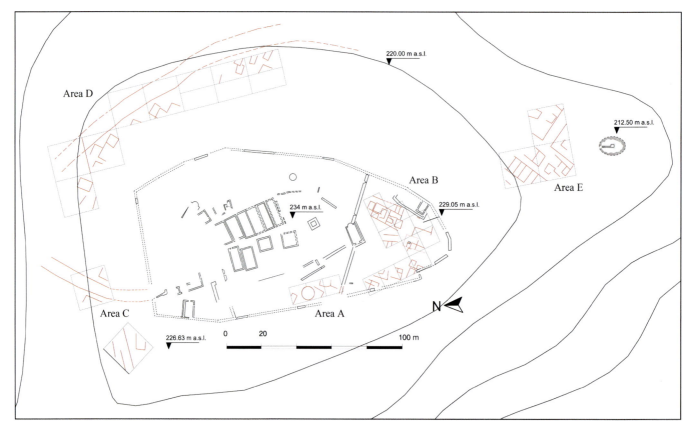

Figure 4.2. Interpretation of the anomalies. Plan by authors.

The research was undertaken in order to determine the stronghold's internal organization (known in part from excavations carried out in the 1970s), identify the principal road system (especially access to the stronghold), and clarify the development of the settlement during the various phases of the site's occupation from the most ancient to the medieval era.

Prospecting was conducted with a Type FM256 Geoscan research fluxgate gradiometer and the data acquired was processed and visualized with Geoplot 3.0 software. Prospecting in the stronghold's interior (Areas A and B) covered a combined area of around 1500 m², which, for reasons of space, was subdivided into 10 m squares on the interior of which measurements were taken every 50 cm along contours that were 50 cm apart. On the other hand, the area outside the stronghold (Areas C, D, and E), approximately 3600 m², was divided into 20 m squares and information was drawn at regular intervals of 50 cm along contours that were 1 m apart.

Area A (c. 300 m²)

This smaller area is situated to the north of the wall that divides the stronghold's interior. The area contains numerous loose stones on its surface, but no visible structures. However, there is evidence of collapsed structures buried underground. The morphology appears fairly regular, save for a large circular pit, which was perhaps created by a bomb explosion in World War II. On account of this, and the extremely irregular nature of the surface, it was extremely difficult to acquire magnetic data.

Area B (1200 m²)

This area is located in the southern portion of the stronghold in a zone separated from the rest of the stronghold by a dividing wall. It is covered in vegetation and contains few standing walls; it drops slightly towards the south and there are many stones scattered over its surface. Present, as well, are many olive trees, which have impeded the collection of data.

Area C (400 m²)

This area is located just north of the stronghold, outside the bailey, close to the north entrance. The particular morphological situation of this zone, characterized by thick vegetation and sizeable stone ruins of the stronghold's bailey, has made prospecting possible solely in a small restricted area, which was nonetheless crucial for identifying the road system that provided access to the stronghold.

Area D (c. 2000 m²)

This area is located to the east of the stronghold, in the vicinity of the bailey. From a morphological point of view, the area's surface is highly irregular, with sharp drops and sudden rises of altitudes, which are caused by rocky outcrops. Despite the wild vegetation, which is very thick and hinders the collection of data, it seemed crucial to investigate this area to verify if there were structures outside of the fortification.

Area E (1200 m²) — Exterior South

This area is in the southern outskirts of the stronghold, close to the oval stone structure. It is a strip of land that is set among numerous olive trees. From a morphological point of view, the surface terrain appears rather irregular, with rocky outcrops in certain areas. The vegetation is wild, with shrubs and grasses that have rendered point readings in this area difficult, as well.

Geophysical Prospecting: Results of the Research and Analysis of the Data (Figs 4.1 and 4.2)

With the exception of the aforementioned foreign objects, which consist primarily of vegetation and fragments of the ruined walls, the results of the prospecting allowed us to give positive answers to the questions posed by the research. Prospecting has revealed part of the inner built-up area of the stronghold, as well as the articulation of the space right outside the bailey. It also distinguished the principal road system and identified a phase prior to the establishment of the stronghold, which probably occurred in the Etruscan era.

Area A

Taking into consideration solely a limited section of the terrain, the results of the magnetic probe seem to attest to the presence of certain linear anomalies with NE–SW and NW–SE orientations, which appear to differ from the orientations of the stronghold's medieval structures. Thus, they suggest the presence of a pre-existent complex, which probably coincided with that discovered in area B. The magnetic data from this area likewise indicates the presence of an anomaly characterized by greatly elevated magnetic values that seem to be attributable to the presence of metal in the subsoil. Perhaps this is a residue of war, since the area around Capalbiaccio was affected by the conflict in 1944.

Area B

Numerous anomalies of linear form with NE–SW and NW–SE orientations were identified in this area, suggesting the presence of masonry structures in the subsoil. The identified anomalies seem to indicate the presence of walls and settings of various shapes and sizes. In the eastern portion of the area, one of the anomalies seems to be a continuation of the elongated and narrow form situated close to the bailey. Meanwhile, in the western zone, the masonry structures detected by the prospecting, aside from having different orientations with respect to the structures of the stronghold, also seem to underlie the bailey and, thus, they probably belong to an earlier phase. Material from the Etruscan and Roman era was discovered on the surface in Area B, which makes one wonder about activity in the area prior to the construction of the stronghold. One cannot dismiss the possibility that the structures detected by the prospecting belong to an earlier, pre-medieval phase of settlement. This would likewise explain the different configuration of this zone in the stronghold, which is almost completely lacks standing medieval structures.

Area C

The results of the magnetic research in this zone make it possible to identify a road on the northern side of the stronghold, the existence of which has been hypothesized by both the entry portal on the north side of the wall and the DEM, whose curves indicate a depression in the ground that corresponds precisely to the area leading north from the stronghold's portal. The prospecting also detected anomalies of a linear shape, which could be read as masonry structures flanking the road and following its direction.

Area D

In this zone too, a road encircling the base of the site, beyond the eastern border of the stronghold, was detected. In this case, the road was also confirmed by the curve obtained through the digital reconstruction of the terrain's morphology (Fig. 4.4a). The road is cut into the virgin rock and the cuts are still visible, while its course is partly assumed by the present path that encircles the stronghold. The road has a NW–SE orientation and seems to veer towards the west, in the direction of the forest, probably to join up with the access road that is situated on the north side of the stronghold. At the road's western end, prospecting detected a series of anomalies that were generated, in all probability, by buried masonry structures, and which seem to constitute tiny rectangular spaces with a NW–SE orientation. These too adapt to the natural contours of the terrain, respecting the course of the road that encircles the stronghold. It is difficult to confirm, solely on the basis of the geophysical data, whether these are structures that are associated with the medieval phase of the site — that is, the same phase as the stronghold — or an earlier one. The materials discovered on the surface in this zone are attributable to various periods of the site's settlement, from the prehistoric to the medieval. Thus, it is probable that this area was already occupied in Antiquity.

Area E

In this area, the study was able to identify numerous anomalies, which are attributable to structures that have the same orientation as those distinguished on the inside of the stronghold in Areas A and B. The magnetic data indicates the presence of numerous linear anomalies that are attributable to masonry structures, which mark off spaces of various sizes. This evidence also suggests the existence of a rather expansive ancient settlement, which developed in the area more towards the south of the hill, where the stronghold was to be built in the Middle Ages.

[LC]

Topography

Satellite surveys using DGPS (Differential Global Positioning System), combined with topographical surveys using Total Station equipment, are assuming ever greater importance in archaeological research and, by this point, they are essential components of preliminary research and the survey.[2] The precision and rapidity with which they provide continuous measurements has led to broad use of the instruments, placing them side by side with more traditional survey methods. The collected data can be managed in a variety of ways, from a vector drawing (CAD), to a database, and, finally, to a GIS platform. Topography, understood as the description of land and an accurate mapping and creation of a

---

2 See the recent contributions on this type of approach (DEM, GIS, 'survey', reconstruction of the territory, etc., which analyses different archaeological contexts: Campana and Francovich 2006; Forte 2003; Gillings, Mattingly, and van Dalen 2000; De Vos 2000.

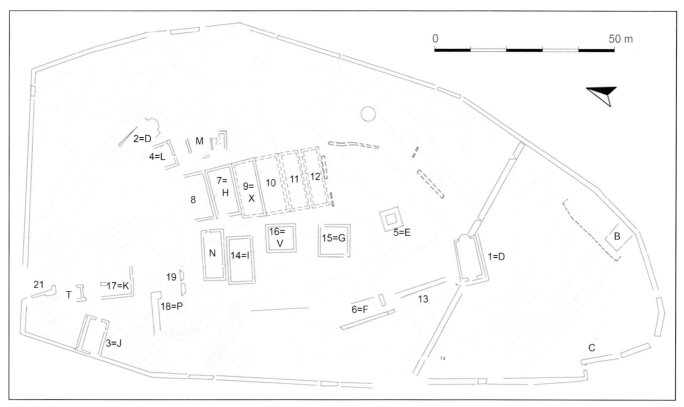

Figure 4.3. Final master plan with Dyson's original excavated structures (letters) and the newly identified structures (numbers). When the line is dotted it is hypothetical. Plan by authors.

digital model of the terrain, is the most significant outcome of this application.[3] All data obtained by these means can be supplemented with archaeological surveys, such as those that reveal obstructions caused by buildings, the positioning of structures, and other findings.

Archaeological DTM (Digital Terrain Model) or DEM (Digital Elevation Model) offers a synthesis of the topography of archaeological remains and the natural morphology of the land. Depending on whether the grid is more or less crowded with topographical points, the survey will show the general course of the land, marking depressions, jumps in altitude, etc. Most of the evidence will derive from the natural orthography (slopes, hills, depressions, etc.); it will be modified to some extent by archaeological stratification and structures that create the final surface on which the archaeologist works. A reading of these two sources of data — significantly different but at the same time, not dissociable — may offer a great deal of information. Surveys of visible structures (done with GPS or Total Station), as well as evidence obtained from geophysical prospecting, are superimposed on this base.

The survey of the terrain in the area of the stronghold was conducted in a first session that was devoted to setting up a topographical system for the expansion — to the extent that it was possible — of the plan, with the integration of newly emerging walls and digital modelling of the surface, which was obtained via magnetometry. In this preliminary phase, a Total Station Leica Tps 400 was used to create a series of stations in an open polygon, which was anchored to certain structures that were present in a prior survey.[4] A 10 × 10 m grid of squares was drawn on this base for the geophysical examination at the eastern end of the site. A second and more extensive session was dedicated to landscape surrounding the site.

Results

In the central part of the settlement, close to the already known buildings, many newly discovered walls were added to the plan (Fig. 4.3).

---

3 The model is three dimensional with contours that have a centimetric isohypse.

4 Environmental factors, such as dense vegetation and imposing ruins, have hindered the imposition of a closed system.

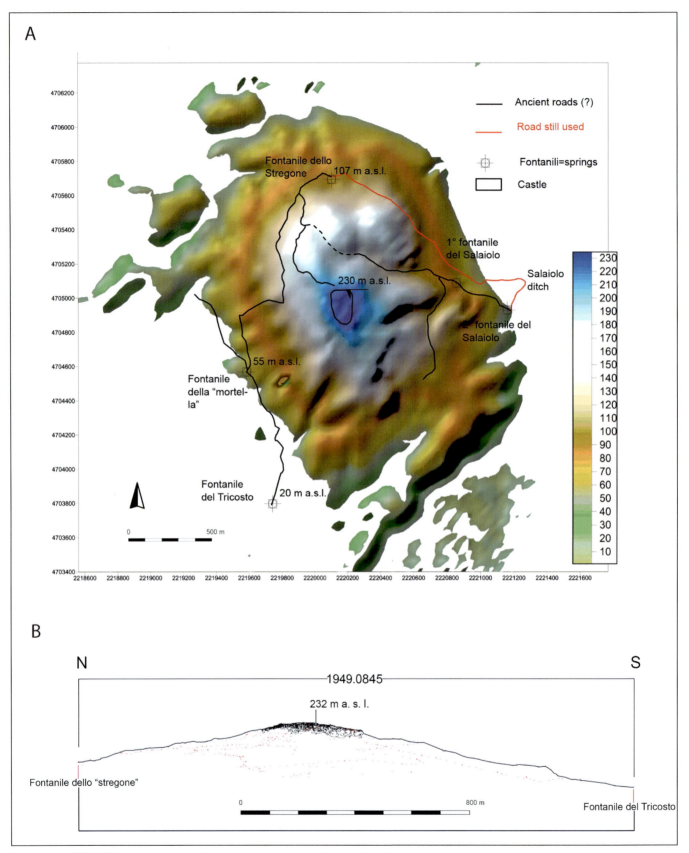

Figure 4.4. a. DEM (Digital elevation model) and cross section of the hilltop of Capalbiaccio showing the roads leading up to the fortified village and the springs (*Fontanili*) surrounding the hilltop. b. Cross Section of the Capalbiaccio hill. Image by Emanuele Mariotti.

The Postern

Significant information has been drawn from a crucial point in the wall: a small portal discovered close to the southern corner, which was probably a secondary entrance related to the thirteenth-century phase. Said portal shows up as a relief, thus indicating an obstruction. This access is characterized by both its position — distinct with respect to the central nucleus and associated with an area that was abandoned in the fourteenth century — and its typology. It is not a direct and frontal entrance simply on a smaller scale, but a well-protected side approach that presupposes some sort of escarpment towards the wall's exterior. The jambs of this postern remain and accommodate an elevation of approximately 1.5–2 m and an aperture measuring 1.25 m. The walls that create this entrance swerve towards the west (that is, towards the outside), thereby opening up a space for the postern. In poliorcetic terms, this type of entrance can be defined as 'tangential', in as much as the linear walls into which the portal is embedded follow parallel courses. Such an access is much easier to defend, as the route of approach is always under the defender's control. Furthermore, the entrance does not permit direct admittance into the settlement's core. This tactical stratagem may shed light on the greater or lesser importance of the site's southern zone. On the other hand, the choice may have been dictated by the terrain's morphology at this particular point, which may perhaps have impeded the construction of a more direct road approaching the site from the south.

Oval Structure

An oval structure facing the coast is set on the front of the hilltop circa 50 mm lower from the top. The area of the base, inside which the dry stone structure lies, is elliptical ($c.\ 15 \times 10\ m^2$) with a perfectly N–S oriented principal axis. Its outer contour, clearly legible in the form at the base, remains covered with earth and vegetation, with only a few stone elements poking through (Fig. 4.2 Oval outside Area E). No substantial collapse of the structure's exterior is visible. The upper portion of the area is 1.5–2 m tall with respect to the present ground level. The interior consists of a narrow corridor (Fig. 4.6) that measures about 0.6 m wide and 5 m deep (though it is not visible in its entirety), which leads into a small, squared inner room (1.5 × 1.5 m). The walls are constructed from well-cut stones and visible to a height of 1–1.5 m. The building technique consists of dry masonry with hewn, partly faced blocks set

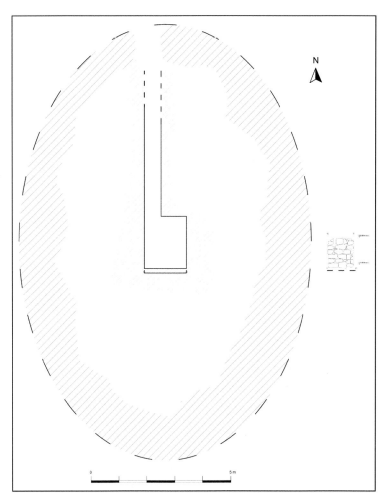

Figure 4.5. Oval Structure outside of Area E (as visible in 2009). Plan by Emanuele Mariotti and Michelle Hobart.

in layers and left rough (Figs 4.7 and 4.8). Wedges of various size, generally chips or scraps left over from handling the stone are often used to respect the levels of the base and fill voids between elements. At the corners, the stones are wedged into alternate levels. The dimensions and form of the building elements vary, but in general they occur in the following sizes: 0.2 × 0.3 m; 0.3 × 0.3 m; 0.3 × 0.1 m; 0.2 × 0.2 m; with extensions of up to 0.4 m in length and 0.15 m in height. In sum, the construction technique seems fairly uniform, with larger squared stones in the exposed walls of the inner chamber.

Although the vegetation and the poor visibility of the remains render a reading of the construction difficult, it seems to be ascribable to a military defensive outlook. The hilltop became a shelter and base against the Allied advancement along the coast during 1944–1945.

The swift erection of the small room, possibly reusing the medieval stones that can be found all over the fortified village, was rather common for German

Figure 4.6. Photo taken in 2010 of the overgrown mound or tomb. Photo by Michelle Hobart.

Figure 4.7. Photo of the wall elevation of the dry stone structure. Photo by Michelle Hobart.

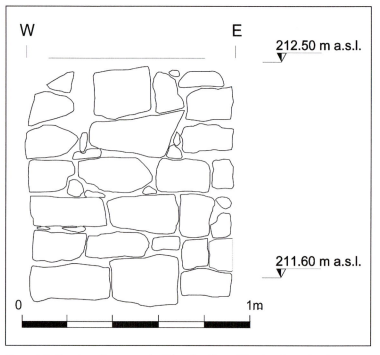

Figure 4.8. Drawing of a segment of the elevation of the dry stone structure. Drawing by Emanuele Mariotti.

engineers during World War II. At Montecassino similar areas have been briefly occupied and organized as a final defence during their withdrawal. The entire hilltop of Capalbiaccio has traces of bomb craters (Fig. 4.2 Area A). That said, it might be tempting to suggest that the elliptical foundation of this small structure may have served in the past for other purposes. The view it commands and its highly strategic position could have been the site for either a sanctuary or a tomb. If the latter were to be confirmed as true after proper investigation, one could further suggest this might have been a known burial type throughout the area of upper Maremma, around Vetulonia, dated to the end of the seventh to early sixth centuries BCE. These burials generally consist of a small tumulus (8–20 m in diameter, as the necropolis of Val Berretta),[5] a *cella* with a rectangular or square plan, a *dromos* — not necessarily axial — providing access, and they are often surrounded by a stone circle. The building technique always consists of dry masonry with blocks of various dimensions, partly cut or dressed and arranged in rows. The roofing normally consists of a corbelled arch or a faux vault. Comparative material in the area is varied and widespread, particularly in the necropolises of Val Berretta, Valle dell'Alma, and Parco dell'Accesa, where it is possible to distinguish evidence very similar to that at Capalbiaccio.[6] Other comparable material for *tombe a camera* (chamber tombs) with tumuli, likewise around Vetulonia, come from the necropolis of Poggio Tondo (near Pian d'Alma-Scarlino), as well as from the necropolis of Poggio Marcuccio (Scansano) in the Vulci region.[7]

Definitive interpretation of the changes of this structure will remain a problem until it can be adequately cleaned or excavated. The walls of the room seem to be well preserved, but offer no indication of where the roofing began, perhaps there was none, at least during World War II. Compared to other examples, though, space is relatively small. There are no traces of vertical beams for enclosure between the *dromos* and the central space, nor any partitioning elements or small pillars visible on the interior of the actual standing walls. The resemblance of the wall technique to some of the medieval ones inside the castle is striking (*infra* Corti). With further analysis it will be clear how this structure has been reused through time. Certainly, the location commanded a key strategic position looking over the entire coast and visible to the people in the valley.

Digital Elevation Model (DEM)

A micro-DEM survey of the terrain in the southern portion of the castle, which is separated from the nucleus of the settlement by a dividing wall, was conducted with the Terminal Station and concentrated on the same area covered by the magnetometry.[8] The surveyed surface was around 1250 m², with around 300 points marked at intervals between 0.5–1 m. The data collected showed the fluctuations in the ground, which were then compared with the results of the prospecting. Unfortunately, this digital model and the contours provide no important evidence except that the terrain regularly declines towards the south. A single well-defined jump in altitude, at the edge of the surveyed area, towards the southwest, is perhaps a testimony of a change in the systematization of the structures. It was most likely influenced by the presence of the postern, as well as the related road system and fortifications.

In a second phase of research, a DGPS Trimble 5700 was used to produce a general, extensive topographical survey, which provided a complex digital model with new contours and altimetric heights (Fig. 4.4). The objective was again to provide a thorough and homogenous reading of the terrain, wherever archaeological remains are scarce. The morphology of the land in the area surrounding the stronghold was able to shape the road system and principal means of access to the settlement and the areas that have been quarried for construction material. A cross section of the Capalbiaccio hill shows the inclination of the slope and provides a better understanding of why when using the old road leading to the castle there is no sense of going uphill.

Trading from the Thermal Camera (UAV)

In the spring of 2021, the Capalbiaccio site underwent a new aerial survey with the UAV system (Unmanned Aerial Vehicle). The survey was undertaken to map the state of the site, compare it with aerial photos from the 1970s, and to verify some working hypotheses. The area immediately outside the walls has always proved difficult to approach with normal survey methods: poor visibility of the ground, mixed collapses, and incoherent accumulations of building materials, in addition to the emergence of the bedrock. Infrequent use of the roads surrounding the fortifications, up to the present day, as well as the growth of vegetation and erosion have also prevented a coherent and comprehensive reading. Compared to the 2009–2010 campaigns, today the site is even more invaded by vegetation, with little archaeological sediment. The collapsed building material, such as rough stones or the like, tends to be confused with the outcropping rock bank and with possible remains of other structures. This is why a new technique was adopted.

At the beginning of April 2021 employment of a drone enabled two new types of investigation to strengthen and expand upon our previous research: one was aerial photogrammetry and the other a thermal sensor. The aim was to capture anomalies derived from the release of heat from the ground,

---

5 Curri 1978, 183–91.
6 For comparisons with chamber tombs with tumuli from the necropolis of Accesa, in Macchia del Monte, which is near Massa Marittima, see Camporeale and Giuntoli 2000, 43–49; Camporeale 2000, 104. On the necropoli of Santa Teresa di Gavorrano, see Donati and Cappuccin 2008, 47–49.
7 Firmati 2011.
8 In this manner, data obtained from the same zone was kept homogenous during the preliminary phase of research.

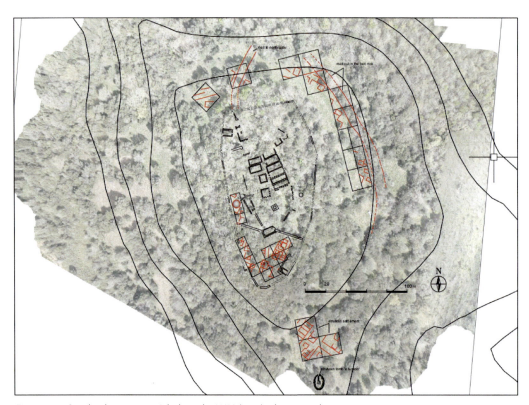

Figure 4.9. Overlap between aerial photo by UAV (2021), the general plan of the site and geophysical anomalies. Image by authors.

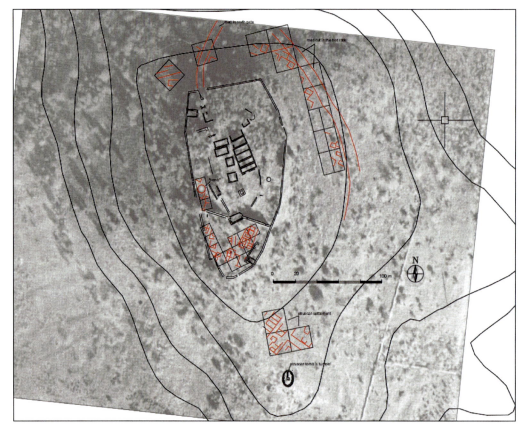

Figure 4.10. Overlap between aerial photo captured in 1970 showing the general plan of the site and geophysical anomalies. Image by authors.

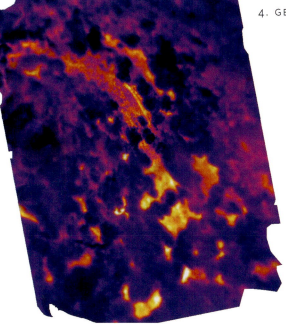

Figure 4.11. Thermal photo of the east side of the site. Photo by Emanuele Mariotti.

based on its composition and the presence of different material on its surface.

Thermal sensing is best undertaken at night or very early in the morning.

Drone photogrammetry highlighted the rapid growth of vegetation, where previously the same areas had been explored by geophysical prospecting, especially in the external parts to the south, northeast and north of the castle (Fig. 4.9). Even more evident is the difference with respect to aerial photos of the 1970s (Fig. 4.10), in which the east, south, and west sides were practically clear, and where one could still appreciate the external stratification. This is not a small detail, if you think about how the vegetation has grown. It is interesting to consider the superimposition of the geophysical anomalies on the current plan, with the aerial photo from the 1970s in which the scarce vegetation evidences the potential growth of the original settlement.

The use of the thermal sensor in the conditions described above did not show any particular new results. Nevertheless, in the clearest areas, the presence of rock material, both collapsed and standing in place, still allowed a thermal reading of the surface (certainly spoiled by solar radiation). The thermal differences between vegetation and soil surface have created natural markers, allowing the construction of a thermal photogrammetry of a large part of the site, in particular of the east and south sides (Fig. 4.11). The rocky outcrops in the cleared areas coincide with those already investigated by magnetometry, showing a chromatic excursion between bright red and yellow (high temperatures according to the range set manually on the camera controller). Also

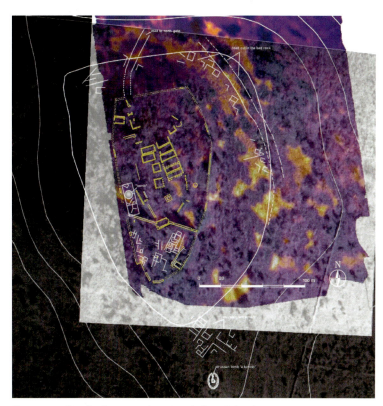

Figure 4.12. Overlap between the general plan of the site, geophysical anomalies and the thermal photo. Image by authors.

in this case an overlap between the general plan of the site, including the geophysical anomalies, and the thermal photo was recorded (Fig. 4.12). Both techniques, geomagnetic and thermal, confirm the presence of structures and anomalies in the areas outside the fortified village: the thermal imaging camera, in particular, underlines the presence of stone material on the surface that is not strictly linked to the natural rock bank and with a distribution compatible with what is highlighted by the geophysics. The presence of the road around the castle in this area is clear, well documented by the same geomagnetic prospecting.

In conclusion, despite the difficult working conditions for this type of investigation, the results show the potential of the site. The thick vegetation which irreparably covers the central part of the castle, could be further analysed with a multispectral sensor. This technique would be especially useful in the areas outside the walls, where the lower vegetation would allow for a better type of reading. The next step in furthering this type of research would be to expand beyond the Capalbiaccio hilltop and look at the wooded areas adjacent to the site.[9]

[EM]

---

9 For multispectral sensing techniques, see Materazzi and Pacifici 2021.

IRENE CORTI

5. Medieval Wall Reading

The Archaeology of Architecture

ABSTRACT The focus of this chapter is the application of building archaeology to the reading of masonry techniques for the standing walls of the fortified village of Capalbiaccio. While a regional database for comparable structures does not yet exist, Corti identifies seven groups of masonry techniques, including variations within each type and dates them creating the first set of records for this southern portion of Tuscany. This vertical matrix provides a relative chronology. By observing how the stones were cut and the tools used therein, the nature of the mortar, and finally comparing them with other examples in the area, a greater understanding of the architectural development of the site is achieved. Dyson's preliminary report discusses two major moments of building — the city walls and the later addition dividing the village in half — correctly indicating the thirteenth century as the high point of the community's life. Corti was able to identify three other major phases (and their variation of sub-categories) which are associated with different workshops operating on site from the twelfth to the fourteenth centuries. All the standing buildings are located on the northern part inside the fortification, while nothing survives from the southern side of the wall. This research provides further data among the many other Aldobrandeschi castles analysed in the region, and it invites new questions about architectural construction in a wider context that includes not only Tuscany and the neighbouring northern Latium, but also Rome. [MH]

Introduction

From the very outset of the project, the site of Capalbiaccio has revealed the potential of the archaeology of architecture to reconstruct the principal historical forces that the Aldobrandeschi initiatives contributed to the castle's character. This new approach to examining the remaining walls, which are well preserved in their elevations, and the planimetric forms, whose original dimensions can be now reconstructed, makes it possible to identify and read the traces of construction left by the builders. If it is possible to identify the phases that marked the completion of the structures in various historical periods one can also compare them with other similar structures in the region.

At Capalbiaccio, the examination of the elevations has yielded information that the former excavations of the 1970s did not, and which, in the case of a future excavation, may provide a historical platform from which to select further areas for investigation. Specifically, the course of research began with a record of the structural stratigraphy of the various constructed entities in order to establish a chronology based on the remains of the masonry. Afterwards, all surviving fragments of the wall were indexed and classified in an analytical manner in order to establish a chronotypology of construction techniques associated with fiducial building types. The study also included a macroscopic analysis of the mortar used in various constructions. Photographic specimens were prepared in scale for each stretch of the wall, indexed, and integrated into a detailed classificatory index of building techniques. Further, a photo-corrected version of stratigraphic readings of the wall was created, making the buildings more legible.

Once fieldwork was completed, the data obtained was modified. The result was a detailed periodization into which all phases of construction identified in the walls of the preserved elevations were inserted. Chronotypology of construction techniques and a classification of the different building types adopted in various centuries were also completed.

Periodization

On the basis of the preserved masonry remains, it is presently impossible to assume the existence of a stone building phase before the twelfth century. The excavation, particularly the examined materials preserved (see *infra* Vaccaro), yielded clear traces of a phase of settlement dating back at least to the central Middle Ages, which can probably be asso-

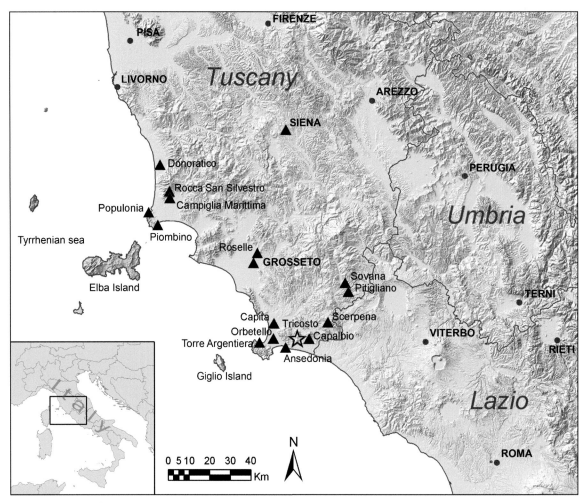

Figure 5.1. Map of places mentioned in the text. Map by Rossella Pansini. Basemap/DTM reproduced with the permission of CTR Regione Toscana.

ciated with structures built of non-durable materials. At the time of Dyson's excavation, the medieval phases were separated into levels (I–III) and there were no traces of the earlier phase (Fig. 5.1).

Phase I (Fig. 5.2)

Among the earliest structures visible at Capalbiaccio are the church (Building 1=2) and the tower (Building 5=E), which are located in the south-central portion of the plateau. We can hypothesize that, in the course of the twelfth century, a settlement consisting of two buildings in stone — a tower (whose reduced dimensions suggest that it served a military, rather than residential, function) and a church — took root here, perhaps over a preexisting one. Given the presence of a sacred building, it is likely that there was a community with residential structures, though they were likely built of perishable materials. It is also plausible to presuppose the existence of a bailey, which might have been made of wood and was probably lower than the stone wall erected later. However, no trace of the bailey remains.

According to Tiziano Mannoni's traditional classification system, the building technique that employed faced stone blocks is attributed to professional masons who were hired by a patron who wished to demonstrate his will to invest financially in the transformation of the settlement.[10] Moreover, numerous parallels can be found in the building techniques of the neighbouring territory and beyond.[11]

---

10 Mannoni 1997.

11 On parallels to neighbouring territories, see the published works on the zone north of Grosseto in Guideri, Parenti and Barbagli 2000; Fichera 2005. On the Amiatino area, see Francovich and others 1997; Citter and others 2002a; and the results of Michele Nucciotti's doctoral thesis (2006). On areas further away, see the works published on the province of Livorno in Bianchi 2003c; Paris 2005. On the territory of Lazio, see Chiovelli 2007; Fiorani 1996.

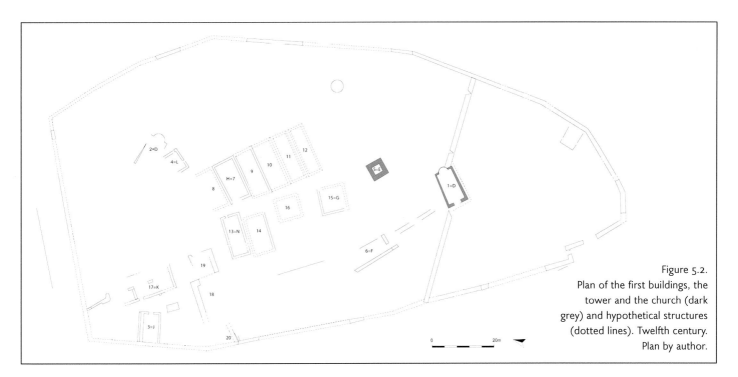

Figure 5.2. Plan of the first buildings, the tower and the church (dark grey) and hypothetical structures (dotted lines). Twelfth century. Plan by author.

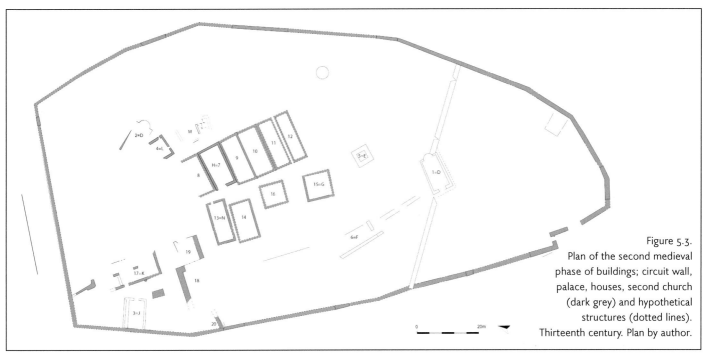

Figure 5.3. Plan of the second medieval phase of buildings; circuit wall, palace, houses, second church (dark grey) and hypothetical structures (dotted lines). Thirteenth century. Plan by author.

Together, they grant us a reliable means of dating this phase, which, on a historical level, corresponds to the oldest surviving documentary testimony that links the ownership of the stronghold to the abbey at Tre Fontane in Rome.[12]

---

12 Farinelli 2007; Cammarosano and Passeri 1985, 28; Collavini 1998.

Phase II (Fig. 5.3)

The moment in which the greatest structural expansion at the settlement took place — in keeping with what has emerged from the preliminary analysis of contextual pottery (see *infra* Valdambrini; Hobart) — can generally be ascribed to the thirteenth century. The most relevant feature of this phase is the extraordinary variety of building types, masonry techniques, and construction methods, visible in both buildings

Figure 5.4. a, b. Building technique with decorative elements in the style *spina di pesce* found in the cloister of the monastery of Sant'Angelo Rovinato (above left) and same style *spina di pesce* in the defensive walls of the fortified site, Torre Argentiera (above right) c. Overall view of the wall at Capalbiaccio. Photos by author.

During the thirteenth century, the settlement grew to occupy the summit of nearly the entire plateau. It was given stone fortifications that were equipped with a communication trench (with a shoe in the northern section as well as two accesses: one each in the north and south spurs). A second church was erected (Building 2=O) in the northern section, perhaps because the preexisting religious building was not ample enough to hold the increased population or had collapsed from disuse (though there is no physical evidence to support the latter hypothesis). The new church was also provided with a small structure (Building 4=L), built nearly under the lee of its southern wall, which possibly functioned as a sacristy.

A series of quality buildings, greatly varied in type, were built in the northwest section of the fortified stronghold including: a structure (Building 17=K) that was notably long and narrow with walls 0.75 m thick and complex internal articulation; an imposing palazzo (Building 18) with brick decoration, joined to another structure (Building 19); a large tower with a residential function. Its original organization has not been preserved, but — based on the quantity of fallen stone blocks — it was presumably quite tall (at least three stories), with walls 2 m thick, and a scarp. The residential structures of the village — aligned in rows and oriented in the same direction — also went up during this phase of construction. They were built in such a way that the sidewalls each rested on that of the adjacent building. This suggests that this phase of building took place over some period of time.

Finally, the building located in the southwest section of the residential area may also be attributed to this phase of development. Given the scarcity of its remains, it cannot be reconstructed in its original dimensions and form, but it was most likely a structure with a residential function. It has a highly unusual foundation (from a technical point of view), with herringbone decorative elements created from small pebbles. With the help of comparative material drawn from the neighbouring area, this pattern can be generically dated to the late thirteenth century (Fig. 5.4, a and b).[14]

of quality (those of the lord and military) and the village's residential structures. This heterogeneity demonstrates a building phase that probably extended over the course of a century and involved many individuals of a certain prominence (based on the number of fine buildings that can be distinguished within the site).

The people who controlled and ran the stronghold, either together or at intervals, were responsible for choosing the types of buildings adopted. Historical testimony show that, in the thirteenth century, the stronghold passed into the hands of the Aldobrandeschi family, which held many fortified sites in the region.[13] It is also possible that a more or less contemporaneous local community took shape on the hill of Capalbiaccio in the thirteenth century or that lesser local nobility directly managed the stronghold for the Aldobrandeschi.

13 Collavini 1998; Farinelli 2007.

14 Thanks to the study that the author is conducting in the area in connection with a doctoral project, interesting comparative

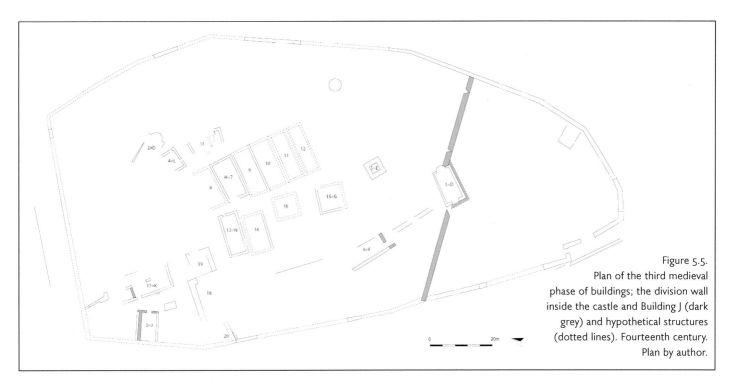

Figure 5.5.
Plan of the third medieval phase of buildings; the division wall inside the castle and Building J (dark grey) and hypothetical structures (dotted lines). Fourteenth century. Plan by author.

Phase III (Fig. 5.5)

The final building activity related to the life of the stronghold belongs to a later phase. For reasons not yet entirely clear, the settlement was reduced in size with the erection of a massive masonry partition that cut across the plateau diagonally from east to west, abutting the bailey on one side and passing over it on the other. This wall excluded the plateau's outer-most southern section, which, having no opening, was no longer accessible. This operation redefined the site's defensive facility and can be linked, with caution, to another change in the stronghold's ownership, when the castle fell into the hands of the Orsini of Pitigliano.

This shift in power is also confirmed by the construction of a new quality building (Building 3=J), which was erected near certain preceding structures, abutting the bailey and a preexistent wall. This structure reveals a certain refinement in typological choices, such as the entrance on the façade, which has a low arch and internal niches in the shape of a hut or beehive, similar to the embrasures in the massive dividing wall. The present state of research has yielded no parallels for this technique in the building typology of the neighbouring region or even beyond. Consequently, the generic fourteenth-century date assigned to the building is solely based on its stratigraphic relationships to the other structures.

Historical Reconstruction

This analytical study of the architecture of the medieval fortified village of Capalbiaccio had two objectives. The first was to define the chief building campaigns and transformations of the site. The approaches by means of a chronotypological grid, listing techniques, and structural typologies were then compared to those of settlements in the surrounding area. The second was to try to define the historical, political, and economic context into which the settlement of Capalbiaccio could be inserted. We sought likewise to identify power groups that controlled the stronghold and their role as principal patrons in the creation of the various structural forms. Indispensable to this end has been a study of the historical sources dealing with the stronghold, as well as a more comprehensive analysis of the surrounding region, based on both documentation and archaeological evidence.

---

data for the stronghold of Capalbiaccio is emerging. Indeed, in the monastery of Sant'Angelo Rovinato (near Orbetello) and at the site of Torre Argentiera (near Porto Santo Stefano), some walls have been found with a particular decorative element — a herringbone pattern — which is associated with a technique in lithic ashlar. It is used in the defensive bailey at both sites. It is curious to note that the aforementioned sites, like Capalbiaccio, were associated with the monastery of Tre Fontane in ecclesiastical documents in the early centuries of the Middle Ages and to the Aldobrandeschi as to building techniques. These mutual bonds and the use of a common work force could have determined some of the architectonic choices made in the construction of these thirteenth-century centres. See Corti 2008–2009.

The stronghold of Capalbiaccio is located in an area that corresponds to the ancient *Ager Cosanus*, which today is made up of the municipalities of Orbetello and Capalbio. In the geography of medieval power, this section of the southern Maremma, which lies between the dioceses of Grosseto to the north, Sovana to the east, and the vast territorial holdings of the Papal States to the south, was without cities. Its geographical position rendered it a self-sufficient area, with respect to the rest of Maremma. From the high Middle Ages onwards it became a frontier land between the Papal States and the lay and ecclesiastical powers that dominated southern Tuscany.[15]

Along with the expansionist aims of the duke and bishop of Lucca during the Lombard period, the historical sources reveal that during the Carolingian and post-Carolingian era, the Papal States were a constantly oscillating power presence in the area.[16] The Aldobrandeschi family, a political actor that played an important role in the formation of the medieval landscape along the coast of southern Maremma, inserted itself into the politics of territorial re-acquisition that was directed against papal expansion in Lombard Tuscia. In 853, Emperor Louis II bestowed authority over a vast portion of southern Tuscia to one member of the family.[17] From the ninth to the twelfth century, the Aldobrandeschi family transformed its vast agrarian holdings into a large earldom, which extended over all of the southern Maremma.[18]

The historical sources also reveal another political player, who had been active in the region since the high Middle Ages. This was the monastery of Tre Fontane, a Roman coenobium that was already involved in papal territorial politics in the seventh century.[19] A document dated 805, of which a copy of the mid-twelfth century survives, speaks of a concession made to the monastery of Tre Fontane by Charlemagne and Leo III, which included the lands of the ancient city of Cosa.[20] The Roman monastery may have been the actual beneficiary of such a donation, which would have occurred between the late eighth and early ninth century. Carolingian sovereigns made donations like this in order to establish the *Patrimonium Petri* in southern Tuscany. What is certain is that in the eleventh and twelfth centuries — as the two papal bulls indicate — the monastery owned those lands and preserved them until the definitive concession in *emphyteusis* to Hildebrand VII at the end of the twelfth century.[21]

Among the possessions of the monastery described in the second bull of 1161 is the stronghold of Capalbiaccio, here referred to as Trecosti. However, in the course of the thirteenth century, the stronghold appears among the baronies within the great countship of the Aldobrandeschi family. The scarcity of documents does not permit one to determine the identity of the actual patrons that founded Capalbiaccio. One may merely guess what role the monastery of Tre Fontane played in the settlement's foundation, without, however, excluding the possibility of the Aldobrandeschi presence as early as the mid-ninth century.

The examination of the region's archaeological evidence does not help us create a clear historical picture of the evolution of the stronghold of Capalbiaccio, in the early and central Middle Ages.[22] Indeed, given the political instability and uncertain

---

15   Fentress and Wickham 2001.
16   Collavini 1998; Biondi 2002.
17   Precise information on which districts is unclear, due to the lack of institutional documents on southern Tuscany. Most likely, they were the districts of Populonia, Roselle, and Sovana (see Collavini 1998, 51–70). With reference to the area surrounding Capalbiaccio, a document from 991 states that there was a Count Oberto (of whom no further mention is made) active in the territory of Sovana (see Collavini 1998; Tabacco 1989).
18   The agricultural legacy of the Aldobrandeschi include fiscal possessions obtained through the title of Count, held by Hildebrand II from the mid-ninth century, and, in the first quarter of the ninth century, through *allodia* holdings connected to the clerical payer of the family. Indeed in 809, the cleric Alperto II of the Aldobrandeschi family obtained the first nucleus of holdings in Sovana: Tucciano, Lusciano and the villages of Mucciano and Valeriano. See Collavini 1998.
19   The monastery, located in *Aquae Salviae*, a small valley along the ancient via Laurentina, was probably founded in the seventh century by Cilician monks. Of notable importance already in that century and closely tied to the papacy, but also the Byzantine empire, it benefited from many donations in the eighth and ninth centuries. In the eleventh century, it was under the rule of the Benedictine order, until Pope Innocent II granted it to the Cistercians, following a crisis. The construction of the monastery in its present form dates back to the thirteenth century. See Luttrell 2001.
20   Collavini 1998, 265.
21   The first papal bull referred to is that of 1080, issued by Pope Gregory VII, who, after the crisis that struck the coenoby, ceded all its holdings to the Roman monastery of St Paul. Five sites are mentioned in the bull: *Simulque Ansedonam civitatem, cum pertinentiis suis et portu suo. Montem qui vocatur Argentarium cum lacu Catamare, ubi est ecclesia S. Angeli; et medietatem castri Orbitelli cum pertinentiis suis; et castrum quod vocatur Elsa, cum omnibus suis pertinentiis* (Trifone 1908, 280). In addition to Capalbiaccio (referred to as Trecosti), the second bull of 1161, issued by Pope Alexander III, also included the new strongholds of Scerpena and Capita, which were added to the old sites mentioned in 1081. See Carandini and others 2002.
22   There are traces of a settlement in the old Roman colony of Cosa (now Ansedonia), datable to the tenth or eleventh century. This settlement is characterized by defensive facilities that are made of perishable materials, some trenches, a fence, two stone churches, each with its own cemetery, and traces of habitations constructed of perishable materials in the zone of the forum and eastern heights. See Hobart 1995.

power relationships that characterized this part of southern Maremma, a not-surprising feature of the region is the limited existence of settlements documented for the early Middle Ages. This scarcity of known settlements is, however, probably partly due to the limited research that has heretofore been conducted in the region, something that this book and its authors are working to rectify.

The evidence derived from a study of the wall elevations at Capalbiaccio confirms the existence of a settlement characterized by a church and a tower at the centre of the plateau (Phase 1, twelfth century). It may have been linked to a residential area comprised of huts and a surrounding wall constructed from perishable material, which have not yet been identified. The same type of settlement seems to develop at Cosa, where a defensive stone citadel, located in the eastern portion of the plateau, enclosed a tower, to which some residential structures were probably linked.[23] In fact, the twelfth century is identified with the beginning of stone building activity, which includes not only sites, such as Capalbiaccio and Ansedonia, but also other contemporary sites that have been documented in the rest of the region.

In the case of Capalbiaccio, there is a true redefinition of the settlement during the twelfth century. By the following century it had become a centre of notable size, with numerous stone buildings. It indicates both a seigniorial zone, with at least three towers and important residential buildings, as well as a village, provided with a second new church. The extraordinary variety in the choice of building typology, masonry techniques, and means of construction, in both the more distinguished structures (seigniorial and military) and the residential ones, indicate the nature of the commission during over much of the century. The variety also suggests the participation of many prominent figures (given the number of distinguished buildings identified within the site), which controlled or managed the stronghold at the same time or at intervals.

In conclusion, Capalbiaccio was one of the few strategic elevated sites created for the sake of controlling and managing territory to develop in the course of the twelfth century in this portion of southern Maremma. This notwithstanding, the physical evidence reveals that the patron(s) who constructed Capalbiaccio did not make a significant investment in the stronghold. They only built structures with a clear defensive or religious purpose (a tower and a church), without constructing buildings such as a residential seat for the lord and the sort of housing that would make us expect the presence of inhabitants within the fortified centre.

Methodology

By this point, the archaeology of buildings is a discipline that has been tested and used for over forty years, beginning with the pioneering studies of the 1970s, wherein the tools used for archaeological digs were first applied to architectural structures.[24] The archaeology of architecture has generated important results in recent years, thanks above all to the work conducted by the Department of Archaeology at the University of Siena. Aware of the discipline's great potential, Riccardo Francovich, with the assistance of several collaborators, such as Giovanna Bianchi and Roberto Parenti, applied these analytical methods at numerous sites in Tuscany. They examined individual monuments, large complexes,[25] and entire historical centres.[26]

Vertical stratigraphic readings of phases of structural activity, visible in the elevations, analyses of building techniques (materials, workmanship, tool types, cement), the study of architectural elements (structural and decorative), location of apertures, and comprehensive architectural typologies created through planimetric reconstructions are the fundamental tools for the study of architectonic remains. The application of such methods has made it possible to identify major construction phases at sites such as the strongholds of Donoratico or Rocca S. Silvestro, and link them to the patrons in charge of planning and erecting buildings, and to specialized workmen, such as the master stonemasons, who were called in to work the stone.

---

23 Hobart 1995; Fentress 2003.

24 For fundamental principles of the archaeology of architecture, see the pioneering studies of Mannoni (1976, 1984, and 1988), as well as the contributions in Francovich and Parenti 1988, and Brogiolo, Zonca, and Zigrino 1988. In addition, see the journal *Archeologia dell'Architettura*, which since 1996 has been demonstrating the evolution of the discipline and offering case studies that have put it to test. For a recent overview, see D'Ulizia 2005; Brogiolo 1996, 1997, 2002; and Cagnana 1994.

25 Donoratico (LI), Rocca S. Silvestro (LI), Sant'Antimo sopra i canali-Piombino (LI), Siena, Campiglia (LI), Piombino (LI).

26 See Parenti 1992b for a reading of the architecture of Siena's centre, as well as Bianchi 2003a 2003b, 2003c. For a reference bibliography on the full context of the coast of southern Tuscany, see Berti and Bianchi 2007.

Analysis of Construction Techniques

Analytical studies of the architecture of Capalbiaccio have led to the identification of seven groups of construction techniques in stone, which are spread across a chronological span from the twelfth to fourteenth centuries. The following criteria were used to classify the masonry techniques: type of building material; the degree and type of labour used to prepare and finish the architectural elements; their setting within the work; profile type; and cement type, accompanied by a macroscopic analysis of their features.

Despite the complete lack of integration between the vertical stratigraphy and the excavated horizontal deposits, it was possible to assign a chronological framework to the format through typological comparisons with other techniques that have been dated through excavations at fortified settlements in the region. Only one masonry technique — with finely finished blocks of local travertine inserted regularly into the structure — has been identified as belonging to the initial phase of the stronghold (twelfth century). The squared and levelled features of this technique required the expertise of specialized stonemasons. On the other hand, analysis of the material remains of the thirteenth century reveals five techniques that use roughly hewn local travertine as their principal material. The variety of techniques can be differentiated according to the degree of precision in the handling of the material and the regularity with which it is inserted into the work.

The principal technical characteristics suggest that only a very small number of specialized workers were employed in the planning and construction of the new settlement. They were likely accompanied by a greater number of simple stonemasons and local manpower. The socio-economic context relegates the so-called 'building industry' to a more local ambit, which currently prevents reliable parallels in a region still poorly studied from an architectural point of view.

Finally, only one fifteenth-century technique has been differentiated. It relies on the same type of local travertine as those techniques from the preceding century: hewn and lightly finished stones placed in a rectangular and quadrangular form. As in the case of the thirteenth-century techniques, it is logical to also attribute this one to a local, non-specialized workforce and stonemasons who were commissioned to build the final structures before the stronghold was abandoned.

Building Technique 1 (Fig. 5.6a)

The first technique was used in the construction of the masonry walls of the church (Building 1=D) and defensive tower (Building 5=E). This technique consists of square, smoothed blocks made from local travertine of uniform lengths, but irregular heights that vary between 0.12 and 0.25 m. For this reason, even the perfectly horizontal and parallel courses vary in their height. The levelling of the blocks' faces, executed with a pointed tool, results in a tight fit between the blocks and a slender and fairly regular thickness — between 0.01 and 0.02 m — of the joints and base. The lime mortar binder is extremely compact and strong, of a light grey colour, with a high ratio of inert particles of small and medium size (maximum 0.05 m), which are chiefly constituted of smooth black pebbles and various types of gravel. On the inner walls of the tower, the mortar flows out from the joints and bases and seems to have been applied with a pointy instrument. The pile presents a filler of regular blocks of a height corresponding to the rows, with medium-small cleft blocks, as well as many lithic chips that serve as infill (Fig. 5.6b). Technique 1 is datable to the twelfth century.

Building Technique 2 (Fig. 5.7a)

This technique was used in the creation of the large habitable tower — now collapsed — in the northwest section (Building 19), in the stronghold's monumental northern gateway (Building 20), and in the stretch of escarpment discovered along the wall of the western bailey of the stronghold (Building 21). It consists of a regular bond with medium-small rectangular blocks of local travertine, extending in length rather than height and lying in parallel horizontal rows with no lithic infill of the kind used mostly for bases. The lithotypes used in the jambs of the apertures are of medium-large size and are, for the most part, square, with smooth surfaces. The joints and bases — given the lack of levelled surfaces — are rather thick (between 0.01 and 0.04 m) and fairly regular, but nonetheless receding due to rains. Having been washed away, the lime mortar used to bind the material is rather friable and not particularly strong; ochre in colour, it is composed of inert particles of sand and variously coloured small-medium gravel, mixed with small clumps of lime. The wall section reveals a heap of chaotic infill, with small-medium size cleft stones incorporated in thick mortar (Fig. 5.7b). Technique 2 is datable to the thirteenth century.

5. MEDIEVAL WALL READING   77

Figure 5.6. A: Technique 1, Buildings 1=D and 5=E (twelfth century). B: Detail of the wall pile for Technique 1. Photos by author.

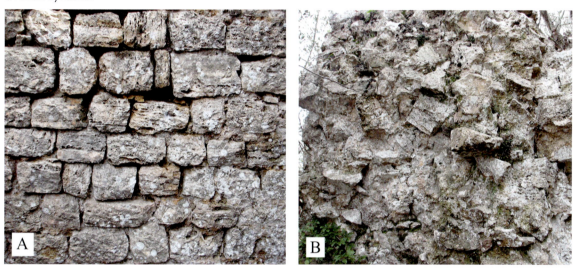

Figure 5.7. A: Technique 2, Buildings 19, 20, and 21 (thirteenth century). Sample not in scale.
B. Detail of the wall pile for Technique 2. Photos by author.

Figure 5.8. A: Technique 2, variant A, in Buildings 2 and 17=K (thirteenth century). Sample 1 × 1 m.
B: Detail of the wall pile for Technique 2, variant A. Photos by author.

Figure 5.9. A: Technique 3, Building 18=P (thirteenth century). Sample not in scale.
B: detail of the wall pile for Technique 3. Photos by author.

Figure 5.10. A: Technique 4, in the city walls and Building 21 (thirteenth century). Sample 1.5 × 1.5 m.
B: Detail of the wall pile for Technique 4. Photos by author.

Building Technique 2, variant A (Fig. 5.8, a and b)

Technique 2, variant A is distinguishable in the second church structure (Building 2) and in the elongated structure (Building 17=K) located in the northwest section. It differs in its greater use of hewn blocks of perfectly rectangular form, which, for the most part, are between 0.25 and 0.35 m long, and are paired with quadrangular rusticated ashlar. The wall pile appears more regular, nearly inclined to form true bases that follow the course. Technique 2, variant A is dateable to the thirteenth century.

Building Technique 3 (Fig. 5.9a)

This technique can be seen in an imposing structure located in the northwest section of the stronghold (Building 18=P). It reveals a regular texture that combines brick with medium-small travertine blocks that are hewn with a certain degree of care and arranged in parallel horizontal rows. The joints and base show a great deal of smooth, overflowing, and, in several places, even dripping mortar that covers the edges and parts of the visible face of the stone nearly to the point of covering it, thus granting it a highly homogeneous appearance. The massive mortar on the external surface of the masonry and joined to the calcareous incrustation prevents the size of the joints and mortar beds from being noticeable. An alternate result is the pile that shows an infill of beds, which follows the rows with cleft, medium-sized blocks that, in some cases, are arranged and lodged obliquely in thick mortar (as in the north church, Building 2) (Fig. 5.9b). The technique of the decorative brick element is characterized by the four horizontal parallel rows at the centre of the wall, which are created by whole bricks, around 0.26 m, and decorative bricks, broken in half, and of around 0.12 m, laid flat. Technique 3 is datable to the thirteenth century.

Building Technique 4 (Fig. 5.10a)

This technique is found on some stretches of the city walls (the bailey) on all slopes, and in the monumental northern gateway (Building 21). It is characterized by summarily hewn or merely broken travertine blocks that are, however, set into the structure in a fairly regular manner, tending towards a rectangular or, in some cases, quadrangular form. The blocks, the dimensions of which vary between small and medium-large, are arranged in horizontal, somewhat parallel, and, in certain cases, double rows. This irregularity, which is caused by the vertical arrangement of the ashlar with respect to the natural sedimentation of the stone, is often resolved by the creation of horizontal rows composed of narrow and long blocks. Recourse to lithic fillers to fill wide foundations is also frequent. The joints and the bases, of ample and irregular thickness, recede significantly. The stone is cemented by lime mortar of a yellow colour, with an extremely fine granulometry composed of sand and tiny inclusions, which can be identified as tiny river-washed pebbles (up to 1 cm in size). With a low ratio of lime, the binding agent appears rather friable and too weak to withstand a heavy downpour or strong wind. The pile seems to consist of a rather chaotic infill of hewn blocks of small and medium size, joined with mortar. In certain areas, hints of regularity can be identified, as in the formation of the beds (Fig. 5.10b). Technique 4 can be dated to the thirteenth century.

Building Technique 4, variant A (Fig. 5.11)

This technical variant was used for the construction of the residential village (Buildings 7, 8, 9, 10, 11, and 12) and for certain stretches of the city walls (the bailey). It includes the same type of material and binding agent as Technique 4 but differs in the use of medium-small blocks that are simply cleft, totally heterogeneous in form, and arranged in highly

Figure 5.11. Technique 4, variant A, in the city walls and Buildings 7, 8, 9, 10, 11, and 12. Sample 1.5 × 1.5 m. Photo by author.

irregular, sub-horizontal rows that tend to split. This irregularity leads to the use of many fillers, both lithic and brick. The mortar, though the same in colour and containing inclusions, seems tougher, with joints and beds that recede less and are less washed away. Technique 4, variant A is datable to the thirteenth century.

Building Technique 5 (Fig. 5.12a)

This technique can be observed in the defensive city walls of the stronghold. It uses only hewn travertine blocks that vary greatly in size and form; the lithotypes vary from medium to small, with extremely irregular forms that approach the rectangular in only a few cases. The bond is articulated in sub-horizontal rows that often tend to lose their horizontality, due to the diversity in the forms and dimensions of the lithotype and the inclusion of smaller blocks set vertically and obliquely. The irregularity of the setting is responsible for the frequent use of horizontal alignments connected to abundant lithic fillers and the use of bricks to fill the spaces between the stones. The joints and the bases are irregular and of notable thickness, with poured, smooth mortar, but no oozing. The binding material uses highly compact and strong light-grey lime mortar with small-

Figure 5.12. A: Technique 5, in the city walls. Technical sample, 1.5 × 1.5 m. B: Detail of wall pile for Technique 5. Photos by author.

Figure 5.13. A: Technique 6 in Building 3=J and the dividing wall. Sample 1.5 × 1.5 m. B: detail of the wall pile for Technique 6. Photos by author.

Figure 5.14. The large collapsed tower, Building 19. Photo by Hermann Salvadori.

and medium-sized inert particles composed of both non-river-washed black gravel and various types of pebbles, mixed with many lumps of lime. The pile displays a chaotic infill of small and medium blocks, with chips of bricks rolled in thick mortar (Fig. 5.12b). The technique is also characterized by circular holes for holding scaffolds, which penetrate the masonry. Technique 5 is datable to the thirteenth century.

Building Technique 6 (Fig. 5.13a)

This technique was used in the masonry partition that divides the plateau diagonally, as well as in building 3=J in the northwest portion of the stronghold. It is characterized by a setting of cleft travertine blocks of heterogeneous size and form — totally irregular and polygonal blocks bound to ones that tend towards the rectangular. On the other hand, more finished blocks, which in certain cases are nearly square and lightly razed, were used for the corners and apertures. The lithotypes were set into the work over sub-horizontal courses. They often split and lose their horizontality because of their heterogeneous form and size, as well as the inclusion of blocks set vertically and obliquely. Numerous lithic fillers and smaller quantities of bricks and tile fragments have been identified along the courses. The joints and the beds are ample and irregular, with a smooth and, in some cases, overflowing mortar. In the corner, on the other hand, thanks to the perfect squaring of the ashlars, the joints and beds are regular and thin. The lime mortar is highly compact, strong, and beige in colour, with a coarse granulometry, due to the high number of inert particles of non-river-washed black gravel of various dimensions (between 0.002 and 0.1 m) present mostly in the binding agent that seeps out of the joints and beds, as opposed to that used on the interior of the wall's nucleus. The wall section reveals a pile full of medium-small stones, which are shimmed with brick and stone flakes, and portions of thick mortar (Fig. 5.13b).

Analyses of Structural Building Typologies

The criteria used to establish a specific classification of an architectural structure include plan type, dimensions, apertures, fittings, and structural elements. As in the analyses of construction techniques, a chronological framework emerged as well through typological comparison with other dated structures at fortified sites in the region. Where a typological parallel was lacking, the date was calculated solely on the basis of the stratigraphical relationships of the buildings.

Structural Typology 1

An 11.5 × 5.3 m building (1=D) with a single semi-circular apse projecting from east to west. Only some of the elevations of the structure, whose planimetric arrangement is plainly visible, are preserved. The building's height and type of roofing cannot be established. It contains two entrances: one on the façade, with an opening of 2.4 m, and another along the north wall. The walls have a thickness of 0.8 m. This is a small religious building, utilizing Technique 1, and datable to the twelfth century.

Structural Typology 2

A building (5=E) with a square plan, an external perimeter of 5.5 × 5.5 m, an internal area of 8.2 m², walls of a thickness of ~1.17 m, and an east-west orientation. The building had several levels, as is demonstrated by the distinctive apertures, which are aligned and positioned at the same height from the ground on the internal perimeter. In view of the poor preservation of the elevations, a reconstruction of the building's initial height and roof-type is impossible.

Its form and reduced dimensions suggest that this tower had an exclusively defensive (non-residential) function. It is built with Technique 1 and is datable to the twelfth century.

Structural Typology 3

A building (17=K) had a north–south orientation. Only ~1 m of the western and southern perimeters' elevations and the ground plan of the eastern wall are preserved. According to a hypothetical reconstruction, this was a rectangular building, considerably more long (over 14 m) than wide (~7 m), with walls 0.75 m thick. The interior appears to have been articulated into naves by rectangular stone piers (of which only two survive) that are set in the centre of the space, around 3.5 m from the eastern and western sides and 5 m from each other. In addition to dividing the space, the piers may have also served as supports for the building's second storey.

A singular aperture, ~1.46 m large, on the northern side of the western peripheral wall, is also related to the initial building. The building features an underground cistern to collect and preserve rainwater midway along the western peripheral wall. The cistern is plastered with a hydraulic red lime and contains a semi-circular aperture of around 0.5 × 0.8 m, with a profile that spreads out, and a conduit that runs beneath the structure. Given the building's dimensions, its internal articulation, and the presence of a

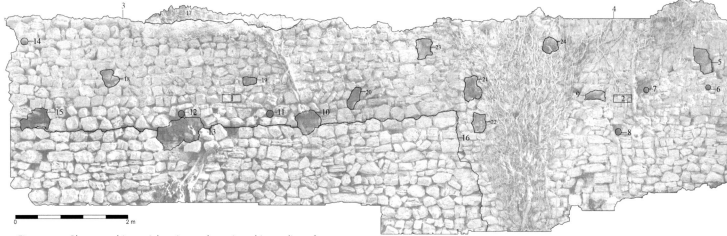

Figure 5.15. Photographic straightening and stratigraphic reading of a section of the wall from the east side of the defensive bailey (city walls). Photo by author.

hydraulic facility of a certain quality, one may assume that this building served an elite residential function. It was built using Technique 2, variant B and can be dated to the thirteenth century.

Structural Typology 4 (Fig. 5.14)

A building (19, the collapsed tower) whose original plan is impossible to reconstruct; the building has collapsed and only three large stumps of masonry are preserved. The majestic quality of the surviving parts and its 2-metre-thick walls lead one to assume that this was an immense tower with a noteworthy interior, capable of serving a residential, as well as a defensive, function.[27] The elevation too must have been tall with at least three floors. There were aligned holes on the internal walls that would have enclosed the beams for the floor. Apertures can also be distinguished. Some narrow, single-lancet windows are located at the heights of the tower's different levels. The tower was built using Technique 2 and can be dated to the thirteenth century.

Structural Typology 5 (Dyson, Fig. 2.8)

A building (18=P) with an east–west orientation, of which only the northern and part of the eastern wall are preserved. Despite its limited remains, the large structure deserves a detailed description. The building has a rectangular plan, walls ~1.4 m thick rising, and at least two floors, in view of the traces of rectangular apertures aligned with each other in the uppermost section of the northern façade. A decorative element, characterized by four parallel, horizontal courses of brick — some whole, some broken in half — laid flat, projects from the centre of the northern wall. In the centre of the uppermost section of the same wall can be seen a narrow embrasure, with two large, squared travertine ashlars for jambs. The presence of ornamentation, as well as the building's dimensions, suggest that it was a quality residential building. It was built using Technique 3 and is datable to the thirteenth century.[28]

Structural Typology 6

A building (7=H, of the residential village) with a rectangular plan of about 16 × 6 m, an east–west orientation, and walls approximately 0.6 m thick. Every side of the structure is preserved in elevation. It must have had two storeys. That is clear from the indentations for crossbeams, which can be identified on the southern wall, and which are aligned with each other and set about 2.6 m from the floor. The entrance into the building is on the short, west side. Its original dimensions cannot be reconstructed, as only the left jamb is preserved. It is possible to imagine a second entrance on the corresponding short wall, though the scanty remains of the structure cannot confirm such a conjecture. Also on the short, west side is a large niche of about 0.94 × 1.2 m, which still preserves part of the wooden crossbeam of its architrave. Traces of preserved plaster are evident in the niche, as well as on the sidewalls, confirming that the entire interior was plastered at one time. Given the presence of the niche and the absence of windows, it is possible that the building served as a storeroom on the ground floor and as a residence on the upper floor.

---

27 Examples of habitable towers can be seen in Parenti 1992a and Bianchi 2004.

28 For other examples of fine quality residential buildings, see Bianchi 2003b.

5. MEDIEVAL WALL READING   83

Figure 5.16. Photographic straightening and stratigraphic reading of the façade of building 3=J. Photo by author.

Structural Typology 8 (Fig. 5.15)

A defensive bailey (city walls), of which a significant portion — equal to 463 m — is preserved, covers an area of 13.360 m². Some remnants of the wall retain their original height of 3.50 m. Visible in the uppermost section are remnants of the original communication platform that was built into the wall and furnished with a stone parapet. Two entrances at the extreme northern and southern ends of the bailey allow access to the settlement. The southern entrance (Building C) is characterized by a corridor running parallel to the bailey, which has a breadth of 1.2 m. Of the northern entrance, only a stretch of wall perpendicular to the stone bailey and creating an L-shape is preserved (Building 21). This was likely the monumental entrance to the stronghold. In the northern section, the bailey created a communication walk about 5 m wide. The bailey was constructed with Techniques 3 and 4; it is datable to the thirteenth century.

Structural Typology 9 (Fig. 5.16)

A building (3=J) with an east–west orientation, built with only two walls (the east and north), whose elevations are still very well preserved. The other two walls were pre-existing: the stone bailey served as the western wall and an older structure, of which only one row remains, completed the building on the southern side. The building is rectangular in form, with dimensions of 8.8 × 4.7 m, and it is articulated into two stories, as is clearly demonstrated by the rectangular holes used for inserting the wooden beams to support the floor above. Said holes are discernible at the same height on the eastern and northern walls. There are also two partly preserved apertures that function as the access to the first floor; one is set up high in the western portion of the northern wall and the other on the façade above the entrance on the ground floor. The latter is chiefly characterized by a shallow arch 1.57 m in size.

Three hut-shaped niches in the uppermost section of the inner northern wall, which corresponds to the first floor of the building, are preserved. The niches, which are more or less equal in size, have monolithic jambs and tympana and a plastered surface. Another larger rectangular niche (1 × 1.30 m) is distinguishable on the lower portion of the same wall,

Flanking this building are other buildings, of which only the ground plan is visible. They are of similar dimensions and plan, oriented along an east–west axis, parallel to each other and facing a common thoroughfare. These rows of houses form the residential village of Capalbiaccio.

The first lot of houses contains six buildings (7=H, 8, 9, 10, 11, and 12) of a rectangular form, with dimensions fluctuating between 4.5–6 m in width and 12.5–14 m in depth. A stratigraphic reading reveals a succession of building campaigns from south to north, with walls progressively supported by one other. The second lot consists of four houses: two of rectangular form (Buildings N and 14=I), with dimensions fluctuating between 11–12 m in depth and 5–6 m in width, which are nearly attached to each other and separated only by a thin strip of earth about 0.7 m thick; and two residences (Buildings 15=G and 16) that are further away and far apart. They are more or less quadrangular in form and noticeably smaller, ranging between 7.4 × 7.4 m and 6.1 × 7 m. All the structures of the village were built using Technique 4, variant A and are datable to the thirteenth century.

Figure 5.17. Section of the dividing wall of Capalbiaccio stronghold. Photo by author.

corresponding to the ground floor of the building. This niche still bears traces of an architrave, probably in wood, which was later stripped away, leaving an opening on its surface.

A nearly square, 0.07 × 0.08 m opening, which may have served as a water conduit, appears to be linked to a second opening, used for drainage, which is positioned right over the larger, 0.2 × 0.15 m niche. This opening directs water straight out to a little channel located along the northern wall, which probably once led to the subterranean cistern for collecting rainwater that lies a short distance away (attached to Building 17=K). It is possible to relate this articulated and unusual water system to a structure that can be identified as a kitchen sink, lying on the ground floor by the northern internal wall. This suggests that running water was available inside the building, which confirms the residential function of this structure, at least in its initial phase. Based on the typology of the structure and the technology used, it is possible to date the building to the fourteenth century.

Structural Typology 10 (Fig. 5.17)

The dividing wall, running along an east–west axis, cutting across the plateau's summit transversely.

This wall serves as a partition and was meant to isolate the settlement's furthest extension (to the south) and fortify the remaining part of the stronghold. The wall survives at its original height of 6 m and still retains its communication platform and a stone parapet, which is of the same thickness as the wall. On the inside of the wall, the communication trench has traces of rectangular openings that do not pierce the masonry. They are arranged along a scale and served to support a wooden system leading up to the trench. The partition wall bears no traces of access into the stronghold, only three embrasures located at its far eastern and western ends, as well as its centre. These embrasures are hut-shaped and placed at the same height as the ground floor, which can no longer be estimated, due to the rise in ground level following a large deposit: 1.1 m² with a depth of 1.5 m. The embrasures are composed of two monolithic blocks, arranged in a hut shape, and set directly upon splayed jambs of well-chiselled and lightly damaged blocks. Only in one case is there a final ornament above this hut-shaped form: an arch composed of small narrow stone blocks set edgewise. The wall was built with Technique 5 and it can be dated to the fourteenth century.

PART III

Material Culture and Survey of Post Medieval Southern Tuscany

MICHELLE HOBART

6. Analysis of the Material Culture

ABSTRACT This chapter presents the methods and codes used by Steve Dyson's team during the earlier archaeological campaigns. The finds were divided by areas and levels and the diagnostic fragments were separated from the rest of the unstudied material. There is only one area that was excavated to the bedrock, known as Building J. The cross section of the trenches clearly shows the thousand-year interval (Level IV) of abandonment below the *terra rossa* of the tenth-century inhabitation. The pottery, the small finds, the coins, and the faunal remains are here introduced.

The 'minimal necessary excavation' to which Tiziano Mannoni refers in the quote which opens Chapter 1 (*infra*), could well become the standard proposition for starting new archaeological projects. Indeed, several pertinent restrictions already constrain large open-area archaeological excavations, such as the political complexities of obtaining permits from governing institutions, a lack of funding, and the high taxes imposed upon the owner of the land when archaeologists find materials. Rather, it appears that emergency excavations or rescue archaeology are becoming more common in situations in which infrastructural intervention collides with ruins that demand to be recorded for posterity.

The future of archaeology seems to have found a fourth dimension in non-invasive techniques, such as ground-penetrating readings and GIS platforms that reorganize the ubiquitous data available online and easily accessible internationally, which is opening the past to unprecedented possibilities of interpretation. Throughout the forty-year span of this project a whole spectrum of traditional archaeological methodologies has been used, from triangulations and theodolites to the latest geophysical survey systems and satellites to show different ways of looking at a precise geographical site.

Returning to historical archaeological sites and the material excavated by others is an approach that is generally avoided. Yet, it can, and should, be done more frequently, as it would help to rectify the lack of adequate publications and the abandonment of material in storage, which is soon forgotten with the passing of subsequent generations. In the most recent campaigns at Capalbiaccio, we approached the site with just such a methodology in mind: not to archaeologically open more trenches, but rather to sift through the material remains from the original excavations and efficiently adopt new geophysical techniques.

The Beginning of the Recording Finds

Steve Dyson's original team (late 1970s) created diaries and logs (now stored in the archives of the SUNY University in Buffalo, New York) during their excavations, which were fundamental to grounding our reinterpretation of the site and the dating of its material culture. They recorded divisions between the stratigraphic layers with Roman numerals (levels), providing exact dimensions (height and width) of each trench in field books that allowed for the reconstruction of the daily activities of the excavation. These notebooks were crucial in alerting us as to what to look for during the analysis of the material. They signalled earlier, not yet visible, settlements with postholes, layers of grey ash, floors, crude pottery, cisterns, and long periods of abandonment under the castle. In total, twelve trenches were opened and all of the material culture was pre-catalogued (partially described) and positioned within the contexts. However — and this is of the utmost importance — only one area, Building J, provided a truly deep stratigraphy, fully excavated to the bedrock, during all three campaigns (Fig. 6.1 with SD plan re-made). The information derived from the material finds from all of the opened areas was sufficient to aid in the reconstruction and dating of the entire site (see Table 6.1).

Particularly important for the understanding of the history of the site is the sequence of Building J (Fig. 6.2). Analysis of the pottery found in the levels of the three campaigns within the building became the guideline to date the contexts described in the notebooks. Below Building J, which abutted one of the fortification walls, there was a village dating to the tenth century. A very long period of abandon-

88 MICHELLE HOBART

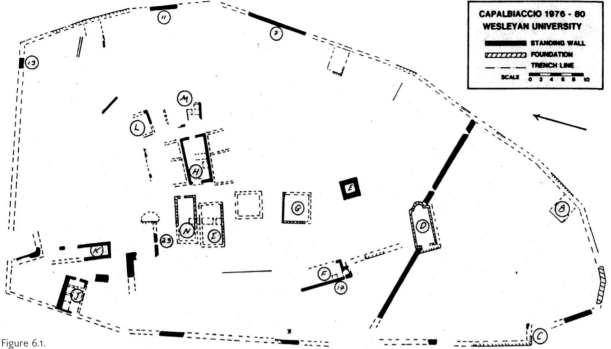

Figure 6.1.
Original plan compiled during the three years of excavation. Plan reproduced from Dyson 1984, with the permission of Western Michigan University.

Figure 6.2. Building J, Pit 1. Cross section with Levels I–IV. Photo by Dyson's Team, reproduced with permission.

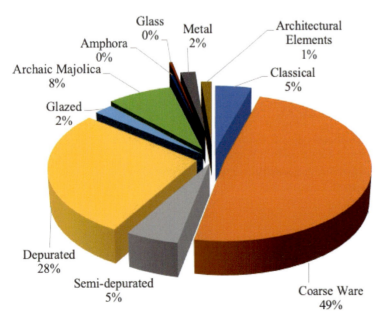

Figure 6.3. Quantitative material culture. Chart by Rossella Pansini, reproduced with permission.

Table 6.1. List of buildings and areas excavated by Dyson's during the three campaigns at Tricosto, Capalbiaccio.

Description of Tricosto Site Designations
1976: Three trenches were opened inside Building J (Trenches 1, 2, and 3) & Church D
1978: Areas D, Wall F, Houses H and I, Pit M, House N and continuation of Building J (Pit I, II, and drain)
1980: Areas B, smaller gate C, tower E, tower G, structure L, structure K with further clearance, and pictures of cisterns, Building J

ment, which produced the *terra rossa* — clear from a drawing of a cross section — with no traces of inhabitation, is interrupted by sparse Roman pottery dated to the late third century, which itself covered an Etruscan community that was founded in the sixth century. What preceded the Etruscan settlement was a prehistoric, Late Bronze Age site, which was abandoned before the Villanovan period.

The following table (Table 6.2) lists the sequence of the hilltop settlements divided by areas and levels=layers. The sections in *italics* are the transcriptions of Dyson's field notebook and the text IN CAPITALS is our interpretation of what it references based on pottery analysis.

Building J (Levels I, II, and III)

Within the same Building J, but in Trench 2, Level II is identified as a step into the last phase of the lavish late medieval residence, which had running water on at least two floors, as well as broad living areas, a rarity — at this point — and an unusual asset in the countryside (Fig. 16.31). This was the last structure inhabited, as shown both by the architecture and the archaeology, before the castle was abandoned and destroyed in the fifteenth century.

Notes on Post Hole Structures (Level IV) based on Steve Dyson's Notebooks

Originally Dyson believed that the *terra rossa* was the Etruscan phase. This description in the notebook preceded the thick layer of about one metre of dirt with no traces or inclusions of handmade artefacts, and interpreted as a long period of abandonment. The abandonment of the entire area is very clear and visible in sketches of the field notebook (Fig. 6.1).

The interval between the medieval and Etruscan period starts with Levels VI and VII. What is evident from the pottery analysis is that the later medieval

Table 6.2. In *italics*, are notes from Dyson's field books; in capital letters are our interpretations of Dyson's levels, based on the pottery found inside.

AREA Building J — Trench 1 and 2
Level I–II–III MEDIEVAL twelfth–fifteenth century. In the first trench (**1**), pottery from the late fourteenth to the twelfth century, with residual classical fragments. In the second trench (**2**) Level II, the latest floor of Building J. The analysis of the pottery found inside Building J led to the realization that during the medieval settlement, the earliest prehistoric material found just below the humus, instead of in the deepest layers, was the result of older pottery having been removed during the excavation of the foundation trenches of the later medieval walls, symmetrically inverting the chronological sequence.
Level IV — *terra rossa (starts at circa 47 cm below surface);* *"Post hole": Discovered 7/8/76. Visible at Level III (terra rossa). Soil was at first thought to be bottom, sterile level. The hole is packed with a burnt loose fill. Oblong shape with major axis N-S. Extreme N end is 90 cm S or N bulk. Extreme E end is 53 cm from W bulk. Major axis: 27 cm; minor axis 19 cm. Depth cuts through terra rossa for at least __ cm and then disappears in lower soil that is sandy with some traces of carbon.* EARLY MEDIEVAL tenth–eleventh century. From the notes it is clear that this description preceded the long phase of abandonment — between the medieval and Etruscan period — and that the medieval foundation trench of Level III also cut through Levels IV and V, which were the layers of the tenth-century medieval village and the abandonment. The sandy and carbon traces preannounce the long phase of almost 1000 years of abandonment, where a thick layer of sediment without any sign of life separates the Etruscan centre from the early medieval village, tenth CE.
Level V — *Residual medieval pottery, mostly carbon and loose strata (the bottom before layer of rock/stones — collapse?) — no pottery from Level V.* ABANDONMENT PHASE from the tenth century CE to the Hellenistic period.
Cuts Into Rocks — ETRUSCAN period, late seventh–sixth century BCE
Level VI–VII — *below rocks: thick layer (50 cm) of carbon loose fill (crude unglazed pottery in fair amounts — 3 bags). Between 60–90 cm: flint chips found at a depth of 90 cm in Trench 1 (no mention of benchmark for height). Change of layers — less charcoal to be found than at depth of cobbles. Soil is loose and a combination of silty dirt and grey ash.* ETRUSCAN life
Level VIII — *new stratigraphic layer: blackish, clay-like soil; little or no ash content. Starts around 113 cm deep. Pottery is remarkably crude in quality [...]* PREHISTORIC — the space of *c.* 23 cm seems to indicate the two hundred years of abandonment of the site as suggested by the analysis of the pre-Etruscan pottery. The 'foundation that continuous down through the *terra rossa* Level IV [...] covered with mortar [...]' refers to the medieval foundation of Building J s which cuts through and into the earlier (LBA) Level VIII found on site.
It is apparent that the structure was not built on top of a previous [site] that would relate to the older horizon [layer] of the crude pottery. This is demonstrated by the fact that the foundation continues down through the terra rossa *(Level IV) to the excavated depth of 125 cm. Much of the foundation below Level IV is covered with mortar. This Trench 1 was closed 7/29/1980 and Finished at 128 cm deep.*

centuries, characterized by glazed pottery found in Levels I, II, and III, were dated between the eleventh and fourteenth centuries, and an earlier production of mostly unglazed pottery imbedded in Levels IV and V were part of a tenth-century village. A prehistoric settlement occupied the site during the late bronze age and is the oldest evident inhabitation at Tricosto. The small amount of excavated pottery related to this period conforms with other similar contexts found in the region and it all comes from one small trench, providing a rather complex amount of evidence.

Brief Description of the Excavated Material Culture

The three years of excavation produced fifty-four cassettes, which contained a total of 15,598 fragments of pottery, metals, glass, and bones, with the exception of amphorae, architectural fragments, and tiles, which are not included and were probably displaced (Fig. 6.3). The large amount of pottery was first divided into two major groups: classical and medieval. During the excavation, the pottery had been originally separated in 'diagnostic' bags by the team, who photographed and divided shards according to their features, rims, bottoms, and handles. The finds were registered with their locations in a code that was recorded in the field notebooks. Every single fragment from the excavation was counted and all of the most relevant 'diagnostic' profiles are included in the catalogues below. Among all the finds collected, glass is the one which left least trace. Eight envelopes with small fragmented pieces suggest that they are medieval.

The Pottery

The pre-Etruscan, Etruscan, and Roman finds described here are partially residual unless identified within the levels and, cannot always be related to definite primary deposit (a house or group of houses, a farm, etc.), but they reveal an historical presence on the hill of Capalbiaccio before the Middle Ages (*infra* Acconcia). The site was inhabited between the late Bronze and early Iron Age, then abandoned until the end of the seventh century BCE, when it was reoccupied. Valeria Acconcia argues that the material evidence from the sixth and fifth centuries BCE mostly relates to Capalbiaccio's role as a defensive site. There is very little evidence at Capalbiaccio from the Roman period onwards. Prehistoric and Etruscan material traces from Capalbiaccio are analysed by Acconcia in the wider context of the lower Albegna Valley (Valle d'Oro) prior to the Roman era.

Early medieval pottery (eighth–tenth centuries) has recently been summarized and published by scholars working in northern and central Tuscany.[1] Elsewhere, Emanuele Vaccaro, who, along with Chiara Valdambrini, analysed all of the pre-glazed early medieval material from Capalbiaccio, has recently reconstructed local histories of pottery production, consumption, and circulation in southern Tuscany and Latium, wherein he evaluates Mediterranean connectivity shifts in dietary habits.[2] Herein, Vaccaro and Valdambrini's analysis, in both dating and comparing the material, is enriched by the inclusion of survey, surface pottery, and, where possible, quantifications on a wider regional scale. The bulk of Vaccaro and Valdambrini's chapters deal with tenth-century domestic productions, making a sub-regional comparison with Poggio Cavolo and other sites.[3] While lots of the material was made locally, two cities are key in the dissemination of their own productions along the coast and into inland central Italy during this period: Pisa and Rome. In Valdambrini's chapter, a second batch of medieval pottery was analysed separately, in order to distinguish it from the tenth-century material treated in Chapter 8, although there are typologies that overlap with both the earlier and the later period. A discussion of the pottery and a catalogue includes levigated and semi-levigated, unglazed ceramics and small amphorae, sparse glazed, red bands, and unglazed coarse ware. The range of their distribution reaches south from the Viterbo area of Latium to Castel d'Asso, Scorano, and as far as Rome; in Tuscany, there are parallels from Ansedonia and Poggio Cavolo. While kiln sites from the seventh–tenth centuries have not yet been identified in the area around Capalbiaccio, surface scatters of pottery suggest that rudimentary wares were produced locally. The fabrics present increasingly fewer inclusions and demonstrate improvements in both material and technique. However, inconsistencies in the degree of oxygen introduced during firing, which is revealed by a grey core typical of this period, suggest that experimentation was taking place.

After the texts in this volume were written, Ariana Briano made an important contribution to the study

---

1 Cantini 2010, 2011; Grassi 2010; Vaccaro 2011; Valdambrini 2010.
2 Vaccaro 2018.
3 The most targeted comparison with the Capalbiaccio material for the early medieval period was Poggio Cavolo, which is not exactly nearby, being closer to Grosseto, but it provides information that allows us to draw conclusions for a still somewhat unknown period.

of sparse and lead glaze in Tuscany. Briano suggested that Capalbiaccio's sparse glaze came from Latium.[4] The conclusive picture that can be drawn sets the standard and the foundation for this crucial period of transition, which precedes the introduction of glazed techniques that will be imported by Pisa and other maritime republics from North Africa and elsewhere in the following two centuries

The peak of life at Tricosto is well represented by archaic majolica, and other types of glazed and unglazed domestic plates, pots, and transportation vessels used between the thirteenth and fifteenth centuries. Michelle Hobart's catalogue (Chapter 10) shows the shift from the earliest Pisan and Sienese products of archaic majolica to the pre-Renaissance blue *zaffera a rilievo* from the northern Latium region. There is a very sporadic presence of imported material that emanated first from North Africa, with cobalt and manganese, and soon after from the northern Italian coastal region of Liguria with *graffita arcaica tirrenica*. Only a few fragments of Spanish lustreware have been found. These are all the common associations found in most of the other castles excavated in Tuscany and central Italy.

Table 6.3. Quantification of material culture from the three campaigns, 1976–1980.

Classical	689
Coarse ware	7591
Semi-depurated	816
Depurated	4294
Glazed	363
Archaic Majolica	1237
Amphora	63
Glass	60
Metal	286
Architectural elements	199

Small Finds

The excavations at Capalbiaccio in the late 1970s produced a total of 575 small finds, which give a picture of the general activities that occupied the community (*infra* Rubegni). These consist of common items found in houses and workshops in medieval Tuscan villages of the thirteenth century, the period of the hilltop's largest occupation. Two objects stand apart from the others, as more unusual: a decorated bone chess piece from one of the houses, which is dated to the twelfth century; and a number of iron plates of armour that belonged to a Brigantina, common in the fourteenth and fifteenth centuries. From a quantitative point of view, nails were the most numerous of finds, followed by glass, which unfortunately survives in a very poor state, and spindles of different sizes, shapes, and materials. The state of the fragments has suffered greatly, especially the metals, whose original shapes have been subject to deterioration. These small finds are published here for the first time.

Coins

The relatively small number of coins (twenty-two samples) were discovered neither through sieving nor a metal detector. Alessia Rovelli, who has greatly contributed to the understanding of currency circulation in the Mediterranean from late Roman to medieval times — with particular focus on the Middle Ages — here addresses what she finds as a commonality between these coins and those from other sites in central Italy. At Capalbiaccio, the earliest presence of coins coincides with the first medieval stone structures (phase 1, *infra* Corti) and not with the tenth-century, early medieval settlement identified by the pottery. On the other hand, Ottonian coins, which are in fact the earliest coins to appear along the Tyrrhenian coast of central Italy, were found at the nearby site of Poggio Cavolo.

While one Roman coin, dated to the second or third century CE was found at Capalbiaccio, the rest of the coins are contemporary with the last two centuries (between the twelfth and fourteenth) of life at the hilltop. All of the coins were minted in central Italy, with the exception of one from Sicily (Messina, 1285–1296). In chronological order, the other coins come from Lucca (second half of the twelfth century), Viterbo (1268–1271), Arezzo (second half of the thirteenth century), Montefiascone (1316–1334), and Pisa (1318–1319). The largest group of seven coins comes from Perugia and is dated to 1321. Two *quattrini* from Florence (1332–1335) were discovered, as well as another from Viterbo, which was minted between 1375 and 1387.

In particular, Rovelli discusses the nature of currency exchange and circulation between the twelfth and fourteenth centuries, offering a rich bibliography for a deeper understanding of the Mediterranean monetary circulation.

---

4 Briano 2020, 18.

Faunal Remains

Diana C. Crader's summary of the archaeozoological remains includes the author's data from Dyson's early campaigns, combined with our new chronology that includes the tenth-century early medieval village (Level IV). This chapter is fundamental for the reconstruction of the food consumption of the town through time. It shows the economy to be rooted in agriculture and livestock, supplemented by occasional hunting.[5] Archaeozoological analyses reveal four major domestic species: sheep, goat, cattle, and pig. Secondary domestic species include horses, donkeys, and chickens. Wild fauna consists of hare, squirrel, hedgehog, several small carnivores, three species of deer (fallow, red, and roe), a few birds, frog, and fish, as well as a significant quantity of tortoise shells.

Faunal remains from Building J count mostly domestic species, predominately pig, cattle, sheep, and goat, along with smaller quantities of horses, donkey, and chicken. Of the three levels excavated, the latest, Level I, shows a prevalence of domestic sheep and goat specimens, while Levels II and III show a great amount of pig specimens, consistent with nearby archaeological sites. The presence of wild fauna shows that the inhabitants occasionally enriched their diet with hunting game. The remaining three other levels of Building J (the tenth-century village, the Etruscan phase and the prehistoric) show the same pattern as the medieval ones: predominance of domestic fauna, with sheep, goat, pig, and cattle, and clear evidence of hunted animals.

The material recovered from four levels in area M, an open space used during the medieval period (tenth to fifteenth centuries), reveals a great amount of both animal bones and pottery. The nature and large amount of faunal and domestic remains in this area has led to the interpretation of it as a midden or a rubbish pit. Since the two upper levels present the majority of specimens, it is evident that area M was mostly used during the later phases of the settlement, from the thirteenth to the fifteenth century, until its abandonment. The species found in this lot are very similar to those registered in Building J, with the exception that goat and sheep abound over pigs. Among the sheep and goat remains, the predominance of adults also indicates that these animals were mostly used for dairy and wool production, and ultimately slaughtered at the end of their useful life.

The small faunal sample in area C is well preserved only in the deepest levels. Cattle remains predominate, while pigs are less common. The evidence from ovicaprines, equids, and tortoises of the more recent life of the site are rare. The bone assemblage from building F comes from four different levels, all dated to the medieval period. Due to the scarcity of evidence, it is not possible to draw any conclusions from this material. Building I was a grain storage area, with little evidence of faunal remains, and probably used for foodstuffs. The presence of canine remains in zone R indicates that this animal was probably used for herding. Faunal evidence in zone T comes from two levels, which both present a predominance of pig specimens. The substantial amount of tortoise remains, with butchery traces, in the whole area indicates that tortoises played a role as food supply at Capalbiaccio.

While the analysis of faunal remains from Capalbaiccio was done before the dating of the pottery, Crader suggests that the evidence of bone material is medieval. However, a number of residual fragments from the Etruscan period were also found (*infra* Acconcia), having probably come to the surface when area M was excavated. Further, it is interesting to note the differences in Crader's Table A3.1 and A3.3 (Appendix 3) between Levels I, II, and III, as opposed to Level IV, which clearly shows stock raising and consumption practices during the medieval period. While sheep and goats dominate the scene, with rare fragments of pig, most of the game animals are missing here and are tied mostly to the earlier prehistoric and Etruscan period, as shown in the levels of Building J. That said, the medieval phases that have been identified by the pottery are consistent in the realm of faunal remains analysed in many of the other medieval settlements excavated in Tuscany.[6]

---

5 Crader. 2003, 161–72. I want to thank Diana Crader for sharing her manuscript 'Cracking the shell: the use of tortoises at late medieval Capalbiaccio'.

6 Valenti and Salvatori 2008; for a recent overview on the zoo archaeozoological exploitation of the region see Aniceti 2020, 121–28.

VALERIA ACCONCIA

7. Pre-Etruscan, Etruscan, and Roman Pottery

ABSTRACT This chapter is one of two contributions in this volume that outlines indicators of the presence of a previous community on the medieval hilltop of Capalbiaccio. The material analysed comes from two different areas, the first in a sealed stratigraphical layer (Building J), and the others from deposits or pits that were disturbed or overturned during the medieval period (Pit M). The chronology dates back to the Late Bronze and early Iron Age, with an interruption lasting until the end of the seventh century BCE. Pottery reappears during the sixth and fifth century BCE, with more sporadic traces dating to the first half of the third century BCE. The material is similar to that discovered at other Etruscan sites in that it was mostly produced locally. The author provides a summary of the settlement patters in the region and the catalogue lists all typologies, including a few notable imports from Corinth and some Etrusco-Corinthian fragments, as well as signs of a Roman presence. [MH]

Pre-Etruscan finds are relatively scarce at Capalbiaccio, compared to the finds from other periods. Diagnostic fragments dated to the late Bronze Age and the beginning of the Iron Age are very few and they can be ascribed to storage vessels or bowls, which are rarely decorated (Plate 2). Some body shards are decorated with typical motifs of incised lines and dots.[1]

The presence of a Bronze Age site at Capalbiaccio has already been attested to by R. C. Bronson and G. Uggeri,[2] and confirmed by the material found in the excavation of Building J. It is dated between the Late Bronze Age and the first phase of the Iron Age. In the nearby area, there is other evidence from the same period, mostly located on the hills along the coastline (Fig. 7.1): surface pottery and funerary evidence were found at Monte Argentario and Orbetello; cremation graves have been found at Torre Argentiera, Torre Capo d'Uomo, Mandrioli, and La Tradita (with another from an unknown area).[3] Traces of settlements have furthermore been identified at Monteti, Monte S. Angelo, and, recently, at Marsiliana d'Albegna on the Poggio del Castello.[4] Some contemporary sites have been identified in the area surrounding Talamone: the promontory of Talamonaccio was probably inhabited until the early Iron Age[5] and another site has been found at Fonteblanda.[6]

The Albegna Valley and Argentario territory seem to have been scarcely settled during the late Bronze Age, in comparison with the typical population pattern of the rest of southern Etruria. The region is characterized by a significant number of small sites on naturally defended positions. The difference is clear with regards to the nearby Fiora Valley, but it could be explained by the characteristics of the landscapes, which change from the tufaceous heights of the Fiora to the mostly flat landscape of the lower Albegna Valley.

Comparing the settlement distribution with the geomorphologic context of the lower Albegna Valley, late Bronze Age sites are located on the few naturally defended places. Furthermore, their positioning along the coastline could have served a specific function in the control of sea traffic between the Tyrrhenian islands, which is attested to by the presence of bronze deposits on the Isola del Giglio-Campese.[7]

---

1 In general, see Dolfini 2005.
2 Bronson and Uggeri 1970, 201; Uggeri 1979, 42.

3 Ciampoltrini 1993a, 494.
4 Bronson and Uggeri 1970, 201; Bergonzi and Cateni 1979, 261; Delpino 1981, 269, n. 7; Ciampoltrini 1993b; Ciampoltrini 1995, 104; for Marsiliana, see Zifferero 2009, 224–25.
5 Negroni Catacchio 1979, 260; Vacano, Crivellari, and Castellini 1985, 35–40; Ciampoltrini 1985, 115–16; Ciampoltrini 1995, 105.
6 Ciampoltrini 1993b; Ciampoltrini 1995; Ciampoltrini 1999; Ciampoltrini 2011b, 19–20.
7 Carancini 1979; Delpino 1981, 261–69; Bietti Sestieri 1985; Ciampoltrini 1995, 105; Giardino 1995, 116–19.

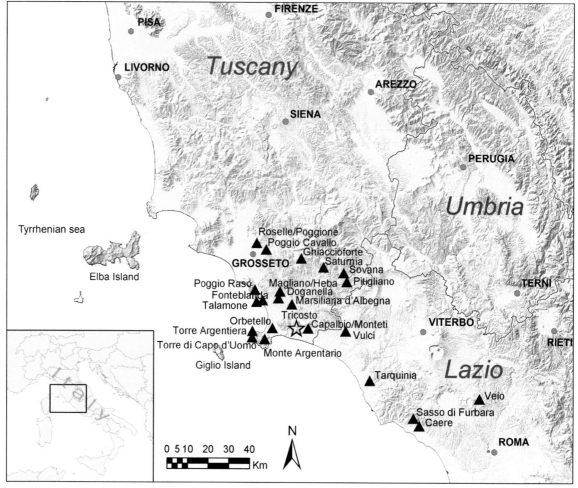

Figure 7.1. Map of Southern Etruria with Proto-historic and Etruscan places. Map by Rossella Pansini. Basemap/DTM reproduced with the permission of CTR Regione Toscana.

Etruscan Period (Fig. 7.2)

The hill of Capalbiaccio was abandoned at the beginning of the Iron Age and then reoccupied at the end of the seventh century BCE by Etruscans. At the time, Capalbiaccio controlled the area between the Radicata Valley and the coastal plain, corresponding to the *Ager Cosanus* (modern-day Valle d'Oro), which, in early Roman times, was under the domination of Vulci.[8] The evidence of an Etruscan occupation of the hill of Capalbiaccio was not recorded by the surveys of the Albegna Valley Project, except for Stephen L. Dyson's excavations in the area of Tricosto.[9]

The residual character of the Etruscan pottery found at Capalbiaccio prevents us from accurately determining the nature of other similar sites, but its position and the prevalence of utilitarian pottery from the seventh to the fourth century BCE suggests that it was, in fact, occupied and presumably fortified. It seems connected to other similar sites in the southern Radicata Valley, which are characterized by the same elevated position, traces of fortifications, and probably by the same chronology, such as Monteti, Poggione and Capalbio.[10]

Other settlements have been discovered nearby:[11] for example, the sites of San Donato, I Poggetti, Torrettina, Polverosa, Binetti, Monte Nebbiello, Settefinestre,[12] and those sites identified by Philip Perkins as 'house or tomb' in the Valle d'Oro.[13] These sites could be related to funerary areas located

---

8   The latter is suggested by Pliny, *Natural History* III, 52 (*Cosa Volcentium*).
9   Dyson 1978b.
10 For the settlement category of the 'fortified hill top', see Perkins 1999, 20–21; Attolini and others 1982, 368–69, 376, 373.
11 Uggeri 1979, 43.
12 Celuzza and Regoli 1982, 35.
13 Carandini and others 2002, 60–61, 80–81, tavs 2 and 6, CAP 2, 24, 31, 32, 52; Perkins 1999, 194–95.

south of the Radicata Valley and in the Valle d'Oro, whose supposed isolation was formerly interpreted as anomalous evidence in a scarcely settled landscape: sites such as Scopetelli, Romitorio, Porcareccia del Conicchio, Cavallin dei Caprai, the slopes of Poggio Torretta, Monte Nebbiello, Giardino, Poggio Tristo, Casetta delle Forane, Mandrioncino della Sotriscia, La Parrina, and Poggio Malabarba.[14]

As previously mentioned, the majority of the Etruscan pottery from the excavation at Tricosto consists of coarse ware utilitarian vessels, such as jars, *pithoi*, and braziers similar to the types known from surveys and excavations in the same area. They show characteristics generally associated with Archaic utilitarian pottery from southern Etruria.[15] Only a few examples of fine wares were found, including some fragments of possibly Corinthian and Attic productions and locally made Etrusco-Corinthian vessels. Bucchero (in black and grey fabric) prevails among the fine wares, which are scarcely diversified in terms of shape, a trait that is typical of the evolution of the type from the end of the seventh century to the fifth century BCE.

Only one fragment, decorated with incised fans (Plate 2, n. 22), must be related to a closed vessel with thin walls, perhaps an *oinochoe*. The other fragments must be assigned to bowls, chalices, or jugs with thicker walls and standardized shapes. Besides coarse ware and Bucchero, few other pottery groups are present. It is important to point out the presence of some Etruscan amphorae of type Py 3 (nos 49–50), which are related to the massive productions located at Doganella and, more recently, at Marsiliana.[16]

The pottery evidence from Tricosto underlines the Etruscan settlement chronology between the end of the seventh and the fourth century BCE, with settlements decreasing from the fifth to the fourth century.[17] In the same period, the area between the Radicata Valley and the *Ager Cosanus*, along with the nearby Albegna Valley, was part of a complex population system, organized around major and minor centres, such as Doganella, Marsiliana, Ghiaccioforte, Saturnia, Talamone, and by villages and rural sites (Fig. 7.3). The area is especially known from nineteenth century excavations of funerary materials.[18]

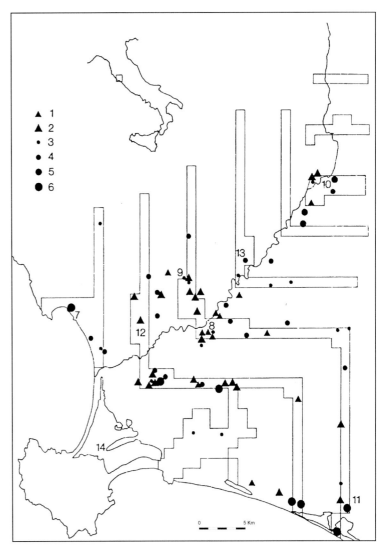

Figure 7.2. Seventh-century BCE places mentioned in the text; 1. Tomb; 2. Necropolis; 3. House or Tomb; 4. Small House; 5. Large House; 6. Village; 7. Talamonaccio; 8. Marsiliana; 9. Magliano; 10. Saturnia; 11. Pescia Fiorentina; 12. Doganella; 13. Ghiaccioforte; 14. Orbetello; 15. Capalbiaccio; 16. Cosa. Lines indicate sampled areas. Open symbols indicate sites of an uncertain date. Map adapted from Carandini and others 2002.

During the second half of the twentieth century, excavations and surveys (especially the *Ager Cosanus/Albegna Valley Project*), identified a number of other settlements.[19]

The main difference between the theories of Etruscan settlement in the area from the mouth of the Chiarone River to the upper Albegna Valley and the Talamone promontory, lies in the definition of Vulci influence. Italian scholars such as G. Colonna

---

14 Levi 1927; Cristofani 1977, 236, 240; Celuzza and Regoli 1982, 35; Perkins 1991, 140; Perkins 2002, 71; Ciampoltrini 1991.
15 Perkins and Walker 1990; Perkins 1999, 115; Michelucci 1991; for a south Etruscan characterization of the pottery found in recent excavations at Marsiliana, see also Zifferero 2009, 243.
16 Acconcia 2005, 609–10; Zifferero and others 2009, 105–06.
17 Perkins 1999, 36–38.
18 Cristofani 1977; Cristofani and Michelucci 1981; Perkins 1999, 12; Perkins 2002.

19 Dyson 1978b; Attolini and others 1991; Perkins 1991; 1999, 15–17; Rendini 1985; Michelucci 1984; Michelucci 1985a; Perkins and Walker 1990. For the Albegna Valley Project, see Carandini and others 2002, 5–12, 15–20.

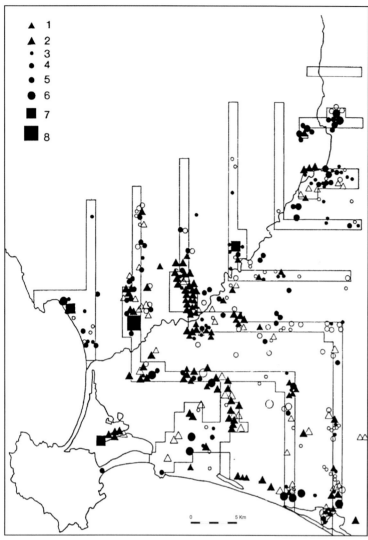

Figure 7.3. Sixth-century BCE places mentioned in the text; 1. Tomb; 2. Necropolis; 3. House or Tomb; 4. Small House; 5. Large House; 6. Village; 7. Minor Centre; 8. Major Centre. Lines indicate sampled areas. Open symbols indicate sites of an uncertain date. Map adapted from Carandini and others 2002.

or M. Cristofani hypothesized that Vulci controlled the whole area from Iron Age onwards.[20] Recently, Philip Perkins, on the basis of a re-appraisal of the role of Doganella, suggested that the region should be divided into three distinct areas with different influences.[21]

During the Iron Age (ninth–eighth century BCE), the Tricosto area developed the typical southern Etruria population pattern, characterized by the abandonment of the late Bronze Age sites, presumably connected to the formation of the cities of Veii, Caere, Tarquinia, and Vulci.[22] This process ended during the second half of the eighth century BCE, when the main sites began to populate their territories, promoting new minor centres, which were probably managed by aristocratic groups.[23] The coastal territory between the Chiarone and the Albegna Rivers was substantially unsettled during the Iron Age, with the exception of a few sites, notably on the Tombolo della Feniglia at Orbetello, at Pescia Romana (Infernetto di Sotto, with burials at Serpentaro),[24] at La Torba, between Pescia Romana and Orbetello (burials),[25] and, north of them, at Talamone (sporadic finds from Bengodi[26] and Talamonaccio).

The period from the late Iron Age to the middle of the seventh century is characterized by the growth of settlements located along the coastline or generally in strategic positions, with burial evidence connected to groups with strong, elite internal hierarchies (Fig. 7.4). This population pattern is typical of the whole Etruscan region and it can be recognized in the Albegna, and also in the Fiora Valley, by the development of new minor centres that were managed by aristocratic elites in well-defended positions, such as Saturnia, Poggio Buco, Pitigliano, and Sovana.[27] In the Valle d'Oro and lower Albegna Valley, some of the settlements known for this period developed from previously recorded sites. The necropolises of Pescia Romana (Serpentaro, Quarto della Moletta, Quarto della Padovella, and Quarto della Capanna Murata) confirm the presence of a concentration of villages very close to one another.[28]

The site of Orbetello was inhabited from the eighth century, as shown by the burials from Il Cristo and Il Grilletto.[29] Settlements at Poggio Raso, in the lower Albegna Valley, and another in the Radicata

---

20 Colonna 1977; Cristofani 1977.
21 Perkins 1999, 137; Acconcia 2005.
22 Colonna 1977, 193; Pacciarelli 1991a; Pacciarelli 2000, 128–79; Ciampoltrini 1995, 105.
23 Iaia and Mandolesi 1993.
24 Cardosa 2005, 533.
25 Ciampoltrini and Paoletti 1995.
26 Mazzolai 1984, 89; Perkins 1999, 22.
27 Some of them overlapped with the LBA sites: Colonna 1977, 198–200; Rendeli 1993, 165–205; Perkins and Walker 1990, 68; Setti 1995. For Saturnia, no traces of settlements area are known until the fifth century BCE. For the necropolies of Sede di Carlo, Pancotta, Prato Grande, Campo delle Caldane, Puntone, Sterpeti, Porta Romana, used from the early seventh century: Minto 1925; Michelucci 1982; Donati and Pacciani 1989; Perkins 1999, 34, 96–100, 177. For Poggio Buco: Bartoloni 1972; Pellegrini 1989; Colmayer and Rafanelli 2000. Pitigliano: Bartoloni 1995, 129–30.
28 Colonna 1977, 198; Cristofani 1977, 238; Attolini and others 1982, 373; Perkins 1999, 32; Tamburini 2000, 39; Casi and Celuzza 2000; Cardosa 2005, 553.
29 Cristofani and Michelucci 1981, 97; Celuzza and Regoli 1982, 34; Iaia and Mandolesi 1993, 34; Perkins 1999, 68. Early Orientalizing tombs from Orbetello have been published by Ciampoltrini and Paoletti 1995.

Valley, testify to a continuity of occupation from the Iron Age to the early Orientalizing period (Fig. 7.2).[30]

In the Albegna Valley, the seventh century BCE is marked by the settlement of Marsiliana, which is known especially for its necropoli (Piani di Banditella, Uliveto di Banditella, and Poggio di Macchiabuia) and the wealth of their funerary furniture. That furniture, dating from the end of the eighth to the third quarter of the seventh century BCE, reflects a strongly aristocratic social order.[31] The corresponding settlement was traditionally localized at the Uliveto di Banditella site, which controlled a natural crossing point of the Albegna River.[32] On the basis of this evidence, scholars have hypothesized that Marsiliana could have acted as an autonomous enclave and there was a strict relationship between the supposed decline of the centre during the last quarter of the seventh century and the growing territorial aims of Vulci from the late Orientalizing period (around 630–620 BCE). Marsiliana may have been destroyed by Vulci, as Colonna suggests, or it could have undergone a slow decline, as shown by burials of the sixth century BCE (Fig. 7.3).[33]

Recently, surveys, and excavations carried out by the University of Siena have hypothesized a different development pattern for Marsiliana. After a new occupation of the acropolis at Piano del Castello at the end of the eighth century BCE, the settlement was extended on the Uliveto di Banditella during the following century (reaching 47 ha of total size). Marsiliana did not decline after the end of the seventh century, but rather, it was inhabited until the fifth century, with the growth of a small 'suburban' settlement nucleus, corresponding to the funerary evidence of the former Orientalizing period (Fig. 7.4). Furthermore, Marsiliana was involved in the production and trade of wine and oil, as evidenced by a late Archaic Period building with storage rooms for amphorae and *pithoi*, and by an amphorae production site located along the Albegna.[34]

In any case, the role and the development of Marsiliana could not be appreciated without considering the whole context of the Albegna Valley. From the last quarter of the seventh century BCE, archaeological data suggests the formation of a new settlement pattern, wherein control of the Valley seems to

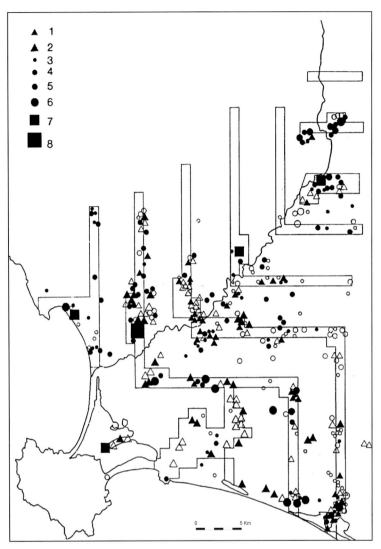

Figure 7.4. Fifth-century BCE places mentioned in the text; 1. Tomb; 2. Necropolis; 3. House or Tomb; 4. Small House; 5. Large House; 6. Village; 7. Minor Centre; 8. Major Centre. Lines indicate sampled areas. Open symbols indicate sites of an uncertain date. Map adapted from Carandini and others 2002.

shift from a nucleated to a centralized system, corresponding to the foundation of Doganella. Surveys recorded the growth of a relevant number of small rural sites (interpreted as villages), small groups of houses, and single houses/tombs, spread throughout the territory, which reveals a new and intensive approach to natural resources.[35]

In the same period, the area of Magliano was occupied by a group of chamber-tomb necropoli dated between last quarter of the seventh and the mid-sixth century BCE.[36] Although scholars have

---

30 Perkins 1999, 32, 195.
31 Minto and Corsini 1921; Colonna 1977, 202–03; Cristofani 1977, 240–46; Cristofani and Michelucci 1981, 98–106; Michelucci 1985a; Iaia and Mandolesi 1993, 21–22; Ciampoltrini and Paoletti 1995, 66; Perkins 1999, 80–90; Zifferero 2009, 226–27.
32 Michelucci 1983, 452–53; Michelucci 1991.
33 Colonna 1977, 202–03, 241.
34 Zifferero 2009, 228–36; Zifferero and others 2009, 104–06.

35 Perkins 1999, 18–20.
36 These were Poggio Volpaio, Le Mollaie, Fortullino, Le Focaie, S. Maria in Borraccia, Il Pisciolo, Le Piantatine, Poggio Bacchino, and Poggio Bestiale.

related the Magliano burials to a centre at the colony of Heba, the tombs do not seem related to any contemporary settlement. To Cristofani, this evidence suggested a rural, nucleated population system. Perkins believes that the funerary areas should be interpreted as the reflection of a social structure based on a scattered rural community.[37]

At the same time, the settlement structure in the Albegna Valley is clustered around the new town of Doganella, which was probably founded at the end of the seventh century and flourished during the sixth and fifth centuries.[38] Compared to other Etruscan cities, Doganella is an anomalous example: its growth is fundamentally recent in comparison with urban Etruscan formation in the Iron Age. Doganella had a bigger extension than other regional centres, a scarcely defendable position in the lower Valley, and a dispersed internal order. All these characteristics identify the centre as a new foundation, a sort of colony, as is proposed for Marzabotto.[39]

The growth of Doganella signalled a clear-cut change in the region and, as suggested by Perkins, the definition of an area clearly distinct from the *Ager Cosanus* or Valle d'Oro, characterized by different approaches to land use. If the *Ager Cosanus* was directly under the control of Vulci, the territory around Doganella reflects a different settlement order, with medium and small rural sites, increasing from the sixth to the fifth century, and reflecting an autonomous and intensive exploitation of land resources.[40] The Albegna Valley Project surveys recorded 30 certain settlements for the seventh century, which grew to 52–54 during the sixth and the fifth centuries, and then collapsed to 20–35 for the fourth and the third centuries BCE.[41]

The sixth-century evidence of a new minor centre at Ghiaccioforte, which has been interpreted as probably developing around a sanctuary and functioned as a centre of control for the internal territories of the Valley, seems to strengthen this system.[42] Along the coastline, Orbetello was continuously settled until the third century BCE and functioned as a harbour. In the Talamone area, the settlement of Bengodi probably had a similar function from the sixth century BCE. At Talamonaccio, the remains of the Archaic Period phase of the temple suggest an analogy with the coastal sanctuaries of Caere and Tarquinia. The site of Portus Telamo, at the Puntata di Fonteblanda, contains a metalworking site with a rich deposit of Py 3 amphorae.[43]

Philip Perkins has recently suggested an alternative interpretation to the model of Archaic and Classical Period development in the lower Albegna Valley. That has traditionally been interpreted as the result of Vulci expansion to the north, removing every possible obstacle to the emerging centre of Marsiliana. Rather, Perkins believes that the lower Albegna Valley was almost substantially autonomous in the late Iron Age, then initially controlled by the aristocratic groups at Marsiliana, who, at the end of the seventh century BCE, probably moved to Doganella, shifting the centre of power.[44]

This reconstruction, although imaginative in its attempt to collect all of the new territorial data, seems to incur some problems of interpretation. For example, from an historical point of view, literary sources did not register, among Etruscan cities, the presence of such a big centre north of Vulci and south of Roselle, which was presumably destroyed at the same time as Vulci, in the first quarter of third century BCE. Furthermore, no toponomastic evidence seems to be connected to this centre. The ancient name of Caletra seems to be linked to Marsiliana.[45] And ancient authors recorded that the *Ager Cosanus* was previously controlled by Vulci.[46]

On the other hand, the archaeological data suggests that Doganella is relatively recent, compared to other Etruscan towns. As Perkins also noticed, it did not exhibit the typical formation phase of the urban social structures of the Iron Age. As previously stated, Doganella must be interpreted as a new

---

37 For a discussion of the necropolis of Magliano as different nuclei or the results of modern landscape use, see Perkins 1999, 90, 175. For Magliano: Minto 1935; Maetzke 1956; Cristofani 1977, 248; Cristofani and Michelucci 1981, 98, 101, 106; Perkins 1999, 90–96.

38 The traditional dating of Doganella to the sixth century BCE is now reconsidered on the basis of the survey's results, and raised to the end of seventh. A history of the research may be found in Perkins 1999, 12; Colonna 1977, 203; Cristofani 1977, 248; Cristofani and Michelucci 1981, 98; Michelucci 1984; Michelucci 1985a; Perkins and Walker 1990; Perkins 1991, 142.

39 Perkins and Walker 1990, 63, 65–66; Walker 2002, 93–94.

40 Perkins 1999, 33–34, 54, 178–90. The necropolis of S. Donato di Orbetello and the nearby site of Parrina could be attributed to the formation of this system: Michelucci 1991; Ciampoltrini 1991; Perkins 1999, 65.

41 Perkins and Walker 1990, 68; Perkins 1999, 30–39.

42 For Ghiaccioforte, see Del Chiaro 1976; Rendini 1985; Talocchini 1986; Firmati 2001; Rendini 2003; Firmati and Rendini 2002; Rendini and Firmati 2005.

43 Cristofani 1977, 249; Cristofani and Michelucci 1981, 101; Michelucci 1985b; Mazzolai 1984, 89; Ciampoltrini 1985, 116; Vacano, Crivellari, and Castellini 1985, 166; Ciampoltrini and Rendini 1992, 985–87; Perkins 1999, 13, 21–22; Ciampoltrini 2003; Ciampoltrini and Rendini 2007; Ciampoltrini 2011b, 19, 21.

44 Perkins 1999, 170–75.

45 On Caletra, see Livy, *History of Rome* XXXI, 55; Pliny, *Natural History* III, 52.

46 For literary sources, see Michelucci 1984; Perkins and Walker 1990, 75–77.

foundation, but it is likely that the impulse to found it belonged directly to Vulci and not to Marsiliana or other minor centres.

The new settlement pattern recorded in the area between the Chiarone and Albegna Valleys from the end of seventh century BCE is not an anomaly in comparison with the development of other regions of southern Etruria, where the growth of a dense new rural system, managed by urban elites, determined a massive land exploitation.[47] This process developed at the cost of the aristocratic enclaves formerly settled in the territory: Vulci at Marsiliana, or Caere at the sites of Ceri or Sasso di Furbara. The recent data recorded at Marsiliana shows a longer settlement for the site, which was neither destroyed at the end of the seventh century, nor collapsed during the sixth. It is possible that it was assimilated into the new influence that Vulci extended over its northern territory, which was strictly connected to Doganella for the production and distribution of amphorae.

Doganella was likely founded as an outgrowth of this system, which joined rural exploitation with the needs of Vulci to control such a distant area.[48] In this sense, the new city could have reached a quite autonomous role in the nearby territory, managing distinctive approaches to natural resources.

Capalbiaccio is among the sites that developed at the end of the seventh century BCE, contemporaneous with the oldest evidence at Doganella, the Magliano cemeteries, and the spread of rural settlements. It flourished during the sixth and fifth centuries and contributed to the strengthening of the Radicata Valley, along with other similar hilltop settlements, such as Poggio Pietricci and Poggio Cavallo.[49] Philip Perkins has already noticed that, together with the other fortified hilltops, Capalbiaccio could exert a coherent system of control over the coastline and the route towards the internal territories (especially the upper Fiora Valley).[50] He hypothesized that the Radicata Valley should be interpreted as a sort of borderline: the northern limit of Vulci, including the land controlled by Doganella. On the other hand, following the hypothesis that Vulci effectively controlled the whole area, the settlements along the Radicata could have had a similar defensive function, but in a much more integrated system that was organized by Vulci in order to shield Doganella on the low side of the *Ager Cosanus* plain.

From the end of the seventh to the fifth century BCE, the lower Albegna Valley, including territories north and south of the river's mouth, seems to be organized as a productive district, with Doganella acting as the main centre. Doganella redistributed resources to the small rural settlements and to other minor centres, such as Marsiliana and Ghiaccioforte, which controlled the route to the upper Valley and the internal territories of other Etruscan cities. At the southern edge of this frontier system, the harbours of Orbetello and Talamone could have been integrated for the export of Vulci wine and oil (Fig. 7.4).

The 'Romanization' Period

The Roman conquest of Vulci around 280 BCE changed the political and settlement order in the *Ager Cosanus*, beginning with the destruction (or the forced displacement of the inhabitants) of the principal minor centres of Doganella, Ghiaccioforte, and Saturnia, and with the acquisition of some strategically located settlements, such as those at Talamonaccio or Orbetello.[51] In 273 BCE, Cosa was founded as a Latin status colony and the site of Saturnia was chosen as the new *praefectura*.[52] The primary aim of these choices was to create new control centres, which shifted the political balance from the former Etruscan, to a new Roman order. At this time, the rural settlement system was also deeply unsettled: as the Albegna Survey Project recorded, during the third century BCE there was a clear decrease in rural sites, which indicates that the Etruscan landscape was being depopulated and the property system that developed during the Archaic Period was coming to an end.[53]

The foundation of Cosa (which received 1000 new colonists in 197 BCE) and Heba in the middle of the second century BCE,[54] along with the implementation of the Centuriation system and the creation of the Via Aurelia in 241 BCE,[55] changed the landscape dramatically and progressively shifted rural possession to the new inhabitants, rearranging the political and territorial axes along the colonial pat-

---

47 On the Ager Caeretanus, see Zifferero 1990; Rendeli 1993, 329–48; Enei 1993, 32–34. For Veii, see Potter 1979, 83–101.
48 Attolini and others 1991, 142; Perkins and Walker 1990, 67–68; Perkins 1991, 141.
49 For Poggio Pietricci and Poggio Cavallo, see Perkins 1999, 21.
50 Perkins 1999, 21.
51 See Regoli 1985, 49–51. For Doganella, see Perkins 1999, 38. For Ghiaccioforte, see Rendini 2003; Rendini and Firmati 2005, 376, 383. On the destruction of the centres of the Albegna Valley, see Celuzza 2002, 104, nt. 21.
52 Celuzza 2002, 104–05; Fentress 2002.
53 On the reduction of rural sites, see Perkins 1999, 38–39; Celuzza 2002, 110.
54 Celuzza 2002, 112, nt. 80; Attolini 2002.
55 De Rossi 1968; Celuzza 2002, 106, 121–23.

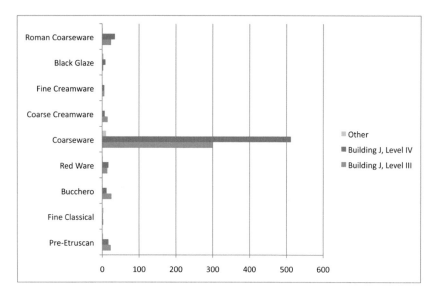
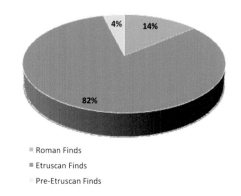

Figure 7.5. Quantification of all classical pottery from Capalbiaccio. Chart and graphic by author.

tern.[56] Thus, the number of rural sites recorded by surveys increased again, along with the rural population, during the second century BCE.[57]

As noted above, only the Etruscan centres that functioned as emporia survived the changes brought by the Roman conquest. Orbetello and Talamone continued to be strategic points, strengthening the coastline, especially during First and Second Punic Wars of the third century BCE. Both harbours were involved in maritime traffic in the Tyrrhenian Sea.[58] The position and role of Talamone were especially strengthened, as suggested by the public engagement in the various decoration phases of the sanctuary, monumentalized during the Hellenistic period.[59]

Capalbiaccio, less than 10 km from Cosa, shows a clear decrease in the number of finds from the Romanization period. The hilltop settlement was abandoned or destroyed during the conquest of the territory, removing one of the controlling agents that strengthened the Etruscan presence in the area. This was typical for those sites closest to the new Roman centres and accentuated when the territorial acquisition occurred through violent means. The character of the settlement during this period cannot be defined from the finds, but the small amount of data from the period between the third century BCE and the first century CE, suggests a sporadic frequentation of the site. Capalbiaccio functioned only marginally within the Centuriation system (stock-raising, wood, refuge during the crisis periods between the second and first centuries BCE) and was probably inhabited by a few Etruscan people.[60]

Among the Classical material, the coarse ware pottery reveals a generic similarity with the typological record for the area (especially from Cosa) and a few black-glaze fragments seem to be connected to the productions of the Ateliers of the *Petites Estampilles*, which were strongly connected to Roman workshops.[61]

There is not any relevant increase or decrease of the finds at Capalbiaccio from the first century BCE, when the Centuriation system of smallholders changed into large- or medium-sized villas and smaller rural sites decreased. However, Capalbiaccio could have been an uncultivated area in the possession of a nearby villa, as suggested by the Albegna Survey Project.[62]

With regard to the Imperial period, no sherds of fine pottery, such as *sigillata* or *pareti sottili* wares, were found in the levels of Tricosto examined herein, although some of the identified shapes can be dated to contemporary phases.

Description of the Pottery Fabrics

The finds presented here show an historical presence at Capalbiaccio before the Medieval phase. The pottery comes mostly from Buildings J and M (Fig. 7.5), but it cannot be related to any primary deposits, having been found in a large dump, mixed with medieval materials. The fragments were so few in comparison with each production, so homogene-

---

56 Castagnoli 1956; Cambi and Celuzza 1985, 104–06, fig. 111; Attolini and others 1991, 144.
57 Perkins 1999, 169, 192.
58 Excavations have discovered imported black-glaze pottery and Greco-italic amphorae; see Ciampoltrini and Rendini 1992. For the new chronology of the polygonal wall of Orbetello, contemporaneous to those of Cosa, Talamonaccio and Saturnia, see also Ciampoltrini 1995. For the battle amongst Roman and Gauls at Talamone in 222 BCE, see Ciampoltrini 2011, 22.
59 For the settlement, see Ciampoltrini 2002; Celuzza 2002, 109, 135–37; for the sanctuary, see Vacano and Freytag 1982; Vacano, Crivellari, and Castellini 1985. On the fictile decoration of the middle of second century BCE, see Gambogi 2000.

60 Cambi and Celuzza 1985, 105.
61 Recently, see Ferrandes 2006.
62 Dyson 1978b, 263; Celuzza 1985, 149, fig. 166.

ously mixed, and in such a fragmentary condition, that a typology has not been defined. Also, due to their residual character, they have been described individually.

Fabric A (Bronze and Iron Age pottery)
Colour: internal: dark brown; external: ranging from black/dark brown to reddish brown depending upon firing conditions. **Inclusions**: small quartzite; medium and small augite; small black. **Fracture**: irregular, with voids. **Surface**: burnished. **Decoration**: incised or cordons. Handmade.

Fabric B (Corinthian pottery)
Colour: light green. **Inclusions**: none; very refined. **Fracture**: regular. **Surface**: powdery. **Decoration**: painted patterns. Wheel-made.

Fabric C (Etrusco-Corinthian pottery)
Colour: light yellowish to light pink. **Inclusions**: none; very well depurated with few black inclusions. **Fracture**: regular. **Decoration**: painted patterns. **Surface**: smooth. Wheel-made.

Fabric D (Attic black figure pottery)
Clay: completely depurated. **Colour**: orange. **Glaze**: thick covering, black with metallic shades. **Fracture**: regular. Wheel-made.

Fabric E (Bucchero pottery)
See Rasmussen 1979, 2–3.

Fabric F (Grey Bucchero)
Colour: light grey. **Inclusions**: very few. **Fracture**: irregular with voids. **Surface**: powdery. Wheel-made.

Fabric G (Red ware)
Colour: internal: pink-orange; external: from red/dark-red to strong orange. **Inclusions**: small/very small quartzite and augite. **Fracture**: irregular with very small voids. **Surface**: slipped. Wheel-made.

Fabric H (Coarse ware)
Colour: internal: dark brown; external: from dark to light brown to reddish brown, depending on the firing conditions. **Inclusions**: small/very small quartzite; medium/small/very small mica; some small stones. **Fracture**: irregular with very small voids. **Surface**: mostly smooth, with a slip; a few examples have a rough surface. Wheel-made.

Fabric I (Cream coarse ware)
Colour: light pink–light yellowish. **Inclusions**: small quartzite; small augite and black; small *chamotte*. **Fracture**: irregular with very small voids. **Surface**: rough. Wheel-made.

Fabric L (Fine creamware)
Colour: light pink–yellowish. **Inclusions**: medium small augite, black, quartzite. **Fracture**: irregular. **Surface**: rough. **Decoration**: some examples are red-painted. Wheel-made.

Fabric M (Etruscan amphorae)
Colour: light yellowish. **Inclusions**: small black and quartzite. **Fracture**: regular with small voids. **Surface**: rough. Wheel-made.

Fabric N (Black-glaze pottery)
Clay: pink, very well depurated. **Glaze**: glossy black, not completely covered. **Fracture**: regular. **Surface**: smooth. Wheel-made.

Fabric O (Black-glaze pottery)
Clay: light grey, very well depurated. **Glaze**: black dull, thick covering. **Fracture**: regular. Wheel-made.

Fabric P
Colour: orange. **Inclusions**: small quartzite, augite, and black. **Fracture**: irregular with medium-small voids. **Surface**: rough. Wheel-made.

Fabric Q (Roman coarse ware)
Colour: varying from yellowish to pink to light grey. **Inclusions**: small black, augite, and quartzite. **Fracture**: regular with small voids. **Surface**: rough. Wheel-made.

Fabric R (Roman coarse ware)
Colour: brown. **Inclusions**: small and medium augite, quartzite, and stony. **Fracture**: irregular with large voids. **Surface**: rough. Wheel-made.

Fabric S (Roman coarse ware)
Colour: light, varying from greyish to pink. **Inclusions**: small black, quartzite, and augite. **Fracture**: regular. Wheel-made.

Fabric T (Roman coarse ware)
Colour: white–light yellow. **Inclusions**: very depurated clay, medium and small black and quartzite. **Fracture**: irregular with small voids. **Surface**: rough. Wheel-made.

Fabric U (Roman coarse ware)
Colour: pink–yellowish. **Inclusions**: small black. **Fracture**: regular. **Surface**: rough. Wheel-made.

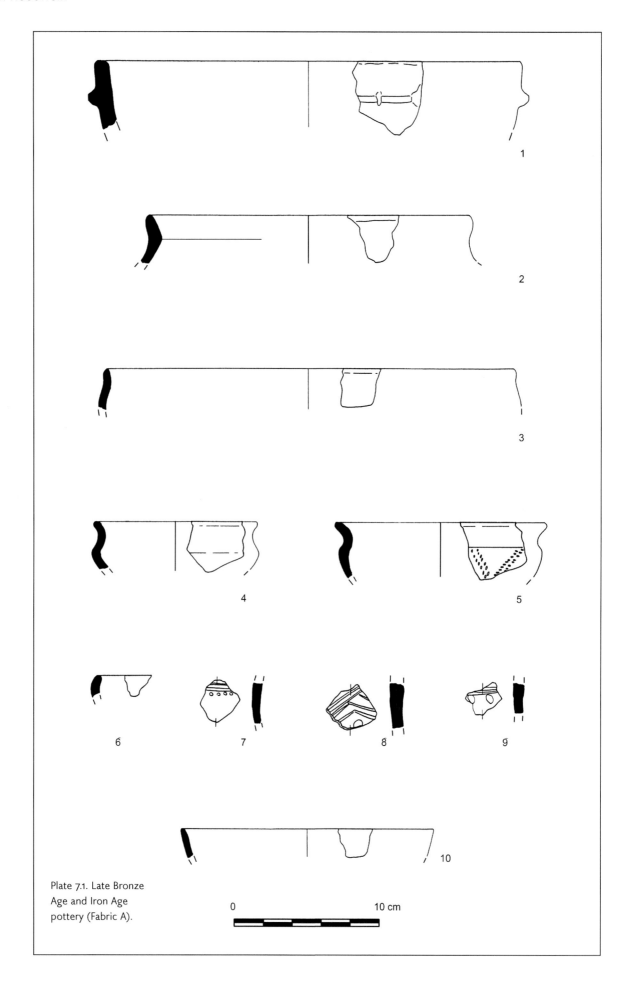

Plate 7.1. Late Bronze Age and Iron Age pottery (Fabric A).

0　　　　　10 cm

CATALOGUE

Late Bronze Age and Iron Age Pottery (Fabric A)

1. Pl. 7.1, no. 1

Description: Fragment of a big jar with a straight and plain rim, decorated with a finger-impressed cordon. This pattern is typical for utilitarian forms (jars, basins, cooking-stands).
Material: Fabric A.
Dimensions: D. 30 cm; H. max. 4.6 cm.
Chronology: Late Bronze Age.
Context: Building J, Level IV.
References: Similar to an example from Podere Tartuchino: Perkins and Attolini 1992, 90, fig. 13.3.

2. Pl. 7.1, no. 2

Description: Fragment of a jar with a slightly everted and thick rim.
Material: Fabric A.
Dimensions: D. 23 cm; H. max. 3.4 cm.
Chronology: Late Bronze Age.
Context: Building J, Level IV.
References: Similar to an example from Podere Tartuchino: Perkins and Attolini 1992, 90, fig. 13.5.

3. Pl. 7.1, no. 3

Description: Fragment of a jar with slightly everted rim.
Material: Fabric A.
Dimensions: D. 29 cm; H. max. 2.8 cm.
Context: Building J, Level III.

4. Pl. 7.1, no. 4

Description: Fragment of a carinated bowl with an 'S' profile. Rounded; rim with internal marking.
Material: Fabric A.
Dimensions: D. 11.2 cm; H. max. 3.3 cm.
Chronology: Late Bronze Age.
Context: Building J, Level I.
References: Similar to a decorated example from S. Giuliano: Di Gennaro 1986, 26, fig. 1B.2 (see for diffusion).

5. Pl. 7.1, no. 5

Description: Fragment of a bowl with an averted rim and strong carination below the rim. The body is decorated with impressed zigzag rope patterns.
Material: Fabric A.
Dimensions: D. 15 cm; H. max. 3.7 cm.
Chronology: Late Bronze Age.
Context: Building J, Level IV.
References: Similar to examples from Monte Tellere: Massari and Sordi 1995, fig. 2, n. 16; and Torrionaccio: Cassano 1978, 224, fig. 47, n. 15 (4th period).

6. Pl. 7.1, no. 6

Description: Fragment of a bowl with an incurving rim.
Material: Fabric A.
Dimensions: H. max. 1.6 cm.
Context: Building J, Level III.
References: Similar to an example from Le Bagnare (Canino): Di Gennaro 1986, 36, fig. 2A.1. This form is diffused between the late Bronze Age and early Iron Age; see Di Gennaro 1986 for diffusion in southern Etruria.

7. Pl. 7.1, no. 7

Description: Fragment of a closed vessel, decorated with horizontal lines and a sequence of small impressed dots.
Material: Fabric A.
Dimensions: H. max. 2.7 cm.
Chronology: Late Bronze Age.
Context: Building J, Level IV.
References: Similar to examples from Poggio Buco: Colonna 1977, fig. 4.8; and Pitigliano: Aranguren and Perazzi 1995, 122, fig. 3, A1.

8. Pl. 7.1, no. 8

Description: Fragment of a closed vessel, decorated with part of a zigzag of incised irregular lines and dots.
Material: Fabric A.
Dimensions: H. max. 3.1 cm.
Chronology: Late Bronze Age.
Context: Building J, Level III.
References: Similar to examples from Poggio Buco: Colonna 1977, fig. 4.9; and Tolfa: Di Gennaro 1986, fig. 28, B.1.

9. Pl. 7.1, no. 9

Description: Fragment of a closed vessel, decorated with horizontal lines and large dots.
Material: Fabric A.
Dimensions: H. max. 2.1 cm.
Chronology: Late Bronze Age.
Context: Building J, Level III.
References: Similar to an example from Pitigliano: Aranguren and Perazzi 1995, 122, fig. 3, C4.

10. **Pl. 7.1, no. 10**

   Description: Fragment of a bowl with a straight, plain rim.
   Material: Fabric A.
   Dimensions: D. 18 cm; H. max. 2 cm.
   Context: Building J, Level IV.

   Some finds, mostly from Levels III and IV of Building J, must pre-date the Etruscan period. They are handmade in a rough ware (Fabric A); some are decorated with incised lines and seem to be dated between the late Bronze Age and the early Iron Age (eleventh – eighth century BCE).

   Unidentified sherds of the same fabric and probably the same period: 19 fragments from Building J, Level III (gr. 185); 12 fragments from Building J, Level IV (gr. 60); and 2 from wall cleaning (gr. 5); probably of closed vessels.

Pottery from the Seventh to the First Half of the Third Century BCE (Etruscan Period)

Corinthian Pottery (?)

11. **Pl. 7.2, no. 11**

   Description: Fragment of a closed vessel, painted with a thin dark-coloured horizontal band. Because of its thinness and the characteristics of the clay, it could be identified as Corinthian pottery.
   Material: Fabric B.
   Dimensions: H. max. 2 cm.
   Context: Building J, Level III.
   Unidentified fragments from the same fabric: 2 fragments from Building J, Level III (gr. 6).

Etrusco-Corinthian Pottery

12. **Pl. 7.2, no. 12**

   Description: Fragment of the bottom of a cup, probably on a stemmed base. Painted with an internal, rounded red band.
   Material: Fabric C.
   Chronology: Late Orientalizing period.
   Context: Building J, Level IV.

13. **Pl. 7.2, no. 13**

   Description: Fragment of a globular bowl with an averted rim. Painted with a dark red band on the external side of the rim and some traces of an unidentifiable figured decoration above. On the inside, the sherd is painted completely dark red.
   Material: Fabric C.
   Dimensions: D. 20 cm; H. max. 3.9 cm.
   Context: Building J, Level I.

Attic Black-figured Pottery

14. **Pl. 7.2, no. 14**

   Description: Fragment of an open vessel (*kylix* cup), painted with a horizontal black band and traces of an unidentifiable figured decoration. With two other fragments from the same vessel.
   Material: Fabric D.
   Dimensions: H. max. 2.5 cm.
   Context: Building M, Level IV.

Bucchero Pottery

15. **Pl. 7.2, no. 15**

   Description: Fragment of a jug with a strap handle and a neck strongly articulated from the shoulder.
   Material: Fabric E.
   Dimensions: H. max. 4 cm.
   Chronology: Last quarter of the seventh to the first quarter of the sixth century BCE.
   Context: Building J, Level III.
   References: The example could be ascribed to Rasmussen 1979, jug type 1b.

16. **Pl. 7.2, no. 16**

   Description: Bottom of a closed vessel with a ring foot and an angular section; maybe a jug.
   Material: Fabric E.
   Dimensions: Base D. 6.5 cm; H. max. 2.8 cm.
   Chronology: Last quarter of the seventh to the first quarter of the sixth century BCE.
   Context: Building J, Level III.

17. **Pl. 7.2, no. 17**

   Description: Fragment of a flared foot, slightly thick and rounded.
   Material: Fabric E.
   Dimensions: Base D. 16.5 cm; H. max. 1.6 cm.
   Chronology: Last quarter of the seventh to the mid-sixth century BCE.
   Context: Building J, Level IV.
   References: Similar to Rasmussen 1979, chalice type 2d.

18. **Pl. 7.2, no. 18**

   Description: Fragment of a carinated *kantharos* with a straight rim, decorated with two horizontal incised lines; carination decorated with diamond notches.

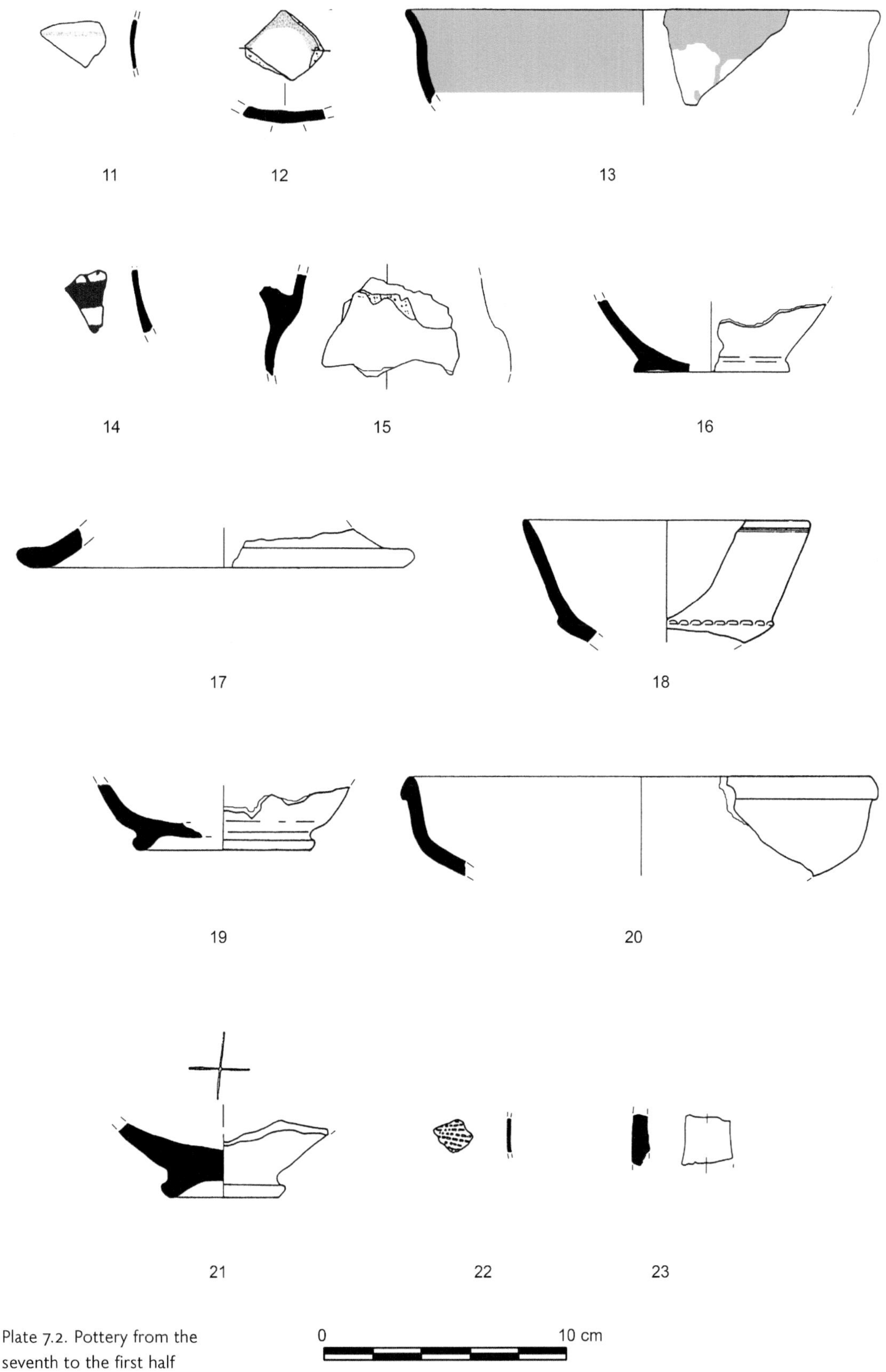

7. PRE-ETRUSCAN, ETRUSCAN, AND ROMAN POTTERY

Plate 7.2. Pottery from the seventh to the first half of the third century BCE (Etruscan Period).

Material: Fabric E.
Dimensions: D. 12 cm; H. max. 5 cm.
Chronology: Last quarter of the seventh to the first half of the sixth century BCE.
Context: Building J, Level IV.
References: Similar to Rasmussen 1979, *kantharos* type 3e.

19. **Pl. 7.2, no. 19**
    Description: Fragment of a deep bowl, with a ring foot and carination above.
    Material: Fabric F.
    Dimensions: Base D. 7.5 cm; H. max. 2.7 cm.
    Chronology: Fifth century BCE.
    Context: Building J, Level III.
    References: Similar to an example from Casale Pian Roseto: Murray Threipland and Torelli 1970, 74, fig. 6.9.

20. **Pl. 7.2, no. 20**
    Description: 2 fragments of a bowl with a beaded rim and a shallow groove below the rim; finished by wheel.
    Material: Fabric F.
    Dimensions: D. 19.5 cm; H. max. 4 cm.
    Chronology: Fifth century BCE.
    Context: Building J, Level IV.
    References: Similar to Rasmussen 1979, 125, bowl type 3.

21. **Pl. 7.2, no. 21**
    Description: Fragment of a probably out-turned bowl, ring foot, graffito cross inside of the bottom.
    Material: Fabric F.
    Dimensions: Base D. 4.5 cm; H. max. 3 cm.
    Context: Building J, Level IV.

22. **Pl. 7.2, no. 22**
    Description: Fragment of a closed vessel, with fan decoration.
    Material: Fabric E.
    Dimensions: H. max. 1.4 cm.
    Context: Building J, Level IV
    References: See Hirschland Ramage 1970, 16–17.

23. **Pl. 7.2, no. 23**
    Description: Fragment of a strap handle, maybe from a *kantharos* or *kyathos*.
    Material: Fabric E.
    Dimensions: H. max. 1.9 cm.
    Context: Building J, Level III.

2 fragments of closed vessel rims (*olpai*? jugs?) from Building J, Level III (Fabric E; 23 gr); 2 fragments of closed vessel rims from Building J, Level IV (Fabric E; 18 gr).

Unidentified sherds of Fabric E: 19 fragments from Building J, Level III (gr. 90); 5 fragments from Building J, Level IV.

Red Ware (Fabric G)

1 fragment of a loop handle from Building J, Level III (12 gr); 1 fragment of a strap handle from Building J, Level IV (24 gr); 2 fragments of averted rims from a jar (1 from Building J, Level III; 1 from Level IV; 33 gr); 1 fragment of a *pithos* rim (45 gr); 1 fragment of a neck decorated with angular incised lines from Building J, Level IV (18 gr).

Unidentified sherds: 12 fragments from Building J, Level III (gr. 123); 14 fragments from Building J, Level IV (gr. 175).

Coarse ware

Jars

A significant number of coarse ware pieces can be ascribed to various types of jar dating from the end of the seventh to the sixth century BCE. Most body and base sherds seem to belong to jars of medium to large dimensions, probably with ovoid shapes and flat bases. This form was useful for cooking or storage.

24. **Pl. 7.3, no. 24**
    Description: Fragment of a strongly averted and thick rim.
    Material: Fabric H.
    Dimensions: D. 15.3 cm; H. max. 1.4 cm.
    Context: Building J, Level III; 3 similar fragments from Level IV.

25. **Pl. 7.3, no. 25**
    Description: Fragment of a plain averted and slightly thick rim.
    Material: Fabric H.
    Dimensions: D. 20.2 cm; H. max. 2.4 cm
    Chronology: Late seventh to sixth century BCE.
    Context: Building J, Level IV. Another similar fragment from the same level.
    References: Similar to Doganella type 1: Perkins and Walker 1990, 35, fig. 29.9.

26. **Pl. 7.3, no. 26**
    Description: Fragment of an averted and cut rim.
    Material: Fabric H.
    Dimensions: D. 20.5 cm; H. max. 2.6 cm.
    Chronology: Late sixth century BCE.

7. PRE-ETRUSCAN, ETRUSCAN, AND ROMAN POTTERY 107

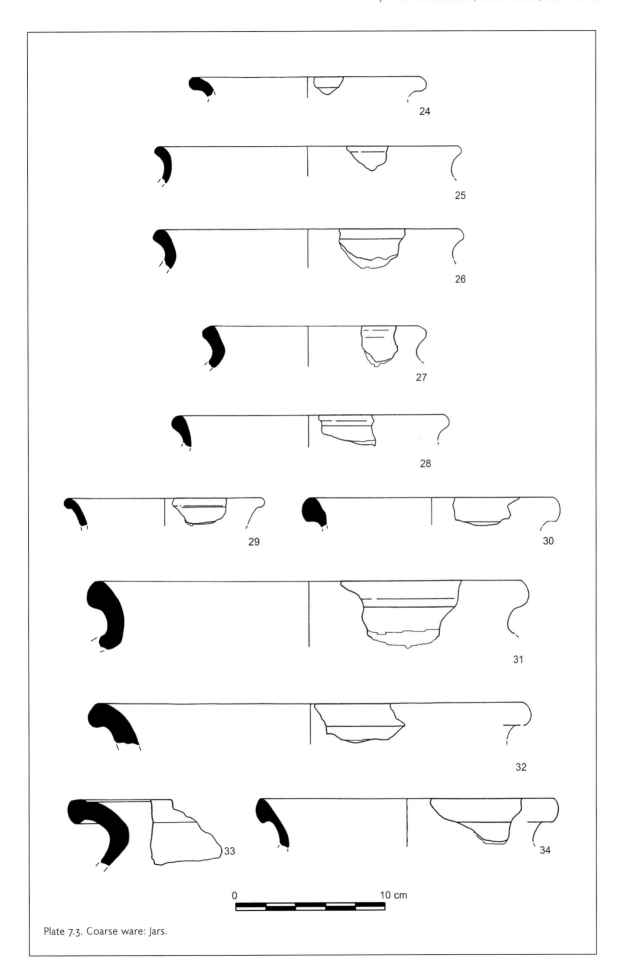

Plate 7.3. Coarse ware: Jars.

Context: Building J, Level III; 1 similar example from Building M, Level I; 1 similar example from the external gate complex.
References: Similar to Doganella type 1: Perkins and Walker 1990, 35, fig. 29.9; and Tartuchino type 1: Perkins and Attolini 1992, 95, fig. 14.1 (see for diffusion).

27. Pl. 7.3, no. 27

Description: Fragment of a thick, averted and shaped rim.
Material: Fabric H.
Dimensions: D. 14.3 cm; H. max. 2.7 cm.
Chronology: Sixth century BCE.
Context: Building J, Level III; 2 similar from the same Level; 3 similar from Level IV.
References: Similar examples from Lago dell'Accesa: Camporeale 1997, 77–83, figs 8.2, 11. For diffusion, see Belelli Marchesini and others 2009, 75, fig. 7.1.

28. Pl. 7.3, no. 28

Description: Fragment of a thick and averted rim. This shape could be a variation of n. 27, although no comparable examples have been found nearby, it is largely diffused in southern Etruria and Latium vetus.
Material: Fabric H.
Dimensions: D. 18 cm; H. max. 2 cm.
Chronology: Late seventh to sixth century BCE.
Context: Building J, Level III; 1 similar from the same Level; 3 similar from Level IV.

29. Pl. 7.3, no. 29

Description: Fragment of a slightly rolled rim.
Material: Fabric H.
Dimensions: D. 13.5 cm; H. max. 1.8 cm.
Context: Building J, Level IV; 1 similar from the same Level.

30. Pl. 7.3, no. 30

Description: Fragment of a thick, averted and slightly rolled rim.
Material: Fabric H.
Dimensions: D. 16.5 cm; H. max. 1.9 cm.
Chronology: Sixth to fifth century BCE.
Context: Building M, Level I.
References: Similar to Doganella type 3: Perkins and Walker 1990, 35, fig. 29.12; Tartuchino type 2: Perkins and Attolini 1992, 95, fig. 14.8; and an example from La Parrina: Ciampoltrini 1991, 265, fig. 7, n. 9.

31. Pl. 7.3, no. 31

Description: Fragment of a strongly thickened, averted, and slightly rolled rim.
Material: Fabric H.
Dimensions: D. 29 cm; H. max. 4.5 cm.
Chronology: Late seventh to early sixth century BCE.
Context: Building J, Level IV.
References: Similar to Roselle 'Casa dell'Impluvium' type I.4: Donati 1994, 111–12, fig. 20, n. 167; and Lago dell'Accesa type IIa, n. 14: Camporeale 1997, 94–95, fig. 11.

32. Pl. 7.3, no. 32

Description: Fragment of a rolled rim.
Material: Fabric H.
Dimensions: D. 29.3 cm; H. max. 2.7 cm.
Chronology: Sixth to fifth century BCE.
Context: Building J, Level IV.
References: Similar to Lago dell'Accesa, type VIIa, n. 6: Camporeale 1997, 84–86, fig. 5.

33. Pl. 7.3, no. 33

Description: Fragment of a rolled and slightly hooked rim with internal marking.
Material: Fabric H.
Dimensions: H. max. 4.3 cm.
Context: Building J, Level IV.

34. Pl. 7.3, no. 33

Description: Fragment of an averted and hooked rim.
Material: Fabric H.
Dimensions: D. 20 cm; H. max. 3.2 cm.
Chronology: Late sixth to fifth century BCE.
Context: Building J, Level IV.
References: Similar to Roselle 'Casa dell'Impluvium' type I.5: Donati 1994, 112, fig. 34, n. 347. For the diffusion, see Belelli Marchesini and others 2009, 80, fig. 11.6.

3 fragments of flat bases from Building J, Level III (Fabric H; 68 gr); 10 fragments of flat bases from Building J, Level IV (Fabric H; 155 gr); 1 fragment of a loop handle from Building J, Level III (Fabric H; 30 gr).

Identified shapes: characterized by rather thick rim, which ascribes them to a period between the end of the seventh and the sixth century BCE. The shape seems to evolve towards an accentuated thickness and curvature of the rim, which probably introduced the hooked version of the fifth century.

Unidentified sherds of the same fabric: 286 fragments from Building J, Level III (gr. 2308); 474 fragments from Building J, Level IV (gr. 2264).

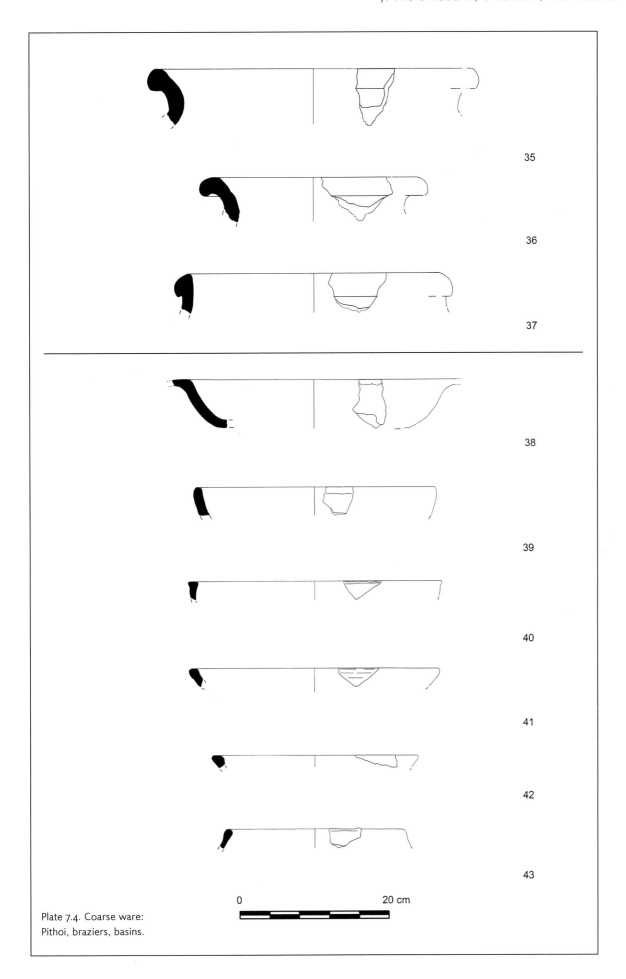

Plate 7.4. Coarse ware: Pithoi, braziers, basins.

Pithoi

35. Pl. 7.4, no. 35
Description: Fragment of a thick and slightly rolled rim.
Material: Fabric H.
Dimensions: D. 43 cm; H. max. 7.4 cm.
Chronology: Late seventh to sixth century BCE.
Context: Building J, Level IV. 1 similar from the same Level.
References: Similar to examples from Doganella: Perkins and Walker 1990, 37, fig. 33.1; and Tartuchino: Perkins and Attolini 1992, 95, fig. 14.6.

36. Pl. 7.4, no. 36
Description: Fragment of a thick, rolled rim with a sinuous internal profile.
Material: Fabric H.
Dimensions: D. 28 cm; H. max. 5.8 cm.
Chronology: Sixth century BCE.
Context: From Building J, Level IV.

37. Pl. 7.4, no. 37
Description: Fragment of a hooked rim with a vertical neck.
Material: Fabric H.
Dimensions: D. 34 cm. H. max. 5.3 cm.
Chronology: Probably fifth century BCE.
Context: Building J, Level IV.

Braziers

38. Pl. 7.4, no. 38
Description: Fragment of a round brazier with an averted rim and incurving wall.
Material: Fabric H.
Dimensions: H. max. 6.4 cm.
Chronology: Sixth century BCE.
Context: Building J, Level III.

Basins

39. Pl. 7.4, no. 39
Description: Fragment of a small basin with hemispherical walls and a plain, incurving rim.
Material: Fabric H.
Dimensions: D. 32 cm; H. max. 3.7 cm.
Chronology: Sixth to fifth century BCE.
Context: Building M, Level I; 1 similar from the same Level.
References: Similar to an example from Doganella: Perkins and Walker 1990, 39, fig. 36.17 (bowl); and Roselle 'Casa dell'Impluvium' type IV.1: Donati 1994, 115, fig. 14, n. 110.

40. Pl. 7.4, no. 40
Description: Fragment of a thick, flat rim.
Material: Fabric H.
Dimensions: D. 34 cm; H. max. 2.4 cm.
Chronology: Late sixth–fifth century BCE.
Context: Building M, Level III.
References: Similar to Doganella type 5: Perkins and Walker 1990, 39, fig. 37.6.

41. Pl. 7.4, no. 41
Description: Fragment of a thick, squared rim.
Material: Fabric H.
Dimensions: D. 32 cm; H. max. 2.4 cm.
Context: Building M, Level III.

42. Pl. 7.4, no. 42
Description: Fragment of a thick, cut rim.
Material: Fabric H.
Dimensions: D. 28.5 cm; H. max. 1.7 cm.
Context: Building J, Level IV.

43. Pl. 7.4, no. 43
Description: Fragment of an hemispherical basin (or large bowl?), with an incurving, thick, and rounded rim.
Material: Fabric H.
Dimensions: D. 24 cm; H. max. 2.5 cm.
Context: Building J, Level IV.

1 fragment of a handle from a large basin from Building J, Level III (Fabric H; gr. 42).

Bowls

44. Pl. 7.5, no, 44
Description: Fragment of a thickened and rounded rim.
Material: Fabric H.
Dimensions: D. 19 cm; H. max. 3 cm.
Context: Building J, Level IV; 1 similar from same Level.

45. Pl. 7.5, no. 45
Description: Fragment of a straight, slightly thickened, and rounded rim.
Material: Fabric H.
Dimensions: D. 16 cm: H. max. 3.3 cm.
Context: Building J, Level III.

46. Pl. 7.5, no. 46
Description: Fragment of an incurving, cut rim.
Material: Fabric H.
Dimensions: D. 16.5 cm; H. max. 2.4 cm.
Context: Building M, Level I.

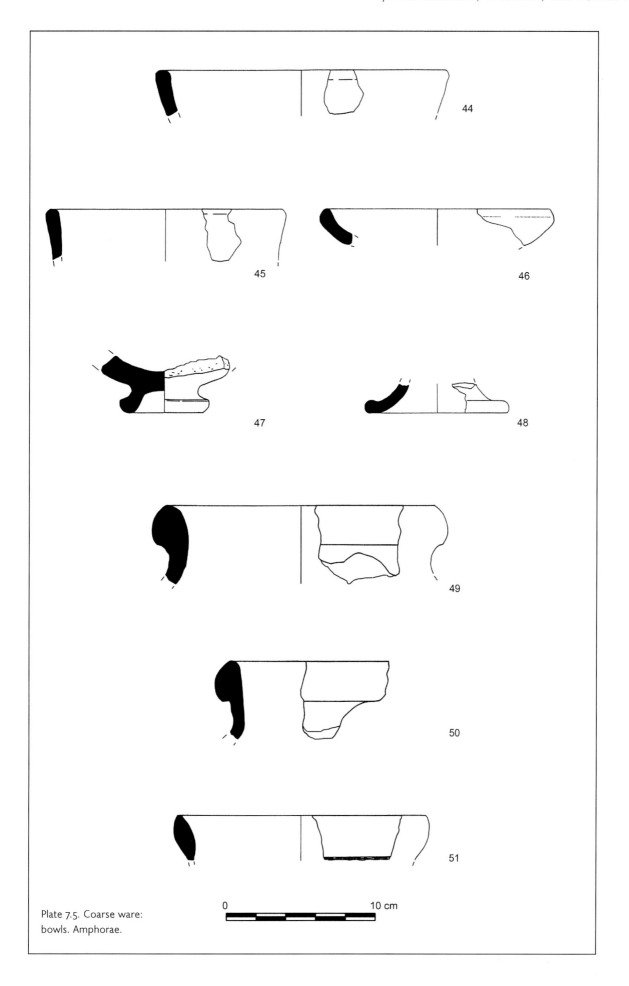

Plate 7.5. Coarse ware: bowls. Amphorae.

47. Pl. 7.5, no. 47
Description: Fragment of a thick ring foot.
Material: Fabric H.
Dimensions: Base D. 5 cm; H. max. 3.7.
Chronology: Late sixth to fifth century BCE.
Context: Building J Level I; 1 similar from Level IV.
References: Similar to an example from Doganella (type 2): Perkins and Walker 1990, 37.

48. Pl. 7.5, no. 48
Description: Fragment of an averted and rolled, flared foot with a sinuous internal profile.
Material: Fabric H.
Dimensions: Base D. 9.5 cm; H. max. 2 cm.
Chronology: Sixth to fifth century BCE.
Context: Building J, Level IV; 1 similar from same Level.
References: Similar to Doganella type 2: Perkins and Walker 1990, 37 fig. 32.9.

Lids

1 fragment of an averted and slightly thick rim, from Building J, Level IV (Fabric H; gr 36).

Amphorae

A small number of amphora sherds have been found at Capalbiaccio. For this class, Perkins has identified a local production at the nearby centre of Doganella. We can suppose that the Capalbiaccio sherds were probably produced at Doganella, on the basis of the comparison of the shapes and the quality of the fabric used for examples 49–50, which are very similar to our Fabric H. Fragment 51 can probably be ascribed to a different area of production, as it is not made of the same fabric (Fabric M).

49. Pl. 7.5, no. 49
Description: Fragment of a hooked rim with a distinct neck.
Material: Fabric H.
Dimensions: D. 18 cm; H. max. 5.2 cm.
Chronology: Sixth century BCE.
Context: Building J, Level III.
References: Similar to Doganella type 2: Perkins and Walker 1990, 42, fig. 38.8, which is related to Py and Py 1974, type 3B; and examples from Tartuchino: Perkins and Attolini 1992, fig. 15.21; and Lago dell'Accesa: Camporeale 1997, 192, fig. 28, nos 4–5.

50. Pl. 7.5, no. 50
Description: Fragment of a hooked rim with a distinct vertical neck.
Material: Fabric H.
Dimensions: H. max. 5.2 cm.
Chronology: Sixth century BCE.
Context: Building M, from Level I; 1 similar from same Level.
References: Similar to Doganella type 2: Perkins and Walker 1990, 42, fig. 38.14; and an example from La Parrina: Ciampoltrini 1991, 265, fig. 8, n. 2.

51. Pl. 7.5, no. 51
Description: Fragment of a thick neck, out-turned at the neck rim.
Material: Fabric M.
Dimensions: D. 17 cm; H. max. 3 cm.
Chronology: Fifth century BCE.
Context: Building J, Level IV.
References: Similar to Py and Py 1974, type 4.

Coarse Creamware

52. Pl. 7.6, no. 52
Description: Fragment of a jar with an averted, thickened, and hooked rim.
Material: Fabric I.
Dimensions: H. max. 2.1 cm.
Chronology: Late sixth to fourth century BCE.
Context: Building J, Level IV.
References: Similar to an example from Doganella: Perkins and Walker 1990, 36, fig. 30.5. Unidentified sherds of the same fabric: 15 fragments from Building J, Level III (gr. 249); 6 fragments from Building J, Level IV (gr. 60).

Fine Creamware

Fabric L; for the class, see Perkins and Walker 1990, 31–33.

2 red-painted fragments from Building J, Level IV (gr. 7); 4 fragments from Level IV (gr. 80); 6 fragments from Level III (gr. 25).

Tiles

3 fragments of tile type Wikander IC from Building J, Level III (gr. 790); 1 fragment from Level IV (gr. 154).

4 fragments of unidentified types from Building J, Level III (gr. 650).

7. PRE-ETRUSCAN, ETRUSCAN, AND ROMAN POTTERY

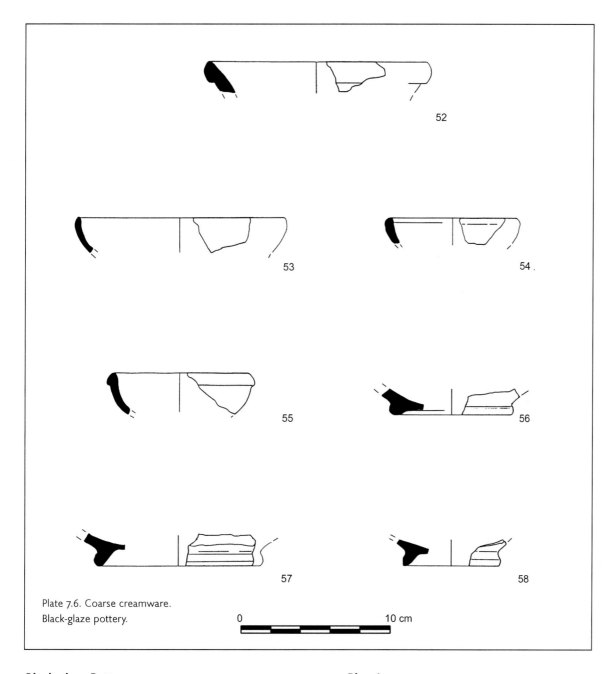

Plate 7.6. Coarse creamware. Black-glaze pottery.

Black-glaze Pottery

Only a small number of black-glaze pottery has been found at Capalbiaccio. Most of the sherds are characterized by pink clay and a shiny glaze, and they seem to be dated to the first productive phases of the class (early third century BCE).

53. Pl. 7.6, no. 53

Description: Fragment of a small bowl with an incurved rim and a rounded shape. Probably a production of the Ateliers des Petites Estampilles.
Material: Fabric N.
Dimensions: D. 14 cm; H. max. 2.4 cm.
Chronology: Early third century BCE.
Context: Building J, Level IV.
References: Similar to Morel 1981, series 2784. Similar to an example from Saturnia in the Ciacci collection: Donati and Michelucci 1981, 99, 175; and examples from Sovana, Monte Rosello, tomb 6: Pancrazzi and others 1971, 100, fig. 45, n. 5; and the acropolis at Populonia: Biancifiori and others 2010, 39, fig. 11, n. 4.

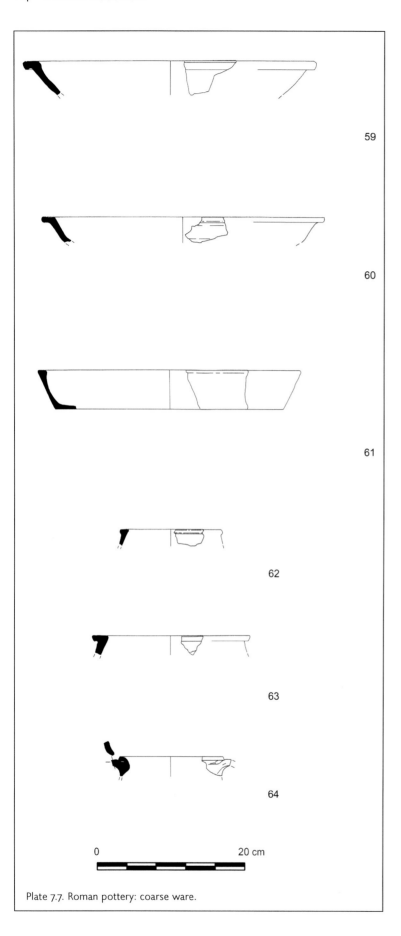

Plate 7.7. Roman pottery: coarse ware.

54. Pl. 7.6, no. 54

Description: Fragment of a small bowl with an incurved, thickened, and shaped rim.
Material: Fabric N.
Dimensions: D. 9 cm; H. max. 1.7 cm.
Context: Building J, Level IV; 2 similar from same Level.

55. Pl. 7.6, no. 55

Description: Fragment of a small rounded bowl and a shallow groove below rim. Wheel made.
Material: Fabric N.
Dimensions: D. 9 cm; H. max. 2.8 cm.
Chronology: 250–25 BCE.
Context: Building J, Level IV.
References: Similar to Morel 1981, series 2537 (diffused in northern Etruria).

56. Pl. 7.6, no. 56

Description: Fragment of a small bowl with a thickened and low ring foot.
Material: Fabric N.
Dimensions: Base D. 8 cm. H. max. 1.8 cm.
Chronology: 300 BCE.
Context: Building J, Level III.
References: Similar to Morel 1981, type 321b3.

57. Pl. 7.6, no. 57

Description: Fragment of a bowl (?) with a shaped ring foot.
Material: Fabric O.
Dimensions: Base D. 11 cm; H. max. 2.2 cm.
Chronology: Early third century BCE.
Context: Building J, Level III.
References: Similar to Morel 1981, type 341a1.

58. Pl. 7.6, no. 58

Description: Fragment of a small bowl with a cut ring foot.
Material: Fabric N.
Dimensions: Base D. 6.5 cm; H. max. 1.7 cm.
Chronology: Early third century BCE.
Context: Building M, Level I.
References: Similar to Morel 1981, type 2621a2.

Unidentified shapes: 1 fragment from Building J, Level III (gr. 3); 4 fragments from Building J, Level IV (gr. 25); 3 fragments from Building M, Level I (gr. 31).

Other Hellenistic Wares

A certain number of body sherds, not related to any definite shape, made in an orange and not very depurated ware, must be ascribed to Hellenistic fabrics, which, when compared with fine productions of central Italy, can be dated between fourth and second centuries BCE (Fabric P).

22 fragments from Building J, Level III (gr. 410); 21 fragments from Building J, Level IV (gr. 235).

Roman Pottery

Coarse Ware

Although already used to describe wares of the Etruscan period, the term 'coarse ware' has been applied to any production of Roman period without covering, made of various fabrics, for kitchen, table, or storage use, according to the definition given by Gloria Olcese in her contribution concerning the *Albintimilium* pottery (1993).

Pans

59. Pl. 7.7, no. 59

Description: Fragment of a flat-bottomed pan with a strongly averted and flat brim, cut and slightly rolled, internally shaped; rounded body.
Material: Fabric Q.
Dimensions: D. 40 cm; H. max. 4.5 cm.
Chronology: First century BCE to the first century CE.
Context: Building J, Level III.
References: Similar to an example from Cosa: Dyson 1976, 22, fig. 1, CF 8, Class 3.

60. Pl. 7.7, no. 60

Description: Fragment of flat-bottomed pan with a strongly averted rim, with a large, hollow, and slightly carinated body.
Material: Fabric Q.
Dimensions: D. 40 cm; H. max. 4.5 cm.
Chronology: First century BCE to the first century CE.
Context: Building J, Level III
References: Similar to an example from Cosa: Dyson 1976, 22, fig. 1, CF 8, Class 3.

61. Pl. 7.7, no. 61

Description: Fragment of a flat-bottomed pan with a straight, slightly thickened, and grooved rim; flat base.
Material: Fabric Q

Dimensions: D. 36 cm; H. max. 5.2 cm.
Chronology: First century BCE to 50 CE.
Context: Building J, Level IV.
References: Similar to an example from Cosa: Dyson 1976, 68, fig. 18, VD5.

Pots

62. Pl. 7.7, no. 62

Catalogue Number: n/a
Description: Fragment of a thickened, squared, and flat rim
Material: Fabric Q
Dimensions: D. 14 cm; H. max. 2.2 cm.
Chronology: n/a
Context: From Building J, Level IV.
References: none listed

63. Pl. 7.7, no. 63

Catalogue Number: n/a
Description: Fragment of an averted, flat, enlarged, and cut rim.
Material: Fabric Q
Dimensions: D. 21 cm; H. max. 2.6 cm.
Chronology: Third century CE.
Context: From Building J, Level IV.
References: Similar to an example from Settefinestre: Papi 1985, 96, tav. 26.4; 100, tav. 27.14.

Jars

64. Pl. 7.7, no. 64

Description: Fragment of a strongly averted rim cut with angular sections, strap handles just under the rim, and possibly an ovoid shape.
Material: Fabric R.
Dimensions: D. 14 cm; H. max. 2.6 cm.
Chronology: From the last quarter of first century BCE.
Context: Building J, Level II.
References: Similar to an example from Cosa: Dyson 1976, 109, fig. 41, PD 160, class 10.

65. Pl. 7.8, no. 65

Description: Fragment of a slightly averted, thickened, and shaped rim with an internally incurving profile.
Material: Fabric Q.
Dimensions: D. 13.5 cm; H. max. 3 cm.
Chronology: Second century BCE.
Context: From Building J, Level IV.
References: Similar to examples from Cosa: Dyson 1976, 72, fig. 20, VD25; Populonia: Baroncelli 1996, 483–83, fig. 44, type 10b; and *Albintimilium*: Olcese 1993, 192, type 18E.

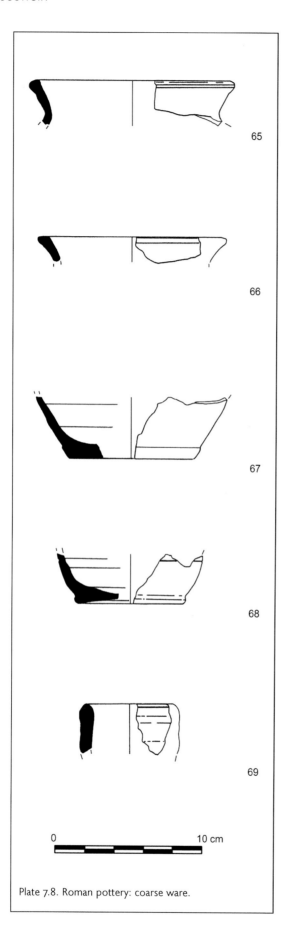

Plate 7.8. Roman pottery: coarse ware.

66. Pl. 7.8, no. 66

Description: Fragment of an averted, flat, and cut rim.
Material: Fabric Q.
Dimensions: D. 13 cm; H. max. 1.7 cm.
Context: From Building J, Level IV.
References: Similar to an example from Populonia: Curti and Tami 1996, 415, fig. 18, type O5.

67. Pl. 7.8, no. 67

Description: Fragment of a flat base, with a shaped band on the bottom.
Material: Fabric Q.
Dimensions: D. 8.5 cm; H. max. 4.1 cm.
Chronology: Third century CE.
Context: Building J; 1 fragment from Level IV.
References: Similar to an example from Settefinestre: Papi 1985, 246, tav. 66.19.

68. Pl. 7.8, no. 68

Description: Fragment of a low, thickened ring foot with an ovoid shape, decorated with an incised horizontal line.
Material: The fabric is different from the previous examples: it is white-yellowish coloured, with small black and quartzite inclusions, irregular fracture and rough, powdery loose surface.
Dimensions: Base D. 7.5 cm; H. max. 3.3 cm.
Context: From Building J, Level IV.

69. Pl. 7.8, no. 69

Description: Fragment of a straight and slightly thickened rim, decorated by a horizontal incised line, possibly from a small-handled jar.
Material: Fabric T.
Dimensions: D. 6 cm. H. max. 3.2 cm.
Context: From Building J, Level IV; 1 similar from same Level.

Fabric Q: 1 fragment of a rim from a jar from Building J, Level III, related to a type known from the first century CE at Settefinestre. Another fragment of a rim from a jar from Building J, Level III, shape known from the third–fourth century at Settefinestre and *Albintimilium*. 1 fragment of a strongly thickened and squared rim of a jar from Building J, Level IV.

Fabric R: 1 fragment of lid with a rounded rim from Building J, Level III; 2 fragments of the same shape from Building J, Level IV. 2 fragments of slightly averted rims from strap-handled jars (1 from Building J, Level III; 1 from Level IV); 1 fragment of a strongly averted rim from Building

J, Level III. 8 fragments of strap handles from Building J, Level IV. 5 fragments of flat bases of jugs from Building J, Level III.

Fabric U: sherds decorated with irregular incised lines, which seem to be related to one-handled jugs, with globular bodies and flat bases, decorated with irregular lines on the shoulder. The shape known from the fourth century BCE at *Albintimilium*, in a similar fabric. 2 fragments from Building J, Level III (gr. 190); 1 fragment from Building J, Level IV.

Unidentified Shapes

Fabric Q: 57 fragments from Building J, Level III (gr. 320); 1 fragment from Building J, Level IV (gr. 10).

Fabric R: 8 fragments from Building J, Level III (gr. 265); 2 fragments from Building J, Level IV (gr. 15).

Fabric T: 21 fragments from Building J, Level III (gr. 97); 11 fragments from Building J, Level IV (gr. 61).

EMANUELE VACCARO

8. Capalbiaccio and Medieval Pottery in Southern Tuscany (900–1000)

ABSTRACT This text started as a larger project about patterns of ceramic production and circulation in southern Tuscany, an archaeological *comparanda* of tenth- and eleventh-century pottery that traced the economic changes and adaptation during the decline of the Roman Empire. This chapter differs from the others as the author compares and analyses aspects of ceramic supply and consumption between three sites: Capalbiaccio, Poggio Cavolo, and Cosa.

After introducing each type of pottery (coarse and semi-depurated wares, levigated, sparse glaze, and Forum ware), the author describes the finds and compares them with material from other known sites to establish if they were local or imported productions. Emmanuele Vaccaro's interpretation is pioneering in using coarse and sparse glazed ceramics to connect Capalbiaccio and other sites to the economic vicissitudes of the Ottonian age and the procurement strategies of emergent towns like Pisa and Rome. These particular typologies, together with those studied in the following chapter by Valdambrini, are among the least-known ceramics, but they provide new data with which to read the early medieval period. Finally, this chapter should be read in tandem with the author's research to the northern part of the coast (see Vaccaro 2018), which provides a perfect introduction to the pottery of this less well-known period.

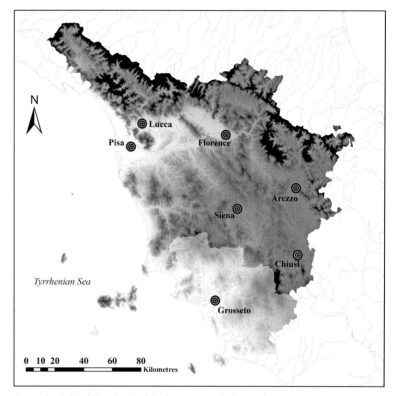

Figure 8.1. Digital Terrain Model of Tuscany with the study area corresponding to the modern Province of Grosseto. Map by author.

Introduction

This chapter discusses a recently rediscovered tenth-century ceramic deposit from Capalbiaccio[1] in the broader context of the production, circulation, and consumption of tenth- to early eleventh-century pottery in southern Tuscany, roughly between the Milia stream, tributary of the Cornia river, to the north and the Valle d'Oro to the south, in what is now the province of Grosseto (Fig. 8.1). Though long poorly understood, the exponential increase in excavations and field surveys over the last three decades in large sectors of southern Tuscany has significantly improved our knowledge of the ceram-

---

* This chapter is intended as a synthesis of patterns of ceramic production and circulation in southern Tuscany in the period 900–1000. It draws upon the large datasets of my research project 'Economics, Adaptation and the End of the Roman Empire: A Comparative Archaeological Study' funded by the Leverhulme Trust and the Newton Trust, carried out at the McDonald Institute for Archaeological Research (University of Cambridge, October 2011–September 2013). I owe a debt of gratitude, for discussions about the research on early medieval pottery, to Andrea Augenti, Graeme Barker, Kim Bowes, Stefano Campana, Federico Cantini, Lisa Fentress, Mariaelena Ghisleni, Michelle Hobart, Richard Hodges, Martin Millett, Alessandra Molinari, Chris Wickham, and Riccardo Francovich. A first draft was completed in 2012 and updated in 2015.

1 Vaccaro 2009.

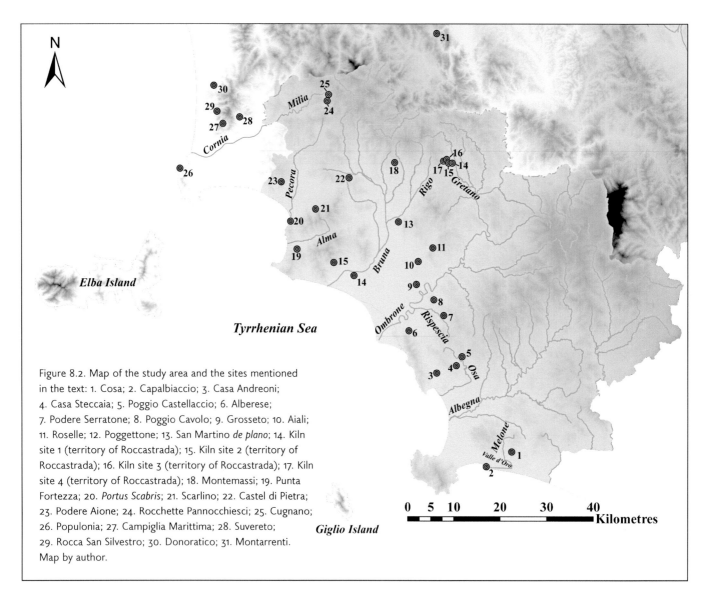

Figure 8.2. Map of the study area and the sites mentioned in the text: 1. Cosa; 2. Capalbiaccio; 3. Casa Andreoni; 4. Casa Steccaia; 5. Poggio Castellaccio; 6. Alberese; 7. Podere Serratone; 8. Poggio Cavolo; 9. Grosseto; 10. Aiali; 11. Roselle; 12. Poggettone; 13. San Martino *de plano*; 14. Kiln site 1 (territory of Roccastrada); 15. Kiln site 2 (territory of Roccastrada); 16. Kiln site 3 (territory of Roccastrada); 17. Kiln site 4 (territory of Roccastrada); 18. Montemassi; 19. Punta Fortezza; 20. *Portus Scabris*; 21. Scarlino; 22. Castel di Pietra; 23. Podere Aione; 24. Rocchette Pannocchiesci; 25. Cugnano; 26. Populonia; 27. Campiglia Marittima; 28. Suvereto; 29. Rocca San Silvestro; 30. Donoratico; 31. Montarrenti. Map by author.

ics of the central centuries of the Middle Ages and their potential, not only as the most valuable tool for dating, but also, even more interestingly, as a tool for exploring technological transformations, economic connections, local trade, and changes in eating habits. With the help of some recent publications[2] and their accurately quantified datasets — both published and unpublished — it is possible to outline a 'potted' sub-regional history and the economic and socio-cultural implications of changes in ceramic repertoires between the tenth and the early eleventh centuries (Fig. 8.2).

This chapter will examine the localization of pottery production and circulation, as well as the simplification of ceramic repertoires, documented throughout the region and particularly marked in the more rural southern areas between the later ninth and early eleventh century CE. Surface assemblages, often considered of little importance and unrepresentative in quantitative terms, will be combined with excavated data to shed light on the later ninth to tenth century circulation of coarse wares and kitchen wares at the local and sub-regional scale. This will help define how 'local' local really is, when dealing with early medieval pottery.

Concerning the evidence offered by excavated sites, a large section of this chapter draws on and discusses the tenth-century pottery assemblages yielded by the recent excavation at the medieval hilltop site of Poggio Cavolo some 35 km north of Capalbiaccio. Through a comparative study of the tenth-century ceramics from the two hilltop villages and the later-ninth-to-early-eleventh-century

---

[2] See Grassi 2010 and Vaccaro 2011 on southern Tuscany, for a regional overview see Cantini 2011; Bianchi and Hodges 2018; Bianchi and Hodges 2020.

pottery from both excavated and surveyed settlements in our area, this chapter aims to tackle issues of production and trade at a sub-regional scale and offers an economic interpretative model.

The tenth century, as demonstrated by using and comparing the ceramic assemblages from the hilltop sites of Capalbiaccio and Poggio Cavolo, represents a possible turning point for the circulation of pottery in southern Tuscany, which is mirrored in central and northern areas, although there it involves different actors.[3] The gradual arrival of some extra-regional pottery in the Ottonian period remains a limited phenomenon with little impact on the composition of repertoires, which continued to be restricted to a handful of functional forms, as in the Lombard and Carolingian periods.

A final methodological point seems in order: the vast majority of the surface and excavated assemblages presented in this chapter, were analysed and quantified using a consistent methodology that allowed for accurate comparisons.[4] All the potsherds belonging to each identified ceramic class were counted and weighed; then the minimum number of individuals (MNI) was calculated. In calculating the latter figure, mostly diagnostic fragments (rims, bases, and handles) were used, while walls were characterized by their fabrics, decorations, or finish, when different from the rest of the assemblage.[5] During the quantification process, a 5× magnifying lens was used to identify the MNI and to determine the main features of fabrics. Subsequently, the hand specimens were analysed using an optical microscope (for descriptions of the main fabrics discussed in this chapter, see Appendix 7.1).[6]

Tenth-Century Ceramic Assemblages from Capalbiaccio

The tenth-century ceramic contexts recently discovered at Capalbiaccio have already been the subject of a summary publication.[7] However, it is worth recapitulating that data here in some detail, in order to compare it with the broader picture of forms of pottery production, circulation, and consumption in southern Tuscany between the eighth and tenth centuries. The material from the Ottonian period mainly comes from two areas excavated by the Wesleyan University project during the late 1970s and early 1980s: Level 5 in Building J and Level 6 in Building T. However, only a small quantity of material was found in Building T, in a highly fragmentary state; this material has been omitted from the analysis, because it turned out to be less informative on pottery consumption at Capalbiaccio in the tenth century.

Table 8.1. In-phase and residual pottery from Level 5 of Building J at Capalbiaccio.

Period	Potsherds	Weight in grams
10th century CE	475	7305
Protohistoric residual pottery	5	240
Archaic residual pottery	43	945
Roman residual pottery (3rd BCE–1st CE)	46	655

Level 5 of Building J yielded a total of 569 fragments, weighing over 9 kg (Table 8.1). As will be seen below, the tenth-century materials immediately revealed some interesting parallels with ceramics documented in Rome and Latium. It was thus considered opportune to compare some fabrics from Capalbiaccio with the materials found during the excavation of the ninth- and tenth-century phases of the *domus solarate* in Rome's Forum of Nerva.[8] Level 5 contained some residual materials belonging to periods of the site's occupation prior to the Middle Ages; these accounted for 16.5 per cent of the total fragments. A total of eighty-seven minimum forms from the tenth century were found. As at other tenth-century sites in southern Tuscany, the number of pottery classes documented is extremely low, just as it was in the eighth- and ninth-century contexts examined in the previous section. These classes are represented by *acroma depurata*, *acroma selezionata*, and kitchen ware, which are accompanied, in this context, by small amounts of red-painted ware (*colature rosse*) (Fig. 8.3). In some cases, a degree of similarity was noted between the purified and selected fabrics, which had similar inclusions, albeit in slightly different quantities, probably indicating that the work-

---

3 On the tenth-century pottery in central and northern Tuscany, Cantini 2011.
4 I refer to the early medieval materials from Podere Serratone, Casa Andreoni, Aialind San Martino de plano, as well as to the tenth-century assemblages from Capalbiaccio and Poggio Cavolo.
5 On quantification see in general Orton, Tyers, and Vince 1993.
6 A Zeiss Stemi 2000-C with magnifications from 6.5X to 50X was used.
7 Vaccaro 2009.

8 On the *domus solarate* of the ninth and tenth centuries in the Forum of Nerva see Meneghini and Santangeli Valenzani 2004, 31–51. I would like to thank Ilaria de Luca, who allowed to examine and sample some fabrics of pottery from building A in the Forum of Nerva in Rome for comparison with those from Capalbiaccio.

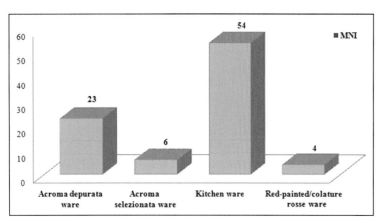

Figure 8.3. Capalbiaccio, Level 5 of Building J (tenth century): ceramic classes and MNI. Graphic by author.

Table 8.2. Medieval small amphorae at Capalbiaccio (tenth century CE): types, fabrics (AD = *acroma depurata* fabric; Sel = *acroma selezionata* fabric), and MNI.

Type	Fabric/MNI
Small amphora 1	AD2 (1 specimen); AD3 (3 specimens)
Small amphora 2	AD3 (1 specimen)
Generic small amphora	AD2 (2 specimens); Sel1 (2 specimens); AD1 (1 specimen)

shops were located in contiguous areas with access to the same sources of raw materials.

The contexts under examination yielded a significant majority of minimum forms in kitchen ware (about 38 per cent), compared to table, storage, and transport wares, made from purified and semi-purified fabrics, including the red-painted ware. The overall number of functional forms is low, with only cooking pots, *testi*, *testelli*, and lids for cooking and bread-making, and jugs, small amphorae, and table amphorae for use at the table, storage, and perhaps for the transportation of agricultural produce.

As at Poggio Cavolo, despite the limited number of forms documented, the functional distinction between forms used for cooking and table or storage is stricter than at the eighth- or ninth-century context of the lowland settlement at Podere Serratone near the Rispescia stream and very close to Poggio Cavolo, where there was occasionally multifunctional use of *acroma depurata* or *selezionata* jugs, which were 'borrowed' for cooking or heating liquid or semi-liquid foods.[9] It should also be stressed that at both Capalbiaccio and Poggio Cavolo, some open forms in *acroma grezza*, such as *testi* and *testelli*, which in some cases presented no significant traces of smoke, may also have been used as a sort of tray for the presentation of food that was to be consumed collectively.

Acroma depurata and selezionata

These two classes are dealt with together, since they present significant affinities in surface treatment and finishing. In particular, there is a similarity between the only selected fabric identified (Sel1) and one of the four fabrics (AD2) used to make *depurata* ware,

which is perhaps an indication that they were manufactured at the same workshop and differentiated merely by a different degree of clay levigation. The *acroma depurata* and *selezionata* wares are generally of very high quality, systematically made on the fast wheel, fine-walled, and carefully finished. Out of a total of twenty-nine minimum specimens, seventeen present an external surface whitening, twenty-one present obvious smoothing with a stick over much of the vessel's surface, including the handles, while ten specimens present a combination of smoothing and whitening. Only in one case were these two techniques associated with a decorative motif consisting of a dense, light ribbing.

Investigation of the presence of a grey core in the purified and selected fabrics revealed that this phenomenon was much less common in the tenth-century wares from Capalbiaccio, than at most of the eighth- and ninth-century contexts of southern Tuscany. Only four out of a total of twenty-nine minimum *acroma depurata* forms and three out of six *acroma selezionata* specimens presented this characteristic: a total of 24.13 per cent. This suggests a greater ability to ensure clay levigation processes and better kiln structures at the production complexes of the tenth century, compared to those of the two previous centuries.

The fragmentary nature of some finds means that at least ten minimum individuals can only be ascribed to generic closed forms, while the remaining specimens of determinate typology are ten small amphorae, eight jugs, and a small table amphora.

The shape of the small two-handled amphora, already documented at several early medieval contexts of southern Tuscany,[10] differs slightly in the tenth-century version, wherein the handles have a thinner strap profile. The latter also loses the light ribbing present on some specimens of the eighth and ninth centuries, although the overall profile remains similar. Additionally, the smoothing frequently found

---

9 Vaccaro 2015, 220–26.

10 Vaccaro 2015, 225–26.

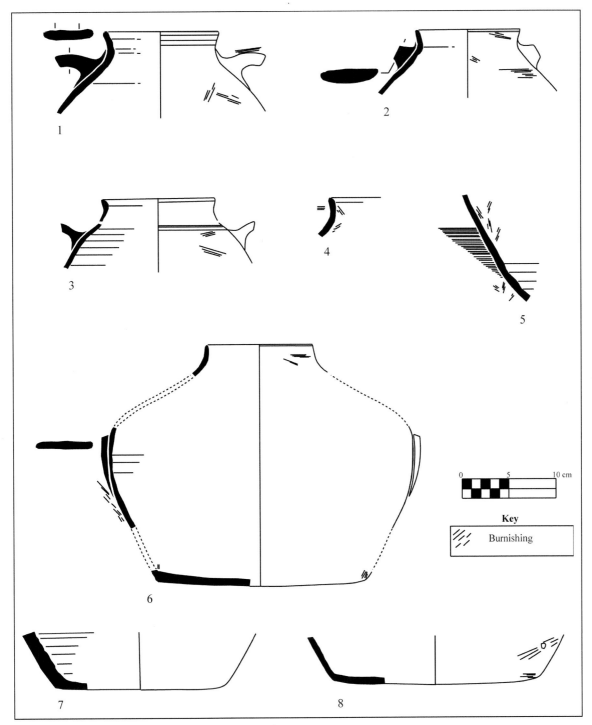

Plate 8.1. Capalbiaccio, Level 5 of Building J (tenth century). *Acroma depurata* and *acroma selezionata* wares: 1–8. Small amphorae.

on the handles appears to be a feature typical of the tenth-century versions. The small amphorae from Capalbiaccio exist in at least two main variants: one, more frequently documented and also common at Poggio Cavolo, has a slightly everted and rounded or occasionally oblique rim set on a short neck; and a second, documented by a single specimen, is characterized by an indistinct vertical rim, globular body, and a strap handle set at the widest point of the body (Table 8.2) (Pl. 8.1, nos 1–6). The base profile is generally convex, while in the eighth- and ninth-century wares made at Podere Serratone it tends to be flat (Pl. 8.1, no. 7). The presence of a repair hole on one of the specimens analysed shows

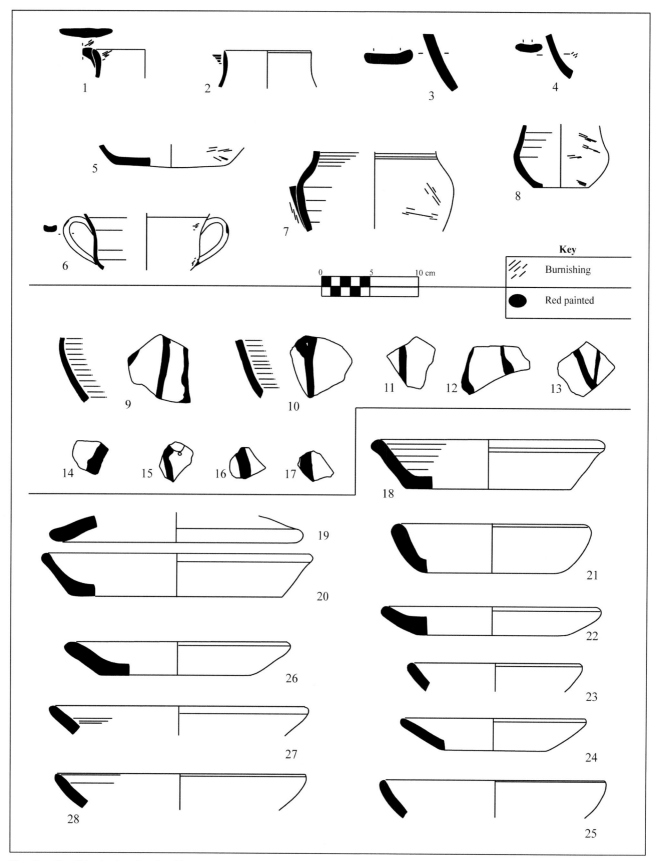

Plate 8.2. Capalbiaccio, Level 5 of Building J (tenth century). *Acroma depurata* and *acroma selezionata* wares: 1–5, 7. Table jugs; 6. Table amphora; 8. Small pitcher. Red-painted/*colature rosse* ware: 9–17. Potsherds of closed forms. Kitchen ware: 18, 19, 20, 21, 22, 26, 27, 28. *Testi*; 23–25. *Testelli*.

that these objects were considered valuable and therefore worth repairing, rather than simply replacing, when they broke (Pl. 8.1, no. 8). As already mentioned, the outer surface whitening and stick smoothing are constants, while a single specimen presents a dense, light ribbing beneath the widest point of the body. This form is made principally from purified fabrics, although two specimens in selected fabrics are also documented.

As well as with the contemporary materials from Poggio Cavolo, there are also similarities with the *acroma depurata* amphorae frequent in the tenth-century deposit at the Crypta Balbi in Rome. Like the specimens from Capalbiaccio, they have short necks, especially compared to the earlier types of the eighth and ninth centuries, and strap handles, which clearly differ from the older specimens that had a more massive morphological structure.[11] However, it should be noted that, in the Roman specimens, the handle is set directly on the neck and not on the junction between neck and shoulder, or directly on the latter, as in those from Capalbiaccio.

It is important to note that three of the ten small amphorae from Capalbiaccio are made from a purified fabric (AD2), which is similar to one from a late tenth century *olla acquaria* (AD36) from Poggio Cavolo, for which a possible provenance of north Latium or Rome has been proposed.[12] Based on the analysis of the fabrics, it seems certain that the rarer type 2 amphora was manufactured with type 1 in a workshop that used fabric AD3. In light of the striking similarities in terms of morphological structure and surface treatment between the amphorae made from purified fabrics AD2 and AD3, it is possible that all the wares made from these fabrics came from the same workshop, or from two workshops that made use of the same formal schemes and had similar technological skills.

Most of the uncoated table, storage, and transport wares are made from fabrics AD2 and AD3: as many as twenty-one minimum forms (seven in AD2 and fourteen in AD3) out of a total of twenty-nine. Of these twenty-one minimum specimens, the medium-sized and small jugs present surface whitening and stick smoothing, as in the larger forms described above. The most significant specimens include a type of jug that is characterized by a vertical rim and a pointed lip, which currently finds no close analogies in southern Tuscan contexts (Pl. 8.2, no. 2). However, the jug with the strap handle set at the widest point of the ovoid body and a neck with light grooves (Pl. 8.2, no. 7) has close parallels in the mid-tenth-century contexts of the Forum of Nerva in Rome[13] and in tenth-century phases of the castle of Scorano.[14] The jug with a slightly everted rim and the broad strap handle that is level with the edge, is made from fabric Sel1 (Pl. 8.2, no. 1). Another interesting form, though it lacks its rim, is a specimen with a 'bag-shaped' profile and flat base, which was perhaps a pitcher. It too appears to be absent from the known pottery assemblages of southern Tuscany, but the form can generically be compared to a small closed form from a context at Tarquinia, which is dated to between the eleventh and the first half of the twelfth century (Pl. 8.2, no. 8).[15] With the exception of the aforementioned specimen, the bases seem to repeat the slightly convex profile of the large forms used for storage and transport (Pl. 8.2, no. 5). The handles are always strap-shaped and vary in breadth and thickness, depending on the size of the jugs to which they belong (Pl. 8.2, nos 3–4).

The only small table amphora from this context made from fabric AD4 (documented only in this specimen) has been included among the *acroma depurata* ware, rather than among the red-painted pottery, even though it has two drops of dark red paint; these are considered accidental given their minute size and the complete absence of red paint from the rest of the body. This type is characterized by a severely flaring neck, small handles, and central grooves set on the widest point of the body and at the base of the neck (Pl. 8.2, no. 6). The outer surface is not whitened, but only smoothed with a stick. This form, hitherto unique in southern Tuscany between the eighth and tenth centuries, is fairly common in the deposits of the Crypta Balbi between the ninth and tenth centuries. It is more frequent in the Carolingian period, when versions with smoothed surfaces, whitened on the outside and adorned with decorative motifs incised on the neck and shoulder, are common.[16] Given its morphology and the absence of decorations, the specimen from Capalbiaccio is more similar to the specimens of the tenth century, rather than those of the ninth, which confirms the dating of Level 5 of Building J to the Ottonian period and suggests that this specimen may have come from workshops active in Rome or, more generally, in Latium.

---

11 Romei 2004, 306, Pl. XVI, no. 97.
12 Vaccaro and Salvadori 2006.
13 Pottery was compared with material studied by Ilaria de Luca.
14 Romei 1998, 131, Fig. 3, no. 4.
15 Bartoloni and Ricci 1995, 103, Fig. 8, no. 3.
16 Romei 2004, 300–06.

Table 8.3. Cooking pots at Capalbiaccio (tenth century CE): fabrics, types, and MNI.

Fabrics	Cooking pot types and MNI
G1 (Rome or Latium)	Type 1 (seven MNI), Type 12 (one MNI), Type 2 (one MNI)
G5 (Rome or Latium)	Type 6 (two MNI)
G2 (Local/subregional), same as G51 at Poggio Cavolo	Type 3 (one MNI), Type 10 (two MNI)
G3 (Local/subregional), same as G54 at Poggio Cavolo	Type 4 (two MNI), unidentified type (one MNI)
G4 (Local/subregional), same as G29 at Poggio Cavolo	Type 5 (one MNI), Type 8 (one MNI), Type 9 (two MNI), unidentified type (five MNI), Type 11 (one MNI)
G6 (Local/subregional)	Type 7 (one MNI)

Table 8.4. Kitchen ware open forms at Capalbiaccio (tenth century CE): fabrics, forms, and MNI.

Fabric	Kitchen ware open forms and MNI
G6	*Testo* (six MNI), lid (three MNI), *testello* (two MNI)
G7, same as G28 at Poggio Cavolo	*Testo* (three MNI), lid (four MNI), *testello* (seven MNI)

Red-painted and colature rosse ware

The distinction between these classes does not pose problems for whole vessels or large fragments, as the decorative pattern — made using a brush to obtain a more or less accurate motif (red-painted ware) or simply by dripping red paint over the surface (*colature rosse*) — is easy to recognize. This is not true of those small fragments for which it is impossible to ascertain whether the red paint forms part of a more complex painted decoration that dripped down or is simply the result of red paint dripped all over the vessel without using a brush.

At Capalbiaccio, this class, which could be described as a hybrid, given the difficulties in developing a more accurate classification, is represented by a total of ten fragments that correspond to four minimum generic closed forms (two of which may be small amphorae, given the thickness of the walls) made from two fabrics: DR1 and DR2 (Pl. 8.2, nos 9–17). Fabrics DR1 and DR2 are identical to AD2 and AD3, respectively, and used to make most of the *acroma depurata* specimens; they can therefore be ascribed to the same workshops that made both uncoated and red-painted wares. The outer surfaces of the few fragments that were discovered are both whitened and smoothed in six cases and only smoothed in four.

Red-painted pottery was common in Rome during the eighth century and seems to subsequently vanish, only to reappear much later, between the mid-twelfth and the thirteenth century.[17] However, at sites in north Latium, this class is also common between the ninth and tenth centuries, as shown by a ceramic context from the urban site of Cencelle, near Tarquinia, where it accounts for 14.54 per cent of all fragments and was probably produced in the vicinity of Rome.[18] Later, it is found with several specimens in an eleventh- or early twelfth-century context at Tarquinia.[19] Early medieval and medieval manufacturing centres for red-painted wares are well-documented in northern Tuscany, including at San Genesio, Pisa, and Lucca.[20] The circulation of these wares appears to be fairly intensive in the Valdarno, while in southern Tuscany, only a few sites yield materials that probably came from workshops active in the northern part of the region.[21]

As regards the few fragments of red-painted and *colature rosse* pottery from Capalbiaccio, it is worth noting that an optical microscope comparison of these two fabrics with that fabric, which characteristic of the pottery belonging to this class at Donoratico (probably imported from northern Tuscany), turned out to be negative.[22] Given this, and above all the fact that the site of Capalbiaccio appears far more similar in terms of ceramic consumption to contexts in Rome and Latium than to those of north-central Tuscany, it is logical that the red-painted and *colature rosse* wares attested to here, came from Latium.

Kitchen ware

Kitchen ware, with a total of 302 fragments or fifty-three minimum forms, is, as previously mentioned, the predominant class. The morphological repertoire documented at Capalbiaccio comprises only a few functional forms, of which the most important is the cooking pot, which was either manufactured locally, sub-regionally, or imported from Rome (Latium), but always made on the fast wheel (Table 8.3). To this is added open forms, *testi*, *testelli*, and lids, all of which probably came from workshops that were active in the Maremma area, given the close similarities of their morphologies and fabrics with some of the tenth-century products from Poggio Cavolo and other sites identified between the Bruna and Ombrone Valleys (Table 8.4).

---

17 Ricci 1990b, 308–13.
18 Prandi and Silvestrini 2004, 185.
19 Bartoloni and Ricci 1995.
20 Cantini 2011, 172–75.
21 Grassi 2010, 20–21.
22 I am grateful to Debora Quaglia of the Laboratory of the University of Siena for showing me samples of red-painted/*colature rosse* ware from the Donoratico excavations.

Particularly noteworthy is the presence of at least eleven cooking pots, belonging to four different types, and made from two similar fabrics (G1 and G5). These probably come from Rome or Latium, given the close similarities between their morphology and fabrics, and those of numerous ninth- and tenth-century cooking pots from the Forum of Nerva. Type 1 (seven MNI) has an everted rim, a slightly pointed edge, and a strap-handle set on the edge. The fragmentary state of the specimens makes it impossible to determine if they had one or two handles, but, in one case, two handles seem more likely on the basis of the materials found (Pl. 8.3, nos 4–5). The handles are often smoothed and present a slight dip; in one case, drops of yellowish-brown glaze are present. This type is similar to mid-ninth- to mid-tenth-century specimens from the Forum of Nerva.[23] It should be noted that, in the Roman specimens, the presence of occasional drops of glaze on ninth- and tenth-century kitchen ware is fairly frequent and has been interpreted as possible evidence that single-fired glazed pottery and kitchen ware were manufactured in the same workshops. This hypothesis is supported by the strong similarities between the fabrics used to make the two classes.[24] Type 12 from Capalbiaccio (one MNI) is also handled and is fairly similar to type 1, except for the less everted rim (Pl. 8.3, no. 17). There are also close morphological similarities between types 1 and 12, and mid-ninth to tenth-century material from Santa Cornelia, in the Agro Romano.[25] Type 2 (one piece) has a strongly everted rim, a slightly pointed edge with a dense light ribbing covering the rim down to the shoulder, and a strip on the body. It is comparable to material from the site of Santa Rufina in the Campagna Romana, which is common in period V, between the early ninth century (or slightly earlier) and the twelfth century (Pl. 8.3, no. 6).[26] The last type of cooking pot from the Rome and Latium area — type 6, with two minimum forms (fabric G5) — has an everted and rounded rim, and presents close similarities with mid-tenth-century material from the *domus solarate* in the Forum of Nerva (Fig. 8.3, nos 10–11).[27]

Moving on to the cooking pots manufactured locally or sub-regionally, it is first worth noting that fabrics G2, G3, and G4 are identical to some of the fabrics used to make the cooking pots documented at Poggio Cavolo in phases dating to the second half of the tenth century. As will be discussed below, in addition to the fabrics, the types of cooking pots discussed in this section are also similar to published and unpublished material from Poggio Cavolo, which dates to the second half of the tenth century.

Cooking pots of types 3, 4, 7, 10, and 11 are characterized by a slightly or moderately inverted rim and a lip of varying shape (in some cases flattened, in others rounded and slightly thickened, and, in yet others, with a forked profile). They are similar to material from the second half of the tenth century, which was found at Poggio Cavolo (Pl. 8.3, nos 7, 8, 12, 15, 16). However, other types of cooking pots (types 5, 8, and 9), though made from fabrics similar to those documented at Poggio Cavolo, are morphologically more similar to products documented in the late ninth- and early tenth-century layers at Grosseto and in the tenth- and eleventh-century layers at Montarrenti. More specifically, type 5, with a strongly everted, thickened, and externally convex rim profile (Pl. 8.3, no. 9), finds a fairly close comparison at Grosseto,[28] while types 8 and 9, with their slightly everted rims that are flat on the upper surface, their slightly hooked lips, and their out-turned edges, which are slightly thickened and rounded, respectively (Pl. 8.3, nos 13–14), are comparable with cooking pots from Montarrenti.[29]

The open kitchen ware forms are made from two different fabrics: G6 and G7. The former was also used to make the only type 7 cooking pot, while the latter, frequently documented among the open kitchen ware forms from Poggio Cavolo, is present at Capalbiaccio only in association with *testi*, *testelli*, and lids. Of the twenty-five MNI, only three *testi* and a *testello*, all made from fabric G6, are made on the slow wheel or by hand, while the remaining specimens are made on the fast wheel. From a functional point of view, the *testi* and *testelli* documented at Capalbiaccio, given their shallow depth, must have been used to make flatbreads. However, in some cases, the absence of smoke and the lack of open forms in the *acroma depurata* and *selezionata* repertoires, suggests that ceramics in these forms were also used to serve food.

In some cases, the lids from Capalbiaccio appear to have narrow rims that are incompatible with the mouths of cooking pots and, therefore, unable to improve the boiling of food. However, in other cases they appear to be too large for the small- and medi-

---

23 De Luca 2006, 104, Fig. 14, no. 27.
24 De Luca 2006, 103.
25 See Patterson 1991, 123, Fig. 24, respectively no. 11 and no. 10.
26 Christie (ed.) 1991, 295, Fig. 94, no. 4.
27 This type of cooking pot yielded by context 1436 of the Foro di Nerva was shown to me and is not illustrated in De Luca 2006.

28 Valdambrini 2005, 46, Pl. 6, no. 9.
29 On type 8 see Cantini 2003, Pl. 14, no. 1.7.52, on type 9 Cantini 2003, 98, Pl. 13, no. 1.7.44.

128 EMANUELE VACCARO

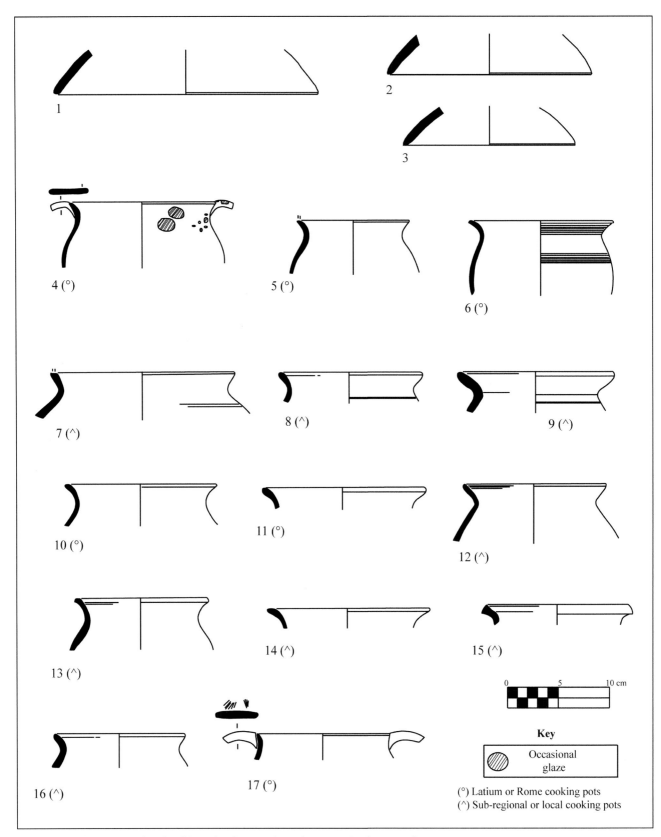

Plate 8.3. Capalbiaccio, Level 5 of Building J (tenth century). Kitchen ware. Cooking pots from Rome or Latium: 4. Type 1; 5. Type 1 *bis*; 6. Type 2; 10. Type 6; 11. Type 6 *bis*; 14. Type 9; 17. Type 12. Local or sub-regional cooking pots: 7. Type 3; 8. Type 4; 9. Type 5; 12. Type 7; 13. Type 8; 14. Type 9; 15. Type 10; 16. Type 11. Local or sub-regional lids: 1–3.

um-sized cooking pots from Capalbiaccio. Thus, their use with *testi* and *testelli* to keep the foods cooked in them warm cannot be ruled out (Pl. 8.3, nos 1–3).

The *testi*, which have thicker walls than the *testelli*, reveal a degree of variety in the morphological structure of the rims and the extent to which the walls flare. Some specimens have slightly flaring walls and rims that may be everted, rounded, and thickened (Pl. 8.2, nos 18, 20, 21). Others have shallower bodies and more flaring walls; the rims may be indistinct or slightly everted and thickened, as in specimens from Poggio Cavolo, dated to the second half of the tenth century (Pl. 8.2, nos 19, 22, 26, 27, 28). Finally, the *testelli* have two main variants: one presenting a slightly convex outer-wall profile (Pl. 8.2, nos 23, 25), similar to Montarrenti specimens from the second half of the eighth to the ninth century;[30] the other has straight walls and an indistinct rim (Pl. 8.2, no. 24).

Tenth-Century Ceramic Assemblages from Poggio Cavolo

The site of Poggio Cavolo, with its large tenth-century ceramic assemblages, is a good case study to compare to Capalbiaccio. The lack of a large representative sample of well-stratified Ottonian material from other sites in southernmost Tuscany at the time in which this text was written[31] prevented us from extending this comparative approach to other settlements in this local context. Poggio Cavolo has provided an extraordinarily clear sequence of pottery from the mid-tenth to the very beginning of the eleventh century, which has allowed for a thorough analysis of the transformation in pottery repertoires and in patterns of ceramic trade and consumption during the Ottonian period. This section discusses in detail the tenth-to-early-eleventh-century pottery from Poggio Cavolo to establish a solid base of data which will be used in the concluding section to develop the comparative study of the two sites in the broader context of southern Tuscany.

The Medieval Village of Poggio Cavolo and its Pottery

The medieval hilltop site of Poggio Cavolo — 182 m ASL and only 5 km, south of Grosseto — was excavated for three seasons in 2005–2007, as part of a broader landscape archaeology project that focused on settlement patterns between the lower Ombrone and Osa Valleys.[32] More specifically, the excavation of Poggio Cavolo aimed at further investigating the topographical and chronological relations between the early medieval lowland village at Podere Serratone, along the Rispescia stream, and the nearby hilltop site, to which the population of Podere Serratone most likely moved after its early abandonment in the late ninth century CE. A GIS-based distance analysis, centred on the site of Podere Serratone, was performed using elevation and slope as the main factors that would have affected the feasible mobility of people through the medieval landscape. It revealed that Podere Serratone's closest neighbour was, indeed, the hilltop village at Poggio Cavolo, which has been known only since the 1990s.[33] Both written sources and surface artefacts suggested that Poggio Cavolo was abandoned early on, between the late twelfth and early thirteenth century.[34] As such, the site appeared particularly promising for an excavation that, in a reasonably short time, could supply some reliable data on the site's initial occupation and, hence, its possible relationship with other early medieval sites in the plains, especially Podere Serratone.

The general layout of Poggio Cavolo is that of a typical medium-sized medieval village (see discussion on villages *infra* Chapter 16). A circuit wall surrounds the hilltop (c. 0.46 ha) and another external feature, probably a terrace wall, rather than an actual defensive structure, in turn marks the perimeter of

---

30 Cantini 2003, 84, Pl. 5, no. I.5.5.
31 The excavation at Cosa revealed that the Arx was occupied as early as the ninth and tenth centuries CE. Only the Forum and Sparse Glazed wares from that area have been published, for the excavation at Cosa see Hobart 1991 and Cirelli and Hobart 2003. The site of Grosseto is likely to have developed as a kind of 'proto-town' probably from as early as 900 CE and would be a significant case study for a comparative approach. Despite this, since the pottery from the recent urban excavation (Citter and Arnoldus-Huyzendveld 2007; Citter 2007a) is still largely unpublished (with the exception of the *acroma depurata* wares in Valdambrini 2006) it cannot properly lend itself to a comparative approach. Also unpublished are the ceramics from the hilltop village of Scarlino, excavated in the late 1970s (Marasco 2002–2003). In other cases, such as that of San Martino in piano, in the middle Bruna valley, the 2008 rescue excavation produced ceramic assemblages dating respectively to between the ninth and early tenth and mid/late tenth to eleventh century CE, although so far only the former have been studied in depth (Vaccaro 2011, 222–27). New detailed sequences of medieval ceramics spanning the ninth to twelfth centuries Bianchi and Hodges 2018; Bianchi and Hodges 2020.

32 Vaccaro 2011, 1–13.
33 The site was first surveyed in the late 1980s and was interpreted as a possible early medieval castrum on the basis of the surface finds (Citter 1995 and Citter 1997). New intensive surface collections revealed that no material earlier than the late ninth-tenth CE was documented in the surface assemblages. To my knowledge, the excavation confirmed the absence of deposits earlier than the late ninth/early tenth CE.
34 Farinelli and others 2008.

Figure 8.4. Aerial picture of the church, the cistern, the tower and the wall circuit at Poggio Cavolo during excavation in 2005. Photo by Stefano Campana, reproduced with permission.

the whole site, covering a total area of roughly 1.2 ha. Poggio Cavolo's location ensured strategic 360-degree visual control over the lower Ombrone Valley, including the former Etruscan town of Roselle, which was occupied in the Middle Ages, and the new regional hub of Grosseto. As emerged from the excavations in 2005–2007, Poggio Cavolo was occupied for a relatively short period of time, from the late ninth to the late twelfth or early thirteenth century.[35]

Particularly worth noting, for the specific purposes of this chapter, is the discovery of a well-built fortification wall, some 1.7 m wide, which represents the earliest feature so far identified at Poggio Cavolo. The chronology of the site has not been fully clarified, although an *ante quem* date has been provided by some well-stratified contexts that served as a foundational level for the new *cocciopesto* floor of a church abutting the wall circuit. This church, with a rectangular plan and a single semicircular apse (oriented northeast–southwest), measured some 12.72 × 5.46 m and did not have a genuine façade; its façade was actually the wall circuit itself. The entrance to the church was identified along the northern wall near the junction between it and the wall-circuit, revealing that it could only be accessed from inside the hilltop area (Fig. 8.4). This church, according to the ceramic assemblages that the foundational levels yielded, dates to the second half of the tenth century CE and, extended and replaced a previous church with a polygonal apse, reusing its main walls as foundations. The earlier church, which was slightly smaller in size (10.42 × 5.26 m), has not been precisely dated, although the pottery excavated from its construction phase does not reveal any marked morphological differences from that of the second half of the tenth century and, above all, does not include the early medieval types in *acroma depurata*, and *acroma selezionata* wares, which were common at the eighth- and ninth-century sites of Podere Serratone and Casa Andreoni. As noted, the chronology of the second church is far more well defined, thanks to the pottery-rich contexts deposited during building works for its construction. Interestingly, these contexts also contained large faunal assemblages, as yet unstudied, which indicate that the building-site was used as a kind of garbage dump.

Mid to Late Tenth-Century Pottery from Poggio Cavolo

Two main pottery assemblages will be discussed here; they were found in the foundational level (context 1522 = 1593) excavated in the area of the semicircular apse, which was particularly rich in ceramic finds, and in the preparation layers for the *cocciopesto* floor, which were identified in the nave (context 1534) and the apse (context 1506). Interestingly, an in-depth analysis of these contexts, which follow one another in direct succession, revealed some typological changes in their ceramic repertoires, which mirrored their slight chronological difference. Although the ceramic material from contexts 1522 and 1593 are discussed together, the two layers were differentiated during the excavation and interpreted as an actual make-up layer (1593) and a levelling layer (1522), which was laid down in the area of the apse in order to construct the new church. The absolute chronology of the contexts was determined by the combination of context 1593's carbon-14 date range of 890–990 CE (68.2 per cent probability) and, in context 1522, the discovery of two *denarii* from either Emperor Otto I or Otto II, which were struck in Pavia between 962–93 CE.[36] As such, a second half of the tenth century date for the two contexts seems certain. A similar date is suggested for context 1600 (the same foundational and levelling activity, but in the nave area), given the presence of three *vetrina pesante/Forum ware* vessels, which were imported from Latium or Rome, and typical of the tenth century. Herein, context 1600 will not be extensively discussed, but only as regards some crucial ceramic classes (*vetrina pesante* and amphorae), which shed more light on patterns of local and extra-regional trade in the tenth century. The sig-

---

35 Farinelli and others 2008.

36 Vaccaro and Salvadori 2006.

nificant change in the pottery repertoire in contexts 1506 and 1534, in addition to the identification of one Sparse Glazed B ware vessel — again possibly imported from Latium — whose date is no earlier than the late tenth or beginning of the eleventh century CE, and their later deposition on completion of the church, suggests a date *c.* 1000 CE (Table 8.5).

As noted, the currently available data supporting an in-depth analysis of pottery consumption patterns at Poggio Cavolo in the second half of the tenth century is mostly based on contexts 1522=1593. No other contemporary assemblage was identified in the few other excavated areas of the village, although this fact is biased given the tiny percentage of the surface area excavated outside of the monumental area hosting the church. Although the characteristics of the ceramic repertoire yielded by contexts 1593 and 1522 cannot be extended to the village as a whole, the large size of these assemblages and their complexity illustrates pottery consumption patterns during the Ottonian period that are suitable for comparison with the ceramic finds from Capalbiaccio.

A total of sixty-one MNI were identified in contexts 1593 and 1522, with kitchen ware (forty-four individuals) being in the overwhelming majority (*acroma depurata* and *acroma selezionata* wares are documented with eight and nine individuals respectively) (Fig. 8.5). The functional identification of vessels was possible in some 66 per cent of cases (forty vessels), while for the rest, it was only possible to ascertain that they belonged to closed vessels, due to the high level of fragmentation of the potsherds (Fig. 8.6).

Acroma depurata and *acroma selezionata* wares

The repertoire of vessels made in levigated and semi-levigated fabrics consists exclusively of closed forms, which reveals their limited functional diversification. Only two main functional categories are documented in the record: table or storage jugs and small amphorae, to which we should add a series of generic closed forms (eight individuals). None of these vessels reveal any trace of smoke, testifying to the marked distinction in the functional make-up of pottery repertoires between table and storage wares, on the one hand, and kitchen wares, on the other. This is an important similarity with Capalbiaccio, where the same pattern was observed. It marks a significant caesura in the multifunctional use of some table and storage wares, which were occasionally 'borrowed' for use in the kitchen in the early medieval period (e.g. at Podere Serratone).[37]

---

37 Vaccaro 2011, 212.

Table 8.5. Number, function, location, and date of the contexts from the church at Poggio Cavolo yielding the ceramic assemblages discussed in this chapter.

Context number	Function	Location	Date
1522=1593	Make-up level for the construction of the Ottonian church	Semicircular apse	Second half of the 10th century CE
1600	Make-up level for the construction of the Ottonian church	Rectangular nave	Second half of the 10th century CE
1506	Preparation layer for the *cocciopesto* floor of the Ottonian church	Semicircular apse	End of the 10th/very beginning of the 11th century CE
1534	Preparation layer for the *cocciopesto* floor of the Ottonian church	Rectangular nave	End of the 10th/very beginning of the 11th century CE

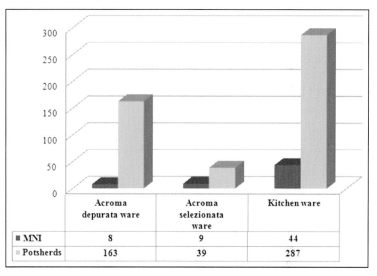

Figure 8.5. Poggio Cavolo, contexts 1522=1593 (second half of the tenth century): ceramic classes, fragments, and MNI. Graphic by author.

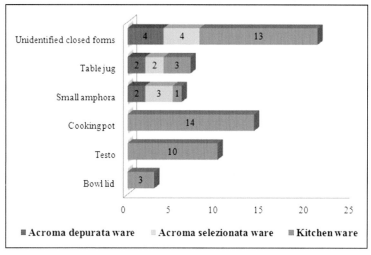

Figure 8.6. Poggio Cavolo, contexts 1522=1593 (second half of the tenth century CE): ceramic classes, forms, and MNI. Graphic by author.

Table 8.6. Poggio Cavolo, contexts 1522=1593 (second half of the tenth century CE): fabrics and MNI in the *acroma depurata* and *acroma selezionata* wares.

Fabrics (*acroma depurata* = AD and *acroma selezionata* = Sel)	MNI
AD30	2
AD33	1
AD35	2
AD36	2
AD37	1
Sel1PCV	1
Sel4	1
Sel8	1
Sel30	1
Sel43	5

The vessels in *acroma depurata* and *acroma selezionata* testify to the good technical skill of the workshops where they were made. All the products are wheel-thrown; they have thin walls that rarely exceed 0.5 or 0.6 cm and well-finished bases, often with string-marks. Another common feature of many vessels is the smoothing of the lower part of the bodies close to and at the junction with the base, which was apparently made using a wooden stick (*steccatura*). A very fine-combed decoration was observed on some walls. It is worth noting that this refined finishing of the external surfaces of table and storage wares seems to increase markedly in the tenth century to become very widespread, whereas it is only occasionally documented in eighth- and ninth-century vessels. Some interesting technological information is also offered by the proportion of grey cores in the fabrics, something which was frequent in the early medieval table and coarse wares from Podere Serratone, where 50.9 per cent of the *acroma depurata* ware and 41.7 per cent of the *acroma selezionata* ware presented this feature.[38] By contrast, at Poggio Cavolo, only a few of the fragments have a grey core: 2.4 per cent of the *acroma depurata* and 10.2 per cent of the *acroma selezionata* wares (Fig. 8.7). The fact that the tenth-century table and storage vessels from Poggio Cavolo are more evenly fired, suggests that various technical solutions, aimed at better refining and finishing the external surfaces of vessels, including the technological advancement of the kilns that supplied the site, were applied. Nevertheless, it is worth noting that two of the fabrics used to make some of the *acroma depurata* (AD30) and *acroma*

selezionata (Sel30) vessels from Poggio Cavolo were already used by the workshop at Serratone, though in association with different forms. This identification is based on the microscopic analysis of hand-specimens, not thin-sections, and may suggest that the same clay source continued to be exploited by a new workshop, as yet unidentified, which took over from that of Podere Serratone after its abandonment (Table 8.6).

Like Capalbiaccio, the Poggio Cavolo excavation revealed some contact with northern Latium or, more specifically, Rome, particularly in context 1600, though to a lesser extent in context 1593. An almost complete *olla acquaria*, a type of small globular or biconical-bodied amphora, common in Latium and Rome from the early Middle Ages, was found in context 1593 (Pl. 8.4, no. 1). The version identified at Poggio Cavolo is double-handled and biconically bodied, with a maximum width *c.* 37 cm; it has a band-shaped rim that is 9 cm wide and a slightly convex base. It appears to be a good-quality vessel with extremely thin walls (0.5 to 0.6 cm) and base (0.6 to 0.7 cm), and a very careful finishing of the external surface, including a thick combed decoration between the shoulder and the handle, and stick-smoothing at the junction of the wall and base. This form is common in Latium and Rome; it was possibly introduced in the ninth century, as evidence from the large rural site of Santa Cornelia suggests;[39] its production continued, albeit with some morphological changes, well into the fourteenth century; it is particularly frequent in eleventh- to thirteenth-century contexts.[40] Nonetheless, some morphological dissimilarities, particularly in the shape of the bases and necks, differentiate the types documented in Rome and those from northern Latium.[41] The type from context 1593 is particularly reminiscent of the slightly convex base of the variants discovered at Tarquinia and Viterbo, which is distinct from the *ombelicato* base that is typical of the Roman specimens. Although thin-section analysis has not been applied to the biconical *olla acquaria* from Poggio Cavolo, its morphological features strongly support a production in northern Latium. Its function was tested by organic residue analysis, which detected no trace of fatty acids or proteins, indicating that the vessel was used to store or transport water or solid foodstuffs, such as cere-

---

38 Vaccaro 2011, 207–15.

39 On the presence of this typology in the medieval pottery from the South Etruria Survey see Whitehouse 1982, 320, Fig. 6.6, no. 19; on S. Cornelia see Whitehouse 1980, 129, 141.
40 Romei 1990, 265–67.
41 On small amphorae from Tarquinia and Viterbo see Bartoloni and Ricci 1995, 104–05 and Güll and others 2001, Fig. 18, no. 1.

8. CAPALBIACCIO AND MEDIEVAL POTTERY IN SOUTHERN TUSCANY (900–1000)   133

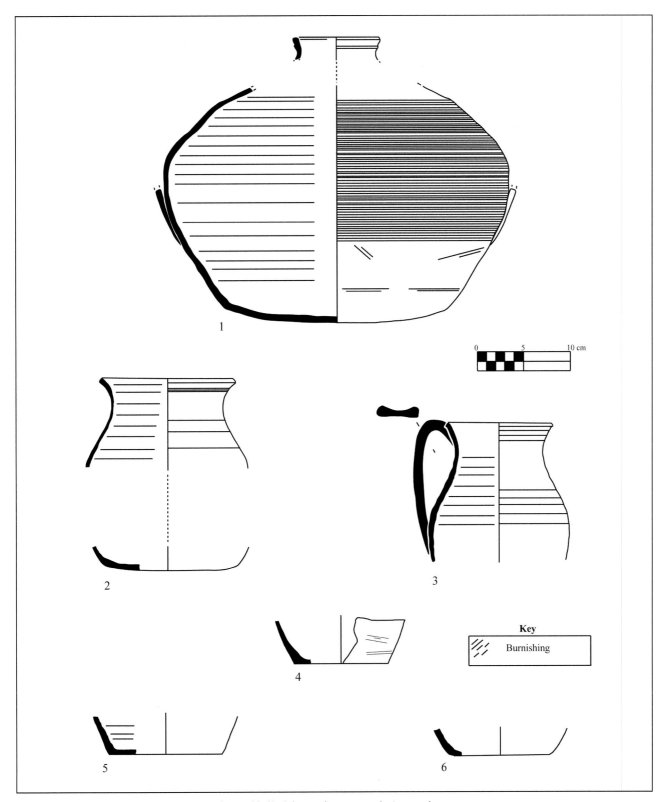

Plate 8.4. Poggio Cavolo, contexts 1522=1593 (second half of the tenth century CE). *Acroma depurata* and *acroma selezionata* wares: 1. *Olla acquaria*-water amphora; 2–3. Table jugs; 4–6. Bases of table jugs.

Table 8.7. Poggio Cavolo, contexts 1522 = 1593 (second half of the tenth century CE): fabrics and MNI in the kitchen ware.

Fabrics (G = kitchen ware)	MNI
G26	6
G28	8
G29	5
G34	1
G51	6
G54	5
G55	3
G56	6
G57	4

als or pulses.[42] A similar result was provided by the analysis of a small tenth-century amphora from the urban excavations at Grosseto.[43]

Except for this form from northern Latium, the remainder of the *acroma depurata* and *acroma selezionata* wares come from local or sub-regional workshops, given their morphological features and fabrics. One jug type, documented both in levigated and semi-levigated fabrics, has a slightly everted rim that terminates in an oblique-cut or thickened lip, a concave base, and one strap-handle with thickened edges (Pl. 8.4, nos 2–3). One flat *acroma depurata* base, characterized by external whitening and smoothing, belongs to a small table jug, which was perhaps manufactured in the Pisan area, given its levigated red-brick fabric (33 CE). It is reminiscent of a class of jugs that is common in the eleventh- and twelfth-century contexts at Poggio Cavolo. The shapes and fabrics of these jugs are identical to specimens from the urban ceramic assemblages at Piazza Dante[44] and Piazza dei Cavalieri[45] in Pisa (Pl. 8.4, no. 4). The possible existence of occasional connections with Pisa as early as the second half of the tenth century, may anticipate, by over 100 years, a far more widespread phenomenon that has been observed in the Maremma, and specifically in the urban context of Grosseto, from the eleventh to the thirteenth century, when the *acroma depurata* repertoires are dominated by Pisan products.[46]

Another interesting feature of the pre-1000 CE *acroma depurata* and *acroma selezionata* wares at Poggio Cavolo, is the presence of both flat and convex bases, whereas the eighth- and ninth-century repertoires from Podere Serratone and Casa Andreoni contained only the former (Pl. 8.4, nos 5–6).[47]

Kitchen Ware

Considering contexts 1593 and 1522 together, kitchen ware accounts for a total of forty-four MNI, with a marked preponderance of closed forms (*c.* 70 per cent), dominated by cooking pots, although other functional forms, such as jugs and small storage amphorae, are also documented. Open vessels include *testi* and bowl-lids, with some 22 per cent and 7 per cent, respectively (Table 8.7).

The technical skill demonstrated by the kitchen ware is comparable to that observed in the *acroma depurata* and *acroma selezionata* wares: vessels are always wheel-thrown and the potters demonstrate significant skill in shaping thin walls, no more than 0.5 cm thick, and flat bases, cut from the wheel using a string. The external surface of the bodies, especially on the neck or between it and the widest point of the body, sometimes bears a ribbed finish, which was made using a wide-toothed comb as the vessel rotated on the wheel. These corrugated walls may have served a dual purpose, both decorative and functional, as in the presence of ribs facilitated the handling of non-handled vessels.

A total of seven different fabrics were identified by a microscopic analysis of hand-specimens (Table 8.9). Despite the many technological similarities between kitchen wares and table or storage wares, one important difference is the higher frequency of the grey core, which was found in a total of 33.8 per cent of fragments, while it was present in only 2.4 per cent and 10.2 per cent of the *acroma depurata* and *acroma selezionata* wares from contexts 1593 and 1522. Notably, the optical-microscope analysis of the kitchen ware fabrics detected mineralogical inclusions similar to those observed in the fabrics of the eighth- and ninth-century pottery from Podere Serratone, which indicates that the workshops that supplied tenth-century Poggio Cavolo were situated in the same local or sub-regional area. Only one fabric (G54) presents a certain amount of pyroxenes, alongside quartz, calcite, and biotite, which means

---

42 I thank Alessandra Pecci (University of Barcelona) for the residue analysis.
43 See Salvini and others 2004.
44 On the decorations and shapes see Menchelli 1993, 484 and 502 (MAC 4); on the fabrics Menchelli 1993, 482, fabric no. 4.
45 On the shapes and decorations see Menchelli and Renzi Rizzo 2000, 136, Pl. II, nos 7.1 and 7.2; on the fabrics Menchelli and Renzi Rizzo 2000, 125, no. 3.

46 For Grosseto see Valdambrini 2006, 476–78.
47 Vaccaro 2011, 207–20.

that it comes from a volcanic area, possibly in Latium. Despite some slight differences in the composition of the fabrics, the typologies of cooking pots refer to similar morphological models, which are found throughout southern Tuscany and some areas of northern Latium.

One type, presenting a slightly everted rim, with a deep groove at the junction with the shoulder, shows some variations in the shape of the rim itself, which is either rounded, externally oblique, or even slightly concave. The body is globular in the wide-mouthed specimens and ovoid in the variants, with a mouth smaller than 15 cm. This group of cooking pots presents close parallels with types documented at Campiglia Marittima in contexts dating to the ninth–tenth and the tenth–eleventh centuries,[48] at Donoratico in the tenth century,[49] and finally at San Pietro (Grosseto) in the late ninth to early tenth century (Pl. 8.5, nos 1–7).[50] The other typologies differ from the first group in their absence of the marked groove at the junction between rim and shoulder; additionally, the rims of the other types present a wide range of variants in terms of shape. One of these types, which has a barely everted rim, a slightly grooved lip, and a globular body, finds some generic parallels in later contexts from medieval Cosa, dating to the eleventh and twelfth centuries (Pl. 8.5, no. 8).[51] An easy-to-make type is that which has an everted and indistinct rim, pointed lip, and globular body; given its uncomplicated morphology, this type may have been produced for a long period (Pl. 8.5, no. 9), although some precise parallels from contexts at Piazza Dante[52] and Piazza dei Cavalieri in Pisa[53] reveal that its peak between the mid-tenth and the mid-eleventh century overlaps with those vessels discovered at Poggio Cavolo. Some slightly later comparisons with eleventh- to twelfth-century cooking pots that are common at Cosa-Ansedonia[54] can be established for two types that have thickened rims, but whose lips differ in shape (pointed or rounded) (Pl. 8.5, nos 10–11). Finally, another type with an everted, thickened, and slightly incurved rim is comparable with a type documented at Montarrenti from the early medieval period (Pl. 8.5, no. 12).[55]

The tenth-century cooking pots at Poggio Cavolo are flat-based and their size varies from 11–12 cm in width, for the smaller specimens, to 15–16 cm in width, for the larger ones (Pl. 8.5, nos 13–14 and Pl. 8.6, nos 1–2). A systematic comparative analysis of the diameters of the mouths and bases of cooking pots distinguished two possible functional categories, on the basis of a palaeo-nutritional study recently applied to a series of medieval contexts in Italy.[56] Though the average size of the mouths of cooking pots is 15.2 cm, they present a fairly broad range of rim diameters, from 11 to 18 cm. Some 64 per cent have rim diameters of less than 15 cm (11 to 14 cm), while the remaining 36 per cent have diameters between 15 to 18 cm. The theory is that the first group, small-mouthed pots, were used by individuals as *pro capite* vessels for boiling and tenderizing dry meat or pieces of bread in wine or water; the second group of larger cooking pots may have been used as communal vessels for boiling larger pieces of meat and preparing soups for family groups.

Among the closed kitchen ware forms, table or storage jugs that were manufactured using the same fabrics (G34, G54 and G56) as the cooking pots, and therefore made by the same workshops, are also documented (Pl. 8.6, nos 3–4). Interestingly, neither the trefoil-mouthed, ovoid-bodied jug, nor that with a coplanar strap handle and a slightly concave base, reveals any trace of smoke on the outer surface opposite the handle, indicating that they were never used for cooking. This clashes with the frequent multifunctional use of eighth- and ninth-century jugs as cooking vessels for warming liquids, as observed in the early medieval ceramic assemblages at Podere Serratone.

One thick flat base, possibly belonging to a storage amphora, is made from the same fabric (G26) as the open forms, such as *testi* and bowl-lids (Pl. 8.6, no. 5). This fabric is never used to manufacture cooking pots or jugs. As such, the very coarse fabrics, rich in large inclusions, which were typical of open vessels, were also occasionally used to make large thick-walled storage vessels that required more 'tooth' in order to avoid breakage during daily use. The absence of any trace of smoke on the base prevents its interpretation as a vessel used for cooking food.

At Poggio Cavolo in the second half of the tenth century, the repertoire of open vessels consists mostly of large, flat-based vessels: the so-called *testi* (ten MNI) used for baking and especially for making flatbreads (Pl. 8.6, nos 6–8); and, to a lesser extent, of bowl-lids (three MNI) (Pl. 8.6, no. 9). It is worth

---

48 Grassi 2003, 281, Pl. II, nos I.2.1, I.2.4.
49 Grassi and Liguori 2004, 121, Pl. I, no. 13.
50 Valdambrini 2005, 46, Pl. 6.
51 Cirelli and Hobart 2003, 337, Fig. 148, no. 1 and Graph 12.
52 Alessi and others 1993, 433 MFAC no. 30.
53 Menchelli and Renzi Rizzo 2000, 184, Fig. 3, no. 3.
54 Cirelli and Hobart 2003, 339, Fig. 149, no. 3 and 337, Fig. 147, no. 4.
55 Cantini 2003, 93, Pl. 10, no. I.7.24.

56 Giovannini 1998, 15–22.

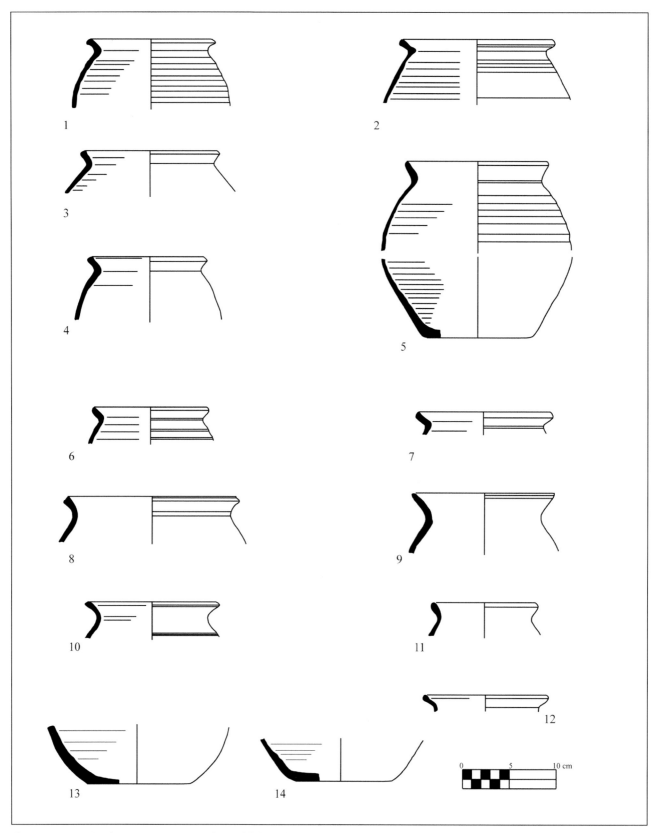

Plate 8.5. Poggio Cavolo, contexts 1522=1593 (second half of the tenth century CE).
Kitchen ware: 1–12. Cooking pots; 13–14. Bases of cooking pots (or other closed forms).

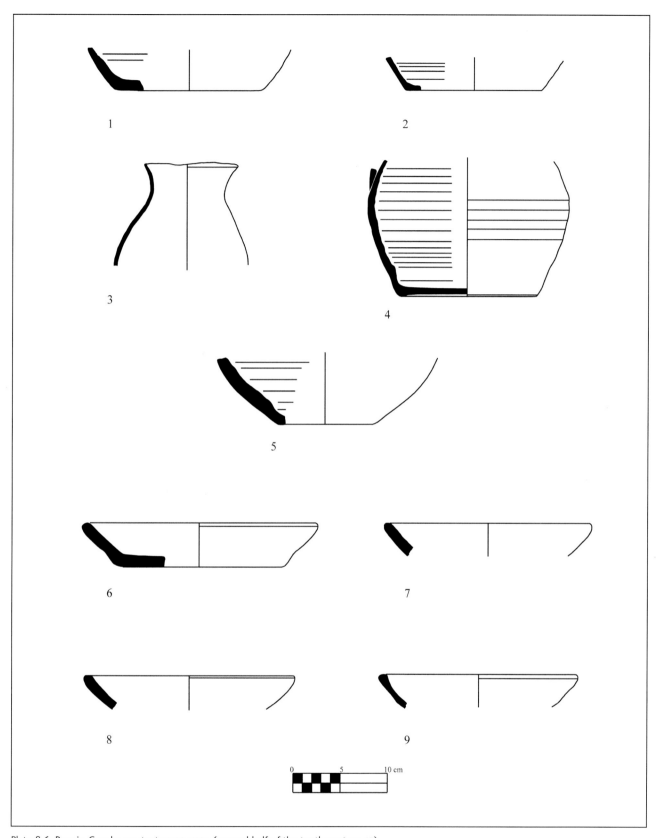

Plate 8.6. Poggio Cavolo, contexts 1522=1593 (second half of the tenth century CE).
Kitchen ware: 1–2. Bases of cooking pots (or other closed forms); 3. Table jug;
4. Table or storage jug; 5. Small amphora (?); 6–8. *Testi*; 9. Bowl-lid.

noting that, though they were manufactured in very coarse fabrics, with a much higher density of larger mineral inclusions, which give the vessels resistance, the open kitchen ware vessels were systematically produced on the fast wheel, rather than by hand, indicating that even the very easy-to-make large open vessels were manufactured by semi-professional potters and not at the domestic level. The absence of any trace of smoke on the outer surface of some *testi*, as at Capalbiaccio, may suggest they were used, at least in some cases, as large plates, possibly for shared food consumption. Given the ease of manufacturing *testi*, they tend not to change markedly through the ages. Indeed, the type with flaring walls, a rounded rim, and a flat base, common at Poggio Cavolo in the second half of the tenth century, continues to be very frequent, even in the eleventh-century contexts at the same site. Although less common at Poggio Cavolo, with only three specimens, the bowl-lid presents a slightly greater morphological variety. Two main types are documented: one with a flattened rim and another with a thickened and rounded rim; in both cases the walls are fairly flaring.

The limited functional variety of the kitchen ware repertoire observed at Poggio Cavolo in the Ottonian period, with the primacy of cooking pots particularly suited for boiling food, closely mirrors eating habits at early medieval rural sites, which are characterized by the prevalence of boiled foods, such as soups made of cereals and pulses, as well as dried salted meat cooked in broths.[57] Since the animal bones from Poggio Cavolo have not yet been studied, it is impossible to establish if and how the model provided by the functional analysis of pottery fits that provided by the archaeozoological remains, which is the most telling evidence for eating habits, at least as concerns animal consumption, at any archaeological site. A recent systematic study of meat consumption in Italy between late antiquity and the Middle Ages indicated the widespread consumption of pigs from the fifth to the tenth or eleventh century CE. Pigs were raised until 2–3 years of age, when they reached the highest meat yield in terms of the ratio of fat to muscle tissue.[58] Though more meat was provided by pigs between 2–3 years of age, it may have been less tender than that of animals under the age of 1 and piglets. As such, the best way of tenderizing these tougher cuts of meat would have been to boil them in cooking pots. This hypothesis may explain why cooking pots are in the vast majority, compared to other kitchen ware vessels at Poggio Cavolo, although this theory should be tested in regards to the animal bone assemblages from the site.[59] The widespread use of cooking pots would also have optimized the consumption of the flatbreads that were prepared in *testi*.[60] Indeed, the more common cereals, unlike wheat, are quite poor in gluten and, therefore, tend to harden rapidly; this made it necessary to tenderize them by heating them in cooking pots with liquids (wine and water). The small-mouthed cooking pots with rim diameters of less than 15 cm may have been used as *pro capite* vessels, entailing their employment for both boiling and eating food directly. It is also worth bearing in mind the simplicity of domestic spaces at early medieval sites, where the presence of a dining table was probably a rarity enjoyed only, if at all, by urban elites and privileged rural landowners. If, in the late Middle Ages, food was consumed at rural sites by people seated in front of the hearth or on a bench near the doorway of the domestic building (to take advantage of the sunlight),[61] it should be no surprise that food was consumed directly from small, more easily handled cooking pots, rather than from large dishes.

Comparative Materials from Context 1600: Vetrina Pesante and Small Amphorae from Poggio Cavolo

In order to provide a broader overview of pottery consumption at Poggio Cavolo in the second half of the tenth century, some ceramic classes (*vetrina pesante* and small coarse ware amphorae) yielded by the excavation of context 1600 will be used to extend the analysis. As previously noted, context 1600 was a foundational levelling layer that was deposited throughout the nave of the church, and thus it serves the same purposes as contexts 1593 and 1522 in the apse area. This context yielded over 1000 potsherds and, on the basis of its stratigraphic position, function, and materials, it is contemporary with contexts 1593 and 1522. Hereafter, only those materials which lend themselves to shedding light on regional and extra-regional trade patterns will be discussed.

---

57 On the diet of early medieval peasants see Montanari 1997, 217–25.
58 Salvadori 2011, 204–10.
59 It is worth considering the early medieval assemblages from the Triconch Palace in Butrint (southern Albania) where kitchen ware is dominated by closed cooking forms (96 per cent) even though meat consumption was mostly characterized by sheep and goat rather than pig (Vroom 2008, 299–303). This example suggests that the relationship between eating habits, meat consumption, and kitchen ware requires specific contextual analysis.
60 For the multiple use of *testi* see Pecci 2009, 28.
61 Piponnier 1997, 408–16.

The *Vetrina Pesante* from Poggio Cavolo and the Distribution of Single-Fired Glazed Wares from Rome (Latium) in the Tuscan context

Some 3.6 per cent of the total fragments from context 1600, corresponding to five MNI, are *vetrina pesante*. Two specimens are likely regional productions that have been identified on the south-central coast of Tuscany,[62] given the similarity of their fabric to that of vessels from the medieval hilltop villages at Donoratico and Campiglia Marittima.[63] Both vessels are very fragmentary and present yellowish-brown (10YR 5/6) glaze drips; the outer surface of the walls has a kind of combed decoration, which is visible underneath the thin glaze and on the uncoated surfaces. One of the two forms is sufficiently well preserved to suggest that it is a small double-handed table jug with an ovoid body (Pl. 8.7, no. 4). Besides these two vessels from regional workshops, three other glazed individuals — two jugs and one small table pot — were identified. On the basis of their shape and fabric,[64] they are *vetrina pesante/Forum ware*, which is well documented in Rome and Latium from the early tenth century. All three individuals are characterized by a fairly bright, thick glaze, which tends to cover most of the vessel's surface. The olive green colour of the glaze (5Y 5/6) is similar to that of glaze no. 3 on vessels from the Crypta Balbi in Rome.[65] A table jug with a short slightly inverted grooved neck and indistinct rim was found almost in its entirety. A fragment of a completely glazed spout definitely belongs to the same vessel, although it could not be joined. The single strap handle is attached directly to the rim and bears a shallow central groove. The body is ovoid and the flat base presents a gentle edge at the junction with the wall. The glaze is well distributed over the vast majority of the surface, leaving the area near the handle joint and the outer surface of the base, uncovered (Pl. 8.7, no. 5). This typology is particularly common in Roman contexts, where it is documented both in Forum ware and Sparse Glazed A and B wares,[66] although it reappeared in the thirteenth century in *acroma depurata* ware.[67] Two flat bases, with the external glaze only on the bottom, belong to a table jug and a tiny table pot, respectively (Pl. 8.7, nos 6–7). Moreover, the large repertoire of spindle whorls from context 1600 (Pl. 8.7, nos 9–15) contains one specimen with a notched biconical body, partially covered by an olive-colour glaze similar to that of the three vessels in *vetrina pesante* from Rome (Pl. 8.7, no. 8). Both the morphology and glaze of this spindle whorl parallel those of specimens from the tenth-century context at the Crypta Balbi in Rome.[68] As such, we cannot rule out that even this artefact was traded directly from Rome or Latium alongside other imported materials, such as the *vetrina pesante* that were found in context 1600 and the *olla acquaria* from context 1593.

In order to better contextualize the presence of *vetrina pesante* at Poggio Cavolo in the broader Tuscan context, it is worth comparing these finds with the glazed vessels from Latium which have been found at other urban and rural sites in the region. A series of new distributional data provided by archaeological research in Tuscany over the last two decades, has expanded and enriched the distribution pattern of single-fired glazed pottery produced in Rome and in the Campagna Romana, which was proposed in 1990.[69]

An overall distributional analysis, based on the data now available, suggests the existence of two probable complementary routes: one along the coast, possibly based on the combined use of *cabotage* routes and the Via Aurelia; and one in the interior, roughly following the Via Francigena. The latter route is quite difficult to explain in light of the very low quantities of single-fired glazed wares from Rome and its environs documented at urban and rural sites located on or near the Via Francigena, such as Chiusi,[70] San Pietro ad Asso,[71] Siena,[72] Poggibonsi,[73]

---

62 The identification of workshops between Campiglia Marittima and Rocca San Silvestro is based on the minero-petrographic analysis of Sparse Glazed ware from both Campiglia Marittima and Donoratico. The outputs of these workshops must have between Donoratico to the north and Grosseto to the south. See Fortina and Turbanti 2003, 337–40, Grassi 2006, 464–65 and Grassi 2010, 19–20.

63 I thank Silvia Liguori for showing me samples of Sparse Glazed ware from Campiglia Marittima and Donoratico for comparanda with Poggio Cavolo.

64 I refer to fabric AD40, associated with Sparse Glazed B ware from context 1506 (late tenth-early eleventh). The optical microscopic analysis of the fabric revealed rare quartz inclusions, possible feldspars, limestone, and biotite. It is light brown in colour (7.5YR 6/4) and recalls fabric no. 18, typical of Sparse Glazed ware from the Crypta Balbi in Rome (Paroli 1985, 221). The examples from Poggio Cavolo were compared with Sparse Glazed ware from early medieval contexts at the Fori Imperiali in Rome. Again I thank Ilaria de Luca.

65 Paroli 1985, 222 (glaze no. 3).

66 Romei 2004, 294–300.
67 Ricci 1990, 288–91.
68 Saguì and others 2001, 527, IV.7.18.20.
69 See distribution pattern in Paroli (ed.) 1992.
70 Paolucci 1992, 314–18.
71 Campana 2004; Hobart and others 2012, Fig. 4.
72 Cantini 2005, 203–04.
73 Francovich and Valenti 2007, 217.

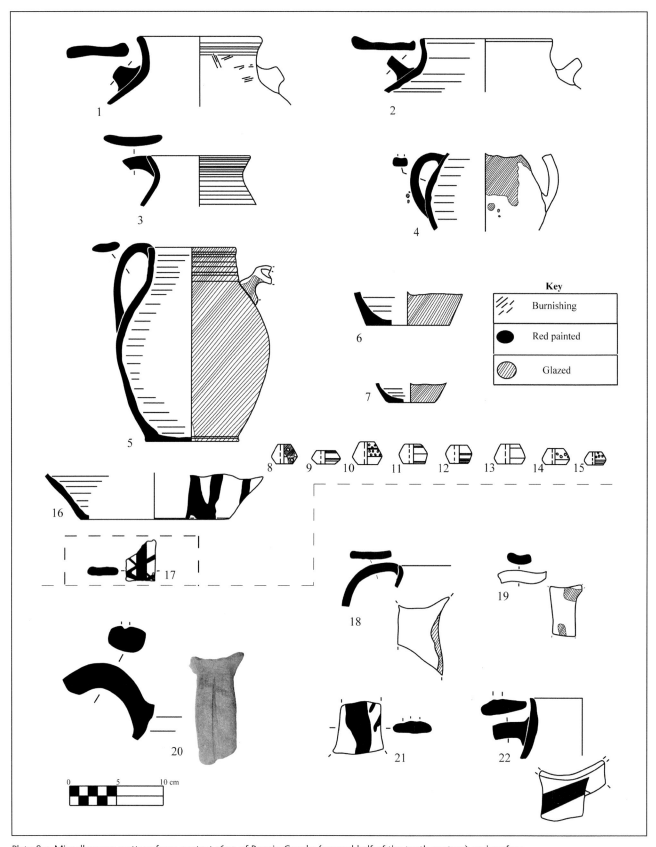

Plate 8.7. Miscellaneous pottery from context 1600 of Poggio Cavolo (second half of the tenth century) and surface sites. Poggio Cavolo: *acroma depurata* ware: 1–2. Small amphorae; 3. Table jug; 9–15. Spindle whorls. Sparse Glazed ware: 4. Handled jug of regional production. *Vetrina pesante/ Forum ware* from Rome/Latium: 5–7. Table jugs and generic closed forms; 8. spindle whorl. Red-painted/*colature rosse* ware: 16. Small amphora; 17. Small table jug (?). Punta Fortezza: Sparse Glazed ware: 18. Table jug. Imported amphorae: 21. *Cannelures* amphora from western Sicily; Poggio Castellaccio: Sparse Glazed ware: 19. Table jug (?). Aiali: red-painted/*colature rosse* ware: 21. Generic closed form; 22. Small amphora (?).

Montefiesole,[74] San Genesio,[75] and Lucca.[76] The low number of finds makes it difficult to interpret these as the result of actual trade. Rather, the intense flows of people — especially pilgrims — travelling along the Via Francigena to visit the holy places of Rome may suggest that these commodities were purchased on the Roman market, as a kind of souvenir, and then taken back to the pilgrims' places of origin.[77]

The distribution pattern of *vetrina pesante* / Forum ware and Sparse Glazed A and B wares along the Tuscan coast is significant: larger quantities of vessels are documented both at Cosa-Ansedonia and Pisa.[78] The excavation of the Arx at Cosa yielded as many as six Forum-ware vessels dating to the ninth and early tenth centuries and one in Sparse Glazed ware, probably from Rome or, more generically, Latium.[79] The concentration at Cosa of several Forum-ware vessels, a class generally very rare outside the Campagna Romana, may reflect direct, proximate economic and political relations between early medieval Cosa and Rome: both the site and much of the medieval *Ager Cosanus* belonged to the landholdings of a Roman monastery. Textual sources attest to the fact that a large portion of the territory around Cosa, including the hilltop village of Capalbiaccio, belonged to the peripheral estate of the monastery of Tre Fontane from the eleventh century — although there is some evidence that this dependence dated back to a much earlier period — to the beginning of the ninth century, if credit is given to the legend of Charlemagne's donation.[80]

An even higher number of individuals was yielded by the urban excavations at Pisa, where as many as twenty-five individuals of Forum ware and Sparse Glazed ware from Rome (Latium) were identified.[81] The two classes of single-fired glazed wares are quite balanced at Pisa, with 13 Forum ware specimens and 12 Sparse Glazed A and B vessels. The chronology of these finds is also significant: they were mostly found in contexts dating to between the tenth and the early eleventh century CE,[82] with the exception of one vessel yielded by a late-ninth-or early-tenth-century context from the Piazza dei Cavalieri.[83] It is evident that the relatively high numbers of single-fired glazed wares documented in Pisa, particularly between the tenth and eleventh centuries, reflects a broader phenomenon of marked re-intensification of maritime trade along central and northern Tyrrhenian routes. Such trade reached levels of vibrancy unknown for some two or three centuries, with Pisa playing a central role as a new Mediterranean hub.[84] It is no coincidence that, beginning in the last quarter of the tenth century, Pisa engaged a series of large-scale maritime connections with Egypt, Sicily, Tunisia, and Spain, as clearly revealed by the ceramic evidence.[85] This slow but progressive intensification of the maritime trade in commodities through the Tyrrhenian Sea, linking west-central Italy, Liguria, Sardinia, Corsica, and southern France, must have begun in the ninth century, as indicated by the distribution of Forum ware that was produced in Rome (Latium).[86]

As regards the site of Poggio Cavolo, it is not easy to explain the nature of the existing connections, trade or otherwise (souvenirs, gift exchange, etc.), given the low overall quantities of imported materials and the site's 'exceptional nature' in the context of the Ombrone Valley. It is worth noting the total absence of single-fired glazed wares from Rome

---

74 Francovich and Tronti 2003.
75 Cantini 2008.
76 Berti and others 1992, 279–94, and especially 287 Fig. 1.
77 See also Molinari 2003.
78 A fragment of Forum ware was also found at the small rural site of Podere Aione (25 × 20 m size), near Follonica; Cucini 1989. And a part of a handle with applied petals and a thick green glaze, belonging to a product of the Roman area, was found near Populonia; see Dadà 2007, 180.
79 Hobart 1992, 304–07.
80 According to legend, Charlemagne was unable to defeat a group of bandits who were holding the site of Cosa-Ansedonia, and dreamt of conquering the stronghold thanks to the miraculous help of Sant' Anastasio's head. At that time the relic happened to be kept by the monks of the Roman monastery of Sant' Anastasio ad *Aquas Salvias* (later known as Sant' Anastasio alle Tre Fontane). The Roman monks brought the miraculous relic to Charlemagne and it caused a sudden earthquake and hence the bandits' death, allowing the king to conquer Cosa. Subsequently Charlemagne, by agreement with Pope Leo III, donated both the ancient town of Cosa and its surrounding territory to the Roman monastery as a mark of gratitude. On the legend and its textual and iconographic sources see Hobart 1995, Luttrell 2001, and Fentress and Gruspier 2003, 95–96.

81 This quantification exploits the data from the urban excavations at Piazza Dante and Piazza dei Cavalieri, Abela 1993b, 419–24 and Abela 2000, 121–22. A premise on the methodology used to quantify the data from Pisa seems in order: in both publications the quantitative analysis of materials from both excavations is based on the number of potsherds, not the minimum number of individuals, making it difficult to determine the absolute number of vessels from the fragments. Further, a systematic distinction between Forum ware and Sparse Glazed A and B wares is challenged by the highly fragmentary nature of the assemblages. As such, the figures suggested here should be considered as a rounding down of the actual numbers as we tried to extrapolate the absolute values of glazed vessels from Latium and Rome using those fragments which, on the basis of their morphology, fabric and glaze, were likely to belong to single individuals.
82 In particular, this is the chronology of contexts yielding single-firing glazed wares from Latium excavated at Piazza Dante, see Abela 1993b, 420.
83 Abela 2000, 121.
84 Tangheroni 1996, 137–47.
85 Berti 2003.
86 Citter and others 1996, 123.

(Latium) at Grosseto (only about 5 km from Poggio Cavolo), a site which, according to the recent urban excavations, experienced a proto-urban development precisely between the late ninth and tenth centuries CE.[87] If there was some kind of regular pottery trade between southern Tuscany and Rome (Latium) in the tenth century, the proto-urban site at Grosseto would yield some single-fired glazed wares, given their presence at the much smaller site of Poggio Cavolo. Nevertheless, although the urban rescue excavation at Grosseto investigated some 3.6 per cent of the area within the Medici walls,[88] it was dependent upon infrastructural works and not a research agenda, and thus it may have failed to identify privileged contexts that are more likely to yield more complex and varied ceramic assemblages.

Apart from Cosa/Ansedonia, whose political and economic links with Rome have been ascertained, the model of distribution for Forum ware and Sparse Glazed ware from Rome (Latium) to southern Tuscany does not mirror the geographical locations of sites near the sea or the Via Aurelia, which was still heavily used in medieval times. Ninth- and tenth-century Forum ware was found at the small rural site of Podere Aione in the coastal area,[89] while fragments of Sparse Glazed B ware were occasionally found during field surveys both at poorly connected sub-coastal sites, such as the hilltop village of Poggio Castellaccio in the upper Osa Valley and Punta Fortezza in the Alma Valley, which faces the sea and is adjacent to the overland route serving the coastal area. The episodic attestation of Sparse Glazed B ware at Capalbiaccio between the eleventh and twelfth centuries demonstrates that the distribution of high-quality pottery from Latium became marginal from the eleventh century onwards, even in the *Ager Cosanus*.[90] The hilltop site at Scarlino, 5 km from the seaport of Portiglioni, also yielded tenth- and eleventh-century Sparse Glazed A ware from Latium.[91] This distribution pattern shows that both well-connected villages (Scarlino, Punta Fortezza, and Capalbiaccio) near seaports and the main coastal roads, and other, more inland sites (Poggio Castellaccio), distant from the coast and major overland routes, occasionally yield isolated fragments of single-fired glazed wares produced in Rome or Latium.

The excavations at Poggio Cavolo are too limited in extension to develop an infra-site distributional analysis of imported commodities, which could depict socio-economic differences within the local community. So far, *vetrina pesante*/Forum ware and Sparse Glazed ware have been found only in the church site (second half of the tenth century) and in the actual preparation of its floor (likely to have been laid down slightly later, between the late tenth and early eleventh century).[92] Similarly, fragments of *olle acquarie* and other small amphorae, possibly imported from northern Latium, were found in the same contexts as the single-fired glazed wares. Given this picture, two hypotheses are possible, though they need to be clarified by the excavation of domestic buildings at Poggio Cavolo. On the one hand, given the location of the finds in the church, specialized workers from Latium may have been involved in its construction after 950 CE. Unfortunately, this hypothesis is based entirely on material culture, as there are no textual sources for tenth-century Poggio Cavolo and its possible *dominus*.[93] If this hypothesis is valid, it would be pertinent to understand whether the pottery was brought directly from Latium by the specialized workers, who used them as their own ceramic equipment, or if the presence of 'foreign' workers stimulated occasional connections with Latium and Rome. On the other hand, a more logical and possibly more plausible explanation is that the variegated and complex ceramic assemblages from the church construction site reflect waste disposal from a privileged domestic building that was located near the church and is, as yet, undiscovered.

Small Amphorae and Other Imported Commodities

Context 1600 also yielded other materials that confirmed that Poggio Cavolo engaged some trade connections, which involved both the episodic purchase of extra-regional pottery and the circulation of small amphorae that derived from early medieval prototypes, which may have been used for a local and sub-regional trade in foodstuffs.

One specimen of table jug, characterized by an everted and indistinct rim with a flattened lip, has a strap handle directly attached to the rim. The outer surface of the vessel was finished with a thick, but shallow, combed decoration, which is reminiscent of that on the *olla acquaria* found in context 1593

---

87 See Citter (ed.) 2005 and Citter (ed.) 2007.
88 Citter (ed.) 2007.
89 Cucini 1989.
90 Hobart and others 2009, 104–05.
91 Marasco 2002–2003.

92 A fragment of a Sparse Glazed B ware jug from Latium was found in context 1534 (*infra*).
93 Citter 2006 tentatively related the construction of the first church at Poggio Cavolo (*pre* 950 CE) to an initiative of the bishop of Roselle, though no textual evidence seems to corroborate this.

(Pl. 8.7, no. 3). The optical microscope analysis of the jug's fabric indicated its similarity with fabric AD36: the same fabric used for the *olla acquaria*. Given the identification of the same fabric and combed surface finish, they are very likely to have been produced by the same workshop, tentatively situated in Latium.

The use of small amphorae to circulate foodstuffs on a local or sub-regional level in the eighth and ninth centuries CE has been proven to continue well into the tenth century, as revealed by the evidence from Capalbiaccio. The small amphorae (at least two) found in context 1600 confirm this pattern. They are both manufactured from a levigated fabric (AD35) and have short cylindrical necks; the rim shape varies from slightly everted and thickened to vertical and indistinct; the strap handles are attached at the junction between the neck and shoulder and present more or less thickened edges, a feature typical of the tenth-century variants, which does not appear in the eighth- and ninth-century specimens, whose strap handles have a thicker profile and no marked edges; one of the two specimens has a more careful finish associating a wide combed decoration with smoothing (Pl. 8.7, nos 1–2).

Finally, it is worth noting the presence of a large flat base from a small amphora or large storage vessel, which, though manufactured in a coarse fabric similar to that of some kitchen wares (G57), has a reddish-brown decoration of drips (red-painted or *colature rosse* ware) (Pl. 8.7, no. 16). No trace of smoke was found on the outer surfaces indicating that it was used as a storage or transport vessel, given its size and shape similar to that of the small amphorae produced in *acroma depurata* and *acroma selezionata* wares. Even the external drips suggest a decorative purpose not in keeping with kitchen vessel. The association of the reddish-brown drips and the fairly coarse fabric is interesting as it suggests that even those fabrics used to produce kitchen vessels, and particularly cooking pots, may have been occasionally adapted to manufacture other ceramic forms for storing and/or transporting foodstuffs.

Late Tenth- to Early Eleventh-Century Pottery from Poggio Cavolo

Thanks to the very clear stratigraphic sequence uncovered in the church area we can observe how the composition of ceramic assemblages varied from the contexts related to the construction site (second half of the tenth century) to the preparation levels of the *cocciopesto* floor of the church, identified both in the nave (context 1534) and in the apse (context 1506), and dating to the late tenth or early

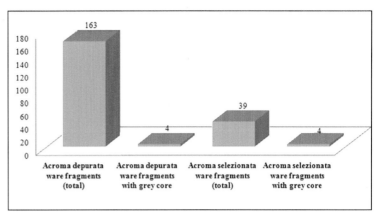

Figure 8.7. Poggio Cavolo, contexts 1522=1593 (second half of the tenth century CE): presence of the grey core in the *acroma depurata* and *acroma selezionata* wares. Graphic by author.

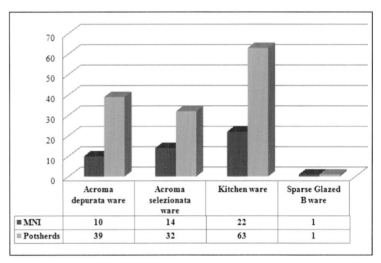

Figure 8.8. Poggio Cavolo, contexts 1506 and 1534 (late tenth/early eleventh century CE): ceramic classes, fragments, and MNI. Graphic by author.

eleventh century. Although the ceramic finds from contexts 1534 and 1506 are less abundant than those from the earlier contexts of the church construction site, they are large enough to allow for some overall observations.

One first significant change is the ratio of *acroma depurata* and *acroma selezionata* wares, on the one hand, to kitchen ware, on the other, which is more balanced than in earlier contexts. *Acroma depurata* and *selezionata* wares now account for some 51 per cent of total specimens, while kitchen ware makes up about 46.8 per cent; interestingly, in contexts 1593 and 1522, kitchen ware was in the overwhelming majority with some 72 per cent of the total individuals (Fig. 8.8).

The presence of the grey core is approximately as low as in contexts dating to the second half of the tenth century as it was in eighth and ninth centuries, which indicates the progressive improvement of the technological skills of the potters supplying Poggio

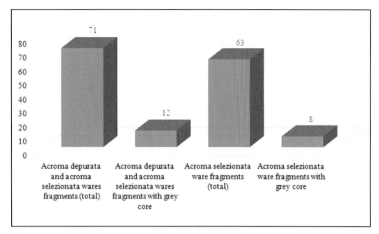

Figure 8.9. Poggio Cavolo, contexts 1506 and 1534 (late tenth/early eleventh century CE): presence of the grey core in the *acroma depurata* and *acroma selezionata* wares and in the kitchen ware. Graphic by author.

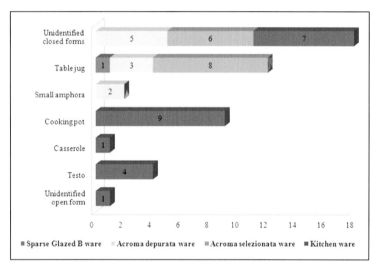

Figure 8.10. Poggio Cavolo, contexts 1506 and 1534 (late tenth/early eleventh century CE): ceramic classes, forms, and MNI. Graphic by author.

Cavolo. The number of *acroma depurata* and *selezionata* wares from the second half of the tenth century (1593 and 1522) that present this feature was just 12.6 per cent, compared to a total of 16.9 per cent for the same classes in contexts 1534 and 1506. Nevertheless, the overall values are more balanced in contexts dating from the late tenth to the early eleventh century, where the 'sandwich' fabric appears in only 12.6 per cent of kitchen ware, as opposed to 33.8 per cent in contexts 1593 and 1522 (Fig. 8.9).

Both table or storage and kitchen wares are good-quality products, which, as in earlier contexts, were made using the fast wheel, had thin walls, and well-finished surfaces. Handmade pottery produced at the domestic scale is as yet undocumented; evidently the demand of the village population and the supply of local and sub-regional workshops were sufficiently balanced, such that production *in situ* was unnecessary.

Sparse Glazed B ware from Rome (Latium)

Unlike context 1600, where at least three vessels and one spindle whorl in *vetrina pesante/Forum ware* were documented, contexts 1506 and 1534 yielded only one sherd of single-fired glazed ware from a small table jug with a strap handle that attached directly to the rim (Pl. 8.8, no. 1). This specimen is made from the same fabric (AD40) as the *vetrina pesante* vessels imported from Rome (Latium) and documented in context 1600. However, the green-yellow glaze, which is much thinner than on the specimens from context 1600, is only represented by a large drop on the handle, while the rest of the fragment is totally uncovered. Given the properties of the glaze and the later date of the context of provenance, this vessel may be Sparse Glazed B ware from Rome (Latium), which has a thinner slip that tends to leave larger portions of the vessels uncovered, completely inverting the ratio of glazed to uncovered surfaces typical of Sparse Glazed A ware in favour of the latter.[94]

Acroma depurata and *selezionata* wares

No significant change was observed in the functional repertoires of *acroma depurata* and *acroma selezionata* wares at the transition between the late tenth and early eleventh centuries. These wares continue to be dominated by two main forms: the table jug, in different sizes, and the *olla acquaria*, which is possibly from Latium. Open forms continue to be absent (Fig. 8.10). The table jugs have three main variants, which differ in morphology and size. One has a slightly everted rim and a lip that varies from pointed to rounded. The single handle, which is attached directly to the rim, has thickened edges; the base is always flat (Pl. 8.8, no. 2). One significant typological change is the decreasing eversion of the rims, which tend to become more sub-vertical compared to the specimens from contexts of the second half of the tenth century (Pl. 8.8, nos 3–5). This pattern becomes even more marked in the eleventh-century types at Poggio Cavolo. Another type, with a pointed vertical rim, clearly anticipates the eleventh-century specimens. In context 1506, a type of jug with a slightly everted, indistinct rim and a shallow combed decoration, has a finish reminiscent of the tenth-century specimens, although it is less marked.

Another *olla acquaria* produced in Latium was documented in the late tenth- and early eleventh-cen-

---

94 On the distinction between Sparse Glazed A and B wares and their respective characteristics, Paroli 1990, 321–23.

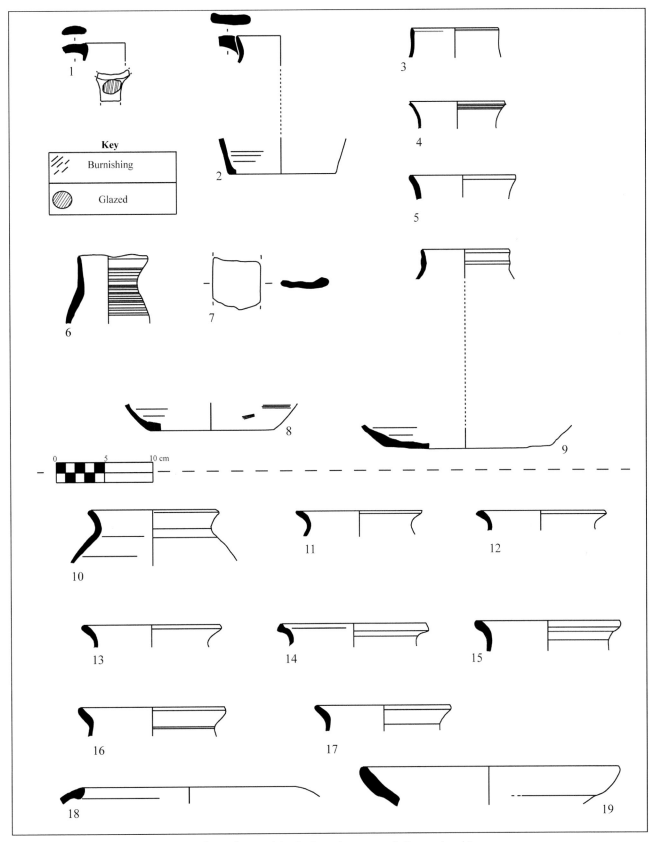

Plate 8.8. Poggio Cavolo, contexts 1506 and 1534 (late tenth/early eleventh century CE). Sparse glazed B ware: 1. Table jug. *Acroma depurata* and *acroma selezionata* wares: 2–6. Table jugs; 7. Table jug handle; 8. Table jug base; 9. *Olla acquaria*/water amphora. Kitchen ware: 10–17. Cooking pots; 18. Casserole; 19. *Testo*.

Table 8.8. Poggio Cavolo, contexts 1506 and 1534 (late tenth/early eleventh century CE): fabrics and MNI in the *acroma depurata* and *acroma selezionata* wares.

Fabrics (*acroma depurata* = AD and *acroma selezionata* = Sel)	MNI
AD1PCV	1
AD34	2
AD37	2
AD39	2
AD40 (Sparse Glazed ware)	1
Sel1PCV	3
Sel4	1
Sel43	7
Sel44	1
Sel45	2

Table 8.9. Poggio Cavolo, contexts 1506 and 1534 (late tenth/early eleventh century CE): fabrics and MNI in the kitchen ware (note that G5PCV and G7PCV are different fabrics than G5 and G7 at Capalbiaccio).

Fabrics (G = kitchen ware)	MNI
G51	6
G7PCV	1
G26	1
G28	4
G29	3
G54	1
G55	2
G56	1
G57	3

tury contexts. Though far more fragmentary than that from US 1593, it resembles said *olla* both in the shape of the rim and the slightly convex base (Pl. 8.8, no. 9). A smoothed medium-sized flat base in fabric AD36 attests to another closed form, which is likely from a jug, rather than a small amphora (Pl. 8.8, no. 8). Finally, the same fabric is associated with a small trefoil-mouthed table jug with an ovoid body and a thick combed decoration between the neck and the shoulder (Pl. 8.8, no. 6).

The optical microscope analysis of the fabrics does not suggest any significant change in production patterns: at least ten fabrics continued to be used to manufacture *acroma depurata* and *selezionata* wares, although they are not the same as those observed in contexts dating to the second half of the tenth century. One possible change is the introduction of five slightly different fabrics: three associated with *acroma depurata* and two with *acroma selezionata* wares. Though they do not look identical to the fabrics documented in earlier contexts, the main mineralogical phases are similar, with the main difference being the ratio of inclusions to clay matrix (Table 8.8). Without systematic thin-section analysis, it is safe to reason that the slight differences observed in the two groups of fabrics reflect the variety of mixing and levigation processes employed by the same workshops and, hence, the continuity of Poggio Cavolo's pottery supply from the tenth to the early eleventh century, rather than actual changes in supply patterns.

Kitchen Ware

The repertoire of kitchen ware in contexts 1506 and 1534 is comprised of a total of twenty-two individuals and presents close morphological and functional similarities with that in use in the second half of the tenth century, with few changes. Given that there is no marked change in the use of fabrics, all of the kitchen ware likely comes from local or sub-regional workshops. As many as sixteen individuals are closed forms: nine of these could be identified as cooking pots, while seven vessels are too fragmentary to be assigned to a specific functional form, such as a cooking pot or kitchen jug (Table 8.9).

Among the cooking pots documented between the late tenth and early eleventh century, there is a type with a slightly everted and rounded rim, which is reminiscent of types already attested to in the second half of the tenth century, although the latter lack the narrowing of the neck, which is seen in the earlier specimens (Pl. 8.8, no. 10). The type with a medium everted rim and pointed lip, already documented in context 1522, is now manufactured in two more variants: one with a rim that tends to flatten on the upper surface and one with a slightly rounded lip (Pl. 8.8, nos 11–13). Similar types have been found in urban Pisan excavations, in contexts dating to the same period as at Poggio Cavolo.[95] A type that makes its first appearance between the late tenth and early eleventh century has a slightly everted, thickened rim and a flattened lip (Pl. 8.8, no. 15). On the other hand, the type illustrated in Pl. 8.8, no. 14 is similar to one already attested in context 1593, though it differs for the pointed lip. Finally, a *pro capite* small-mouthed cooking pot, with rims varying from 14 to 15 cm in width, is the same typology as one specimen from 1593 (Pl. 8.8, nos 16–17).

---

95 Contexts from the urban excavation at Piazza Duomo, dating to the mid-tenth–early eleventh century CE; Alessi and others 1993, 433, MFAC 29 and 436, MFAC 32.

Open forms are present with a total of five vessels: two *testi of* the same type seen in contexts dating to the second half of the tenth century, one new type of *testo* with flaring walls, a shallow body and rounded rim, used for baking as revealed by the abundant traces of smoke (Pl. 8.8, no. 19), one generic open form, too fragmentary to be identified and finally a completely new functional form: the casserole (Pl. 8.8, no. 18). The introduction of the casserole is telling as it may reflect the emergence of new cooking practices based on water evaporation (rather than water retention as in the cooking pots) such as braising and frying. This functional form, frequent in the late Roman contexts of the Ombrone valley,[96] seems to be common at other early medieval rural sites of central-southern Tuscany such as Montarrenti[97] and Montemassi,[98] while in the Ombrone valley it does seem to have been reintroduced before the late tenth century, as the evidence from Poggio Cavolo[99] and Grosseto[100] indicates. The type attested in context 1534 is characterized by a markedly inverted and rounded rim reaching *c.* 22 cm in width.

Tenth-Century Pottery in Southern Tuscany: An Interpretative Model

The two sites of Capalbiaccio and Poggio Cavolo, about 35 aerial km apart, and both well connected with the coastline and a major overland route, the Via Aurelia, yielded some varied and representative ceramic assemblages dating to the tenth century, which lend themselves to a close comparison that aims to shed light on aspects of ceramic supply and consumption at the two medieval hilltop villages. Given the shortage of systematically quantified and published ceramic contexts dating to the Ottonian period[101] in the coastal and sub-coastal areas of southern Tuscany, the comparative analysis of the two datasets from Capalbiaccio and Poggio Cavolo can help to write a 'potted' history of this area and reveal the range of economic connections indicated by the ceramic evidence between 900 and 1000 CE. This final section focuses on similarities and differences between contemporaneous pottery assemblages from the two sites, with special emphasis on the relations between ceramic classes, the variety and complexity of the repertoires, their functions, the possible contribution of extra-regional sources to the pottery supply of the two sites, and the potential socio-economic implications of these differences. Moreover, in comparing the tenth-century pottery of Capalbiaccio and Poggio Cavolo, we will refer to the period 700–900 CE to pinpoint typological and technological changes in pottery production in the longer term.

Given the absence of any tenth-century kiln site identified in the field, any assumptions regarding patterns of ceramic production must be based on the visual analysis of the vessels and the study of their fabrics. Though systematic thin-section analysis has not yet been undertaken,[102] some preliminary data has been extrapolated from the systematic optical microscope study of hand-specimens. Combined with the morphological study, this microscopic data is able to define the possible local (sub-regional) or extra-regional location of the workshops that supplied the two sites.

A first observation is the generally high quality of both the *acroma depurata* and *acroma selezionata* wares distributed to the two sites. These two classes, which account for most of the repertoire of table and storage vessels, though differing in the process of clay levigation, were made by professional or semi-professional potters who were able to shape forms with thin walls, rarely exceeding 0.6 cm in thickness. One fabric (AD2=AD36) that was used to manufacture small amphorae, *olle acquarie*, and

---

96 Vaccaro 2011, 99–103.
97 Cantini 2003, 79–81.
98 Grassi 2006, 463.
99 At Poggio Cavolo the casserole with an inverted rim is also attested in some eleventh-century contexts in the metal-working district uncovered immediately to the east of the church (Area 2000), which are not presented here. For an overall discussion of the metal-working area at Poggio Cavolo see Farinelli and others 2008.
100 On the absence of the casserole in the early medieval contexts excavated in the area of S.Pietro in Grosseto see Valdambrini 2005.
101 The large medieval ceramic assemblages excavated at Scarlino, whose publication was announced some time ago, remain unpublished (see in general Marasco 2002–2003); some preliminary reports on the medieval hilltop village at Montemassi and the medieval village to proto-urban site at Grosseto are currently available, although an analytical publication of the pottery, including the tenth-century materials, is lacking. For the two sites see respectively Grassi 2006; Grassi 2010 and Valdambrini 2005; Valdambrini 2006. On the other hand, the medieval excavation at Cosa, recently published, did not identify new contexts dating to the early Middle Ages, and the evidence for that period is limited to a few materials from Brown's earlier excavations on the *Arx*. As such, the well-quantified medieval evidence refers to the periods between the eleventh and fourteenth centuries CE (see Cirelli and Hobart 2003) and cannot be used for our purposes.
102 So far, thin-section analysis has mainly been applied to mid and late Roman pottery from both coastal and inland sites in southern Tuscany as part of a comparative study of patterns of ceramic production, circulation, and consumption by the author, see Vaccaro 2013.

Table 8.10. Summary of the incidences of the grey core in the ceramic classes from Capalbiaccio and Poggio Cavolo.

Site	Period	MNI in *acroma depurata* and *acroma selezionata* wares with a grey core (%)	MNI in kitchen ware with a grey core (%)	Average (MNI) (%)
Capalbiaccio	10th century CE	24.13	9.4	12.26
Poggio Cavolo	Second half of the 10th century CE	12.6	33.8	23.2
Poggio Cavolo	Late 10th/early 11th century CE	16.9	12.6	14.75

Table 8.11. Frequencies of vessels in *acroma depurata* ware and red-painted/*colature rosse* ware manufactured with fabric AD2=AD36=DR 1 attributable to a source in (northern?) Latium.

Site	Period	*Acroma depurata* ware (MNI)	Red-painted/*colature rosse* ware (MNI)
Capalbiaccio	10th century CE	7	2
Poggio Cavolo	Second half of the 10th century CE (only including contexts 1522=1593)	2	0
Poggio Cavolo	Late 10th/early 11th century CE	3	0
MNI total		**12**	**2**

table jugs was apparently discovered at both sites. It will be discussed in detail below, as the identification of the morphological repertoire made from this fabric helped locate the workshop in Latium in which it was probably produced.

First, some interesting differences between the other workshops that supplied Capalbiaccio and Poggio Cavolo can be detected by observing the surface finish of table and storage vessels. The material from Poggio Cavolo was made by potters who frequently used a combed tool to create an even decoration on the external surfaces of their vessels. They also tended to smooth the lower part of their products, particularly at the junction between the base and walls. Only one base of a table jug, tentatively interpreted as an early import from the Pisan area on the basis of the fabric, has surface whitening. By contrast, at Capalbiaccio, the combed decoration of the walls, widely witnessed at Poggio Cavolo, is documented only in one case. The potters who produced the table and storage wares that reached Capalbiaccio made frequent use of surface whitening and stick smoothing, which is present on about 58 and 72 per cent of the total individuals, respectively, and altogether on some 34 per cent of vessels. The use of different techniques to finish vessels suggests that, apart from the workshop using fabric AD1=AD36, the other production sites that supplied Capalbiaccio were different. The workshops supplying Capalbiaccio and Poggio Cavolo must have taken advantage of different trade circuits (possibly one in the Ombrone Valley and one in northern Latium) and probably did not significantly compete with each other to extend their respective spheres of distribution.

The potters from the workshops supplying both Capalbiaccio and Poggio Cavolo demonstrate a similar level of technological skill in the careful levigation of their clays and the management of the firing temperature. This results in a lower frequency of the grey core in the fabrics of *acroma depurata* and *selezionata* wares, as well as in those of kitchen ware, compared to early medieval pottery.[103] Remember that Podere Serratone's eighth- and ninth-century pottery presented a high frequency of the 'sandwich' fabric: 46.3 per cent of the *acroma depurata* and *selezionata* wares; and 34.5 per cent of the kitchen ware. At San Martino de Plano, in the middle Bruna Valley, where some well-stratified ninth- and early tenth-century ceramic assemblages were analysed, the number of *acroma depurata* and *acroma selezionata* vessels with a grey core was much lower than at Podere Serratone, with only some 20.7 per cent of total specimens.[104]

The data from Capalbiaccio and Poggio Cavolo differs significantly from that collected at Podere Serratone: at the former, the grey core was identified in some 24 per cent of the MNI in *acroma depurata* and *selezionata* wares and 9.4 per cent of the kitchen wares; while at the latter, in contexts dating

---

103 Vaccaro 2011, 208–15 and Vaccaro 2015.
104 Vaccaro 2011, 222–27.

to the second half of the tenth century, the 'sandwich' fabric was identified in 12.6 per cent of the *acroma depurata* and *selezionata* wares and in 33.8 per cent of the kitchen vessels. This technological improvement is generalized, though it appears far more marked in the production of table and storage wares. It must be stressed that at Poggio Cavolo, the transition between the late tenth and early eleventh centuries is associated with a further reduction of the grey core in kitchen vessels which, by then, accounts for some 12.6 per cent (Table 8.10).

A similarly higher frequency of the grey core in early medieval pottery has recently been emphasized in a regional overview of ceramic production, trade, and circulation,[105] though with some possible variations between kilns supplying urban sites and those that mainly produced vessels for rural sites: the latter are more affected by firing defects than the former.[106] The study of ceramic assemblages from southern Tuscany presented here further corroborates this regional pattern and, in addition, provides a series of analytically quantified data, with a systematic observation of fabrics and possible defects. This data demonstrates that the potters' technological skills, both in levigating clays and constructing more efficient kilns, improved in the tenth century.

Further data on the organization of pottery production can be extrapolated from the combined study of fabrics and the different wares manufactured with them. One fabric from Capalbiaccio (AD2) that was used to manufacture *acroma depurata* wares was associated with two red-painted vessels, though the fabric was initially catalogued as DR1. Later, the optical microscope analysis revealed the close similarity between the two fabrics AD2 and DR1, which suggested that the workshop that produced *acroma depurata* vessels occasionally made red-painted vessels too. This is important for several reasons. First, it is evidence of the diverse ceramic classes output by the workshop that made the closed vessels, such as small storage or transport amphorae and table jugs, which were found at Capalbiaccio. Second, the identification of specific similarities between fabric AD2=DR1 at Capalbiaccio and fabric AD36 at Capalbiaccio is telling. The analysis of hand-specimens suggests that these fabrics are one and the same (hence AD2=DR1=AD36). It is interesting to note that at Poggio Cavolo this fabric is associated with the almost-complete *olla acquaria*, a generic closed form from context 1593, a jug from context 1600, another *olla acquaria*, and two table jugs from contexts dating to the late tenth and early eleventh century. The *olla acquaria* specimens from Poggio Cavolo have been ascribed to a production in Latium, given the morphological similarities with the products of that region. Similarly, the materials from Capalbiaccio present a series of close links with Latium, and thus this workshop (AD2=DR1=AD36) was likely located in that region, possibly in the north (Table 8.11).

At Capalbiaccio, even some kitchen ware, specifically cooking pots, comes from workshops in Rome or Latium: some 39 per cent (eleven of twenty-eight) of the pots was attributed to that source on the basis of both fabrics and morphology. By contrast, none of the kitchen ware from Poggio Cavolo appears to come from a workshop outside the local or sub-regional context. Their differing access to extra-regional kitchen ware is plausibly due to Capalbiaccio's very southerly geographical location, near the border with Latium, and the fact that the *Ager Cosanus* belonged to the landholdings of the Roman monastery of Sant' Anastasio, possibly from the ninth century onwards. Despite that, Capalbiaccio and Poggio Cavolo also reveal some similarities in their access to local and sub-regional kitchen ware. Five out of seven kitchen ware fabrics from Capalbiaccio can be ascribed, on the basis of their mineral inclusions, to generic local or sub-regional workshops; these supplied the site with some 79 per cent of the total kitchen ware vessels (forty-two out of fifty-four) documented in the tenth-century context of Building J. Four of these (G2=G51, G3=G54, G4=G29 and G7=G28) are identical to some of the fabrics used to make the kitchen ware found at Poggio Cavolo in the second half of the tenth century. Three fabrics are used to manufacture cooking pots (G2=G51, G3=G54, G4=G29) and one is used to produce open vessels, such as *testi*, *testelli*, and large lids (G7=G28), which were distributed to both sites.

The morphological similarity of some of the kitchen ware from Poggio Cavolo and Capalbiaccio, and the likely identification of the same fabrics, tentatively suggests that one or more local or sub-regional workshop supplied both hilltop settlements in the tenth century. At Poggio Cavolo, other fabrics and other functional kitchen ware vessels are also documented, including kitchen jugs, which are so far absent at Capalbiaccio. At Capalbiaccio, one fabric (G6) used to manufacture open vessels, and only episodically to make cooking pots, seems to use clay sources located either in southernmost Tuscany or in Latium. What is interesting is the use of this fabric to produce mostly wheel-thrown vessels, though a handful of open forms are probably handmade or manufactured on the slow wheel. Two plausible explanations can be advanced for this

---

105 Cantini 2011, particularly 178–79.
106 Cantini 2005, 245–48.

phenomenon: either the fabric was used by both a workshop using the wheel and a homemade production or the production context contemporaneously employed both manufacturing techniques. Whatever the case (no definitive conclusion is possible), it is significant that a few open kitchen vessels at Capalbiaccio were not produced on the fast wheel, while at Poggio Cavolo, similar products have not been identified for the tenth century.

This means that, although 21 per cent of the repertoire of kitchen ware from Capalbiaccio was imported from Rome or Latium, the vast majority of vessels used for cooking came from workshops that were operating at a local or sub-regional scale. The range of circulation of these vessels appears quite wide in comparison to the early medieval standards exemplified by the wares produced at Podere Serratone, which seem to have circulated only between the lower Ombrone and Osa Valleys. The same kitchen ware fabrics from Capalbiaccio were not only identified at Poggio Cavolo, but also in the surface assemblages dating to the late ninth to eleventh century, which were found in Aiali and Poggettone, in the Ombrone and Bruna Valleys, respectively.[107] This distribution pattern suggests that the 'market' for these kitchen wares covered at least some 60 km of the coastal and sub-coastal belt, considering the aerial distance between the two furthest-flung sites: Poggettone in the north and Capalbiaccio to the south.

Also of interest, as it confirms the existence of trade connections between Tuscany south of the Ombrone River and Latium in the tenth century, is the picture offered by single-fired glazed and painted wares. Production centres for early medieval and middle medieval red-painted and *colature rosse* wares have been identified at many sites in northern Tuscany, which are mostly concentrated in the Arno Valley, and include San Genesio, Pisa, and Lucca. There was a significant circulation of these wares in the same areas[108] and a limited penetration of low-value products to some sites in southern Tuscany, such as Donoratico, Campiglia Marittima, Rocchette Pannocchieschi, and Scarlino in the tenth to the eleventh century.[109] One exception is the tenth- to twelfth-century contexts at Populonia, where red-painted and *colature rosse* wares produced in northern Tuscany represent almost 1/3 of total specimens.[110]

Strikingly, south of the Ombrone River, painted and *colature rosse* wares are only episodically found at a handful of medieval sites (Fig. 8.11).[111] As regards the early medieval period, the only site that yielded a single red-painted specimen is Casa Andreoni, where two fragments (a base and a handle) of the same jug, which is manufactured in a levigated yellow fabric, were found in the eighth- and ninth-century surface assemblage.[112] The ceramic assemblages analysed at the Roman to medieval surface site of Aiali yielded as many as thirty vessels from the late ninth to eleventh centuries, two of which are red-painted. They are both made from the same hard levigated fabric with a grey core that is similar to one documented at Poggio Cavolo (AD37), where it is associated with *acroma depurata* wares. Both vessels are closed forms and one is probably a small storage amphora (Pl. 8.7, nos 21–22). On the basis of the fabric, these vessels are probably a local or sub-regional production, though an import from elsewhere (the Arno Valley, perhaps) cannot be ruled out. At Poggio Cavolo, a small amphora base in red-painted and *colature rosse* ware is made from a very coarse fabric, likely by a local or sub-regional workshop, given the similarity of its fabric with that of some of the mid-tenth- and early eleventh-century cooking pots found at the site. An eleventh-century context excavated below the tower at Poggio Cavolo yielded a small strap handle with a red-painted decoration. It has a geometric motif that consists of a longitudinal strip and a crisscross; a tiny, possibly occasional drop of yellow-green glaze overlapping the red-painted decoration was also observed (Pl. 8.7, no. 17).[113] The fabric of this vessel appears similar to that of a fragment of Sparse Glazed B ware from Latium in context 1534, but without thin-section analysis, this similarity cannot be conclusively proven. However, neither the carefully made motif, nor the fabric can be ascribed to a Tuscan production, and it was probably imported from another region in central or southern Italy. The last site to yield painted and *colature rosse* ware is tenth-century Capalbiaccio, already discussed in detail.

---

107 Data from these two sites is not presented in detail here; the study of surface ceramics was carried out by the author, in general on the site of Aiali see Vaccaro and others 2009 and Vaccaro 2011, 185–86, on Poggettone see Vaccaro 2011, 195–96.
108 Cantini 2011, 172–75.
109 Grassi 2010, 20–21, particularly Fig. 16, where it is clear that the highest values for red-painted and *colature rosse* wares are some 3 per cent at Scarlino in the tenth and at Campiglia Marittima in the eleventh.
110 Dadà 2007, 175–79.
111 By contrast, late antique *colature rosse* ware was well documented between the lower Bruna and Ombrone valleys, including the urban site of Roselle in contexts dating from the sixth to the early seventh century CE (Vaccaro 2011, 63–71), the cave-sites of Scoglietto and Spaccasasso between the mid-fifth and mid-sixth CE (Vaccaro 2011, 96–105) and the 'transformed' villa at Paduline in the mid-sixth–early seventh CE (Vaccaro 201, 105–10).
112 Vaccaro 2011, 216–17.
113 Vaccaro and Salvadori 2006, 482–83.

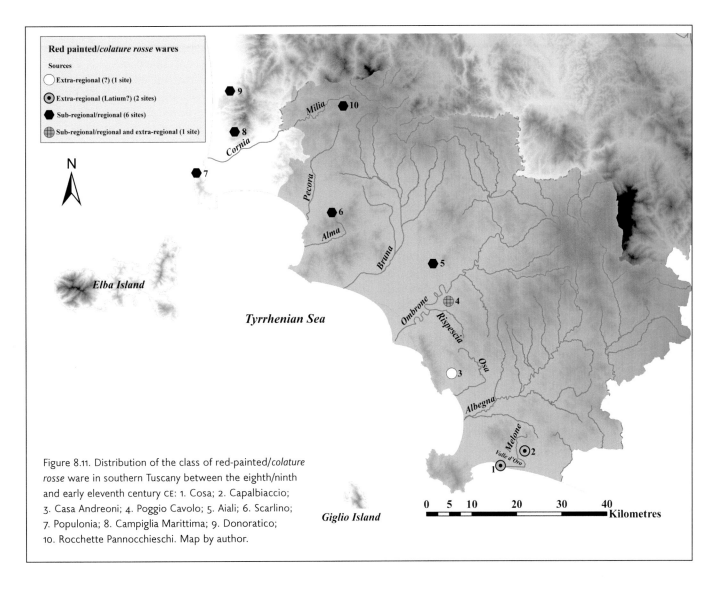

Figure 8.11. Distribution of the class of red-painted/*colature rosse* ware in southern Tuscany between the eighth/ninth and early eleventh century CE: 1. Cosa; 2. Capalbiaccio; 3. Casa Andreoni; 4. Poggio Cavolo; 5. Aiali; 6. Scarlino; 7. Populonia; 8. Campiglia Marittima; 9. Donoratico; 10. Rocchette Pannocchieschi. Map by author.

This brief overview clearly shows that, as we approach the southern part of Tuscany, the quantity of painted and *colature rosse* wares falls. Up in the Pecora Valley, where the hilltop site of Scarlino is located, the circulation of red-painted and *colature rosse* wares from northern Tuscany, though low, appears quite widespread, while the Ombrone Valley seems to represent a kind of barrier to the further penetration of such products. Indeed, with the exception of the two vessels from Aiali, whose source is unknown, neither the painted closed form in a yellow fabric from early medieval Casa Andreoni, nor the four vessels from tenth-century Capalbiaccio, come from northern Tuscany. Rather, they seem attributable to workshops located in Latium or, more generally, in south-central Italy. The red-painted products of Rome and Latium only occasionally reached a few sites in the southernmost coastal stretch of Tuscany, such as Capalbiaccio, in the tenth century, and Cosa, where a few fragments were identified in contexts dating to the eleventh century.[114]

Also of interest is the distribution pattern for the Sparse Glazed products manufactured in some areas of northern Tuscany, as it presents close parallels with that for red-painted and *colature rosse* wares. Archaeological research has identified a series of workshops specializing in the production of Sparse Glazed ware, mostly established in the tenth century, at Lucca, Pistoia, Camerelle di Chiusi, and other sites in northern and eastern Tuscany.[115] A slightly earlier production of single-fired glazed wares operated in Pisa between the ninth or early tenth century and the eleventh centuries.[116] Finally,

---

114 Personal communication from Enrico Cirelli, whom I thank.
115 Cantini 2011, 175.
116 On the single-fired glazed wares from the urban excavations at Piazza Dante and Piazza dei Cavalieri in Pisa, including local products, see Abela 1993a and Abela 2000.

an aforementioned workshop in the coastal areas of south-central Tuscany, between Rocca San Silvestro and Campiglia Marittima, made Sparse Glazed ware between the late ninth and the eleventh or twelfth century.[117] Sparse Glazed vessels manufactured at this workshop have been identified at several sites in south-central Tuscany, such as Donoratico, Campiglia Marittima, Suvereto, Rocca San Silvestro, Cugnano, Rocchette Pannochhieschi, and Castel di Pietra, though it accounts for a higher proportion of pottery in the assemblages from Donoratico and Campiglia Marittima from the late ninth to the eleventh century.[118] Despite the widespread circulation of these products in the area between Donoratico and Scarlino, with a higher concentration in the vicinity of the workshops, they are virtually absent south of the Alma Valley. With the exception of the two-handled closed form and another generic closed vessel from context 1600 at Poggio Cavolo, which is tentatively ascribed to that production.

Overall, this picture reveals that pottery not directly supplied by local or sub-regional workshops was imported from sources in Rome and Latium, while pottery connections with northern and central Tuscany were far less than occasional. As we have demonstrated, this pattern did not just characterize the circulation of fine wares, such as Sparse Glazed pottery, or the highest quality tableware, such as red-painted and *colature rosse* wares; some *acroma depurata* wares, such as that made from fabric AD2=AD36 at Poggio Cavolo and Capalbiaccio, a double-handled table amphora in fabric AD4 from Capalbiaccio, and some 39 per cent of the tenth-century cooking pots from Capalbiaccio, were also imported from Latium and Rome.

All these observations suggest a significant change in pottery in the second half of the tenth century, compared with the early medieval period. In the coastal areas between the Alma and Osa Valleys, which have been studied in depth through both field surveys and focused excavations,[119] the eighth and ninth centuries have supplied no evidence for a terrestrial circulation of extra-regional commodities, while the harbour at Portus Scabris yielded a few amphorae, which indicates the possibly occasional use of north-central Tyrrhenian routes for maritime trade. The second half of the tenth century seems to have seen a slight recovery of the interregional trade in bulk-goods and Latium is by far the most important interlocutor. The existence of *vetrina pesante*/Forum ware at Cosa, Poggio Cavolo, Poggio Castellaccio (Pl. 8.7, no. 19), and Punta Fortezza (Pl. 8.7, no. 18), that of red-painted and *colature rosse* wares at Capalbiaccio, and, even more interestingly, that of *acroma depurata* wares and kitchen wares at Poggio Cavolo and Capalbiaccio, respectively, strongly supports a fairly broad range of 'pottery connections' with Latium and Rome (Fig. 8.12).

Given the limited number of extensively excavated medieval sites in the southernmost part of Tuscany, it is not easy to develop a socio-economic model to explain the distribution pattern for commodities from Rome and Latium. Sites located in the medieval *Ager Cosanus*, such as Cosa and Capalbiaccio, definitely enjoyed some 'privileged' connections with Rome, thanks to the economic influence of the monastery of Sant' Anastasio ad Aquas Salvias. The case study of Poggio Cavolo, with its mid-tenth- to early eleventh-century connections with Latium and Rome, demonstrated not just by the *vertina pesante* and Sparse Glazed ware, but also by some *acroma depurata* products, hitherto represents an exception in the broader context of the Ombrone Valley. Not even Grosseto, which gradually rose to be a central place in the ninth and tenth centuries, enjoyed a similar range of connections. There, a series of small amphorae and *olle acquarie* that share some morphological features with products of northern Latium has been ascribed to a possible local production supported by kiln wasters.[120] At Poggio Cavolo, the possible 'privileged' nature of the artefacts dumped in the church construction site, after 950 CE, may be supported by the presence of two *denarii* of the emperor Otto I or Otto II. If we interpret the mid-tenth- to early eleventh-century assemblages deposited in the church construction site as domestic rubbish that was dumped by a privileged domestic context in the village, it is easy to explain the variety of pottery and specifically the presence of some imported commodities. This is certainly a fascinating possibility, although great caution should be exerted in using pottery as a socio-economic marker, particularly in the medieval period, as high-quality products may sometimes have been available to the lower and middle classes too; on other occasions, the distribution of low-quality products, if incorporated into a well-structured system of exchange, may have circulated widely to all social groups.[121]

The failure to identify production sites dating to the tenth century CE does not allow us to draw any conclusions regarding the actual organization of

---

117 Grassi 2010, 19–20.
118 Grassi 2010, Figs. 13–14.
119 Vaccaro 2011, 202–31.
120 Valdambrini 2006, 474.
121 See in particular Gelichi 2007, 66.

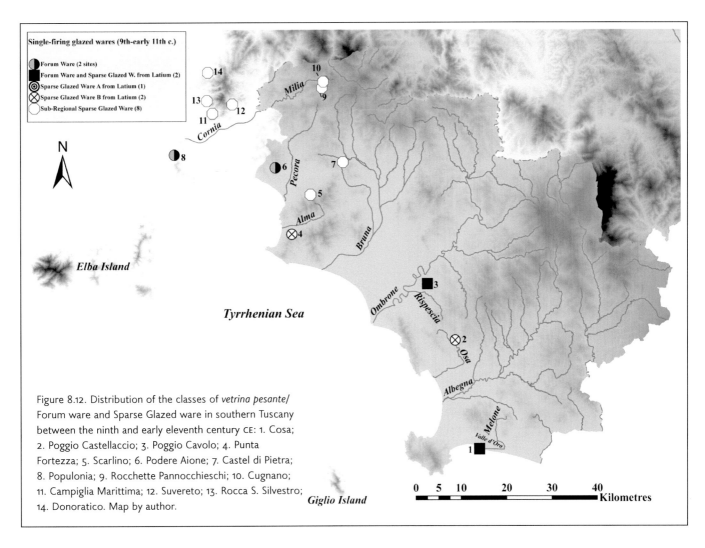

Figure 8.12. Distribution of the classes of *vetrina pesante*/Forum ware and Sparse Glazed ware in southern Tuscany between the ninth and early eleventh century CE: 1. Cosa; 2. Poggio Castellaccio; 3. Poggio Cavolo; 4. Punta Fortezza; 5. Scarlino; 6. Podere Aione; 7. Castel di Pietra; 8. Populonia; 9. Rocchette Pannocchieschi; 10. Cugnano; 11. Campiglia Marittima; 12. Suvereto; 13. Rocca S. Silvestro; 14. Donoratico. Map by author.

the workshops. Nevertheless, the combined study of morphological repertoires and fabrics, and the spatial distribution of the different ceramic classes emerging from consumption sites, may support some preliminary hypotheses:

- At Poggio Cavolo, in the second half of the tenth century (contexts 1593 and 1522), the percentage of *acroma depurata* and *acroma selezionata* wares is similar (13.1 per cent and 14.75 per cent of the total, respectively) at Capalbiaccio in the tenth-century contexts of Building J (they account for 24.6 per cent and 6.89 per cent). As only one fabric recurred at both sites (AD2=AD36), it can be assumed that different workshops supplied the two hilltop sites with table and storage vessels. Interestingly, at both sites some ceramic types occur both in *acroma depurata* and *selezionata* wares, which indicates that they may have been made by the same workshops. The same pattern was observed at the early medieval workshop of Serratone, which specialized in the production of table and storage vessels in levigated and semi-levigated fabrics, and possibly also kitchen ware. At Capalbiaccio, the larger amount of well-levigated fabrics compared to semi-levigated ones may indicate that the workshops producing these fabrics employed better techniques for levigating their clays than those supplying Poggio Cavolo. Despite this, the generally high quality of the tenth-century table and storage vessels at both sites indicates that they were made by at least semi-professional, if not professional, potters. Using David Peacock's model,[122] we can ascribe part of the *acroma depurata* and *selezionata* wares from Poggio Cavolo and Capalbiaccio to single workshops, where pottery was made by semi-professional potters, who systematically used the fast wheel and a series of techniques to finish their products, such as smoothing, combed decorations, and whiten-

---

122 For the model, developed on the basis of ethno-archaeological data and mostly applied to Roman pottery, see Peacock 1982, 8–11.

ing. These workshops also had more well-constructed kilns than at early medieval production sites like Podere Serratone, which were able to guarantee a more even firing of vessels.

- Two groups of products associated with fabrics AD2=AD36=DR1 and AD3=DR2 must have been made by even more specialized potters, who produced *acroma depurata*, red-painted, and *colature rosse* wares. They knew how to produce the liquid clay mixture (rich in iron oxides and hydroxides extracted from red ochre) used for painted decorations, which was an additional skill that distinguished them from those potters who were only able to manufacture unpainted wares. Products made from both fabrics characterize the repertoires at Capalbiaccio, while fabric AD2=AD36=DR1 is only documented at Poggio Cavolo in limited quantities. The overall quality of these products seems even higher than the rest of the repertoires of table and storage vessels. The technological investment of workshops that specialize in both painted and unpainted wares is unquestionably more than that of those producing only unpainted products and, though both groups can generally be ascribed to David Peacock's model of the single workshops, a differentiation is evident. Thus, it appears that two different typologies of single workshops — variant 1 (only high-quality unpainted levigated wares) and variant 2 (both painted and unpainted pottery in levigated fabrics) — which, though producing wares of generally high-quality, with a certain degree of standardization, differed in their use of painted decorations. Another assumption regarding the workshop producing vessels in the AD2=AD36=DR1 fabric relates to the range of distribution of these materials. Their workshop of origin has tentatively been located in northern Latium and, the fact that its products were found as far away as Poggio Cavolo, may mean that traders were involved in the distribution of these artefacts, either through forms of commerce or on the basis a barter economy. Similarly, at Capalbiaccio, the presence of relatively large quantities of cooking pots produced either in Rome or Latium, possibly by the same workshops that made glazed wares (the occasional glaze drop on a cooking pot is telling), suggests the existence of a trade network that probably involved merchants.

- Other workshops, assumed to be local or sub-regional, distributed their vessels throughout a large coastal area of southern Tuscany c. 60 km in breadth, between the Bruna Valley and the Valle d'Oro. These workshops certainly made cooking pots, but the production of some table and storage wares cannot be ascertained without systematic thin-section analysis of the specimens and, above all, the identification of kiln-sites in the field. All this kitchen ware (fabrics G2=G51, G3=G54, G4=G29, and G7=G28) is characterized by a high technological level and possibly relates to Peacock's model of a household industry,[123] which implies organization based around semi-professional potters who resorted to ceramic production as a way of supplementing their income from other sources, such as agriculture. The actual location of these workshops is unknown, but to ensure the profitability of this supplementary activity, they must have been located in or near a settlement, at a conveniently short distance from clay sources and the refractive minerals used to give 'tooth' to the vessels. It is of great interest that, despite the relatively limited investment supporting this production, vessels made from the aforementioned fabric circulated in a fairly wide, sub-regional radius. This data further corroborates Sauro Gelichi's model of the wide distribution of medium- and even low-quality ceramic products in well-established systems of exchange, such as the large estates of the eighth to tenth centuries in central and northern Italy, which ensured the functionality and efficiency of trade connections.[124] One question that consequently arises concerns how this widespread circulation throughout the coastal areas of southern Tuscany was possible. A potential explanation is the semi-specialization in pottery production of one or more rural communities living in the tenth-century villages of the area and taking advantage of the trade opportunities offered by the local demand for high-quality cooking pots. Their products then progressively conquered large portions of the local and sub-regional market, thanks to their efficiency. What remains unclear is how all these pots were transported: this case, too, suggests the presence of traders who guaranteed transport and probably purchased pottery at the production site for resale to other consumption sites.

---

123 Peacock 1982, 17–25.
124 Gelichi 2007, 59–60 and 66.

Another few final aspects that require further discussion concern the functional analysis of tenth-century ceramic repertoires, their relationship with eating habits, and elements of continuity with the early medieval period. A progressive reduction in the variety of functions performed by ceramic repertoires throughout the western Mediterranean after the seventh century CE has been ascertained.[125] Italy is no exception, although there is a marked difference between south-central regions, where ceramic production maintained both a higher technological quality and a wider functional repertoire, and most of northern Italy.[126] Tuscany, as a whole, is in line with the overall pattern for many central and southern areas of the peninsula: despite a decrease in pottery sophistication and complexity, compared to late antiquity, production maintained some variety in terms of ceramic classes and functions between the eighth and tenth centuries.[127] Nevertheless a closer examination reveals some significant differences, both at a micro-regional scale and between urban and rural sites located in the same area. For example, the mid-seventh- to ninth-century urban contexts excavated in Siena yielded a certain variety of beakers and table jugs, which were generally in *acroma depurata* ware and occasionally in red-painted and *colature rosse* wares, storage vessels in the form of jars, funnels, and basins, while the kitchen ware repertoire was composed of *testi*, basin-lids, casseroles, and cooking pots.[128] During the same period, at Montarrenti, a few kilometres away, table and storage vessels basically consisted of jugs, rare jars, and basins that were mostly made in *acroma depurata* ware (no painted ware is documented), whereas the repertoire of kitchen ware included casseroles, basins, bowls, *testi*, and cooking pots.[129]

As has been demonstrated, the ceramic assemblages from early medieval sites in southern Tuscany indicate a trend paralleling that of Montarrenti, with a significant reduction of ceramic classes (almost exclusively unpainted) and functional vessels. Notably, most of the contexts south of the Ombrone River between the eighth and tenth centuries yielded an even more limited number of functional vessels, both in table or storage and kitchen ware. The presence of *acroma depurata* basins is occasionally documented at Casa Andreoni between the eighth and ninth centuries, at Grosseto in the ninth,[130] and at San Martino de Plano in the ninth or early tenth century. This ceramic type is absent from both Poggio Cavolo and Capalbiaccio, where no open table or storage vessel has been found. Another form that probably disappeared in the tenth century is the table jar, which was fairly common at early medieval Casa Andreoni[131] and, again, absent from both Poggio Cavolo and Capalbiaccio. As regards kitchen ware, it is interesting to note that the casserole, frequently documented at Montarrenti, does not appear at the rural sites south of the Ombrone River until the late tenth or early eleventh century, when it is documented at Poggio Cavolo for the first time. This picture shows that the repertoire of functional vessels in use at the rural sites of southernmost coastal Tuscany between the eighth and tenth centuries is likely to have been even smaller than at inland villages like Montarrenti, with a possible further reduction after 900 CE, when table jars and basins in table or storage ware disappear.

To summarize, a closer examination of the tenth-century assemblages from the area between the Pecora River to the north and the Valle d'Oro to the south indicates a repertoire limited to jugs and small amphorae for table and storage purposes, and cooking pots, lids, and *testi* for cooking food and baking. This reduction of functional vessels to a handful of forms has been correctly related to a change in eating habits, while the complete absence of open table vessels in most of the eighth- to tenth-century ceramic assemblages of Italy may be the consequence of the use of perishable materials (such as wood), which are poorly preserved (if at all) in the archaeological record.[132] But how exactly did eating practices change at early medieval rural settlements in southern Tuscany? The medieval sites analysed here have offered a broad morphological and dimensional range of cooking pots, grouped into small-mouthed (diameter under 15 cm) and large-mouthed (diameter over 15 cm) specimens. The interpretative model assumes the use of the former as *pro capite* vessels for individual consumption and of the latter to prepare food for larger groups, such as the household. Small-mouthed cooking pots may have been used to directly consume both semi-liquid foods, such as soups, and solid ones, like dried meat that was tenderized and heated in water or wine. In addition, the tenth-century assemblages at Capalbiaccio and Poggio Cavolo revealed the presence of some large *testi* with no trace of smoke, which means that they might have been employed as platters for present-

---

125 Arthur 2007a.
126 Wickham 2005, 728–41.
127 Cantini 2011; Vaccaro 2011, 202–03 and Vaccaro 2015, 220–27.
128 Cantini 2005.
129 Cantini 2003.
130 On Grosseto see Valdambrini 2006.
131 Vaccaro 2011, 218–19.
132 On these explanations see Arthur 2007a.

ing large meat or fish cuts, as well as vegetables, and consuming them collectively.[133] The versatility of the kitchen ware repertoire may thus have filled the gap left by the absence of dishes and large bowls in tableware for direct food consumption. As such, the contribution of storage and table vessels, systematically represented by closed vessels at Capalbiaccio and Poggio Cavolo, was limited to food storage and transport (small amphorae), to water supply (*olle acquarie*), and to storing, pouring, and possibly drinking liquids (table jugs). At the same time, as regards cooking practices, boiled food was absolutely predominant in the tenth century, with the exclusive presence of cooking pots, suitable for cooking by water retention. On the other hand, open kitchen vessels, such as casseroles, which were employed for braising and roasting food by water evaporation,[134] and were common at Montarrenti from the mid-seventh to the eleventh centuries,[135] are completely absent at Capalbiaccio and do not appear at Poggio Cavolo until the late tenth to early eleventh century, when they play a very minor role in cooking food, as the dominance of cooking pots is still overwhelming. Both at Capalbiaccio and Poggio Cavolo, the presence of small percentages of open kitchen vessels, such as bowl-lids, may testify to their use for braising and roasting foods. The absence of the form typically used for this purpose (the casserole) should be emphasized as clear evidence of the minimal impact of roasted and braised meat, compared to boiled meat, on the local diet. This model suggests that, though much simplified and reduced to a very limited number of functional vessels, the tenth-century ceramic repertoire was still able to meet, by itself, the demand for food preparation, cooking, and consumption, without the need to resort to wooden vessels to explain the absence of bowls and dishes for food consumption, as was the case up until the seventh century.

---

133 Such a scenario is now confirmed by residue analysis applied to a sample of *testi* from excavated urban and rural sites in Tuscany. The presence of markers of cabbage (one *testo* from the medieval hilltop village at Donoratico), leak (one *testo* from medieval contexts in Florence) and fish (several *testi* from the same contexts in Florence) would confirm their use as platters and not just as baking vessels, see Pecci 2009, 28.

134 On the different use of cooking pots and casseroles and the implications on the late Roman and early medieval eating habits in the Mediterranean context see Arthur 2007b.

135 Cantini 2003, 79–81.

APPENDIX 8.1: CATALOGUE OF THE RELEVANT CERAMIC FABRICS

Key: AD = levigated fabrics; Sel = selected fabrics;
G = coarser fabrics (mostly for kitchen ware)

Fabric	Possible source	Occurrence	Description
G1	Rome or Latium	Capalbiaccio (10th century CE)	**Hardness**: quite hard; **breaking**: from regular to conchoidal; **texture**: hiatal and homogeneous; well-sorted; inclusions 10–15%; **description of inclusions**: limestone, calcite, feldspars (?), volcanic inclusions and very rare muscovite. Inclusions measure from 0.1 to 0.6 mm, mean size 0.2–0.3 mm. Granules sub-rounded and lowly spherical; **porosity**: 10%, pores are mostly rounded, pore size is prevalently <0.1 mm; **colour**: from 2.5YR 6/6 light red to 2.5YR /1 reddish black.
G2 (Capalbiaccio) = G51 (Poggio Cavolo)	Local or subregional	Capalbiaccio (10th century CE) Poggio Cavolo (second half of the 10th century CE) Poggio Cavolo (late 10th/ early 11th century CE)	**Hardness**: hard; **breaking**: slightly irregular; **texture**: hiatal and homogeneous; well-sorted; inclusions 25–30%; **inclusions**: quartz, rare feldspars and very rare calcite; they are sub-angular and highly spherical; inclusions measuring between 0.1/0.2 and 0.6 mm, mean size 0.2/0.3 mm; **porosity**: 10/15%. Pores prevalently elongated and orientated measuring on average 0.2/0.5 mm; **colour**: grey core (gley 2 4/1 dark greenish grey) in some fragments; surface 5YR reddish brown 5/4.
G3 (Capalbiaccio) = G54 (Poggio Cavolo)	Subregional (or northern Latium?)	Capalbiaccio (10th century CE) Poggio Cavolo (second half of the 10th century CE) Poggio Cavolo (late 10th/ early 11th century CE)	**Hardness**: hard; **breaking**: slightly irregular; **Texture**: hiatal and homogeneous. Inclusions to matrix ratio 30–40%. Well-sorted fabric; **inclusions**: absolute predominance of calcite crystals and quartz, very rare biotite, a few fragments of aggregates of several minerals with an association of quartz and biotite. Rarer pyroxenes, rare iron oxides. Inclusions measuring between 0.3 and 1 mm, mean size 0.5 mm, sub-rounded with low sphericity; **porosity**: in the order of 5/10%, prevalently rounded pores measuring 0.1/0.2 mm; **colour**: grey core: gley1 6/1 grey; surface: 2.5YR 5/6 red.
G4 (Capalbiaccio) = G29 (Poggio Cavolo)	Local or subregional	Capalbiaccio (10th century CE) Poggio Cavolo (second half of the 10th century CE) Poggio Cavolo (late 10th/ early 11th century CE)	**Hardness**: quite hard; **breaking**: irregular; **texture**: hiatal and homogeneous; well-sorted; **inclusions**: in the order of 15%; calcite, quartz and biotite; inclusions measuring between 0.2 and 1 mm, rounded with low sphericity; **porosity**: in the order of 5–10%; rounded pores measuring 0.1 mm in diameter; **colour**: often two-coloured, from red to reddish grey (2.5YR 5/8 red to 2.5YR 3/1 dark reddish grey).
G5	Rome or Latium	Capalbiaccio (10th century CE)	**Hardness**: quite hard; **breaking**: from regular to conchoidal; **texture**: hiatal and homogeneous; quite well-sorted; **inclusions**: in the order of 10%; very rare limestone, rare muscovite and biotite, occasional volcanic inclusions and iron oxides. Inclusions measuring between 0.1 and 0.5 mm, sub-rounded with high sphericity; **porosity**: in the order of 5%; prevalently rounded pores measuring <0.1 mm; **colour**: from 2.5YR 6/6 light red to 2.5YR /1 reddish black.
G6	Very southern Tuscany or Latium	Capalbiaccio (10th century CE)	**Hardness**: quite soft; **breaking**: very irregular; **texture**: hiatal and homogeneous; quite well-sorted; **inclusions**: in the order of 30%; frequent calcite, augite and quartz are more rare; angular and lowly spherical; from 0.1/0.2 to 1 mm; **porosity**: in the order of 5%, prevalently rounded pores measuring <0.1 mm; **colour**: 10R 5/6 red.

Fabric	Possible source	Occurrence	Description
G7 (Capalbiaccio) = G28 (Poggio Cavolo)	Local or subregional	Capalbiaccio (10th century CE) Poggio Cavolo (second half of the 10th century CE) Poggio Cavolo (late 10th/ early 11th century CE)	**Hardness**: quite hard; **breaking**: irregular; **texture**: hiatal and heterogeneous, moderately well-sorted; **inclusions**: in the order of 15%; inclusions measuring between 0.5 and 1 mm, mean size 0.5 mm, sub-rounded and highly spherical. Prevalence of quartz, with some biotite, an aggregate of several minerals with an association of quartz and biotite; **porosity**: 15/20%, pores prevalently round measuring 0.2/0.3 mm. Some elongated and orientated pores measuring between 0.5 and 1 mm; **colour**: 5YK, yellowish-red 5/6.
G26 (Poggio Cavolo)	Local or subregional	Poggio Cavolo (second half of the 10th century CE) Poggio Cavolo (late 10th/ early 11th century CE)	**Hardness**: quite hard; **breaking**: quite irregular; **texture**: hiatal and homogeneous; moderately well-sorted; **inclusions**: in the order of 30–35%. Inclusions measuring between 0.2 and 1.5 mm, mean size 0.5–1 mm, sub-rounded with low sphericity. Abundant quartz and feldspars (including some polycrystalline); to a lesser extent calcite crystals and clasts of biotite, numerous iron oxides; **porosity**: in the order of 10–15%, prevalently rounded pores measuring 0.5 mm; **colour**: 5YR, 5/6 yellowish red.
G34 (Poggio Cavolo)	Local or subregional	Poggio Cavolo (second half of the 10th century CE)	**Hardness**: quite hard; **breaking**: quite irregular; **texture**: hiatal, inhomogeneous granulometry; moderately well-sorted; **inclusions**: in the order of 25–30%. Quartz grains measuring 0.5–1 mm. Feldspars 0.2–1 mm. Presence of an iron oxide. Inclusions from sub-angular to sub-rounded; porosity: in the order of 10–15%. Pores measuring between 0.5 and 1 mm, elongated and orientated; **colour**: grey core: gley 2 5/1 bluish grey; surface: 2.5YR 6/8 light red.
G7PCV (Poggio Cavolo)	Local or subregional	Poggio Cavolo (late 10th/ early 11th century CE)	**Hardness**: quite hard; **breaking**: quite irregular; **texture**: hiatal and homogeneous; well-sorted; **inclusions**: in the order of 15%; prevalently quartz, calcite and numerous iron oxides; inclusions sub-rounded with low sphericity, measuring between 0.2 and 1 mm, prevalently between 0.2 and 1 mm; porosity: in the order of 5–10%, rounded pores measuring 0.1 mm in diameter; **colour**: 10YR 6/3 pale brown.
G55 (Poggio Cavolo)	Local or subregional	Poggio Cavolo (second half of the 10th century CE) Poggio Cavolo (late 10th/ early 11th century CE)	**Hardness**: quite hard; **breaking**: slightly irregular; **texture**: hiatal and homogeneous; **inclusions**: in the order of 15%; well-sorted. Inclusions measuring between 0.2 and 1 mm, mean size 0.5 mm. Angular and highly spherical. Quartz, muscovite and rare calcite; **porosity**: in the order of 10–15%; pores both elongated and orientated and rounded, measuring between 0.2 and 2 mm; **colour**: 2.5Y, 2.5/1 black.
G56 (Poggio Cavolo)	Local or subregional	Poggio Cavolo (second half of the 10th century CE) Poggio Cavolo (late 10th/ early 11th century CE)	**Hardness**: quite hard; **breaking**: quite irregular; **texture**: hiatal and homogeneous; **inclusions**: in the order of 20–30%; moderately well-sorted, measuring between 0.2 and 1 mm, mean size 0.5 mm. Sub-rounded and highly spherical. Inclusions: mainly quartz and calcite, rare iron oxides; **porosity**: in the order of 5–10%; pores both rounded and elongated and orientated, measuring between 0.1 and 0.5 mm; **colour**: surface: 2.5YR, 5/8 red; grey core: 2.5YR, 5/1 reddish grey.
G57 (Poggio Cavolo)	Local or subregional	Poggio Cavolo (second half of the 10th century CE) Poggio Cavolo (late 10th/ early 11th century CE)	**Hardness**: quite hard; **breaking**: quite irregular; **texture**: hiatal and heterogeneous; well-sorted; **inclusions**: in the order of 25–30%; inclusions measuring between 0.2 and 1.5 mm, mean size 0.3/0.5 mm, rounded and highly spherical. Calcite, feldspars, quartz, biotite, and muscovite. Larger quantities of quartz, feldspars, and calcite; **porosity**: in the order of 5/10%, prevalently rounded pores measuring 0.1/0.3 mm; **colour**: 2.5YR 4/3 reddish brown.

Fabric	Possible source	Occurrence	Description
AD1 (Capalbiaccio)	Local or subregional (?)	Capalbiaccio (10th century CE)	**Hardness**: hard; **breaking**: regular; **texture**: serial and homogeneous, sorted fabric; **inclusions**: in the order of <5%; prevalence of quartz and limestone; inclusions measuring between 0.08 and 0.2 mm, generally very tiny, rounded and highly spherical; **porosity**: in the order of 5%, prevailingly rounded and measuring <0.1 mm; **colour**: 10YR 5/1 reddish grey.
AD2 (Capalbiaccio) = AD36 (Poggio Cavolo)	(Northern?) Latium	Capalbiaccio (10th century CE) Poggio Cavolo (second half of the 10th century CE) Poggio Cavolo (late 10th/ early 11th century CE)	**Hardness**: hard; **breaking**: from regular to conchoidal; **texture**: serial and homogeneous. Well-sorted fabric; **inclusions**: in the order of < 5%. Inclusions measuring on average 0.2/0.3 mm, they are rounded and highly spherical. Prevalence of tiny quartz, rare calcite and biotite and very occasional dark inclusions (of volcanic nature?); **porosity**: 5–10%. Prevalence of rounded pores measuring 0.1/0.2 mm, some elongated and orientated pores measuring 0.3/0.5 mm; **colour**: 10YR 6/8 brownish yellow.
AD3	(Northern?) Latium or subregional	Capalbiaccio (10th century CE)	**Hardness**: hard; **breaking**: regular; **texture**: serial and homogeneous; sorted fabric; **inclusions**: in the order of <5%; limestone-rich fabric with occasional quartz and iron oxides; Inclusions measuring on average 0.2 mm, they are sub-rounded and highly spherical; **porosity**: in the order of 5%. Prevalence of rounded pores measuring <0.1 mm; **colour**: 10YR 6/8 light red.
AD4	Latium (?)	Capalbiaccio (10th century CE)	**Hardness**: quite hard; **breaking**: slightly irregular; **texture**: hiatal and homogeneous; well-sorted fabric; **inclusions**: in the order of 5–7%; sub-rounded and highly spherical inclusions. Presence of limestone, quartz, muscovite and rare augite. inclusions measuring between 0.08 and 0.5 mm; **porosity**: in the order of 5%. Prevalence of rounded pores measuring <0.1 mm; **colour**: 2.5YR 5/6 red.
AD1PCV (Poggio Cavolo)	Local or subregional	Poggio Cavolo (late 10th/ early 11th century CE)	**Hardness**: quite hard; **breaking**: regular; **texture**: serial and homogeneous, absence of inclusions, very fine fabric; **porosity**: in the order of 10%. Pores elongated and rounded measuring between 0.1 and 0.5/0.6 mm, prevalence of those measuring 0.2/0.3 mm; **colour**: 2.5 YR light red 6/6.
AD30	Local	Poggio Cavolo (second half of the 10th century CE) Podere Serratone (8th and 9th century CE)	**Hardness**: medium hard; **breaking**: slightly irregular; **texture**: serial and homogeneous; sorted; **inclusions**: in the order of <5%. Sandstone fragment (?), oxides, secondary calcite; **porosity**: in the order of 20%. Pores elongated and orientated, measuring between 0.25 and 0.5 mm. Secondary calcite around some pores; **colour**: surface: 2.5 YR 5/8 red; grey core: gley 1 5/1 greenish grey.
AD33	Regional (Pisan area?)	Poggio Cavolo (second half of the 10th century CE)	**Hardness**: quite soft; **breaking**: regular; **texture**: serial, homogeneous distribution of inclusions; very well-sorted; **inclusions**: in the order of <5%, measuring between 0.2 and 0.4 mm, they are sub-rounded and highly spherical. Presence of limestone granules measuring between 0.2 and 0.5 mm, some iron oxides; **porosity**: in the order of 5–10%, pores both round and elongated in the direction of the wheel measuring between 0.1 and 0.5 mm; **colour**: 7.5 YR 5/6 strong brown.
AD34	Local or subregional	Poggio Cavolo (late 10th/ early 11th century CE)	**Hardness**: medium hard; **breaking**: quite regular; **texture**: serial, heterogeneous; **inclusions**: in the order of 5%. Inclusions measuring between 0.1 and 0.3 mm. The inclusions are biotite and calcite, with rarer quartz. They are sub-rounded with low sphericity; **porosity**: in the order of 5–10% with a mean pore size of 0.1/0.2 mm; some elongated and orientated pores measuring 0.5 mm; **colour**: 5YR 5/3 reddish brown.

Fabric	Possible source	Occurrence	Description
AD35	Local or subregional	Poggio Cavolo (second half of the 10th century CE)	**Hardness**: quite hard; **breaking**: quite regular; **texture**: hiatal, heterogeneous granulometric distribution; moderately sorted; **inclusions**: in the order of 5–10%. Inclusions measuring between 0.2 and 2 mm, mean size 0.5 mm. Angular inclusions with low sphericity. Mineral phases identified: scarce muscovite, 0.2 mm; moderate presence of quartz grains measuring 1 to 2 mm; dominant limestone measuring between 0.2 and 1 mm; rounded iron oxides 0.5 mm; **porosity**: in the order of 20–25%. Pores prevalently rounded or elongated and orientated in the direction of the wheel. Pores measuring between 0.1 and 0.5 mm. The smallest pores are generally elongated; **colour**: 5YR 5/8 yellowish red.
AD37	Local or subregional	Poggio Cavolo (second half of the 10th century CE) Poggio Cavolo (late 10th/early 11th century CE)	**Hardness**: hard; **breaking**: slightly irregular; **texture**: hiatal, heterogeneous granulometric distribution; well-sorted; **inclusions**: in the order of 5–10%; inclusions measuring between 0.2 and 0.7 mm, mean size 0.4–0.6 mm. Granules angular and highly spherical. Inclusions: quartz 0.4–0.5 mm, calcite 0.4–0.6 mm, muscovite 0.6–0.7 mm, iron oxides 0.3–0.5 mm, secondary calcite around some pores, feldspars 0.3–0.4 mm. Predominant calcite; **porosity**: in the order of 10–15%, mean pore size of 0.2 to 0.5 mm, prevalently 0.2–0.3 mm; pores both rounded and elongated in the direction of the wheel; **colour**: surface: 5YR 6/8 yellowish red; fracture: gley 2 5/1 bluish grey.
AD39	Local or subregional	Poggio Cavolo (late 10th/early 11th century CE)	**Hardness**: medium hard; **breaking**: conchoidal; **texture**: serial and homogeneous; well-sorted; **inclusions**: in the order of < 5%. The inclusions present are calcite granules measuring on average 0.2 mm, only one measures 7 mm in diameter and may be an accidental presence. The inclusions are rounded and highly spherical; **porosity**: in the order of 5–10%, generally elongated and orientated pores measuring 0.2/0.3 mm. Some rounded pores < 0.1 mm; **colour**: 7.5YR 6/8 reddish yellow.
AD40 (Sparse glazed A and B ware from Rome/Latium)	Rome or Latium	Poggio Cavolo (second half of the 10th century CE) in context 1600 Poggio Cavolo (late 10th/early 11th century CE) Medieval hilltop village of Poggio Castellaccio (Osa valley) Medieval hilltop village of Punta Fortezza (Alma valley)	**Hardness**: hard; **breaking**: quite regular; **texture**: serial and homogeneous; very well-sorted; **inclusions**: in the order of 5–10%; size between 0.1/0.2 mm and 0.5 mm, with a mean size of 0.2 mm. A fragment of rock with an association of quartz and feldspar has a section of 1 mm. Presence of quartz grains, followed by feldspars, biotite and rare calcite, including secondary calcite; occasional dark inclusions (volcanic?) and rare iron oxides. Inclusions sub-angular and highly spherical; **porosity**: in the order of 10%, pores both round and elongated, measuring between 0.1 and 0.3 mm; **colour**: 7.5YR 6/8 reddish yellow.
Sel1 similar to AD2 (?)	(Northern?) Latium or subregional	Capalbiaccio (10th c. CE)	**Hardness**: quite hard; **breaking**: conchoidal; **texture**: hiatal and homogeneous; well-sorted; **inclusions**: in the order of 7–10%; inclusions measuring between 0.1 and 0.8 mm. Presence of quartz, iron oxides, calcite and feldspars, very occasional dark inclusions (volcanic?); **porosity**: in the order of 5%; prevalence of rounded pores measuring <0.1 mm; **colour**: 2.5YR 6/8 light red; occasional grey core 2.5YR 7/1 light reddish grey.
Sel1PCV (Poggio Cavolo)	Local or subregional	Poggio Cavolo (second half of the 10th century CE) Poggio Cavolo (late 10th/early 11th century CE)	**Hardness**: medium-hard; **breaking**: slightly irregular; **texture**: hiatal and homogeneous; very well-sorted; **inclusions**: in the order of 15–20%. Inclusions measuring between 0.5 and 2 mm, prevalently between 0.5 and 1 mm, sub-rounded and highly spherical. Quartz, including polycrystalline quartz, and rare iron oxides are attested; porosity: in the order of 15–20%, essentially rounded pores measuring on average 0.2–0.5 mm; **colour**: grey core: gley 2 6/1 bluish grey; surface: 2.5 YR 5/8 red.

Fabric	Possible source	Occurrence	Description
Sel4 (Poggio Cavolo)	Local or subregional	Poggio Cavolo (second half of the 10th century CE) Poggio Cavolo (late 10th/early 11th century CE)	**Hardness**: quite hard; **breaking**: quite regular; **texture**: hiatal and homogeneous; very well-sorted; **inclusions**: in the order of 10%. Inclusions measuring between 0.2 and 1.5 mm, prevalently between 0.5 and 1 mm, sub-rounded and highly spherical. Mainly quartz, with some feldspars; **porosity**: in the order of 20–25%, pores measuring between 0.2 and 2 mm, mainly elongated and orientated. The smallest pores are rounded. Mean size of 0.5 mm; **colour**: 7.5 YR light brown 6/4.
Sel8 (Poggio Cavolo)	Local or subregional	Poggio Cavolo (second half of the 10th century CE)	**Hardness**: quite hard; **breaking**: quite irregular; **texture**: hiatal and homogeneous; well-sorted; **inclusions**: in the order of 15–20%. Inclusions measuring between 0.5 and 1 mm, prevalence of those measuring 0.5 mm. Inclusions sub-rounded and highly spherical. Quartz and iron oxides; **porosity**: in the order of 25–30%, pores prevalently rounded and measuring 0.2–0.3 mm; **colour**: 5Y 7/3 pale yellow.
Sel30 (Poggio Cavolo)	Local or subregional	Poggio Cavolo (second half of the 10th century CE)	**Hardness**: hard; **breaking**: quite regular; **texture**: hiatal and homogeneous, well-sorted fabric; **inclusions**: in the order of 10–15%; inclusions measuring between 0.2 and 0.5 mm, prevalently 0.5 mm. Rare quartz measuring 1 mm. Inclusions sub-angular and highly spherical. Prevalence of quartz with some calcite crystals; porosity: in the order of 10–15%. Pores both rounded and elongated and orientated, measuring between 0.2 and 0.5 mm, prevalence of those measuring 0.2 mm; **colour**: grey core: gley 2 5/1 bluish grey; fracture and surface: 2.5 YR, 6/6 light red.
Sel43 (Poggio Cavolo)	Local or subregional	Poggio Cavolo (second half of the 10th century CE) Poggio Cavolo (late 10th/early 11th century CE)	**Hardness**: medium-hard; **breaking**: quite regular; **texture**: hiatal and homogeneous; well-sorted; **inclusions**: in the order of 10–15%. Inclusions measuring between 0.2 and 1 mm, mean size between 0.5 and 0.6 mm, sub-rounded and highly spherical. Larger quantities of quartz and feldspars, with some biotite and muscovite and secondary calcite. Rare iron oxides; **porosity**: in the order of 10–15%. Pores both rounded and elongated and orientated measuring between 0.1 and 0.3 mm; **colour**: 5YR 6/6 yellowish red.
Sel44 (Poggio Cavolo)	Local or subregional	Poggio Cavolo (late 10th/early 11th century CE)	**Hardness**: medium hard; **breaking**: quite irregular; **texture**: hiatal and homogeneous; well-sorted; **inclusions**: in the order of 15–20%. Inclusions measuring between 0.5 and <1 mm, mean size 0.5 mm, angular and highly spherical. Predominance of quartz, with some calcite crystals, chalk, feldspars and some iron oxides, muscovite (very rare); porosity: in the order of 10–15%. Pores elongated measuring between 0.5 and 1 mm, prevalence of those measuring 1 mm; **colour**: 10 YR 6/4 light yellowish brown.
Sel45 (Poggio Cavolo)	Local or subregional	Poggio Cavolo (late 10th/early 11th century CE)	**Hardness**: medium-hard; **breaking**: quite irregular; **texture**: hiatal and homogeneous; very well-sorted; **inclusions**: in the order of 15–20%. Inclusions measuring between 0.2 and 1.5 mm, modal value 0.5 mm. Abundance of calcite crystals, both quartz and feldspars are very well attested, mineral associations of quartz and feldspar and of feldspar and biotite were found, some iron oxides; porosity: in the order of 20%. Pores both round (0.1–0.2 mm) and elongated (0.3–0.5 mm) and orientated; **colour**: grey core: gley 2 6/1 bluish grey; surface: 5YR 6/6 reddish yellow.

APPENDIX 8.2: RATIO AMONG CERAMIC CLASSES FROM EARLY MEDIEVAL SITES

Site	Date of the analysed contexts	Ratio of *acroma depurata* and *acroma selezionata* wares versus kitchen ware	Predominant ware	Source
Donoratico	9th–11th CE	Among a total of 2132 processed potsherds, kitchen ware is overwhelming with some 1200 fragments	Kitchen ware	Grassi 2010
Campiglia Marittima	9th–10th CE	46% kitchen ware, 41% *acroma depurata* ware, 13% single-firing Sparse Glazed ware and painted ware altogether. Quantification based on a unspecified number of potsherds.	Balanced	Grassi 2010
Populonia, Acropoli	7th–9th CE	Only 18 *acroma depurata* vessels.	*Acroma depurata* ware	Grassi 2010
Rocchette Pannocchieschi	8th–10th CE	62% *acroma depurata* ware, 36% kitchen ware, 1% single-firing Sparse Glazed ware. Quantification based on 3750 potsherds.	*Acroma depurata* ware	Grassi 2010
Montemassi (data from four timber buildings and a rubbish dump)	8th–10th CE	62 fragments of kitchen ware, 24 fragments of storage vessels in purified fabrics, 15 fragments of table vessels in purified fabrics, and 12 fragments of spindle whorls. Quantification based on MNI.	Kitchen ware	Grassi 2010
Kiln sites near Roccastrada	8th–10th CE	265 fragments of *acroma depurata* and *acroma selezionata* wares, 17 fragments of kitchen ware, and 10 generic kiln wasters. Quantification based on the number of potsherds.	*Acroma depurata* and *selezionata* wares	Basile and others 2010
Podere Serratone	8th–9th CE	101 MNI of *acroma depurata* and *acroma selezionata* wares and 48 MNI of kitchen ware. Based on MNI	*Acroma depurata* and *selezionata* wares	Vaccaro 2011
San Martino *de plano*	9th–early 10th CE	66 MNI of *acroma depurata* and *acroma selezionata* wares and nine MNI of kitchen ware. Based on MNI	*Acroma depurata* and *selezionata* wares	Vaccaro 2011
Casa Andreoni (all four surface assemblages)	8th–9th CE	72 MNI of *acroma depurata* and *acroma selezionata* wares, 55 MNI of kitchen ware and one MNI of painted/*colature rosse* ware. Based on MNI	*Acroma depurata* and *selezionata* wares	Vaccaro 2011
Farmstead near Alberese	8th–9th CE	9 MNI of *acroma depurata* and *acroma selezionata* wares and 2 MNI of kitchen ware. Based on MNI	*Acroma depurata* and *selezionata* wares	Vaccaro 2011
Casa Steccaia (three dispersed houses)	8th–9th CE	17 MNI of *acroma depurata* and *acroma selezionata* wares and 2 MNI of kitchen ware. Based on MNI	*Acroma depurata* and *selezionata* wares	Vaccaro 2011

CHIARA VALDAMBRINI

9. A Comparative Study of Pottery from Southern Tuscany and Latium (1000–1200)

ABSTRACT This chapter, together with the previous chapter by Emanuele Vaccaro, deals with early medieval pottery from the late tenth century. Chiara Valdambrini discusses the pottery that signals a radical transition in the sphere of productions, in particular the treatment of the fabric, the use of decorative elements, and the appearance of sparse glaze, which are also symptoms of shifting tastes in vessel forms. The widening range of shapes, and the different types of inclusions in the fabric, indicate a demand for more varied products in the markets in which such wares circulated. Some fragments also evidence early forms of unglazed vessels that will lead to the double process of firing. These changes reflect the socio-economic transformation of the tenth century, setting the stage for glazed techniques. The sparse glazed wares are the early signs of contact with Rome, North Africa, and the Middle East in central Italy. Yet, it is premature to talk about trade, for another century passed before imported glazed pottery appeared in the archaeological record. The early attempt to cover the surfaces with glaze is a sign of new standards of hygiene, which demanded beautifully coloured, impermeable pottery as a substitute for wood and rough coarse fabrics. [MH]

Eleventh- and Twelfth-Century Pottery from Tricosto

Many issues germane to the study of the medieval pottery found at Capalbiaccio have already been addressed in the contribution to the discussion of tenth-century pottery (*infra* Vaccaro), particularly those related to the type of wares used and their dissemination and trade in southern Tuscany. Many trends from the tenth century can likewise be traced into the next two centuries, though certain new aspects arise. It is precisely in these two centuries (the eleventh and twelfth) that changes start to appear in the range of unglazed pottery, which will become more evident with the technical revolution that introduced tin-glazed products, as well as those that are lead-glazed and fired twice (*infra* Hobart).

According to the documents, Tricosto seems to have been dependent on Rome from 1152, with the Aldobrandeschi appearing to have arrived on the scene only in 1269.[1] However, archaeological data reveals even more details. Indeed, even before the tenth century, the same types of pottery were circulating in Pisa, Rome, and Capalbiaccio: there are close similarities between the ceramic fabrics of Tricosto and those found in the Forum of Nerva in Rome (*infra* Vaccaro). This situation also defines the next generation of ceramics from the eleventh and twelfth centuries. The eleventh- and twelfth-century material comes, above all, from Building J, Levels 3 and 4, but also from other samples, such as those from Buildings C, M, and T. It indicates that the same Aldobrandeschi circuits that passed through other areas of Tuscany also began appearing in Tricosto in the eleventh century, when the Aldobrandeschi family, originally from Lucca, was already deeply settled in southern Tuscany.

The second half of the twelfth century not only witnessed the complete reorganization of Aldobrandeschi rule, which culminated in the creation of their earldom, but also its territorial expansion. Historical research reveals that, although the Aldobrandeschi claimed rights of a varied type and magnitude over certain centres in northern Latium in the 1170s (pre-dating the death of Ildebrandino VII), these rights had different implications in rural areas of the Aldobrandeschi territory. In the centres, the rights of the count remained strong, even in the thirteenth century. However, due to the dearth of sources on the region (the area to the south and east of the Talamone-Magliano-Semproniano-Castell'Azzara line), it is difficult to determine whether the Aldobrandeschi family had already inserted itself there before the twelfth century.

---

1 Collavini 1998, 263.

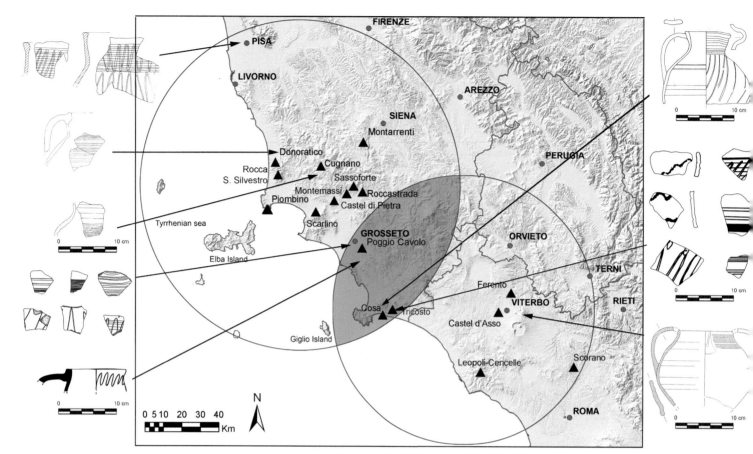

Figure 9.1. Comparative provenance from Latium and Tuscany. Map by author. Basemap/DTM reproduced with the permission of CTR Regione Toscana.

In the passage between the eleventh and twelfth centuries, products from the area of Pisa, such as storage jars, began to appear at Tricosto. Such evidence increases more consistently in the twelfth and thirteenth centuries, as the influence of the Aldobrandeschi grew in southern Tuscany. The Aldobrandeschi family contributed greatly to the proliferation of Pisan products in many of the excavated sites under their control. In this period, Pisa dominated the production and commerce of pottery vis-à-vis all other Tuscan cities, such as Siena (at least until the twelfth century). Pisan material, which has been found in many of the Tuscan strongholds examined, is datable to between the second half of the eleventh and the thirteenth century. Therefore, the presence of these products from Pisa at Tricosto does not seem accidental. The Pisan material shows that the pottery exchanges evident at Capalbiaccio in the eleventh through the thirteenth centuries reflect relatively long-distance and wide-ranging networks in central Italy, as well as other areas of the Mediterranean. In addition to this material, it would seem that the connection between Rome and Tricosto was also consistent throughout the period of the Aldobrandeschi family's presence at Capalbiaccio and beyond.

The eleventh and twelfth centuries represent a particular moment of radical change in pottery production. That moment is characterized by a shift between the production of local and mostly functional pottery to an increasingly larger scale, standardized production of pottery for export. The growth of strongholds transformed land seigniories into agents for this change in ceramic form between the eleventh and twelfth centuries. Such changes slowly built up through such formal experiments and, in the thirteenth century, resulted in the revolution of glazing techniques. The environment in which these changes took place resulted from a reorganization of the microeconomic system of manufacturing, combined with a sharp transformation in food production (Crader *infra*), which was, in turn, caused by the conversion of much pasture and wooded terrain into arable soil, leading to a significant addition of grain to the local diet.[2]

---

2 Grassi 2010, 28.

Ceramic Categories

What follows demonstrates and proportionally quantifies the documented transformation in the range of unglazed ceramic goods in the eleventh and twelfth centuries. It is notable that there is no record of significant formal change in vessels used for cooking and dispensing until the mid-twelfth century.

The various categories of ceramics used in daily life at the castle of Tricosto are here listed with their specific functions. Ceramics for cooking food — unpainted clay with inclusions in its fabric — are comprised of jugs (with single and double handles), plates for cooking bread (*testi* and *testelli*), *olle*, and lids. Ceramics for food preparation — unpainted and untreated in fabric without inclusions (levigated and semi-levigated clay) — consist only of colanders. Ceramics for dispensing and/or storing food — unpainted, untreated, and in semi-levigated clay — are made up of pitchers, jugs, and small amphora. Sparse glazed and red-painted wares are only represented by a small number of fragments related to closed forms (*infra* Vaccaro).

The Eleventh Century

Table and storage wares from the eleventh century are, for the most part, semi-levigated. Closed forms, such as three-lobed pitchers and small amphora (*amphoracei*), predominate within the morphological range. On the other hand, the kitchen ware exhibits both closed forms (*olle*) and open ones (*testi*). The products meant for storage are often burnished, either internally or externally, and, in some cases, a light glaze was applied to the terminal point of the vase or in threads that generally cover the vase's entire surface. Without archaeometric analyses, it is difficult to determine the exact provenance of these products, which, on a macroscopic level, reveal various levels of refinement in their ceramic bodies. Nonetheless, it seems plausible that they came from Latium or southern Tuscany, via a short-range system of circulation. On a technical level, one finds that the prevalence of products with a grey core starts to dwindle in the twelfth century, when they are replaced by objects fired in an oxidized environment with uniform colouration (Vaccaro *infra*).

In the eleventh and twelfth centuries, besides the more popular types of pottery, such as coarse ware and unglazed, purified ceramics, there were also objects decorated with dripped glazes. Fragments of such productions were few at Tricosto and all related to closed forms of small to medium size, displaying the influence of Latium (*infra* Vaccaro). The low incidence of these materials seems symptomatic of the marginal penetration of these products, which was possibly due to Capalbiaccio's distant location from principal centres of distribution. Sparse glazed follows a pattern of distribution similar to that found in other Tuscan contexts. While documented mainly at sites such as Campiglia Marittima[3] in the eleventh century, it is also found in small quantities at Scarlino, Donoratico, Rochette Pannocchieschi, Cugnano, and Rocca San Silvestro.[4] Despite the scant number of Sparse Glazed forms found at Capalbiaccio, they can be linked to two other nearby Tuscan sites, which reveal a significant presence of products from Latium: Cosa/Ansedonia[5] and Poggio Cavolo.[6] It would thus seem possible to draw a boundary between the areas south of Grosseto, where Sparse Glazed from Latium has been documented, and those to the north, where the technological and formal characteristics of pottery, combined with archaeometric surveys, point towards a provenance in regional ateliers instead, perhaps the same ones that produced levigated pottery in this period.

Samples of Sparse Glaze from other excavations suggest that there are no open vessels, lids, or pans. These single fired glazed products with strap handles were mostly used for domestic storage.

The lead glazes are normally yellow and randomly cover the exterior surface, leaving most of the vessel's fabric exposed. The shape of the spout suggests a provenance of Latium. However, identifying Sparse Glaze can be challenging due to the similarity of the levigated fabrics.

This particular practice is found also in other contexts, such as northern Latium when in the twelfth century most of the depurated wares were produced with a very similar fabric used for the sparse glazes. Similarly, in nearby Cosa the local shapes discovered have parallels, not only in Tuscany but to the north of Rome as well.[7] These productions end around the mid-thirteenth century.[8] Therefore, one can assume a sort of ideal separation between the coast with Latium shapes and those that formally recall contemporary local Tuscan productions.[9]

---

3 Grassi 2006.
4 Scarlino, Donoratico, Rochette Pannocchieschi, Cugnano, and Rocca San Silvestro.
5 Hobart 1992.
6 See *infra* Vaccaro, and Vaccaro and Salvadori 2006.
7 Hobart 1992.
8 Ricci 1990a, 288.
9 Grassi 1999.

The Twelfth Century

From the twelfth century, a record of the first profound redefinition of the Capalbiaccio's urban and political organization exists. Such changes had an impact on the range of pottery circulating in the region, which, at the century's close, was augmented by the addition of unrefined wares exported from Pisa, which were manufactured in shops that were most likely located in the countryside. In fact, Pisa had already developed its own form of industrialization by the eleventh century, building strong mercantile bases in areas outside of its direct political influence.[10] The aforementioned techniques, such as burnishing and threading, which appear in the pottery intended for external distribution, continue to appear. Examples of bleached surfaces and other decorative elements, such as long ripples (sinusoids) or parallel horizontal lines incised repeatedly with a sharp point, are not lacking.

The earliest forms of decoration incised before firing appear at Capalbiaccio in the eleventh century. These incisions can be either wavy or sinusoidal (a), and in a few cases with a sequence of U elements (b) which can be both intermittent and combined. Finally, there is also the more common decoration of incised parallel lines. The rims are tri-lobed.

Stamped impressions of a saw-toothed wheel (*infra* Hobart) and rosettes, which are sometimes repeated, are found on jug handles that are datable to the late twelfth century and throughout the thirteenth.[11] It is also noteworthy that smaller closed forms were developed only from the thirteenth century onwards. Typological changes occurred within the domain of the kitchen ware, but no differences in range were recorded.

One striking feature of the general traits of the morphological panorama lies in the absence of ceramic forms meant for the table. This lack could be imputed either to the fact that dishes of this sort were made from wood, or that into the twelfth century, people consumed food directly from kitchen ware. Tableware became widespread only in the thirteenth century, both at Capalbiaccio and throughout Tuscany (*infra* Hobart).

---

10 Berti and Menchelli 1998; Boldrini and others 2003.
11 Berti and Gelichi 1995; Boldrini and Grassi 1997. Sparse Glaze is found until the end of the thirteenth century along the Tyrrenic coast in Pisa, in Piazza Dante and Piazza dei Cavalieri (Abela 1993b and Abela 2000); Cosa (Hobart 1992); Scarlino and Rocca San Silvestro (Bernardi, Cappelli, and Cuteri 1992); Grosseto (Francovich and Gelichi 1980, 190).

CATALOGUE

Sparse Glazed Pottery

1. Pl. 9.1, no. 1

    Description: The side of a closed-form vessel, decorated with dripped yellow glaze.
    Material: Sparse Glazed pottery.
    Chronology: Eleventh–twelfth century.
    Context: Building J Pit M Level IV.
    References: In Rome (Paroli 1990), Sparse Glazed B, dated to the early eleventh century. On upper Latium, see Romei 1998, 138, dated to the eleventh–twelfth century.

2. Pl. 9.1, no. 2

    Description: 'Pelican' spout of jug, ovular shape and traces of olive-green lead glazed only on the body.
    Material: Sparse Glazed pottery.
    Chronology: Eleventh century.
    Context: OS 106.
    References: Material from Umbria and Latium. Hobart 1992, 5, 8, p. 305. Tav. 12 n. 1; Crypta Balbi 1985 p. 197.

Pottery Painted with Red Bands

3. Pl. 9.1, no. 3

    Description: The side of a closed form, decorated with three red bands.
    Chronology: Eleventh–twelfth century.
    Context: Building J Pit M Level IV.
    References: In Rome (Ricci 1990a), the type appears between the twelfth and thirteenth century, later than in Tuscany. In northern Lazio (Luttazi 1995), its date falls between the tenth and twelfth century. In Pisa, at the piazza Dante and piazza dei Cavalieri (Abela 1993b, 417, nos 8 and 9; Abela 2000, 120, no. 3), the type can be dated to the tenth–eleventh century. The ornamental bands are random and do not follow any pattern. For general survey (Cantini 2011).

9. A COMPARATIVE STUDY OF POTTERY FROM SOUTHERN TUSCANY AND LATIUM (1000–1200) 167

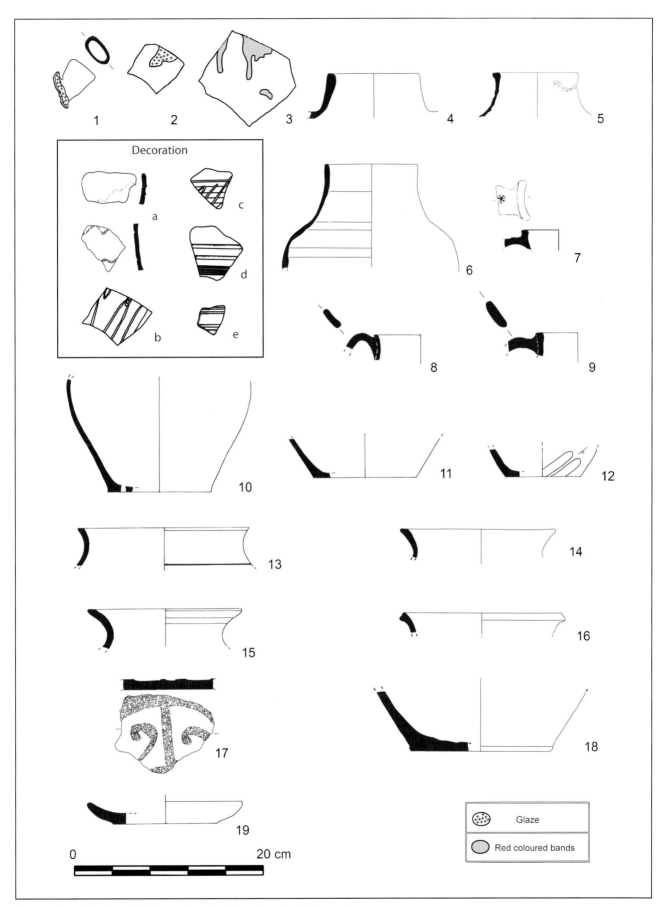

Plate 9.1. Capalbiaccio castle. Pottery from the eleventh and twelfth centuries.

Levigated and Semi-levigated, Unglazed Ceramic

4. Pl. 9.1, no. 4
Description: A water olla with a rim that is thicker on the inside and a short neck inclined towards the interior.
Dimensions: ⌀ jug, 9.5 cm.
Context: Building J Pit M Level IV.
References: Similar to Romei 1990, 268, no. 168, dated to the eleventh–twelfth century; on upper Latium, see Romei 1998, 131, dated to the eleventh–twelfth century; and Bartoloni and Ricci 1995, 104, no. 1, dated to the eleventh–twelfth century.

5. Pl. 9.1, no. 5
Description: Jug with flattened larger spout on an outward fleering neck, with thin body with thrown traces. It is decorated with incised horizontal undulated lines.
Dimensions: ⌀ jug, 10 cm.
Chronology: Eleventh century.
Context: Building J Pit M Level IV.
References: Paganelli, Mandarini, 'Note preliminari sulla ceramica commune', in *Le ceramiche di Roma e del Lazio* vol. III, p. 28, fig. 4.11.

6. Pl. 9.1, no. 6
Description: A pitcher with a barely swollen rim, tall conical neck, and distinct back.
Dimensions: ⌀ rim 9 cm.
Chronology: Twelfth century.
Context: Building J Trench 1 Level VI.
References: Similar to Ricci 1990a, 292, nos 231 and 232, dated to the twelfth century.

7. Pl. 9.1, no. 7
Description: A pitcher with a flat, rectangular rim, and a handle with an impressed seal 'a rosetta' with eight triangular petals. Parallels type IIIc (Berti Gelichi 1995).
Context: Building J Pit M Level IV.
Dimensions: ⌀ rim 8 cm; handle: breadth: 3.5 cm, thickness: 1 cm.
Chronology: Eleventh–twelfth century.
References: Similar to Menchelli 1993, 488, n. 13, dated to the late tenth–twelfth century; Liguori 2004, 127, pl. 2, no. 15, dated to the eleventh century; Cirelli and Hobart 2003, 333, fig. 147, no. 7.

8. Pl. 9.1, no. 8
Description: A jug with an everted rim, which is flat on top, a straight neck, and a raised handle strap.
Context: Building J Pit M Level IV.
Dimensions: ⌀ rim, 8 cm; handle: breadth: 2.5 cm; thickness: 0.6 cm.
Chronology: Tenth–twelfth century.
References: Similar to Menchelli 1993, 488, no. 13, dated to the late tenth–twelfth century; Liguori 2004, 127, pl. 2, no. 10, dated to the tenth–eleventh century; Berti and Gelichi 1995, type c; Boldrini and Grassi 1997, 356, nos 15, 17, 19; Boldrini and others 2003, 289, pl. VI; Valdambrini 2006, 476, no. 22, dated to the thirteenth century.

9. Pl. 9.1, no. 9
Description: A pitcher with a flat, rectangular rim, and a handle with a portion of its strap set beneath the rim.
Dimensions: ⌀ rim 10 cm; handle: breadth: 3.5 cm, thickness: 1 cm.
Chronology: Eleventh–twelfth century.
Context: Zone T Trench 8–10 Level IV.
References: Similar to Menchelli 1993, 488, n. 13, dated to the late tenth–twelfth century; Liguori 2004, 127, pl. 2, no. 15, dated to the eleventh century; Cirelli and Hobart 2003, 333, fig. 147, no. 7.

10. Pl. 9.1, no. 10
Description: A colander with no base, with perforations made in raw clay.
Dimensions: ⌀ rim 11 cm.
Chronology: Twelfth–thirteenth century.
References: Similar to Frazzoni and Vatta 1994, 78, fig. 7, nos 4–7, dated to the thirteenth century; Cantini 2003, 131, pl. 29, I.10.1 and I.10.2, dated to the twelfth–thirteenth century.

11. Pl. 1, no. 11
Description: A closed form with flattened base and slightly everted sides.
Dimensions: ⌀ rim 11 cm.
Context: Building J Pit M Level III.
Chronology: Twelfth century.
References: Similar to Ricci 1990a, 289, no. 220, dated to the twelfth century; Valdambrini 2006, 476, no. 22; Cantini 2003, 131, pl. 29, II.8.14; Liguori 2004, 127, pl. 2, no. 8.

12. Pl. 9.1, no. 12

Description: A closed form with flattened base and slightly everted sides; it has thin ribs and burnishing close to the base.
Dimensions: ⌀ rim 8 cm.
Context: Zone T Trench 8–10 Level IV.
References: Similar to Ricci 1990a, 289, no. 220, dated to the twelfth century; Bartoloni and Ricci 1995, 103, no. 2, dated to the eleventh–twelfth century; Cantini 2003, 131, pl. 29, II.8.9, dated to the twelfth–thirteenth century; Liguori 2004, 127, pl. 2, no. 4.

See insert in Pl. 9.1 for the 'Decorations'

a) **Description**: Decorated with undulated lines either horizontally or slanted, fashioned with a pointed tool before firing.
Context: Building J Pit M Level III.

b) **Description**: Decorated with sinusoidal lines fashioned with a pointed tool.
Context: Building J Pit M Level III.

c) **Description**: Decorated with a single, thin dotted sinusoidal line with fine filleting on the sides of the neck.
Context: Building M Level III.

d) **Description**: Decorated with bands of horizontal lines, with alternating comb-like rows.
Context: Building C Level III.
References: On the decoration, see Cirelli and Hobart 2003, 333, fig. 147; Liguori 2004, 128; Cantini 2003, 142; Boldrini and Grassi 1997, 356; Menchelli 1993, 484; Boldrini and others 2003, 294; Francovich and Gelichi 1980a, 131, pl. 29, no. 9; Valdambrini 2006, 476; Vaccaro and Salvadori 2006, 483.

e) **Description**: Decorated with intermittent bands of horizontal lines.
Context: Building C Level III.

Unglazed Coarse Ware

13. Pl. 9.1, no. 13.

Description: An olla with a flat border, elongated neck, and a globular body; comb-like border on the exterior.
Dimensions: ⌀ rim 18 cm.
Chronology: Tenth–late thirteenth century.
References: Found in many parts of Tuscany: one from a tenth–thirteenth-century context in Montarrenti (Roncaglia 1986, 272; Cantini 2003, 89, type I.7.7); in Campiglia Marittima (Grassi 2003, 281, pl. II, types 5 and 5a); in Rocca San Silvestro from the twelfth–thirteenth century (Boldrini and Grassi 1997, pl. I, no. 6); in Pisa, in the Piazza dei Cavalieri, dated to the first half of the eleventh century (Abela 2000, 184, figs 12 and 13, C.3.2); it is also documented at Castel di Pietra and Grosseto (unpublished).

14. Pl. 9.1, no. 14

Description: An olla with a flat rim and a short, straight neck.
Context: Zone T Trench 8–12 Level III.
Dimensions: ⌀ rim 17 cm.
Chronology: Eleventh–thirteenth century.
References: Found in Rocca San Silvestro, dated from the late eleventh–late thirteenth century (Boldrini and Grassi 1997, pl. I, no. 9); in Pisa, in Piazza Dante (Menchelli 1993, 433, fig. 21) from strata dated to the tenth–thirteenth century; and in Piazza dei Cavalieri between the late eleventh and the late twelfth century (Abela 2000, C.3.3, p. 184, fig. 17); it is also documented at Castel di Pietra (Gavorrano, GR) and Grosseto (unpublished).

15. Pl. 9.1, no. 15

Description: An olla with an everted rim and a barely noticeable indentation for a lid.
Dimensions: ⌀ rim 16 cm.
Chronology: Ninth–late twelfth century.
Context: Zone T Trench 8–12 Level III.
References: In Tuscany, similarities exist from Cosa (Cirelli and Hobart 2003, 333, fig. 149, no. 3); Montarrenti (Cantini 2003, 91, type I.7.8, and 98, type I.7.44); and in Donoratico (Grassi 2004, 121, pl. 1, no. 14).

16. Pl. 9.1, no. 16

Description: An olla with an everted and swollen rim.
Context: Building J Pit M Level III.
Dimensions: ⌀ rim 16 cm.
Chronology: Tenth–fourteenth century.
References: Found in Tuscany at Montarrenti (Cantini 2003, 100, type I.7.57, dated to the twelfth–fourteenth century); Poggibonsi (Francovich and Valenti 1997, 130–31, type M, dated to the mid-ninth–early tenth century); and in Sienese Chianti (Valenti 1995, 172, pl. XCII, no. 2, dated to ninth–eleventh century).

17. Pl. 9.1, no. 17

Description: *Testo* flattened with finger traced decoration made before firing.
Context: Building J Pit M Level IV.
Dimensions: NA.
Chronology: Twelfth century
References: Similar typologies are found in southern Maremma: Grosseto (Citter 2007b), Poggio Cavolo (Salvadori 2006).

18. Pl. 9.1, no. 18

Description: An olla with an apodal base and everted sides.
Context: Building J Pit M Level III.
Dimensions: ⌀ base 15 cm.
Chronology: Twelfth–fourteenth century.
References: Found in Tuscany at Montarrenti, although it is purified (Cantini 2003, 132, type II.8.16, dated to twelfth–fourteenth century).

19. Pl. 9.1, no. 19

Description: *Testo* with a wide flaring rim.
Dimensions: ⌀ cm 11; ⌀ with rim cm 16.
Context: Zone T Trench 8–12 Level III.
Chronology: Eleventh century.
References: Similar typologies are found for a long period; in Montarrenti are dated to the ninth century (Cantini 2003, type I.5.6 p. 84); while in Donoratico in the eleventh century (Grassi 2004 p. 121, Tav. 1, n. 28).

Conclusions

In order to better illustrate the changes and obvious signs of transformation, it can be suggested that two different cultures were present at Capalbiaccio in the final two decades of the twelfth century. The first relies on a local production basis and the second that was imported from northern Latium. With that said, it was possible to identify the picture of circulation of the goods, or at least the workshops, at different sites. In the case of Latium, the selected sites lay north of the capital, such as Viterbo,[12] Castel d'Asso,[13] Scorano,[14] as well as Rome itself.[15] In southern Tuscany, the sites analysed were Cosa/Ansedonia and Poggio Cavolo.[16] Distributional charts illustrating the various wares discovered at the sites were compared with published data with the chronotypology that emerged from the study of Tricosto.

To facilitate the analysis of the differences and similarities between the various wares, the distributional chart was subdivided into ceramic categories — levigated wares (*acroma depurata*)— and type of vessel — closed or open forms (Fig. 9.1). The agents of Tricosto's ties with other sites from the eleventh and twelfth centuries onward, visible in the aforementioned map, demonstrate that at first Tricosto was strongly influenced by the rising communal republic of Pisa and the powerful family of the Aldobrandeschi, who together initiated substantial networks of exchange, even over the borders of their territorial reach, and at places such as Cosa/Ansedonia and Capalbiaccio.[17]

---

12 Güll and others 2001, 286.
13 Güll and others 2001, 292.
14 Romei 1990.
15 Ricci 1990a.
16 Vaccaro and Salvadori 2006; Valdambrini 2010.
17 Cirelli and Hobart 2003; Hobart 1992.

MICHELLE HOBART

10. Medieval Pottery (1200–1400)

ABSTRACT The previous two chapters deal with the analysis of the early medieval village with tenth- to twelfth-century non-glazed pottery: the data from this chapter covers all of the later material from the thirteenth and fourteenth centuries. Before presenting the catalogue, a brief introduction of each typology will provide some background, followed by conclusive remarks contextualizing the findings. Most of the ceramics imported to Tricosto were from Pisa and Siena. By the middle of the thirteenth century a shift is evident, wherein production shifts from cities in the interior to those in the south, such as Orvieto and Viterbo. The most distant productions including some sporadic Ligurian Archaic graffita, came from the sea, North Africa (CoMn) and Spain (lustreware).

Most of the pottery excavated and herein presented reflects daily life in medieval Tuscany, and is found in both rural and urban contexts. The variations in productions show little differences if compared to other sites in Tuscany, and which are key to identify the provenance within quite a precise chronology. The sequence of the early medieval typologies of coarse and fine wares begins with the ninth and tenth century, and ends with imported and locally coarse, fine ware and glazed productions. Most of the pottery has striking parallels with the nearby settlement of Cosa-Ansedonia (eleventh to fourteenth century) and many other contemporary medieval settlements.[1]

Coarse ware productions served mainly as cooking vessels. The most common shapes are the *testi* and the *olle*, differing in function, depending on the type of food they contained. The most common find, the *testo*, was normally used for cooking bread and meats, and the shape differs depending on whether they were made by hand or on the wheel.[2] The shape generally consists of a flattened plate, varying slightly in the nature of the rim. One typical variation of *testi* found at Tricosto is distinguished by an engraved cross and a circle or a semicircle inside the plate, carved out with either a finger or a large, rounded stick. Most likely a local production, this decoration can be found all over the region, starting from the tenth until the thirteenth century (Fig. 10.1).

The closed and round cooking vessels, called *olle*, are similarly found all over central Italy. These pots were used for boiling and cooking soups and stews, and their variation in shape is established by the degree of roundness of their body, as well as the inclination and shape of their rims. These pots have slight variations to the standard type. They are covered by lids made from the same clay as the vessels, which could be adapted to fit over both *olle* and *testi*. Some lids were flat with a knob in the centre, while others were rounded with handles in the centre (Pl. 10.3). Contemporary to the coarse ware were other productions that served as fine tableware, with a levigated fabric and hardly any inclusions (Fig. 10.2).

By the thirteenth century, in central Italy, as in most of the Mediterranean, people's eating habits were radically changed by the use of glazed-ware products that provided for a new hygienic standard due to its impermeable surfaces. This revolutionary glazing process was re-introduced in Italy at the end of the tenth century from the Islamic world, mainly by Pisans who had vast trade contacts in the Mediterranean.[3] A handful of new typologies were imported from different areas, among them the cobalt and manganese (CoMn) frequently found in Tuscany, which arrived in Sicily and Pisa from the Maghreb and distributed far and wide in the Mediterranean, and was distinguished by the strong contrast between its black and blue glaze over a white slip. This North African production was traded all over the Tyrrhenian Sea, providing secure dating (1175–1250) of sealed archaeological

---

1 Hobart 1991; Hobart 1992; Cirelli and Hobart 2003.
2 Pecci 2004; Pecci 2009.

3 Berti, Renzi Rizzo, and Tangheroni 2004; Berti, 2003; Berti, Gelichi, and Mannoni, 1997.

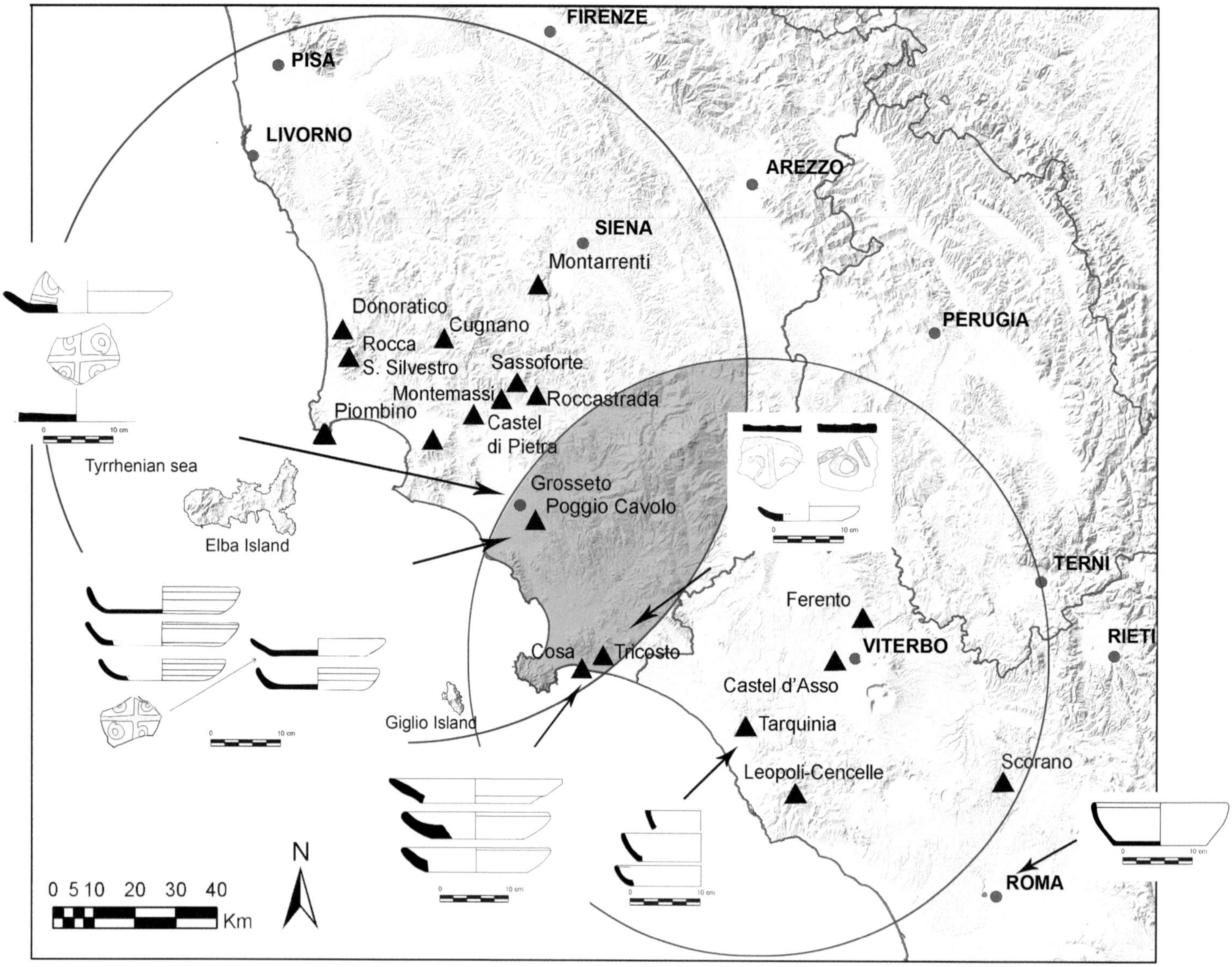

Figure 10.1. Map of Tuscany and Latium kitchen coarse-ware open shape. Figure by the author. Map by Chiara Valdambrini. Basemap/DTM reproduced with the permission of CTR Regione Toscana.

deposits containing such material.[4] Between Cosa and Ansedonia, not more than a handful of fragments have been found. CoMn is consistent in most excavations along the Tyrrhenian coast, although in small quantities.

It took a few generations for local Italian productions to increasingly substitute the imported glazed pottery, by inverting the trend and flooding Mediterranean harbours. Pisa became among the first major centres for archaic majolica, producing its own glazed pottery starting in the early thirteenth century (1210–1230). Pisan majolica thus became the most common circulating table ware, especially in central Italy, and increasingly replaced imports from other Mediterranean countries.[5]

Glazed pottery made out of a finer fabric and a double-firing technique was meant for serving and entertainment, and in smaller amounts to decorate Pisan, Tuscan, and Sardinian churches (*bacini*). Unlike the locally produced coarse ware, all of the glazed ceramics excavated at Tricosto were purchased elsewhere and imported to Capalbiaccio. The glaze

---

4 Cobalt and Manganese appeared at first as an architectural element on churches, both in Tuscany and in Sardinia, but soon after it was found in private domestic contexts and ecclesiastical institutions in both cities and in the countryside. Hobart 2010.

5 Berti and Giorgio 2011.

10. MEDIEVAL POTTERY (1200–1400)   173

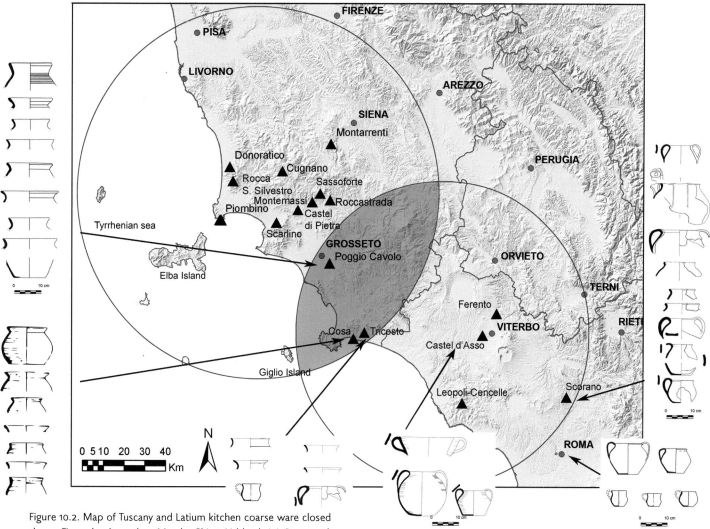

Figure 10.2. Map of Tuscany and Latium kitchen coarse ware closed shape. Figure by the author. Map by Chiara Valdambrini. Basemap/DTM reproduced with the permission of CTR Regione Toscana.

covering the surface consisted of either lead (*majolica*) or tin glaze (*graffita*), the difference being that the lead glaze was applied immediately over the *biscotto*, while the tin glaze was cooked twice — the first after the graffito decoration, and the second with the painted decoration.[6]

Another common transportation vessel — also from Pisa and often associated with archaic majolica — were the small, unglazed amphorae or *brocchette pisane*. These liquid containers were made out of fabrics with hardly any inclusions and a strap handle frequently marked with easily recognizable, impressed seals. The seals indicate different workshops and have a long history, as can be seen in the previous pottery chapters (*infra* Vaccaro, Valdambrini). Besides Pisan pottery, at Capalbiaccio there was also a significant group of green archaic majolica from Siena (*famiglia verde*; (Fig. 10.3a,b). This style of pottery was soon after substituted by other archaic majolica productions when trade shifted south towards Orvieto and Viterbo (Fig. 10.4).

These southern products replaced northern Tuscan pottery with new decorative patterns. However, towards the end of the thirteenth or early fourteenth century, another new technique was introduced, which used a thick layer of cobalt blue pigment over white tin slip; called *zaffera a rilievo*, and most likely produced in Viterbo, this was the last glazed product that served the inhabitants of Tricosto before the destruction and abandonment of the castle.

While archaic Pisan majolica became the common tableware in the thirteenth century, another new

---

6 For an introduction to the glazing techniques used in Italy during the Middle Ages, see Berti, Gelichi, and Mannoni 1997, 383–403.

174 MICHELLE HOBART

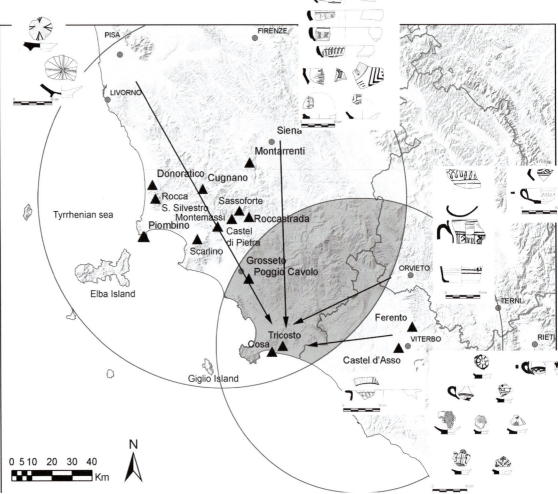

Figure 10.3. Map of Tuscany and Latium Archaic majolica drawings. Figure by the author. Map by Chiara Valdambrini. Basemap/DTM reproduced with the permission of CTR Regione Toscana.

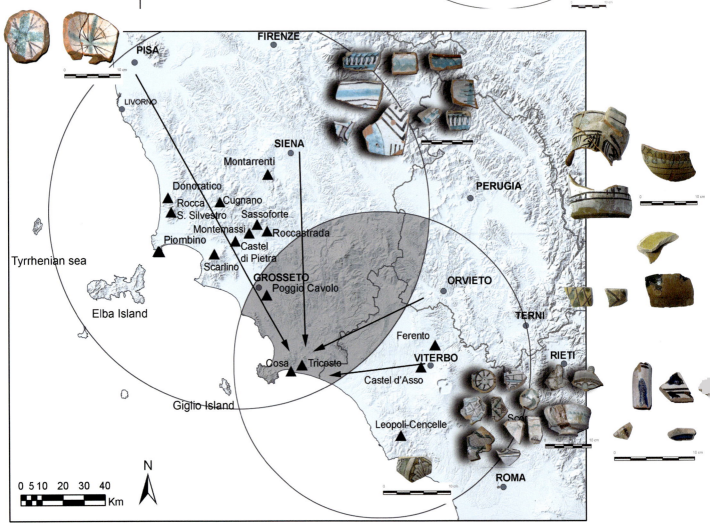

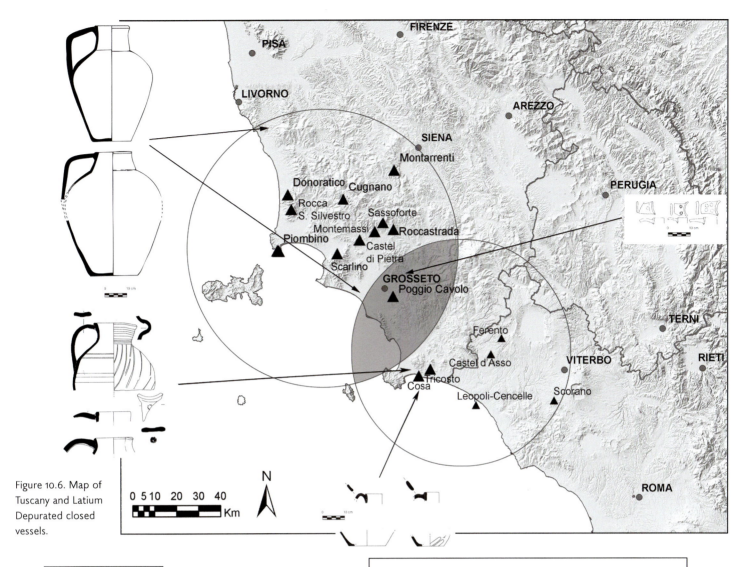

Figure 10.6. Map of Tuscany and Latium Depurated closed vessels.

Figure 10.4. Latium Archaic majolica from Viterbo. Photo by author.

Figure 10.5. Spain lustreware from Manises and Paterna. Photos by author.

Figure 10.7. Tuscany Archaic majolica handles. Photos by author.

Figure 10.8. Viterbo *zaffera a rilievo*.

Italian production appeared rather commonly in the markets from the maritime republics of Genoa and Savona. The Ligurian *graffita arcaica*, made with a double firing process typical for this tin-glazed, graffito plate, competed in smaller numbers and scale with Pisa, but circulate around the same trade routes. Archaic majolica and *graffita tirrenica* became the two major domestic products found in excavations, both in urban contexts, as well as in the countryside in central Italy and further abroad.

The distribution and associations of the different pottery typologies excavated on site are consistent with those found in other southern Tuscan settlements, such as those around Siena (Montarrenti,[7] Poggibonsi[8]) and in the Grosseto region,[9] (Poggio Cavolo,[10] Scarlino,[11] Campiglia Marittima,[12] Rocca San Silvestro[13]), to name a few.

Other imports from Spain are frequently found on archaeological sites on the Tyrrenian coast. The hard-to-replicate formulas used to fabricate Spanish lustreware resulted in imitations that were not always successful. Lustreware, also known as primitive Malagueño, was mainly imported from two centres in the Valencia area (Manises and Paterna), and dated to the end of the fourteenth century (Fig. 10.5). Ansedonia, as well as many of the other excavated castles along the coast, also had a few similar pieces.[14]

POTTERY CATALOGUE

Coarse Ware

Each sample was analysed macroscopically and described with its inclusions, by the texture of the fabric, the surface, the glazes, the type of fracture, and the technique — either on a wheel or by hand. The variance of the colour is described in broad terms, since the distinction may be subjective and is not necessarily an identifying element. In fact, most of the coarse ware was overly exposed to fire, changing and altering the original colour of the surfaces. The basic differences, however, are worth mentioning, because it helps to identify the original source of the clay: red/orange if containing ferrous elements (iron), or whitish/beige if the clay was taken from a limestone or calcareous quarry. The ideal procedure would integrate this data with proper mineralogical analysis, but this did not take place. Unfortunately, no whole vessel survives, so that distinctions rely exclusively on the fabric and their shape and known parallels. A brief description of each fabric will summarize the main characteristic that distinguishes one from the other. Finally, there may be some overlap or repetition with some of those fabrics researched by Vaccaro and Valdambrini (*infra*), as some of the local productions tend to last through the centuries.

---

7 Cantini 2003.
8 Valenti 1996.
9 Citter 2007a.
10 Salvadori and others 2006.
11 Francovich 1985.
12 Bianchi 2003c.
13 Grassi 1999.
14 Berti and Tongiorgi 1985; Molinari 1990; Hobart 1991.

Testi

Fabric 1 (Pl. 10.1–10.2). A very porous clay with random small inclusions of calcite, augite, and quartz. The colour ranges from dark orange to dark leather. The shape of the *testi* varies from completely flat to almost vertical rims, which are both rounded and pointed. The technique is mixed: thrown, and in some cases, while finished by hand in others. The large amount of this fabric suggests a local workshop and a common source of clay. One type of rimless *testo* stands out for the cross decoration placed inside the plate, which has many parallels from other excavations (see above notes 7–13). The fact that different fragments have been found in two different levels (II and IV) suggests that in some cases the two levels can be unified. This particular fabric (no. 1) has been found in all medieval layers (Levels I–IV). Many of these shapes are also found at Ansedonia.

Pl. 10.1, no. 1

Description: Testo 0S71. Rounded rim. Thick bottom and rim, with a traced line on the exterior.
Material: Coarse ware.
Chronology: Thirteenth century.
Context: 8S 145=Bld. M Pit 16 Wall cleaning.

Pl. 10.1, no. 2

Description: Small testo, rounded inwards, with a slanted rim.
Material: Coarse ware.
Chronology: Thirteenth century.
Context: 8S142=Bld. M Level I.

Pl. 10.1, no. 3

Description: Testo 0S71. Flattened, slanted rim. Thick bottom and rim, with a traced line on the exterior.
Material: Coarse ware.
Chronology: Thirteenth century.
Context: 8S 145=Bld. M Pit 16 Wall cleaning.

Pl. 10.1, no. 4

Description: Testo, large with pointed rim.
Material: Coarse ware.
Chronology: Thirteenth century.
Context: 8S 111=Bld. M Pit 9 W. ext. Level II (466–78 cm).

Pl. 10.1, no. 5

Description: Large testo and thick bottom.
Material: Coarse ware.
Chronology: Thirteenth century.
Context: 0S127=Zone R Level II (storage pit).

Pl. 10.1, no. 6

Description: Testo with a tall flaring rounded rim.
Material: Coarse ware.
Chronology: Thirteenth century.
Context: 8S4=Bld. J Level III.

Pl. 10.1, no. 7

Description: Testo with a tall flaring rounded rim.
Material: Coarse ware.
Chronology: Thirteenth century.
Context: 8S162=Bld. J Pit I/II Level III.

Pl. 10.2, no. 1

Description: Testo with a flaring rim.
Material: Coarse ware.
Chronology: Thirteenth century.
Context: 0S32=Zone M Trench 8–1 Level IV.

Pl. 10.2, no. 2

Description: Testo with very thick bottom and pointed, almost vertical rim.
Material: Coarse ware.
Chronology: Thirteenth century.
Context: 8S82=Bld. J Pit II Level III.

Pl. 10.2, no. 3

Description: Testo, practically flattened with rounded borders.
Material: Coarse ware.
Chronology: Thirteenth century.
Context: 0S71=Zone J Trench 8–11 Level III.

Pl. 10.2, no. 4

Description: Testo, flat bottom with incised grooves. Four quadrants with a simple motif inside.
Material: Coarse ware.
Chronology: Thirteenth century.
Context: Bld. J Pit 11–1 Level III (638–66 cm).
References: Similar testo with only a cross was found at Poggibonsi and dated to the thirteenth or early fourteenth century. See Valenti 1996, Tav. XXV, 1, p. 278; *infra* Valdambrini.

Pl. 10.2, no. 5

Description: Testo, flat bottom with incised grooves. The decoration seems to divide the plate in quadrants, with a circle inside.
Material: Coarse ware.
Chronology: Thirteenth century.
Context: 0S15=Bld. J Pit 11/1 Level IV.

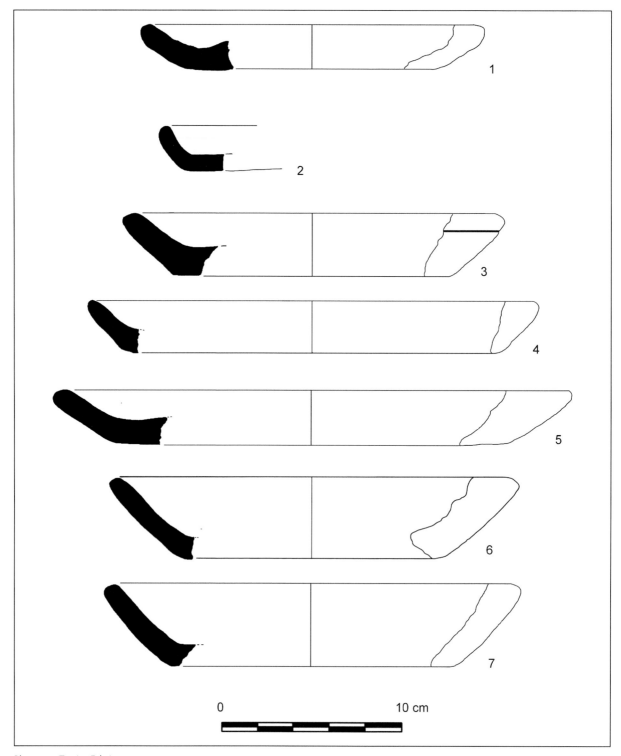

Plate 10.1. Testi – Fabric 1.

10. MEDIEVAL POTTERY (1200–1400) 179

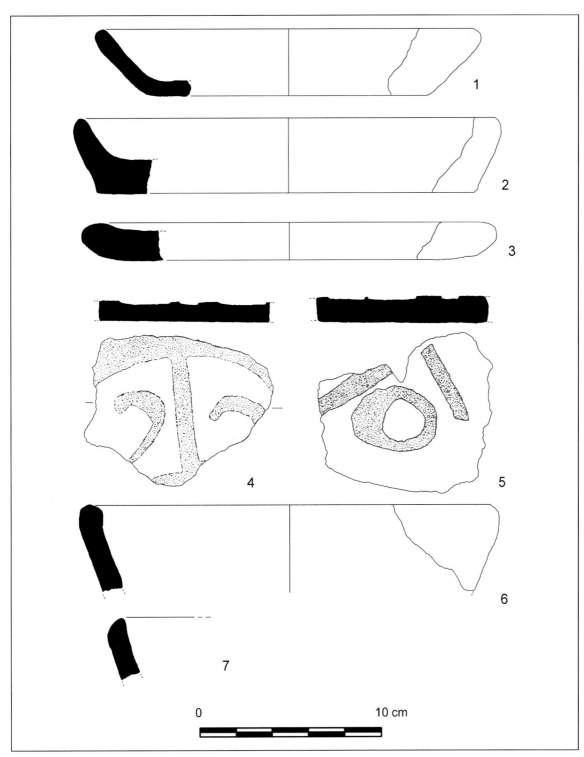

Plate 10.2. Testi – Fabric 1.

Pl. 10.2, no. 6

Description: Testo or lid with a vertical rim rounded inwards.
Material: Coarse ware.
Chronology: Thirteenth century.
Context: 8S85=Bld. J Pit 11 Level IV.

Pl. 10.2, no. 7

Description: Testo or lid with an almost vertical rim slanted outwards.
Material: Coarse ware.
Chronology: Thirteenth century.
Context: Bld. J Trench 1 Level VI.

Lids and Closed Shapes (Pl. 10.3)

Fabric 2 (Pl. 10.3–10.4). This is a variation of fabric no. 1 with larger inclusions, and a hard and less porous fabric, but similar to fabric no. 1 in texture. The colour is dark leather leading towards rust or dark orange. The surface is smooth with traces of fingerprints. Both internally and externally there are traces of fine lines or *filettatura*. Thrown technique. There are *testi*, lids, and smaller closed containers (*ollette*). All of the lids are similar in shape, made from the same fabric, and in most cases their diameter could cover pots (*olle*) and pans (*tegami*). Unfortunately, traces of the lids' handles do not survive. These profiles were generally rounded or square and differ slightly from the *testi* (of fabric 1) in height (taller) and thickness (reduced). The fact that the clay is not burnt, like the rest of the *testi*, strengthens the lid hypothesis. However, there is a chance these were unused *testi*. Certain pieces (Plates 10.3.9, 10.3.10, and 10.4.6) have been overcooked, as can be seen in the grey section, while the exterior colour is again orange with evenly burnt traces. This fabric is found on the surface and Levels I–V. Of 17 fragments, 9 (the majority) come from Level II.

Pl. 10.3, no. 1

Description: Angled, flaring, rounded rim.
Material: Coarse ware.
Chronology: Thirteenth century.
Context: 8S85=Bld. J Pit 2 cleaning.

Pl. 10.3, no. 2

Description: Rounded testo with inwards rim.
Material: Coarse ware
Chronology: Thirteenth century.
Context: 8S131=Bld.5 Pit 14 W. ext. Level I.
References: Grassi 2010, fig. 32, n. 5a, b, c.

Pl. 10.3, no. 3

Description: Lid facing inwards with an almost vertical rim.
Material: Coarse ware.
Chronology: Thirteenth century.
Context: 8S99=Bld. M Pit 9 Level II.

Pl. 10.3, no. 4

Description: Small closed container (*olletta*) with vertical, pointed rim flaring outwards.
Material: Coarse ware.
Chronology: Thirteenth century.
Context: 8S146 Bld. M Pit 17, Level II; another similar closed fragment was found in 8S146=Bld. M Pit16, Level II (ex. S7).

Pl. 10.3, no. 5

Description: Large rounded lid with an almost vertical rim, flattened and slanted outwards. Three incised lines are traced on the exterior.
Material: Coarse ware.
Chronology: Thirteenth century.
Context: 8S99=Bld. M Pit 9 Level II.

Pl. 10.3, no. 6

Description: Small lid of an *olletta* with rounded rim.
Material: Coarse ware.
Chronology: Thirteenth century.
Context: Bld. J Pit 17 W. ext. Level II.

Pl. 10.3, no. 7

Description: Open lid with pointed rim slanted outwards.
Material: Coarse ware.
Chronology: Thirteenth century.
Context: 8S142=Bld. M Pit 16, Level II (ex S7).

Pl. 10.3, no. 8

Description: Small *olle* or *olletta* with an outwards pointed or hooked rim.
Material: Coarse ware.
Chronology: Thirteenth century.
Context: 8S85=Bld. J Pit 2 Level II.

Pl. 10.3, no. 9

Description: Small *olle* with flaring rim.
Material: Coarse ware.
Chronology: Thirteenth century.
Context: 8S154=Bld. J Pit 17 Level II.

10. MEDIEVAL POTTERY (1200–1400) 181

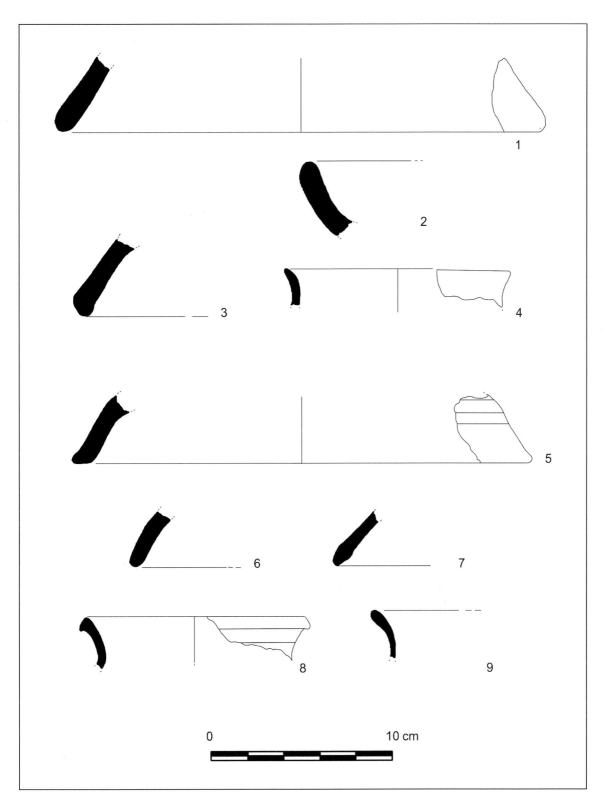

Plate 10.3. Lids and closed shapes – Fabric 2.

Pl. 10.4

This family of *testi* are variations of the same type listed above and probably from the same workshop. The best parallels come from the area around Campiglia Marittima.[15] These productions appear by the end of the twelfth century and continue to be produced in the thirteenth century.

Pl. 10.4, no. 1

Description: Testo with pointed rim slanted outwards.
Material: Coarse ware.
Chronology: Thirteenth century.
Context: 0S151=NA.

Pl. 10.4, no. 2

Description: Testo with rim slanted outwards.
Material: Coarse ware.
Chronology: Thirteenth century.
Context: 0S 118=Zone M Trench 8–2 Level II.

Pl. 10.4, no. 3

Description: Testo with pointed and flattened rim. Line across the middle on ext.
Material: Coarse ware
Chronology: Thirteenth century.
Context: 0S101=Zone R storage pit Level II.

Pl. 10.4, no. 4

Description: Testo; complete profile with rounded rim. Fabric similar to fabric 1, but the inclusions are larger and the surface is less porous. The colour shifts from dark leather to rusty. Finger prints are visible on the smooth surface both internally and externally, with lines traced by the thrown technique.
Material: Coarse ware.
Chronology: Thirteenth century.
Context: 8S57=Bld. J Pit 1S Level II (722–33).

Pl. 10.4, no. 5

Description: Testo, profile with pointed and faceted rim.
Material: Coarse ware.
Chronology: Thirteenth century.
Context: 0S43=Zone J Trench 8–6 Level V (1.4 m).

---

15 Grassi 2010, fig. 9 I.1 and 29.

Fabric 3 (Pl. 10.5). The small inclusions of quartz, augite, and calcite differ only in colour between fabric 1 and 2, being a clearer beige and leading towards pink. The clay is compact and less porous than fabric 1. Different styles of lids, pans, and pots (*olle*) are made out of this fabric. The shape of Pl 10, no. 2 (the flattened lid) is extremely practical, as it fits with every type of pot and pan, but it differs from the more traditional rounded type seen in Pl. 10.4 and found in other contexts on site. The rim shapes of the *testi* are similar in this group, being squared and flattened. Two *testi* have a complete profile, and could have been made by wheel and finished by hand. The bottom is very thick, compared to the vertical rims, which are thinner towards the ends. The other shape made in this fabric consists of low, thick pans and small pots (*tegami* and *ollette*). Some of the fragments of this group show calcareous residuals. They are present in Levels I, II, and III.

Pl. 10.5, no. 1

Description: Large pan with flattened rim. A flat lid could have covered the top. Similar clay to Fabric 1 and 2, but the colour differs, being quite clear beige leading towards pink. It is more compact and less porous than fabric 1. It was thrown quickly with almost invisible craft lines.
Material: Coarse ware.
Chronology: Thirteenth century.
Context: 8S112=Bld. M Pit 9 W. ext. Level II (478–83 cm).

Pl. 10.5, no. 2

Description: Flat lid for pans or *olle*.
Material: Coarse ware.
Chronology: Thirteenth century.
Context: 8S147=Bld. M Pit 16 Level II (494 cm).

Pl. 10.5, no. 3

Description: Pan with flattened rim.
Material: Coarse ware.
Chronology: Thirteenth century.
Context: 8S147=Bld. M Pit 16 Level II.

Pl. 10.5, no. 4

Description: Pan slightly larger than the previous, with flattened rim.
Material: Coarse ware.
Chronology: Thirteenth century.
Context: 8S147=Bld. M Pit 16 Level II.

Pl. 10.5, no. 5

Description: Testo profile with pointed and flattened rim.
Material: Coarse ware.
Chronology: Thirteenth century.
Context: 8S143=Bld. M Pit 16 Level I.

10. MEDIEVAL POTTERY (1200–1400) 183

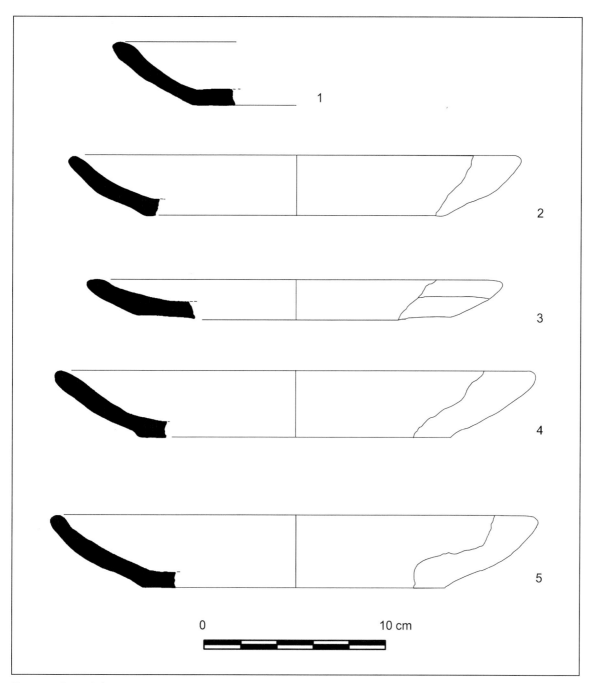

Plate 10.4. Testi – Fabric 2.

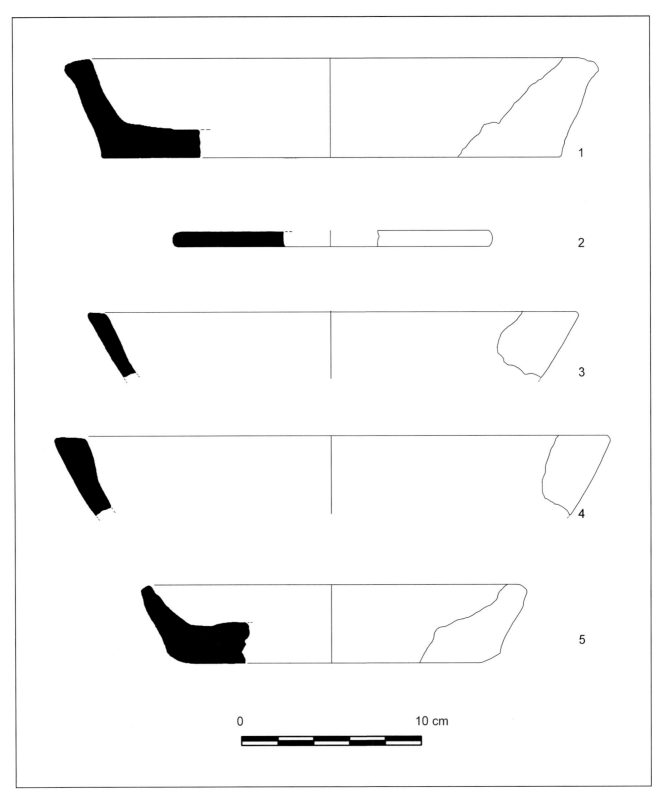

Plate 10.5. Lids and closed shapes – Fabric 3.

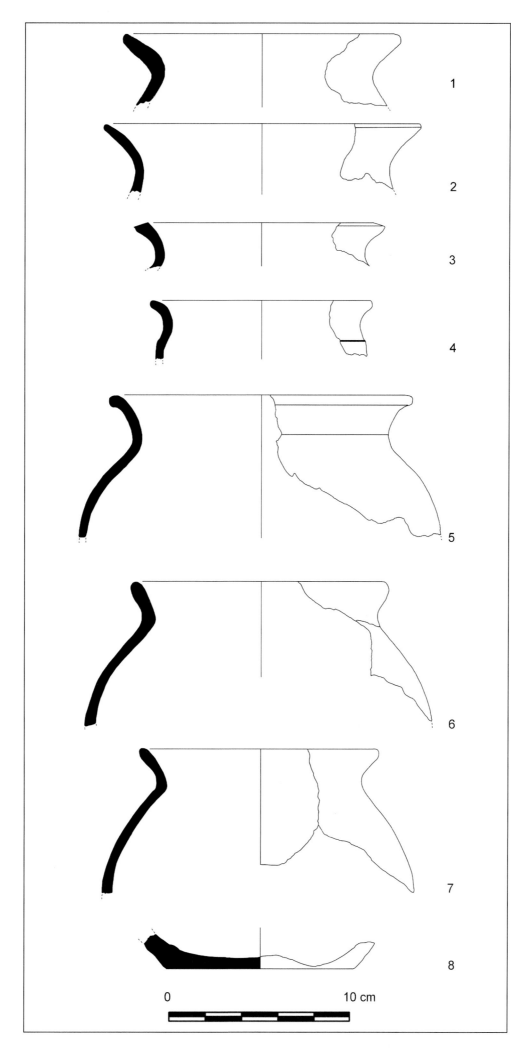

Plate 10.6. Closed shapes: *Olle* – Fabric 4.

Fabric 4 (Pl. 10.6). This fabric is mixed with small and medium augite, calcite, and quartz inclusions. Both internal and external surfaces have thin and frequent lines over the entire body, which is a result of the thrown wheel technique. The clay has a reddish exterior and has burnt black traces inside. All of the samples have flared rims and are either cut horizontally or rounded. Distinct is the way the rims of some of the *olle* are decorated with a tool. Fabric 4 is present in Levels III, IV, and VI.

Pl. 10.6, no. 1

Description: Olla with flaring rim.
Material: Coarse ware.
Chronology: Thirteenth century.
Context: 8S 143=Bld. M wall cleaning.

Pl. 10.6, no. 2

Description: Olla with pointed rim defined by tool, with a line around the neck.
Material: Coarse ware.
Chronology: Thirteenth century.
Context: 8S80=Bld. J Pit III Level IV (673–77 cm).

Pl. 10.6, no. 3

Description: Small olla with thick, flaring rim, cut horizontally by a tool.
Material: Coarse ware.
Chronology: Thirteenth century.
Context: 0S57=Zone J Trench 8–6 cleaning surface of previous year's excavation.

Pl. 10.6, no. 4

Description: Small olla with an exterior line below the neck. Similar to the larger Pl. 6 no. 6, but on a smaller scale.
Material: Coarse ware.
Chronology: Thirteenth century.
Context: 0S38=Zone J Trench 8–6 Level III.

Pl. 10.6, no. 5

Description: Large olla with outwards rounded rim with two exterior lines, one defining the rim and the second at the tightest point of the neck of the vessel.
Chronology: Thirteenth century.
Context: 8S80=Bld. J Pit III Level IV (673–77).

Pl. 10.6, no. 6

Description: Olla with flaring rim. The internal and external surface has undetectably thin lines over the entire body. The rim is rounded and the colour of the clay is reddish outside and black inside, with burnt traces all over.
Material: Coarse ware.
Chronology: Thirteenth century.
Context: Bld. J Pit II/I Level IV.

Pl. 10.6, no. 7

Description: Olla with flaring rim, similar to the composition of the sample above.
Material: Coarse ware.
Chronology: Thirteenth century.
Context: 6S38=Trench 2 Level VI.

Pl. 10.6, no. 8

Description: Base of an olla.
Material: Coarse ware
Chronology: Thirteenth century.
Context: 0S57=Zone J Trench 8–6 cleaning. Another olla with no drawing comes from 8S 157. Bld. J Pit 17 (1, W. Ext.) wall cleaning.

Fabric 6 (Pl. 10.7). The colour of the clay is beige. Very similar to fabric 3, it has the same quartz, augite, and calcite inclusions. The rough surface wears out in a more porous way and the dimension of the inclusions are larger. There are traces of fingerprints from the throwing wheel. All of the pottery comes from Levels IV and V. While the profiles of the finds appear to be of a later date, the fabric is clearly different from fabric 3, which is associated with thirteenth- and fourteenth-century pottery.

Pl. 10.7, no. 1

Description: Pointed rim of an olla.
Material: Coarse ware.
Chronology: Thirteenth century.
Context: 8S111=Bld. M Pit 9 W. ext. Level II (466–78 cm).

Pl. 10.7, no. 2

Description: Rim of an olla flared outward.
Material: Coarse ware.
Chronology: Thirteenth–fourteenth century.
Context: Bld. J Bulk I/II Level IV.

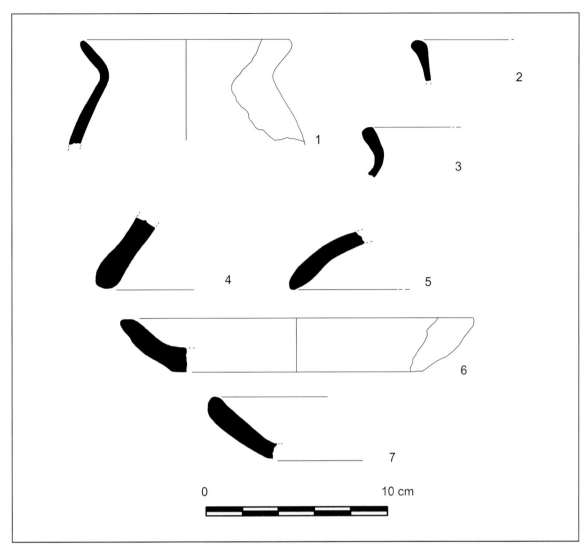

Plate 10.7. Lids and closed shapes – Fabric 6.

Pl. 10.7, no. 3

    Description: Rounded rim of an olla.
    Material: Coarse ware.
    Chronology: Thirteenth–fourteenth century.
    Context: Bld. J Bulk I/II Level IV.

Pl. 10.7, no. 4

    Description: Rim of a lid.
    Material: Coarse ware.
    Chronology: Thirteenth century.
    Context: Bld. J Bulk I/II Level IV (666–79 cm).

Pl. 10.7, no. 5

    Description: Rim of a lid, rather similar to fabric 6.7 and 6.8 (above).
    Material: Coarse ware.
    Chronology: Thirteenth century.
    Context: Bld. J Bulk I/II Level IV.

Pl. 10.7, no. 6

    Description: Testo, complete profile. While the fabric is similar to fabric 3 (Pl. 5) the surface is rough and porous and erosion exposes the inclusions. Almost vertical, the rim is cut horizontally and smaller towards the end. Traces of fingerprints are visible on the exterior.
    Material: Coarse ware.
    Chronology: Twelfth–thirteenth century.
    Context: 6S28=Bld. J Level V.

Pl. 10.7, no. 7

    Description: Testo, complete profile with rounded rim.
    Material: Coarse ware.
    Chronology: Twelfth–thirteenth century.
    Context: Bld. J Trench 6–8 Level V.

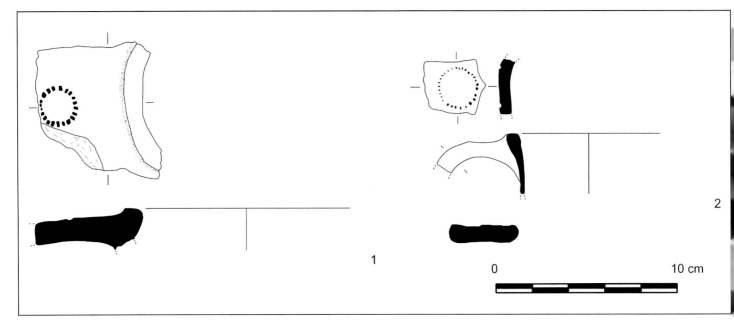

Plate 10.8. Fine wares or Depurated Fabrics.

Fine Wares or Depurated Fabrics (Pl. 10.8)

This type of container, a pitcher, often with trefoil spout, was produced for over three hundred years and is found frequently in central Italy (*infra* Valdambrini). Pisa, in particular, but also Siena, exported similar vessels, which are normally identified (due to their long-lasting production cycle) by the pottery they are associated with as well as by the impressed stamp, which was more or less deeply applied against the surface of the rim before firing. These seals, or workshop signatures, vary in diameter and symbol. The earlier stamp is comprised of a circle with small triangles meeting at the centre (Pl. 10.9, no. 3) and dates to the late twelfth or early thirteenth century. The most common stamp is called the *rosetta* type (*infra* Valdambrini, Pl. 9.1, no. 7), and dates to the middle of the thirteenth century. The nearby site of Cosa also has a large number of these pitchers, which have been divided into sub-types and different sizes. These variants are decorated with wavy lines incised along the neck and sometimes the body, as well.[16]

Berti and Gelichi (1995), who have classified among the largest groups of similar finds from Pisa and elsewhere, provide parallels for the stamped impressions, the most common of which is type Ia: a wheel made out of teeth pointed towards the centre (Fig. 10.6). On site at Capalbiaccio, two samples vary in the number of teeth (21 and 30). Another similar type is IIIb, a small, stylized five-pointed 'rosetta', thus the name. It seems plausible to date this common production to the thirteenth century, while the earlier types (*infra* Valdambrini) start at the end of the eleventh or twelfth century and are dated mainly by their association with pre-glazed productions.[17]

Pl. 10.8, no. 1

Description: Pitcher with flat rim and attachment of a strap handle. Stamp of an indented circle on the upper side of the handle.
Material: Coarse ware.
Chronology: Thirteenth century.
Context: (0S 69=Zone C Trench 8–3, cleaning Gate).
References: Made in Pisa, thirteenth century. Berti, Gelichi 1995, Tav. 1, 2; 13 tipo 1a (Tav. 13, n. 1).

Pl. 10.8, no. 2

Description: Handle of a liquid container smaller than the one above, but with same stamp, not as deeply impressed.
Material: Coarse ware.
Chronology: Thirteenth century.
Context: (0S 45=Zone M Trench 8–9 Level II).
References: Pisa, thirteenth century. Berti, Gelichi 1995, Tav. 1, 2; 13 tipo 1a (Tav. 13, n. 2).

---

16 Cirelli and Hobart 2003, 331–33.

17 For Donoratico, see Grassi 2010; for Rocchette, see Grassi 2013 and Vaccaro 2011; and for Grosseto, see Valdambrini 2010.

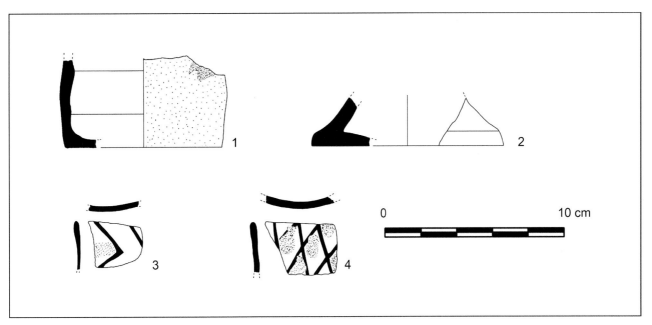

Plate 10.9. Painted under glaze or *dipinta sotto vetrina*.

Painted Under Glaze or Dipinta sotto Vetrina (Pl. 10.9)

Only a few fragments of painted under glaze (*dipinta sotto vetrina*) come from Orvieto and the northern Lazio (Viterbo) area. A transparent lead glaze covers the fabric and the decorative motifs are made in manganese or copper (green). The shapes are closed, with the exception of one small cup bottom. This typology had a very brief life, and preceded archaic majolica. This unpractical type is rather expansive and is associated with similar shapes in the more convenient, one-process production of archaic majolica. This type is normally attributed to the thirteenth century, contemporary with archaic majolica. Similar pieces were found in nearby Cosa-Ansedonia.

Pl. 10.9, no. 1

Description: Flat bottom of a closed vessel, decorated with thick green drops of glaze.
Material: Painted under glaze.
Chronology: Thirteenth century.
Context: 0S 169=NA.
References: *Tuscania* 1972, fig. 9, 1, Orvieto, end of thirteenth century.

Pl. 10.9, no. 2

Description: Flaring bottom of pitcher with transparent lead glaze over the fabric.
Material: Painted under glaze.
Chronology: Thirteenth century.
Context: 0S 169=NA.
References: Ward-Perkins and others 1972, fig. 9,10 (This might be a jug or *versatoio* of archaic majolica; see Sconci 2001, 72 p. 112).

Pl. 10.9, no. 3

Description: Body shard of a cup, decorated with pointed arrows in manganese around the centre.
Material: Painted under glaze.
Chronology: Thirteenth century.
Context: 8S 101=Bld. M Pit 9 Level II.
References: Similar pieces are found in Ansedonia. Cirelli and Hobart 2003, fig. 145 nos 1–3, 326.

Pl. 10.9, no. 4

Description: Body shard of a cup (similar to Pl. 10.11, no. 3) decorated with black cross lines that form rhomboids, filled in with green dots.
Material: Painted under glaze.
Chronology: Thirteenth century.
Context: OS 163.
References: Similar in Ward-Perkins and others 1972, 8, 9 p. 221.

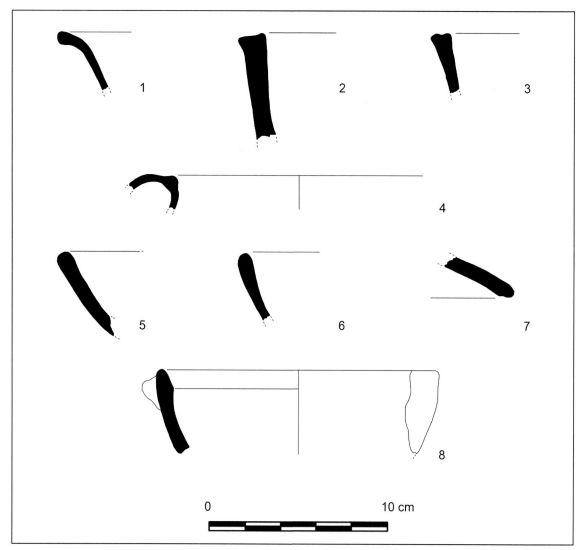

Plate 10.10. Lead glazed pottery.

Lead Glazed Pottery (Pl. 10.10)

Three different shapes of lead glazed or *invetriata da fuoco* were found in Buildings J and M. The fabric has inclusions and there are traces of cooking on the surfaces. While green glaze is used for dining sets, the colour shifts to brown when the vessels are used in the kitchen. This rather homogenous group is always associated with archaic majolica and is present in the most recent contexts. It is worth noting that the thickest fragments come from the most recent layers (Level I), while the others come from the layer immediately preceding it (Level II). A similar chronology was noted for the *invetriate da fuoco* found in Rome at the Crypta Balbi. The date for this type of production ranges from the second half of the fourteenth to the early fifteenth century.

Pl. 10.10, no. 1
Description: Flaring rounded rim of a small open vessel (*ciotoletta*).
Material: Lead glazed.
Chronology: Late thirteenth century.
Context: 8S 143=Bld. M Level I (430–54 cm).
References: Saguí and Paroli 1990, pp. 250–59; Grassi 1999.

Pl. 10.10, no. 2
Description: Thick vertical rim of pan (*tegame*).
Material: Lead glazed.
Chronology: Late thirteenth–fourteenth century.
Context: 8S 117=Bld. J Level I (578–601 cm).

Pl. 10.10, no. 3
Description: Smaller vertical rim of pan (*tegame*).
Material: Lead glazed.
Chronology: Late thirteenth–fourteenth century.
Context: 8S 149=Bld. M surface.

Pl. 10.10, no. 4

Description: Rim and handle attachment of a closed vessel (cooking pot), thicker at the rim level.
Material: Lead glazed.
Chronology: Late thirteenth century.
Context: 8S 76=Bld. J Pit 2 Level I (624–26 cm).
References: Saguí and Paroli 1990.

Pl. 10.10, no. 5

Description: Rounded rim of bowl/lid.
Material: Lead glazed.
Chronology: Late thirteenth century.
Context: 8S 121=Bld. I Level II.

Pl. 10.10, no. 6

Description: Rounded rim of bowl/lid.
Material: Lead glazed.
Chronology: Late thirteenth century.
Context: 8S 108=Bld. M Level II (450–67 cm).

Pl. 10.10, no. 7

Description: Large flaring lid to cover a pan.
Material: Lead glazed.
Chronology: Late thirteenth century.
Context: 8S 153=Bld. J Pit 17 Level II (635–49 cm).

Pl. 10.10, no. 8

Description: Open vessel with pinched handles.
Material: Lead glazed.
Chronology: fourteenth century.
Context: 8S 142=Bld. M Pit 16 Level I (to 430 cm).
References: Grassi 1999.

Archaic majolica (Pl. 10.11–10.15)

This is the largest group of glazed medieval pottery on site. The production centres for this period are mostly from central Italy, particularly the cities of Pisa, Siena, Volterra, Orvieto, and Viterbo. As seen above, when the first glazing techniques were introduced, archaic majolica began to be produced in Pisa at the end of the twelfth and early thirteenth century.[18] About the same time, many other production centres flourished in central Italy.[19]

Each significant fragment is either drawn, or photographed, or both. This typology is consistently present in the highest levels (Levels I, II, and III) in all of the excavated areas, except for the rubbish pits (M), where the material was not ordered in chronological sequence. Some parallels can be drawn with Cosa-Ansedonia, at least for the earlier period (thirteenth century), with material from Siena and Volterra, but when the former was destroyed (about a century before Tricosto), by then the imports came from markets centred in Orvieto and Viterbo.[20]

White Archaic Majolica, or Monochrome with Rays (Pl. 10.11)

The white archaic majolica is one of the most basic glazed productions that appear in Pisa. The white slip glaze occasionally serves as a background for very plain and simple decorations, such as crosses, letters, or symbols, mostly placed in the centre of a plate or jug. Another frequently encountered group of plates has a green cross and black rays in the centre. This common typology was produced in Pisa for about a century and exported all around Tuscany, Rome, central Italy, and the Mediterranean. The earliest examples date from the mid-fourteenth to the first half of the fifteenth century.

Pl. 10.11, no. 1

Description: White monochrome plate (tin glaze), with wide rims.
Material: Archaic majolica.
Chronology: Fourteenth century.
Context: 0S 111=Zone J Trench 8–6 Level III.
References: From Pisa: Grassi 1999; Berti 1997, Tav. 48b2 (type Ba R 1.33) p. 98.

Pl. 10.11, no. 2

Description: White plate with a ring foot and decorated with a black central motif of either a cross or a letter.
Material: Archaic majolica.
Chronology: Thirteenth–fourteenth century.
Context: Bld. J Trench 8–6 (Level III).
References: From Pisa: Berti 1997, Tav. 104, p. 148; Baldassarri and Milanese 2004.

Pl. 10.11, no. 3

Description: Plate without a visible rim, with a ring foot decorated with a central green cross and three black rays in each quadrant.
Material: Archaic majolica.
Chronology: Thirteenth–fourteenth century.
Context: 8S 152 Bld. J Pit 17, W. ext. Level II (628–35 cm).
References: From Pisa: Berti 1997, Tav. 71a, p. 112, and fig. 23, p. 113.

---

18 Berti 1993; Berti and Gelichi 1995; Berti, Cappelli, and Francovich 1986; Berti 1997; Berti, Gelichi, and Mannoni 1997.

19 For Pisa, see Berti 1997; for Piombino, see Berti and Bianchi 2007; for Siena, see Luna 1999; Cantini 2005; Cantini 2011; Cantini and Grassi 2012; for Volterra, see Pasquinucci 1987; and for the rest of Tuscany, see Grassi 2010; Berti and Giorgio 2011.

20 Fentress and others 1991; Hobart 1991, 71–89, Cirelli and Hobart 2003.

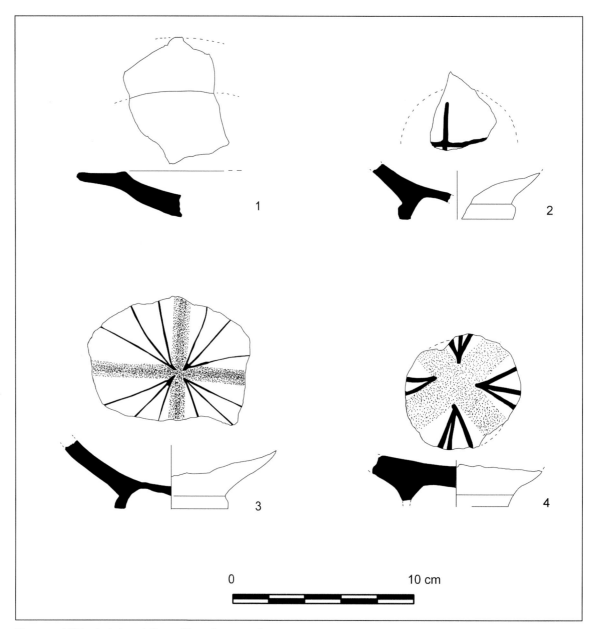

Plate 10.11. White Archaic majolica or Monochrome and rays.

Pl. 10.11, no. 4

Description: Plate with ring foot and larger green cross and black rays; Same plate as above, but with larger rays in manganese. The edge of the plate is missing.
Material: Archaic majolica.
Chronology: Thirteenth–fourteenth century.
Context: Bld. J Level III (633–56 cm).
References: Berti 1997, Tav. 71 a2, p. 113. Other fragments of monochrome come from Zone C Trench 8–3, cleaning gate area.

Archaic Majolica from Pisa (Pl. 10.12; Fig. 10.7)

Pl. 10.12, no. 1

Description: Plate with a flat, wide rim, decorated with black squares and an adjacent green line on its left side. This decoration seems to be a variation of the grid motifs used frequently in Pisa on closed vessels.
Material: Archaic majolica.
Chronology: Second half of the fourteenth century.
Context: 0S 4=Zone J, Trench 8–6 Level II.
References: Berti 1997, MA.I. VIIth group, Tav. 81, a2; Tav. 131 a2.1, p. 191.

10. MEDIEVAL POTTERY (1200–1400) 193

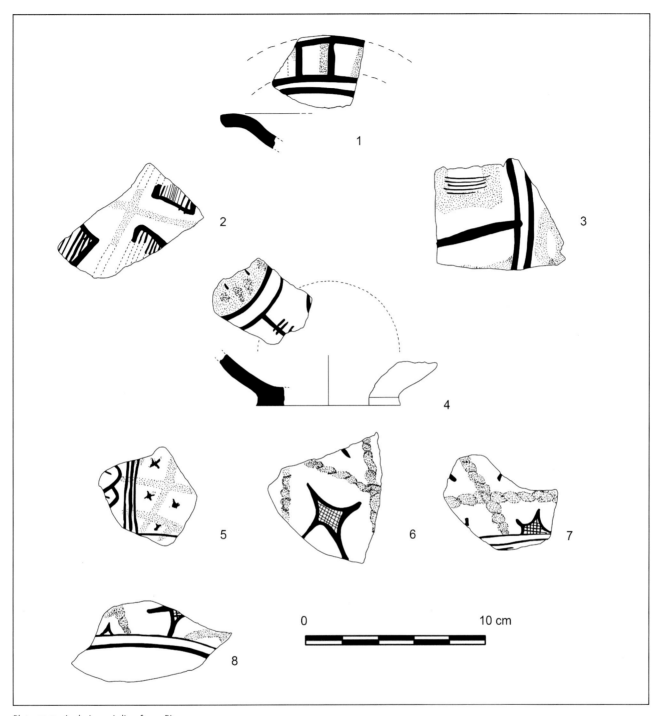

Plate 10.12. Archaic majolica from Pisa.

Pl. 10.12, nos 2–3

Description: Body shard of a pitcher, with decoration based on a series of intersections of square grids in green and black. The grid has green squares filled with black parallel lines.
Material: Archaic majolica.
Chronology: Second half of the fourteenth century.

Context: oS 4=Zone J, Trench 8–6 Level II.
References: Berti 1997. The motif belongs to the MA.I. VIth group pp. 118–23. A similar plate comes from the church of S. Martino dated 1210–1240. These are Pisan productions from the first decades of the thirteenth century.

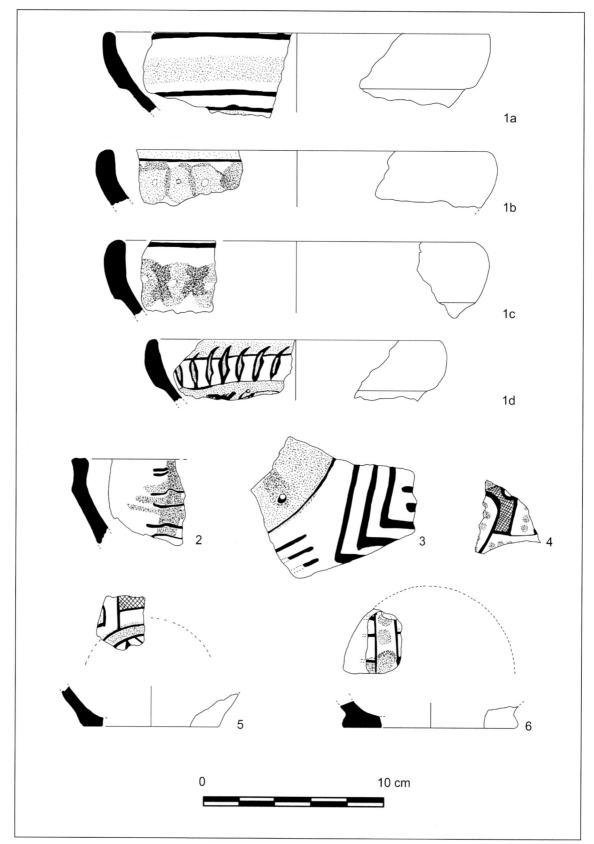

Plate 10.13. Ceramics from Siena 'Famiglia Verde'.

Pl. 10.12, no. 4

Description: Bottom of a plate with central motif in black, connected to large stylized leaves filled in green.
Material: Archaic majolica.
Chronology: Second half of the fourteenth century.
Context: OS 30=Bld. M Trench 8–1 Level IV (rubbish pit).
References: Despite the small dimension of the fragment, we can assume that the decoration belongs to Berti's third group MA.III type Ac or Bc; see Berti 1997, fig. 100, pp. 214, 218. This fragment would help identify more precisely the uncertain date for this group. Berti suggests, with reservation, a date in the middle of the fifteenth century, but does not exclude an earlier date (the first part of the century). This is in fact confirmed at Capalbiaccio, which offers an *ante quem* date of 1410, when the site was abandoned.

Pl. 10.12, nos 5–8

Description: Three body shards of a jug with narrow green chains and a four-point star with a black grid inside. Part of the body of a pitcher has a green grid filled with crosses in each square. This very common Pisan motif is found in trading posts all over the Mediterranean.
Material: Archaic majolica.
Chronology: Fourteenth century.
Context: 0S 111 and 0S99=Bld. M Pit 9 West Ext. Level II (rubbish pit).
References: Berti 1997.

Ceramic from Siena 'Famiglia Verde' (Pl. 10.13)

This next group differs from the rest of the archaic majolica, because of its distinguished colour: turquoise green or the so-called *famiglia verde*. All of the pieces come from open vessels and are fragmentary. The decorations inside the thick, rounded rims show three different patterns: the plain horizontal decoration (1a), the common green chain (1b, 1c) and the repeated elongated leaf-like shapes (1c). Smaller fragments show green dots between lines and filled black grids. The fabric is made of dark orange depurated clay. Their fragmented state does not allow much speculation about the rest of the pattern. This particular group seems to have been produced in Siena between the end of the thirteenth and the fourteenth century.[21] The *contrada* of the Civetta Museum in Siena displays the same productions. Similar examples can also be found at Volterra in the early fourteenth century.[22] Volterra seems to have produced its own form by importing the technique and borrowing many of the themes from the larger nearby production centre of Siena.[23]

Pl. 10.13

Material: Archaic majolica/
Chronology: Fourteenth century

Pl. 10.13, no. 1a

Description: Rounded and thickened rim of a plate, decorated with horizontal lines in black and filled with a green brush stroke. The shape is found in Siena and Volterra.
Context: 0S 111 and 0S99=Bld. M Pit 9 West Ext. Level II (rubbish pit).

Pl. 10.13, no. 1b

Description: Rounded and thickened rim of a plate, decorated with a green chain motif framed in black and green.
Context: 0S 20=Bld. J Trench 8–6 Level II.
References: Pasquinelli 1987, Tav. IX, 1, p. 47.

Pl. 10.13, no. 1c

Description: Rounded and thickened rim of a plate, decorated with a darker green chain motif framed in black.
Context: 0S 20=Bld. J Trench 8–6 Level II.
References: Pasquinelli 1987, Tav. IX, 4, p. 47.

Pl. 10.13, no. 1d

Description: Rounded and thickened rim of a plate, decorated with a series of vertical elongated green leaves outlined in black and framed by green borders.
Context: 0S 4 Bld. J Trench 8–6 Level II. Sienese production early fourteenth century.
References: Luna 1999. p. 48; Francovich 1982, fig. 84, p. 78, fig. 126, 2; Pasquinelli 1987, Tav. X, 9.

Pl. 10.13, no. 2

Description: Flattened vertical rim and angled profile, decorated with a green brush stroke with perpendicular black lines.
Context: 0S 20=Bld. J Trench 8–6 Level II.

---

21 Luna 2002.
22 Pasquinelli 1987, 81.
23 Francovich 1982; Bojani 1992; Luna 1999; Luna 2002.

Pl. 10.13, no. 3

Description: Fragment of plate, decorated in the interior with a geometric motif with black lines and a green area on a white surface. The pierced hole could have either served for hanging or simply as a restoration to hold the pieces together.
Context: oS 12=Zone C Trench 8–3 Level II.
References: Francovich 1982, M.I.8. p. 144; Pasquinelli 1987, Tav. VII, 11, p. 45.

Pl. 10.13, no. 4

Description: Body shard of a plate, decorated with the knot of Salomon with green dots and a cross-hatched motif.
Context: oS 4=Bld. J Trench 8–6 Level II.
References: Francovich 1982, M.I.1, p. 139, fig. 186, 1 p. 198; Pasquinelli 1987, Tav. V, 2, 5, p. 43.

Pl. 10.13, no. 5

Description: Bottom of a plate, decorated with areas in green framed by black lines and filled with black crosshatching.
Context: 8S 131=Bld. J Pit 14, W ext. Level I (510–50 cm).

Pl. 10.13, no. 6

Description: Bottom of a plate, decorated with a pattern of green dots between black lines.
Context: oS 147=??? It is the same type of decoration as Pl. 10.5, no. 4.
References: Pasquinelli 1987, Tav. V, 2, 5 1, p. 43.

Ceramics from Orvieto and Viterbo (Pl. 10.14)

Besides the archaic majolica from Pisa and Siena, the other large group of well-known glazed ceramics comes from Orvieto. Both the lead glazed and tin glazed productions found at Capalbiaccio come from Umbria and Northern Lazio and date between the thirteenth and the fourteenth century. The decorative repertoires and the large production suggest that majolica use was becoming more standardized, which is also visible in the abundant parallels and variations. The samples below have a lighter colour and a thinner fabric. In Capalbiaccio both secular and religious decorative motifs are invariably present, probably indicating their wide range of use in domestic contexts.[24]

Material: Archaic majolica.
Chronology: thirteenth–fourteenth century.

Pl. 10.14, no. 1

Description: Bottom of a cup. The centre is decorated with a manganese circle divided in rays, centred around a smaller green circle.
Context: oS 20=Zone J Trench 8–6 Level II. Orvieto thirteenth century.
References: Sconci 2001, 105, p. 146; and for the pattern only 16, p. 56.

Pl. 10.14, nos 2–3

Description: Cup with possibly two small, oval handles. Decorated in green and manganese, with the symbols of the passion in the centre.
Context: 2a (Zone R pit; 2b (8S 49=Bld. J Pit 2 north level? (631–32 cm). Orvieto thirteenth–fourteenth century.
References: Satolli 1981, fig. 34, p. 61; fig. 62, p. 129. Sconci 2001, 114–23, pp. 155–64.

Pl. 10.14, nos 4–8

Description: Bottom of a cup. Central motif with a green floral element, filled in with a thick grid in manganese. These are variations of the same type. No. 7 is different from the others, lacking a ringed foot. Note the different profiles.
References: Sconci 2001, 109–11, pp. 150–52. Ward-Perkins and others 1972, fig. 10, ORV 5, p. 222. 3a (Bld. J Pit 14 n. ext. Level I); 3b (8S 121=Bld. J, Pit; 13c 8S 121; 3d (oS 111=Bld. J Trench 8–6, Level III).

Pl. 10.14, nos 9–10

Description: Bottom of cup or *ciotola* decorated with four flowers at the end of a central cross. Two are filled in green, while the other two have a cross-hatched pattern inside. No. 9 is a variation of a similar cup (oS 111=Zone J Trench 8–6 Level III).
References: These Orvieto productions belong to the family with a central vegetal motif in Sconci 2001, 157, pp. 198 or 160, 201.

---

24 Common Umbrian vessels from Orvieto can be found in Guaitini 1981, schede 35, 44, 52, 56, 61, 69, 71, 92, 96, 105; Satolli 1983–1985, schede I–II, 10, 96, 100, 104, 118–22, 127–28, 169, 197; Satolli 1983–1985; Sconci 2001, schede 1, 3–5, 12–13, 31–46. From Todi, see Guaitini 1981, 169, fig. 128; from the Latium and Viterbo regions, see Mazzucato 1975, tav. 66, n. 5; Mazza 1983, schede 88–89, 96, 98, 101, 109; from Tuscania, see Ward-Perkins and others 1972, tav. XLIIIa, XLIVa-b; Ricci and Portoghesi 1972, fig. 2, n. 9; Romei 1994, 89, fig. 4, n. 8; 92; from Celleno, see Raspi Serra and Picchetto 1980, tav. LXVII, a-b; and from Rome, see Saguì and Paroli 1990, 433, tav. LXIII, nos 491–92. A very common shape, typical of this area, is the small cup decorated with symbols of Christ's passion, the so-called *Agnus Dei*.

10. MEDIEVAL POTTERY (1200–1400)

Plate 10.14. Ceramics from Orvieto and Viterbo.

Pl. 10.14, no. 11

Description: Full profile of cup with floral decoration in the centre and zig-zag lines on the exterior of a vertical rim.
Context: 0S 20=Bld. J Pit 9 Level II.

Pl. 10.14, no. 12

Description: Partial profile of cup with a green chain motif on the exterior centre part of the body, with yellow and green.
Context: 8S 99=Bld. M Pit 9 Level II.

Pl. 10.14, no. 13

Description: Exterior decoration of body part with a framed chain motif filled in yellow, over a green background. The shape of the cup differs from the other.
Context: Bld. M Pit 9 Level II.

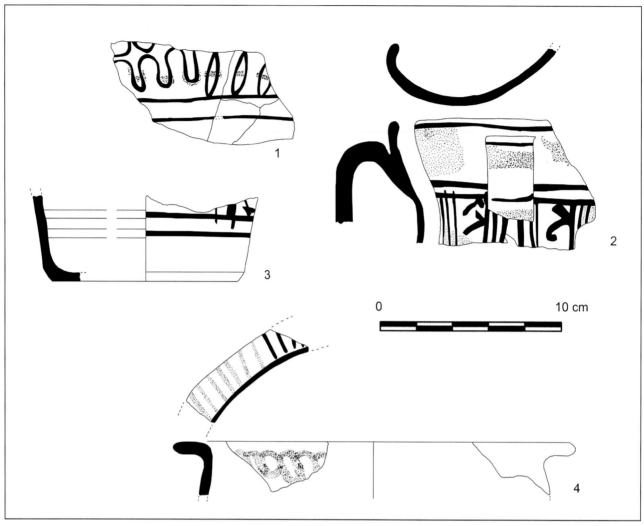

Plate 10.15. Ceramics from Latium and Orvieto.

Archaic majolica from Latium and Orvieto (Pl. 10.15)

Pl. 10.15, no. 1

Description: Body part of a closed jug (*boccale*) decorated with a pointed oak leaf, filled in black.
Material: Archaic majolica.
Chronology: Fourteenth century.
Context: Bld. J Pit 13 Level II.
References: Francovich and Gelichi 1980a, p. 49 n. 36.

Pl. 10.15, nos 2–3

Description: Rim and bottom of a jug, probably part of the same vessel. The rim is trilobed with a strapped handle. The decoration that survives framed the central image and has a sequence of small, slanted, vertical Vs in black. The bottom is flat with no foot.
Material: Archaic majolica.
Chronology: Fourteenth century.
Context: Bld. J Pit 13 Level II
References: Francovich 1982.

Pl. 10.15, no. 4

Description: Horizontal rim of a large rounded serving bowl. The rim is decorated with alternating groups of green and black lines, while in the inner part of the vessel, below the rim, a green chain frames the plate.
Material: Archaic majolica.
Chronology: Fourteenth century.
References: Francovich and Gelichi 1980a, p. 36 n. 24.

10. MEDIEVAL POTTERY (1200–1400)

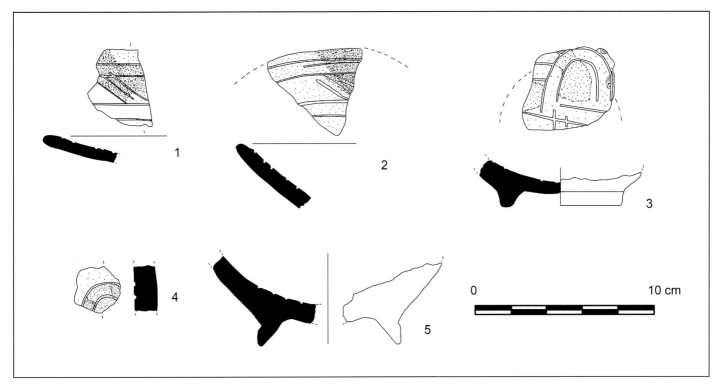

Plate 10.16. Graffita arcaica tirrenica.

Graffita arcaica tirrenica (Pl. 10.16)

Graffita arcaica tirrenica was produced mainly in Liguria. It differs from the archaic majolica technique in the type of cover, called *ingobbio*: a thick whitish tin glaze that once applied provides a contrast to the incised decoration. A second firing with a lead glaze gives the pot the impermeable coat it needed. Savona was a major production centre, which started to export at the end of the twelfth century and continued to produce graffita arcaica tirrenica until the fifteenth century.

Pl. 10.16, no. 1

Description: Rim of plate (*bacino*) with incised parallel and oblique lines created before firing. Decorated in green and yellow; the interior is covered with lead glaze. The exterior has no revetment. Produced in Liguria, probably Savona.
Material: Graffita arcaica tirrenica.
Chronology: Thirteenth century.
Context: 8S 104. Zone J Trench 8–6 Level V.
References: Varaldo 1997, p. 440, fig. 1, tipo l; Liguori 2007, p. 261, n. 194.

Pl. 10.16, no. 2

Description: Rim of plate (*bacino*) with incised parallel and oblique lines created before firing. Decorated in green and yellow; the interior is covered with lead glaze. The exterior has no revetment. Produced in Liguria, probably Savona.
Material: Graffita arcaica tirrenica.
Chronology: Thirteenth century.
Context: Bld. M Pit 9 w ext. Level II (466–78 cm, 464–75 cm).
References: Varaldo 1997, p. 440, fig. 1, type n; Liguori 2007, p. 261, n. 197.

Pl. 10.16, no. 3

Description: Bottom of a small bowl with a foot ring. The central decoration, a knot of Salomon, was incised before the first firing and coloured with yellow and green. Same provenance and parallel as above.
Material: Graffita arcaica tirrenica.
Chronology: Thirteenth century.
Context: Bld. M Pit 9 w ext. Level II (466–78 cm, 464–75 cm).
References: Varaldo 1997, p. 440, fig. 7, n. 6; Liguori 2007, p. 265, n. 207.

Pl. 10.16, no. 4

Description: Same as above: fragment of a body part of a plate. The exterior has no revetment. Produced in Liguria, from Savona.
Material: Graffita arcaica tirrenica.
Chronology: Thirteenth century.
Context: Bld. M Pit 9 Level II (471–93 cm).
References: Varaldo 1997, p. 440, fig. 7, n. 6; Liguori 2007, p. 265, n. 207.

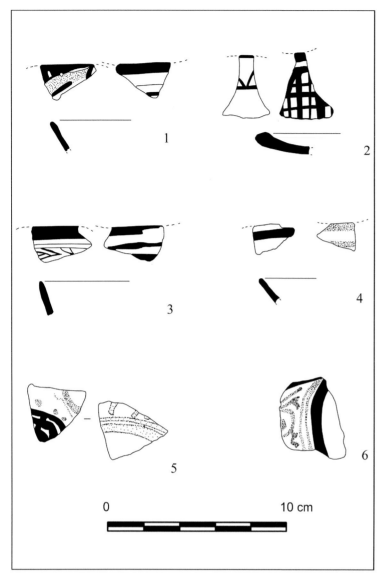

Plate 10.17. Imported pottery from Spain and North Africa; Cobalt and Manganese (n. 6).

Pl. 10.16, no. 5

Description: Bottom of plate with a foot ring, decorated with a circular shape and a grid at the centre, with touches of green points. The exterior has no revetment. Produced in Liguria, probably Savona.
Material: Graffita arcaica tirrenica.
Chronology: Thirteenth century.
References: Varaldo 1997, p. 440, fig. 7, n. 6; Liguori 2007, p. 261, n. 200.

Imported pottery from Spain and North Africa (Pl. 10.17)

Lustreware (Pl. 10.17, nos 1–5)

Pl. 10.17, nos 1–2

Description: Rims of plates decorated with blue and red. Spain, Valencia fourteenth century.
Context: Bld. J Pit 2, Levels II–III.

Pl. 10.17, nos 3–5

Description: Rims of plates decorated with blue and red. Spain, Valencia fourteenth century.
Context: Bld. I Pit 13 Level II

Cobalt and Manganese (Pl. 10.17, no. 6)

Pl. 10.17, no. 6

Description: Fragmented rim of a plate decorated with cobalt blue stylized motif and Manganese. Very common in Tuscany.
Chronology: 1150–1250.

Zaffera a Rilievo

Zaffera a rilievo starts to appear in Romagna, Tuscany, and Lazio at the end of the fourteenth and the start of the fifteenth century. This technique, which maintains the same form of the archaic majolica, replaces the traditional copper green glaze by using a thicker polychrome layer of yellow (*antimonio*), as well as a cobalt blue glaze.[25] The random frequency and small dimensions of both fragments from Capalbiaccio and outside the castle around the later *casolari* do not allow much speculation about the shape of the vessel. The round handle of the jugs, with a thick blue drop interrupted by horizontal lines, suggests that the decoration might have included 'oak leaves',[26] like those found in Viterbo.[27] This type of zaffera a rilievo is found mostly in Tuscany[28] and northern Lazio,[29] and also in small quantities in Rome.[30]

Fragment of a jug 8S 125=Bld. I Pit 13 (N.ext.) Level I (to 48 cm below surface).

Body shard from Jug 'oak leaf' with a diluted light blue or *zaffera diluita*. 8S 49=Bld. J Pit 2 N. Level II.

---

25 Cora 1973, 74, Tav. 321, 322a, b, c, 323a; Conti and others 1990; Francovich and Gelichi 1980b, 137–53; Francovich 1982; Moore 1984.
26 Fragment of a jug 8S 125=Bld. I Pit 13 (N. ext.) Level I (to 48 cm below surface).
27 Luzi 1990.
28 Montarrenti, among other Tuscan castles. Cantini 2003.
29 Mazza 1983.
30 Saguí and Paroli 1990.

Conclusion

The pottery has provided essential information and rather precise chronology for the first medieval settlement on the hilltop of Capalbiaccio around the tenth century. It took another two centuries (1200–1400) to see the maximum expansion of the community and the highest population density. By the second half of the thirteenth century, the population started to shrink, which lead to the abandonment and final destruction of the castle of Tricosto in 1417.[31]

The largest group of medieval pottery are the coarse wares, most likely produced locally, while the glazed pottery consists of archaic majolica, lead glaze, painted under glaze, and slip glazes, such as the graffita arcaica tirrenica from Liguria and the zaffera a rilievo from the area around Viterbo (Fig. 10.8). These associations are consistent with many other excavations in both rural and urban Tuscany.[32] It is now clear that Pisa was the major pottery distributor of not only local productions of both archaic majolica and small amphorae, but also the North African CoMn. The maritime republic, which commanded a privileged position in the Mediterranean, was also exporting its own products of archaic majolica and other medieval types available in other markets. Siena, Volterra, and Orvieto soon after became production centres, but on a smaller scale.

Like at most other sites on the Tyrrhenian coast, no eastern productions were found at Tricosto. There was an ideal and physical geographical line — the Apennine Mountains — that separated the Italian peninsula, impeding circulation and resulting in absolutely no traces of Byzantine zeuxippus ware, or the thirteenth-century Adriatic production of RMR (ramina, manganese, and rosso). Further, the absence of southern productions, such as protomajolica, green lead wares, and spiral wares also testifies to the different trading patterns among nearby sites along the Tyrrhenian coast, such as Rocca San Silvestro[33] or Ansedonia.[34]

As seen in the previous pottery chapters (Vaccaro and Valdambrini), most of the early medieval, unglazed vessels were either produced locally or at nearby production centres, with some imports from the Grosseto area and a few possibly from Rome. It would take larger resources and new forms of elites settling in the area to bring goods from more distant geographic areas. Pisan ceramic products start arriving at Capalbiaccio from the second half of the twelfth century, and for the entire thirteenth century, just like at many other Aldobrandeschi settlements.[35] However, with the increasing tension between the two rising communes of Orvieto and Siena over land to grow their *contadi*, and the increasing fragmentation of the powerful Tuscan family, the channels of trade moved east and southwards. The countryside was eventually absorbed into the Sienese *contado*, and the agriculture resources used to sustain its citizens. The pottery found from surveys, dated from the fourteenth century onwards, comes from the *casolari*, large farmhouses built half way up to the top of the hill. These structures still survive and well restored in many cases today, features of one of the most beautiful landscapes along the Mediterranean coast.

Less is known of the ceramics used outside of the fortified village. From the surveys in the Albegna valley, the medieval and post-medieval material found is little compared to the classical periods of Etruscan and Roman settlements. The countryside *casolari* are the only habitations for the later periods in this part of the Maremma and were probably seasonal. The small amount of medieval pottery found in surveys dates mostly from the fourteenth and fifteenth century, and was mostly imported from Siena, Orvieto, and Viterbo, or made locally. The small community of Ansedonia was destroyed a century before Tricosto.

---

31 Dyson 1979. Cammarosano and Passeri 1984.
32 Grassi 2013; Cantini and Grassi 2012; Grassi 2010.
33 Boldrini, Grassi, and Molinari 1997, 101–27.
34 Hobart 1993.

35 Collavini 1998, 396.

ELISA RUBEGNI

11. Small Finds

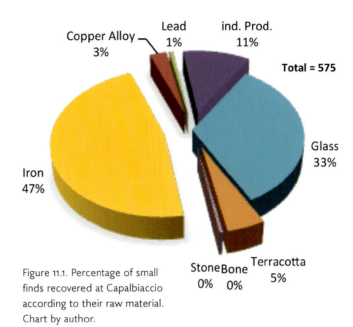

Figure 11.1. Percentage of small finds recovered at Capalbiaccio according to their raw material. Chart by author.

ABSTRACT The excavations at Capalbiaccio in the late 1970s produced a total of 577 small finds, which provides a picture of the community's general activities. The finds consist of common items found in houses and workshops in medieval Tuscan villages of the thirteenth century, the period of the hilltop's largest occupation. Two objects stand apart from the others, as more unusual: a decorated bone chess piece from one of the houses and dated to the twelfth century; and a number of iron plates of armour that were part of a *Brigantina*, common in the fourteenth and fifteenth centuries. From a quantitative point of view, nails were the most numerous of finds, followed by glass, which unfortunately survives in a very poor state, and spindles of different sizes, shapes, and materials. The state of the fragments has suffered greatly, especially the metals, whose original shapes have been subject to deterioration. These are published here for the first time. [MH]

Overview

The relatively low number of small finds recovered from the early campaigns at Capalbiaccio reflects only the 1978 campaign. However, some materials, such as metal objects, especially those made of iron, were, despite substantial restoration, imperfectly preserved and remain unidentifiable. On the other hand, glass objects were in better condition, but often fragmented and relatively scarce. It is worth noting that objects fashioned from metal and glass are susceptible to reuse through fusing, which must be considered when taking into account the percentages of these two classes of materials found onsite. Terracotta spindles did not reveal any sign of decay and appeared perfectly well preserved. The two stone objects, a spindle and a tiny decorative element were in perfect condition. One item stands out from the others, a chess piece in carved bone. This has already been published, albeit erroneously, as being from Cosa. In total, 575 finds were recovered, of which about 70 per cent were identifiable (Fig. 11.1).

The majority of the small finds were made of iron and produced by forging and beating. Unfortunately, iron is the most perishable and unstable metal, and its most frequent form of decay is chemical: exposure to atmospheric agents (carbon, hydroxyls) can transform iron into a sort of mineral conglomerate, compromising its structure. Thus, it was impossible to calculate the exact amount of iron fragments, due to this typical 'scaling' decay. The iron objects found at Capalbiaccio likewise reveal other typical forms of decay (exfoliation, cracking, corrosion, flaking). However, despite their state most items are still identifiable.

A large percentage of the 290 metallic objects are nails, for which there is evidence of various types (circular, squared, or rectangular heads and shafts), sizes, and usages (carpentry and furniture); yet, their lack of links to other types of substantial finds, as well as the poor state of their preservation, make functional distinctions for the most part impossible. Only one very small nail (Cat. 27), which belongs to the shoeing type, could be linked to three horseshoe fragments (Cat. 26) and a buckle (Cat. 28), although the latter pieces were found in different contexts. Other iron objects have been identified, including several pieces of plate armour of various sizes (Cats 40–44), blades, handles, keys, locks, and other objects (Fig. 11.2).

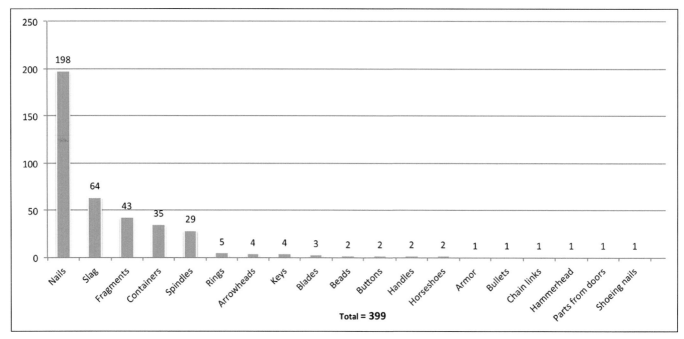

Figure 11.2. Quantity of functional objects from Capalbiaccio. Chart by author.

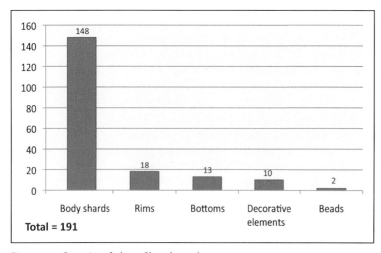

Figure 11.3. Quantity of glass. Chart by author.

There are sixteen copper objects, primarily comprising personal effects, which have all been termed alloys due to the absence of chemical analyses to clarify their exact composition. Among these, a thimble (Cat. 15) with punched decoration attests to activities revolving around cloth production at domestic level. Lead objects are even more rare, apart from an acorn missile (Cat. 45), which was found in good condition, and three other unidentifiable fragments. Unfortunately, only part of the rim of a vessel, in copper alloy, is preserved.[1] Its precise shape is impossible to make out, as a result of warping. The rim seems to have been created simply by folding, and a tiny handle was attached to the rim. If this was the case, then the thinness of the plate and the rim's tiny diameter suggest that it belonged to a swinging lamp.[2]

A fair amount of slag was recovered from the site, amounting to a total of sixty-four pieces. As of yet, no chemical analyses have been performed, but it is possible to distinguish them with a microscope. A good clue as to the type of the final product is provided by the size of the slags: the dimensional relationship between the slag and the final product is proportional. At Capalbiaccio, the dimensions of the slags are all small and show simple repairs, providing another clue as to the identity of their products. Three different types have been distinguished:

- Strained slag: a sign that the slag overflowed the walls of the kiln when it was in a viscous state and solidified in threads with smooth surfaces.
- Cap slag: a type of slag usually associated with drip slag (see below) and hammering waste but foreign to the forging process and to metal refinery. It generally has a smooth, concave surface and is usually characterized by glass-siliceous, dirt, clay, or charcoal inclusions, as a result of contact with other surfaces.
- Drip slag: generally small and drop-shaped with a glazed external surface and a porous inner surface. This type of slag is very fragile.[3]

---

1 Not in this catalogue published here but referenced in the excavation catalogue: number 8F.754, which was found in context Pit 11, Building. J, Level I.

2 La Salvia 2005, 93.
3 La Salvia 2005, 92–94.

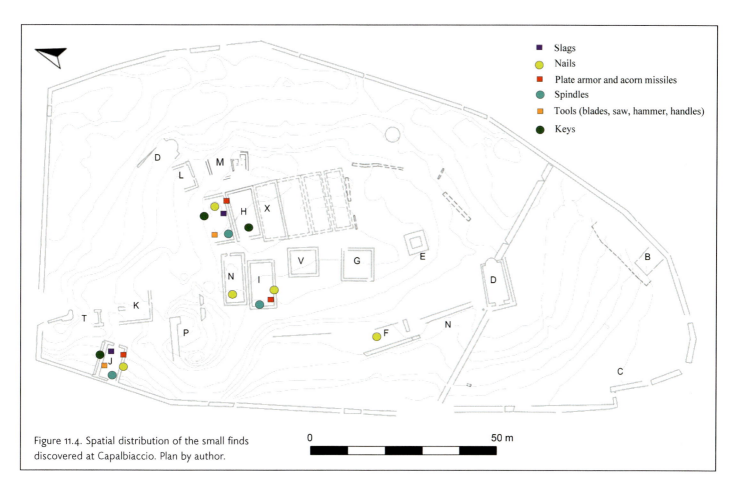

Figure 11.4. Spatial distribution of the small finds discovered at Capalbiaccio. Plan by author.

Of these sixty-four slag fragments, fifty-three were from Building J, and were concentrated on Levels II (34 fragments) and III (16 fragments). It is therefore possible to argue that, at a certain point, some form of production took place in this building, despite the fact that other signs of manufacturing, such as tools, crucibles, anvils, or warped objects, are unfortunately missing.

As mentioned, some of the most well-preserved of the small finds recovered from Capalbiaccio are spindles: at least twenty-nine, most of which are intact (Cats 6–14). One of the spindles is of stone, while the rest were terracotta, and in two cases (Cats 9–10) it is impossible to dismiss the possibility that they are necklace beads. In addition to the stone spindle, one other stone object was found: a tiny necklace bead or element of a pendant.

The glass material is numerous (191 pieces), but extremely fragmentary compared to the other materials. Two small round beads (Cat. 2–3), probably part of a necklace, and a light green drinking vessel are the few clearly identifiable shapes. The vessel was made with a free-blowing technique and decorated with a *bugnette* decoration, created by pulling the vitreous mass out towards the exterior with a tool, thus producing a cavity on the inner wall.[4] A glass vessel survives in fragments and is very poorly preserved. The rest of the glass material (a total of 191 fragments) is not identifiable (Fig. 11.3).

Finally, only one object made of bone was found: the chess piece, which is finely decorated with a dice-eye motif (Cat. 47). Chess was possibly invented in northern India in the sixth century CE, if not earlier, and was introduced to western Europe in the course of the tenth century. This form of decoration is quite common on bone or ivory objects, such as combs or boxes. The shape resembles gaming pieces found in Northern Europe, but similar pieces have been found also in Italy, at Molise and in the castle of Miranduolo, Tuscany.

---

4   Uboldi 1999, 293.

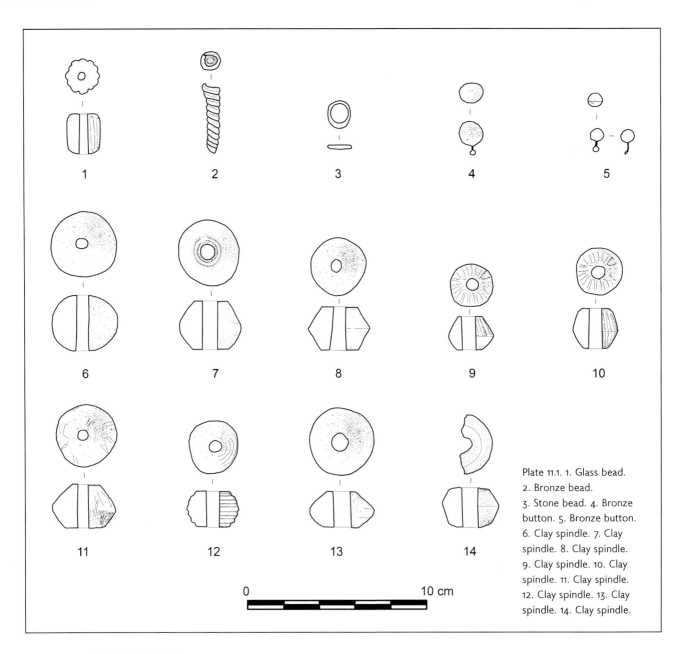

Plate 11.1. 1. Glass bead. 2. Bronze bead. 3. Stone bead. 4. Bronze button. 5. Bronze button. 6. Clay spindle. 7. Clay spindle. 8. Clay spindle. 9. Clay spindle. 10. Clay spindle. 11. Clay spindle. 12. Clay spindle. 13. Clay spindle. 14. Clay spindle.

CATALOGUE

The objects in this catalogue are divided into five groups and are organized by function rather than material. This method makes it easier to visualize the small quantity of objects and offers a more efficient means of noting the co-existence of the different materials that were used in daily activities.[5] The groups include beads and buttons, spindles and thimbles, knives, hammers and nails, animal shoes, and slags, domestic objects such as vessels, studs, rings, locks and keys, arrowheads, a bell, war items, such as armours and missiles, and a game piece. Only well-preserved objects are shown in the plates and listed in the catalogue. Parallels are given only in cases in which resemblance is certain, and specific differences are highlighted. The original catalogue numbers (campaign 1978), when known, are also given.

Objects Pertaining to the Individual

Beads and decorative elements

These objects may be plain or decorated and made of various materials (glass, bronze or stone). They constitute necklaces, bracelets, earrings, pendants, and ornaments applied to clothing.

---

5 This subdivision is obviously subjective, as there are multiple categories into which some objects may be classified (i.e. nails or blades both belong to everyday life and working activities).

1. **Pl. 11.1, no. 1**

    Catalogue Number: 8F-758
    Description: Tiny tubular bead created by the helical wrapping of a copper wire; Type Légoux 5. Complete.
    Material: Copper alloy, moulded with tools.
    Dimensions: Length: 2.9 cm; Diameter max: 0.8 cm.
    Date: seventh–sixth century BCE.
    Context: Pit 11, Building J, Level III.
    References: Bartoloni 1972, 35, n. 28; Bruschetti, Cecchi, Giulierini, and Pallecchi 2012, 180, n. 135; De Santis and Giuliani 1998, 225, pl. 292, 16; Falcetti 2001, 519, pl. 71, 2 (the latter is glass, type Légoux 5).

2. **Pl. 11.1, no. 2**

    Description: Large cylindrical bead with vertical ribs; a multitude of brown surface stains makes any exact identification of the colours impossible.
    Material: Glass, moulded with tools.
    Dimensions: Diameter: 1.4 cm; Length: 1.7 cm; Thickness: 0.6 cm.
    Date: third century BCE – third century CE.
    References: Bierbrauer 1994, 33, fig. I.12, 1 (dated from the late second–third century CE); Brogiolo 1999, 646, pl. CXXX, 12 (troncoconical profile; early Imperial period onwards); Urlacher, Passard, and Manfredi-Gizard 1998, pl. 13; Simpson 2003, 225, fig. 109, 4–5 (third–first century BCE; parallel but not precise).

3. **Pl. 11.1 no. 3**

    Catalogue Number: 8F-628
    Description: Tiny annular, irregular bead, similar to Type Légoux 7.
    Material: Glass.
    Dimensions: Diameter max: 0.9 cm.
    Context: Pit 11, Building J, Level IV.
    References: Falcetti 2001, 519, pl. 71, 3; Bierbrauer 1994, 105, fig. I.168.

Buttons

Elements of this type were used for clothing, as well as accessories or harnesses. On female dress, they were applied mainly on the forearm or shoulder, either as fasteners or simply as ornaments.[6] Parallels can be found in Rome and Nocera (Umbria). Wide circulation is recorded from the fourteenth century onwards.[7]

4. **Pl. 11.1, no. 4**

    Catalogue Number: 37
    Description: Spherical head, with a shank consisting of a tiny eye-folded bar welded onto the head.
    Material: Copper alloy, casted and welded.
    Dimensions: Height: 1.4 cm; Diameter of head: 1 cm.
    Date: Thirteenth–fourteenth century.
    References: Bandini, Cicali, and Felici 1996, 331, pl. XLIV, 6–7 (thirteenth century); Belli 2000a, 142, fig. 112, 17 (seventeenth century); Belli 2003, pl. 1, 1–2 (thirteenth–fourteenth century); Belli 2004, 111, fig. 6 (second half of the thirteenth–second half of the fourteenth century); Cantini 2003, 174, pl. 41, 23 (thirteenth–fourteenth century); Ceppatelli 2008, 421, fig. 187, 5; Dadà 2005, 364, pl. 5, 18 (fourteenth century); Panichi and Ceppatelli 2007, 246, 1–2 (thirteenth–fourteenth century); Viara 2001, 449, fig. 205, 1585 (late thirteenth–fourteenth century).

5. **Pl. 11.1, no. 5**

    Description: Spherical head, with a shank consisting of a tiny eye-folded bar welded onto the head.
    Material: Copper alloy, casted and welded.
    Dimensions: Diameter of head: 0.6 cm; Height: 1 cm.
    Date: Thirteenth–fourteenth century.
    References: Bandini, Cicali, and Felici 1996, 331, Pl. XLIV, 6–7 (thirteenth century); Belli 2000a, 142, fig. 112, 17 (seventeenth century); Belli 2003, pl. 1, 1–2 (thirteenth–fourteenth century); Belli 2004, 111, fig. 6 (second half of the thirteenth–second half of the fourteenth century); Cantini 2003, 174, tav. 41, 23 (thirteenth–fourteenth century); Ceppatelli 2008, 421, fig. 187,5; Dadà 2005, 364, tav. 5, 18 (fourteenth century); Panichi and Ceppatelli 2007, 246, 1–2 (thirteenth–fourteenth century); parallel but not precise. The heads of these buttons are silver with a smooth or convex shape); Viara 2001, 449, fig. 205, 1585 (end of the thirteenth–fourteenth century).

---

6 Belli 2003, 442.
7 Dadà 2005, 366.

Objects Related to Working Activities

At Capalbiaccio, tools pertaining to labour seem to be related mostly, if not solely, to the spinning of wool, and include a thimble. On the other hand, needles and reels are absent. Other signs of working activities include a hammerhead and a fair amount of nails, which indicate that carpentry and some metallurgical activities occurred *in situ*; this is confirmed by the corresponding amount of slag, above all at Building J.

Spindles

Used since the Neolithic period, the spindle is related to the practice of spinning and is used either as a loom weight or, more likely, by being attached to a wooden shaft to maintain constant rotation and a better tension in the thread. Traditionally, it was assumed that spinning was a skill strictly limited to women, but spindles have been found within male funerary contexts, suggesting that men too could have engaged in this activity, at least since late antiquity.[8] The spindle's shape is strictly functional, and its weight, which places a strain on the thickness of the thread produced, is not limited to a particular profile or type of material. Spindles in terracotta, stone, bone, wood, and metal have been used throughout the centuries, making it difficult, if not impossible, to establish a precise chronology. The variety of materials and shapes in which they were made suggests a morphological causality.[9] Clay or terracotta spindles are especially common, and were made entirely by hand, with the help of both a wheel and moulds. Spindles can be variously shaped (discoid, conical or bi-conical, globular) and decorated, but they all have a central hole, which is created by shaping the clay with a wooden stick. It is sometimes possible to recognize traces of usage or exposure to fire on their surface, as in an example published here (Cat. 11). Spindles are frequently found also in southern Tuscany, both in quotidian contexts and burials, where they appear to function as symbolic objects. In the case of Capalbiaccio, the spindles all come from the village. Moreover, the absence of spinning weights suggests that the workshops here used horizontal spinning frames. Seven spindles (twenty-nine pieces in all) were recovered during the excavation, all of which are described below and illustrated (Pl. 11.1, nos 6–14).

6. Pl. 11.1, no. 6

Description: Spherical spindle, regular, made of a pinkish-orange compact material with very small inclusions. Complete. Type I and represented by this unique example.
Material: Terracotta, hand- or wheel-made.
Dimensions: Diameter: 2.9 cm; Height: 2.4 cm.
Date: fourteenth–seventeenth century.
Context: Pit 11, Building J, Level III.
References: Mandolesi, 2007, 228, Pl. 2 (early fourteenth c.); De Vingo 2001, 462, fig. 207, 1623; Giannotti 2005, 389, pl. 3, 2 (parallels from the first half of the fifteenth to the beginning of the seventeenth century).

7. Pl. 11.1, no. 7

Description: Symmetrical, bi-conical spindle of a bright material with several inclusions. A circular groove lies next to the hole in the upper portion. Complete. Type II.[10]
Material: Terracotta, hand- or wheel-made.
Dimensions: Diameter max: 2.8 cm; Height: 2 cm.
Date: A type used for a long time, from the eleventh to the sixteenth century.
References: De Marchi 1999, 331, 653, pl. CXXXVII, 3 (568–680 CE); Piuzzi and others 2003, 113, 157 (sixteenth century); Giannotti 2005, 389, pl. 3, 5 (eleventh–sixteenth century). Mandolesi, 2007, 228, Pl. 2, 8 (early fourteenth century).

8. Pl. 11.1 no. 8

Description: Spindle of a bright and pinkish material, bi-conical shape. Complete. Type III. This type differs from the latter for its more balanced relationship between height and diameter; three elements belong to this type, of which the only one entire is presented in this catalogue. The other two were found in Pit 1 south, Building J, Level III and Building J, Trench 8–6, Level IV.
Material: Terracotta, hand- or wheel-made.
Dimensions: Diameter max: 2.5 cm; Height: 1.8 cm.
Context: Pit 17 (external), Building J, south wall.
Date: Twelfth–fourteenth century.
References: De Vingo 2001, 462, fig. 207, 1628; Giannotti 2005, 389, pl. 3.1 (twelfth–fourteenth century); Mandolesi 2007, 228, Pl. 2, 8 (early fourteenth century).

---

8 De Vingo 2001, 460.
9 Giannotti 2005, 383 and footnotes.

10 This is represented by two other examples beyond the one in this catalogue and described above (both belonging to Building J, Trench 8–10).

9. Pl. 11.1, no. 9

Description: Spindle of the same shape as the previous item, but smaller in dimension. Half of the surface was made with a mould and decorated with vertical ribbing. The material is depurated, pinkish in colour. It might belong to a type of spindle described by De Vingo (2001, 460), which was used as a necklace bead or a fastener for small purse. Complete. Type III. A.[11]
Material: Terracotta, moulded.
Dimensions: Diameter max: 1.9 cm; Height: 1.4 cm.
Context: Pit 2, Building J, Level III.

10. Pl. 11.1, no. 10

Description: Similar to the previous spindle, but with a double valve, decorated with the same ribbed motif on a vertical axis. This one too could have been used as a necklace bead or as a fastener for small purses. Complete. Type III.B. This is the only element belonging to this sub-category.
Material: Terracotta, hand- or wheel-made.
Dimensions: Diameter max: 2 cm; Height: 1.7 cm.
Context: Building J, Trench 8–11, Level III.

11. Pl. 11.1 no. 11

Description: Irregular and rounded, this type of spindle has a less markedly bi-conical shape. This particular object shows signs of wear. The material is a darker orange than the others. Type IV.[12]
Material: Terracotta, hand- or wheel-made.
Dimensions: Diameter max: 2.7 cm; Height: 1.9 cm.
Context: Area around Building R, storage pit.
References: De Marchi 1999, 331, 653, pl. CXXXVII, 7 (568–680 CE). Non-parallel: Sfligiotti 1990, 531, pl. LXXVIII, 692; Mandolesi 2007, 288, Pl. 2, 8 (early fourteenth century).

12. Pl. 11.1, no. 12

Description: Spindle of an oval shape, made of a yellowish material and decorated with horizontal ribs that highlight its flat profile. Type V.A. Complete.[13]
Material: Terracotta, wheel-made.
Dimensions: Diameter max: 2.1 cm; Height: 1.5 cm.
Date: Thirteenth–seventeenth century.
References: Giannotti 2005, 389, pl. 3, 3 (thirteenth–seventeenth century CE); Sfligiotti 1990, 531, pl. LXXVIII, 686.

13. Pl. 11.1 no. 13

Description: Spindle with a flat profile, incisions and concentric circles around the holes. Differs from the other types in the finish of its wall, at the height of its maximum breadth. Type VI. Complete.[14]
Material: Terracotta, wheel-made.
Dimensions: Diameter max: 2.8 cm; Height: 1.5 cm.
Context: Area around Building R, Level II.
References: Sfligiotti 1990, 531, pl. LXXVIII, 694; Mandolesi 2007, 288, Pl. 2, 10 (early ninth to tenth century).

14. Pl. 11.1, no. 14

Description: Spindle with acute cusped corners both at its centre and on its upper and lower edges. Made of a depurated, compact material of a lively orange colour; it retains traces of firing. Type VII. Half is preserved.
Material: Terracotta, wheel-made.
Dimensions: Diameter max: 2.5 cm; Height: 1.7 cm.
Context: Pit 11 south, west exterior, Building J, Level III.
References: De Vingo 2001, 462, fig. 207, 1628; Sfligiotti 1990, 531, pl. LXXVIII, 689; Mandolesi 2007, 288, Pl. 2, 10–11 (fifth–eighth c.).

---

11 This is the only object belonging to this sub-category. For this and the following spindles, the decoration type and reduced dimensions could indicate that they are necklace beads.

12 Only one other element shares the same characteristics (Pit 1 south, Building J). A variant is attested (IV A), decorated with thin, concentric circles, three set in the upper part and three others set in the lower part of the spindle (Building M, Trench 8–1, Level II).

13 Type V spindles, distinguished by the sharp relationship between height and diameter, are the most common at Capalbiaccio: there is a portion of one made from stone (Building J, Trench 8–6, Level IV); the other 6 are in terracotta, but with no decoration (Pit 2 north, Building J, Level II; Building J, Trench 8–11, Level III; Pit 17, Building J, Level II; Pit 16, Building M, cleaning of the wall; Pit 13, Building I, Level II; Pit 14, Building J, north wall).

14 Two other spindles (Pit 17 west ext., Building J, Level III; Pit 11, Building J, black oval) belong to this category. They are both entire, but seem to be more decayed than the one chosen for the catalogue.

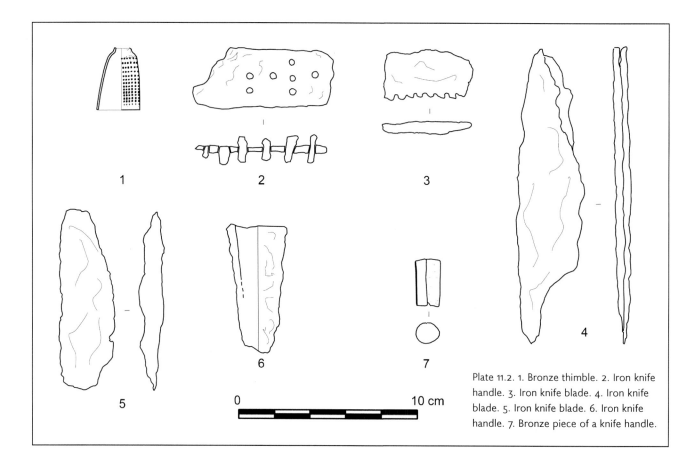

Plate 11.2. 1. Bronze thimble. 2. Iron knife handle. 3. Iron knife blade. 4. Iron knife blade. 5. Iron knife blade. 6. Iron knife handle. 7. Bronze piece of a knife handle.

Thimble

This type of tool, known both in metal and bone since the Roman era, is related to the domestic and manual preparation of leather and textiles. Its production in bronze can be in one of three different processes: casting in moulds; the hammering and welding of two plates; and deep drawing, the process of punching a circular plate to create a shape. In each case, the final phase consists of the punching and carving of the surface. Thimbles come in two forms: caps and rings. As the object found at Capalbiaccio is neither completely closed, nor a simple band, it falls somewhere in between, marking a transitional phase between the two types. Its functional decoration is common to both types, with closely and regularly inset punches. It differs from other thimbles that have been found nearby in the southern Maremma, in which the triangular- or lozenge-shaped punched indentations follow a more chaotic pattern.

15. Pl. 11.2, no. 1

Description: A cap thimble, open on top, decorated with a jagged punched motif that is neatly set in a vertical register and framed by carved horizontal lines at the edges.
Material: Copper alloy, rolled and punched or incised.
Dimensions: Diameter of upper edge: 0.8 cm; Diameter of lower edge: 1.9 cm.
Date: Second half of the fourteenth–fifteenth century.
Context: Pit 14 exterior west, Building J, Level I.
References: Fossati and Murialdo 2001, 720–21, pl. 101, 16–17 (dated generally to the medieval and modern eras); Sogliani 1995, 75, fig. 39 (thirteenth–fourteenth century); Direct parallels include: Belli 2003, 426, pl. 2, 1 (dated to the second half of the fourteenth–fifteenth century); Viara 2001, 447, fig. 204, 1566 (second half of the fourteenth century).

Knife Handles and Blades

Blades and knife or dagger handles are included into this category, bearing in mind that with the exception of saw blades, these objects pertain as much to use in combat as to everyday domestic activities. Only the metal parts of handles survive, the presence of tiny nails still *in situ* offering evidence of attachments in wood or other lost materials. These tiny nails or rivets are typical of the type of knife blade known as a 'scale-tang', which is characterized by a broad, large, flat tang joined to the blade, which is sandwiched between strips of another softer material to form the grip (wood, bone, or leather) and is fixed with rivets. The other type, not present at Capalbiaccio, is known as the 'whittle-tang', in which the tang is longer and tapered so that it can be inserted directly into a handle in another material. It is very difficult to establish a chronology for these kinds of objects, because their basic function does not lead to variations in type over the centuries.[15]

16. Pl. 11.2, no. 2

Catalogue Number: 8F.938
Description: Part of a handle of the 'scale-tang' type, in which seven iron rivets are preserved.
Material: Iron, forged.
Dimensions: Preserved width: 2.4 cm; Preserved length: 6 cm; Thickness: 0.2 cm.
Context: Pit 9, Building M, Level II.
Date: Thirteenth–fifteenth century.
References: Belli 2003, 424 (second half of the twelfth–second half of the fourteenth century); Sogliani 1995, 73, fig. 31 (fourteenth–fifteenth century).

17. Pl. 11.2, no. 3

Catalogue Number: 8F.742
Description: Piece of a saw blade with notches.
Material: Iron, forged.
Dimensions: Preserved width: 2 cm; Preserved length: 3.8 cm; Thickness: 0.5 cm.
Context: Pit 9, Building M, Level II.
Date: Thirteenth–fifteenth century.
References: Ricci 2001c, 347, II.4.245; Piuzzi and others 2003, 71, 36 (thirteenth–early fifteenth century); and 81, 15.

18. Pl. 11.2 no. 4

Catalogue Number: 8F.720
Description: Fragment of a knife blade with a curved cutting edge and convergent spine.
Material: Iron, forged.
Dimensions: Length of blade: 10.5 cm; Total length: 12.4 cm; Maximum width of blade: 2.9 cm.
Context: Building J, Level III.
Date: Thirteenth–fifteenth century.
References: Ricci 2001c, 349, II.4.269–73; Belli 2004, 108, fig. 5, 1.

19. Pl. 11.2, no. 5

Catalogue Number: 8F.741
Description: Fragment of a knife blade with a straight, sharp edge and a curved spine.
Material: Iron, forged.
Dimensions: Length max: 7.6 cm; Width max: 2.3 cm; Thickness max: 1 cm.
Context: Pit 9, Building J, Level II.
Date: Thirteenth–fifteenth century.
References: Belli 2004, 108, fig. 5, 1 (late thirteenth–early fifteenth century); Ricci 2001c, 349, II.4.274–79; De Vingo and Fossati 2001c, 543, Pl. 77, 5.

20. Pl. 11.2, no. 6

Catalogue Number: 8F.758
Description: Circular fragment of a handle, heavily rusted.
Material: Iron, forged.
Dimensions: Diameter max: 2.5 cm; Height: 5.5 cm.
Context: Pit 11, Building J, Level III.
Date: Sixteenth–nineteenth century.
References: Dadà 2005, 369, pl. 9.63.

21. Pl. 11.2, no. 7

Catalogue Number: 8F.710
Description: Tiny tubular element, possibly part of a handle. Created by folding a bronze plate.
Material: Copper alloy, forged.
Dimensions: Diameter: 1 cm; Height: 2 cm; Thickness: 0.1 cm.
Context: Pit 2 south, Building J, wall clearing.

---

15 Sogliani 1995, 38–39, suggests a transition from the 'whittle tang' type (twelfth – first half of the fourteenth century CE up to the early fifteenth century CE) to the 'scale tang' type (first half of the fourteenth century), due to a qualitative evolution of the coating typology.

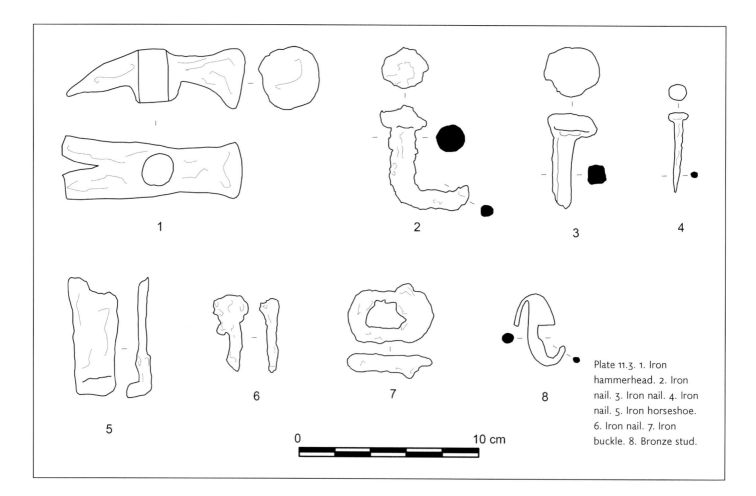

Plate 11.3. 1. Iron hammerhead. 2. Iron nail. 3. Iron nail. 4. Iron nail. 5. Iron horseshoe. 6. Iron nail. 7. Iron buckle. 8. Bronze stud.

Hammerhead

This hammerhead, identifiable as the nail-driver type, was designed for small carpentry works, or a saddler's or a cobbler's activities (Cat. 22). Its purely functional shape has seen little change since the Middle Ages.

22. Pl. 11.3, no. 1

Catalogue Number: 8F.758
Description: The complete head of a small hammer ('nail-driver' type) with a flat, short, and strong percussion face and a bifurcated claw. The central eye for the handle is well preserved.
Material: Iron.
Dimensions: Length: 7.8 cm; Width: 2.4 cm.
Date: thirteenth–fifteenth century.
Context: Pit 11, Building J, Level III.
References: Belli 2004, 108, fig. 5, 10; Panichi and Ceppatelli 2007, 249, 4; Sogliani 1995, 94.122.

Nails

Here, only a few examples of all the nails recovered during the excavations are presented, due both to their poor state of preservation and the impossibility of establishing a useful chronology for these tools, given their basic and common function (Fig. 11.4).

23. Pl. 11.3, no. 2

Catalogue Number: 8F.720
Description: Nail of medium size, with circular shaft and head. The ridge, set some centimeters from the head, suggests that this nail was used for planking. At the very least, it has features that are not truly consistent with those of others nails found on the site.
Material: Iron, forged and beaten.
Dimensions: Diameter of head: 2 cm; Maximum thickness of shaft: 1.2 cm.
Context: Building J, Level III.
References: De Vingo and Fossati 2001b, 555, pl. 81.

24. Pl. 11.3, no. 3

Catalogue Number: 8F.769
Description: Fragment of a large iron nail, possibly with a square, flat head, and with a squared shaft.
Material: Iron, forged and beaten.
Dimensions: Diameter of the preserved head: 2.3 cm; Thickness of the shaft: 0.8 cm.
Context: Pit 14, Building J, Level I.
References: Saguì and Paroli 1990, 515, n. 602 (early twelfth–early fifteenth century); Sfligiotti 1990, 515, pl. LXXIII, 602; Viara 2001, 447, fig. 203, 1545; De Vingo and Fossati 2001b, 555, pl. 81.

25. Pl. 11.3, no. 4

Catalogue Number: 37
Description: Small nail, consisting of a rounded head and a circular shaft. Complete.
Material: Iron, forged and beaten.
Dimensions: Diameter of head: 0.8 cm; Length: 3.3 cm.
References: Sfligiotti 1990, 515, pl. LXXIII, 591; De Vingo and Fossati 2001b, 555, pl. 81.

Horseshoes, Shoeing Nails, and a Buckle

26. Pl. 11.3, no. 5

Catalogue Number: 37
Description: Fragment of a horse- or mule-shoe; only a tiny portion is preserved. The surviving part has a rectangular section and a linear edge. The crampons end with the heel.
Material: Iron, forged.
Dimensions: Length preserved: 4.9 cm; Thickness: 0.5 cm.
Context: Pit 11, Building J, Level IV.
Date: Eleventh–fifteenth century, and eighteenth century.
References: Belli 2000b, 213, pl. I, 13 (eleventh–fifteenth century); Belli 2000a, 145, pl. 113, 4 (eighteenth century); Belli 2003, 426, pl. 2, 2 and 4 (second half of the eleventh century onwards); Dadà 2005, 364, pl. 5, 9, 11; and 369, pl. 9, 58 (dated to the fourteenth century and the sixteenth–nineteenth century, respectively); Mascagni 2006–2007, 89, n. 4 (second half of the fourteenth century).

27. Pl. 11.3, no. 6

Catalogue Number: 8F.703
Description: Tiny nail, identified as a treble clef, i.e. with a semicircular head with a flat rectangular section. Complete but heavily corroded.
Material: Iron, forged and beaten.
Dimensions: Length: 3.2 cm; Thickness: 0.5 cm.
Context: Pit 1 south, Building J, Level III.
References: Dadà 2005, 364, pl. 5, 5 (dated to the fourteenth century); Belli 2003, 426, pl. 2, 1–2 (second half of the eleventh–fifteenth century); Belli 2000b, 213, pl. I, 14 (late fourteenth–mid-sixteenth century); Belli 2004, 102, fig. 3, 6 (eleventh–mid-twelfth century); Piuzzi and others 2003, 43, 9 (late seventh or early eighth century–eleventh century); Tremlett and Coutts 2001, 323, fig. 13:41.

28. Pl. 11.3, no. 7

Description: Rectangular buckle-ring, the prong missing. This may be part of a buckle belonging to a horse's harness. Complete but corroded.
Material: Iron, forged.
Dimensions: Length: 3.7 cm; Width 2.2 cm; Thickness: 0.7 cm.
Context: Pit 2 south, Building J, Levels II–III.
Date: Fourteenth century.
References: Ricci 2001d, 393, pl. II.4.715–16 (seventh century); Sogliani 1995, 119, n. 256 (fourteenth century).

Objects Pertaining to Everyday Life

Furniture Stud

Elements of this type are attested on doors and furniture.

29. Pl. 11.3, no. 8

Catalogue Number: 8F.714
Description: Stud with a cap head and circular shank. Complete.
Material: Copper alloy, forged and beaten.
Dimensions: Diameter of the head: 1.8 cm; Thickness of the shank: 0.4 cm.
Context: Pit 2, Building J, Levels I–II (wall cleaning).
References: Belli 2000b, 213, pl. I, 9 (mid-fourteenth–early fifteenth century).

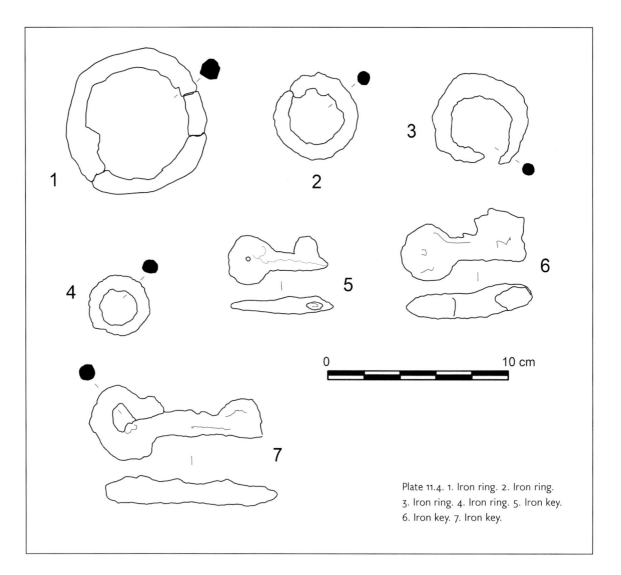

Plate 11.4. 1. Iron ring. 2. Iron ring. 3. Iron ring. 4. Iron ring. 5. Iron key. 6. Iron key. 7. Iron key.

Rings

30. Pl. 11.4, no. 1

Catalogue Number: 8F.753
Description: Iron ring, heavily corroded and in 3 fragments; circular section. Given its dimensions, this conceivably may have been a ring from a horse's harness.
Material: Iron, forged.
Dimensions: Diameter: 4.5 cm; Thickness: 0.7 cm.
Context: Pit 11, Building J, Level I.
Date: Late thirteenth–early fifteenth century.
References: Belli 2004, 106, fig. 4, 10 (late thirteenth–early fifteenth century); De Marchi 2001, 393, pl. LI, 15.

31. Pl. 11.4, no. 2

Catalogue Number: 8F.740
Description: Given its modest dimensions, this tiny ring with a circular section could have been part of either a piece of furniture or a buckle.
Material: Iron, forged.
Dimensions: Diameter: 2 cm; Thickness: 0.5 cm.
Context: Pit 9, Building J, Level II.
Date: Late thirteenth–early fifteenth century.
References: Belli 2004, 108, fig. 5, 2 (late thirteenth–early fifteenth century); Sfligiotti 1990, 515, pl. LXXIII, 608.

32. Pl. 11.4, no. 3

Catalogue Number: 8F.740
Description: This fragmented, circular section ring, like the previous one, may have been either an element in a piece of furniture or most likely a buckle, given the light and not perfectly circular shape.
Material: Iron, forged.
Dimensions: Diameter: 2.5 cm; Thickness: 0.7 cm.
Context: Building M, wall cleaning.
Date: Late thirteenth–early fifteenth century.
References: Belli 2004, 108, fig. 5, 2 (late thirteenth–early fifteenth century).

33. Pl. 11.4, no. 4

Catalogue Number: 8F.7
Description: Tiny ring with a circular section. Like the latter, it could have served as a buckle. Complete.
Material: Iron, forged.
Dimensions: Diameter: 1.5 cm; Thickness: 0.5 cm.
Context: Pit 2 north, Building J, Level II.
References: Belli 2004, 108, fig. 5, 2 (late thirteenth–early fifteenth century); Sfligiotti 1990, 515, pl. LXXIII, 608.

Keys

Keys can be made by forging, casting solid iron bars (as in the case of bit keys known as *maschie* or *bernarda*), or by rolling plates on a given shape, as in the case of hollow cylinder keys. At Capalbiaccio, the keys may all be bit keys of small and medium dimensions. Unfortunately, the poor state of conservation does not allow certainty using macroscopic analysis. Extreme oxidation renders precise morphological identification difficult, especially in the case of the bit, which is not preserved. Basically, these keys appear to have been used to open chests, boxes, or other articles of furniture.

34. Pl. 11.4, no. 5

Catalogue Number: 8F.745
DescriptionTiny *bernarda* key, with a gently tapered linear cylinder, containing a circular section that ends with a sharp bump. Disc-shaped bow with a tiny central hole. Rectangular U-shaped bit, attached along its entire height to the cylinder.
Material: Iron, forged.
Dimensions: Length: 4.3 cm; Thickness: 0.6 cm.
Context: Pit 9, Building M, Level IV.
References: Belli 2004, 108, fig. 5, 4 (late thirteenth–early fifteenth century).

35. Pl. 11.4, no. 6

Catalogue Number: 8F.715
Description: *Bernarda* key, with a linear profile cylinder and a circular section, and a flat bow, completely filled and circular. It is impossible to distinguish the bit, possibly U-shaped and rectangular.
Material: Iron, forged.
Dimensions: Length: 5.4 cm; Thickness: 1 cm.
Context: Pit 2 north, Building J, Level II.

36. Pl. 11.4, no. 7

Catalogue Number: 8F.729
Description: *Bernarda* key, with a cylinder with a linear and rectangular profile and a circular section. Circular bow, made by folding the bar. The bit is corroded.
Material: Iron, forged.
Dimensions: Length: 7.5 cm; Thickness: 1.1 cm.
Context: Pit 3, Building H.
Date: Late thirteenth–fourteenth century.
References: Sogliani 1995, 83, fig. 69 (fourteenth century) indirect parallel; Piuzzi and others 2003, 43, 8 (late seventh or early eighth–eleventh century); Simpson 2003, 248, fig. 118, 24 (twelfth–fourteenth century).

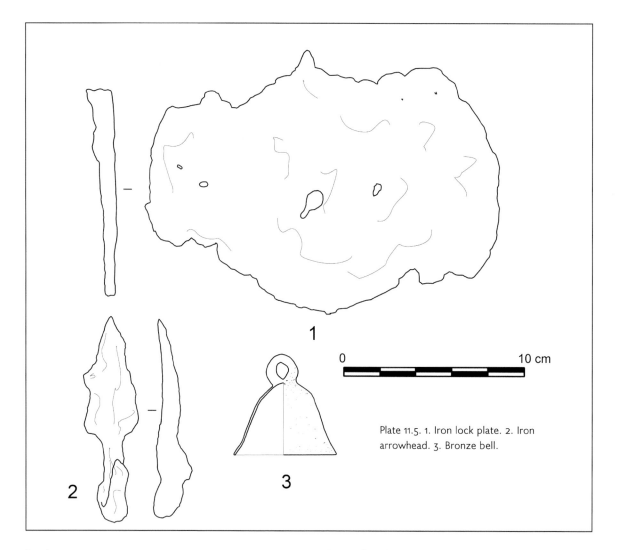

Plate 11.5. 1. Iron lock plate. 2. Iron arrowhead. 3. Bronze bell.

Lock

In addition to the lock described here, there is another element, possibly related to a door latch. It is impossible to show the element due to its high decayed state of preservation.[16]

37. Pl. 11.5 no. 1

Catalogue Number: 8F.718
Description: An iron plate for a lock, with a keyhole probably of a discoid shape, with a central hole for inserting the key and some other holes (at least 6) for nails used to fix the object.
Material: Iron, forged.
Dimensions: Preserved length (probably the diameter): 15 cm; Thickness: 1 cm.
Context: Pit 2 north, Level II.
References: Sogliani 1995, 79, fig. 53 (thirteenth–fourteenth century).

Arrowhead

The two basic medieval types of projectile weapons, the bow and the crossbow, were used either for hunting or military purposes. The bow was the less expensive of the two, being made of wood (preferably yew, but also nut, elder, elm, ash, oak, or maple), and a string, hemp, or sinew cord; the points of the arrows were made of iron or wood, with little wings at the end (made of bird feathers or other material). Medieval bow and arrows generally fall into three categories: the 'simple' bow constituted from a single piece of wood, tapered in the centre (the grip) and sometimes at the ends (to which is attached the cord); the 'composite' bow, assembled of different parts in such a way as to create a sharp curve; and 'longbows', typical of English archers, which were introduced to Italy in the fourteenth century.[17] Crossbows, which had been used in the Roman period, were rediscovered in the early elev-

---

16 But see parallel Sfligiotti 1990, 518, n. 617.

17 De Luca 2000, 216.

enth or twelfth century, and developed into a myriad of variants. In medieval documents they were generally referred to as *balestra grossa*, *a due piedi*, *a girella*, *a staffa* (large crossbow, on two legs, with a pulley, with a clamp). The arrowheads found at Capalbiaccio are flat and large, suggesting that they were designed for hunting.

38. Pl. 11.5, no. 2

Catalogue Number: 37
Description: Arrowhead for a bow, with a *lanceolata* and *gorbia* head, possibly conical (it is too corroded and folded to be precisely described). This particular type may have been used as a military weapon, but most likely it was used for hunting large animals. Due to corrosion, it is impossible to estimate the weight of this piece, which is a really important factor pertinent to the understanding of this group of weapons.
Material: Iron, forged.
Dimensions: Preserved length: 8.3 cm; Width: 2.4 cm; Thickness: 0.8 cm.
Date: Twelfth–fourteenth century.
References: Ricci 2001b, 399, pl. II.4.743 (sixth–seventh century); De Luca 2003, 404–05, pl. I, 4 (thirteenth–fourteenth century).

Bell

Bells were hung from the necks of lead-animals of a herd (oxen, cows, or goats), so as to control them in open spaces. Usually, bells were made by folding an iron plate to create an elliptical opening. A hook and a clapper were then added. The bell found at Capalbiaccio is slightly different from this type; made of copper alloy, it has a circular opening and a flared mouth. For this reason, it most likely belongs to the domestic rather than the agricultural sphere.

39. Pl. 11.5, no. 3

Description: Bell with a circular section and flared mouth; tubular, ring-shaped handle. Complete but missing the clapper.
Material: Copper alloy, forged.
Dimensions: Diameter: 4.3 cm;
Height max: 4.2 cm.
References: Ricci 2001d, 391, Inv.422915.
Context: Pit 2 sout.

Objects Pertaining to War

Armour Plates

Medieval armour was a development of the Roman *lorica*. In the thirteenth and fourteenth centuries, an earlier form of armour, known as the hauberk or chain mail (falling into two categories: made of loops or *grano di orzo*, depending on the dimensions of the links), has been documented. In the period between the fourteenth and fifteenth centuries, it was accompanied by a kind of armour plate, which was attached with rivets to a leather undergarment. In the late fifteenth or early sixteenth centuries, this type of armour evolved into a true and proper, complete armour plate. One type is characterized by the small dimensions of its plates. The other type, which is prevalent at Capalbiaccio, is known as 'brigantina', with thin plates that come in a variety of shapes to suit different bodies. The plates are made to overlap slightly and are folded into cloth or leather.[18] They are generally thicker on the exterior, thinner on the interior, and fixed by rivets (or nails) set on the upper edge of each plate in a continuous series, or at least at short intervals, usually in order to create a sort of a geometric motif. In the early fifteenth century, the leather fold was gradually abandoned and the metal parts became visible.[19] A number of these plates has been recovered from Building J at Capalbiaccio.[20] Unfortunately, their poor state of preservation makes the identification of the associated cloth fragments and the reconstruction of the armour on a mannequin impossible. Usually other parts of the soldier/knight armour would include a protection for the hands, a pair of leather gloves with iron defensive spikes and the head with iron helmets or visors. These other parts have been found in northern Italy. Armature parts similar to those found at Capalbiaccio have been discovered in the collapse at the entrance of the castle of Ripafratta. They have been found in other areas of Italy, such as Rome,[21] Satriano,[22] Brucato and in the north.[23]

This early form of armature starts to appear during the second half of the thirteenth century.

---

18 Giorgetti 1961, 55; see also Saguí and Paroli 1990, 513–52.
19 Zagari 2005, 152; Amici 1989, 463.
20 Building J: Pit 1 south, Level I; Pit 17, Level II; Pit 2, Levels II and III; Pit 14, Levels I and II; Pit 11, Level III; Building I: Pit 13, Level II.
21 Sfligiotti 1990, 536.
22 Whitehouse 1970.
23 Brucato: Piponnier 1984; and in the northern Italy: Piuzzi, Biasi, and Costantini 1994, 541–54.

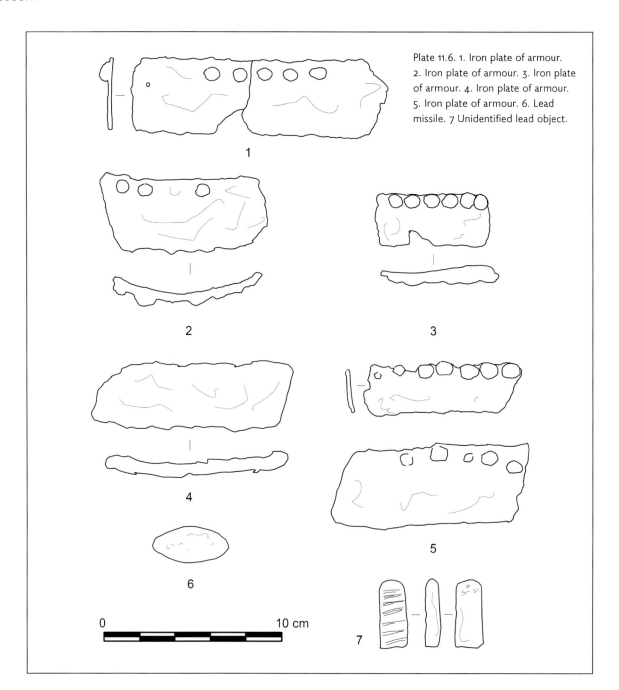

Plate 11.6. 1. Iron plate of armour. 2. Iron plate of armour. 3. Iron plate of armour. 4. Iron plate of armour. 5. Iron plate of armour. 6. Lead missile. 7 Unidentified lead object.

40. Pl. 11.6, no. 1

Description: Plate of armour on which 5 rivets are still *in situ*. Fragmented and corroded.
Material: Iron.
Dimensions: Length: 11 cm; Width: 3.4 cm; Thickness: 0.3 cm.

41. Pl. 11.6, no. 2

Description: Plate of armour on which 3 rivets are still *in situ*. The flexed profile may relate to the anatomical part that it originally protected. Fragmented and corroded.
Material: Iron.
Dimensions: Length: 7 cm; Width: 3 cm; Thickness: 0.5 cm.
Context: Pit 14, Building J, Level I.

42. Pl. 11.6, no. 3

Description: Plate of armour; 6 rivets are still *in situ* and thickly arranged on the upper edge of the actual plate. Fragmented and corroded.
Material: Iron.
Dimensions: Length: 4.9 cm; Width: 2.4 cm; Thickness: 0.6 cm.
Context: Pit 11, Building J, Level I.

43. Pl. 11.6, no. 4

Description: Plate of armour; 6 rivets are still *in situ* and thickly arranged on the upper edge of the actual plate. Fragmented and corroded.
Material: Iron. Giorgetti 1961, 55; see also Saguí and Paroli 1990, 513–52.
Dimensions: Length: 4.9 cm; Width: 2.4 cm; Thickness: 0.6 cm.
Context: Pit 11, Building J, Level I.

44. Pl. 11.6, no. 5

Description: Two plates of armour, each with 5 rivets still *in situ*, though heavily rusted and nearly invisible. Fragmented and corroded.
Material: Iron, forged and beaten.
Dimensions: Length: 6.6 cm; Width: 2.2 cm; Thickness: 0.2 cm; Length: 7.9 cm; Width: 3.2 cm.
References: Belli 2004, 106, fig. 4, 8 (late thirteenth–early fifteenth century); De Luca 2000, 219, pl. II, 1–5 (fourteenth century); Piuzzi and others 2003, 82, 24 (fifteenth–early sixteenth century); Piuzzi and others 2003, 120, 273, 278 (sixteenth century); Sfligiotti 1990, 536, pl. LXXIX, 709.

Acorn missile

Known to the Romans as *glans plumbea*, this type of missile was used with a sling instead of the more common stone pebble. Made of molten lead, it could carry inscriptions, such as ones identifying the wearer's *legio*. This missile exists in three forms: bi-conical (second century BCE–first half of the fourth century CE); ovoid (late second century BCE–second century CE) and finally globular (second half of the second century CE–first half of the fourth century CE).[24]

45. Pl. 11.6, no. 6

Description: Ovoid acorn missile. Complete.
Material: Lead, melted.
Dimensions: Length: 3.3 cm; Width max: 1.5 cm.
Date: Late second century CE–second half of the second century CE.
Context: Bulk I–II, Building J, Level V.
References: Bartoloni 1972, 28, fig. 108, 75–76 (seventh–sixth, and second-first century BCE); Sannibale 1998, 93, fig. 107 (late second century BCE – second half of the second century CE); Simpson 2003, 241, fig. 115, 74 (first century BCE–first or second century CE); *Settefinestre* (Trajanic-late Antonine period).

Arrowheads

Arrow heads appear frequently from the thirteenth century onwards and will be substituted with the *balestra* the following century. Similar material has been found in excavations of castles, in general in the *cassero*, of the Aldobrandeschi and other powerful families settled in the senese contado and the Maremma region. For a general picture of the nature of objects associated with arrowheads derived from both the archaeology and documents in Tuscany (De Luca and Farinelli 2002).

46. Pl. 11.6, no.7

Description: Arrowheads.
Material: Iron(?).
Dimensions: Length: 6–8 cm; Width max: 1.5 cm. central base of point.
Date: Fourteenth–sixteenth century.
References: Ermeti and others 2008, Tav. 1, 5, p. 163; Favia 1992, p. 266; De Luca and Farinelli 2002, pp. 474, 476–79; Cantini 2003, pp. 173, 175; Amici 1989, p. 461.

Objects Pertaining to Games or Entertainment

Chess Piece

Chess has been played in India since at least the sixth century CE, but it appeared in Europe only in the course of the tenth century, thanks to the Arabs. The word 'chess' derives from a Persian term (Shatranj), and also used in Arabic and evolved into the game that has become known in Sicily, the entire Mediterranean and the North Sea islands. The name is based on the game's objective, which is to capture the king, the most important piece. This game of strategy is played on a square board divided into sixty-four squares of two different colours, on which there are thirty-two pieces. The piece documented at Capalbiaccio has not been assigned a specific role, as only its face is clearly visible. Its decoration, consisting of ring-dots, is typical of the Lombard period, but was used extensively over the centuries.[25] From simple one-eyed schemes, to the most complex (with a series of ring-dots set into bands or concentric circles, with crosses or much more elaborate motifs), this type of ornament was applied to metal objects, but mainly to bone, ivory, and horn ones, such as combs, game pieces, dice, weapon handles, wooden sticks, and folding lids

---

24 Sannibale 1998, 93–94.

25 Tozzi 2000, 239.

Plate 11.7. Photograph of chess piece.

Plate 11.8. Photograph of end of clay smoking pipe.

for boxes or chests.[26] The finish of the ornamentation applied to this example suggests an elite owner.

47. Pl. 11.7

Description: A chess piece, rounded conical shape with flat base and a stylized head protruding forward. The head has 2 circles for the eyes and a bar for the mouth. Two narrow horizontal bands of ring-dots encircle the cope at its base and in the middle of the body. In the centre six crosses created by four ring-dots decorated the figure. The top rear is adorned with the same motif, but with a vertical band and the same four ring-dots in the central field. On the top there is a small hole that might have held some other decorative element.
Material: Bone.
Dimensions: Altezza: 7.6 cm., larghezza base: 4.2 cm.
Date: Tenth–fourteenth century.
Context: Zone M Trench 8–1 Level IV
References: This piece was erroneously published in a catalogue of small finds from Cosa 5 (Fentress 2003). Simpson 2003, 248–49. See also Valente 2009; Ferlito 1994 (eighth–tenth century CE). Demains d'Archimbaud 1980, 424 ff., figs 410.4 and 412.15 (twelfth–fourteenth century); On the decoration, De Marchi 1999, 330, 652, pl. CXXXVI, 7 (568–680 CE); Murialdo 2001a, pl. 72, 1; Murialdo 2001b, pl. 73, 3–4; Bonomi Ponzi and von Hessen 1997, 189, figs 39–40; 197, fig. 62; von Hessen 1997, 133, fig. 1 (here the ornament is applied to a bronze buckle from the mid-sixth–seventh century); Ricci 2001a, 402, II.4.789; 416–19, II.4.949–59, II.4.974–89 (late sixth–seventh century); 543, IV.10.8–12 (eighth–ninth century); IV.10.44 (eighth century); 399, II.4.754; Valenti 2008.

Pipe

48. Pl. 11.8

Description: Shank part of the foot of a pipe. The earliest examples appear in the sixteenth century in England, France, and Holland, to mention a few, but also in Eastern Mediterranean countries. In Italy, these pipes were produced in regions such as Emilia Romagna, Tuscany, Abruzzo, Sicily and Sardinia. This type of pipe was very common in the 1800s; simple ones like this cost 1 cent while those with decoration cost 2 cents. A proper classification of these objects is not available yet, however general histories of pipes offer images on the variety of decorative patterns and their circulation.
These were made with a mould made out of either wood or led and the object would be finished with the fine terracotta shank that held the wooden mouthpiece. Decorations were on the terracotta

---

26 As for example in Venafro (Molise), or Albano (Rome), and the Sicilian chess piece, now at the British Museum; but also at Ponferrada (Spain), Witchampton-Dorset, Wallingford Museum, Museum of St Albans Hertfordshire, and the Thames set (England); the pieces from Louvre Museum, Cluny Museum, Gironde set, Isère set (France), TØnsberg (Norway), Norimberg- Germanisches Nationalmuseum (Germany), Sandomierz set (Poland), The Metropolitan Museum of Art (USA) where bone chess pieces with projecting parts, but substantially different shapes, exist. See Sorbo 2020.

part and were either stamped or in bas-relief in elaborate abstract or figurative forms.

This fragment is missing its decorative element, yet it appears to be that of Scoglietto, which was dated to the mid of the 1800s (Chirico and Sebastiani 2011).

Material: Terracotta
Dimensions: Height 5 cm, diameter 2 cm.
Date: Nineteenth century
Context: Uncertain.
References: These differ from the earlier thinner pipes as those found at the Pretorio Palace in Prato (Francovich and others 1978) or at Fiesole (Francovich 1990, 292, pl. 69, nn. 1–2). For an introduction to pipes see Oswald 1975; Ayto 1979; Previato 2009.

Conclusions

Perhaps the most characteristic feature of the small finds from the site of Capalbiaccio was their spatial distribution: a notable concentration of the small finds came from Building J, while scarcely any were discovered in the other excavated buildings (Fig. 11.5). In most cases, the small quantity and various types of objects and materials make it virtually impossible to propose specific practical interpretations of the functions of the buildings at Capalbiaccio. However, Building J does offer some evidence for its use, in the large number of finds it contained:

- Level I: 1 thimble, 1 key, 1 fragment of the rim of a vessel, 1 stud, 12 nails, 1 ring, and several fragments of plate armour.
- Level II: 37 pieces of slag, 2 rings, several fragments of plate armour, 25 nails, 1 key, 1 blade, and 2 spindles.
- Level III: 16 pieces of slag, 1 hammerhead, 1 blade, 1 piece of a handle, 1 latch, 1 arrowhead, 40 nails, and 10 spindles.
- Level IV: 6 nails, a fragment of a horse iron, and 2 spindles.
- Level V: 1 lead projectile and two nails.

All this clearly indicates the presence of some sort of artisanal activity related to metalwork (almost certainly iron and/or lead, given the absence of the globular slag that typically characterizes the handling of bronze), which was pursued during the time period represented by Levels II and III. The large quantity of nails in these strata (a high concentration with respect to all the other Buildings and Levels investigated here; Fig. 11.5) could indicate that nails, as a particular type of finished product, were being produced on a massive scale.

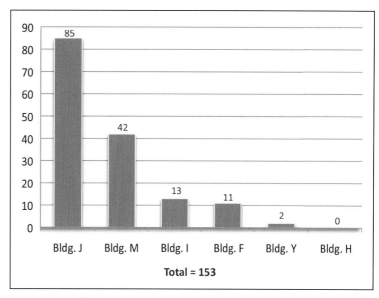

Figure 11.5. Distribution of nails from excavated areas. Graph by author.

The picture that emerges from this analysis bears a strong affinity with the repertory of manufactured metal goods that have been found at other sites in the Maremma: Donoratico,[27] Campiglia Marittima,[28] Rocca San Silvestro (insofar as concerns the coastal region),[29] Rocchette Panocchieschi,[30] Montemassi,[31] and Castel di Pietra (in terms of the hinterland).[32] All these sites have some common factors that are also found at Capalbiaccio:

- A clear prevalence of objects made of iron, as opposed to other alloys.
- Little representative evidence of life in the stratigraphy.
- A prevalence of material datable to more recent phases, as opposed to the initial occupation of the site.

Regarding the items connected with building practice, it is likely that structural elements (joints or binding systems) made of wood or some other perishable material were in widespread use, insofar as the number of carpentry nails, hinges, hooks, and other objects is limited and decidedly lower than would be required for the construction of various buildings.[33] Though numerous, the nails discovered do not all belong to the 'carpentry' type, and in any

---

27 Bianchi 2004.
28 Bianchi 2003c.
29 Francovich 1991.
30 Bianci, Boldrini, and De Luca, 1994.
31 Guideri, Parenti, and Barbagli 2000.
32 Citter 2009b.
33 Belli 2004, 100–01.

case they do not amount to the quantity that would have been required to build the structures uncovered.

Finally, the more or less consistent presence of spindles on Level III (at least 10 forms out of a total of 28, which probably pertain to a horizontal loom), suggests a heavy (and typologically variegated) use of Building J in a fairly restricted chronological span, in comparison to all the other areas. These conclusions thus raise a few questions. How was the working space used and organized between the metalsmith and the spinning activities during the same time in Level III under Building J? Was this type of workshop limited to Building J? and were these different productive occupations repeated in other houses producing similar objects inside the fortification?

ALESSIA ROVELLI

12. Coins

ABSTRACT The relatively small number of coins (twenty-two samples) discussed in this chapter were discovered throughout the three years of excavation in the late 1970s. Neither sieving nor a metal detector were used. Alessia Rovelli, who has greatly contributed to the understanding of currency circulation in the medieval Mediterranean, here addresses what she sees as a common pattern between these coins and their association with other sites in central Italy. At Capalbiaccio, the earliest presence of coins coincides with the first medieval stone structures (phase 1, *infra* Corti) and not with the tenth-century, early medieval settlement identified solely by the pottery. On the other hand, Ottonian coins, which are in fact the earliest coins to appear along the Tyrrhenian coast of central Italy, were found at the nearby sites of Cosa/Ansedonia, Poggio Cavolo, and San Pietro d'Asso, Montalcino.

While only one Roman coin, dated to the second or third century CE, was found at Capalbiaccio, the rest of the coins are contemporary with the last two centuries of life at the hilltop (between the twelfth and fourteenth centuries). What makes this interesting is a large range of connections evidenced by coins minted outside of central Italy: one from Sicily (Messina, 1285–1296); others from Lucca (second half of the twelfth century); Viterbo (*Patrimonium Sancti Petri*, 1268–1271); Arezzo (second half of the thirteenth century); Montefiascone (1316–1334); and Pisa (1318–1319). The largest group of seven coins comes from Perugia and is dated to 1321, along with two *quattrini* from Florence (1332–1335), and one from Viterbo, which was minted between 1375 and 1387. In particular, Rovelli discusses the nature of currency exchange and circulation between the twelfth and fourteenth centuries, offering a rich bibliography for a deeper understanding of monetary circulation in the Mediterranean. [MH]

Historical Context of the Finds

The excavation of the castle of Tricosto on the hill of Capalbiaccio has led to the discovery of twenty-one coins, to which can be added some altogether illegible 'pulverized' fragments. Though this is a small amount of coins, it is altogether in keeping with the mode of excavation adopted which was not, in fact, extensive, consisting of the opening of some trenches, and subsequently aided by geophysical surveys, which made it possible to clarify the characteristics of the settlement.[1] The limited quantity of the samples does not hinder our understanding of the principal features of local coin circulation, since it is possible to integrate this data with that found at the more extensive excavation of Cosa, just a few kilometres away. This is particularly true for the Middle Ages, when Cosa/Ansedonia and Tricosto shared similar functions and fates, while in the Roman era the two sites experienced quite different situations well represented in our finds.[2] At Cosa, initially a colony and then a Roman *municipium*, 770 coins, datable between the third century BCE and fifth century CE, were recovered at Tricosto only a single sample came to light (an *as* or *dupondius* dated to between the second and third centuries CE).[3] The pottery from the late Republican and Imperial periods excavated at Tricosto is similarly sparse, represented by only 4 per cent of the total (689) fragments (*infra* Acconcia). This scarcity suggests that the site in the classical era was slightly populated.[4]

Coinage reappears on our site with a billon Luccan *denaro* of the second half of the twelfth century. At Cosa we notice a similar situation: the earliest medieval coin found is a *denaro* struck in the name of Henry IV of Franconia (1056–1106).[5]

This picture reflects a well-known feature that portrays Lucca as an hegemonic mint in central Italy from the eleventh century onwards.[6] After all, the

---

* I would like to thank Andrea Sacocci for his ever-helpful suggestions and Flavia Marani for the photographic documentation.

1 Dyson 1984, 270; Hobart and others 2009, 52–54.
2 For an analysis of medieval numismatic finds from Cosa, see Rovelli 2003, 260–65.
3 Buttrey 1980, 111–53; Buttrey 2003, 250–59.
4 Hobart and others 2009, 50.
5 Buttrey 2003, 260 n. 83; Rovelli 2003, 261, no. 3.
6 Since bibliography on this issue is vast, I will mention the few key items: Toubert 1973, 584–95 and Matzke 1993; while on the

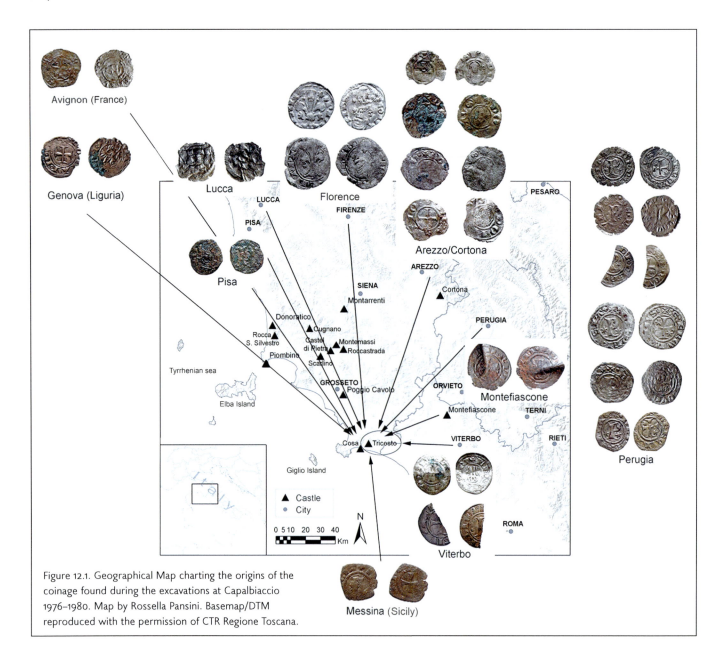

Figure 12.1. Geographical Map charting the origins of the coinage found during the excavations at Capalbiaccio 1976–1980. Map by Rossella Pansini. Basemap/DTM reproduced with the permission of CTR Regione Toscana.

mint of Lucca, which was founded in the Lombard period (seventh century) and continued to be active during the Carolingian and Ottonian eras, was the only present mint in the eleventh century in central Italy.[7] Since Rome lacked a mint, what further contributed to the Luccan *denari* fame was that these were the most frequently used currency by the papacy and known as one of the 'official' issues of the First Crusade. As far as Italy is concerned, the circulation of the Luccan *denari* through Tuscany reached the borders of Lombardy and extended to Marche, Umbria, and southern Latium. Thus, the *Liber Censuum* testifies to the fact that a significant portion of the census dues owed to the Curia was paid in *lucenses*. In the first decades of the existence of the Latin States, the *denari* from Lucca were included, along with the deniers of Poitiers, Chartres, Le Mans, Valence, Melgueil, and Le Puy, among the issues that constituted the '*moneta nostri exercitus [Dei]*', which made them among the most widely diffused coins in the Holy Land.[8]

---

latest evidence on archaeological findings and its written sources see Cicali 1996; Rovelli 2000; Travaini 1992; Saccocci 2001–2002; Degasperi 2003; Saccocci 2004; Gambacorta 2009; Rovelli 2009b, 171–94; Baldassarri 2011.

7 Grierson and Blackburn 1986; Arslan 2011, 397–99; Rovelli 2008; 2009c; Rovelli 2012b; Vanni 2011, 785–88.

8 Matzke 1995, 109.

That said, in the sample of coins from Capalbiaccio the Luccan *denaro* remains a *unicum*; nearly all of the other finds date from the period 1250 to 1350. This data finds a clear correspondence in the convergence of two different matters, the first of which is tied to the history of castle of Tricosto. On the basis of the pottery analysis and the surviving architectural structures, the thirteenth century coincides with the highest expansion of the settlement that occupies most of the hilltop plateau protected by city wall fortification. To this period dates also the construction of a second church to serve the obviously growing community.[9] From a monetary point of view, by the mid-thirteenth century, coin production and circulation had profoundly changed from what it had been in the years when the Luccan *denaro* enjoyed unrivalled circulation. The middle decades of the thirteenth century were a crucial period of transformation, marked by the rise of new local mints, including those of Perugia, Cortona, Orvieto, and Viterbo (Fig. 12.1). Focusing on central Italy, it is worth keeping in mind that these mints joined those already active in Pisa (opened circa in 1150), Volterra, Ancona, Siena, and Rome that started in a rapid succession in the second half of the twelfth century.[10]

After more than a century-long process of reforms and innovations, a fundamental step of which was the creation of large silver coins or *grossi*, the monetary system reached full maturity thanks to a return to gold coinage around the mid-thirteenth century. The pioneers in this process were Genoa and Florence that began coining the first Genovini and Florins in 1252.[11] The considerable increase in the supply of money led to the rapid monetization of the economy, even in rural areas, which is likewise clearly visible in the sample of coins from Tricosto.[12] The multiplication of mints and, consequently, the striking of coins with different intrinsic values fostered the rise of different monetary areas, each of which was characterized by the prevalence of a dominant coinage.[13] At Tricosto, between the thirteenth and fourteenth centuries, small change was initially dominated by debased Aretine *denari* or *piccioli* (issued by the bishop either in Arezzo or the nearby Cortona), and subsequently by *denari* from the pontifical mints of the *Patrimonium Beati Petri* (Viterbo and Montefiascone) and from Perugia.

As for the small coins from Arezzo and Cortona, this sample confirms their prevalence in a large portion of Umbria and northern Latium.[14] Thus far, Tricosto and Cosa are the northernmost points at which these piccioli have been found along the Tyrrhenian coast. Judging from their significant presence in our limited sample their importance in the area's circulation may also have been favoured by the politico-economic network of the Aldobrandeschi family which extended from the coast to the inner region.[15]

Regarding the fourteenth century and continuing our comparisons with the Cosa finds, the fourteenth-century coins from Tricosto are consistent with the coins discovered in a small hoard in one of the cisterns of the ancient Roman colony, whose medieval castle was destroyed during the Sienese attack of 1329. The purse, which was probably hidden on the occasion of these dramatic events, consisted predominantly of *denari* issued in the papal territories: out of a total of thirty-two items, fourteen coins are in the name of John XXII and were probably coined at Montefiascone; another ten items were coined in Perugia, the second-most important mint from a quantitative point of view. As noted elsewhere, analogies likewise exist between the material from the small purse of Cosa/Ansedonia and those found at Capalbiaccio with the much more consistent treasure discovered in Fontana Antica (close to Tarquinia), as well as with the larger group of coins preserved in the National Etruscan Museum in Tarquinia.[16] This museum contains over 800 items from local excavations, which are datable from the twelfth (represented once again by a *denaro* struck at Lucca in the name of one of the Henry's Emperors) to the sixteenth century.

It is striking that in this important group of coins in the National Etruscan Museum of Tarquinia we also notice that in the fourteenth-century issue, there is a significant presence of coins issued at Montefiascone and Perugia.[17] Further, it is noticeable — in both, the small group from Capalbiaccio and in the more conspicuous samples from Tarquinia, the ancient Corneto — the random presence of issues from the papal mint of Avignon, particularly those in the name of Pope Urban VI (1378–1389).

---

9 Hobart and others 2009, 58–60.
10 For a general point of view, see Spufford 1988, 187–201; on the principal mints handling the materials examined here, see Bernocchi 1974–1986; Stahl 1988; Finetti 1997; Bellesia 2007; Baldassarri 2010.
11 Spufford 1988, 225–39; Grierson 1991, 105–38. On some aspects of the early *grossi* struck by Tuscan mints, see Stahl 2000.
12 In the case of Italy, the theme has recently been addressed by Delogu and Sorda 2002; see also Dyer 1997.
13 On these issues, with respect to Tuscany, see Travaini 2000, 25–42.
14 Finetti 1999, 72–75.
15 Hobart and others 2009, 81; *infra*, Hobart on Medieval pottery.
16 Rovelli 2012b, 191–94.
17 Gambacorta 2009.

A series of factors helps explain the dominance of these mints in a scenario that remains highly variegated. From a strictly monetary point of view, Perugia's mint notably increased the volume of its issues as it profited from the significant decline in the production of *piccioli* in Cortona and Arezzo that were the prevailing currency in the second half of the thirteenth century. Further, the vitality of the mint in Perugia was also assisted by the consolidation of commercial routes that originated, at least in part, on the ancient paths used for transhumance.[18] In the coastal stretch along the border between Latium and Tuscany, the spread of Perugian coinage is notable and well attested not only in Cosa and in Tricosto, but, as we just mentioned, by samples now in the Tarquinia Museum. Of these 185 *sestini* are dated between 1340 and 1395. Connections with Umbria are further confirmed by the ceramic evidence from Capalbiaccio in the second half of the fourteenth century.[19]

Finally, it is necessary to note the existence of specimens that seem anomalous with respect to the chief protagonists in the local situation, but which nonetheless clearly reflect monetary circulation along the coast. These are the *denario* of James I from the mint of Messina and the *quartaro* from Genoa, to name a few. A Genovese *quartaro* has also been documented at Monte Romano, not far from Tarquinia, and in Sicily, at Brucato.[20] The *denaro* from Messina at Capalbiaccio constitutes tangible evidence of reciprocal movement between Sicily and central Italy along the heavily trafficked Tyrrhenian coast.

CATALOGUE

Roman Empire

1. Pl. 12.1

Description: AE, *as* or *dupondius*.
Obv. Illegible legend. Traces of a female bust.
Rev. Illegible legend. Traces of a standing figure.
Dimensions: 25.30 mm; 9.61 g.
Mint: **Origin**: Rome.
Date: second–third century CE
Context: Campaign 1980, Building M, Level 4, Trench 8–1.

Republic of Lucca

2. Pl. 12.2

Description: Billon, *denaro*.
Obv. Illegible legend. In field, 'monogram' of Henry with two 'T's bound to form an 'H'.
Rev. Illegible legend. In field, LV/CA.
Dimensions: 14.90 mm; 0.47 g.
Mint: Lucca.
Date: Second half of the eleventh c.
Context: Campaign 1978, Building J, Pit 11.
References: Matzke 1993, 190, no. 43; 191, nos 44 and 47; *Corpus Nummorum Italicorum* 1929, 70–71, no. 3f; pl. IV, no. 33.

---

18 Finetti 1997, 88; Gambacorta 2009, 148.
19 Hobart and others 2009, 81.
20 Scapaticci Perfetti 2000, 224. On the circulation of coins from Genoa, see Baldassarri 2009. On mercantile activity along the Tyrrhenian coast and the role of local grain production, see Abulafia 1974; from the Scarlino material one *grosso* from Genoa dated to the thirteenth century, and a *denaro* from Turin (torinese) of Guillaume I or Guy II de la Roche form Athens mint (1280–1308) and finally a *denaro* of Alfonso V of Aragon from the mint of Messina (1416–1458), Rovelli, 1996, 225–54.

Patrimonium Beati Petri

3. Pl. 12.3

Description: Billon, *denaro paparino*.
Obv. + PATRIMONIV'. In field, cross fleury.
Rev. + BEATI PETRI. In field, two keys.
Dimensions: 17.40 mm; 0.47 g.
Mint: Viterbo, Vacant seat.
Date: 1268–1271 (or later).
Context: Campaign 1978, Building M, Level II, Pit 9.
References: *Corpus Nummorum Italicorum* 1933, 271, no. 6, pl. XIX, 20; on the chronology, see Rovelli 2009b, 185–89.

James I, King of Sicily

4. Pl. 12.4

Description: Billon, *denaro*.
Obv. + […]A. In field, crowned head left.
Rev. Illegible legend. In field, cross potent.
Dimensions: 13.20 mm; 0.50 g.
Mint: Messina.
Date: 1285–1296.
Context: Campaign 1978, Pit 11/1.
References: Grierson and Travaini 1998, 696, pl. 42, no. 769.

Arezzo (Communal or Episcopal Authority)

5. Pl. 12.5

Description: Billon, *denaro*.
Obv. […]E A[RI]TIO[.]. In field, cross potent.
Rev. + S DON[AT]VS. In field, frontal, bearded bust in blessing gesture, with halo, mitre, and crosier (both 'S's are horizontal).
Dimensions: 16.70 mm; 0.43 g; fragmentary.
Mint: Arezzo (?), Cortona (?).
Date: Second half of the thirteenth c.
Context: Campaign 1978, Building M, Level II, Pit 9.
References: *Corpus Nummorum Italicorum* 1929, 4–6, nos 24–44. On the chronology, see Finetti 1997, 41. On the mint of Cortona and the *denarii cortonenses*, see Stahl 1988, 483–93; Finetti 1993, 17, note 14; Finetti 1997, 39–45; Vanni 1997; Vanni 2005; Travaini 2011b, 624–26.

6. Pl. 12.6

Description: Obv. + · *vertical crescent* D[E ARIT] IO *horizontal crescent*. In field, cross potent.
Rev. + […]TVS *vertical crescent*. In field, frontal bust as above (the 'S' at the end of the legend is horizontal).
Dimensions: 17.50 mm; 0.40 g.
Context: Campaign 1978, Building M, Level II, Pit 16.
References: *Corpus Nummorum Italicorum* 1929, 5, no. 33.

7. Pl. 12.7

Description: Obv. [+ .] *crescent* D[E ARI]TIO[.]. In field, cross potent.
Rev. + S DO[NA]TVS *vertical crescent*. In field, frontal bust as above (both 'S's are horizontal).
Dimensions: 16.60 mm; 0.33 g.
Context: Campaign 1978, Building M, Level 4, Pit 9.
References: *Corpus Nummorum Italicorum* 1929, 4–6, nos 24–44, pl. I, no. 9.

8. Pl. 12.8

Description: Obv. […]A[…]. In field, cross potent.
Rev. + *vertical crescent* S D[ONA]TVS. In field, frontal bust as above.
Dimensions: 14.40 mm; 0.29 g; fragmentary.
Context: Building M, Level II, Trench 8–1.
References: *Corpus Nummorum Italicorum* 1929, 4–6, nos 24–44, pl. I, no. 9.

John XXII

9. Pl. 12.9

Description: Billon, *denaro paparino*.
Obv. [+] IO[...]XII *star*. In field, two keys.
Rev. [...]RI'M[...]. In field, cross fleury.
Dimensions: 16.90 mm; 0.34 g.
Mint: Montefiascone.
Date: 1316–1334.
Context: Campaign 1978, Building M, Level II, Pit 9.
References: *Corpus Nummorum Italicorum* 1933, 264, nos 13–14.

Republic of Pisa in the Name of the Emperor Frederick

10. Pl. 12.10

Description: Billon, *denaro*.
Obv. Illegible legend. In field, large P, a crossbow (?) on the left.
Rev. Illegible legend. In field, crowned eagle with outspread wings standing on a capital.
Dimensions: 12.40 mm; 0.53 g.
Mint: Pisa.
Date: *c.* 1318/19–1330.
Context: Campaign 1978, Building J, Level II, Pit 2.
References: *Corpus Nummorum Italicorum* 1929, 311, no. 93 (but as a fifteenth-century *quattrino*). On the denomination and chronology, see Rovelli 1985, 379–87; Finetti 1999, 76; Baldassarri 2010, 311.

Republic of Perugia

11. Pl. 12.11

Description: Billon, sestino. Obv. + : DE : PERVSIA *small quatrefoil cross*. In field, large P between two stars.
Rev + : S : ERCVLANVS *rosette*. In field, cross with six-rayed star in 1st and 4th quarters.
Dimensions: 19.10 mm; 1.26 g.
Mint: Perugia.
Date: Ordinance of 25 August 1321.
Context: Campaign 1978, Building M, Level II, Pit 9.
References: Finetti 1997, 183, no. 45; *Corpus Nummorum Italicorum* 1933, 190–92, nos 23–35, pl. XIII, 21 (but based on a chronology following the ordinances of 1471 and 1482).

12. Pl. 12.12

Description: Billon, *denaro*.
Obv. + · D[...]IA *rosette*. In field, large P between two six-rayed stars.
Rev. [...]RCVLA[...]. In field, cross potent with six-rayed star in 1st and 4th quarters.
Dimensions: 15.50 mm; 0.43 g.
Mint: Perugia.
Date: Ordinance of 25 August 1321.
Context: Campaign 1978, Building M, Level II, Pit 9.
References: Finetti 1997, 181–82, nos 39–43; *Corpus Nummorum Italicorum* 1933, 192–93, nos 38–43, pl. XIII, no. 23 (but as a *quattrino*, and following the chronology of the ordinances of 1471 and 1482).

13. Pl. 12.13

Description: Obv. [+] · DE PERVSIA[.]. In field, large P, as above.
Rev. […] ERCVLA[…]. In field, cross potent, as above.
Dimensions: 14.30 mm; 0.42 g.
Context: Campaign 1978, Building M, Level II, Pit 9.

14. Pl. 12.14

Description: Obv. […] DE PERV[…]. In field, large P, as above.
Rev. + : S : ERCVL[…]. In field, cross potent, as above.
Dimensions: 14.30 mm; 0.27 g; fragment amounting to about half.
Context: Campaign 1978, Building M, Level I, Pit 9.

15. Pl. 12.15

Description: Obv. […] · DE · PERVSI[…]. In field, large P, as above.
Rev. […] ERCV[LA]NVS[.]. In field, cross potent, as above.
Dimensions: 14.40 mm; 0.36 g.
Context: Campaign 1978, Building I, Level II, Pit 6.

16. Pl. 12.16

Catalogue Number: R 1
Description: Obv. […] DE PE[R]VSIA[…]. In field, large P, as above.
Rev. +[.] S : ERCVLANVS :. In field, cross potent, as above (reversed 'N').
Dimensions: 15.20 mm; 0.22 g.
Context: Campaign 1978, Building M, Level II, Pit 9.
References: Finetti 1997, 182, no. 43.

Republic of Florence

17. Pl. 12.17

Description: Billon, *quattrino*.
Obv. […]ENTIA · . In field, Florentine fleur-de-lis with flowers intersecting a pearled border.
Rev. […] · IO[…] · B. In field, Half bust of St John.
Dimensions: 18.40 mm; 1.10 g.
Mint: Florence
Date: 1st semester 1332–2nd semester 1335.
Context: Campaign 1978, Building M, Level I, Pit 9.
References: Bernocchi 1974–1986, III, pl. LV.

18. Pl. 12.18

Description: Billon, *quattrino*.
Obv. + FLO[…]NTIA. In field, Florentine fleur-de-lis with two flowers, no border.
Rev. S IOHA – N[…]. In field, St John with cape partly covering his tunic. Privy mark: tusk (?).
Dimensions: 17.10; 0.65 g.
Mint: Florence.
Date: 1st semester 1372 (?).
Context: Campaign 1980, Building J, Level IV, Trench 8–6.
References: Bernocchi 1974–1986, II, 228; III, pl. LVIII.

Francesco di Vico, Prefect of Rome

19. Pl. 12.19

Description: Billon, *quattrino*.
Obv. + [...]RBIO [leaf?]·. In field, large P between two bezants.
Rev. + S L[...]TIVS [leaf?]. In field, cross potent.
Dimensions: 18.60 mm; 0.47 g; fragment, half.
Mint: Viterbo.
Date: 1375–1387.
Context: Campaign 1978, Building J, Level 4, Pit 2.
References: *Corpus Nummorum Italicorum* 1933, 273, nos 4–6, pl. XIX, no. 24 (but with the head of an eagle).

Urban VI

20. Pl. 12.20

Description: Billon, *denaro*.
Obv. *small, decussated keys* · V[...] PP · SE[..] VS ·. In field, mitre.
Rev. [...]AN[...] · E [...]. In field, cross potent, with small decussated keys in 2nd and 3rd quarters.
Dimensions: 17.80 mm; 0.78 g.
Mint: Avignon (?).
Date: 1378–1389.
Context: Campaign 1980, Building J, Level III, Trench 8–6.
References: Muntoni 1972, 34, no. 1, pl. 7.

Republic of Genoa

21. Pl. 12.21

Description: Copper, *quartaro*.
D/ [...]Q°V°A°[...]R•.
In field, rampant griffon to right.
R/ [...]T°O°M°A°I°N°V[...].
In field cross potent.
Dimensions: 15.10 mm; 0.49 g.
Mint: Genoa.
Date: Fourteenth century
Context: Campaign 1978, Building M, Level II, Pit 9.
References: *Corpus Nummorum Italicorum* 1912, p. 40, nos 30–31, pl. II, 25 (pre-1339); on current dating, and analyses of its area of circulation, see Baldassarri 2009, 331–71, esp. 339–40, pl. IV, IV.

Illegible Fragments

22. Pl. 12.22

Dimensions: 0.27 g.
Context: Campaign 1978, Building J, Level III, Pit 2.

DIANA C. CRADER

13. Archaeozoological Remains

ABSTRACT Diana C. Crader's study of faunal remains from samples excavated in the 1970s is fundamental for the reconstruction of the economy of the town. It shows an economy rooted in agriculture and livestock, and supplemented by occasional hunting. Zooarchaeological analyses reveal four major domestic species: sheep, goat, cattle, and pig. Secondary domestic species include horses, donkeys, and chickens. Wild fauna consists of hare, squirrel, hedgehog, several small carnivores, three species of deer (fallow, red, and roe), a few birds, frog, fish, and a significant quantity of tortoise shells.

Faunal remains of Building J count mostly domestic species, predominately pig, cattle, sheep, and goat, along with smaller quantities of horses, donkey, and chicken. Of the three levels excavated, the latest, Level I, shows a prevalence of domestic sheep and goat specimens, while Levels II and III show a great amount of pig specimens, consistent with other nearby archaeological sites. The presence of wild fauna shows that the inhabitants occasionally enriched their diet by hunting game. The remaining levels of Building J (the tenth-century village, the Etruscan phase, and the prehistoric) show the same pattern, with a predominance of domestic fauna, together with clear evidence of hunting.

The other analysed area, Area M, an open space used during the medieval period and dating from the tenth to the fifteenth centuries, reveals large quantities of both animal bones and pottery. This has been interpreted as a garbage dump. Of the four identified levels, the two uppermost present most specimens, suggesting that Area M was mostly used during the later phases of the settlement (thirteenth to the fifteenth centuries, until its abandonment). The species found here are very similar to those registered in Building J, although with greater quantities of goat and sheep compared to pigs. Of these, the predominance of adult remains indicates that these animals were mostly used for dairy and wool production before being slaughtered at the end of their 'useful' life.

The small faunal sample in Area C is well-preserved only in the deepest levels. Cattle remains are dominant, while pigs are less common. The evidence of ovicaprines, equids, and tortoises from more recent periods of the site is rare.

The bone assemblage of Building F comes from four different levels, all dated to the Medieval period. Due to the scarcity of evidence, it is not possible to draw any conclusions. Building I was a grain storage area, with little evidence of faunal remains, and was probably used for foodstuffs. The presence of dog remains in zone R indicates that this animal was probably used for herding. Faunal evidence in zone T comes from two levels, with pig specimens predominant in both.

The substantial amount of tortoise remains with butchery traces from across the whole area indicates that tortoises played a big role within food supply and had an important economic role.[1]

Although the Capalbiaccio bone analysis was carried out before the pottery dating evidence, Crader suggests that the bone material is medieval. However, a number of residual fragments from the Etruscan period have also been found (see Acconcia's chapter and the Appendix); these probably came to the surface when the dump area was excavated. It is interesting to note the differences shown in Table A3.3 (Building M) between Levels I–III and Level IV, which clearly shows stock raising and consumption practices for the medieval period. For this level, sheep and goat finds are dominant, pig fragments only rare, and remains of game animals are missing. Game remains are tied mostly to the earlier prehistoric period, as shown in the oldest levels of Building J. [MH]

---

* I am particularly indebted to Stephen L. Dyson, my colleague and friend, who made my work on the Capalbiaccio fauna possible. He introduced me to Italian archaeology, provided access to the bone specimens, and has given me immeasurable support and encouragement during all stages of the analysis. Special thanks are due to Graziano Bonnino, caretaker of the Cosa Museum in Ansedonia, who facilitated my work in Italy and introduced me to many beautiful aspects of life in Tuscany. I benefitted greatly from correspondence with Graeme Barker and Gillian Clark, who taught me about medieval Italian zooarchaeology. Over the years, several students at Wesleyan University and at the University of Southern Maine helped with various parts of the identification and analysis, and provided technical assistance, especially Melissa Gates and Matt Rowe, and more recently Mica Jones, who assisted with the analysis of the Etruscan fauna. Finally, this work could not have been completed without the help of my husband, Bob Johnson, who assisted me with the analysis in Italy, always supports my 'bone work', and shares my love of Italy. I take responsibility for all errors.

1 Crader and Rowe forthcoming.

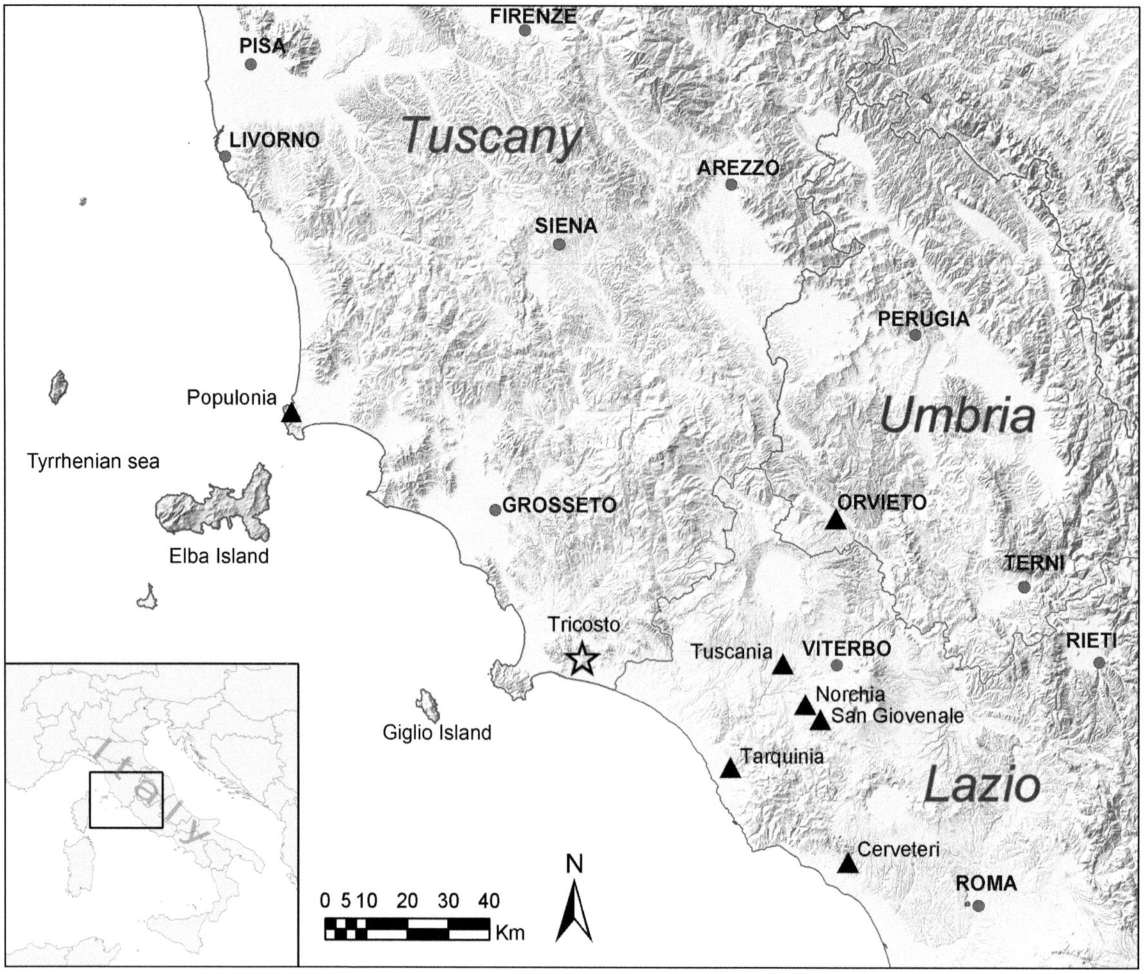

Figure 13.1. DEM of Tuscany and the sites mentioned in the chapter. Map by Rossella Pansini. Basemap/DTM reproduced with the permission of CTR Regione Toscana.

Introduction

Excavations at the site of Capalbiaccio produced a large sample of animal bones and teeth. This report focuses on the faunal material recovered from several areas at the site (designated with letters) in secure stratigraphic contexts, comprising a total of 5752 specimens. The bulk of the faunal remains were recovered from Building J and Area M, with smaller samples from Areas C, F, I, R, and T (Fig. 13.1). The vast majority of the fauna is from late medieval contexts, covering a time range from the late thirteenth to the early fifteenth centuries, but a small sample of earlier Etruscan material was recovered from the area known as Building J and is also described here.

Methodology

The animal remains were initially organized and studied between 1982 and 1987, first in Italy and later in the United States, where many additional specimens were shipped for further analysis. This preliminary work focused on basic identifications of the species present in the medieval levels of Building J and Area M. A hiatus in the faunal research ensued until 1999, when specimens housed in the United States were de-accessioned from where they had been stored and study could resume again.[2] The latest round of research on the animal remains has included detailed attribute analysis, a special study focused on the tortoise remains,[3] and an analysis of the fauna from the Etruscan levels.

---

2 Crader 2003.
3 Crader and Rowe, forthcoming.

Each specimen was identified to taxon and body part, following common practice.[4] The following attributes were also recorded for every specimen: age, sex (if known), symmetry, epiphyseal fusion, tooth wear (where applicable), and surficial markings including burning, butchery marks, gnaw marks, weathering, pathologies, bone condition, and other human modifications. Metrical analysis was completed on some specimens. This primary data was then used to generate secondary data, including the minimum number of individuals (MNI) for each species, estimates of meat weight, and demographic profiles. Full details of the methodology used to study the animal remains can be found elsewhere and will not be repeated here.[5] However, it is important to highlight a few methodological issues and conventions used in zooarchaeological research for this region and time period.

A major problem in the analysis of domestic stock involves the identification and separation of similar species when specimens are fragmentary, especially sheep and goat; cattle and horse. Although each of these domestic species has some diagnostic morphological features, identification is further complicated at Capalbiaccio by the presence of wild species, especially three species of deer, whose sizes overlap with sheep, goat, and pig, at the small end, and with cow and horse, at the large end. Thus, it is not always possible to distinguish among these similar species. Therefore, when fragmentary specimens could not be identified to the species level, higher taxonomic categories and size groups were used. For example, medium-sized artiodactyl refers to a specimen that could belong to either sheep, goat, pig, or fallow deer.

Sheep and goat bones are difficult to distinguish, but new criteria for teeth were used for the Etruscan specimens,[6] in addition to the more traditional criteria.[7] Similarly, the distinction between domestic swine and wild boar is tenuous and usually based on the larger size of the latter.[8] A suid specimen was only designated as wild boar if it was extremely large. The distinction between horse and donkey is usually based on size and, when *Equus* specimens were very small, they were designated as donkey (*Equus asinus*). Cattle (*Bos taurus*) can vary in size, depending on whether a cow or ox is represented.

Interpretation

A basic part of any zooarchaeological analysis is quantification of the relative proportion of identifiable versus non-identifiable specimens. Due to animal processing activities, which tend to break up bones and render them non-identifiable, a larger proportion of non-identifiable specimens is usually found at archaeological sites. However, at Capalbiaccio there is a smaller proportion of non-identifiable bones than would normally be expected (Appendix 3, Table 1). This is probably due to the excavation methods employed in the 1970s, which failed to recover the many small fragments that would ordinarily result in a larger non-identifiable sample.

The relative proportion of the major domestic animals is an important aspect of medieval Italian zooarchaeological studies, because it reveals how different stock raising and consumption strategies were practised in different contexts. A variety of patterns has been found in medieval Italy, due to the different types of settlements (for example, urban centres or small towns) and factors such as ecological conditions or politics.

In this summary report, results are presented using NISP (number of identifiable specimens) and MNI (minimum number of individuals), despite the problems of using the latter for assemblages from medieval Italian market economies, where joints, rather than whole animals, may have entered a site.[9] A reasonable approach recognizes that each type of quantification yields a different kind of data and a different assessment of the assemblage, and both are valuable, once the context of the site is understood. Capalbiaccio was a rural town where most on-site animal production was small and for on-site use, not intended for a market economy. Here, selected animal parts may have occasionally been obtained from elsewhere.

Although the fauna from each level was analysed and presented separately, the results from all of the medieval levels are combined here for purposes of providing a summary of the important trends.[10] The MNI was determined by taking into account the symmetry, age, and size of every skeletal element of each species in each level and then adding the results together. Additionally, in order to assess the relative meat contribution of the main domestic stock animals (sheep, goat, pig, and cattle), meat weight conversion factors were applied to the data:

---

4 Reitz and Wing 2008.
5 Crader 2003 and Crader and Rowe, forthcoming.
6 Halstead, Collins, and Isaakidou 2002.
7 These are outlined in Boessneck 1969 and Hildebrand 1955.
8 Baker and Clark 1993.

9 Baker and Clark 1993.
10 For further details, see Crader 2003.

27 kg for sheep and goat; 46 kg for pigs; and 227 kg for cattle.[11]

Age profiles can be used to reveal how animals were used and the activities that took place at the site. The age of the fauna at the time of death was determined using epiphyseal fusion stages, tooth eruption, and tooth wear.[12] Gillian Clark's summary of the meaning of different age profiles has been applied to the Capalbiaccio data.[13] In general, evidence of meat production is suggested by a large number of deaths at prime sub-adult age, whereas animals raised for dairy production would have been killed at older ages, after yields begin to decline. Sheep raised for wool would also be kept until they were older, while animals used as beasts of burden would have lived to old age. A combined economic strategy would show mixed characteristics.

Differential body-part representation and cultural marks on bones, such as butchery marks and burning, reveal how animals were processed and any additional animal-related activities that took place at the site. Carcass dismemberment, secondary butchery, cooking techniques, culinary practices, eating habits, and bone-working activities can be reconstructed by analysis of the number, type, and location of modifications to the bones.

The Medieval Animal Economy at Capalbiaccio: Overview

Zooarchaeological studies of faunal remains from medieval sites in Italy have contributed to understanding several key issues about stock rearing and herding practices in the region.[14] The animal remains from Capalbiaccio contribute to this body of knowledge about medieval animal economies in several major areas, including: the range of animals used, both domestic and wild; the relative proportion of the primary domestic species; changes in stock raising and consumption practices through time; the role of stock raising in the overall economic system (in relation to cereal crops), as important sources for meat, wool, milk, labour, and other products; and the role of wild species in an otherwise domestic-based economy.

As a small, rural, hilltop town, Capalbiaccio was supported by an agrarian economy that included raising crops and rearing domestic animals, but the residents also occasionally supplemented their diet with wild game. Zooarchaeological analyses revealed that the animal-based economy was focused on four major domestic species: sheep, goat, cattle, and pig.[15] Other domestic animals recovered from the site include horse, donkey, and chicken. Wild species include hare, squirrel, hedgehog, several small carnivores, three species of deer (fallow, red, and roe), a few birds, frog, fish, and a significant quantity of tortoise remains. Tortoises were common domestic animals in some areas of the site and were the subject of a separate study.[16]

An initial study of the fauna focused on the assemblages recovered from two areas of the site: Building J and Area M.[17] These areas were of particular interest because the assemblages were relatively large and they represent different habitation and depositional contexts in the town. The results of the analysis provide insight into the habitation history of the site, the economic workings of the town, and differences in the use of the buildings and areas of the site. From the animal remains, a clear picture of the medieval meat economy at Capalbiaccio can be reconstructed, including changes through time, given the postulated two-phase medieval occupation of the town. The results of the analysis of the medieval fauna from Building J and Area M are summarized below, followed by a summary of specimens from other areas of the site (C, F, I, R, and T), a separate section on the tortoise remains, and, finally, a summary of the animal remains from the earlier Etruscan levels.

Building J

As previously noted, Building J was a 10 × 6 m structure located along the northwestern part of the outer defensive wall (*infra* Corti). It is one of the most well-preserved structures at Capalbiaccio, with an arched doorway and one wall rising to the second floor.[18] Excavations of Building J revealed three levels of medieval occupation, spanning a time period from the late thirteenth to the early fifteenth centuries, underlain in most places by the hard-packed *terra rossa*. Beneath these levels, there was evidence of a deeper stratified pre-Roman or Etruscan occupation (60–70 cm), which is discussed below in a separate section.

A total of 1786 bone fragments were recovered from the three medieval levels of Building J, which

---

11 For these standard weight conversion factors, see Bedini 1995.
12 Grant 1975; Silver 1969.
13 Clark 2003.
14 For reviews, see Clark 1987; Baker and Clark 1993.
15 Crader 2003.
16 Crader and Rowe, forthcoming.
17 Crader 2003.
18 Dyson 1978a; 1979.

included 1210 (67.7 per cent) identifiable and 576 (32.3 per cent) non-identifiable specimens (Appendix 3, Table 1). Far fewer specimens were recovered from the uppermost level of Building J, compared to the two deeper medieval levels, which suggests less frequent use of the building near the time of abandonment of the town.[19] Perhaps the structure was completely abandoned once the construction of the outside defensive wall destroyed its main drain.[20]

Spatially, the bone specimens from Building J were recovered from trenches along the north wall of the building, the eastern side (where the doorway was located), and also in the southwest corner. Thus, they represent bone refuse found in the interior of the building. Taphonomically, the bones have modifications that contribute to understanding the depositional history of Building J and the living conditions inside the structure. Of the specimens, 63 (3.5 per cent) were gnawed by carnivores, presumably dogs, which were kept as pets by the inhabitants. Another 11 bones (0.6 per cent) bore rodent gnaw marks, revealing the presence of these unsavoury critters inside the building with the inhabitants, an image that reinforces popular notions about living conditions during the Middle Ages. Most of the bones were very well preserved, but some were pitted and crumbly, and some were discoloured, either with grey mottling or an orange stain.

As a group, domestic species dominate the assemblage at Building J in all levels, with pig, cattle, sheep, and goat predominating, along with smaller quantities of horse, donkey, and chicken. Wild animals include three species of deer (fallow, red, and roe) and some very large pig remains, which may belong to wild boar, indicating that the residents occasionally supplemented their diet by hunting wild game. Other small species are represented, including otter, hare, rodents, wild or domestic cat, birds, fish, and a relatively large number of tortoise remains.

At Building J, there is a clear dominance of pigs over the other domestic species, both in terms of NISP and MNI. The predominance of pig over sheep, goat, and cattle is a pattern seen at earlier sites in the area, from Roman times onwards.[21] This pattern is also seen in the earlier medieval (late twelfth- to mid-fourteenth-century) levels at the nearby site of Tarquinia,[22] as well as at other medieval sites, such as Castello di Manzano.[23] However, this differs from the pattern shown at the later levels of Tarquinia and at the neighbouring town of Tuscania, where sheep and goat dominate over pig.[24] But, although pigs dominate in the lower two medieval levels of Building J, there is a gradual decrease in their relative proportion through time, until, in Level I, they are actually outnumbered by sheep and goat.[25] This suggests a small shift in stock raising or consumption patterns during the later stages of occupation at Capalbiaccio, at least as regards Building J. This shift also occurs at Tarquinia, where pigs dominate in the lowest levels, but then decline through time and are outnumbered by sheep and goat in the later levels.[26]

The overall fewer number of sheep and goat remains (compared to those of pigs) at Building J suggests their lesser role in the agricultural economy of the town. Given the grazing requirements of sheep and goat (compared to pigs), it may have been more difficult to keep large flocks, since arable land near the town would have been needed for farming. Pigs, on the other hand, could have eaten household scraps and may have been kept in sties or been allowed to roam freely in the town or on hillsides, and they may have fitted more easily into the overall agrarian pattern. It has been suggested that, in some areas, sheep and goat may have been raised only in the context of transhumance, with the localized movement of flocks exploiting available grazing lands.[27] But, it is also possible that rural communities such as Capalbiaccio could have kept small flocks year round.

Cattle rank last in importance among the major stock animals at Building J in terms of NISP and MNI, although meat weight conversions suggest that they were more important in the meat economy than the raw data indicates.[28] The apparently larger relative meat contribution of cattle should be viewed with scepticism in the context of a market economy, where whole carcasses may not have been present. Large-scale cattle husbandry was probably impossible at Capalbiaccio, given the confines of the town and its hilltop setting, although this region of Tuscany is known for its cattle production. Like sheep and goats, cattle would have competed with the arable lands needed to grow crops for human consumption.

Mortality data was used to establish age profiles for each of the domestic species and thus, they revealed patterns about how each species was used — whether for meat or for other products, such as

---

19 Crader 2003.
20 Dyson 1978a; 1981b.
21 For example, see Dyson 1981b; King 1999.
22 Clark 1987.
23 Bedini 1995.

24 Barker 1973; 1978; Clark 1989a.
25 Crader 2003.
26 Clark 1987; 1989a.
27 Barker 1973; 1995; King 1999.
28 Crader 2003.

milk or wool, or for labour. At Building J, pigs of all ages are represented from neonates to 2-year-olds to very old adults. Given that pigs were raised almost exclusively for meat (and not for milk or other products, such as wool), it is not surprising to find this wide age range. Young pork and suckling pig were probably highly desirable and, although animals of all ages are represented, half of the individuals present were around 2 years of age when they died, which was probably a critical culling point when they reached their maximum weight.[29] The ages of the sheep and goats suggest multiple uses. Over half of the individuals (6 out of 11) were adults over 2–3 years old, suggesting that they were kept for milk or for wool, while one third (4 out of 11) were 12–24 months old when they died, suggesting that they were used for meat. The small sample size of cattle from Building J precludes the development of a clear picture of their role in the overall economy. Mortality data indicates the presence of only one younger animal, less than 2 years old. The other four were all adults over 3 years old, suggesting that they were kept for milking or labour, and only later were they perhaps used as a source of beef. None of the cattle remains at Building J belonged to extremely large individuals, so the presence of oxen is not indicated here.

Area M (also known as Building M)

With few fragmentary architectural features, the structure originally referred to as Building M was more likely an open space that was probably used as a garbage pit or dumping ground for the town or surrounding buildings. Excavations revealed numerous animal bones and a considerable quantity of medieval pottery, which were recovered from four levels, with no indication of any earlier pre-Roman occupation. Based on the pottery and coins, the medieval occupation probably spans the time period from the late thirteenth to the late fifteenth centuries.

A total of 2432 bone specimens were recovered from Area M, including 1585 (65.2 per cent) identifiable and 847 (34.8 per cent) non-identifiable (Appendix 3, Table 1). This is the largest faunal assemblage at the site, despite the fact that the excavated area here was eight times smaller than the area excavated at Building J. This suggests a very dense bone heap, consistent with the notion that Area M served as a garbage dump, rather than a dwelling. Additionally, while the same proportion of bones at Area M and Building J had carnivore gnaw marks (3.5 per cent), a higher proportion of bones at Area M had rodent marks (1.9 per cent compared to 0.6 per cent at Building J), which suggests that there was more rodent activity among the bone refuse here. This further supports the idea that Area M served as a refuse dump, since rodents could have more readily visited or lived at the town dump than in the interior of a residence, as at Building J.

Here, as for Building J, the specimens from each level were originally analysed and presented separately, but the results are combined for purposes of this summary and changes through time are noted.[30] Faunal remains are most numerous in the upper two levels at Area M, which yielded over 95 per cent of the specimens, then taper off dramatically in the deeper deposits.[31] This pattern contrasts with the paucity of specimens found in the uppermost level at Building J and suggests very different depositional histories and uses for the two areas, at least during the later phases of the occupation of the town. Area M apparently continued to be used as a repository for bone refuse right up until the town was abandoned, whereas Building J may have fallen into disuse sometime earlier.

The species represented at Area M are consistent with those found at Building J, again showing the predominance of sheep, goat, pig, and cattle. Horse, donkey, and chicken are present, along with a variety of other species, including dog or wolf, hare, squirrel, and hedgehog. Three species of deer (red, fallow, and roe) are present and tortoise remains are common, indicating that wild game sometimes supplemented the diet. Finally, among the pig remains is evidence for the presence of two wild boars, based on the extremely large size of some specimens, including a canine.

The Area M assemblage differs from Building J in the relative proportion of the major domestic stock animals. Sheep and goat, rather than pig, are more common, both by NISP and MNI, but pigs are still well represented. Here, however, the relative proportions of these domestic species do not change through time, as they do in Building J.[32] It is possible that the fauna in the upper levels of Area M represent the culmination of the trend toward more sheep and goat than pig, which was revealed at Building J, so that here, by the later stages of occupation of the town, sheep and goat dominate the remains. This reflects the general trend toward a predominance of sheep and goat in late medieval contexts at sites in Italy, compared to earlier times,[33] and it is

---

29 Cartledge, Clark, and Higgins 1992.
30 Crader 2003.
31 Crader 2003.
32 Crader 2003.
33 Clark 1987.

also the pattern seen at the nearby site of Tuscania[34] and in the main levels at the neighbouring town of Tarquinia.[35] At Tuscania, sheep and goat are overwhelmingly dominant (as high as 87.6 per cent of the stock animals in one pit), so that it appears that this neighbouring town may have been involved in small-scale stock production.[36] Meat weight conversions of the domestic species reveal the same pattern as Building J, where cattle are less common numerically, but may have contributed more meat to the diet. However, as noted above, this pattern should be viewed cautiously in the context of market economies in medieval Italy.

Age profiles for the sheep and goats indicate a clear predominance of adults over sub-adults — more so than at Building J — a pattern that suggests that they were raised primarily for dairy products and wool, rather than meat. Almost 75 per cent of the individuals were over 2.5 years old when they died. This variation may relate to different uses of these areas at the site: Building J probably reflects the multiple uses of an individual household, whereas Area M may reveal the important role of sheep and goats in dairy and wool production for the town as a whole. At the nearby site of Tuscania, the majority of the sheep and goats were adults over 2 years old, suggesting that there they were also raised primarily for products other than meat. This contrasts with the pattern found in the main levels at Tarquinia, where most of the individuals were young when they died, suggesting that they were killed for their meat.[37] Tarquinia may have been involved in some kind of sheep- and goat-meat production, given its location and size, which was not the case for Capalbiaccio. Instead, at Capalbiaccio, it is more likely that small flocks of sheep and goats were simply kept at the town year round.

At Area M, pigs are once again represented by individuals of all ages, from three piglets only 6 weeks old to two very old adults (based on extremely worn teeth). The majority of animals (nine individuals) were 2–3 years old when they died, which was probably the optimum time for their meat weight. Cattle are represented in the same low proportions that they are in Building J and at many other medieval Italian towns.[38] Among the remains are several extremely large specimens, undoubtedly belonging to two adult oxen. The remaining four individuals include two cows under 2.5 years old and two over 2.5 years old. The small sample size again precludes fully understanding their role in the economy of the town, but multiple uses are suggested, including milk, beef, and labour.

Cultural Patterns: Comparison of Building J and Area M

Cultural behaviours relating to processing animals for food or other products can be seen in superficial modifications to the bones, especially burning and butchery marks. Evidence for burning showed dramatic differences between the two areas. At Building J, a total of 148 bones (8.3 per cent) were burned, whereas at Area M, only 78 specimens (3.2 per cent) were burned. Such variations are usually interpreted as differences in cooking methods: stewing or boiling in a pot causes little burning damage to bones, whereas roasting over an open fire may scorch exposed bones. Here, however, another explanation seems more likely, especially given ethnographic observations about how and when bones actually become burned and the different functions of Building J and Area M at the site. It seems more likely that this pattern reveals different treatment of the bones after consumption in the two areas. It has been observed that a significant amount of burning actually occurs not during cooking, but during household clean-up activities, when bones are swept or thrown into the fire, which is undoubtedly the situation at Building J. The higher proportion of burned bone there probably results from on-site housekeeping inside the structure, an activity that would be absent in the garbage dump at Area M.

Butchery marks were present in equivalent proportions on bones from Building J (n=164; 9.2 per cent) and Area M (n=242; 9.9 per cent), suggesting that butchery patterns and practices were generally similar throughout the site. Four types of butchery marks were recorded: cuts (fine, incised lines), chops (deeper, wedge-shaped marks), shears (flat, planar surfaces), and saws (fine, parallel marks made by a back-and-forth motion). The location and number of butchery marks on specimens reveal patterns typical of both primary and secondary butchery, and it is possible to reconstruct how animals were processed. Evidence of butchery is found on almost all body parts of domestic species, attesting to different phases of the butchery process; similar patterns were found on deer.

Initial processing included removal of the skin (except on pigs), removal of the head, ribs, and feet, division of the vertebral column, and separation of the limbs. These activities are clearly seen in cuts on

---

34 Barker 1973.
35 Clark 1989a.
36 Barker 1973.
37 Clark 2000.
38 Barker 1973; Clark 1987: 2000.

the distal tibia, metatarsals and tarsals (skin removal), and in chops, shears, and saws on distal radii, tibiae, fibulae (pigs only), tarsals, and proximal metapodials (foot removal). The removal of the head by blows to the neck left chops and shears on the rear of skulls, on occipital condyles, and on atlas and axis vertebrae. Shears and chops also appear on many other cervical, thoracic, and lumbar vertebrae, some chopped entirely in half, as the vertebral column was divided. Finally, initial processing also included the separation of limbs, as seen by chops and shears on the scapula and on the acetabulum of the pelvis.

Secondary processing of carcasses included the disarticulation of limbs, the removal of meat from limb bones, division of the pelvis and mandible, removal of the tongue, and removal of bone for use as a raw material. The articular ends of limb bones (humerus, radius, ulna, femur, and tibia) exhibited chops, shears, and saw marks where joints had been disarticulated, and the shafts of these bones also bore cuts and scrapes where meat had been removed. The pelvis was divided, as seen by chops, shears, and saws on ilium and ischium specimens, and pig mandibles were divided by chops near the symphysis. Tongues were apparently removed, due to the many cuts seen on the interior of the mandibles of pigs and cows. Bone was also used as a raw material for making other objects, as evidenced by horn cores of sheep and goats, which were chopped off at the base, and a pig femur that was completely sawn obliquely across the shaft.

Other Areas of the Site: C, F, I, R, and T

Five other areas at the site yielded faunal remains that were subsequently examined and identified. These include Areas C, R, and T, and Buildings F and I (Appendix 3, Table 2 and *infra* Dyson Appendix 4, Fig. 5). All of the specimens from these areas are in the medieval contexts and the analysis revealed the same species and general patterning that was found at Building J and Area M, where the faunal remains were more numerous. Each assemblage is described briefly below, with unusual features noted.

Area C

This area yielded a small faunal sample (NISP=126), recovered from two levels in two trenches, one near a gate area. The specimens from the upper level are weathered and pitted, while those below are well preserved. Cattle dominate the remains (52.4 per cent), with at least three individuals represented (two adults and a juvenile). What appears to be the entire skull of an adult cow is present, broken into many pieces; cut marks and chops on the frontal bone and a sheared surface at the base of one horn core fragment suggest removal of the horns. Other body parts of cattle, including limb bones and foot bones bearing butchery marks, are also present. Although pig specimens are less common, at least five individuals are represented, including a fetal or neonate, a juvenile, and three adults. Ovicaprines, equids, and tortoises are present, but rare.

Building F

This structure contained an extremely small bone assemblage (NISP=18), recovered from four excavated levels, all in medieval contexts. Several different species are present among the scant remains, represented by just one or two specimens each, and any conclusions are purely speculative, due to the small sample size dispersed throughout the levels. Two pigs, two sheep, one goat, a juvenile cow, and two chickens are represented. Wild species include roe deer, vole, and tortoise.

Building I

Very few bones (NISP=27) were recovered from this small rectangular structure, which appears to be a food storage area for grain. The condition of some of the miscellaneous animal parts recovered here suggests that they were used for food. Sheep and goat specimens include a rib and radius with cut marks. Some burnt cow bones and various parts of a skull from a very old pig were present, along with a donkey toe bone. Finally, eight tortoise carapace bones, representing two individuals, attest to the potential use of this species as a food resource.

Zone R

This faunal sample (NISP=159) was recovered from two levels in a stone-lined storage pit. The assemblage is interesting because of the numerous bones belonging to two species that are uncommon elsewhere on the site: dog and toad. Three dogs are represented by two young puppies, less than 4–5 months old (one of which appears to be almost a complete skeleton), and one adult, represented only by a few bones. Their occurrence may be fortuitous (they do not appear to be food remains, since dogs were not commonly eaten and the bones bear no butchery marks or burning), but their presence does indicate that the residents of Capalbiaccio kept dogs, which they probably used for herding. The toad specimens belong to two large individuals. They could be a food source (toad's legs?), but their presence could also simply be accidental. The remaining specimens belong to domestic and wild species also found at other areas of the site: sheep and goat (including a juvenile less than three years old), three pigs (an adult and two juveniles), a cow, and a chicken. Wild species include fallow deer, vole, hedgehog, a small carnivore, and tortoise.

Zone T

After Building J and Area M, Zone T yielded the largest sample of medieval animal remains from the 'other' areas of the site (NISP=325). The assemblage is associated with a rectangular structure near a road and cistern. Specimens were recovered from two levels (II and III), with the majority coming from Level II. The assemblage is typical of those found at other areas of the site. Pig specimens are most common in both levels: six individuals are represented, including four adults (one of which is very old, based on tooth wear), one under 2 years old, and one approximately 6 months old. Almost all body parts are present among the pig remains, including crania fragments, mandibles, teeth, vertebrae, ribs, girdles, long bones, and feet; several specimens have cuts, chops, and shears, indicating butchery. The sheep and goat remains include two adult sheep and two adult goats, as well as two additional adults, only identifiable as ovicaprine. Cattle remains belong to two adults, who are represented by mostly teeth and cranial bones, including two horn core fragments. Wild animals include two adult red deer; two adult roe deer and one juvenile; and one adult fallow deer. Several small antler fragments are present, but too small to identify to species. One specimen is burnished and rounded on the end, as though it was fashioned into some kind of handle. Finally, a single carnassial tooth belonging to *Canis* is present and its large size suggests that it belongs to a wolf.

Tortoise Remains

Although the inhabitants of Capalbiaccio relied on domestic stock as the basis for their meat economy and for other products, such as milk and wool, the site also revealed a large quantity of tortoise remains (see Appendix 3, Tables 1 and 2). The tortoise specimens were the subject of a separate, detailed study, the results of which are briefly summarized here.[39]

The presence of tortoise remains in faunal assemblages from medieval sites in Italy is well known, because they are easily identified due to their distinctive morphology. However, they have generally been excluded from serious study, in favour of a focus on domestic stock and also because they are considered a commensal species. Their ubiquitous presence at Capalbiaccio and elsewhere in medieval Italy raises questions about how they were used and suggests that they were economically important.

The tortoise remains from Capalbiaccio belong to *Testudo hermanni* (Hermann's tortoise), a species that inhabits central Italy today. They were recovered from seven excavation areas around the site but were most densely concentrated in Building J and Area M, which, as already noted, yielded the largest faunal assemblages at the site. The large number of identifiable specimens (NISP=660) suggests their relative importance and is supported by an analysis of the MNI. Such large numbers of individuals were unexpected, because most workers assume that the relatively large number of tortoise specimens on medieval sites is due to the presence of just a few individuals whose shells have broken apart, resulting in large NISP numbers that inflate their relative importance. The Capalbiaccio data indicate that not only were tortoise specimens numerous, but a substantial number of individuals were present. Meat weight conversions[40] applied to the data suggest that the tortoises constituted 19076.48 g of usable meat, which is not a huge amount, but certainly enough to be a supplementary source of protein, especially if the tortoises were cooked in a broth or formed the basis of a soup or stew.[41]

Body part analysis revealed that shell pieces were substantially more common than cranial and postcranial bone elements, which suggests the destruction of the latter through cooking, disposal, and other taphonomic processes. The butchery marks on carapace and plastron specimens reveal activities that involved prying open the shell to gain access to the body meat, while additional cut marks on postcranial elements suggest removal of meat or secondary processing. Burning patterns show that tortoise shells may have been used as cooking vessels over open-hearth fires.

---

39 Crader and Rowe, forthcoming.

40 Wing and Brown 1979.
41 Crader and Rowe, forthcoming.

Etruscan Levels

Until recently, the fauna from the Etruscan levels of Capalbiaccio had not been analysed. Preparation of this summary chapter provided the opportunity to conduct a detailed study of these specimens in order to present, for the first time, some insight into the pre-Roman use of animals at what later became the medieval town of Capalbiaccio. Substantial, well-collected faunal samples from Etruscan sites are rare, because these materials have not been given priority, and they are often poorly preserved in the volcanic soils of central Italy. Thus, most accounts of the Etruscan diet have relied on descriptions by classical authors, such as Pliny and Livy.[42] However, samples from sites such as Cerveteri[43] and Populonia[44] do provide some comparisons.

The pre-Roman fauna at Capalbiaccio was recovered below the *terra rossa* in the excavated area known as Building J. Three levels (designated IV, V, and VI from top to bottom) showed decreasing overall numbers of specimens in the deeper deposits (Appendix 3, Table 3). This suggests that the initial settlement of the hilltop was quite small, although it may have been related to the large nearby Etruscan city of Tarquinia.[45] Generally, the same species are present in the Etruscan levels and in the medieval levels and this assemblage is no different: dominated by domestic stock, including sheep, goat, pig, and cattle. Like the medieval fauna, there are fewer non-identifiable specimens than would normally be expected in a zooarchaeological assemblage, which may be due to excavation methods. A summary of the finds from each level is provided hereafter.

Level IV

The uppermost Etruscan level produced the largest faunal assemblage (NISP=492) and the greatest variety of species, compared to the lower levels. Pig, sheep and goat, and cattle are most common, but wild species are also well represented. The assemblage also included evidence of a dog, which was probably kept as a pet and used in herding. Chickens are well represented and would have provided eggs, as well as a source of meat. Sixty bones (12.2 per cent) had butchery marks and 47 (9.6 per cent) were burned.

The assemblage is clearly dominated by pig remains, both in terms of NISP (143) and MNI. twelve individuals of all ages are present, including two neonates, two aged 1–1.5 years, three 2-year-olds, three aged 2–3 years, one adult over 3 years, and one extremely old individual. Pigs, unlike sheep or goats, do not provide milk products or wool. This age pattern is consistent with their use as meat, including an apparent culling at 2 or 3 years of age, when the animals were fattened enough to provide a good amount of meat. Graeme Barker and Tom Rasmussen note that Etruscan pigs undoubtedly matured later than modern pigs, so an age of 2–3 years probably represents the optimum age for meat.[46] The older *suid* individuals probably represent breeding males or sows, and one very large adult may be a wild boar. All body parts are present, including skulls, teeth, vertebrae, girdles, limb bones, and feet; butchery marks reveal regular processing of carcasses on-site. Shears and chops on the underside of the skull, rear of the mandible, and on cervical vertebrae suggest removal of the head. Vertebrae are also sheared in half, probably as the spine and ribs were segmented, and a pelvis had multiple chops where the hind limb was removed. Finally, the distal end of a humerus shaft was burnished smooth, as though being prepared for use as a handle or some other bone tool.

Sheep and goat comprise the next largest portion of the assemblage. Three sheep are present, all mature adults aged 4–5 years, which indicates a 'wool' pattern, that is, keeping animals longer for their wool, rather than slaughtering them for meat when they are younger. This pattern is also found at the Etruscan site of Cerveteri.[47] The goats include two juveniles aged 3–6 months, two adults aged 2–3 years, and one older animal aged 4–5 years. This mixed age group is consistent with a pattern that suggests an unspecialized herd in which females are kept for breeding and milk, and some surplus males might be killed young for meat. Barker and Rasmussen note that mortality profiles for sheep and goats are highly variable at Etruscan sites, which may relate to whether the site was a population centre or a smaller rural farm.[48] The entire range of body parts for sheep and goats is present; cuts and chops on limb bones and feet, as well as sheared-off upper molars, demonstrate carcass processing on-site.

Cattle remains include evidence for one sub-adult aged 2–3 years, one adult aged 4–5 years, and one very large adult (probably an ox). Other Etruscan sites, such as Cerverteri, Populonia, and San Giovenale, also have evidence for two size groups of cattle,[49]

---

42 Barker and Rasmussen 1998.
43 Clark 1989b.
44 De Grossi Mazzorin 1987.
45 Barker and Rasmussen 1998; Haynes 2000; Leighton 2004.

46 Barker and Rasmussen 1998.
47 Barker and Rasmussen 1998; Clark 1989b.
48 Barker and Rasmussen 1998.
49 Barker and Rasmussen 1998.

and depictions of oxen pulling carts and wagons are known in Etruscan art.[50] All cattle body parts are present, including crania, teeth, vertebrae, girdles, long bones, and feet. Many cattle specimens have spectacular butchery marks that reveal how the animals were processed. A skull frontlet is chopped where the horn and horn core were removed, leaving part of the horn core base intact on the skull. An atlas vertebra has chop marks, probably inflicted when the head was removed, and four additional vertebrae are sheared longitudinally, probably from splitting the body in half. Cuts and chops on a scapula and pelvis indicate separation of the front and hind limbs, while large chops on an astragalus suggest cutting off the hooves.

In addition to domestic animals, it is clear that the Etruscans also hunted, trapped, and captured a variety of wild game. Three species of deer are present (fallow, red, and roe) and other wild animals include badger, otter, and a single tooth of a brown bear. Bears are known in the hills of central Italy and may have been hunted in Etruscan times. Mouse, tortoise, lizard, and fish also occur in the assemblage. There is a variety of species of avifauna. As noted above, domestic chickens are most common, but there is also evidence for domestic goose or greylag, mallard duck, a wading bird, wood pigeon, and sparrow hawk. The pigeon is an interesting find, because Etruscan pigeon roosts or coops (square holes hewn into rock) are still seen today, carved into the tufa of Tuscan towns, such as Orvieto and Norchia. Pigeons were probably used as food.

Level V

Level V yielded a good-sized faunal assemblage (NISP=338), with a variety of species. Sixty-six specimens (19.5 per cent) bore evidence of butchery and 45 (13.3 per cent) were burned. Pigs are again the most common domestic animal, but sheep or goat and cattle are also well represented. Other domestic animals include a chicken and a donkey, which was probably used as a beast of burden in the countryside. Although Barker and Rasmussen indicate that equids were common on Etruscan sites, this apparently was not the case here.[51] Only a single, small equid phalanx was present among all the Etruscan specimens.

The pigs include at least six individuals: a very young piglet aged 2–3 months, a juvenile under 1 year, a 2-year-old, a 2–3 year-old, an adult over 3 years, and one additional, very large adult (possibly a wild boar or a big male). Among the pig tooth specimens are some unusual finds: a burned lower incisor, a lower incisor with a notch cut out of it (intentionally modified?), a huge male upper canine, a female upper canine, and two sheared-off molars. One mandible specimen is scraped and sheared off, and a premaxilla and parietal are burned. The damage to cranial parts and teeth suggests tongue removal and the grilling of pigs' heads on open fires.

Two adult sheep and four goats are represented among the remains, in addition to a young neonate, identifiable only as ovicaprine. The goats include three 3-year-old adults and one sub-adult, about 2 years old. These ages are consistent with a mixed-use pattern, where goats were used for milk and also for meat. Evidence of processing includes a goat mandible with chops underneath and burned cranial parts.

Cattle were represented by few specimens, but the remains include evidence for at least three individuals, all of whom were relatively old when they died: one was 4–5 years old (based on tooth eruption), one was much older (based on extreme tooth wear), and one was a very large adult (probably an ox). The advanced age of these individuals suggests that they were used as meat after their use for dairy products or as beasts of burden ended, a pattern also seen at Cerverteri.[52] One cervical vertebra is sheared in half from a powerful blow, perhaps in the process of removing the head.

Wild game includes fallow deer and the larger red deer, indicating that the diet was supplemented with venison. Specimens include an antler that was chopped and sawn off the skull and a cervical vertebra that was sheared transversely across the centrum, probably when the head was removed. The birds present are greylag (or domestic goose) and pigeon. Two fish fragments are also present. The tortoise remains from this level are impressive in terms of NISP. Several carapace and plastron specimens could easily be fitted back together, and four fitting sets belonging to two different individuals were reconstructed. Tortoises can be easily captured and were undoubtedly used for meat and a variety of other products. Two carapace specimens were burned, perhaps when the shell was used as a cooking vessel over the fire.

---

50 Haynes 2000.
51 Barker and Rasmussen 1998.
52 Clark 1989b.

Level VI

The lowest Etruscan level had very few specimens (NISP=49), but all of them were identifiable to some taxonomic level. Fourteen specimens (28.6 per cent) had butchery marks and three (6.1 per cent) were burned. This small assemblage is also dominated by pig remains. At least two individuals are represented: a very large adult (probably a wild boar, as evidenced by a very large scapula and tibia) and a sub-adult aged 2–3 years. The pig remains derive from a wide variety of body parts, including several cranial fragments belonging to one skull. This suggests on-site processing; several specimens reveal butchery marks. One skull fragment has cut marks near the cheek and a frontal fragment is burned. An atlas vertebra has deep cuts, probably from separating the head from the body, and cuts also appear on the proximal end of the large tibia, probably from separating the joint or removing meat. A metacarpal bone is sheared transversely through the shaft, which probably occurred when the foot was removed.

Other species represented in the small assemblage from Level VI include a sheep, a goat, and two cows (one juvenile and one very old individual, indicated by an extremely worn molar). Wild species include a red deer, a very large tortoise, and a wood pigeon.

Summary of Etruscan Use of Animals

The picture that emerges from the analysis of the Etruscan fauna at Capalbiaccio shows that the early, pre-Roman diet included pork, lamb, mutton, beef, and poultry, as well as deer, wild boar, small carnivores, various birds, tortoise, and fish. Besides meat, the domestic animals also provided milk, cheese, other dairy products, and eggs, and they were also used for their wool and hides, as well as for labour. The evidence at Capalbiaccio is consistent with the notion that the Etruscans used a wide range of domestic and wild species and clearly made full use of the seasonal resources available in the area.[53] According to Vedia Izzet, the actual range of animals increased from earlier times, as did the use of secondary animal products.[54]

The Etruscan occupation at Capalbiaccio was apparently fairly small. The site may represent a temporary outpost or small farm that was connected to the larger population centre at the nearby Tarquinia. The faunal remains suggest that domestic animals were raised for consumption at the site, rather than for any large-scale production and distribution, and the presence of all body parts supports the idea of slaughtering on-site. It has been suggested that Etruscan butchery was standardized[55] and the patterns seen at Capalbiaccio are almost identical to those described for sheep, goat, and cattle at Populonia: the head was removed by cuts or blows to the cervical vertebrae, the forelimb and hindlimb were separated from their girdles, and sections of the limb were then disarticulated.[56]

The dominance of pigs in all Etruscan levels at Capalbiaccio is an interesting pattern, one that is not well known at Etruscan sites, perhaps due to the lack of data. For example, cattle, are more common at Cerveteri.[57] However, the dominance of pigs is also found in the medieval levels of Building J at Capalbiaccio and, as noted previously, this pattern occurs in the general area from Roman times onward.[58] It is now documented here even earlier. Given the grazing requirements of sheep, goats, and cattle, it is much easier to raise pigs in this rural setting, since they could roam freely, eat household scraps, and do not compete for arable land. If the Etruscan occupation at Capalbiaccio was a small farm, pigs would have fit easily into the agrarian pattern.

Discussion and Conclusions

Capalbiaccio is an important site for understanding the evolving nature of medieval communities in central Italy. It provides evidence for how a small rural fortified town fitted into the changing Italian countryside, since this was a time of important alterations in community form.[59] An examination of the faunal remains reveals the role of animal production and consumption in the overall economic system. In this context, it is difficult to be certain about the relative self-sufficiency, autonomy, or connectedness to a market economy of a town like Capalbiaccio. Polydora Baker and Gillian Clark have noted that zooarchaeologists working on medieval faunas from Italy need to be conscious of the difference between production and consumption, and must consider the role of animals always in terms of the wider economic system of which they were only a part.[60]

Like other towns in the area, such as Tuscania and Tarquinia, the animal economy at Capalbiaccio

---

53 Barker and Rasmussen 1998.
54 Izzet 2007.
55 Izzet 2007; Barker and Rasmussen 1998.
56 De Grossi Mazzorin 1987.
57 Clark 1989b.
58 For example, see Dyson 1981b; King 1999.
59 Dyson 1979; 1984; Hodges, Wickham, and Barker 1995.
60 Baker and Clark 1993.

was dominated by domestic animals.[61] The medieval (and Etruscan) faunal assemblages are comprised primarily of sheep, goat, pigs, and cattle, but the relative proportions of these groups differ in the various areas of the site and through time. In Building J, which appears to be a residence, pigs dominate, but decrease through time as sheep and goat become more common. This suggests a small shift in stock raising or consumption practices during the latter part of the occupation of the town. In Area M, the quantity of animal refuse increases through time and the fauna is dominated by sheep and goat, rather than pigs. This area appears to have been used as a garbage dump by residents of the town, until it was abandoned. Differences in the proportions of sheep and goat and pig in Building J and Area M could be due to variations in how these two spaces within the town were used, but may instead indicate a small change in animal exploitation patterns through time.

The meaning of the apparent shift through time, away from pigs and toward more sheep and goat, is not entirely clear, because a number of complex factors may influence stock raising choices, including geography, economy, environment, and politics. The changes may be related to the two-phase medieval occupation of the town envisioned by Dyson.[62] Documentary evidence for the region suggests a general increase in sheep and goat herding during this time, perhaps in connection with raising more sheep for wool production.[63] The predominance of pigs in the earlier levels probably represent an important strategy the town used as it initially developed. Pigs are easier to raise, compared to sheep, goats, and cattle, who require grazing lands or fodder, and thus would have competed with cereal crops or with arable land where such crops could be grown.

Mortality profiles for domestic stock suggest that sheep, goats, and cattle were primarily raised for their secondary products, such as milk, wool, or labour, rather than for meat, whereas pigs were primarily used for meat, as would be expected. In terms of the overall economy, the faunal remains do not suggest any large-scale production of stock for market exchange. Rather, it seems more likely that the consumers of the animal products represented by the faunal remains were largely also the producers, and that no large-scale meat, dairy, or wool production was taking place in the town.

A significant aspect of the animal economy at Capalbiaccio also involved the use of wild species for meat and other products. Deer were undoubtedly hunted for meat, while their skins and antlers also provided useful products. A range of small carnivores, rodents, birds, and fish also supplemented the diet. The quantity of tortoise remains demonstrates the importance of this species as a supplement to the meat diet and as a source for raw materials. Such supplemental sources of protein may have been important during the later stages of occupation of the town, as the Bubonic Plague spread throughout Europe and resources became scarce.

Through an analysis of the faunal remains recovered from the site, the animal economy of Capalbiaccio can be reconstructed. This includes the range of species used, changes through time, butchery and processing patterns, the amount of available meat, and the use of animals for other resources, including milk, wool, hides, and as sources of raw material for artefacts. The results presented here are a critical part of reconstructing the economic history of the town in the context of understanding the larger picture of medieval communities in central Italy.

---

61 Barker 1973; 1978; Clark 1989a; 2000.
62 Dyson 1979; 1981b; 1984.
63 Barker 1978.

APPENDIX: FAUNAL REMAINS TABLES

Table 13.1. Summary of faunal remains from Building J and Area M by NISP (number of identifiable specimens). Minimum number of individuals (MNI) is given in parentheses. All levels at each area have been combined. See Crader (2003) for details; some figures differ, because additional specimens, not previously available, are herewith included.

	Building J		Area M	
Ovis aries, sheep	5	(2)	6	(1)
Capra hircus, goat	8	(2)	22	(4)
Ovicaprines, sheep/goat	77	(7)	140	(14)
Sus scrofa, pig	132	(16)	139	(18)
Medium artiodactyl, sheep/goat/pig	556	—	579	(1)
Bos taurus, cattle	36	(5)	40	(6)
Equus caballus, horse	5	(2)	22	(5)
cf. *Equus asinus*, donkey	2	(1)	8	(1)
Large ungulate, cattle/horse/red deer	69	—	86	(1)
Cervus dama, fallow deer	19	(4)	24	(2)
Cervus elaphus, red deer	3	(2)	1	(1)
Capreolus capreolus, roe deer	5	(2)	10	(2)
Cervidae indet.	2	—	3	—
Canis sp., dog/wolf	0	—	4	(2)
Felis sp., wild/domestic cat	4	(2)	0	—
Lutra lutra, otter	1	(1)	0	—
Medium carnivore	19	(2)	0	—
Small carnivore	1	—	0	—
cf. *Lepus capensis*, brown hare	4	(2)	2	(2)
cf. *Sciurus* sp., squirrel	0	—	3	(2)
cf. *Erinaceus europaeus*, hedgehog	0	—	1	(1)
Rodentia indet.	3	(2)	2	-
Medium mammal indet.	0	—	30	(1)
Small mammal indet.	3	—	32	(1)
Gallus gallus, chicken	14	(3)	14	(2)
Bird indet.	22	(3)	27	(5)
Testudo hermanni., tortoise	212	(13)	379	(22)
Emys orbicularis, pond turtle	2	(1)	5	(2)
Fish indet.	6	(2)	6	(3)
Total Identifiable (%)	1210	(67.7)	1585	(65.2)
Non-identifiable (%)	576	(32.3)	847	(34.8)
GRAND TOTAL	**1786**	**(100.0)**	**2432**	**(100.0)**

Table 13.2. Faunal remains from Areas C, F, I, R, and T by NISP (number of identifiable specimens). Minimum number of individuals (MNI) given in parentheses. Some data may differ from other published reports due to re-analysis or addition of specimens not previously available.

	C		F		I		R		T	
Ovis aries, sheep	0	—	2	(2)	1	(1)	1	(1)	5	(2)
Capra hircus, goat	0	—	1	(1)	1	(1)	15	(2)	7	(2)
Ovicaprines, sheep/goat	2	(1)	3	(2)	2	(—)	4	(1)	16	(2)
Sus scrofa, pig	15	(5)	2	(2)	5	(2)	12	(3)	39	(6)
Medium artiodactyl, sheep/goat/pig/deer	9	—	0	—	0	—	0	—	46	(3)
Bos taurus, cattle	66	(4)	2	(1)	3	(1)	2	(1)	12	(2)
Equus caballus, horse	1	(1)	0	—	0	—	0	—	0	—
cf. *Equus asinus*, donkey	2	(1)	0	—	1	(1)	0	—	0	—
Large ungulate, cattle/horse/red deer	0	—	0	—	1	(—)	5	(—)	12	(—)
Cervus dama, fallow deer	0	—	0	—	0	—	2	(1)	9	(3)
Cervus elaphus, red deer	0	—	0	—	0	—	0	—	4	(2)
Capreolus capreolus, roe deer	0	—	1	(1)	0	—	0	—	6	(2)
Cervidae indet.	0	—	0	—	0	—	0	—	4	—
Canis familiaris, dog	0	—	0	—	0	—	48	(3)	0	—
Canis sp., dog/wolf	0	—	0	—	0	—	0	—	1	(1)
Small mustelid	0	—	0	—	0	—	1	(1)	0	—
Small carnivore	0	—	0	—	0	—	0	—	1	(1)
Erinaceus europaeus, hedgehog	0	—	0	—	0	—	1	(1)	0	—
Cleithironomys glareolus, bank vole	0	—	1	(1)	0	—	4	(1)	0	—
Medium mammal indet.	0	—	0	—	0	—	0	—	3	—
Small mammal indet.	0	—	0	—	0	—	0	—	6	—
Gallus gallus, chicken	0	—	2	(2)	0	—	3	(1)	7	(3)
cf. *Alectoris graeca*, rock partridge	0	—	0	—	0	—	0	—	1	(1)
Columba palumbus, wood pigeon	0	—	0	—	0	—	0	—	1	(1)
Columba sp., dove	0	—	0	—	0	—	0	—	1	(1)
Small bird indet.	0	—	0	—	0	—	0	—	2	—
Testudo hermanni, tortoise	2	(1)	3	(1)	8	(2)	8	(3)	48	(8)
cf. *Bufo bufo*, common toad	0	—	0	—	0	—	28	(2)	0	—
Total Identifiable (%)	97 (77.0)		17 (94.4)		22 (81.5)		134 (84.3)		231 (71.1)	
Non-identifiable (%)	29 (23.0)		1 (5.6)		5 (18.5)		25 (15.7)		94 (28.9)	
GRAND TOTAL	**126 (100)**		**18 (100)**		**27 (100)**		**159 (100)**		**325 (100)**	

Table 13.3. Faunal remains from the Etruscan levels at Building J by NISP (number of identifiable specimens). The minimum number of individuals (MNI) is given in parentheses.

	Level IV		Level V		Level VI		Total	
Ovis aries, sheep	15	(3)	9	(2)	5	(1)	29	(6)
Capra hircus, goat	30	(5)	9	(4)	6	(1)	45	(10)
Ovicaprines, sheep/goat	23	—	6	(1)	1	—	30	(1)
Sus scrofa, pig	143	(12)	38	(6)	19	(2)	200	(20)
Medium artiodactyl, sheep/goat/pig/deer	23	—	74	—	0	—	97	—
Bos taurus, cattle	53	(3)	17	(3)	9	(2)	79	(8)
cf. *Equus asinus*, donkey	0	—	1	(1)	0	—	1	(1)
Large ungulate, cattle/horse/red deer	6	—	10	—	3	—	19	—
Cervus dama, fallow deer	21	(2)	9	(2)	0	—	30	(4)
Cervus elaphus, red deer	12	(1)	9	(1)	2	(1)	23	(3)
Capreolus capreolus, roe deer	4	(1)	0	—	0	—	4	(1)
Canis familiaris, dog	1	(1)	0	—	0	—	1	(1)
Ursus arctos, brown bear	1	(1)	0	—	0	—	1	(1)
Meles meles, badger	1	(1)	0	—	0	—	1	(1)
Lutra lutra, otter	1	(1)	0	—	0	—	1	(1)
Small mustelid	1	(1)	0	—	0	—	1	(1)
Small carnivore	2	(1)	0	—	0	—	2	(1)
Lepus capensis, brown hare	3	(1)	0	—	0	—	3	(1)
Mus musculus, house mouse	5	(1)	0	—	0	—	5	(1)
Rodentia indet.	1	(1)	0	—	0	—	1	(1)
Large mammal indet.	2	—	0	—	0	—	2	—
Medium mammal indet.	17	—	12	—	0	—	29	—
Small mammal indet.	4	—	3	—	0	—	7	—
Gallus gallus, chicken	28	(4)	1	(1)	0	—	29	(5)
cf. *Anser anser*, domestic goose/greylag	1	(1)	1	(1)	0	—	2	(2)
cf. *Anas platyrhynchos*, mallard	2	(1)	0	—	0	—	2	(1)
Ciconiiformes, wading bird	3	(1)	0	—	0	—	3	(1)
Columba palumbus, wood pigeon	8	(1)	1	(1)	2	(1)	11	(3)
cf. *Accipter nisus*, sparrow hawk	1	(1)	0	—	0	—	1	(1)
Bird indet.	8	—	0	—	0	—	8	—
Testudo hermanni, tortoise	18	(2)	49	(2)	2	(1)	69	(5)
Reptile, small lizard	2	(1)	0	—	0	—	2	(1)
Fish indet.	22	(2)	2	(1)	0	—	24	(3)
Total Identifiable (%)	462 (93.9)		251 (74.3)		49 (100.0)		762 (86.7)	
Non-identifiable (%)	30 (6.1)		87 (25.7)		0 (0)		117 (13.3)	
GRAND TOTAL	492 (100.0)		338 (100.0)		49 (100.0)		879 (100.0)	

HERMANN SALVADORI

14. Field Survey of the Post-Medieval Settlement Patterns in Southern Tuscany

ABSTRACT The first of its kind on Southern Tuscany, this chapter focuses on the post-medieval transformation of the landscape and the countryside surrounding seven castles, including Tricosto. Salvadori compares archaeological data with historiographical models to understand how modern settlement patterns changed. The absence of important urban centres or failed cities in southern Tuscany, with the exception of Grosseto and Massa Marittima, makes this study of the countryside even more relevant. Salvadori outlines two buffer zones for each castle (a larger and a smaller one) and surveyed each settlement and its surroundings, which allows him to reconstruct the wider evolution of these local communities and their continuation and/or abandonment. By combining the collected finds with geographical dictionaries and public records of land ownership, Salvadori then reconstructs the local history of each site. He uses two well-known sources, the *Dizionario Emanuele Repetti*, which is now available online (Repetti 1833–1845) and the Catasto Leopoldino, which was ordered by the Grand Duke of Tuscany, Leopoldo, in 1823 and provides a wealth of relatively recent information on how properties were organized in the landscape, with the rivers, canals, roads, and boundaries of Tuscany as they existed at the beginning of the nineteenth century.

Siena's expansion in the fourteenth century, with large investments in infrastructure along the coast, did not last long before another wave of abandonments took place and crystallized the picture of the landscape that can still be found today in Maremma. Salvadori's reconstruction of the territory from the early nineteenth-century land records leads him to conclude that the nature of the agrarian settlements has its roots in the early fourteenth century and has not changed through time. This seems to be a representative situation, especially around communal cities, such as Siena, and in the nearby Valle d'Asso (Salvadori has undertaken similar work for the area around Montalcino and Arezzo). [MH]

Introduction

This chapter is subdivided into four sections: historiographical questions and the geographic scope of the research; the applied methodology and the relationship between documented archaeological data and the existent historiographical model; a description of the data that has come to light in the area surrounding the castle of Tricosto; and a comparison of the settlement model developed herein with that of other areas in Tuscany.

One of the most important historiographical themes in medieval archaeology has been the multiple facets of the process of *incastellamento*, a topic which has almost become a field of its own (*infra* Hobart, ch. 1). The research group specializing in medieval archaeology at the University of Siena's Department of Archaeology has paid particular attention to southern Tuscany (including the provinces of Siena, Grosseto, and the southern part of the provinces of Livorno and Pisa), beginning with the excavation of Scarlino in 1977 and continuing with more recent projects at Donoratico, Castel di Pietra, and Cugnano.[64] A total of eight castles have been subject to excavations and many others have been investigated using non-invasive methods (surveys, reconnaissance, surface collecting, and, more recently, geo-physical studies and remote sensing). These studies have helped shed light on key factors precipitating the structural alteration of agrarian land in late antiquity and the formation of early medieval elevated landscapes, centred first on the *curtis* and then on the castle. They have also helped to define the forms of power (through a hierarchy of urban structures and domiciles) and, not least of all, the economic bases of social life (through material indicators, shifts in urban assets, construction techniques, and the use of productive technologies).[65]

---

64 On Scarlino, see Francovich 1985; on Donoratico, see Bianchi 2004; on Castel di Pietra, see Citter 2009b; and on Cugnano, see Belli and Dallai 2005.
65 Francovich, Ginatempo, and Augenti 2000.

Historiographical Questions

The development of themes related to life at fortified castle sites, which differ according to the subject tackled and the depth and intensity of the historiographical questions posed, has led to a comprehensive project of cataloging all fortified sites in Tuscany.[66] The aim of this project has been to reconstruct fundamental settlement patterns in historical epochs, which are crucial for reconstructing extensive periods of the land's occupation.[67] The data gathered in thirty years of research allows us to affirm that *incastellamento* was not a monolithic, but a dynamic phenomenon, characterized by premature abandonment between the eleventh and twelfth centuries (the first de-*incastellamento*) followed by new foundations and re-foundations of settled castles from the early thirteenth century onwards (the so-called second *incastellamento*).

Fortified castles assumed the function of central places in a geo-political context in which the city, after many centuries, returned to play a determining role in the dynamics of settlement and confronted the power of territorial seignories.[68] The debate remains open on various points, such as whether the dynamics were regional or whether each site had its own particular dynamic within a broader process of transformation. However, the research conducted to date seems to suggest that at each site, the situation differed greatly from both an urban-architectural and demographic perspective.[69] Regardless, the result was that a select number of villages became population hubs by the thirteenth century.

This new cognitive phase of research into individual castles and their territorial settings has made it possible to hypothesize the existence of a 'Tuscan model' of settlement, which attempts to describe the dynamics at work in the formation of high-altitude sites. The same intensity has not been applied to the problem of abandonment and its consequences on forms of settlement organization. Also still remaining to be clarified are the final results of these long-term processes and the extent to which evidence of these transformations can be identified in indicators recovered through archaeological investigations.

This research examines de-*incastellamento*, or rather the final phases in the life of the castles, as well as changes in settlement patterns in the territory surrounding them. Save for certain areas where investigations were approached diachronically, there has been no penetrating study of the dynamics that transformed settlement patterns between the Middle Ages and the Modern era, from an archaeological perspective.[70] The general picture that emerges is the outcome of information drawn from written sources, such as data on demographics or types of agricultural contracts, which can rarely be confirmed or refuted by archaeological evidence. Field research is therefore aimed at identifying those material elements that can help understand the process of transformation in the forms of settlement. Only after identifying those material indicators is it possible to compare them with existing historical models.

Southern Tuscany is distinguished by the absence of important urban centres, with the exception of Grosseto and Massa Marittima, which have been cities in the full sense of the word for little more than two centuries, but have never played a role comparable to that of Siena or Pisa. The crisis of the mid-fourteenth century exists as a significant watershed moment, which has led some scholars to consider 1348 as the virtual end of the Middle Ages.[71] Many of the excavated castles in the region were in fact abandoned during the course of the fourteenth century. With that said, even the final phase of the medieval landscape may have been more complex than it is currently thought to have been.

While research into written sources presents a diversified panorama of the area between Siena and the Maremma, many of the communities attested to have not yet been identified.[72] This gives rise to the first question: did castles still serve as central places, or is it reasonable to assume that it was precisely in the fourteenth century that the re-fragmentation of rural areas began with the resumption of sparse settlements, of which there is no archaeological trace in the preceding centuries? Nevertheless, archaeological data reveals a considerably more articulated panorama than written sources, suggesting that this dynamic period of abandonment be approached with caution. References to the desertion of castles describe not so much the complete interruption of any human habitation, but rather the cessation of socio-residential and institutional functions in the twelfth and thirteenth centuries. However, temporary or seasonal occupations may not have been recorded in sources, but they can be brought to light through archaeological investigation. This study deals with the phases in which fortified castles were deserted,

---

66 Francovich 1999.
67 Francovich and others 1997.
68 Farinelli and Giorgi 2000.
69 Bianchi, Fichera, and Paris 2009, 412–17.

70 On those investigations that were approached diachronically, see Milanese and Baldassarri 2004; Arthur and Bruno 2007; Citter 2009b.
71 Bergdolt 1997; Herlihy 1997.
72 Pinto 1982.

the identification of the forms of their successive reorganization (either in the case of abandonment and subsequent frequentation, or transformations that were caused by changes in political power, which occurred between the sixteenth and seventeenth centuries), and the degree of legibility of these transformations in both written and archaeological sources.

The Current Historiographical Model for Southern Tuscany in the Post-Medieval Period

The historical period into which this study falls — from the late thirteenth through to the nineteenth century, generally defined as post-medieval — is not considered a proper academic discipline in historical studies or other scholarly fields that deal with the history of civilization.[73] Rather, it is always regarded as belonging to specific, mutually distinct areas of study: the Middle Ages, on the one hand, and the Renaissance and Modern eras, on the other.[74] Historiography has always considered the post-Medieval period a transitional period, and the schism between Medievalists and Modernists exclusively binds subjects to their own chronological horizon. The current historical debate is characterized by the affirmation of less extreme positions that hinge on the idea that continuity and rupture alternate — a chronological distinction useful only on a scholastic, pedagogical level. There are no fixed or universally accepted dates that mark the end of the Middle Ages and the beginning of the Modern era; depending on the criteria and the given country, not to mention the discipline to which the designation is applied, there are as many cardinal dates as there are national or disciplinary schools.[75] The principal historical and archaeological issues concerning the post-medieval era are virtually still in the embryonic stage, especially compared to the transitional period between late antiquity and the early Middle Ages. 'Transition', as it is used here, seems to be the most appropriate term for emphasizing the gradual change in the management of a territory's resources and the structure of the landscape.[76]

The historian Jacques Le Goff has underscored a position in which every transformation is a factor that acquires value only if considered within a broader context.[77] Le Goff preferred to speak of continuity and shifts rather than rupture, since *caesurae*, though important and quantifiable, do not constitute disruption, but rather a series of shifts that signal transformations. Only when these shifts — in areas as diverse as economics, politics, and the sciences — interact among themselves to the point of constituting a system, is it possible to speak of a new period. Analysis of this transformative process at the castle of Tricosto — archaeologically distinguished above all by the various forms of its rural population — begins with the moment in which the administration of the territory became the exclusive prerogative of the castle's 'system', managed by the rural communities bound to Siena.

If the Black Plague of 1348 is rightly considered the principal sign of the medieval crisis, the symptoms of the demographic and economic crisis in the province of Grosseto can be traced back through historical sources to the final decades of the thirteenth century.[78] Demographic analyses drawn from Sienese fiscal records of the second half of the thirteenth and early decades of the fourteenth century reveal that the concentration of settlements around a few major castles occurred within the context of a general population decline. The net drop in population, evident around the late thirteenth century, seems to foreshadow the abandonment of minor centres between the fourteenth and fifteenth centuries. Although zones closer to the city, such as the foundation of Castelfranco di Paganico, expanded, this general trend was indicative of the Maremma. It is not possible to qualify the aforementioned expansion of Paganico as settlement reorganization; rather it seems that the foundation was an attempt to stem the area's depopulation, given the flight of the population towards major castles in the surrounding area.[79] In the first decades of the fourteenth century, the corresponding demographic drop seems moderate, putting no crucial strain on levels of population. Despite the absence of quantitative data on the population of southern Tuscany, sparse human presence and its negative economic consequences does emerge in the normative sources. Unfortunately, the dearth of specific archaeological studies aimed at understanding these issues makes it impossible to provide a comprehensive picture based on material evidence from excavations and surveys.

The first significant famine occurred in 1328–1330, followed by the first great plague in 1340. These were the earliest symptoms, with the most severe blow to the population being the 'Black Death' of 1348,

---

73 Milanese 1997.
74 Heers 1992, 9.
75 Heers 1992, 52.
76 Fourquin 1971, 19; Heers 1992, 51; Vitolo 2000, 37.
77 Le Goff 2003, 33.

78 Giorgi 1994; Pinto 1982.
79 Giorgi 1994, 260 ff.

which was succeeded by numerous other grave epidemics. The worst effects were felt in zones in which settlement was less concentrated and population sparser, chief among them being the Maremma. For this reason, the revival of the late 1400s was slower and more strenuous in this area.[80] With the onset of the fifteenth century, the harsh circumstances that had deeply impressed the previous half century were hardly over; famines, pestilence, and, above all, wars broke out with an ever greater frequency, even if they were less intense. Some historians, such as Maria Ginatempo, claim instead that the principal characteristic of the late medieval revival was that it occurred despite the never-ending impact of negative conditions, especially high rates of mortality.[81] Without comprehensively listing the 'misfortunes' suffered by Tuscany and Siena, it is worth noting that epidemics, pestilence, famines, wars between Siena and Florence, as well as between Siena and the counts of Pitigliano, raids by mercenary cavalry, and armies crossing the territory are recorded with nearly regular cadence in every decade until 1500. The situation naturally caused the usual problems, such as a lack of manpower and the consequent impossibility of cultivating fields, which had the inevitable result of raising the price of wheat.

In order to curb the crisis, the commune of Siena took fairly limited measures in their territories, such as tax reductions and certain 'allowances' to the petitions of communities and smaller communes, which were growing perceptibly. This manifested itself in affirming these smaller settlements and, in certain cases, even in the reconstruction of dwellings and walls, as well as the exploitation of an influx of migrants from the Florence area. Assessments of the effects of these events are more difficult for other parts of the dominion. It is not easy to sketch a clear picture of what happened in the Maremma, although its vast stretches of deserted terrain and sparse population were likely a favourite destination of rapacious mercenary companies.

Siena watched the depopulation of the Maremma with anxiety, but correctional interventions were not forthcoming. Some centres, especially principal ones (the seats of the *podestà*, for example) enjoyed a privileged position and saw short-lived population booms (Grosseto, Massa Marittima, and Talamone, but also Sovana, Pereta, Gavorrano, and Monterotondo); others faced a relentless decline in population, attaining some privileges after 1461 (Manciano and Istia).[82] Other communities, such as Cinigiano and Batignano, which were beyond efforts at re-population, enjoyed good provisions. However, settlements that enjoyed privileged positions did not immediately experience prosperity. Multiple items in petitions and accounts from the 1470s and 1480s indicate a revival in the Maremma. This data suggests that pandemics were abating, if not in frequency, then at least in intensity, which forced the inhabitants to continue to cope with misfortunes. The birth of colonies that were administered by Siena and fed by a steady flow of migrants (Corsicans in the Maremma and Pisans in Grosseto), suggests that in the Maremma it was common to abandon castles in order to escape disease, especially in avoiding the risks associated with malaria.[83]

In the post-medieval period, the social structure of the Maremma appears to have been highly complex and, at the same time, unstable due to the impact of the crises of the mid-fourteenth century on the fundamentally fragile region, whose population was more exposed to unfavourable conditions than elsewhere.

The picture in the mid-fifteenth century is that of a borderland with transhumant shepherds, breeders of local animals, specialized and unspecialized labourers of various origin, often without fixed habitation. The presence of mercenary soldiers and pirates along the coasts heightened the instability and sense of insecurity. To this may be added the periodic return of epidemics and the spread of malaria, which rendered the depletion of agricultural and other resources in the so-called realm of Siena even more problematic.[84]

The historical picture reconstructed here is drawn solely from written sources. This makes the creation of a practical archaeological databank, which can produce an organic and all-inclusive model, as well as propose an orientation and methodology for future research, all the more exciting and, at the same time, urgent.

In the late Middle Ages, the province of Grosseto, in which the castle of Tricosto lies, was largely subject to the political power of Siena. The borders of the Sienese state were never as extensive as they are today. The communes of Follonica, Scarlino, Castiglione della Pescaia, Santa Fiora, Castell'Azzara, Pitigliano, as well as parts of Sorano, Semproniano, and Scansano were not included in the Sienese territory (Fig. 14.1). The territories of S. Fiora, Castell'Azzara, Pitigliano,

---

80 Pinto 1982, 79 ff.
81 Ginatempo 1988, 261, 263, n. 6.
82 Ginatempo 1988, 302–06.
83 Ginatempo 1988, 343 ff.
84 Pinto 1982, 448–49.

Sorano (save the part pertaining to Sovana), and parts of Semproniano and Scansano remained autonomous and under the dynasty of the Aldobrandeschi family, whose dominion was undermined by Siena only in the Quattrocento, thus replacing one sovereign with another.[85]

The mid-fifteenth-century Sienese fiscal records paint a picture of settlement in the Maremma as characterized by a centralized but slack population, which basically lacked the smaller communes typical of other areas politically closer and subject to Siena. Amiata, on the other hand, displays the same type of centralized settlement, but within a much tighter grid.[86]

Methodology and Description of the Data

The following research is focused upon mutations in settlement structure, the relationship between city and country, and the determination of archaeological evidence that facilitates the understanding of this transition. In examining the borders of the high medieval landscape, it is possible to observe that the settlement pattern underwent a gradual selection process: next to sites that were abandoned at the beginning of this period (e.g. all the castles that reveal no traces of occupation after the mid-fourteenth century, as exemplified by Rocca San Silvestro), stand other castles that survived the initial moment of crisis, but were abandoned in the following decades (such as Castel di Pietra and Rocchette Pannocchieschi). Others were abandoned in the Modern era (Cotone and Selvena, for example), and some were never abandoned at all (e.g. all the historical centres, which, like Campagnatico and Arcidosso, still retain their function as communal seats).

The second objective of this study is to identify the dynamics of transformation in relations between city and country through a comparative study of the region's organization and the centres of economic and institutional power. Indeed, this part of Tuscany is known, not by chance, as that 'of the powerless cities (*delle città deboli*)'.[87] The crisis of Roman urbanism did not give rise to a new articulated system of urban centres, except in the case of Siena, even though — at least between the twelfth and fourteenth centuries — Grosseto and Massa Marittima, which inherited the functions of Roselle and Populonia, were considered cities. This was an early point of comparison with the other parts of Tuscany, those of the 'powerful cities', and the role that they played in the ongoing process of transformation in the countryside. Although Siena's involvement in southern Tuscany, as well as Pisa's along the coast, is documented from the mid-fourteenth century onward, Siena was the only true urban centre in this vast region. The foundation of new territories, such as Talamone, Roccalbegna, and Paganico,[88] the project for a dam on the Bruna River, the construction of a new road connecting Talamone to Grosseto and Siena, the drafting of a valuation (the Table of Possessions), and the interest in the extraction of salt, are just some of the indicators of a new approach to the territory that constituted a definitive shift of scale vis-à-vis the 'seigneurial' era. This renewed interest was intertwined with, and perhaps to some extent conditioned settlement patterns and, particularly, the network of castles. The same period also saw profound modifications in systems of producing and distributing pottery. The expansion of manufacturing centres (it is here that the problem

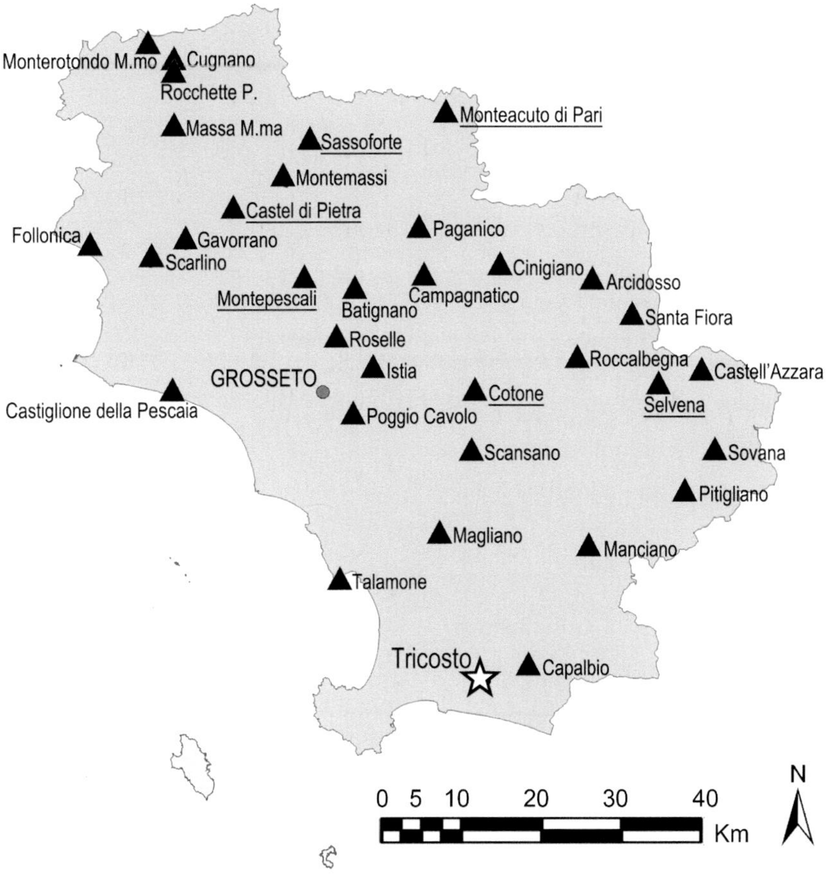

Figure 14.1. Map of the modern Grosseto Province with sites mentioned in the text. Map by author.

---

85 Ginatempo 1988, 168.
86 Ginatempo 1988, 184 ff.
87 Citter 1996c; Citter and Vaccaro 2005; Farinelli 2007.
88 Farinelli 2003.

Table 14.1. The seven sites examined in this chapter and the data available from texts before fieldwork began.

Castle	Commune	Type of examination	Data from examination	Present condition	Abandonment
Tricosto	Capalbio	Excavation/ ASFAT Survey	Pottery (1970s and early 1980s)	Abandoned	1416
Castel di Pietra	Gavorrano	Excavation	Fragmentation of the summit area; open-air frequentation; halt in the use of seigniorial land	Abandoned	Early fifteenth century
Cotone	Scansano	Exploration and survey	Potsherds, census of walls	Abandoned	Seventeenth century
Monteacuto di Pari	Civitella Paganico	Census ASFAT	No data	Abandoned	1320
Montepescali	Grosseto	Survey and examination of historical centre's walls	Renaissance adaptation of walls and reconstruction of buildings	Inhabited centre	—
Roccaccia di Selvena	Castell' Azzara	Excavation	Halt in the use of seigneurial land; partitioning of the castle; construction of buildings within the seigneurial area; reinforcement of the bailey	Abandoned	Early nineteenth century
Sassoforte	Roccastrada	Excavation	Late frequentation of the seigneurial area; construction and refacement of buildings in the seigneurial area and village	Abandoned	1329/1438

of the production of archaic majolica in the areas of Siena and Valdarno enters the picture), the existence of centres directly controlled by cities (for example, Montelupo, the artisanal area of Florence), and the appearance of new types of manufactured goods, such as glazed slipware and majolica, can all be used as further indicators of the ongoing process of transformation in cities and the countryside.

This study focuses on a sample of various types of sites with relation to the phase of either their abandonment or continuity, up until the present, in order to come to an understanding of the strong and weak points of late medieval settlement patterns, as a whole. Archival material, such as the Catasto Leopoldino of 1823 and Emanuele Repetti's dictionary of Tuscany from the same period, suggest that the process that formed the agrarian landscape had deep roots that were already evident in the early phases of the fourteenth century, as well as others that could have developed much later.[89] An assessment of those castles, like Selvena, which survived the medieval crisis, only to be abandoned in the course of the Modern era, but which assumed the very different functions of military fortresses, rather than population centres, is also amongst the historical inquires herein.

During this project, archaeological literature on the period in question, as well as historical publications on the crisis of the seigneurial territories, the new role of the city and aristocratic citizens in the countryside, the new assets of the rural population, and the emergence of regional states, were all assembled and considered. Since archaeological documentation is the principal source for information on the final days in the life of any site, the by-products of the final phases of the castles' lives (waste, strata of abandoned material, traces of temporary occupation and frequentation in the phase of early disintegration) were examined. Data drawn from masonry structures, which can be viewed as interventions in the transformation of the urban structure (efforts to contract or expand stone baileys, the partitioning of residential units, and the decommissioning of seigneurial lands), were combined with information derived from the horizontal stratigraphy.

The example of Grosseto and its role as a city was gauged from an examination of the stratigraphic sequences of the fifteenth and sixteenth centuries, which were recorded during the excavations of its historical centre. This made it possible to make highly detailed and direct comparisons with castles excavated in the province of Grosseto. Moreover, data derived from the exploration of areas immediately surrounding Castel di Pietra and Roccaccia di Selvena were also compared to those drawn from the castle of Tricosto.[90] Non-invasive methods of examination used in the most recent campaigns at Capalbiaccio, though providing a less detailed type of information, produced important data for formulating hypotheses about the dynamics of shifts in settlement patterns.

---

89 Repetti 1833–1845.

90 Citter 2002a; Francovich 2000; Citter 2005b.

The castles documented in the archives of ASFAT (*L'Atlante dei Siti Fortificati d'Altura della Toscana*) were subdivided on the basis of the period in which they were abandoned and grouped in categories appropriate to the subjects of the research: castles abandoned before the crisis of the mid-fourteenth century; those abandoned at various moments after the crisis, yet before the end of the fifteenth century; sites that survived the crisis, but were abandoned in the following centuries; and those that still exist as population hubs today (Fig. 14.2).[91] These categories have been supplemented with additional parameters that pertain to geographical distribution.

It was necessary to choose a sample of castles that would make it possible to cover all territorial regions that characterize the present province of Grosseto: the central plain, the metal-rich hills, Ardenghesca, the southern hills, Monte Amiata, and the southern plain. Not only were castles that offered ample archaeological evidence (excavation and identification, or only excavation) chosen for this study, but also those sites that had never been subject to investigation, but which had been partially studied using non-invasive methods (surveys). In the end, interest in each site being equal, a selection of those sites with the best environmental conditions for conducting surface explorations was made based on a combination of data on the use of the soil and ortho-photocard displays.

The data was inserted into a GIS base to which was added information drawn from field exploration. For the selected sites, two buffer zones, centred within each castle, were planned on the GIS base: one had a radius of 1.5 km; the other a radius of 5 km (Fig. 14.3). An examination of different degrees of intensity was conducted within the two areas: intensive within the former and focused in the latter. Investigations proceeded in the areas surrounding the farmhouses listed in the Catasto of 1823. The evidence that emerged after this first stage of exploration necessitated a change of strategy: in the first four castles examined, no archaeological evidence was found that could aid in the comprehension of the issues addressed by this study. Hence, the research was focused on the remaining sites mentioned solely in the Catasto Leopoldino.

The Catasto of 1823–1835 was used as the project's principal cartographic basis, since it is the source for the old territorial organization that is chronologically closest to ours. In fact, the Catasto offers a picture of the territory that is already partly structured, it being the result of the earliest reclamation

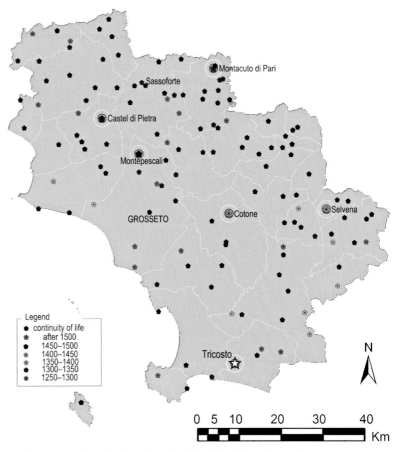

Figure 14.2. Map of 128 castles identified in the Grosseto province (ASFAT) and their approximate date of their decline. Map by author.

activity, which anticipated the interventions that substantially modified a major portion of the province of Grosseto between the mid-nineteenth and mid-twentieth century. The definitive picture of the transformations that followed this activity can be found in the territorial organization evident in the standard maps prepared by the *Istituto Geografico Militare* in 1966 (IGM 1:25000 scale). A more recent view of the areas studied was provided by the digital ortho-photocards from the 1976 EIRA flight, which were used in the planning stage of this study in order to evaluate the sites to be investigated and identify anomalies within the buffer zones (see Table 14.1).

The archaeological databank can thusly be used to determine a general trend, even in terms of broader or different territorial settings. The existence of fragmented rural settlements, whose chronology did not necessarily coincide with the abandonment of the castles, but rather with their final phase, could then be determined.

What emerges from this general picture is a continuity of settlement types, centred on the presence of castles between the late thirteenth and mid-fourteenth centuries. The sparse forms of habitation that

---

91 Augenti and others 1997; Farinelli 2007.

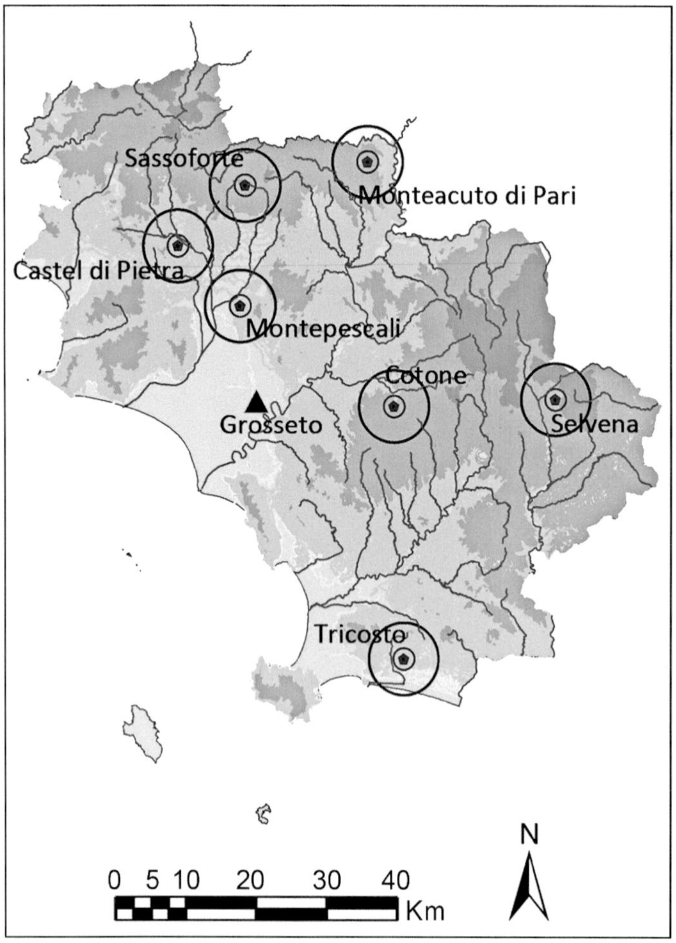

Figure 14.3. The seven castles surveyed inside two buffer zones (one with a radius of 1.5 km and the other a radius of 5 km). Map by author.

arose starting in the mid-fourteenth century, transformed and became characteristic of the landscape of southern Tuscany only in the late fifteenth century. The lack of an active administrative centre in a region that had been covered almost exclusively with medieval castles until the mid-fourteenth century was partly the cause of the irregular inhabitation of southern Tuscany in the post-medieval period.

Nevertheless, archaeological surface exploration grants merely a partial view — heavily conditioned by environmental factors and other variables — of the forms of population. In this case, the 'other variables' principally consisted of the intensity of the fieldwork, the time limits of the actual research, and the interpretation of the data. The first two are tightly bound, precisely because the intensity of the exploration strongly affects the amount of evidence found: 'as intensity increases, the number of sites discovered increases indefinitely'.[92]

---

92 Cambi and Terrenato 1994.

Limitations of the Study

The data obtained constitutes only the first level of documentation — proofs on which to build interpretative hypotheses — as it is impossible to conduct explorations at all times of year. However, this does not pose a cognitive limit, since the evidence emerging from fieldwork is enough to answer most of the historical questions raised by the project.

However, it is always pertinent to consider the inherent limits of archaeological exploration: visibility, the subjectivity of oral sources, and discontinuity in written sources, as well as their interpretation. Among these, visibility is the most important limiting factor in the reconstruction of historical events based on surfaces finds, for which evidence must always be considered fragmentary, partial, and subordinate to multiple factors. The identification of archaeological evidence is frequently determined by external factors related to surface conditions: existent vegetation, intensity of agricultural activity, and pedological dynamics. While the impact of pedological phenomena on visibility is more difficult to determine, they are typically related to the planting of new types of crops, changes in use (from cultivation to pasture), or the abandonment of agricultural terrain. Other factors affecting the surface include the integral reorganization of structures and the changing of place names, especially of minor settlements such as country farms, homesteads, or built-up rural areas.

Nonetheless, material data contributes to an overall critical re-reading, not only of the written sources, but also of its own meaning in a broader context. For instance, the Catasto utilized in this study was not able to furnish either quantitative data, nor provide a sense of the actual distribution of structures. Similarly, when reworking the data it is necessary to take into account the amount of absent evidence and the risk that often arises from interpreting it as proof of non-existence. Whatever the nature of the factors determining absence, it is important not to let the elaboration of interpretative reasoning overshadow reality. Evidence and lack thereof rival each other in the formulation of interpretative hypotheses that can affect strategies of intervention, which may be detracted or confirmed by more intense research.

This is not the place to elaborate upon an issue that has been debated for over forty years, let alone reduce the argument to the simple problem of visibility, even though during surface exploration it is much simpler to consider non-evidence as non-existence and to offer partial and thus inexact interpretations of the subject of the research.[93] For example, in the region around the city of Grosseto, the abandonment of many sites on the plain has been dated to the seventh century due to a lack of indicators. However, the recent acquisition of new data and a revision of the materials have demonstrated continuous frequentation, even in the early Middle Ages, and thus the existent interpretative trends regarding the absence of people in the area were modified.[94]

The same problems confront archaeological excavations. For example, the data that has emerged from work at the castle of Sassoforte seems to stress the dissonance between evidence and its absence.[95] On the one hand, the ceramic findings counter what written sources relate about two phases of abandonment (the first, in 1330, was followed by a re-population attempt; in the second, from 1438, the castle was defined as 'broken and abandoned', or deserted). On the other hand, the presence of strata antedating the thirteenth century suggests that Sassoforte was occupied over a very broad chronological span from the sixth to the early sixteenth century.[96] The same can be said for Castel di Pietra, where residual material datable to the eighth through the tenth centuries constitutes an indirect source of a stable habitat. However, the periodization of the excavation has conjured a void that lasts from the early sixth to the second half of the eleventh century.[97]

Nonetheless, visibility is the fundamental factor that determines the organizational strategies that guide the exploration of a site. Once again, Castel di Pietra can be taken as an example: the results that emerged from the excavation confirmed that another period in the life of the site was partially visible. Although the abandoned site is plagued by poor visibility due to vegetation, frequentation in the fourth to second centuries BCE can now be conjectured as a result of the discovery of fragments of black varnish during the explorations that preceded the dig, which led to the identification of two habitable structures datable to the third or second century.[98]

The region under question is also faced with ever-present changes that risk distorting the historical-archaeological resources present in the landscape. Intense reclamation efforts in the mid-nineteenth and mid-twentieth centuries have altered the current appearance of the territory, which deviates greatly from the Catasto Leopoldino.[99] The nearly total abandonment of agriculture since the mid-1950s has given way to other forms of exploitation of the landscape: agritourism and the establishment of agricultural farms *ex novo*, which affect not only the settlement patterns, but also the cultural inclination of an area. The ever more widespread seasonal frequentation of these zones also affects the reorganization and evolution of the landscape. This project proceeds from the assumption that similar transformations began to occur simultaneously with the final phases of the castles and continued from the second half of the fourteenth through the sixteenth century, only to explode in the first half of the seventeenth century.

Results of the Study

An examination of the fourteenth-century phase in the life of the castle of Tricosto, which marks the final moment of construction prior to the destruction of the castle in 1416, has already been published.[100] In this period, the settlement decreased in size, with the construction of a massive dividing wall that sliced the plane diagonally from east to west, abutting on the bailey on one side and passing through it on the other (Corti, Fig. 5.5). The wall excluded the southern ramification of the settlement, which, having no aperture for passage, was no longer accessible. It is with extreme caution that this redefinition of the site's defensive system could be related to the conveyance of the castle's property, which, prior to the Sienese conquest, appears to have been among the holdings of the Orsini of Pitigliano. The final generation of buildings in the northwest portion of the stronghold, close to the castle's access gate, is likewise related to the fourteenth-century phase.

The elevated plain across which the castle extends has been the object of intensive exploration, which divided it into the three micro-areas: a zone to the north of the bailey, one south of it, and the buffer zone outside of it. The material discovered on the surface was comprised mostly of ceramic fragments that can be dated between the twelfth and the first half of the fourteenth century. The presence of two fragments of black glaze and one fragment of pre-historic *impasto* causes some irregularity on the quantitative level, but it is nonetheless possible to delineate the various phases of frequentation at the site. The data collected at this stage of research seems to clash slightly with what is related by written sources. The

---

93 Sagan 1997; Holdaway, Fanning, and Shiner, 2005; Morgan 2011.
94 Citter and Arnoldus-Huyzendveld 2007; Vaccaro 2008.
95 Salvadori and Valdambrini 2009.
96 Fichera 2005, 191–200.
97 Citter 2009b.
98 Bernardini 2009.
99 La Carrubba 2003; La Carrubba and Macchi 2005.
100 Hobart and others 2009.

Table 14.2. Summary of the Farm houses (C. = casolari) and the traces found in the survey inside the buffer zones around the Tricosto castle.

IGM Place names	Leopoldine Place names	Typologies	Dates	Dating elements	Current State
Cava del Salaiolo (quarry)	Il Salajolo	Pottery	1st–4th century CE	Pottery	Tilled field
Cava del Salaiolo	Il Salajolo	Pottery, stones, bricks and roof tiles	13th – 20th century	Pottery	Tilled field
Buranello	C. Burano	Structure	NA		Abandoned
Forte di Burano (fort)	Torre di Buranaccio	Structure (inaccessible)	16th century	Written sources	WWF Oasis
Forte di Macchia Tonda	C. Macchiatonda	Structure	17th century	Written sources	Abandoned
Megarozzo	Capanne di Macarozzo	Pottery and Structure	4th BCE – 3rd CE	Pottery	Tilled field
F.sso di Fonte Picchio	Le Fornaci	Pottery concentration	14th – 19th century	Pottery	Olive grove
Fonte Picchio – Sicilia	La Cicilia	Concentration of pottery, stones, bricks and roof tiles	3rd century BCE – 1st CE	Pottery	Tilled field
c/o C. Tricosto	Porcareccia	Structure and abandoned quarry	NA		Restored
C. Tricosto	Il Tricosto	Structure	15th century	Written sources	Under restoration
C. Tricosto	Il Tricosto	Dispersed pottery	Prehistoric – 20th century	Pottery	Tilled field
C. Marotti	Lo sbratto	Dispersed pottery	3rd BCE – 1st CE	Pottery	Untilled
C. Marotti	Lo Sbratto	Structure / dispersed pottery	13th – 19th century	Pottery	Abandoned
Le Tombe	Le Tombe	Structure	NA		Restructured compound
Le Mortelle	Molinaccio, Molino diruto	Residual Structure	NA		Ruins
C.ta delle Forane	Capanna Forane	Structure	NA		Restructured compound
Villa la Pinciana	Il Barzontino	Structure	NA		Restructured compound
Poggio Dolce	Torre del Dolci	Structure	NA		*Agriturismo*
Torre Palazzi	La Torre di Palazzi	Structure	NA		Conglomeration
c/o Barucola	Casetta di Barucola	Structure	NA		Farm

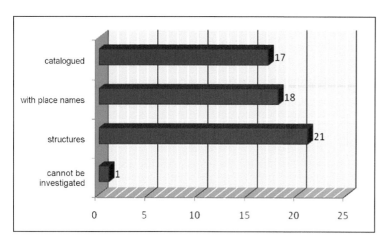

Figure 14.4. Farmhouses in the Catasto Leopoldino present in the territory of Tricosto. Graphic by author.

documents report that in 1417, the General Council of the Republic of Siena deliberated over a proposal to destroy the fort of Tricosto, while material indicators of the frequentation of the site between the second half of the fourteenth and the early fifteenth century do not exist.[101] Such evidence opens the field to multiple interpretations, not least of all being a consideration of the degree of visibility at the moment that the material was gathered. Tricosto was described as 'inconveniente et con spesa senza niuno utile' (inconvenient, costly, and having no function), and the possession of it would only bring 'piuttosto danno' (certain damage), which is what motivated the Sienese to destroy it.[102] Thus, it is pos-

---

101 Angelucci and Bellettini 2006, 31.
102 Angelucci and Bellettini 2006, 31.

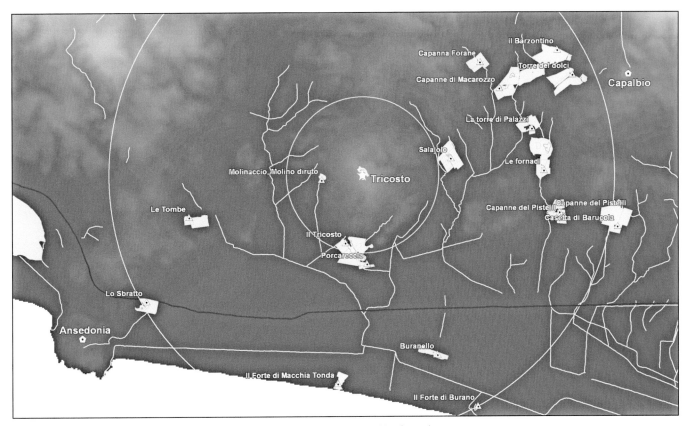

Figure 14.5. Distribution map of the farmhouses investigated in the Tricosto area. Map by author.

sible that Capalbiaccio was already in the process of being depopulated or even deserted, and at risk of being re-occupied by unknown forces. It may not be an accident then, that the explorations carried out at the two country houses closest to the castle — identified as Salajolo and Casale of Tricosto on the Catasto Leopoldino of 1823 — reveal evidence of habitation at by the beginning of the fourteenth century and perhaps even earlier.

A further and a more extensive phase of research aimed at understanding the road used to access the hilltop of Capalbiaccio and the possibility of hydraulic resources. The road follows the sides of the slope and gradually rises in height, continuing north, skirting the eastern slope of the mound, and leading to the sole access to the fortification on the north wall (*infra* Cerri and Mariotti, Fig. 4.4). Surrounding the hill, with the exception of the southern slope towards the coast, five fountains, corresponding to springs, were found. Close to the Fontanile della Strega (107 m above sea level), the course of the road changes direction and heads south towards the castle. The evidence suggests that the course was chosen on the basis of two basic needs: facility of access, which is affirmed by the absence of sharp slopes, despite the greater distance covered; and the location of the springs.

Tricosto's Micro History

The Catasto Leopoldino mentions twenty-one pieces of evidence related to structures in the region surrounding the castle of Tricosto, of which eighteen are distinguished by place names (Fig. 14.4). Of these, all but the fort of Burano were investigated, since it lies in an oasis protected by the World Wildlife Fund and is inaccessible. The zone under examination covers 2.1 km²; it yielded three pieces of evidence that cover the entire chronological spectrum addressed by this study. One piece has been identified as Roman a manufacture and is published elsewhere.[103] Another finding from the area south of Torre Palazzi, along the western banks of the moat of Fonte Picchio, testifies to the inhabitation of the area between the fourteenth and eighteenth centuries. And in the field of the Casa Marotti, ceramics manufactured in Siena or northern Latium[104] in the late fifteenth and early sixteenth century were discovered.[105] Other finds have been documented in the immediate vicinity of the castle, right at the foot of the hill (Fig. 14.5).

---

103 Regoli 2002, 219; Celuzza and Zona 2002, 248.
104 Farnese 1985; 1991.
105 Milanese 1997, 96–99.

Figure 14.6. View from the west coast of the hilltop of Capalbiaccio with the Spanish Tower under restoration (scaffolding) and the modern farmhouse called 'Torre/Casale di Tricosto'. The Tricosto Castle was moved during the Spanish occupation downhill and renamed Tricosto Tower. Photo by author.

Figure 14.7. Pottery concentration near the Salaiolo quarry. In the background on the right is the medieval town of Capalbio. Photo by author.

Figure 14.8. Areas that have been surveyed inside the buffer-zone of the Tricosto castle: Casale Tricosto, il Salaiolo, La Sicilia, Casa Marotti. Photo by author.

In the territory around Tricosto, all the findings related to the period addressed by this study were associated with or were topographically very close to traces of frequentation from an earlier period, which was the case with Castel di Pietra as well. At Casale Tricosto, the farm house was identified southwest of the castle, an area of frequentation from proto-historic times to the twentieth century (Fig. 14.6). The pottery found in the survey dates from prehistoric times to today with no interruption affirming a continuous agricultural richness and exploitation in the area around the Salaiolo farmhouse; at Salaiolo, a concentration of material datable to the first through fifth centuries CE was identified to the southwest of the late medieval seasonal occupation (Fig. 14.7); in Sicilia, about 350 m north of the area known as Le Fornaci, a site (where the concentration extends 1500 m^2) with material datable between the third century BCE and the first century CE, was identified; and around the Casa Marotti,[106] materials ascribable to the period between the third century BCE and the first century CE, as well as a rectangular structure that could be interpreted as a cistern, were discovered (Fig. 14.8; Table 14.2).

The topographical distribution of the identified sites shows that Salaiolo is located near a quarry that has been known since Roman times. The other site of Le Fornaci, equidistant from the castles of Tricosto and Capalbio, is not documented as being related to Tricosto in the early and high Middle Ages. What is interesting is the existence of a settlement in the vicinity of the Casale Tricosto at the bottom of the hill (Fig. 14.9). Here, it seems that the ancient settlement coexisted with that on the hilltop (between the eleventh and eighth centuries BCE), then, between the tenth and thirteenth century, it was to a large extent absorbed by the castle of Tricosto (Table 14.3). The Casale Tricosto coexisted with the final phases of the castle from the fourteenth century on, and it finally outlived the castle (Fig. 14.10).

Further findings make it possible to determine the diachrony of human activity and transformations that affected the area surrounding the castle (Fig. 14.11). As noted above, the exploration of the farmhouses and the land immediately around them enabled the identification of unpublished findings from the Classical period. In the vicinity of

---

106 Carandini and others 2002.

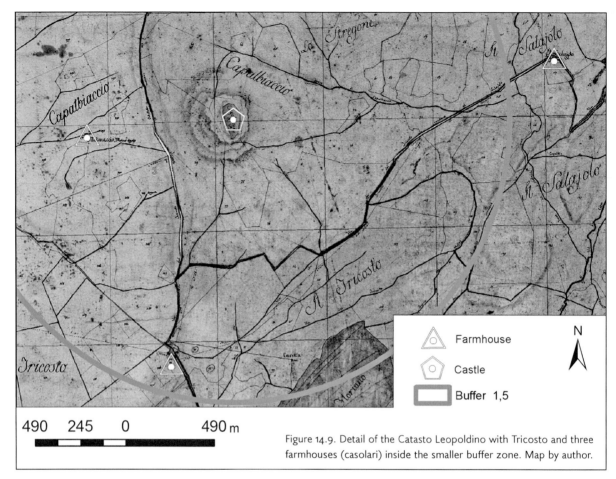

Figure 14.9. Detail of the Catasto Leopoldino with Tricosto and three farmhouses (casolari) inside the smaller buffer zone. Map by author.

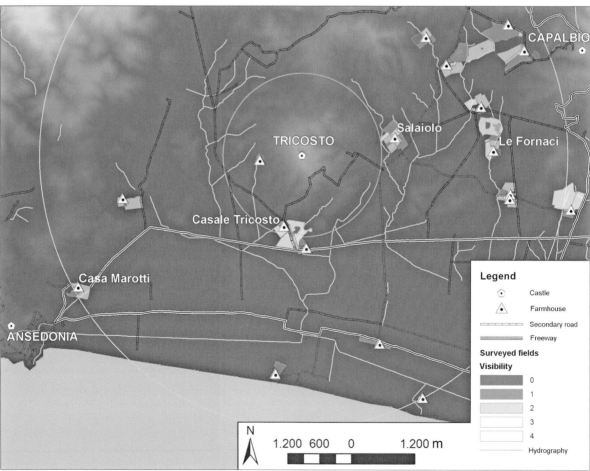

Figure 14.10. Map of the castles and farmhouses identified during the field survey in the buffer zone of the Tricosto castle dated between the end of thirteenth and the sixteenth century. Map by author.

the quarry of Salaiolo, a concentration of ceramic material was discovered together with a structure that covers around 970 m², datable to the first to fourth centuries CE. This chronology coincides with trends evidenced in the entire area.[107] In the area of Megarozzo ('I Barzanti' in the Catasto Leopoldino), ceramic material suggests human activity from the fourth century BCE to the third century CE, which may fall into a broader chronological period. Site 3, which covers an overall area of 5000 m², was identified with the help of a build-up of stone material and four concentrations of ceramic material and bricks. It could be related to a residential structure (ruling out the hypothesis about villa CAP 260, according to which material was dispersed over an area beyond 10,000 m²) that does not seem to have reappeared among the findings documented in the 1980s (Fig. 14.12).[108]

The site identified in the vicinity of Fonte Picchio and SicilіI ('La Cicilia' in the Catasto Leopoldino) can also be related to the Classical period, even though the material findings fall into a narrower time frame compared to the preceding cases. Its overall dimensions are over 15,300 m², suggesting that it was a settlement — probably a village — inhabited between the third century BCE and the first century CE.[109] This site was found in an area that was not included in the explorations carried out in the 1980s, while the other findings (Casale Tricosto and Casa Marotti) are related to sites that were already identified in earlier studies of the region (Fig. 14.13).[110]

The Post-Medieval Settlement Model

The data reported above, especially when it pertains to sites examined stratigraphically, reveals the existence of traits common to all the sites analysed, both in terms of their phases of greatest development and their ultimate phases of existence, notwithstanding the fact that they were characterized by various moments of abandonment (Table 14.1). In a wider geographical spectrum, Sassoforte was acquired by Siena in 1330 and subsequently depopulated; an attempt to repopulate it was undertaken, but it failed, and a century later the castle was described as lying in ruins, the site abandoned.[111] Castel di Pietra survived the crisis of the mid-fourteenth century, but it was abandoned at the beginning of the fifteenth

Figure 14.11. Two examples of the transformation of the landscape resulting from human activity: an abandoned farmhouse (above) is contrasted with the removal of earlier settlements for agricultural purposes (below). Photos by author.

century,[112] while Selvena was transformed into a fortress and survived until the eighteenth century, though losing its function as a population hub.[113]

Excavations in the wider northern region have attested to the peak of the sites' development in an intensive phase of construction between the thirteenth and the first half of the fourteenth century, which may have ended before the Black Death of 1348. This was the case at castles such as Montemassi,[114] Rocchette Pannocchieschi,[115] Castigliocello del Trinoro,[116] and Rocca Ricciarda.[117] Others were abandoned in the course of the thirteenth century, or entered a phase of decline, such as Poggio Cavolo,[118] Miranduolo,[119] and Poggio della Regina.[120] The new urban organization of the seigneurial areas and the

---

107 Regoli 2002.
108 Regoli 2002.
109 Fentress 2002.
110 Carandini and others 2002, 44–45.
111 Salvadori and Valdambrini 2009.

112 Citter 2009b.
113 Citter 2002a.
114 Guideri, Parenti, and Barbagli 2000.
115 Bianchi, Boldrini, and De Luca 1994, 253.
116 *Castiglioncello*.
117 Vannini 2009, 23.
118 Salvadori and others 2006, 274.
119 Valenti 2008, 232.
120 Vannini 2002, 39.

Table 14.3. Evidence collected between the thirteenth and sixteenth century during the field survey done inside the two buffer zones centred on the castles and including the land surrounding the farmhouses represented in the Leopoldine census.

Castle	IGM Place Name	Leopoldine Place Name	Traces	Date	Location/use
Tricosto	c/o cava del Salajolo	Il Salajolo	Concentrated pottery	13–20 c.	Proximity to spring and quarry
Tricosto	F.sso di Fonte Picchio	Le Fornaci	Concentrated pottery	14–19 c.	Road Tricosto Capalbio
Tricosto	C. Tricosto	Il Tricosto	Dispersed Pottery	Prehistoric – 20 c.	Proximity to the castle
Tricosto	C. Marotti	Lo Sbratto	Structure/ Dispersed Pottery	13–19 c.	Road Aurelia
Castel di Pietra	Porcareccia di Casteani	Porcareccia	Concentrated pottery	12–13/ 15–19 c.	Proximity to River Bruna
Castel di Pietra	C.Campotondello	Pod. Campo Tondello	Dispersed Pottery	end 14–19 c.	Proximity to River Bruna
Castel di Pietra	Mulinaccio	Molinaccio diruto	Dispersed Pottery	13–14 c.	Proximity to River Bruna dam
Castel di Pietra	C. Muccaia	La Muccaja	Dispersed Pottery	s.h. 14–19 c.	Proximity to River Bruna dam
Castel di Pietra	C. Petraio	Casetta del Petraj	Dispersed Pottery	14–20 c.	Proximity to River Bruna
Cotone	c/o Castello di Cotone	###	Dispersed Pottery	12–18 c.	Road
Cotone	Poggio Vicerano	###	Dispersed Pottery	16–20 c.	Road
Cotone	c/o Pod. La Poderina	###	Concentrated pottery	13–16 c.	Road
Cotone	c/o Pod. C. Acquarello	###	Concentrated pottery	mid 14–20 c.	Road
Cotone	Fosso del Romito	Romito	Structure/ Dispersed Pottery	14–16 c.	Road
Cotone	c/o Pod. Palazzetto	###	Concentrated pottery	14–15 c.	Road
Monteacuto di Pari	M. Acuto	M. Acuto Podere	Dispersed Pottery	14–19 c.	Proximity to the castle
Monteacuto di Pari	Ferraiola	Podere di ferrajola	Dispersed Pottery	14–20 c.	Agriculture area/ road
Monteacuto di Pari	Pod.E S. Ansano	Pod. di S. Ansano	Concentrated pottery	13–20 c.	Road
Monteacuto di Pari	Pod.E Colombaio	Pod. del Colombajo	Dispersed Pottery	14–20 c.	Agriculture area/ road
Monteacuto di Pari	Pod.E Vignali	Pod. di Vignali	Dispersed Pottery	11–14 c.	Agriculture area
Monteacuto di Pari	Fercole	Fercole Osteria	Dispersed Pottery	13–20 c.	Road
Monteacuto di Pari	Pod.e Gellino	Gellino Pod.	Dispersed Pottery	16–20 c.	Agriculture area/ road
Montepescali	Pod. Tondicarlo	Tondi Carlo osteria	Concentrated pottery	14–20 c.	Road
Montepescali	C. Dosso	C. del Dosso	Concentrated pottery	15–20 c.	Road
Montepescali	La Pescaia	Tenuta della Pescaja	Concentrated pottery	15–20 c.	Road
Sassoforte	c/o il Poggio	Querceto	Dispersed Pottery	15–20 c.	Agriculture area/ road
Sassoforte	Pagiano	Casetta Chelini	Dispersed Pottery	Medieval	Agriculture area/ road
Sassoforte	Pod. Bettarello	Pod. di Bettarello	Dispersed Pottery	13–20 c.	Proximity Giugnano /road
Sassoforte	Il Poggio	Casettine	Dispersed Pottery	12–20 c.	Agriculture area/ road
Sassoforte	Il Casalone/ Pozzacce	San Fabiano	Dispersed Pottery	13–20 c.	Proximity to parish of Caminino
Sassoforte	Poggio Paolo	Fagiano	Dispersed Pottery	13–16 c.	Agriculture area/ road
Roccaccia di Selvena	Selvena	###	Dispersed Pottery	14–20 c.	Road

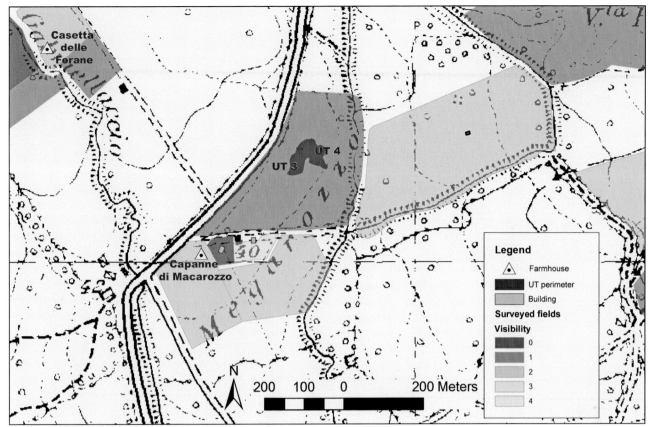

Figure 14.12. Detail of the IGM map showing different visibility established by the field survey in the Megarozzo area (UT is the topographical unit). Map by author.

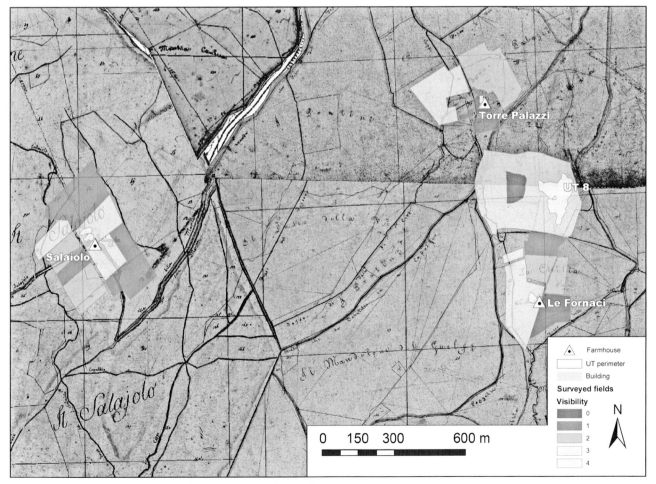

Figure 14.13. Detail of the Catasto Leopoldino with the newly identified sites of Salaiolo, Le Fornaci and Cicilia in the vicinity of Tricosto. Map by author.

construction of villages during this developmental peak is evidence of the gentry's involvement in this phase, which is the situation that was documented at the castle of Tricosto. Each of the three sites investigated changed perceptibly, well into the fourteenth and early fifteenth centuries: the area of the keep at Castel di Pietra was divided into two residential units; the palazzo in Selvena was restructured and some working spaces, as well as a three-storey house, were built; at Sassoforte, a winepress belongs to this phase. Similarly, at Castel di Pietra and Sassoforte, areas that had been abandoned earlier were still frequented.

Quantitative and qualitative analyses of ceramic material further contributed to the idea of development and the vitality of relations. Information on the circulation of goods can, in a certain way, signal areas of economic and cultural influence within which the centres developed and gravitated. A clear preponderance of Sienese products was evident at all the sites: they account for nearly all the ceramics from Castel di Pietra, while at Selvena, material from Umbria (Orvieto) and Latium is also present. At Sassoforte, there was a greater variety of ceramics, including goods from Pisa, Volterra, Latium, and imports from the western Mediterranean basin.

Thus, in all these castles, the final phases of existence reveal signs of human activity that portray their phases of abandonment as a more complex than what might have been deduced from written sources. The one counterexample being Castel di Pietra, for which there is a significant concurrence between the date of its abandonment, as reported by the sources, and the ceramic findings. Indeed, in the absence of more definitive evidence, the only ceramic findings from fifteenth-century Castel di Pietra proper, may be related to seasonal and occasional activities. On the other hand, the reoccupation of structures and the existence of a wine press at Sassoforte in the period between the late fourteenth and early fifteenth centuries provide a more complex view of the effects of repopulation than that reported by sources. Furthermore, the presence of material datable to the second half of the fifteenth and early sixteenth centuries reveals a real discrepancy between physical and written sources.

To this end, it is necessary to take into account the ideological component of written sources that refer to abandonment or repopulation, and to contextualize it within the framework of ongoing changes brought about by the ever-greater presence of the urban aristocracy.[121] The period between the late thirteenth and the early fourteenth centuries was characterized by a great increase in land holdings by Sienese magnate families.[122] Such protagonists enabled the city's domination of the countryside, urbanizing and expanding it so as to create a vaster institutional space. It was only between the fourteenth and fifteenth centuries that the definitive 'return to the land' took place as a result of an irreversible crisis in mercantile and banking activity, which forced many people to fall back on revenue from land.[123] At this point, central interest was no longer placed upon individual castles, but rather the territory in all its complexity. And it is precisely within the context of such an urban initiative that regional reorganization began. Surface explorations have identified habitation in cites, castles, and the countryside, which suggests a historical model other than that proposed by written sources.

It is necessary to specify that the material data documented herein is not an indicator of a settlement typology *per se*, but is rather regional evidence, particularly pertaining to the area surrounding the farmhouses included in the Catasto Leopoldino. In the absence of further information, which could be gathered through additional archaeological research, the partial information available from the presence of ceramic material is a relevant indicator of settlement patterns. Nonetheless, as already indicated in the literature, these areas may have been used as seasonal or temporary residences that served as lodgings for transhumant shepherds or agricultural labourers,[124] who have already been identified in other zones of the Maremma.[125] Only in a later phase, due to a change in political and social conditions, or merely thanks to the continuity of human activity in the area, were these residences converted into country houses or farms stable enough to accommodate direct management of the surrounding region. It is by this route they would come to be registered in the Catasto Leopoldino.

Can archaeology tell us if and how settlement patterns changed when the castle's role — either as a pole attracting population or as an entity administering the territory's resources — diminished? Comparing the data that emerged from the field to the historical sources and models, it seems that the medieval city, once it won over the territorial gentry, engaged in a general process of redefining the entire territory's political, economic, and social administration

---

121 Citter 2009c.

122 Cammarosano 1979, 220; Piccinni 1992, 15; Cherubini 2009, 590.
123 Cherubini 1974, 236; Pinto 1990, 440; Piccinni 1992, 13 n. 6.
124 Cherubini 1974, 15; Pinto 1982, 58; Piccinni 1992, 151–52; Cantini 2003, 243.
125 Citter 2009c.

from the thirteenth century onwards. When it came to the general reorganization of the territory, of the population, and of forms of settlement, everything revolved around the interest of the medieval city and its new elites, who focused their interests not so much on the individual castles, which maintained their role as population hubs and became the seats of new districts, but rather on those that had been conquered.[126] It is precisely in this sense that the transformations in castles between the fourteenth and fifteenth centuries, along with the appearance of settlement forms that coexisted and outlived the final phases of castles, can be read. If interpreted in this light, then the topographic distribution of findings documented during this research, albeit not representative of all the sites frequented between the late thirteenth and the sixteenth centuries, may not appear completely arbitrary.

Farmhouses and the Reorganization of the Countryside

At Monteacuto di Pari, the sites identified occupy a tillable strip of land close to the road system that links Siena to the Maremma, at the foot of the elevation from which the castle rises. A very similar situation existed at the castle of Tricosto, where farmhouses and a new tower were constructed around the slope of Capalbiaccio, possibly built in the mid-fifteenth century (Fig. 14.14).

At Montepescali, the scanty findings were compensated for by the features of the inhabited centre that still maintains its role as a population hub and is, in this study, the sole example of a castle in which life continues (Fig. 14.15). Sassofortino, the site which the inhabitants of Sassoforte moved to after the abandonment of the castle, becomes the proof of a village from the post-medieval period which testifies that a new area, endowed with its own forms of resources, was established. The findings from the strip of land to the south of Sassofortino, along the roads that connected the village to the plain, demonstrated its great agricultural potential and prime location (Fig. 14.16). At Castel di Pietra, all the evidence from the fourteenth to the sixteenth centuries was located in the northern zone of the castle, along the Bruna River, while the zone chosen for the late fifteenth-century dam that supplied Siena with fish, offered no material remains (Fig. 14.17). Exceptions to this were the regions around the castles of Selvena, Tricosto (from the moment that

Figure 14.14. Detail of the Tricosto farmhouse with Capalbiaccio Castle in the background. Photo by author.

Sienese rule solidified in the period following that documented by the findings), and Cotone (two sites — in the northwest, along the road that connected the castle with Montorgiali, and in the southwest, corresponding to the road connecting Cotone to Montepò — were, however, inhabited in the fourteenth century). Thus, between the fourteenth and fifteenth centuries, civic power over seigneurial territories was fully affirmed. Frustration with the castle system could be interpreted as an impetus for the new forms of settlement that are documented in this study by farmhouses. Certainly, these new forms of settlement were not a direct expression of civic will, but a consequence of a different utilization of the territory, which had already blossomed in other zones that benefitted more from external factors. This change may have resulted in the diffusion of sharecropping, a system of agricultural management based on contractual agreements between landowners and peasant families that were charged with running the former's farm complexes. Because of environmental and economic conditions, as well as reasons related to the management and control of the territory, this system of managing property was not adopted in the Maremma until the Modern era.[127] However, documents confirm that, in other areas of Tuscany, sharecropping was not an exception.[128] The same is affirmed in the archaeological map of the Province of Siena, which provides numerous exam-

---

126 Citter 2009c.

127 Cherubini 1979a, 137; Pinto 1990, 434; Bonelli Conenna 1980, 225; Rombai 2002, 13.
128 Cherubini 1979a; Isaacs 1979; Pinto 1990; Piccinni 1992; Pirillo 2002, 175.

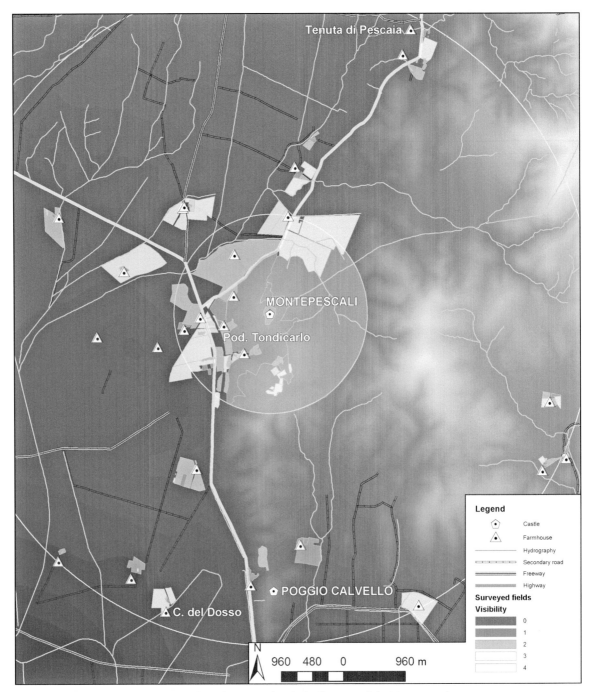

Figure 14.15. Map indicating all castles and farmhouses within the buffer zone of the Montepescali castle between the end of thirteenth and the sixteenth century. Map by author.

ples of sharecropping throughout the Sienese territory.[129] Other examples have been found in the area between Arezzo and Florence, emerging from explorations around Poggio della Regina[130] and Rocca Ricciarda.[131] In the areas of Pratomagno, closest to the Arno River, as well as the new centres along the Via Aretina, settlement types were notably influenced by the diffusion of sharecropping and the division of land into small estates in the fourteenth century.[132]

---

129 Valenti 1995, 411; Valenti 1999, 349; Nardini 2001, 180; Campana (ed.) 2001, 315 and 319; Felici 2004, 333, 337; Botarelli 2005, 231; Cenni 2007, 366, 379, 382.
130 Vannini 2002, 14.
131 Vannini 2009.
132 Cimarri 2009, 87.

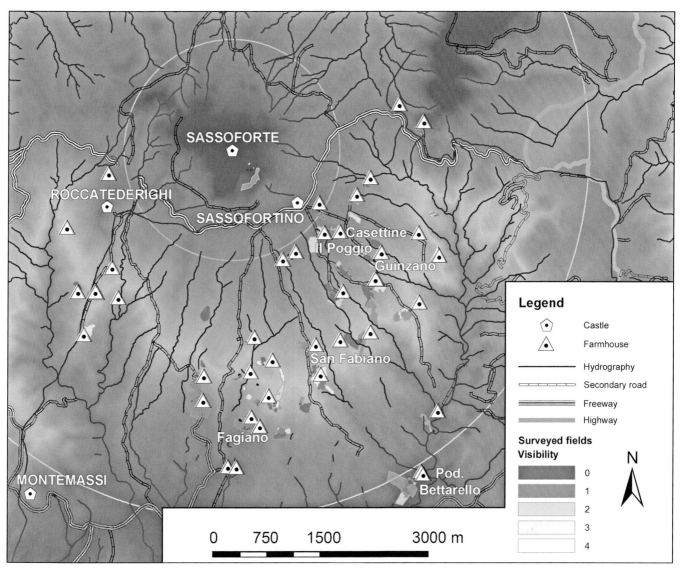

Figure 14.16. Map indicating all castles and farmhouses within the buffer zone of the Sassoforte castle between the thirteenth and the sixteenth century. Map by author.

The expansion of Siena towards the Maremma, combined with the crisis that culminated in the Black Death, clearly transformed the settlement of the region, a process which can be archaeologically documented. On the one hand, these transformations stripped some castles of their function as population hubs (even if in some cases they continued to be frequented) and brought more activity to the plains and the elevated terrain immediately surrounding them. This research uncovered a chronology that coincides not so much with the desertion of castles, but with the final phases of their existence. Thus, at the outset of the fourteenth century, it is possible to imagine a settlement situation still centred on the presence of castles, but clearly not exclusively characterized by their existence. It would appear that castles evolved to take on exclusively administrative roles and they coexisted with other settlement types, whose significance in the landscape came to be visible only two centuries later.

How does this data relate to the historical models developed on the basis of written sources? The results of this research have helped to determine the forms of rural population in quantitative and qualitative terms. The absence of scattered populations does not clash with the evidence of late medieval frequentation in areas that later became farms in the Modern era. Indeed, such establishments can be traced back to seasonal sites that served as residential quarters for transhumant shepherds or relief stations for peasants, who worked the fields, but continued to inhabit castles. Survey work cannot reveal the intensity and duration of this frequentation, but systematic excavations might be able to.

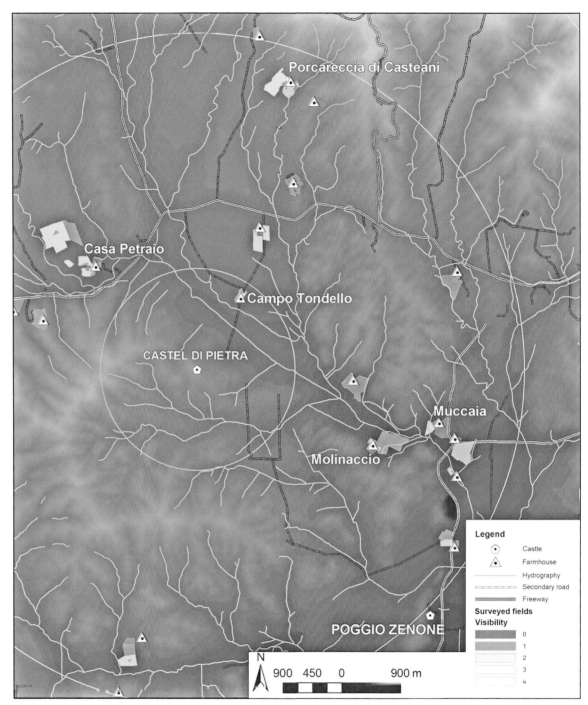

Figure 14.17. Map indicating all castles and farmhouses within the buffer zone of the Castel di Pietra castle between the end of the thirteenth and sixteenth century. Map by author.

Nevertheless, the coincidence between this physical evidence and that mentioned in the Catasto of 1823 delineates the emergence of a new agrarian landscape. It is not out of question that these structures, often invisible, either because written sources do not refer to them or because there are few traces of them in the field, contributed to the formation of the farm system that developed between the sixteenth and nineteenth centuries.

Similar examples have come to light from investigations conducted in regions surrounding the castles of Montemassi, Castel di Pietra, and Scarlino. In each case, the characteristic feature at the threshold of the fourteenth century was an extensive network of castles. The demographic crisis and the politics of Sienese exploitation caused the gradual disappearance of the population and transformations in settlement patterns. Prior to the crisis, the landscape was characterized by a scarcity of people on the farms, which was the consequence of the meagre diffusion of sharecropping leases in the region and progressively greater exploitation of the land, thanks to the ever stronger and more pervasive spread of transhumant animal herding. The surveys carried out at Scarlino have produced evidence of small agglomerations within broad networks, which existed concurrently with castles.[133] There was also a population within a large network in the Pecora Valley, which had counterparts all over the Maremma, and which existed in a natural landscape that was not yet the overgrown and inhospitable place it became in the following centuries.

Conclusions

The results that have emerged from this study make it possible to document a typology of frequentation in areas outside of castle habitats, which coincided with and outlasted the latter, even though the Province of Grosseto is actually characterized by a high percentage of medieval castles that continued to serve as centres of population (Fig. 14.18). Starting with the homesteads listed in the Catasto Leopoldino of 1823–1824, it was possible to identify zones in which to analyse the chronology of homesteads in the territory, as well as human frequentation prior to their firm establishment in the physiognomy of the landscape (since sharecropping was only fully instituted in Maremma at the end of the sixteenth century). This was accomplished principally through the recovery of ceramic material and the investigation of surviving walls.

The ceramic material that was recovered confirmed what had already emerged from the excavations and surveys of the Province of Grosseto: the prevalence of products from Siena and its environs (archaic majolica, with graffiti and glaze over slip) stood out in the entire chronological timeframe of the study (late thirteenth–sixteenth century). The number of products from Pisa and Valdarno, though fewer percentage-wise, increased in the fifteenth and sixteenth centuries, especially in terms of slipware and polychrome graffiti ware. Pottery from the area of Umbria and upper Latium was documented solely around castles located in the southern region: Selvena, on Monte Amiata, and, naturally, Tricosto.[134]

---

133 Cucini 1985, 267–314; Ceccarelli Lemut 1999.
134 For more in-depth detail on such information, see the publications already cited in this chapter on the excavations and surface explorations of the castles of Tricosto, Selvena, Castel di Pietra, Sassoforte, Montemassi, and Scarlino.

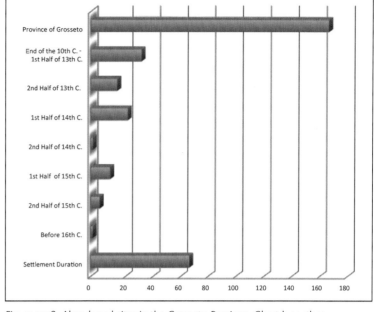

Figure 14.18. Abandoned sites in the Grosseto Province. Chart by author.

The spatial distribution of the documented frequentation likewise provides a picture of the basic continuity of settlement in 'strategic' zones in the region, above all, along road systems (Tricosto, Sassoforte, Castel di Pietra, Cotone), streams and rivers (Castel di Pietra and Montepescali), or in the vicinity of springs and fertile areas (Tricosto, Sassoforte, Monteacuto di Pari, Selvena).

Inserted within these very general parameters, which became normalized in crucial areas of the region, lie the documented findings from the area surrounding the castle of Tricosto. Southeast of the castle, in the vicinity of the spring of Salaiolo (the place-name also signals the existence of a quarry, for which no elements have been identified to assist in its dating), ceramic findings superimposed over a settlement from the Roman period provide a chronology that runs uninterrupted from the thirteenth to the twentieth centuries. Around the moat of Fonte Picchio, at the site of the kilns, along the road system that connects Tricosto to Capalbio, the materials discovered revealed human frequentation in the area from the fourteenth century. Medieval and late medieval materials were also found in the flat area presently occupied by Casale Tricosto, where the Roman villas belonging to the Giardino and Colonna families are recorded to have stood. The final finding related to the chronological span of the transition from the Middle Ages to the Modern era, and it was documented along the Via Aurelia near the Casa Marotti. The signs of frequentation that have emerged from precise explorations of the areas around the Castle of Tricosto confirm the same tendencies encountered in the regions around the other castles investigated. The documented findings are thus attributable to a settlement model that, though not excluded *a priori* from archaeological research, has never actually been applied to the province of Grosseto.

Even though the view offered by this study focuses on only part of the region, and the findings may clash with the settlement model proposed by historiography, it nonetheless provides a reconstruction of settlement patterns in the territory that evidences settlement continuity. However, we cannot exclude — and this is one of the many incentives driving this research — that the evidence gathered may, in part, be attributable to a completely different model, one characterized by sparse houses distributed more or less organically, larger nuclei based on the model of eighteenth-century farms, or by yet another more complex settlement system — excluding the hypothesis that these types of settlements resemble open villages. At this point, despite the material traces, it is impossible to determine the typology of the findings. However, it is plausible that they are attributable to temporary inhabitation, such as service buildings that stored tools or served as shelters for agricultural labourers that resided in or around the castle, but who moved on a daily basis according to the plots of tillable land, returning to the inhabited centre only at the end of the day, as was the custom in other areas of the Maremma.

Part IV

Historical Reconstructions and Conclusions

MICHELLE HOBART

15. Reassessing the Etruscan Valle d'Oro

ABSTRACT The first chapter in the final discussion of the book locates the hilltop site of Capalbiaccio in the immediate vicinity of the ancient port of Cosa and its hinterland, as well as the broader Etruscan *Ager Cosanus*, demonstrating why it was a significant place for Stephen Dyson and his team to explore in the late 1970s. The historical reconstruction of the Etruscan and subsequent Roman period is bolstered by modern geophysical techniques, unavailable to the original excavator, and forty years of celebrated research that has developed in the meantime. It elucidates what is currently understood about this enigmatic period in Italian pre-history, and how the place in question fits into the regional context. Without a doubt, the Capalbiaccio hilltop was home to a mid-sized Etruscan precursor settlement, and this archaeological discovery allows certain gaps in our knowledge to be addressed and pressing historical questions to be tentatively answered for what is arguably one of the most significant sub-regions in Italian classical archaeology. In summary, the addition of the Etruscan hilltop site at Capalbiaccio to the regional picture, which encompasses the extensively excavated Roman coastal colony of Cosa and the slave-run villa at Settefinestre, pinpoints a presence within what previously appeared to be a vacuum in an otherwise essential territory. In the end, the chapter proposes a new angle on settlement patterns in the southern Maremma area and the story of Cosa's proximate historical interlocutors. [MH]

This chapter is about what we have learned from the archaeology and geophysics for pre-Roman and Roman Etruria. After analysing the earliest pottery excavated at Capalbiaccio, it became obvious that a geophysical survey of the hilltop was necessary to understand the size and nature of the pre-medieval compound. The anomalies identified with the magnetometry — stone foundations organized in mostly squared alignments — revealed an extension that went beyond the medieval standing castle which was determined to be early medieval and pre-Roman. Among all the finds collected during the three archaeological campaigns (1976–1980), medieval ceramics and early medieval represented the largest group, followed by the Etruscan fragments; the two periodizations clearly mirror the settlements. Any temptation to see a Roman presence was excluded, given the lack of Roman pottery, except for a few fragments and bricks found just outside the walls. The evidence from the late bronze age is deduced from the pottery as well as the Etruscan pottery while no late antique traces have emerged until the early medieval tenth-century village.

To present knowledge, the earlier site of Capalbiaccio appears a typical hilltop small Etruscan fortified centre. The confirmation derives from both the geophysical investigations and the pottery, found in the lower layers, without visible structures from the excavation.

This finding is corroborated by the extension (about 4.5 ha), the dominating position, and the chronology of the material. There are a number of similar findings at Castel di Pietra (territory of Vetulonia) where there is an example of a Final Bronze Age site, on which a Late Orientalizing Period site is superimposed and was abandoned in the second to the first century BCE, both lying under the structure of the castle, as at Capalbiaccio.[1] Other hilltop settlements also existed within Populonia's territory.[2]

While a fuller excavation of the hilltop would help clarify the nature of the site, the geophysics show enough to ponder the presence of an Etruscan community. The discovery of another Etruscan settlement on the hilltop of Capalbiaccio, in such a strategic part of the Roman economic landscape, allows to rethink of the Valle d'Oro in southern Etruria. This newfound presence also informs the nature of the dynamics between farming and village, fortifications and larger centres, before the Romans settled in their new colony at Cosa.

---

1 Citter 2009b, 72–98.
2 Di Paola 2018, 273–92 and other examples of oppida see Cambi 2012.

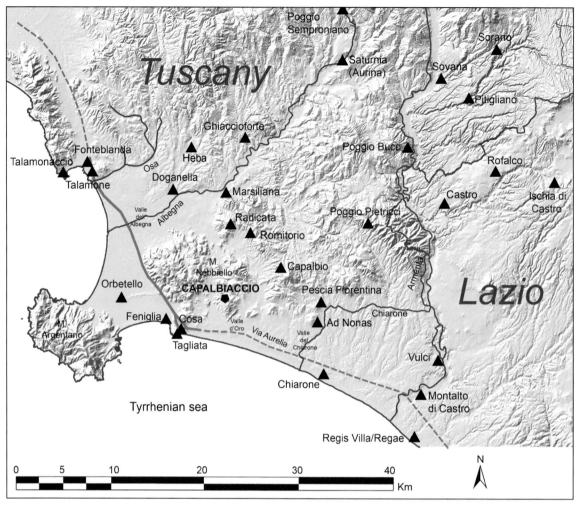

Figure 15.1. Map of Etruscan settlements around Capalbiaccio. Map by Rossella Pansini. Basemap/DTM reproduced with the permission of CTR Regione Toscana.

The Landscape

A large triangular shaped area extends between the Albegna River and the coastal strip between the Albegna and Fiora Rivers. The Albegna Valley is generally considered to include the extensive Etruscan farming communities of Doganella and Marsiliana, on the northern side, while the region surrounding the city of Vulci to the south has been less investigated. The valleys are protected by hills, upon which agricultural settlements have existed since the earliest traces of human presence in the area. The sandy coastline is interrupted by the large rocky peninsula of the Monte Argentario, which is tied to the mainland by two strips of sand dunes (the Giannella and the Feniglia), which protect Orbetello.[3] At the north-western limit, the harbour of Talamone was protected by a small gulf while the southeastern boundaries are traced by the Fiora river and the Etruscan city of Vulci (Fig. 15.1).

On the southern side of the Argentario promontory, the Roman port of Cosa — also known as the *Tagliata Etrusca* — a slit in the rocks that creates a natural conduit into a pool to capture fish — was occupied up to the imperial era.[4] South of the peninsula of Monte Argentario, the coast, which was once a lagoon, lies low with no other interruption down to the Tolfa hills beyond Tarquinia.

The hilltop of Capalbiaccio sits in the centre of a smaller triangular valley, called Valle d'Oro (Fig. 15.2). During the Roman period, this geographic agricul-

---

3   For a general introduction and bibliography of the region, see Celuzza and Luzzetti 2013; Carandini and others 2002; and, for Orbetello, see Ciampoltrini 1991; Cardosa 2019.

4   McCann and others 1987; Ciampoltrini and Rendini 2004b.

15. REASSESSING THE ETRUSCAN VALLE D'ORO 275

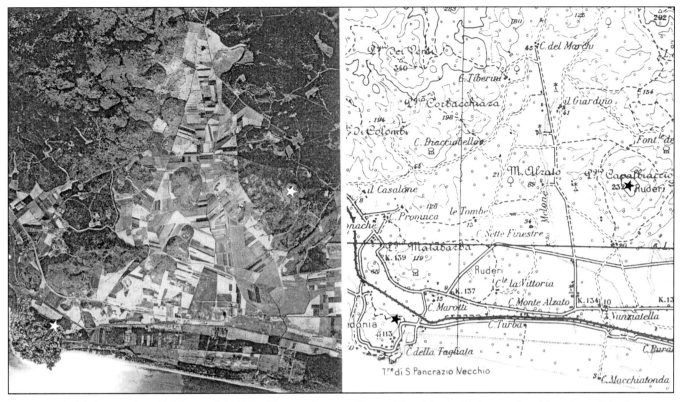

Figure 15.2. Aerial photograph and IGM map of the Valle d'Oro area between Cosa and Capalbiaccio. Photo reproduced from Carandini 1985.

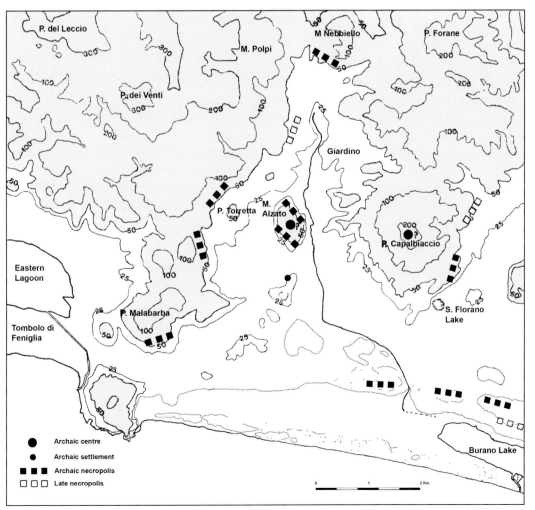

Figure 15.3. Archaic burials around Capalbiaccio and its surroundings. Adapted from Celuzza and Regoli 1982, 36. Map adapted from Celuzza and Regoli 1982, 36.

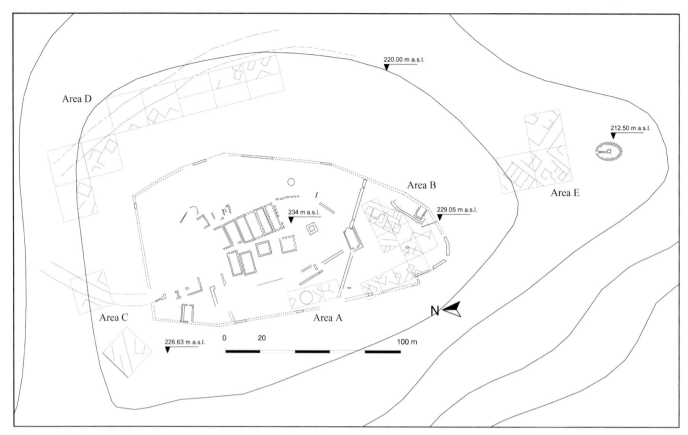

Figure 15.4. Geophysical survey of Capalbiaccio hilltop and castle. Image by Laura Cerri and Emanuele Mariotti.

tural area was variously referred to by its correlated town, such as the *ager Caletranus* (an unknown location), *ager Cosanus* (a newly founded Roman colony), *ager Hebanus* (no longer visible), and *ager Saturninus* (re-founded Roman town).[5]

Surveys and excavations in the region have established that, before the Roman colonies of Cosa, Saturnia, and Roselle, concentrations of people were gathered on the valley's northern hilltops opposite Capalbiaccio. Despite the identification of Etruscan burials in the 1970s (Fig. 15.3), a wide vacuum stretching from the coast to the interior of the Valle d'Oro is visible on maps of current Etruscan settlements.[6] This open space between Vulci and Doganella is unusual according to Etruscan settlement patterns, which otherwise occupied every high point at regular intervals in the landscape. The regular distribution of sites every 10 km in the Albegna Valley suggests that there was a deliberate intent to plan, control, and defend settlements between the end of the seventh and the sixth century BCE.[7] Thus, some form of condensed habitation on the hilltop of Capalbiaccio, at an expected distance from other known sites, provides a more complete picture of the Valle d'Oro, and may explain a settlement for the Etruscan tombs in the area.

The community of Capalbiaccio is situated between Vulci (c. 22 km) to the south, and it faces Doganella (c. 12 km) and Marsiliana (c. 10 km) to the north and northeast. From the height of the hilltop, the settlement commands its *ager*, which extends between the coast, the inland region of Saturnia, and the Radicata Valley. Within the natural geographic triangle of the Valle d'Oro, Capalbiaccio occupies a remarkably central position in one of the most fertile regions of central Italy. The plain of the Valle d'Oro is surrounded by springs and defined by rolling hills dotted with regular, although sparse, fortifications, making a larger settlement nearby on a defensible hilltop a distinct possibility.

---

5 On the *ager Cosanus*, see Cambi 1986, 528, 533.

6 While they are not currently visible, the burials have been documented by Bronson and Uggeri 1970, and later recorded on the *Carta archeologica* by Torelli 1992, folio 135, 533–60; Celuzza and Regoli 1982, 35; Perkins 1999; and Celuzza and Luzetti 2013.

7 Perkins 2010.

The New Archaeological Evidence

Magnetometry

While the flattened extension of the hilltop consists of about 3 hectares of land, the medieval castle covered only 1.2 hectares. This area was reduced to 1 hectare when a second fortified wall was built, separating and excluding 0.2 hectares in the northern portion of the fortification. This smaller area on a slightly lower terrace has no standing structures and was possibly used for agriculture and pasture during the Middle Ages. It is here where we started the geophysical survey that identified the earlier settlements (Fig. 15.4).

The reading of the geophysical survey indicates that the earlier community was much larger than that of the medieval fortification, occupying the entire plateau (at least 300 × 200 m, or 4.5 ha), and it most likely extended further down the sloping hill. The layout of the early dwellings can be likened to a form of a communal domestic life. The structures consist of different groups of three or four rooms, measuring approximately 5 × 10 m. These are arranged in rows that share a loose orientation: NE–SW and SE–NW. Towards the apex of the hilltop, there is a denser concentration of close-knit structures (Area B in Fig. 15.4). Further from the centre, small groups of nucleated houses are tied together by what appears to be a larger road cut into the bedrock, which winds around the plateau (Areas C and D). In the area around a still unclear oval structure, south of the medieval fortification (Area E), the settlement seems to border on orthogonal, with a medium density and larger rooms, compared to the other two areas. These alignments suggest a plan of a wider scale, based on the connected layout of these buildings, which visibly differs from what we can deduce inside the medieval wall.

Pottery

While no surface structure from the Etruscan period is visible, the analysis of the pre-medieval pottery found on the Capalbiaccio hilltop led to the identification of at least one if not two pre-Roman phases of occupation.[8] The chronological sequence outlined by the excavated finds starts in the late Bronze and early Iron Age, and goes to the third century BCE, with an interruption during the eighth and part of the seventh century BCE. This period of abandonment of almost two centuries is inferred from

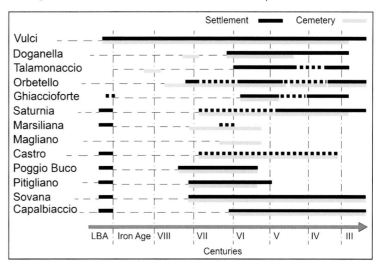

Table 15.1. Timeline of settlement in southern Etruria, adapted from Perkins 2010.

the lack of late Iron Age and minimal Orientalizing period pottery. Small Bronze Age sites were abandoned for a time during the ninth and most of the eighth century on the Tyrrhenian coast in southern Etruria, when large proto-urban centres, such as Vulci, Veio, Caere, and Tarquinia developed.[9] On the basis of the pottery excavated in the late 1970s, life re-emerged at Capalbiaccio in the late seventh and early sixth centuries, similar to a large number of smaller centres that were re-founded, inaugurating a new configuration of inhabitation in the archaic period (Table 15.1).

The Etruscan finds from Capalbiaccio revealed that, at its apex, this community might have been sizable, and it may have continued to prosper into the sixth century BCE. They also indicate that the area was in contact with other Etruscan cities and that it traded and imported goods from places as far away as Greece. Relative to the brief archaeological seasons carried out in the late 1970s, the quantity of Etruscan pottery that was discovered was not enough to measure the size of the site and establish the length of the Etruscan phase at the site. Yet, it must be emphasized that only two of all the excavated areas reached all the way to the bedrock, uncovering the earliest layers of occupation at Capalbiaccio (Buildings J and M (a pit]). Only further investigation would confirm if the Etruscan settlement covered the entire hilltop. Valeria Acconcia, who studied the pottery before the discoveries of the

---

8 In addition to her chapter *infra*, see Acconcia 2005.

9 On the development of urban settlements, see Pacciarelli, 1991b; Perkins 1999; Pacciarelli, 2000; Paoletti, 2005; Bonghi Jovino 2005; Perkins, 2014. For Marsiliana, see Colonna 1976; Colonna 1977, 198; Cristofani 1977; Michelucci 1977; Zifferero, 1990. For Vulci, see Pacciarelli, 1991a, 11–48; Pacciarelli, 1999; Tamburini 2000, 39; Carandini and others 2002.

geophysical survey, is naturally cautious in determining the nature and sequence of the site, given the small overall sample at her disposal. However, Acconcia underlines 'the position and the prevalence of utilitarian pottery from the seventh to the fourth century BCE', and suggests that, at the time, the site was 'presumably fortified'.[10]

The Oval Foundations

The structures identified in the geophysical survey show the demarcation of an oval building (Area E in Fig. 15.4; *infra* Cerri, Mariotti). This foundation was visible on the ground in 2009–2010, and contained standing walls inside, built with locally quarried limestone. More than 300 m south of the medieval walls of the fortified village, at a level lower than the plateau on which the Etruscan community lived (212.5 m above sea level; 16–17 m lower than the hilltop), this exterior elliptical alignment was made of square-faced stones, and measured 15 × 10 m, with a corridor running in a L shape. The structure has repeatedly fallen victim to looting and no excavation or cleaning has yet to take place, but it still occupies a prominent position on the hillside (Fig. 15.5).

While the visibility of this structure in the recent campaign allowed our team to sketch its foundations and inner structure, by 2015 no trace of its perimeter was evident, except for the interior corridor and a room. This structure has created confusion and challenged some of the reports done in the past.[11] If this oval structure turns out to be a tomb, then its presence within proximity to an Etruscan village is not common, but it is likewise not totally unique. Although from a much earlier period, circular burials outlined with stones, the so-called *tombe a circolo* variety, have recently been discovered in the Albegna Valley, as well as north, in areas around Vetulonia, Marsiliana, and the Apennines, both in the opposite direction and quite a distance from Vulci. The Marsiliana 'chamber tomb in a stone circle' is dated to the late seventh century Orientalizing period of which almost no traces are present at Capalbiaccio.[12] Early variations of the *tombe a circolo* have been found and excavated at the nearby sites of Macchiabuia,[13] and the chamber room tombs (*tombe a camera*) from Poggio Marcuccio, near Scansano, are similar in design.[14] Both sites' chronologies range between late seventh and early sixth century BCE. In each case, the tomb is located on the hillside, close to inhabited areas and visible to those looking up from the valley. The structure found at Capalbiaccio differs as the stones were carved more regularly and resembles a tumulus tomb, like the one found in Roselle.[15]

On the geophysical survey, the wall surrounding the oval structure seems to be enclosed by a larger rectangular wall, which could suggest a sanctuary.[16] If the oval structure at Capalbiaccio is indeed a tomb, then its location, both visible from the valley, as well as commanding a significant vantage point over the landscape, would seem to be relevant. An alternative interpretation, based on a comparison of the masonry technique and type of stone used, suggests that the oval structure could have been a medieval defensive base used for a catapult, as excavated in the nearby Ansedonia/Cosa.[17] If these remains served as a medieval form of defensive structure, sitting on a remarkable position on the hillside, it seems that this location had the same function at the end of World War II, when the scattered stones fallen from the hilltop circuit walls were assembled in haste by the Germans to place their firing weapons over the valley facing the small lake of Burano as the allies liberated Italy.[18]

The Well

In the 1970s, the excavations of Dyson's team documented the presence of a well within the fortified medieval town (Fig. 15.4 the round structure on top of the 234 m asl). The well was not cleared out

---

10 Acconcia 2005. A similar situation is found at Castel di Pietra; see Citter 2009b.
11 This phenomenon has happened before in Tuscany on the same southern hill of Capalbiaccio, Levi in 1927 and later Bronson and Uggeri in 1970, identified in their survey tombs that are no longer visible in both the Radicata valley and the Valle d'Oro. Similarly, a drawing made from aerial photographs outlined the urban plan of Heba which was no longer visible when the site was recently surveyed. I thank M. G. Celuzza for her comments see also Carandini 1985b, 125; Attolini and others 1982; Attonlini and others 1983; Attolini in Carandini 1985b. Graham Barker, during his pioneering multi-period field surveying around the castle of Montearrenti, in the early 1980s (with Riccardo Francovich and Richard Hodges) noticed that when returning to the same rural landscape findings changed year by year and that the presence and absence of settlements or simply pottery gave never the same result. Which of course is problematic and might be why, to my knowledge, it was never published.

12 Perkins 1999, 79–81, fig. 4.3.2.
13 Giuntoli 2009; Zifferero and others 2011b; Pallecchi 2011; Tofani and Zifferero 2011.
14 Firmati 2008; Firmati 2011.
15 Celuzza 2017, 64.
16 Recently, new theories regarding sanctuaries and their role in defining territorial boundaries have been proposed by Andrea Zifferero and accepted by others. See Zifferero 1995; Zifferero 1998; Zifferero 2002. On *oppida*, see Cambi 2012.
17 Fentress and others 1991.
18 I thank Andrea Zifferero who has noticed similar structures built by Germans hiding at Montecassino during World War II.

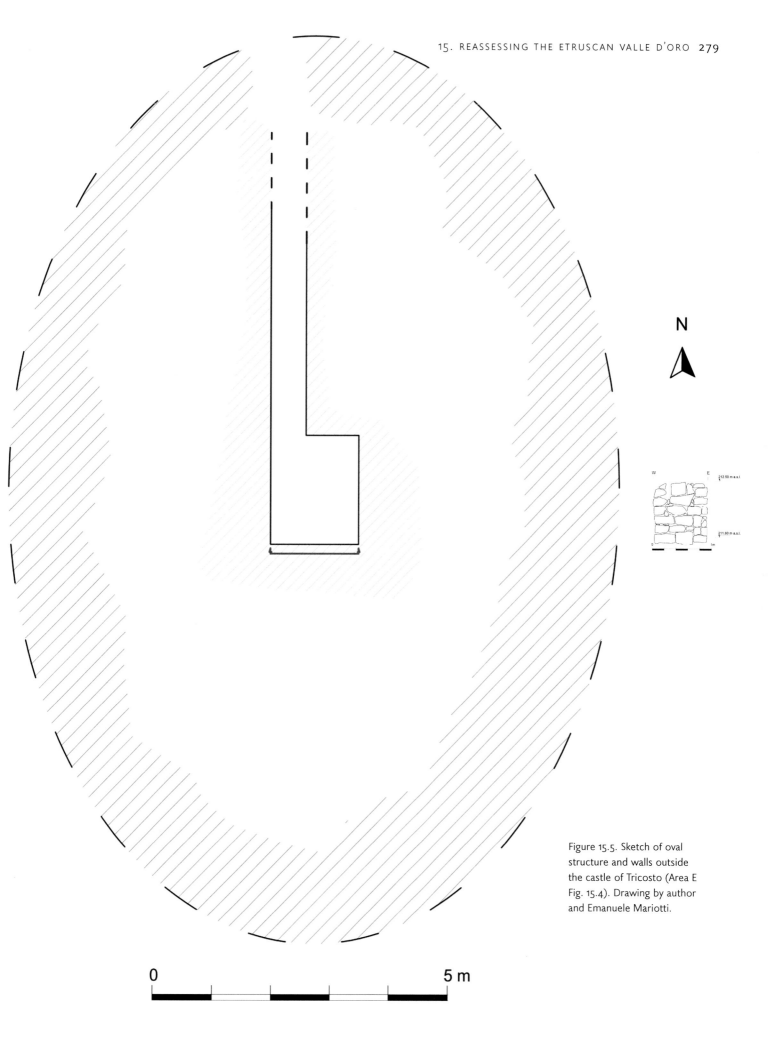

Figure 15.5. Sketch of oval structure and walls outside the castle of Tricosto (Area E Fig. 15.4). Drawing by author and Emanuele Mariotti.

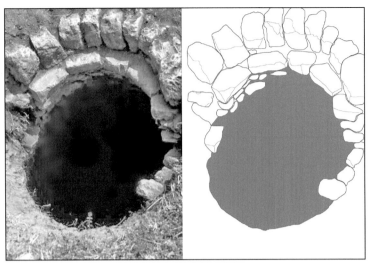

Figure 15.6. Well within the city walls and reused since the pre-Roman period. Photo by Dyson's Team, reproduced with permission. Drawing by Rossella Pansini, reproduced with permission.

during the excavations, and thus remains undated. The opening of the well is currently flush with the ground level. It is perfectly rounded in shape and built out of squared stones placed radially (Fig. 15.6).

As the well descends into the ground, it widens, but there are no longer traces of impermeable mortar. At this time, the well can only be dated based on its wall construction, which is complex. A similar, but smaller scale well has been found at Fonteblanda in the 'house of the blacksmith', which dates from the late sixth or early fifth century BCE.[19] This dating is comparable to the Etruscan pottery discovered during excavations at Capalbiaccio, and it is likely that the well was first active during the same time period. Another parallel comes from the Garfagnana excavation of the Etruscan roadway, near Lucca.[20]

Historiography

During the last forty years, scholars have focused on a wide variety of aspects of the history, archaeology, landscapes and settlement patterns, necropolises, and topographical research by foot and with machines in southern Etruria. Particular attention has been placed on the Albegna and the Valle d'Oro Valleys.[21] Further, Etruscan necropolises in general have been researched far more extensively than settlements linked to the everyday life.

A conspicuous presence of burials around the Capalbiaccio hill and across the valle d'Oro have been found but not their communities. Roman documents mention several unidentified sites, such as Cusa, Caletra, and Kalousion, whose locations have been proposed through time as an attempt to address the lacunae.[22] Searching for locations to match these names has become a sort of proxy for the missing urban community. Attempts to find them go back to the late nineteenth century, when local prince Tommaso Corsini started excavating on his own lands in the area around Marsiliana. He excavated the rich necropolises nearby, finding, among other things, the famous Fibula Corsini, a treasure of Etruscan jewellery, which is now housed in the Archeological Museum of Florence. However, Corsini found no traces of the fabled Caletra. In the early decades of the twentieth century, Antonio Minto followed in Corsini's footsteps and continued to excavate the area around Marsiliana, suggesting that the hills around the city's medieval castle were part of Caletra's fortification system.[23] In the early 1970s, Luisa Banti examined the possibility of this attribution, but concluded that the town of Marsiliana was not an urban centre, nor Caletra, but rather a possible Etruscan farm.[24] Yet, the many necropolises in the territory around Marsiliana — the hilltops of Poggio Petricci, Banditella, Perazzeta, and Macchiabuia — still offered enough evidence for Mauro Cristofani, Maurizio Michelucci, and Mario Torelli to believe that an urban centre, such as Caletra, should have been located in the Marsiliana area.[25] Their attention was mainly focused on the many hypogeal burials in the area, which date to the late seventh and sixth centuries BCE, leading them to speculate that the valley could have been the *ager Caletranus*. Similarly, tombs were found around the hill of Capalbiaccio, but they were neglected because no associated nuclei had been identified nearby, and now they are no longer visible (Fig. 15.3).[26]

In 1970s, Bronson and Uggeri, and before them Doro Levi, in the early twentieth century, were the first to suggest that the hilltop had been occupied

---

19 Ciampoltrini and Firmati 2002, 32; Ciampoltrini 2003, figs 9, 12.
20 Ciampoltrini 2006, 23–28. Closer to Tricosto, under the *domus* of Impluvium at Roselle, another well has been studied by Donati 2012.
21 Dyson 1978b; Attolini and others 1982; Attolini and others 1983; Celuzza and Regoli 1985; Carandini 1985b; Cambi 1986; Attolini and others 1991; Cambi and Fentress 1988; Carandini and others 2002; Celuzza and Luzzetti 2013; Celuzza 2017; and for the pottery, see Perkins 1998.
22 Michelucci 1984; Di Gennaro 1986.
23 Minto and Corsini 1921; Zifferero and others 2016.
24 Banti, 1973, 112–13.
25 Zifferero 2009; Zifferero 2016; Zifferero and others 2016; Cristofani 1977; Michelucci 1981; Torelli 1984, 116.
26 Carandini and others 2002.

in pre-medieval times.[27] After them, Philip Perkins added that the hilltop of Capalbiaccio, together with Poggio Pietricci, Poggione, Poggio Cavolo, and other similar sites, were part of a strategic military strip that guarded the Albegna Valley between the sixth and third centuries BCE.[28] Perkins and others suspect that these settlements signalled the boundary between the large city of Vulci and the site of Doganella. On the other hand, Acconcia, and many others, prefers the more traditional interpretation of this area, which holds that such fortified sites in southern Etruria were evidence of a strategic expansion on the part of Vulci, alone.[29] This strategy of territorial control was used by Vulci, and later Rome, in the interior and along the coast, eventually leading to the establishment of Roman colonies, such as Cosa, Heba and Luni.[30] Recently, one of the points in this defensive system was excavated: although dated later, Rofalco, a small ex-novo fortified outpost (fourth to third century BCE) near Ischia di Castro, was abandoned after the 280 BCE defeat of Vulci by the Romans.[31] Tucked in a hilltop and naturally well defended, Rofalco embodies the type of defensive site described by Acconcia and others.

Other defensive sites were often re-occupied in order to control agricultural activities and establish military dominion over southern Etruria. According to the most recent accepted classification of settlement typologies of villages in rural Etruria, these fortified outposts are called *oppida*, ranging in size between 3–5 ha. and occupying naturally defensible heights.[32] The walled settlement at Giaccioforte occupied two hilltops and *c.* 3.7 hectares and fits into this category.[33] The idea that these new, smaller sites were autonomous from a larger centre and a localized power has been suggested by the northern American scholars. These forts, or as *castella*, 'may have represented an antithetical power structure' to regional centres like Vulci.[34] This notion, further, reinforces an earlier proposal for Etruscan settlement patterns on a smaller scale, where *castella* that may have 'functioned autonomously, at least in part, and that [they] had [their] own sphere of influence over the farms and villages in [their] immediate vicinity'.[35] While Capalbiaccio could well have served in this system for the strategic defence of the countryside, the community was undoubtedly larger.

When the pioneering edited volumes on the 'Romanizzazione of Etruria' came out in 1985, the one explicitly about the city of Vulci published a map of the 'colonized' *regio VII* showing only Vulci in the geographic outline of Etruria. Of course, the map reflected the topic of the book, but it also created the visual premises that all the rest of the future findings in the region were secondary to it. Vulci was the topic, as an important central Etruscan city north of Rome that was in control of the territory along the coast going north, but the volume left a legacy which has informed a generation of scholars. It seems also key to underline that, at the time, little in southern Etruria had been excavated, while field surveys were just starting to explore the Maremma landscape. The success of this national initiative to validate a pre-Roman culture was in response to another important project: the unprecedented excavation of a large-scale Roman slave-driven villa of Settefinestre, which came out the same year. The chronology from documents and confirmed by archaeology, tells the story of a series of conquered cities, systematically taken by Rome that set a safe space for them to to build their new centrally positioned colony of Cosa in 273. The dissolution of the Leagues of the Etruscan cities exposed a crisis which led to Rome's defeat of Vulci and soon after Roselle.[36] The expansions start early in the fourth century, with a military expedition against Veio by Rome, followed soon after by Roselle in 294, and by Vulci and Volsinii in 280 BCE. The first official colony north of Rome was placed just below the large promontory of the Argentario, which provided protection from weather and, more importantly, a series of docking sites tucked in calm bays, such as Porto Ercole, and the port Santo Stefano. Orbetello, an Etruscan community, even more protected, and built with polygonal walls as Cosa is seems to have been the most important place along the coast, according to the large financial effort in the construction of these centres. Recently the dating of these large fortifications has been attributed with large consensus, but I personally suggest that more research

---

27 Levi 1927, 477–85; Bronson and Uggeri, 1970, 201–14; and accepted by subsequent surveys; see Attolini and others 1982, 368, fig. 2; Celuzza and Luzzetti 2013.
28 Perkins 1999, 21. In the early 1980s, the survey of the *ager Cosanus* had already established such a defensive alignment, made up of Poggione and Monteti; see Attolini and others 1982, 369, fig. 3.
29 Acconcia 2005; *infra* Acconcia. Marco Rendeli, one of the strongest proponents of the dominant position of Vulci in the valley, has argued for the dependency of the many smaller fortified nuclei disseminated along the coast and in the hinterland; see Rendeli 1993; Rendeli 2002.
30 On pre-roman and roman fortifications in Etruria, see Michetti 2017; Cerasuolo and Pulcinelli 2013, 113; Maggiani 2008.
31 Frazzoni 2012; Cerasuolo and Pulcinelli 2010; Cerasuolo 2009.
32 Cambi 2012.
33 Firmati 2002; Del Chiaro 1976.
34 Vander Poppen 2008, 80.

35 Becker 2002, 92.
36 Carandini 1985b.

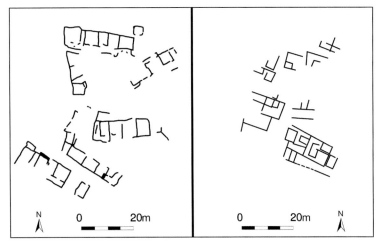

Figure 15.7. Comparison between the settlement plans of Lago dell'Accesa. Left: Plan reproduced from Camporeale 1997. Right: Plan by Laura Cerri.

be done, as the early stages of Cosa and Orbetello are still unknown.

If the Etruscan settlement at Capalbiaccio did spread beyond the plateau to occupy part of the hillside, then its size would elevate it to being a minor centre of roughly 6 to 12 ha. Minor centres were normally situated about 20 km from a major city (in this case, Vulci), were almost always fortified, had religious structures, flourished between the seventh and fifth centuries BCE, and were then abandoned or absorbed into the system of municipal Roman colonies.[37] Capalbiaccio seems to adhere to these criteria, and its still uncertain pre-Roman settlement history suggests that a village of sparse huts was replaced, after a period of abandonment, by rectangular stone structures and planned streets that may also have been fortified. The hypothesized plan derived from the magnetometry appears to represent a number of buildings knitted together in groups of different sizes but following a similar orientation. Minor centres similar to Capalbiaccio, which likewise have prehistoric and archaic phases, as well as alignments of orthogonal buildings in stone, dating from the late seventh and early sixth centuries BCE, have been identified at Sovana,[38] Acquarossa,[39] and San Giovenale.[40]

Regional Comparisons

Despite the recent increase in attention to the archaeology of Etruscan settlements in the Albegna Valley, few open-area excavations have yet occurred, and therefore the analysis of the Etruscan contexts at Capalbiaccio lacks strong comparisons.[41] That said, one site which demonstrates similarities with the structures extrapolated from the anomalies in the magnetometry at Tricosto, is the community found at Lago dell'Accesa: a non-planned village with stone foundations, clustered together, each room measuring approximately 5 m² (Fig. 15.7).[42]

Besides finding other parallels, it would be interesting to place a trench in a similar area and connect the two proposed in the comparison

The major exceptions to these smaller settlements are the two extensive farming communities of Doganella and Marsiliana. A survey of the site of Doganella by Philip Perkins and Lucy Walker has shown that a huge area (covering more than 280 ha) was made up of nucleated groups of farms, within a large circuit wall.[43] Similar groupings of these agro-towns, many of which have been identified, existed about every 10 km in the Albegna Valley. While Perkins and Walker identified several orthogonal buildings and streets within a fortified circuit around Doganella, the fragmented configuration of the settlement, and the evidence provided by a general overview of the plan, led them to be cautious in affirming such a conclusion.

Recently, another team from the University of Siena under the direction of Andrea Zifferero has examined Marsiliana and its surroundings, located 7–8 km directly due east of Doganella, with a combination of survey and excavation. To date, their research has uncovered many farming settlements with terraced fields and burials.[44] The formation of sparse and large communities, better defined as agro-towns, subsisted on agriculture as the core source of sustenance. When Paola Rendini, noticed the absence of urban centres in proximity to the tombs in the Albegna Valley, she indicated large estates in the region around Marsiliana and a fair number of settlements around Magliano.[45] In any case, while Doganella's subsequent rise seems to have mir-

---

37 Vander Poppen 2008; Perkins 1998.
38 Negroni Catacchio 2005.
39 Pallottino and Wikander 1986; Camporeale 1985, 170.
40 Pallottino and Wikander 1986.

41 On Marsiliana, see Zifferero 2009; Zifferero 2011a; on Ghiaccioforte, see Firmati 2001; and on Fonteblanda, Ciampoltrini 2003.
42 Camporeale 1997.
43 Perkins and Walker 1990; Perkins 2010.
44 Zifferero 2009; Zifferero 2011a; Zifferero 2016; Zifferero and others 2016.
45 Rendini 2011.

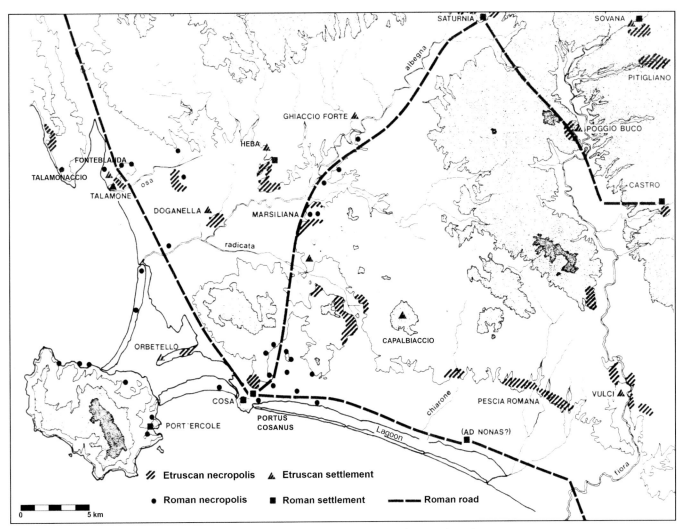

Figure 15.8. Etruscan and Roman Settlements in the Valle d'Oro. Although this map was drawn in the 1980s and is therefore no longer fully up-to-date, it gives a good indicaton of the burial sites of Etruscans and where the Roman burial and the location chosen to settle. Map reproduced from Carandini and Cambi 2002.

rored settlement pattern identified at Marsiliana, these farms coincided with the rebirth of new settlements in the greater Albegna Valley. Around the sixth century BCE, a series of more concentrated *oppida* and minor/medium centres, perhaps similarly to Capalbiaccio, arose on defensive hilltops around the region.[46]

As mentioned above, past historiography of the Etruscan Albegna Valley posited the region as under the control of Vulci, which is mostly accepted. Other options have also been explored especially after the unusual wide scale sites were identified. Perkins wonders if Doganella could have been autonomous from Vulci, due to the expansion of the agricultural compound. The lack of urban markers in the archaic period, which are normally present in cities like Veio, Tarquinia, and Vulci, rich in monumental architecture, elite material culture, and imports from distant locations confirm the suspicion.[47] The expansive agro-towns of the fertile Albegna Valley, in combination with wine production and amphorae kilns along the coast demonstrate an economic vitality that begs the question of dependency or local autonomy. The presence of polygonal walls seems a rather autonomous action rather than a colonial pursuit. Was this richness and the surplus produced the reason of conquest and colonization in the third century? Or was it, as recently suggested, simply a need to protect the land under possible attacks from Carthage (see Cardosa 2019)? Or did the defensive posture relate to aggressive demands by Rome or those of some other external force?

---

46 Perkins 1999; Carandini and others 2002; Cambi 2012.

47 Perkins 2014.

We know that the Valle d'Oro, the area around Capalbiaccio, did attract attention from Rome. Why was this area selected for the construction of the Cosa colony in 273? If Vulci was the centre point of reference that it is assumed to have been, why did not Rome place a colony over the city when it conquered it (eventually inheriting its agency)? Archaeology has shown that both the Albegna and d'Oro Valleys were already extracting, producing, and exporting goods — providing therefore a ready-made economy that was fundamental for the growth of the republican seat, while also lucrative for wider range trade (Fig. 15.8).

What is certain is that there were many types of settlements and different types of communities, and it seems that striving to understand if it was Roman or Etruscan is no longer important, if we were to envision a distant exurb of Rome where families consistently move to and from with economic interests shared on both sides. It has been recently argued that the massive system of polygonal walls was erected and restored along the Etruscan coast during the rising tensions between Carthage and Rome.[48] What I am trying to suggest here is that while trade between Rome and Etruria was long standing, it took many forms, and was not subject to constant rules found in bilateral trading regimes.

After the disintegration of the Etruscan league, its members likely reacted differently towards Rome. Those who rejected Rome had one response resulting in conflict and others, if more agreeable to persuasion, avoided disruptive intervention from Rome, going on to become colonies. Features of the Roman republic territorial administration included civic recognition, competition, voting rights and favouritism, all motivated to consolidate the notion of *Romanitas* at the expense of resistant communities. This strategy was consolidated in newly annexed communities after the social war (90–89 BCE).[49] The confirmation for said strategy will be found case by case, but the record so far for 'Romanization' suggests as stated above that some communities resisted while others like Cosa and Paestum joined Rome and became prosperous colonies.

Identities of the Pre-Roman Settlements in Etruria

It is tempting to imagine that the concentrated settlement at Capalbiaccio served as a rural administrative centre for its community, which was supplied by nearby farms that produced grains, amphorae, fish paste, and oil, among other goods. The housing concentration underlying the medieval village at Capalbiaccio, a road cut into the ground, and the presence of some sort of ceremonial burial place, present a site that is notably larger than the small, unplanned, nucleated settlements of Lago dell'Accesa and Macchiabuia. At the same time, the community at Capalbiaccio had a different character and role in the region than that of the extensive farming settlements around Doganella and Marsiliana.[50] And, while Etruscan Capalbiaccio seems too small to be considered a city since as a hilltop it has not the room to extend like an agro-town, its lack of defensive walls suggest it cannot be a fortification. The geographic location is telling and perfectly centred amid all that represents the Mediterranean culture. The water supply is also an extraordinary asset as compared to, say, the waterless Cosa. One could therefore hypothesize the need for an aggregation centre to maintain the irrigation and hydraulic networks imbedded in the rolling hills of the larger Albegna Valley and the Valle d'Oro. Thus, the identification of an Etruscan settlement, in a location as significant as that of Capalbiaccio, somewhat changes the regional picture. By virtue of not fitting the mould of an agro-town, fortification, or a sanctuary, Capalbiacco presents yet another typology.[51]

Ongoing archaeological excavations in southern Tuscany continue to provoke ideas about Etruria's relationship to Rome. The history of settlements in this region date from the late Bronze Age and continued, with brief interruptions, until the fall of the Roman empire between the fifth and sixth century CE. At this point a long period of about five centuries occurred when the area was mostly abandoned until the early medieval villages appear again between the ninth and the tenth century. The proximity to Rome has led to profound connections, which are hard to prove because of the myth of the foundation of Rome. The last three of Rome's seven legendary kings were reputed to be Etruscans from Tarquinia, indicating how two different cultures came together in leading the Roman monarchy. More traditional

---

48 Cardosa 2019.
49 Roselaar 2011, 527–55.

50 Firmati 2001; Firmati, Rendini, and Zifferero 2011.
51 Torelli 2002, regarding settlements patterns said that 'there are as many settlement models as there are different Etruscan sites', which seems to be confirmed through time.

accounts describe Rome as a forceful and violent conqueror against a reluctant Etruria, but as research progresses the encounter between the two spheres reveal a more complex relationship, that of possible collaborations that entrusted individuals with governing their burgeoning city. That notwithstanding, the impact of Roman expansion on Etruscan culture needs to be reassessed and understood within the context of the variability of settlements, the agency for construction and maintenance of infrastructure, and, in some cases, their destruction.

As discussed above, colonial narratives for Roman control of the area are no longer adequate to explain what the archaeology tells us. Rather than binary domination of Rome over Etruria we see through the finds evidence for possible symbiosis, collaboration, and exchange of cultures and goods. There is no denying that suppression, destruction, and reconstruction and abandonment did also occur as with Doganella, Ghiaccioforte and the slow decline of Vulci.

What is clear is the many differing outcomes among the multitude of landscapes in Southern Maremma. A place that was once sought-after became a rural backwater when the long arm of Rome reached wider horizons in North Africa.

Capalbiaccio defies easy categorization. And while it was affected by a marginal Roman presence it is not clear what happened to its past central position and how the use of the hill changed. Most of our investigation was limited to the tallest of the three hills that surround the fortified village, but it would not be surprising to find further communities or necropolis. The long wall that protects the community is on its own a large, monumental, and efficient defence. It could have been also a central place, as important as the ports along the coast, which need to be also better understood, and certainly trading with the Mediterranean since prehistoric times.

The attention to Vulci as the most important city in Southern Etruria for its size, elaborate artefacts, monumental structures, and necropolis is taken for granted. Rome may have shaped this sweeping vision to its advantage. By unifying a wide variety of settlements and resources under the broad heading of Vulci, it was easier to control them militarily bureaucratically, and geographically. Most of the historiography, including the work of some of the authors in this volume, agrees that the Etruscan city of Vulci was the central place for the Albegna valley and the Valle d'Oro within the geographic territorial subdivision of the *regio VII, Etruria*.

Nevertheless, this view of Etruria being subsumed into Vulci is too reductive and convenient. It is precisely the kind of propaganda Rome wanted. Instead, the picture is much more decentralized with a variety of settlements and towns with relative degrees of autonomy, each with its own history of continuity and discontinuity before and after the Roman Empire.

It is at this point that a post-colonial approach might provide a new language for the mixed and complex social relationships, both in the form of elite connections, mercantile exchange, and human labour, rather than examining a fabricated relationship between Romans and natives or colonizers and colonized.[52]

When Roman Cosa was built in the early third century BCE to control the export of wine and grains, and started to extract salt and make fish paste, the settlers likely intended to control an economic system that was already entrenched. There was already in place a tradition of amphorae production and export since the sixth century BCE, if not earlier, as can be seen at Albinia, in Fonteblanda, the port of Telamon, and the agro-towns of Doganella.[53] The Albegna Valley and the Valle d'Oro were highly productive regions, which prompted their physical occupation by Rome, as well as its appropriation of the lucrative businesses based therein.

It is tempting to propose that the lost Etruscan city of Caletra, which gave name to its own *ager*, originally attracted the attention of Romans interested in expanding their empire. The question that remains is, which Etruscan city commanded the area of the *ager Caletranus*?

If Capalbiaccio was indeed the city that gave its name to the territory, but ceased to exist after Cosa was built, then the Roman's choice of another location nearby could have been seen as a replacement of that presence, which commanded a key position over the agricultural resources.

The dating of the polygonal walls, in the past considered to be Etruscan, has been revised in the past few years to Roman. I disagree. The Romans may have rebuilt polygonal walls, but it is not their style to build them ex-novo. Apart from Roselle, the walls of Etruscan cities are not older than the fourth century. As far as Orbetello is concerned, it was recently suggested that the walls are Roman and contemporary to those of Cosa. In Cosa, it is generally believed that there is no previous Etruscan settlement but only the Roman colony and the various later occupations of the site.[54] What seems to

---

52 Terrenato 2005.
53 Ciampoltrini and Rendini 1992; Ciampoltrini and Rendini 2007.
54 For recent work on the dating of local polygonal walls see Cardosa 2019.

Figure 15.9. Photograph showing how Cosa's *decumanus maximus* was connected to the valle d'Oro through still visible alignments part of the centuriation land redistribution. In some case these subdivisions were also roads, such as that to the Settefinestre Villa. Photograph adapted from Castagnoli 1956 by Rossella Pansini.

occur is that there was an earlier community that pre-dated the Roman intervention, and if we believe the sources, it could be Cusa. If the polygonal walls of both Orbetello and Cosa, were indeed older, as I believe, once Rome controlled most of the Maremma, what need would it have for building new hilltop fortifications? In other words, *Ager Caletranus* was replaced by the *Ager Cosanus* and absorbed by Rome into a territory encompassing all the arable lands (*agers*) between the coastal larger cities of Vulci, Roselle and Populonia. The argument that these huge walls were built to protect the Roman coast from Punic attacks has been recently revised and widely accepted by scholars who have seen the mark of Roman building techniques therein. I wonder if what we are seeing is rather a Roman restoration of an earlier system of fortifications.

Why would the Romans build polygonal walls while becoming the new controlling power? The Romans would not have built huge walls like this because they controlled all the agers. Why do so many of the Tyrrhenian cities have polygonal walls that are dated generally to the sixth or fifth century? And how are they now redated to the Roman con-

quest of the region? Could the traces that have been offered as a possible Roman intervention be instead a restoration when Carthage was threatening to get closer to Rome? Were the walls of the coastal settlements instead protecting the raw materials that Capalbiaccio and the other centres were administrating, controlling or re-distributing?

Excavated areas, like Doganella, Marsiliana and other sites in the regions (skilfully summarized above by Valeria Acconcia), elucidate the organization of the production and distribution system was already in place in pre-Roman times. Further, wider networks existed and are confirmed by a handful of findings from this area in other parts of the Mediterranean.[55] More attention is given to the Etruscan ports and it is convincingly argued that Orbetello could have been one of the ports for Marsiliana and Doganella. I will add Orbetello as the port for farms at Cusa and Capalbiaccio, too.[56]

It stands to reason that life did not entirely stop at the hilltop of Capalbiaccio when the colony of

---

55 Perkins 1998.
56 Zifferero, De Angelis, and Pacifici 2019; Cardosa 2019.

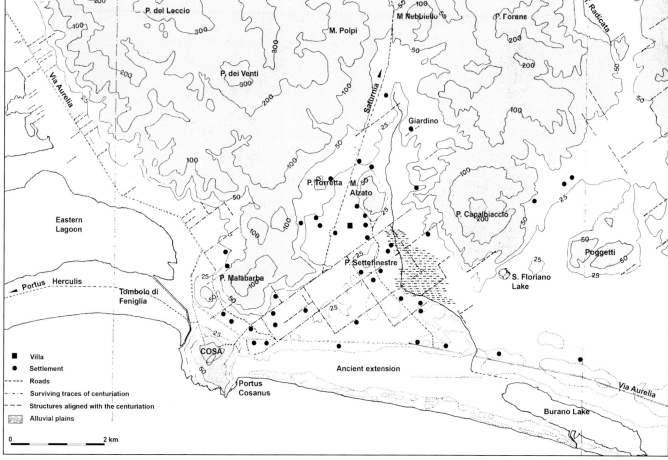

Figure 15.10. Centuriation of the Valley d'Oro at the foot of the Capalbiaccio hill. Map adapted from Carandini and others 1982.

Cosa was founded, which is attested to by minimal findings of Roman pottery and bricks on the surface. Undoubtedly, the plateau was slowly abandoned, but the path of the *decumanus maximus*, which reached from Cosa to the foot of Capalbiaccio, suggests that the Capalbiaccio continued to be a place of some importance to the Romans (Figs 15.9 and 15.10).[57] We know for example that in the first century several slave-run villas were built around the base of the Capalbiaccio hill. The few fragments of Roman pottery suggest that some form of continuity between the Romans and the local farmers took place, as the new settlers might have used the manpower and the local experience of those working the land. These resources seem to be the reason and too valuable to allow destruction of the infrastructure in place.

Our understanding of the nature of the Etruscan settlement at Capalbiaccio grows. Clearly not a large urban centre, neither does it fit the model of the agro-towns found on the opposite side of the Albegna valley, like Doganella and Marsiliana, and finally there are no signs of a defensive fort. With further excavation it will be possible to understand why this site — surrounded by springs over vast fertile planes and close to the sea — did not attract the Roman settlers, who decided instead to build its first colony on a waterless abandoned Etruscan town, called Cusa.

---

57 From the aerial view in Fig. 15.9, Castagnoli identified the centuriation boundaries between the two sites of Cosa and Settefinestre which if extended would naturally reach the base of the hilltop of Capalbiacccio.

MICHELLE HOBART

16. Builders of Landscapes

The Aldobrandeschi and the Castle of Tricosto

ABSTRACT This chapter combines the archaeology with a thorough historical reconstruction of the Capalbiaccio hilltop in the medieval period in order to describe the site's second life as a fortified village with two churches and towers. Occupying a liminal position in the long-running political struggle between the Aldobrandeschi family, the communal cites of Siena and Orvieto, and later the papal state to the immediate south, Capalbiaccio is again shown to have played a crucial role in regional power dynamics. The events outlined herein largely transpired over the tenth to fourteenth centuries, before the hilltop castle was effectively destroyed by Siena. Here, historiography receives a healthy amount of contextual assistance from the far-reaching amount of archaeological research conducted in Maremma to date, but which is almost exclusively published in Italian with limited syntheses. As such, this chapter serves as an introduction to the region for an English-language audience interested in the Tuscan Middle Ages more broadly.

The history of Tricosto cannot be completed without discussing the role of the Aldobrandeschi family in the region. In medieval Florence, at the time of Dante's *Divine Comedy*, the Aldobrandeschi were immortalized as the quintessential feudal family against whom communal cities fought with members of both Ghibelline and Guelph factions. Founded upon an anti-aristocratic form of government, communal cities, such as Siena, defined their new identity in contradistinction to the traditional order represented by families such as the Aldobrandeschi. Dante places members of the Aldobrandeschi family in both the *Purgatorio* and in the *Inferno* (the *fiero Tosco*) to illustrate the sin of 'Pride' among families with *l'antico sangue* (old blood). A Castle like Tricosto is one of more than one hundred settlements built by this family who immortalized the Maremma landscape. Their land, the infrastructure, and their resources were confiscated by Siena piece by piece starting in the thirteenth century. Some castles developed into larger towns, others were abandoned and some destroyed, especially when they represented a threat to the new Tuscan Republic.

The Maremma region and the growing town of Grosseto were part of the Aldobrandeschi influence and possessions that included the hilltop castle of Tricosto at Capalbiaccio. Tricosto lies at a good distance from the seats of any of the powerful Tuscan cities, towns, or monasteries, and far enough from Rome (circa 140 km) to just exceed the Eternal City's grasp. The analysis of centuries of fortifications and material culture at Tricosto reveals the specific strategic intention of the Aldobrandeschi, who controlled most of the large network of castles all over Tuscany.[1] The Aldobrandeschi were dealing politically, securing alliances, exerting their power, and asserting themselves on an increasingly wide geographical scale. Their positioning had a clear plan that covered every aspect of the region from the point of view of both economic and political advantage. At the height of their power in the twelfth century, the Aldobrandeschi inserted themselves into political and territorial relationships with the other newly formed communes of Orvieto, Viterbo Perugia, and Siena, as well as towns and budding cities all over the Maremma region. They were also able to create strong ties with other powerful families and later also the Church, further extending their domain. Their political ability derived from a great wealth of experience from exercising power in every activity that contributed to developing their feudal sphere. The family's diplomatic skills are further evident in the way they negotiated with both imperial figures and ecclesiastic rulers, whom they treated as peers.

Settled along the southern and eastern boundaries of modern Tuscany, the Aldobrandeschi extracted goods that included raw materials, salt, and grain, and redistributed them by land and through coastal har-

---

[1] The most significant publications on the Aldobrandeschi family are Collavini 1998, Ciacci 1935, and Rossetti 1981.

bours.[2] Their economic interest was initially geared towards mineral extraction, but then focussed mostly on agriculture as they moved south towards Rome occupying the land around Capalbiaccio. Their journey is a long one that increased their power consistently, beginning in Lucca during the ninth century and continuing to expand until the middle of the thirteenth century, mostly in the Maremma, building castles that were tactically planned to control the land resources and farming activities in the region. Eventually, after many generations of strong leadership, the Aldobrandeschi were weakened by issues of inheritance and property subdivision. This diffusion of power among strong but divided heirs eventually eroded the family's structure into more branches. The long resilience of the Aldobrandeschi, whose leaders held and maintained strategic powers and locations for more than four centuries, was exceptional as compared to other rural or urban elites like the Ardengheschi, the Peruzzi, and, later, the Medici whose lineage was briefer. Documents from the ninth century do not always help in identifying the agents behind the first forms of stone building emerging in Tuscany, although it is known that the Aldobrandeschi family members were involved in some of the earliest phases of the first *incastellamento* process closer to Pisa and Lucca. That said, their most significant contribution was shaping the medieval landscape when they expanded into southern Maremma during the twelfth and thirteenth century.

There are great differences between the northern part of Tuscany and its southernmost Maremma region, especially in the way they have been settled. The Maremma is usually considered a backwater of marshes lacking in cities, although small to mid-range castles and villages start appearing around the tenth and then the twelfth century. Only in rare cases did these grow into larger communities, such as Grosseto, Massa Marittima, Piombino, and Campiglia Marittima. The failure of many of these communities to survive, these so-called 'weak cities' which were soon abandoned, represents a testament to the challenges of settling in the Maremma's marshy and malaria-prone coastline.

The cause of the shift of settlements to hilltops from lowlands is widely debated.[3] It is generally accepted for the early medieval period that the wide-ranging imperial estates controlled by senatorial Roman villas evolved naturally into smaller villages, which at first were scattered along the plains.[4] The actors of this process, a 'new, long golden age of peasants', were no longer bound to the imperial taxation, and increasingly developed more complex autonomous communities. The migration toward hilltops continued to evolve with early forms of villages and fortifications between the tenth and eleventh century, with ditches and wood fences, as found also on the Eastern height in Ansedonia, the closest medieval settlement to Capalbiaccio.[5] The communities at both Capalbiaccio and Ansedonia started to expand in the twelfth century, in what is known as the *incastellamento* process. But it was only later, when the *signoria fondiara* started investing resources, that a stone village took shape. A handful of local aristocratic families, some descended from the Lombards, were not opposed by the new regime but, rather, were anointed by the Carolingians, confirming officially their land and increasing their power as landholders. The early elite families were small in number and many of these interrelated. The Aldobrandeschi, the Ardengheschi, and the Berardeschi, to mention the earlier ones documented, were transforming the landscape and building towers and castles, the first forms of *incastellamento*.

The tenth-century hilltop reoccupation at Tricosto began with a village made out of perishable materials (huts) and perhaps some stone structures and a defensive wall.[6] The presence of a skilled architectural workshop on site suggests that new resources were invested. The castle of Tricosto belongs to and was built by the Aldobrandeschi, the only family recorded in both ecclesiastical and family records since the twelfth century.

The Aldobrandeschi family gained power under Carolingian patronage at the start of the ninth century, and quickly expanded their holdings, from Lucca to the Tyrrhenian coast, building castles on the metal-rich hills (*colline metallifere*) between Siena, Volterra, and Grosseto. It is commonly argued that the family favoured non-urban locations, but that might simply be tied to the lack of documentation of their urban palaces at this early date. The Aldobrandeschi family also had palaces in every significant Tuscan rising city, but they pursued a fierce strategy of establishing a ubiquitous presence in the countryside.

---

2 For the history of the coastal settlements and ports see Ceccarelli Lemut 2004; Ceccarelli Lemut 2014.
3 Francovich and Hodges 2003; Valenti 2004.
4 In general, see Costambeys 2009. In particular, see Celuzza and Regoli 1982; Celuzza 2002 [1993]; Carandini and others 2002.
5 Fentress 2003. For a general summary of the situation in Tuscany, see Bianchi 2012; Valenti 2004, and for a case study, see the hypothetical reconstructions of Miranduolo in Valenti 2008. This last settlement has recently shown that the migration to hilltops started since the eighth–ninth century, even earlier than most of the other cases.
6 Hobart and others 2009.

16. BUILDERS OF LANDSCAPES   291

Figure 16.1. View of *Ager Cosanus* facing the Argentario Mountain. Photo by Hermann Salvadori.

Figure 16.2. Post hole inside Building J Pit 1 and cross section of Dyson's levels. Photo by Dyson's team, reproduced with permission.

Figure 16.3. Tower 1: Exterior. Photo by Hermann Salvadori.

Figure 16.4. Tower 1: Interior. Photo by Hermann Salvadori.

Figure 16.5. Church 1: Overview. Photo by Dyson's team, reproduced with permission.

Figure 16.6. Church 1: East End Apse. Photo by Dyson's team, reproduced with permission.

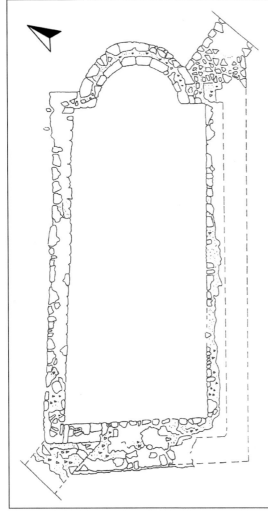

Figure 16.7. Church 1: Plan. Note the intersection of the church predating the division that cut the castle in half. Plan by Dyson's team, reproduced with permission.

It became clear to them that to grow and control territory, one needed to spread out to distant geographic areas. The family's early territorial investments were focused on extracting metals such as silver and iron from the mining hills around Volterra. Once revenues from mining metals were not producing enough to justify costs, and with the population increasingly moving to towns and cities, which offered more amenable living conditions and social mobility, the Aldobrandeschi expanded into the south and the interior of Tuscany, where salt, grain, and other metals were available. This move south was also precipitated by competition with other local families, such as the Guidi, the Pannocchieschi, or the della Gherardesca.[7] The hilltop of Capalbiaccio seems to represent one of the many places where their plan for long-term territorial control could prosper (Fig. 16.1). It counted among the family's last coastal fortified villages, at the end of their legacy.

Before weaving together the surviving records it is necessary to provide a detailed description to help visualize the context.

Description of the Castle of Tricosto

Occupation of the Capalbiaccio hilltop restarted after a long period of abandonment from the third century BCE to the tenth century CE. The archaeological evidence of an early medieval village are slim, and emerge from one particular area that was excavated to the bedrock revealing a thick, sealed layer, approximately 1 m deep, with no traces of life.

The original tenth-century village populated the hilltop with huts, as well as what seems to have been a circuitous form of defence. Dyson's 1978 excavation identified post-holes and an abundance of tenth-century pottery in the earliest medieval, red-earth layers (Fig. 16.2). Thereafter, it took almost two hundred years to shift from huts to stone buildings, according to the reading of the construction techniques for the second medieval phase of the hilltop's re-habitation. Evidence drawn from other early medieval excavations in Tuscany show that villages of the same time period were made out perishable materials, such as mud and brambles. It has also shown that the average size of their extension fluctuates between one half to two hectares large (1 hectare = 2,471 acres; and 1 acre = 43,560 square feet).[8]

The continued development and growth of the early medieval village between the tenth and eleventh centuries is particularly evident in the pottery. At the current stage of research, what is harder to speculate about is the size of the village, because only diagnostic fragments were analysed (it being impossible to quantify the material). However, it is safe to say that the early inhabitants of Tricosto were most likely producing their material locally. Nonetheless, they began long-range exchange with places as far away as Pisa and Rome, setting the stage for future expansion. This economic revival has been tied to Ottonian policy that promoted a new wave of building techniques and trading activity, from which Capalbiaccio benefited.[9]

During the twelfth century, a radical change in early medieval settlement patterns took place all over southern Tuscany, when diversified stone buildings reveal a more complex society with the basis for

---

7 For the Guidi family history see Guidi 1941; for the Pannochieschi see Ceccarelli Lemut 1991; for the Gherardesca see Ceccarelli Lemut 1995.

8 For a recent overview on early medieval housing in central Italy, see Valenti 2004; Bianchi 2012.

9 Bianchi 2012; Ceccarelli Lemut, 1985; Ceccarelli Lemut 1999.

hegemonic, stratified communities, both in urban and in rural contexts. A large number of initiatives spread all over the region and the evolution of the second *incastellamento* started to shape a new landscape. Between the eleventh and twelfth century, on the highest part of the Capalbiaccio hilltop, the small village started building a tall stone tower (Fig. 16.3) with a beautifully built masonry technique that still is visible partially inside the tower (Fig. 16.4) and a basic single-apse church of which hardly any decorative aspects survives (Figs 16.5, 16.6, and 16.7). The pottery evidence associated with this period shows local trade, as well as imports, from Pisa. Precisely faced squared stones and well-constructed building required the presence of skilled stonemasons, which indicates that substantial resources were intended for the village. However, it is premature to say if the site was already fortified, and if a long, stone wall, made out of irregularly squared blocks discovered just below the smaller gate of Capalbiaccio, was part of this or an earlier pre-medieval phase, as found in other sites, such as the castle of Scarlino, further north along the coast.[10]

The reconstruction of the castle (Fig. 16.8a) is the result of the elaboration by Paul Henderson who created a three-dimension digital elevation modelling, DEM (Fig. 16.8b) of the compounded plans added to Dyson's original mapping of the site (Fig. 16.8c). The diachronic 3D reconstruction also shows the pre-medieval elevation alignments of the anomalies (in red) found during the magnetometer survey (see this volume, Chapter 4). The dark green represents the first stone buildings after the long phase of abandonment, which was surrounded by a village built from perishable materials. The height of the castle expansion is documented with housing and a second church (with lighter green). The circuit walls and two gates also have two phases, showing when the castle was divided for defensive purposes in the fourteenth century.

The hilltop of Capalbiaccio experienced its most significant growth in the thirteenth century, notably erecting a massive perimeter wall (463 m, covering an area of 13,360 m²) that enclosed the flat area of the hilltop. The oval shape of the Capalbiaccio plateau dictated the plan of the settlement, where two or more parallel roads served housing blocks on the southern side, while the residential bailey fortified by towers occupied the northern part. The original urban conception of how space was organized inside the city walls of Tricosto was straightforward, functional, and typical of the Aldobrandeschi castles.

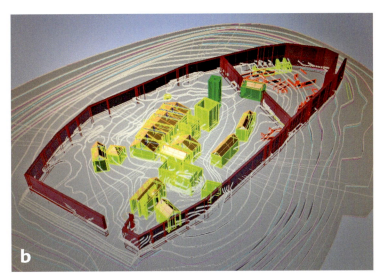

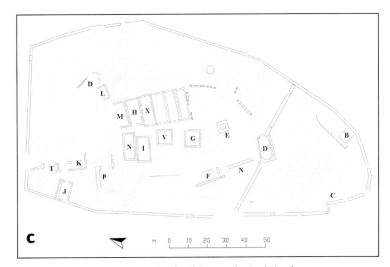

Figure 16.8. a: Reconstruction: Castle of Tricosto by Paul Henderson, reproduced with permission. b: DEM Reconstruction: Castle of Tricosto by Paul Henderson, reproduced with permission. c: Castle of Tricosto compounded plan by Emanuele Mariotti.

---

10   Francovich 2002–2003. Francovich 1995; Marasco 2002–2003.

Figure 16.9. Exterior face of Church B. Photos by Hermann Salvadori.

Figure 16.10. Long side of Church B.

Figure 16.11. Residential palace.

Figure 16.12. Residential palace: slit window.

Figure 16.13. Residential palace: corner.

The newly fortified thirteenth-century village erected a second church, perhaps dedicated to S. Angelo, as indicated in the records.[11] The church was placed in a central area where the housing alignments and two parallel roads came together. The ecclesiastical building which partially survives, has lost its face stones, that once covered the exterior walls, revealing the filling of how it was built, called *muro a sacco*. The plan is similar to the earlier church, with one long nave and an apse facing east, however the masonry technique is not as refined as the previous building (Fig. 16.9 Ext wall). That said, the ruins of the church still attracted looters who left fragmented

---

11 Farinelli 2007.

unusable stones, as can be seen on the long eastern side of the wall (Fig. 16.10).

The most monumental building is the residential palace (Fig. 16.11) with a defensive role suggested by the slit window (Fig. 16.12). The palace corner demonstrates the skill at work, joined by the essential decorative element of an alignment of a few rows of bricks on the northern face, perhaps an Aldobrandeschi feature? (Fig. 16.13). The residential palace could have been much taller with one or more towers. It is impossible to identify the position or the height from the massive collapse that covers the surroundings (Fig. 16.14a, b, c). One tower was butting against the southern circuit wall of the castle and was supported by a scarp (Fig. 16.15). The scarp framed the southern side of a tower, built against the fortification wall to the right of Building J, as can be seen in the reconstruction.

The community lived in alignments of two-storey houses as suggested in the reconstruction of the castle (Fig. 16.16). The pitched roofs and floors of these houses were held by beams, the holes for which are still visible inside the standing walls (Figs 16.17–16.18). Two areas were excavated to the bedrock (Figs 16.19–16.20). These houses were placed along the main road (south–north) leading to the monumental palace and towers facing the northern main gate (Fig. 16.21). At the exterior of that main gate, along the northern edge of the wall, a scarp strengthened the fortification and provided a narrow walkway that could have been used for maintenance (Fig. 16.22). The northern gate connected a wide, curving road to the valley below the hill facing the promontory of Ansedonia/Cosa (Fig. 16.23), and a much smaller southern gate provided a secondary entrance to the lower terrace that served the rest of the community (Fig. 16.24).

What became clear from reading the building archaeology in Tricosto is that the bulk of the thirteenth-century project was built as a whole, with a clear design for the occupation of the areas within the wall circuit. The similarity of the masonry techniques, which were repeated with minimal variations over the entire site, as well as one single master urban plan for a period that lasted about one hundred years, confirms this idea. The buildings from (phase II *infra* Corti) the major development of the village show that different campaigns occurred in a relatively short period of time that were built by specialized workshops, which produced different details, but kept the same standards and modular system. An anomaly is the long wall which runs below the main road which seems to have been restored through time and presents different type of masonry. The slanted *spina di pesce* stones are usually associated

Figure 16.14. a, b, c. Tower: collapsed. Photos by Hermann Salvadori.

296 MICHELLE HOBART

Figure 16.15. Scarp supporting the tower butting against the western circuit wall, to the right of Building J. Photo by Dyson's team, reproduced with permission.

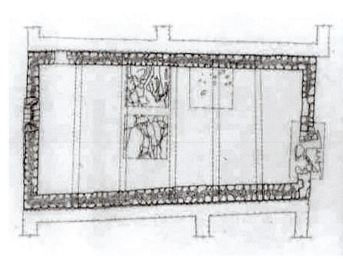

Figure 16.16. Plan of Building H. Drawing by Dyson's team, reproduced with permission.

Figure 16.17. House. Photo by Hermann Salvadori.

Figure 16.18. House wall: interior. Photo by Hermann Salvadori.

Figure 16.19. Building H: Pit 3. Photo by Dyson's team, reproduced with permission.

Figure 16.20. Building H: Pit 5. Photo by Dyson's team, reproduced with permission.

16. BUILDERS OF LANDSCAPES 297

Figure 16.21. Main Gate: northern side.
Photo by Hermann Salvadori.

Figure 16.22. Scarp of northern circuit wall: exterior.
Photo by Hermann Salvadori.

Figure 16.23. View of the promontory of Cosa.
Photo by Hermann Salvadori.

Figure 16.24. Smaller southern service gate.
Photo by Dyson's team, reproduced with permission.

Figure 16.25. a. Long wall (no. 17 on Dyson map on p. 318 of ths volume). b. Long wall showing horizontal length. Photos by Hermann Salvadori.

with early medieval masonry, but at this stage it is premature to suggest that it belonged to the tenth–eleventh century (Map Fig. 16.8c, F; Fig. 16.25a, b).

The high fortification walls and the impressive masonry reflect the political tensions caused by the expansion of the communal cities of Siena and Orvieto into Southern Tuscany (Fig. 16.26). In the fourteenth century, the community was reduced in size by building a new massive division wall (Fig. 16.27), that severed the city nearly in half. A series of diagonal post holes allowed access to the top of the defensive wall to enable security lookout. The scale of the wall and the thickness can be appreciated in a window with the practical design of being opened from the inside for visibility while presenting on the exterior a thin vertical slit (Fig. 16.28).

Almost a century later, a new residence abutting the north-western circuit wall was excavated to the bedrock (Fig. 16.29). Still standing today, Building J was two stories tall, with large beams that held the second floor, containing windows on each of the two long interior walls (Fig. 16.30). A particularly interesting feature is a sink with running water fed by a clay pipeline that was built inside the walls connecting the two floors (Fig. 16.31).[12] Water was evidently collected from the roof in a cistern and the spouts

---

12 On top of the building, a reservoir must have collected rainwater, which then flowed down to both floors and was flushed out below the sink into a drainage channel that is visible outside the northern wall of the palace. The water would then travel in between Buildings J and K into a larger cistern.

Figure 16.26. Fortification wall: East interior. Photo by author.

Figure 16.27. Division wall with post holes for stairs. Photo by Hermann Salvadori.

Figure 16.28. Division wall: Detail. Photo by Hermann Salvadori.

Figure 16.29. Building J. Photo by Hermann Salvadori.

Figure 16.30. Building J: From the interior looking east towards Structure K. Photo by Hermann Salvadori.

Figure 16.31. Building J: Interior – niche with sink against the northern wall. Photo by Hermann Salvadori.

Figure 16.32. Building J: Exterior – drainage system. Photo by Dyson's team, reproduced with permission.

Figure 16.33. Area K: Water collector – drainage system (cistern). Photo by Dyson's team, reproduced with permission.

Figure 16.34. Area K: Wall facing Building J with opening into the rounded drainage system (Fig. 16.33). Photo by Dyson's team, reproduced with permission.

were plugged with cork or similar material to stop it from running. Water from the sink travelled to the drainage channel (Fig. 16.32), carved outside along the northern exterior of the building, culminating in a larger cistern, of Area K (Fig. 16.33). Complex K faced Building J and presents standing walls built with a peculiar masonry technique of stones that do not appear elsewhere on the hilltop (Fig. 16.34). The wall covers the water system with a larger structure facing the second church. The Area K was excavated during two seasons and reached structures below which had a different axial orientation built with calcareous local stones (Fig. 16.35). There were two wells, possibly providing drinking water from the springs that surround the hill and which have likely been reused and restored through time. The remarkable architecture of Building J, and the nearby Area K, represents the last chapter in the life of Tricosto

Figure 16.35. Area K: Open trench revealing axial alignments below the walls. Photo by Dyson's team, reproduced with permission.

before it was destroyed in the early fifteenth century by the Sienese.

For the post-medieval era at Capalbiaccio, Hermann Salvadori compared Tricosto with seven other castles in the countryside by analysing archaeological data and historiographical models, with the goal of understanding how modern settlement patterns changed.[13] The absence of important urban centres in southern Tuscany, with the exception of Grosseto and Massa Marittima, makes this study of the countryside even more relevant. Salvadori outlined two buffer zones (a larger and a smaller one) and surveyed each castle and its surroundings, which allowed him to reconstruct the expanding evolution of these settlements and their continuation and/or abandonment. By combining pottery with geographical dictionaries and public records of land ownership, he then reconstructed the local history of each site and provided information about how properties were organized in the landscape, with the rivers, canals, roads, and boundaries of nineteenth-century Tuscany.[14] Salvadori's reconstruction of the territory led him to conclude that the agrarian settlements have their roots in the early fourteenth century and have not changed through time. This seems to be characteristic of other communal cities, such as Siena, and most of southern Tuscany making the region into one of the most coveted tourist attractions in the country as it has remained untouched through time.

Historical Context of the Aldobrandeschi and the Castle of Tricosto

In 844, when Charlemagne's grandson Louis II the Younger became the King of Italy, he officially gave a member of the Aldobrandeschi family authority over a large part of Tuscany. Southern Tuscany was an unusual type of peripheral region, both out of the reach of Rome and too distant from the rising communal cities of northern Tuscany to control, at first. During this period, the Aldobrandeschi also extended their control over the Amiata Mountain (also rich in minerals).

Between the tenth and the eleventh centuries, countryside migration took place towards larger villages or new cities. The Aldobrandeschi were often protagonists in the political and economic decisions starting with Lucca where they first appear as clergy members, but then also in other towns, such as, Massa Marittima, Grosseto, and Roselle, and in other smaller towns in southern Tuscany.[15] While Grosseto was laying the foundation for an early urban development by 973, the Aldobrandeschi continued to exert their power there until the early twelfth century by controlling the town's fisheries (*piscaree*) and salt extraction.[16] The Aldobrandeschi also had interests and properties in Roselle, however the nature of the site and the demographics of its community are under scrutiny.[17] It is generally accepted that the ancient diocese of Roselle was moved to Grosseto in 1138, adding prestige to the growing town and that the Aldobrandeschi played a role in this move.[18]

The Aldobrandeschi family's territorial interests spread further south, abutting and forcefully penetrating into the Church's properties in Latium, such as the *curtis* in Castro and Montalto, and the port of Corneto (near Tuscania). According to documents in Southern Tuscany there were three bishoprics, that of Roselle, Populonia, and Sovana. Although, there is much debate on how and when this happened, little if any material traces confirm the argument.[19] Traditionally, the Lombard kings are said to be responsible for building monasteries, churches, and baptisteries in most of the territories they occupied in central Italy.[20] In this particular coastal region there is no sign of Lombard presence. The most prominent, but in the interior, was the seventh-century monastery of San Salvatore on the Amiata Mountain, along the Cassian Way, just north of the boundaries of the *Patrimonium Beati Petri*. The monastery existed from

---

13 The Ager Cosanus and the Valle dell'Albegna survey project started in the 1977 tied to the Roman villa Settefinestre excavation (Caradini 1985a) and it was later expanded to a much wider territory experimenting with 'sampling' landscape archaeology deriving from the *New Archaeology* ideas developed in the England and the States that introduced a more scientific approach to the collection of data and called and later called 'processual archaeology'. See Cambi 1986 for the intellectual background of the project.
14 He used two well-known sources, the *Dizionario Emanuele Repetti*, which is now available online (Repetti 1833–1845), and the Catasto Leopoldino, which was ordered by the Grand Duke of Tuscany, Leopoldo, in 1823.
15 Collavini 1998; Ciacci 1935.
16 Redon 1999 [1994]. Citter and Arnoldus-Huyzendveld 2007; Citter 2007; Farinelli 2009, sito 5.3; Citter and Arnoldus-Huyzendveld 2011.
17 Celuzza and Luzzetti 2013.
18 Citter 2005a.
19 Rizzitelli 1999; Kurze and Citter 1995.
20 The conversion of elite Goths and Lombards to Christianity had the double purpose of, on the one hand, tying them to the legacy of imperial Rome, while, on the other hand, justifying the construction of religious settlements to advance the interests of Rome. In becoming part of the Roman legacy, the Germanic kings avoid being perceived as occupiers, while, de facto, they were expanding and occupying land and thus legitimizing their actions.

the eighth century. The news we have of this originally Lombard monastery is that it suddenly felt threatened by the expansion of the Aldobrandeshi, and the monks' letters provide an extensive, detailed record of the family's early manoeuvres in southern Tuscany.[21] For elaborate reasons, the Church invested more resources in this region, but the extent of its control is not yet established. In papal documents, San Salvatore and smaller monasteries, oratories, and castles of Lombard foundation were claimed by the Church later in the thirteenth century and assigned to the Cistercian order.

In the Maremma, Roman ecclesiastical presence appears to have been practically absent for much of the first millennium. Rome, by proxy of the Church, showed a formal interest in the region, evidenced by an increased number of documents. The Roman monastery of Saint Paul Outside the Walls issued the first two official claims that showed territorial ownership in southern Tuscany starting in 1080. This statement was followed by a papal bull from Gregory VII (1073–1085), who listed the names of the five sites in southern Tuscany, which were declared to be under the monastery's custody: the *civitas* of Ansedonia, its properties and port; Monte Argentario; Sant'Angelo; Orbetello; and the castle of Elsa.[22] Tricosto was not yet included.

All the aforementioned sites in southern Maremma, and those subsequently, were claimed by the Church starting in 1080 by virtue of the so-called 'Carolingian donation'. In both Ansedonia and Capalbiaccio, the archaeology confirms that there were no settlements on either site at the time when the supposed donation took place. The pottery shows that the first traces of early medieval life post-date the eighth and ninth century, but precede the eleventh century.[23] That said, this is no place to debate the legendary donation and the role of the Carolingian's ties to Rome. While it is now generally accepted that the original donation was false, it was certainly used to formalize the rights over this part of coastal Tuscany, *possessio Tuscie*, by the Roman monastery.[24] Although the Church undoubtedly maintained some presence in the region and in what survived of the ancient Roman cities, it seems to have played a marginal role in southern Tuscany from the fifth to the tenth centuries. The rise of the communal cities and the burgeoning power of aristocratic families, such as the Aldobrandeschi, operated autonomously as an independent power building and investing of in the public domains that were abandoned for centuries. These borders were at the mercy of the constantly shifting alliances among families, and Rome was too distant to wield any real local power or presence. Archaeological evidence helps to clarify some of the sources of the historiography that has crystallized in the region.

While Tricosto is not mentioned in Church documents until the 1116 *privilegio* by Alexander III, its historical events are closely linked to those of the nearby *civitas* of Ansedonia.[25] Ansedonia appears in each one of the documents and it is the only name that carries the status of ancient Roman *civitas*, in contrast to the other castles, towers, and land mentioned in the documents. While it is frequently used, the Latin term of *civitas* seems to enable the Church to claim authority over extended properties that once were part of the Roman empire, or colonies, despite their long state of abandonment. As an example, the excavation of medieval Cosa/Ansedonia shows that life returned on site in the tenth century as determined by pottery analysis.[26] Visual evidence of the Carolingian donation was paraded in Rome to a much later date (the second half of the thirteenth century). The frescoes inside the gatehouse of the Roman monastery of the Santi Vincenzo and Anastasio at Tre Fontane depict the 'legendary' belief that Charlemagne was there and that he reclaimed the territory from enemies.[27] The frescoes, like the papal orders that claim such a patrimony, have recently been dated and seem to have served the same purpose: to provide historical facts to prove ecclesiastical ownership. In Monte Cassino, one of the earliest Benedictine monasteries in Campania, an exemplary piece of ecclesias-

---

21 Ascheri and Niccolai 2002; Kurze 2008; Ascheri 1989; Kurze 1989.
22 Ciacci 1935: *Ansedonam civitatem, cum pertinentiis suis et portu suo, Montem ... Argentarium cum lacu Catamare, ubi est ecclesia S. Angeli castri, Orbitelli cum pertinentiis suis; et castrum ... Elsa, cum omnibus suis pertinentiis.*
23 Hobart 1995; Hobart and others 2009.
24 The historian Simone M. Collavini believes that there was most likely an imperial donation dated to the Carolingian period and tied by fiscal heritage to the monastery of Santi Vincenzo and Anastasio at Tre Fontane (or ad Aquas Salvias)'s in Rome, but there is uncertainty as to what was included in the text and which territories were targeted. By comparing the different properties listed for the monastery, the author patiently reconstructed the changes and new additions to the list through time. In sum, all of the texts mention the *civitas* of Ansedonia, Tricosto, the port of Feniglia, the Monte Argentario, and Orbetello (originally half and then whole), Collavini speculates that these may well be the same properties contained in the Carolingian donation; Monteti and Marsiliana, along with the two islands of Giannutri and Giglio, were instead added later when the Church formally acquired them, demonstrating that the land was not always considered part of the *Patrimonium Beati Petri*. Collavini, 1998, 266, n. 105; 268.
25 Collavini 1998, 270.
26 Hobart 2003; Hobart 1992; Hobart 1991.
27 On the frescoes, see Barclay Lloyd 1997; Barclay Lloyd 2006, 230–31; Luttrell 2001; Fentress and Wickham 2001.

tic propaganda is found on the bronze doors of the original monastery, which contained a long inscription of place names and properties either donated or acquired by the monastery.[28] This long list was placed at the entrance to the church to remind the churchgoer of the power of Monte Cassino and the extent the *Terra Sancti Benedicti*. This visible 'exemplary' promotion of the donations was emulated elsewhere confirming through time the Church's ownership of land, while stimulating further forms of gifts. These two examples to the north of the south of the roman *Patrimonium Beati Petri* show visually the makings of active expansion by affirming locally the centrality of the Church and a new centre, Rome for the 'western' universality of Christianity. The Aldobrandeschi were one of the actors who the Church both targeted and allied with to gain privileges and eventually their land as the family declined.

In Lucca and in northern Tuscany, early medieval documents abound, but comparatively fewer documents exist that mention Tricosto and Ansedonia, the properties of the Aldobrandeschi and their vassals.[29] The best known are the ecclesiastical records, in the form of requests for revenue (or *emphitheusis*) to the Aldobrandeschi family for having settled in land that once belonged to Rome, according to the donation of Charlemagne. Here, the Church appears to have carried out a different form of relationship with the landowners. The documents primarily attempt to establish an economic exchange and a desire (on the part of the Church) to rent a portion of the castle (a percentage) and subordinate families such as the Aldobrandeschi. Despite their proximity to the *Patrimonium Beati Petri*, these once 'public lands' were instead distributed, by those rulers that ascended towards Rome — the Carolingians and then the Germanic kings — to families that granted them loyalty, beginning at least by the ninth century. The development of villages in the tenth century in this area and the increasing draw to exploit the many natural resources with which Tuscany was endowed, brought together initiatives that not only augmented mining initiatives and fostered the agricultural revolution, but also brought about the formation of the early communal cities and the entrepreneurship of the maritime republics during the eleventh century. Tuscany was thriving not only through international ports such as Pisa, and communal cities such as Siena and Florence but was establishing relationships with other countries and powers that Rome was not always matching.

As stated before, the spread of the Aldobrandeschi family to the fullest extent of their power was a result of their ability to master multiple specializations in the local exploitation of raw materials — from mining, fisheries, salt collection, agricultural cultivation, etc. — whose revenues allowed them to invest broadly across southern Tuscany. Diversification was their formula for success, because it generated constant growth and balanced the risk of loss or failed investments. This approach allowed them to set apart surplus, which was then reinvested locally to solidify ties with their allies. However, this method necessitated abandoning regions, such as the mining hilltops around Siena, when competition did not reward their projected expectations. Instead, huge revenues from the salt marshes played a large part in the Aldobrandeschi moving their operations south and settling in Grosseto.[30] But there is another unspoken resource that the plains in between Grosseto and Tricosto provide for profitable returns. Although not visible in the documents, grains and wheat have always represented an important area of provisions for this part of the region. Tuscany's primary resources, such as minerals and salt have been targeted and analysed for the last forty years, at the expense of grain and wheat. This basic daily good which plays a huge role in the local and regional economy is finally under scrutiny.[31]

Not only were the Aldobrandeschi concerned with natural resources: they pursued political dominion (expressed through the construction of castles in many different localities), and managed packaging, distribution, and conservation. The presence of a number of Aldobrandeschi ports — from Talamone, those surrounding the Monte Argentario promontory (Santo Stefano, Orbetello, Port'Ercole, Feniglia), and further south to Corneto (Montalto di Castro) — indicate that their goods travelled not only in the region but also, along the coast, and by sea, north to Pisa and Genoa, and possibly south to Rome.

The Aldobrandeschi were also large investors in real estate and built and organized communities in the Maremma with three standard types of developments. According to their size and the geomorphological potential for growth, these can be summarized as:

1. a single, tall tower or small castle with a settlement around it (e.g. Argentiera and perhaps the early phase of medieval Cosa/Ansedonia), with or without a wall around it;

---

28 Bloch 1993.
29 Ciacci 1935; Collavini 1998.
30 Redon 1999 [1994].
31 Collavini 2013; Bianchi and Grassi 2013; Buonincontri and others 2017.

2. a larger castle with a proto-urban plan (village with defence), containing both housing and a palace, with at least one or two churches (similar to Capalbiaccio) and the potential to be enlarged;
3. a *fortilitiaea*, a major fortification which would accommodate a large community with a more ambitious plan for expansion (Pitigliano, Arcidosso, and Santa Fiora).

These three types of distinction are confirmed by records of the Aldobrandeschi properties, that list the various subdivisions, mainly those of 1216 and 1276. There was no fear of failure. To the contrary, it seems that the family followed a clear design on how to build their new settlements, expressing determination and rationale in the building of communities. The repetition of the proto-urban housing plans inside the castles and settlements guaranteed the Aldobrandeschi continuity between ruling heirs and allied families, while shaping communities and contributing to the economic growth for both the population and the activities tied to the local resources. Fixed to their persistent 'standard' plan, the family knew how to run and defend their settlements. In this region, even to this day, remnants of medieval masonry are referred to as *opera aldobrandesca*. Capalbiaccio fits between the second and third type listed above: a fortified village that had all the potential to grow into a medieval town, yet never did, although it lasted longer than the rest.

Once the Cistercian order asserted itself with the Pope Eugene III at the helm of the Church, Rome became interested in southern Tuscany. In 1152, the stronghold of Capalbiaccio was referred to as *Trecosti* in a papal bull stating its dependence on Rome, which was reconfirmed in 1161.[32] However, the Church was not the only authority making claims to this region: rising communal towns were also challenging the seigniorial hegemony of the Aldobrandeschi, setting the economic premises for future conflicts. The large investment in castles, towns, and their local resources by the Aldobrandeschi family and their vassals came under threat by the end of the twelfth century with Siena and Orvieto's expansion into the county. Documents show that properties were exchanged for varied reasons, including favours, which increasingly undermined the family's control. For instance, in 1168 Ranieri di Bartolomeo, a vassal of the Aldobrandeschi family, transferred his dominion of the Guiniccesca properties to Orvieto.[33] The same was happening with some of the castles built by the Aldobrandeschi, which were given, exchanged, or lost to Siena, or other competing families. Similarly, the Ardengheschi properties were kept in the family and donated to one of their own monasteries, such as Castelleraccio on the nearby hilltops of Paganico, north of the Ombrone River.[34]

The beginning of the thirteenth century was defined by a struggle for control over the salt marshes outside Grosseto, in which the Aldobrandeschi suffered great losses. Ildebrandino VIII made an alliance with the commune of Siena in 1203, creating a pact to monopolize the salt from Grosseto. A representative, Locterengo de Tricosto, perhaps a vassal of the Aldobrandeschi family, was present and witnessed the negotiations between Ildebrandino and the commune of Siena. Nevertheless, the pact was revoked a year later, when a document, the *Charta Libertatis*, shows that the Aldobrandeschi may have forfeited half of their control over the salt works in Grosseto to the monastery of San Salvatore on Monte Amiata. When Ildebrandino VIII died in 1208, his will bequeathed all of his salt revenue to two small ecclesiastical centres that were in debt to Siena, thereby surrendering their interests in the salt production of the region.[35] Less than two decades later, Siena ceased in its diplomatic attempts to control the coast when she attacked Grosseto in 1224, officially driving the Aldobrandeschi out of that area.[36]

The larger 'European' context helps put the Aldobrandeschi narrative in perspective. Between 1220–1250, Emperor Frederick II's alliance with the papacy and the creation of the Lombard League solidified the Roman Church's involvement in its declared territories, through the insertion of churches into towns and rural areas, which it sought to control. This was another period in which the Carolingian donation was productively used by the Church to stake its claims. The Lombard League was particularly successful in sprawling across northern Italy, through its support of commercial initiatives and growth of the individual cities. As a result, Frederick II was able to re-appropriate some of the land that had been listed as part of the *Patrimonium Beati Petri*. After his death in 1250, while the castle of Tricosto was experiencing its most significant growth and transforming into a fortified village, internal conflicts among papal families revealed frailties within the Church,

---

32 Ciacci 1935.
33 Collavini 1999, 367.
34 Cammarosano and Passeri 2006; Cardarelli 1924–1925; Angelucci 2000.
35 Farinelli 2009, 110.
36 To reinforce the ostracization of the family, a combined revolt of citizens from Grosseto and Siena was launched against the Aldobrandeschi and its leader, Count Guglielmo, in 1236; see Redon 1999 [1994], 134; Farinelli and Pellegrini 2009, 166.

Figure 16.36. Castle of Tricosto, Capalbiaccio — Reconstruction as it would have appeared in the fourteenth century by Paul Henderson, reproduced with permission.

not only in Rome, but also beyond the Alps. Each subsequently elected pope did not last long and the strategy of excommunication increased the tensions and led the papacy to flee to Avignon (1309–1377) leaving a vacuum in Rome and fierce competition among prominent families, such as the Colonna, the Orsini, and the Caetani.[37] Meanwhile, the conflict of investitures was at its height in central Italy. As in Rome, alliances with filo-imperial Ghibelline or pro-papal Guelphs often shifted, causing instability among the ruling families. The north and central Italian communal towns increasingly used the tensions between these factions to their advantage and flourished as a result. These independent 'city states' expanded their *contadi* and became fundamental agents in the provision of financial resources by lending to the papacy, which had not yet established a sound form of currency, nor a solid position in southern Tuscany.[38] With the move of the Papacy to Avignon, many of the elite families fought to regain control over the land they lost to the expanding communal towns and resisted paying the *decime* which was starting to assert itself in a conspicuous form of papal control.[39]

The decline of the Aldobrandeschi family began shortly after the death of Ildebrandino VIII at the beginning of the thirteenth century and suffered a major blow in 1216, with the bifurcation of their wealth and property into two branches, those of Santa Fiora and Sovana.[40] Whereas the success of the family had always been a function of their miraculous ability to maintain filial unity, the Aldobrandeschi

---

37 Watt, 1999, 138; Watt 1965.

38 The Germanic empire had minted coins for generations in the Italian peninsula, starting from Pavia in the eighth century in both silver coins and other metals. The Hohenstaufen even had the golden Augustalis Federiciano, while Rome was just starting to reactivate its mint. Abulafia 1992; Rovelli 2012b.

39 Guidi 1932; Lanconelli 1998.

40 Collavini 1998, 259.

county became too large to be administered by a united family, let alone a single individual.

Albeit slowly, the house of the Aldobrandeschi was beginning to decline. Nevertheless, Tricosto thrived in the thirteenth century, due in part to the distance from larger centres and the strategic placement of Capalbiaccio. In particular, it was its location at the heart of the fertile Valle d'Oro, overlooking the coastal Aurelian highway and its harbours, which interested the growing communal cities of Siena and Orvieto. Both cities sought to gain control over the wealth of different grain fields surrounding the hilltop and to secure safe access to the sea. In order for them to expand their *contadi* and assert their power in ever-broader territories, the communal cities appropriated land by acquisition or by force, from families that had been settled in the countryside for generations. The communal cities also vied with the papacy by making claims to ecclesiastical properties and collecting revenues that otherwise went to the Church. For example, by 1221 Siena had acquired enough power to negotiate fees and boundaries with the Aldobrandeschi by isolating their allies, the Ardengheschi, on the other side of the Ombrone River. In a process of territorial reorganization that seriously undermined the Aldobrandeschi family, Orvieto established the Albegna River as the boundary between its commune and that of Siena.[41] In 1223, Guglielmo and Bonifacio Aldobrandeschi lost Castiglione al Trasimeno to the village of Val del Lago and Orvieto. Documents describe that members of the Orvieto commune were allowed into Tricosto, despite a papal bull by Pope Alexander IV that recognized the 'castrum Tricostum' as part of the monastery of Santi Vincenzo and Anastasio at the Tre Fontane.[42] These official accounts indicate that communal and ecclesiastical institutions expressed formal interest in establishing ownership or control over the Tricosto castle at this critical juncture. It was, perhaps, at this crucial moment in the early thirteenth century that the expanding village on the hilltop of Capalbiaccio built a major fortification around the entire plateau to protect its local community in the event of a military skirmish with Orvieto (Fig. 16.36).

In 1251, when central Italian communal cities were siding with opposing factions, Guglielmo Aldobrandeschi supported the Emperor, signing a treaty with Florence and Orvieto against Grosseto, Siena, and all of its allies.[43] Tricosto was still part of lists of properties belonging to the Aldobrandeschi family in records claiming rent from Rome in two other documents dated 1269 and 1286. Called upon to reestablish papal order, Charles of Anjou headed south into Tuscany in 1273, where he somewhat upset the balance of power.[44] The Aldobrandeschi family was forced to readdress their possessions at this time, either for defensive reasons or to establish land that they could use for negotiation. A second subdivision is evidenced in a 1274 list of the properties, *fortilictie, domini diretti, baronie, affictus et iura*, of the Aldobrandeschi, as well as in a papal bull of 1286, which counts Tricosto castle as a possession of the Aldobrandeschi family.[45] A grand effort was made, through the marriage of Margherita, the last heir of the Sovana branch of the Aldobrandeschi, to Guy of Montfort, a representative of Charles of Anjou in this region, to retain her inheritance in the late thirteenth century, against the pressure from the rising communal cities and Rome. The papacy wanted to assure that Margherita's assets would be part of the *Patrimonium Beati Petri* and pressured her into a second marriage with a member of the Roman Orsini family, who became the new lord of the *fortilitia* of Pitigliano, ending this branch of the Aldobrandeschi family's control. Margherita's father, Ildebrandino XI, had already given the majority of his estate to many ecclesiastical institutions in southern Tuscany (Sovana, Grosseto, San Galgano, San Salvatore, Santi Vincenzo and Anastasio at the Tre Fontane, etc.) in 1284. The Aldobrandeschi, who for generations were reminded of their ecclesiastical submission to the *emphitheusis*, now, through marriage, became part of a papal family. Thus, Pope Bonifacio VIII was now able to count among the papacy's possessions, a good portion of southern Tuscany.[46]

Subject to fierce conflicts between powerful communal, imperial, and ecclesiastical forces, the fourteenth century saw southern Tuscany decline economically and suffer from depopulation. Many castles in the region around Grosseto were abandoned and large landholdings were broken up into small estates. Others, such as the nearby castle of Ansedonia, which was destroyed in 1329 by the Sienese, were ransacked as part of the wider political conflicts. The dawn of the fourteenth century found Siena aggressively pursuing territory in the Maremma, to achieve safe access to their newly annexed port of Talamone, north of the promon-

---

41   Redon 1999 [1994], *Lo spazio di una città*, 130–33.
42   Farinelli 2009.
43   Siena (29 July 1254) subjects the lords of Sticciano, Sasso, Cinegiano, and those of the Ardengheschi of Fornoli, Civitella and Pari; Redon 1999 [1994], 134–36.
44   Terlizzi 1950, nn. 507, 268–69; 323, 329.
45   Collavini 1998, 362–64.
46   Collavini 1998, 340–53; Farinelli 2009.

tory of Mount Argentario. They were locked in competition with Orvieto in the Maremma. Any castle that resisted, or whose politics were antagonistic, were eventually destroyed or annexed as part of the growing communes. Many of the castles in question were part of the Aldobrandeschi family's formerly extensive county.

Experiencing these pressures, Capalbaiccio survived by reducing its urban plan to almost half of its original perimeter. A new, massive defensive wall was placed in the centre of the fortified village, cutting the church and the community in half. This area included the towers, the palatial residence, a church, and a new building (Building J), which was probably the chosen living quarters of the landlord who built an extravagant feature, at the time, rooms with running water on both floors. Burnt traces of ashes were found during the excavation. In 1313, a fire destroyed the village inside the city walls.[47] Around the same time, Tricosto was 'occupied' by Orvieto with six 'sergeants', who held more than twenty prisoners (the same fate had befallen Ansedonia before it was sacked by Siena).[48] The inhabitants at first revolted, but then agreed to submit to Orvieto, only on the condition they would receive rights and obligations as communal citizens. At this point, the lordship of Tricosto shifted to Mancino Calzolari, who was likely a vassal of the Orsini family from Pitigliano. In 1335, the grandson of Margherita Aldobrandeschi, Guido of Orso Orsini, now count of the Sovana's Aldobrandeschi committee, submitted Tricosto to the commune of Orvieto, while granting himself the feudal income rights. A few years later he conceded (*in accomandigia*) the 'castrum Atricosti' to the commune of Perugia.[49] A substantial presence of coins from Perugia (dated 1321), together with ceramics produced in Orvieto and Viterbo, testify that the markets serving Capalbiaccio had shifted from Pisa and northern Tuscany to towns closer better connected to Rome along the Cassian Way.

The entire coast of the Maremma has been described as the region of 'weak cities' (*città deboli*), not because they were built hastily or without purpose, but rather because self-sustainability was not an option.[50] Not even coastal Grosseto, which was once controlled by the Aldobrandeschi and had rich natural resources, as well as the potential to grow, became a larger city or port.[51] Southern Tuscany continued to struggle into the mid-fourteenth century, when the Black Plague and other misfortunes, such as malaria, caused a dramatic population decline in 1348. The beginning of the fifteenth century saw a crisis in both the mercantile and banking sectors, which resulted in civic powers being fully affirmed over seigniorial territories. Further plagues and epidemics (in 1411–1412; 1417–1419; 1430) reduced what was left of the local rural population.[52] In 1416, the Sienese took advantage of this instability and attacked the hilltop fortification of Tricosto, where they encountered fierce resistance. The following year, the General Council of the Republic of Siena deliberated upon the destruction of the fort of Tricosto, ultimately deciding to abandon the site, as it was found to be '*inconveniente et con spesa senza niuno utile* (inconvenient, costly, and having no function)', and the possession of it would only bring '*piuttosto danno* (certain damage)'.[53] In Sienese documents from 1430, the census records the castle of Tricosto under the name *torre di Malfollia* (tower of bad folly), an appellation which encapsulates the commune's distaste for the site, as well as its diminished capacity.[54] The tower mentioned is the one at the foot of the hill today, and called Casolare of Tricosto. It faces the agricultural planes towards Ansedonia.[55]

The fate of Tricosto was shared by several other former Aldobrandeschi castles in the *contado* of Siena in the second half of the fifteenth century. Documents from 1433 and 1461 define Capalbiaccio (or Alticosto) as an abandoned castle whose lands were being rented for pasture, so as to avoid the risk that 'bandits' might inhabit them.[56] An attempt by the nearby town of Capalbio to revive Alticosto in the late fifteenth century was rejected, but seems to have been part of repopulation petitions, which indicate some form of use, probably tied to transhumance, foraging, and logging. After centuries of conflict, in 1432 this land became the theatre for the ultimate clash between Siena and the Orsini family, as representatives of Rome and the Church. In prevailing, Siena finally expanded its *contado* to southern boundary that is now Tuscany.

---

47 Dyson 1994.
48 Giorgi 1878, 61–63; Farinelli 2007.
49 Farinelli 2009.
50 Farinelli 2007.
51 Carlo Citter and Antonia Arnoldus-Huyzendveld explain why Grosseto was condemned to remain small, by analysing the self-sustainable capacity for the town by calculating the amount of food the Grosseto countryside could produce; they quantified the city's maximum capacity based on constraints upon local agricultural resources that would not allow for further growth. See Citter and Arnoldus-Huyzendveld 2007.
52 Ginatempo 1988, 265–66, 270.
53 Angelucci and Bellettini, 2006, 31.
54 Farinelli 2007. This was built over another Roman villa recently excavated by the local Soprintendenza.
55 Chirico 2018.
56 Ginatempo 1988, 85; 283; 308. On the abandonment of the Maremma, see Redon 1975 and Cammarosano and Passeri 1985.

MICHELLE HOBART

17. Concluding Remarks and Open Questions

Returning to the archeological site at Capalbiaccio, after decades and working on material that none of us had excavated was at first a challenge, but gradually examination of that material yielded worthwhile results. The three years of excavation and trenching in the 1970s provided a wide spectrum of much of what transpired on the site. Our 2009–2010 non-invasive campaign sought to contextualize what was impossible to do some three decades earlier. The research of medieval pottery in the 1970s was just starting to provide the data that we now take for granted. Our team was able to recreate the chronological sequence from the pottery and contextualize the nature of the settlement with more precision. Similarly, wall reading, geophysical surveys and GIS generated mapping systems have allowed us to augment the information available in the late 1970s. This publication hopes to show the merits of returning to past excavations and reinvigorating prior work when new information and technologies become available.

The 2009–2010 campaigns now confirm that the hilltop of Capalbiaccio had been occupied from the late Bronze Age to the Iron Age. The geophysical evidence suggests that traces of different settlements covered the whole plateau and part of the hilltop in the Etruscan era with a proto-urban community. The dating of the pottery fragments, from the 1970s excavations, confirms the existence of a pre-Roman settlement which is incontrovertible proof of an Etruscan community at Capalbiaccio, which peaked in the sixth century BCE. There is also an earlier Neolithic community although only a small sample of material was found disturbed in a rubbish pit and not *in situ*. On the other hand, by interpreting the anomalies of the magnetometry we could rule out the possibility of an early medieval stone community where huts and stone foundation were finished with perishable material. The proposed hypothetical reconstruction provides two reasons.

The first is based on the different axis, visible from the anomalous alignment of the group of structures, which are not aligned with the standing medieval plan with the castle. If there was an early medieval stone community, the castle would have respected the orientation of its previous generations. The second reason was made on the basis of the quantitative statistics offered by the pottery analysed and their periodization (See Table 6.3 in ch. 6).

Throughout the fourth century BCE, the Romans expanded at first in the interior of central Italy and soon after into the Regio VII (Etruria), when in the third century they began to establish their rule, first with the construction of colonial settlements, and soon after, with the distribution of land (centuriation) and the foundation of major road system network — the Cassia, the Clodia, the Emilia and the two Aurelian ways. What happened before the Republican period at Capalbiaccio is not known to due to lack of more precise archaeological evidence, but what is clear is that during the late Republican period there was a demographic decline or an out migration toward the new nearby Roman colony of Cosa, founded in 273 BCE. We know this once again from the pottery and the lack of architectural remains or traces. Assorted and random pottery fragments — Roman bricks and tiles — dating from the late second and early part of the first century BCE, were discovered on the southern part of the hill attest to the minimal presence of people, perhaps a farm, a look out, a refuge? Capalbiaccio from the late Republican and Imperial Roman period, when slave-driven villas, such as Settefinestre, populated the Valle d'Oro seems abandoned and nothing has been found at this stage and the hilltop was not re-occupied for a long period.[1]

What happened in the Mediterranean midway through the first millennium is still being debated after the provocative catastrophic vision of the fifth-century fall of Rome by Bryan Ward-Perkins. He depicted the momentous, bleak circumstances in central Italy, reminiscent of pre-historic times.[2] Tuscany was no exception; centralized power dissolved, and towns fell into ruin. Roman towns and colonies that had been founded in Etruria, such as Roselle, Volterra,

---

1 Carandinie and Settis 1979; Carandini 1985a; Dyson 2002; Carandini and others 2002; Fentress 2003; Celuzza and Luzzetti 2013.
2 Ward-Perkins 2005, 183.

Figure 17.1. Photo of Capalbiaccio, with a view of Cosa and the Argentario. Photo by Michelle Hobart.

Siena, Pisa, Lucca, Arezzo, and Florence, were abandoned or reduced to small enclaves by the fourth or fifth century CE.[3] In the region of Capalbiaccio, the disintegration of cities has been well documented at post-Roman Cosa,[4] Heba,[5] Saturnia, and Roselle,[6] where stages of adaptive redevelopment, including the reoccupation of monumental architecture, have been delineated. The classic examples of reoccupation from within Rome — the Crypta Balbi theatre and the Nerva forum — perfectly illustrate how people reused Roman walls to create monumental compounds for communal living.[7] If that is what happened in the seat of the Empire, it should provide a glimpse of what was happening elsewhere in the Italian peninsula. Other large Roman cities, including Milan, Bologna, Catania, and Verona, succumbed to a similar fate, where large structures were downsized into small village compounds.[8] The rise of slave-driven villas between the first centuries BCE and CE greatly transformed the economy of southern Tuscany, but did not last much longer. Similar to Roman towns, these imperial villas, which were once great producers of wine, oil, fish paste, salt, grain, and amphorae, also suffered the fate of their urban counterparts, with small families inhabiting the once-large centres of production well into the fifth or even the sixth century CE.[9]

The catastrophic image of the fall of Rome is now being integrated with a more fluid new archaeological evidence identified in the late-antique countryside.[10] Thus, while the nature of the shift from the city to the countryside is still being assessed, extra-urban contexts reveal a gradual occupation of rural landscape as a better choice for sustainable living, even on a minimal scale. It appears that life in rural Maremma continued in reduced settlements, where small farms were scattered across the countryside distant from larger centres in both the fifth and sixth centuries.[11] The fertile Albegna Valley's ample grain, oil, wine, pasture and woodland resources continued to support these smaller scale communities.

It is widely accepted that, with the decentralization and fragmentation of the Roman Empire, long-range exchange came to an end, while short-range material circulation continued virtually unchanged for the majority of the late-Roman population.[12] The presence of Tunisian amphora and African Red Slip wares, found along the coast and in the countryside in small quantities, can be explained as residual, imbedded trade patterns that continued into the sixth century, despite the economic and political changes that took place when the Roman system collapsed.[13] The late-Roman peasantry was not involved in this international trade, but the existence of African pottery in domestic contexts, including some as primitive as the cave shelter at Scoglietto, testify to the continued reception on a minimal scale, or perhaps just the reuse, of these trade goods.[14] Despite the suggestion of small Byzantine re-settlement of cities such as Cosa, Roselle, and Luni, which could demonstrate the lack of interest in the

---

3 Augenti 2010.
4 De Giorgi 2019; Fentress 2003.
5 Micheluuci 1984; Attolini 2002.
6 Mazzolai 1960; Bocci 1978; Celuzza 1987; Citter 1996a; Nicosia and Poggesi 1998; Rizzitelli 1999.
7 Arena and others 2001; Manacorda 1982, 45, fig. 47; On the Nerva forum, see Brogiolo 2011, 176, fig. 82.
8 Saguì, Ricci and Romei 2001; Bruttini 2013. Augenti 2010.
9 Carandini 1985b; Cambi and Fentress 1989; Carandini and others 2002; Dyson 2003. For a more recent assessment of the Roman countryside, see Terrenato 2000.

10 Bowes and others 2017; Terrenato 2012; Grey 2011.
11 Ghisleni 2010; Ghisleni, Vaccaro and Bowes 2011.
12 Augenti 1998a; Cantini 2011; Vaccaro 2011.
13 Vaccaro 2013.
14 Cygielman, and others 2010; Sebastiani and others 2015.

Tyrrhenian coast from the imperial seat, the exchange that would have brought this type of material culture was minimal, if not totally suspended after the sixth century. It may be worthwhile to mention at this point that the notion of a Byzantine presence on the Tyrrhenian coast is associated with the assumption that the Byzantine army was in place to defend a region that was not particularly active, an idea that seems increasingly hard to believe. It is probably better to simply describe the persistence of local families on small, continuous or intermittent settlements, rather than the political effort to control the area by a centralized government. It is also hard to believe that any central government would invest resources in an area as depressed as southern Etruria was in the wake of the Roman Empire. With the ascendance of the empire in the east, the focus and economic interests of Rome, or what had survived of it, had shifted from the Tyrrhenian the Adriatic coast,[15] but mostly towards North Africa as confirmed by archaeology. The protagonist is no longer Rome but the Mediterranean Sea.

In the fifth century CE, the Gallic senator Rutilio Namaziano, who was returning to his original estate from Rome, sailed up the coast of Tuscany through the Albegna Valley and Luni, describing the area as depopulated.[16] Geographically, the key factor in the reversing the fortunes of settlements in the coastal Maremma has been the extent to which its inhabitants have been able to contain the spread of the marshes and the safety of circulation. The recurrent land reclamations during the Roman era, the Renaissance, and the early twentieth century have enabled the area, although with interruptions, to re-flourish agriculturally, but when the marshes were left untamed caused significant depopulation and stagnation: in other words, a backwater.

It would take this once rich and prosperous coastline a long time to regenerate interest sufficient enough for settlement to return. The same can be said for the former Roman colony of Cosa, which, by the end of the fifth–early sixth century, had lost most of its original features. There is still hardly any trace of the seventh–eighth century anywhere in the region, and it will take another two centuries for communities to come together and eventually grow into cities.[17] One provocative theory about this gap, where no substantial traces allow for identification worthy of attention, is that some devastating climate change occurred, during which life was put on hold.[18] Otherwise, the abundant research done in Tuscany would have borne evidence if there was indeed something to show.

For some forty years, rural Tuscany has been subjected to every available cutting-edge archaeological technique. Early on, medieval archaeology benefitted from a remarkable amount of documents artefacts, and architectural history. It was no mistake that a classical art historian from Tuscany, Ranuccio Bianchi Bandinelli, used his expansive viewpoint to combine archaeology and architectural studies.[19] Similarly, Tiziano Mannoni, although a Ligurian, was the father of archaeometry. He experimented and developed scientific methods becoming the pioneer of the making, that is the archaeology of production of all sorts of material culture (pottery, bricks, stone cutting and its site and territory. The *homo faber* was both an *art-igiano* and an art-ist, and whatever she produced was a matter of a unique endeavour, be it functional or decorative, where the object's value, before standardization, was its use, void of protagonism.

Tuscany provides the active laboratory to analyse the medieval past since the awareness thereof lies just below the surface in the minds of its citizens and above the surface in its architectural legacy. Interdisciplinary approaches like Bandinelli's or Mannoni's happen more frequently for classical — than medieval — studies given the greater interest in the classical period and the artefacts still surviving. But the medieval period is quickly catching up in this light, given the abundance of documents and a landscape punctuated by buildings and infrastructure, like those of the Aldobrandeschi. Another fortuitous example, is the first monograph on Montemassi (Guideri, Parenti, and Barbagli 2000), where archaeology and architecture are measured against the frescoes painted on the walls of the Public Palace in Siena. The book shows well how each medium can inform the other. The more scientific approach now available with new radar and satellite technologies allows for depths that were unimaginable when Medieval Archaeology was founded in the late 1970s. At this juncture it is worth mentioning the multi-disciplinary approach used by historian Dario Gaggio in his 2017 book, *The Shaping of Tuscany: Landscape and Society between Tradition and Modernity*. The author investigates our often-mistaken assumptions about how static the Tuscan landscape appears or is portrayed, as he delves into the factors that shaped it from 1870 to 1970. Blessed with testimonials from

---

15 Gelichi and Hodges 2012.
16 Celuzza 2015.
17 Augenti 2000; Abela 1999.

18 Cheyette 2008; Hodges 2010a.
19 Bianchi Bandinelli 1976.

the peasant perspective unavailable to a medieval reader, we come to appreciate how twentieth-century peasants, stuck largely in feudal arrangements made in the late Middle Ages, are awakened to their own agency by the disruptions of the First and Second World Wars. The sharecropper soldiers returned from these wars with an understanding that institutions and arrangements were not eternal but negotiable: compliance with authorities was undermined and subordination to the *mezzadria* pacts and their associated behavioural norms were no longer granted. Sharecropper pacts are now in flux as peasants push back firmly with union help on the imbalances in cost sharing. From here spatial relationships mutate (be they: town to country, farm to estate, travel and communications, mixed subsistence agriculture to monocrops, cows to goats). The social isolation and docility of peasants is no longer tolerable to them. Even as the clay domes are flattened; rivers are dammed and channelled; lands are smoothed; hillsides are horizontally terraced and farm houses improved, the reclaiming of the peasants themselves is largely ignored. Nothing less than feudalism itself is ended in the mid- twentieth century, despite seventy years of ruralizing reforms that smoothed the landscape and reclaimed the marshes, but never fundamentally challenged the supremacy of the landlords. The relationship with the national government is critical as Central and Southern Tuscany go from neglect to the focus of Rome's agrarian and national policies. Ultimately, the landlords and their political sponsors can no longer hold back modernity. Tragically, just as peasants are able to dismantle the unfair sharecropping pacts and obtain power and ownership of small farms, and attract capital for farm equipment, and separate their living quarters from the farm animals, their desires for improved living conditions, education, and material goods leads the majority to abandon the countryside to seek these goods in the cities. The vacuum they leave behind is eventually filled by the landlords, wine for export, and agro-tourism. Chianti is branded and the Orcia valley is UNESCO protected as part of a heritage tourist industry that claims Tuscany's soft rolling lands as eternal.

While we don't have as large a data set for our period, in particular testimonies from peasants themselves, we can imagine that Gaggio's portrayal of the factors influencing the Tuscan landscape's physical transformations from 1870–1970 have analogues in Etruscan, Roman Classical, Medieval, and Renaissance periods.

What can we learn from all of this work and how can one put to use this micro local history to learn from in a region that has seasonal shifts in demography raising prices that seem unfair to the local communities that work there all year round? The inevitable tensions between year-round farmers and Roman summer vacationers played out in the difficulties in enlarging that highway, the Via Aurelia, that crosses and separates the coast from the inland fields and hills. Decades have gone by and slowly from the Northern coast pieces of the road have been built, but still part of the coast needs approval in a constantly shifting game of local power and Rome. Or from an identarian distinction the proud Tuscan identifies still today with the refined Etruscans against the corrupted Roman patricians.

Of course, the reality can be found to be different chapter by chapter but the polarity between these neighbouring territories continues to show two parallel lives that hardly ever meet.

APPENDIX — STEPHEN L. DYSON

Castle and Countryside

Capalbiaccio and the Changing Settlement History of the Ager Cosanus

My intention here is to describe the history of settlement in the Cosanus, the territory of the ancient Roman colony of Cosa, as it has been reconstructed by the Wesleyan survey team. Emphasis will be on the Middle Ages, which are the concern of this volume; however, in order to place medieval patterns in context, one must first consider the long-term relationship between human communities and the region, and, therefore, a brief history of Roman Cosa will precede my discussion of the medieval period.

According to ancient sources, Cosa was an Etruscan city. Decades of excavation by the American Academy in Rome have failed, however, to turn up any substantial traces of Etruscan occupation at the site, a hilltop in Ansedonia generally linked to Roman Cosa (Fig. A.1).[1] The Etruscan centre may have been located elsewhere, perhaps at modern Orbetello. Archaeological excavation and survey have demonstrated that the four- to five-hundred square kilometres of land set aside as the *territorium* of ancient Cosa was sparsely inhabited when the Romans arrived. The latest evidence from excavations at Capalbiaccio may force some re-evaluation of this point, about which I will withhold discussion until later.

The Romans founded Cosa in 273 BC on a coastal point some one-hundred miles north of the city now known as Ansedonia.[2] Founded to watch over the recently-rebellious Etruscans and, more importantly, the inhabitants of the major centre at Vulci, Cosa was a Latin colony. Its population of several

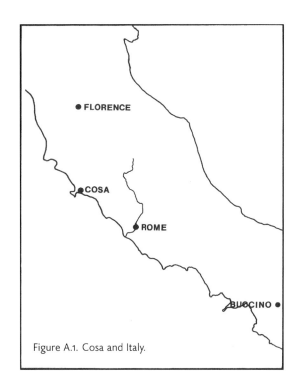

Figure A.1. Cosa and Italy.

thousand families was settled partly in the city and in greater numbers in the surrounding countryside. Excavations by the American Academy have shown that, although the urban centre prospered in the second and first centuries BC, the city suffered some disaster toward the end of the first quarter of the first century BC, and, while occupation continued at the site until the end of the fourth century AD, the city never recovered its former vigour.[3]

Literary evidence for Cosa's transition from Antiquity to the Middle Ages is very limited. Religious legends suggest some occupation during the Carolingian period,[4] probably centred on

---

* This chapter was originally published as Stephen L. Dyson, 'Castle and Countryside: Capalbiaccio and the Changing Settlement History of the *Ager Cosanus*,' in *Archaeological Approaches to Medieval Europe*, ed. by Kathleen Biddick, Studies in Medieval Culture, 18 (Kalamazoo: Medieval Institute Publications, 1984), 263–78. It is reprinted here by kind permission of the editor and Medieval Institute Publications, Western Michigan University. [MH]

1 The best account of Cosa and its excavations is now F. E. Brown, *Cosa: The Making of a Roman Town* (Ann Arbor: Univ. of Michigan Press, 1980). It contains a full bibliography of previous work.

2 *Cosa: The Making of a Roman Town*, 1–30; E. T. Salmon, *Roman Colonization Under the Republic* (Ithaca: Cornell Univ. Press, 1970), 29–39.

3 *Cosa: The Making of a Roman Town*, 72–76; R. T. Scott, 'A New Inscription of the Emperor Maximinus at Cosa,' *Chiron*, 11 (1981), 309–14.

4 The written evidence for the history of the Cosa area during the Middle Ages has been collected and analyzed by Cardarelli. For his reconstructions see R. Cardarelli, 'Confini fra Magliano e Masiliana; fra Manciano e Montuto Scerpenna Stachilagi; fra Tricosto e Ansedonia; fra Orbetello e Marsiliana; fra Port Ercole

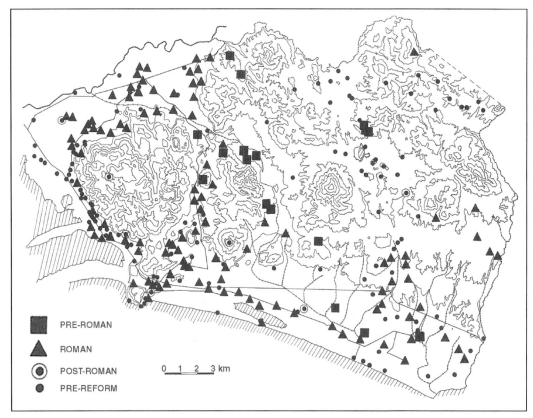

Figure A.2. Archaeological Sites in the *Ager Cosanus*. Courtesy of the Wesleyan University Survey.

the settlement of Succosa, which grew up below the town, between the small harbour which served the area and the line of the Via Aurelia, the Roman trunk road. The monastery of the Tre Fontane near Rome claimed the zone and continued to play an important role in the medieval history of Cosa.[5]

By the twelfth century, written documentation is more abundant. The centre of Orbetello had probably been continuously inhabited from the Etruscan era, through the Roman period, into the Middle Ages. In the thirteenth century, it became a commune.[6] In the territory of the old Roman colony were established several castles or fortified centres, including one on the *capitolium*, or religious centre, of the old Roman colony, which recall the process of *incastellamento* in southern Lazio described by the French medievalist Pierre Toubert.[7] This castle-dominated landscape can still be seen in the first views we have of the Cosa area — the maps in the Vatican's sixteenth century *Galleria delle Carte Geografiche*.

Politically, the Cosa area was a border zone in which the diverse interests of the Papal States — Orvieto, Siena, and even Pisa — came into conflict; political uncertainty allowed local magnates to establish at least a temporary hold over the area. In spite of these inevitable difficulties, the area seems to have enjoyed a reasonable degree of prosperity in the twelfth and thirteenth centuries. In the fourteenth century came the economic decline and depopulation for which, traditionally, malaria has been blamed.[8] Certainly, throughout the nineteenth century, the malarial swamps kept most people out of the area, particularly during the summer months.[9] However, fourteenth-century accounts clearly place more blame for this decline on growing political insecurity.[10] By the fifteenth and sixteenth centuries, most of the castles had been dismantled or abandoned, and the area gradually assumed the deserted appearance described by eighteenth- and nineteenth-century travellers.[11]

This brief history of the rise and fall of Cosa has been assembled from the sources and from excavations at the ancient city site. Before turning to the ways in which the Wesleyan survey has modified this picture, some general observations on the geography of the area should be made. The landscape around Cosa is extremely varied (Fig. A.2). A reasonably wide coastal plain along which the Via Aurelia passed borders the territory on the southwest and provided fertile farmland and access to the sea. It was also dotted with coastal swamps which could become a breeding ground for the mosquito. The northern border of the colony, formed by the Albegna River,

---

e Monte Arsgentario (28 dicembre 1508–2 marzo 1510),' *Bollettino delle Societe Storice Maremmana*, 1 (1924), 131–42, 155–86, 205–24; 2 (1925), and, for the reference to the Carolingian period (1925), 89–92.

5   R. Cardarelli (1924–1925), 88, 96–100.
6   R. Cardarelli (1924–1925), 117–28.
7   For the whole question of incastellamento in Lazio see P. Toubert, *Les structures de Latium médiéval* (Rome: Ecole Frangaise de Rome, 1973).

8   R. Cardarelli (1924–1925), 147.
9   G. Dennis, *Cities and Cemeteries of Etruria*, 3rd edn (London: J. Murray, 1883), ch. 42.
10 R. Cardarelli (1924–1925), 160–61.
11 R. Cardarelli (1924–1925), 147–88.

provided a communication route to the interior. Several other highly fertile valleys linked the coast with the hill country behind, and even today they provide some of the best farmland in the area. The northeast, however, is hilly and sometimes rugged; the land is relatively poor in quality and the ground cover often dense.

One may observe, in the twentieth-century pattern of settlement in the *Ager Cosanus*, two distinct landscapes — the first is the early modern, the second a post-World War II development. To the former, the city of Orbetello represents continuity. Toward the interior, the fifteenth century hilltop city of Capalbiaccio reflects an inland shift of population during the later Middle Ages. Topographic maps of the 1930s show its farmsteads still grouped in a late-medieval pattern: a number are clustered along the line of the Via Aurelia, especially near its juncture with the road to Orbetello. Another concentration of settlements is to be found in the northeast highlands, where the elevation and distance from the coast provided protection from malaria, piracy, and passing armies. Complementing these survivors of the Middle Ages are the ruins of several castles, monasteries, and hermitages.

The second landscape, a post-World War II development, uncannily reproduces the pattern of the Roman period. The Italian government undertook extensive land reforms in the area after the war, creating numerous small farmsteads,[12] the locational pattern for which is very close to that of the Roman farms and very different from the settlement structure of the medieval countryside. Furthermore, the coastal region has, in recent years, become a popular vacation spot, and the Ansedonia area is crowded with sumptuous summer homes — an interesting parallel to the phenomenon found during the Roman period when several large pleasure villas were built below the city.

In 1974, Wesleyan University began a systematic survey of the Cosa area with the aim of producing a settlement history based on archaeological evidence. Our model was the series of surveys undertaken by the British School at Rome around Veii, the results of which have been summarized in Timothy Potter's *The Changing Landscape of South Etruria*.[13] For nearly three seasons we have investigated by car and on foot all accessible areas of the *Ager Cosanus*. Among many advantages offered by the area for such a survey is the quality of farmland: extensive tilling of the land by mechanical means has resulted in the type of deep soil disturbance so useful for the survey archaeologist. Our inventory of nearly 150 sites, while not massive, is still a great improvement over few more than a dozen known when our work began; our methods and results have been summarized in previous publications.[14]

The survey showed that for areas presently under cultivation, Roman sites are most dominant; almost no Etruscan sites were turned up, although a few Etruscan tombs have been recorded in the past. The Roman evidence was of special interest, since it related to the question of the decline of the Roman small farmer in the wake of the Hannibalic War and the rise of the large slave estates. In the past, this development has often been associated with the Cosa region, particularly since Tiberius Gracchus, while passing along the Via Aurelia, supposedly drew inspiration for his reforms from the deserted, slave-dominated landscape he saw from the road.[15]

Contrary to previous research linking the desertion of the area around Cosa to the second century BC, our survey demonstrated that, in actuality, settlement was relatively dense at this time, with a mixture of medium and small estates. Later in the century, large villas appeared, but these were probably resort estates mainly confined to a limited coastal area and did not threaten the demise of smaller farms (Figs A.3 and A.4). Some consolidation of farm holdings did take place in the early Empire, but the area continued to support a healthy mixture of agricultural estates.

In the second century AD, the rapid process of desertion began, which, by the late third century AD had spread not only to farms and other small estates but to the largest villas as well. Excavations at Le Colonne and Sette Finestre suggest that these large villas were, for the most part, in ruins early in the century.[16] To date, archaeological research cannot supply the reasons for the rapid desertion of the

---

12 For the routine and process of this reform, see C. Retzleff, *Kulturgeographische Wandlungen in der Maremma* (Kiel: Selbstverlag des geographischen Instituts der Universitiit Kiel, 1967).

13 T. Potter, *The Changing Landscape of South Etruria* (New York: St Martin's Press, 1979).

14 The results of this survey have been summarized in S. L. Dyson, 'Settlement Patterns in the Ager Cosanus: The Wesleyan University Survey, 1974–1976,' *Journal of Field Archaeology*, 5 (1978), 251–68; S. L. Dyson, 'Settlement Reconstruction in the Ager Cosanus and the Albegna Valley: Wesleyan University Research, 1974–1979,' in *Archaeology and Italian Society*, ed. by G. Barker and R. Hodges, BAR International Series 102 (Oxford, 1981), 269–74; and S. L. Dyson, 'Survey Archaeology: Reconstructing the Roman Countryside,' *Archaeology*, 34 (1981), 31–37.

15 Plutarch, *Tiberius Gracchus* 8.7; D. B. Nagle, 'The Etruscan Journey of Tiberius Gracchus,' *Historia*, 25 (1976), 487–89.

16 For the recent work on Sette Finestre see A. Carandini and S. Settis, *Schiavi e Padroni nell' Etruria Romana* (Bari: De Donato, 1979). The information on the villa at Le Colonne is based on the Wesleyan University excavations at the site which now is in process of publication.

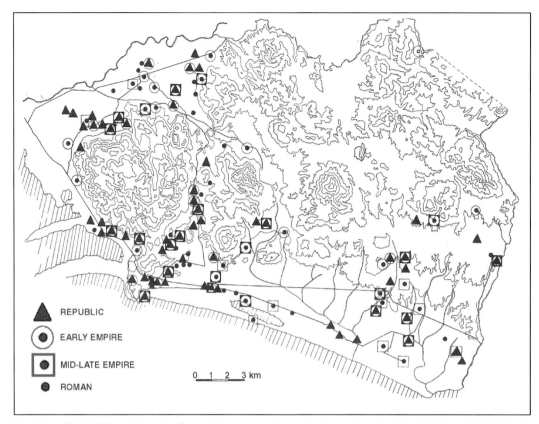

Figure A.3. [Original legend is unclear].

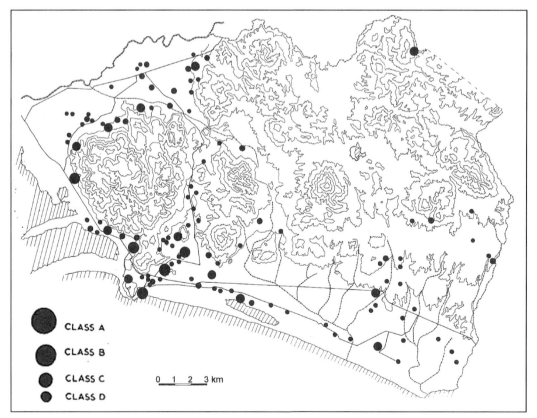

Figure A.4. Variation in Villa Size in the *Ager Cosanus*.

countryside in a period well before barbarian pressures were felt in Italy. One is therefore tempted to look to the spread of malaria as a factor, particularly since all socio-economic groups seem to have joined in the flight.

Survey evidence for the medieval period in the Cosa region is sparse. Almost no true medieval sites were found in the lowland agricultural zones; in the interior, a few ruined early modern farmhouses were discovered. If any deliberate attempt was made to resettle the *Ager Cosanus* in the early medieval period, such as happened around Veii, we have not found the traces.[17] However, the survey did investigate the major standing medieval ruins, most of which are located on hills, well above the zone of cultivation. These sites are usually unploughed and are often covered with thick vegetation that makes normal survey impossible. Nevertheless, since they were an important part of Cosa's settlement history, we felt that our research would not be complete until at least one had been cleared, mapped, and selectively excavated.

The site selected was a hilltop settlement known as Capalbiaccio, in many respects the medieval equivalent of Roman Cosa. Located on a hill 4.5 km. from the sea, at an elevation of 231 m, it commands a view of the coastal plain and two of the larger valleys which lead into the interior. The elevation provided some protection from malaria, while the inland location decreased the danger of sudden pirate raids.

The plan of Capalbiaccio differs from other, smaller castles and watchtowers scattered about the *Ager Cosanus* (Fig. A.5). The outline of the fortification is oval in form, and there is a wall that bisects the enclosed area, which measures roughly 94 × 180 m. Both aerial photographs and detailed ground surveys clearly show that the smaller section contains no internal building, while the larger part is crowded with structures. Thus, Capalbiaccio appears to have been more of a fortified village than a military outpost.[18] The distribution of structural surface remains suggests that a small community permanently inhabited one part of the fortress, while the other section was left free as a place of refuge for men and beasts in times of temporary danger. Subsequent archaeological investigations, however, have shown that the evolution of the settlement and its defence system was far more complex.

Documentary evidence for Capalbiaccio is sparse; the site is mentioned for the first time in 1161. It is tempting to connect its foundation with *incastellamento*, the process of concentrating population in controllable fortified centres known to other areas in medieval Italy.[19]

Our intention was to reconstruct in detail a history of the site and, thus, to illuminate the material aspects of medieval community life in this part of central Italy. Unfortunately, the difficulties of the site, with its heavy cover of underbrush and thick layers of rubble from the fallen walls, and our limited financial resources, forced us during this phase to limit excavation to what seemed key areas.

One puzzling aspect of the fortification system at Capalbiaccio was a break in the central area of the division wall (Fig. A.6). Wall foundations and mounds of earth suggested that there had been a gate in the area which had been levelled when the site was abandoned. However, when this section was excavated, the remains of a small church were discovered. This structure was probably the church S. Frediano, mentioned as being located at Capalbiaccio (Fig. A.7).[20] Although churches built into walls are known from other medieval Italian sites,[21] in this case the church clearly preceded the fortification system, and the building of the wall led to the destruction of the church: foundations of one cross wall were built across the entrance of the church, and in the apse area, the division wall abutted the church apse. Although construction of the division wall clearly came after the building of the church, the next question was whether this was true for the rest of the fortification system.

It was possible that the division wall was a secondary addition to the circuit of walls and that the outer fortifications had been built when Capalbiaccio was first settled. However, careful study of the juncture points of outer fortifications and the division wall shows that they were in fact contemporary: the construction of the walls appeared to postdate the foundation of the settlement. To test further this relation between the fortifications and the buildings within the circuit, we excavated one large building (J on Fig. A.4) which abutted the outer wall in the

---

17   For the resettlement efforts in the area around Veii, see T. Potter, *The Changing Landscape of South Etruria*, 138–67.
18   The best recent study of medieval fortification in central Italy is D. Andrews, 'The Archaeology of the Medieval Castrum in Central Italy,' in *Archaeology and Italian Society*, 313–34. Other useful articles are: A. W. Lawrence, 'Early Medieval Fortifications near Rome,' *Papers of the British School at Rome*, n.s. 19 (1964), 89–122; and D. Andrews, 'Medieval Masonry in Northern Lazio: Its Development and Uses for Dating,' in *Papers in Italian Archaeology*, vol. 1, ed. by H. Mc. Blake, T. W. Potter, and D. B. Whitehouse, BAR International Series 41 (Oxford, 1978), 391–422.

19   See R. Cardarelli 1925, 95 for first references to Capalbiaccio, or Tircoste as it is called in the medieval texts.
20   R. Cardarelli 1925, 96.
21   D. Andrews, 'The Archaeology of the Medieval Castrum in Central Italy,' 318–19.

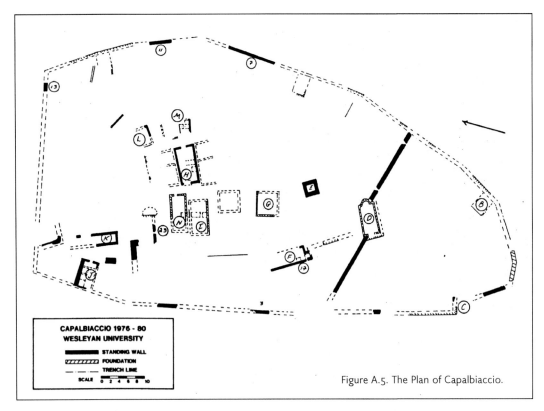

Figure A.5. The Plan of Capalbiaccio.

Figure A.6. Capalbiaccio Church.

northwest area. The soundings showed clearly that the west wall of Building J had been destroyed when the fortifications had been started. Other evidence suggests that the attempt to build the very ambitious defence system represented the very last phase of occupation at Capalbiaccio but that it never completed. Today the outer circuit has a very disjunctive quality: the division wall is preserved to nearly its original height, and certain segments of the outer wall are almost totally intact. These sections are located at key positions around the perimeter of the hill and provide excellent observation points. The parts in between are usually not preserved much above the foundations.

One explanation for this discrepancy, that later inhabitants of the area robbed the stone for building purposes, is insufficient. Between the sixteenth century and the 1950s, few people lived in the area. Since stone is abundant close to the zone of settlement, there is little reason to assume that people went up in great numbers to rob material from Capalbiaccio. A more logical explanation is that the fortification was never finished. The great division wall was complete enough to provide not only a good lookout but also to give the impression, to anyone coming in from the sea or coastal plain, of massive fortification. Other wall sections were constructed at key intervals, but the connecting parts were never completed. Before the possible events behind this aborted fortification scheme are discussed, it seems appropriate to review briefly the history of the earlier unfortified community.

There is no reason to doubt documentary evidence that Capalbiaccio was settled in the twelfth century, although most of the pottery recovered from the excavations dates from the thirteenth through the early sixteenth centuries. The central features of this early community would have been the church and the large keep tower (P on Fig. A.5), the remains of which are still among the most impressive on the site (Fig. A.8). The variety in the construction details of individual buildings suggests a gradual expansion of the community. This reconstruction of a largely open settlement dependent for its protection on the central keep tower, its natural location, and perhaps some ditches and banks not yet discovered, greatly varies from theories of the evolution of fortified settlements in Italy as proposed by such scholars as David Andrews.[22] However, most of the analysis of building typology has been based on examination of standing structures and has not been tested by excavation. Clearly, Capalbiaccio has shown the importance of both archaeological investigation and examination of above-ground features.

The decision to adopt a more ambitious scheme of fortification at Capalbiaccio came relatively late and may have resulted, in part, from a disaster that eliminated the keep tower as a fortification. Large sections of the tower are scattered around the site today, as if thrown down by a very powerful force. An earthquake is the only reasonable cause for such destruction. The Capalbiaccio region is still active geologically and there have been earthquakes in the general area in recent years.[23] The smaller buildings do not show the same degree of destruction, but they could have been repaired more quickly and easily than the tower.

At present we do not have any stratified deposits which allow us to date the construction of the outer walls. We do have a key reference that traces the abandonment of the site to 1417, when the Sienese, who controlled the area by that time, ordered the demolition of Capalbiaccio.[24] Pottery and coins found at the site, however, show that occupation continued until the early sixteenth century. Among the artifacts was a series of coins from Perugia which can be dated to the 1480s. As Capalbiaccio is well removed from Perugia and was historically more dependent on Siena and Rome, the number of Perugian coins is interesting and points to patterns of contact and influence that require more investigation.

Why, then, was the fortification plan abandoned when only partially completed? In part, this was probably due to the widespread abandonment of *castella* in the fifteenth and sixteenth centuries. For Capalbiaccio, the observations of Judith Hook on the changes in Sienese military policy seem relevant.[25] She observes that for such fifteenth- and sixteenth-cen-

Figure A.7. View of Capalbiaccio Church.

Figure A.8. The Keep Tower at Capalbiaccio.

tury city-states as Siena, new and more expensive fortification systems were urgently needed to meet the changes in siege tactics produced by introduction of artillery, at a time when the financial position of these outdated political units was becoming increasingly precarious. Although it is tempting to associate the decision to stop construction of the already-outmoded fortifications of Capalbiaccio to these developments, the decision to leave the site may have had more local causes. Security in the area was not improving, and presumably the problem of malaria was increasing. Cosa was quickly slipping into the wilderness condition described by George Denis in the early nineteenth century.

Before some closing observations, the cycle of settlement at Capalbiaccio, and in the *Ager Cosanus* in general, should be taken back to its Etruscan ori-

---

22 D. Andrews, 'Medieval Masonry in Northern Lazio,' and 'The Archaeology of the Medieval Castrum in Central Italy'.
23 My own hypothesis on an earthquake causing the destruction at Capalbiaccio was supported by on-site studies during the 1980 field season by Professor Jelle de Boer of the Wesleyan Earth and Environmental Sciences Department.
24 R. Cardarelli 1925, 157–59.
25 J. Hook, 'Fortifications and the End of the Sienese State,' *History*, 62 (1977), 372–87.

gins. I have noted above the lack of Etruscan sites in the lowland areas. However, deep soundings in two of the buildings at Capalbiaccio revealed clear traces of an Etruscan occupation, including *bucchero* pottery. At present, we cannot determine how extensive the settlement was, but the findings suggest that we must seek our missing Etruscans on the high places, in sites which were later inhabited during the Middle Ages; this pattern of Iron Age settlement on the heights, a move during the *Pax Romana* down to the more accessible agricultural areas, and then a return during the Middle Ages to the high points, is one that is found elsewhere on sites in Europe.

Here, an effort to profile one small part of the Italian peninsula which played an important role during the Roman Republic and an increasingly marginal one during the Empire and the Middle Ages has been made. For both periods, the reality of settlement history as revealed by archaeology is more complex than the documents suggest. I have also attempted to show the relative value of survey versus excavation in illuminating that history: for the Roman period where the settlement pattern is closely related to areas of modern cultivation, survey is a most effective technique. David Andrews and other scholars working out of the British School at Rome as well as the older topographers such as G. and F. Tomassetti have shown how much is to be learned about the settlement patterns of the Middle Ages from the careful examination and recording of standing monuments. Excavations at sites such as Capalbiaccio show that much is to be learned by selective digging — not only about the material history of a community, but also about its structural evolution.

One final observation about this project is in order, especially in this period of rising costs and limited funding. Any archaeology is expensive relative to other historical investigatory techniques. However, the Wesleyan Cosa project has been run at a minimal cost and, in addition to its research goals, has provided valuable field training for students in archaeology.[26] Emphasis on survey and on carefully-defined excavation goals has kept the cost down. The potential of such projects is, we feel, worth consideration by others interested in investigating the landscape history of Europe and the Mediterranean.

---

26 The survey and excavations were conducted by Wesleyan University, in cooperation with the American Academy in Rome. The surveys were conducted by the author, together with teams of two to five undergraduates. Undergraduates (about fifteen per session) were used to carry out the excavations at Capalbiaccio. Funding came from Wesleyan and in 1978 from the National Endowment for the Humanities. Total annual budget for the project reached $17,000 in the final year.

Works Cited

Abela, Elisabetta. 1993a. 'Ceramica dipinta in rosso (DR)', in *Pisa: Piazza Dante. Uno spaccato della storia pisana: la campagna di scavo 1991*, ed. by Stefano Bruni (Pisa: Cassa di Risparmio di Pisa), pp. 413–18

——. 1993b. 'Ceramica a vetrina pesante. Ceramica a vetrina pesante a macchia', in *Pisa: Piazza Dante. Uno spaccato della storia pisana: la campagna di scavo 1991*, ed. by Stefano Bruni (Pisa: Cassa di Risparmio di Pisa), pp. 419–24

——. 1999. *Archeologia urbana in Toscana: La città altomedievale* (Mantua: SAP)

——. 2000. 'Ceramica dipinta a bande rosse', in *Ricerche di archeologia medievale a Pisa. I. Piazza dei Cavalieri, la campagna di scavo 1993*, ed. by Stefano Bruni, Elisabetta Abela, and Graziella Berti (Florence: All'Insegna del Giglio), pp. 119–21

Abulafia, David. 1974. 'Corneto-Tarquinia and the Italian Mercantile Republics: The Earliest Evidence', *Papers of the British School at Rome*, 42: 224–34

——. 1992. *Frederick II: A Medieval Emperor* (New York: Oxford University Press)

——. 2014. *The Great Sea: A Human History of the Mediterranean* (London: Penguin)

Acconcia, Valeria. 2005. 'Aspetti archeologici e produttivi della Bassa e Media Valle dell'Albegna', in *Dinamiche di sviluppo delle città nell'Etruria meridionale: Veio, Caere, Tarquinia, Vulci: atti del XXIII Convegno di studi etruschi ed italici: Roma, Veio, Cerveteri/Pyrgi, Tarquinia, Tuscania, Vulci, Viterbo, 1–6 ottobre 2001*, ed. by Orazio Paoletti (Pisa: Istituti editoriali e poligrafici internazionali), pp. 603–11

Ademollo, Alfonso. 1881. 'Il lago di Orbetello nelle epoche antiche fino a noi', *L'Ombrone*, 13: 36–41

Alessi, Donatella, Patrizio Bonet, and Paola Spinesi. 1993. 'Vasellame da fuoco privo di rivestimento: forme chiuse', in *Pisa: Piazza Dante. Uno spaccato della storia pisana: la campagna di scavo 1991*, ed. by Stefano Bruni (Pisa: Cassa di Risparmio di Pisa), pp. 427–44

Alföldi, Andreas. 1965. *Early Rome and the Latins* (Ann Arbor: University of Michigan Press)

Allegrezza, Franca. 1998. *Organizzazione del potere e dinamiche familiari. Gli Orsini dal Duecento agli inizi del Quattro-cento* (Rome: Istituto Storico Italiano per il Medio Evo)

Amici, Silvia. 1989. 'I reperti metallici e non metallici delle campagne di scavo 1983–1984', *Archeologia Medievale*, 16: 460–79

Andrews, David. 1977. 'Vetri, metalli e reperti minori dell'area sud del convento di S. Silvestro a Genova', *Archeologia Medievale*, 4: 162–207

——. 1978. 'Medieval Masonry in Northern Lazio: Its Development and Uses for Dating', in *Papers in Italian Archaeology I: The Lancaster Seminar: Recent Research in Prehistoric, Classical and Medieval Archaeology*, ed. by Timothy W. Potter, David Whitehouse, and Hugo Blake (Oxford: British Archaeological Reports), pp. 391–422

——. 1981. 'The Archaeology of the Medieval Castrum in Central Italy', in *Archaeology and Italian Society: Prehistoric, Roman and Medieval Studies*, ed. by Graeme Barker and Richard Hodges (Oxford: British Archaeological Reports), pp. 313–34

——. 2011 'Remembering Medieval Archaeology in Italy in the 1970s', *PCA: Postclassical Archaeologies*, 1: 493–95

Angás Pajas, Jorge. 2005. 'Santuarios como indicadores de frontera en el territorio noroccidental de Vulci (siglos VII–III a.C. Italia centro-Tirrénica)', *Salduie: Estudios de prehistoria y arqueología*, 5: 65–94

Angelucci, Paoloa. 2000. *L'Ardenghesca tra potere signorile e dominio senese, secoli XI–XIV*, XVII (Perugia: Studi e Ricerche)

Angelucci, Valentina and Barbara Bellettini. 2006. *Capalbio. Aspetti della sua storia dal medioevo all'età moderna* (Siena: Betti)

Aniceti, Veronica. 'The Zooarchaeological Analyses from Vetricella (Scarlino, Grosseto): An Overview of Animal Exploitation at the Site', in *The nEU-Med project: Vetricella, an Early Medieval Royal Property on Tuscany's Mediterranean*, ed. by Giovanna Bianchi and Richard Hodges (Florence: All'Insegna del Giglio), pp. 121–28

Antonelli, G. 1870. *Sulle condizioni del lago di Orbetello dall'anno MDCCCLIX all'anno MDCCCLXIX* (Pitigliano: ATLA)

Aprili, Sara. 1999–2000. 'L'abbazia romana di S. Anastasio ad Aquas Salvias e i suoi domini maremmani' (Laurea diss., University of Florence)

Aranguren, B. M. and P. Perazzi. 1995. 'La rupe di Pitigliano (GR): Scavi e ricerche topografiche', in *Preistoria e Protostoria in Etruria: Tipologia delle necropoli e rituali di deposizione. Ricerche e scavi*, ed. by Nuccia Negroni Catacchio (Milan: Centro studi di preistoria e archeologia), pp. 121–24

Arena, Maria Stella and others 2001. *Roma dall'antichità al medioevo. Archeologia e storia nel Museo Nazionale romano Crypta Balbi* (Milan: Electa)

Arslan, Ermanno A. 2011. 'La produzione della moneta nell'Italia ostrogota e longobarda', in *Le zecche italiane fino all'Unità*, ed. by Lucia Travaini (Rome: Istituto poligrafico e zecca dello Stato), pp. 367–413

Arthur, Paul. 1992. 'Amphorae for Bulk Transport', in *Excavations at Otranto*, II: *The Finds*, ed. by Francesco D'Andria and David Whitehouse (Galatina: Congedo), pp. 199–217

——. 1999. 'Riflessioni intorno ad alcune anfore tra la Calabria e la Puglia in età medievale', in *Contenitori da trasporto e da magazzino tra tardo antico e basso medioevo: atti [del] XXX Convegno internazionale della ceramica: Albisola, 16–17–18 maggio 1997* (Albisola: Centro ligure per la storia della ceramica), pp. 9–18

——. 2007a. 'Form, Function and Technology in Pottery Production from Late Antiquity to the Early Middle Ages', in *Technology in Transition A.D. 300–650*, ed. by Luke Lavan, Enrico Zanini, and Alexander Sarantis (Leiden: Brill), pp. 159–86

——. 2007b. 'Pots and Boundaries. On Cultural and Economic Areas between Late Antiquity and the Early Middle Ages', in *LRCW2. Late Roman Coarse Wares, Cooking Wares and Amphorae in the Mediterranean. Archaeology and Archaeometry*, ed. by Michel Bonifay and Jean-Christophe Tréglia (Oxford: Archaeopress), pp. 15–27

Arthur, Paul and Brunella Bruno, eds. 2007. *Muro Leccese. Alla scoperta di una terra medievale* (Lecce: Mario Congedo)

Arthur, Paul and Helen Patterson. 1998. 'Local Pottery in Southern Puglia in the Sixth and Seventh Centuries', in *Ceramica in Italia: VI-VII secolo*, ed. by Lucia Saguì (Florence: All'Insegna del Giglio), pp. 511–30

Ascheri, Mario, ed. 1989. *L'Amiata nel medioevo* (Rome: Viella)

——. ed. 2001. *Siena e Maremma nel Medioevo* (Siena: Betti)

Ascheri, Mario and Lucio Niccolai, eds. 2002. *Gli Aldobrandeschi: La grande famiglia feudale della Maremma toscano* (Santa Fiora: Lions Club International)

Attema, Peter, Albert Nijboer, and Andrea Zifferero. 2005. *Papers in Italian Archaeology*, VI: *Communities and Settlements from the Neolithic to the Early Medieval Period* (Oxford: Archaeopress)

Attolini, Ida. 2002. 'Heba', in Andrea Carandini, Franco Cambi, Mariagrazia Celuzza, and Elizabeth Fentress, *Paesaggi d'Etruria: Valle dell'Albegna, Valle d'Oro, Valle del Chiarone, Valle del Tafone: progetto di ricerca italo-britannico seguito allo scavo di Settefinestre* (Rome: Edizioni di storia e letteratura), pp. 126–29

Attolini, Ida, Franco Cambi, M. Castagna, Mariagrazia Celuzza, Elizabeth Fentress, Philip Perkins, and Edina Regoli. 1991. 'Political Geography and Productive Geography between the Valleys of the Albegna and the Fiora in Northern Etruria', in *Roman Landscapes: Archaeological Survey in the Mediterranean Region*, ed. by Graeme Barker and John A. Lloyd (London: British School at Rome), pp. 142–52

Attolini, Ida, Franco Cambi, Mariagrazia Celuzza, Elizabeth Fentress, Maria Letizia Gualandi, Marinella Pasquinucci, Edina Regoli, A. Ricci, and Lucy Walker. 1983. 'Ricognizione nell'Ager Cosanus e nella valle dell'Albegna. Rapporto preliminare 1982/83', *Archeologia Medievale*, 10: 439–65

Attolini, Ida, Franco Cambi, Mariagrazia Celuzza, Elizabeth Fentress, Marinella Pasquinucci, and Edina Regoli. 1982. 'Ricognizione archeologica nell'Ager Cosanus e nella valle dell'Albegna. Rapporto preliminare 1981', *Archeologia Medievale*, 9: 365–85

Augenti, Andrea. 1998a. Introduction to *Continuity and Discontinuity from Late Antiquity to the Early Middle Ages in Europe and Across the Mediterranean Basin*, ed. by Mark Pearce and Maurizio Tosi (Oxford: Archaeopress)

——. 1998b. 'Continuity and Discontinuity from Late Antiquity to the Early Middle Ages in Europe and across the Mediterranean Basin', in *Papers from the EAA Third Annual Meeting at Ravenna 1997*, II: *Classical and Medieval*, ed. by Mark Pearce and Maurizio Tosi (Oxford: Archaeopress, 1998), pp. 88–90

——. 2000. 'Dai Castra tardoantica ai castelli del X secolo: Il caso della Toscana', in *La Roccaccia di Selvena. Rapporto preliminare degli scavi e della ricognizione archeologica 1999*, ed. by Riccardo Francovich (Florence: All'Insegna del Giglio), pp. 25–66

——. 2010. *Città e Porti dall'Antichità al Medioevo* (Rome: Carocci)

——. ed. 2011. *Classe. Indagini sul potenziale archeologico di una città scomparsa* (Bologna: Ante Quem)

Augenti, Andrea and others 1997. 'L'atlante informatizzato dei siti fortificati d'altura della Toscana: Un progetto in corso di svolgimento', in *Sistemi informativi e reti geografiche in archeologia: GIS-INTERNET*, ed. by Antonio Gottarelli (Florence: All'Insegna del Giglio), pp. 89–111

Baccarini, Alfredo. 1873. *Sul compimento delle opere di bonificazione e sulla definitiva regolazione delle acque nella Maremma Toscana* (Rome: n.p.)

Baglioni, Astorre. 1984. *Mi chiamo Enrico Stoppa: Il brigante di Talamone dai documenti autentici* (Pitigliano: Azienda tipolitografica)

Baker, Polydora and Gillian Clark. 1993. 'Archaeozoological Evidence for Medieval Italy: A Critical Review of the Present State of Research', *Archeologia Medievale*, 20: 45–78

Bakirtzis, Charalambos. 1989. 'Byzantine Amphorae', in *Recherches sur la céramique byzantine*, ed. by Vincent Déroche and Jean-Michel Spieser (Athens: EFA), pp. 73–77

Baldassarri, Monica. 2009. 'I denari della zecca di Genova e i loro frazionari tra il XII e il XIV secolo: Alcune osservazioni su datazioni, seriazioni ed ambiti di circolazione', *Numismatica e Antichità classiche. Quaderni ticinesi*, 38: 331–71

——. 2010. *Zecca e monete del Comune di Pisa. Dalle origini alla Seconda repubblica, XII secolo-1406* (Ghezzano: Felici Editore)

———. 2011. 'L'uso della moneta in Lunigiana tra X e XIV secolo ed il problema dei denari imperiali di Luni', *Numismatica e Antichità Classiche. Quaderni ticinesi*, 40: 347–83

Baldassarri, Monica and Marco Milanese. 2004. *Archeologia in Chinzica: insediamento e fonti materiali (secoli XI–XIX) dagli scavi nell'area di Santa Cristina in Pisa* (Pisa: Plus)

Bandini, Francesca, Cristina Cicali, and Cristina Felici. 1996. 'Manufatti in metallo', in *Poggio Imperiale a Poggibonsi: dal villaggio di capanne al castello di pietra*, ed. by Marco Valenti (Florence: All'Insegna del Giglio), pp. 327–36

Banti, Luisa. 1973. *The Etruscan Cities and Their Culture* (London: Batsford)

Barclay Lloyd, Joan. 1997. 'The Medieval Murals in the Cistercian Abbey of Santi Vincenzo and Anastasio ad aquas salvias at the Tre Fontane, Rome in their Architectural Settings', *Papers of the British School at Rome*, 45: 287–348

———. 2006. *SS. Vincenzo e Anastasio at Tre Funtane Near Rome: History and Architecture of a Medieval Cistercian Abbey* (Kalamazoo: Cistercian Publications)

Barker, Graeme. 1973. 'The Economy of Medieval Tuscania: The Archaeological Evidence', *Papers of the British School at Rome*, 41: 155–77

———. 1978. 'Dry Bones? Economic Studies and Historical Archaeology in Italy', in *Papers in Italian Archaeology*, 1: *The Lancaster Seminar: Recent Research in Prehistoric, Classical and Medieval Archaeology*, ed. by Timothy W. Potter, David Whitehouse, and Hugo Blake (Oxford: British Archaeological Reports), pp. 35–49

———. 1995. *A Mediterranean Valley: Landscape Archaeology and the Annales History in the Biferno Valley* (London: Leicester University Press)

Barker, Graeme and Tom Rasmussen. 1998. *The Etruscans* (Oxford: Wiley-Blackwell)

Baroncelli, A. 1996. 'Ceramica acroma grezza. Le olle', in *Studi sul territorio di Populonia: In memoria di Antonio Minto* ed. by G. Capecchi and A. Romualdi (Florence: All'Insegna del Giglio), pp. 475–84

Barsanti, Danilo. 1980. 'Caratteri e problemi della bonifica maremmana da Pietro Leopoldo al Governo Provvisorio Toscano', in *Agricoltura e Società nella Maremma grossetana del'800*, ed. by Giovanni Spadolini (Florence: Olschki), pp. 39–64

———. 1987. *Allevamento e Transumanza in Toscana, pastori, bestiami e pascoli nei secoli XV–XIX* (Florence: Medicea)

Barsanti, Danilo and Leonardo Rombai. 1986. *La "Guerra delle acque" in Toscana: Storia delle bonifiche dai Medici alla riforma agraria* (Florence: Medicea)

Bartoloni, Gilda. 1972. *Le tombe da Poggio Buco nel Museo Archeologico di Firenze* (Florence: Olschki)

———. 1995. 'La rioccupazione della Rocca di Pitigliano', in *Preistoria e Protostoria in Etruria: Tipologia delle necropoli e rituali di deposizione. Ricerche e scavi*, ed. by Nuccia Negroni Catacchio (Milan: Centro studi di preistoria e archeologia), pp. 129–30

Bartoloni, Valeria and Marco Ricci. 1995. 'Produzioni ceramiche da un contesto dei secoli XI–XII a Tarquinia', in *Le ceramiche di Roma e del Lazio in età medievale e moderna, II*, ed. by Elisabetta De Minicis (Rome: Kappa), pp. 100–06

Basile, Laura, Francesca Grassi, Elena Basso, and Maria Pia Riccardi. 2010. 'Gli scarichi di fornace di Roccastrada (GR): nuove analisi tipologiche e archeometriche;, in *LRCW3. Late Roman Coarse Wares, Cooking Wares and Amphorae in the Mediterranean. Archaeology and Archaeometry. Comparison between Western and Eastern Mediterranean*, ed. by Simonetta Menchelli, Sara Santoro, Marinella Pasquinucci, and Gabriella Guiducci (Oxford: Archaeopress), pp. 387–91

Becker, Hillary W. 2006. 'The Etruscan *Castellum*: Fortified Settlements and Regional Autonomy in Etruria', *Etruscan Studies*, 9.1: 85–96

Becker, Helmut and Jorg W. E. Fassbinder. 2001. *Magnetic Prospecting in Archaeological Sites*, Monuments and Sites, 6 (Paris: International Council on Monuments and Sites)

Bedini, E. 1995. 'I reperti faunistici del Castello di Manzano (XI–XIII secc.)', *Padusa Quaderni*, 1: 341–47

Beex, Willem. 2004. 'Use and Abuse of Digital Terrain/Elevation Models', in *Enter the Past: The E-Way Into the Four Dimensions of Cultural Heritage: CAA 2003, Computer Applications and Quantitative Methods in Archaeology: Proceedings of the 31st Conference, Vienna, Austria, April 2003*, ed. by K. F. Ausserer, W. Börner, M. Goriany, and L. Karlhuber-Vöckl (Oxford: Archaeopress), pp. 240–42

Belelli Marchesini, Barbara. 2013. 'Considerazioni sull'abitato etrusco di Pyrgi', in *Riflessioni su Pyrgi. Scavi e ricerche nelle aree del santuario*, ed. by Maria Paola Baglione and Maria Donatella Gentili (Rome: L'Erma di Bretschneider), pp. 245–60

Belelli Marchesini, Barbara, Laura Ambrosini, Gabriele Colantoni, B. Giuliani, M. R. Lucidi, and M. Merlo. 2009. 'Il contributo degli scavi di Piano di Comunità alla conoscenza dell'abitato di Veio: materiali dal riempimento di un pozzo sul pianoro sommitale', in *L'Abitato etrusco di Veio: Ricerche dell'Università di Roma La Sapienza*, ed. by Gilda Bartoloni (Rome: IUNO), pp. 66–123

Bellesia, Lorenzo. 2007. *Lucca. Storia e monete* (Serravalle: Nomisma)

Belli, Maddalena. 1997–1998. 'I reperti metallici provenienti dal castello di San Silvestro' (Laurea diss., University of Siena)

———. 2000a. 'I metalli', in *Archeologia e storia di un castello apuano*, ed. by Juan Antonio Quirós Castillo (Florence: All'Insegna del Giglio), pp. 140–46

——. 2000b. 'I reperti metallici', in *Archeologia a Montemassi: Un castello fra storia e storia dell'arte*, ed. by Silvia Guideri, Roberto Parenti, and Francesco Barbagli (Florence: All'Insegna del Giglio), pp. 211–15

——. 2003. 'I metalli', in Giovanna Bianchi, *Campiglia: Un castello e il suo territorio* (Florence: All'Insegna del Giglio), pp. 414–37

——. 2004. 'Gli oggetti in metallo: Indizi per l'analisi funzionale degli spazi', in Giovanna Bianchi, *Castello di Donoratico: i risultati delle prime campagne di scavo, 2000-2002* (Florence: All'Insegna del Giglio), pp. 99–114

Belli, Maddalena and L. Dallai, eds. 2005. *Archeologia di un castello minerario: Il sito di Cugnano, Monterotondo M.mo (Gr)* (Florence: All'Insegna del Giglio)

Bergdolt, Klaus. 1997. *La peste nera e la fine del Medioevo* (Milan: Piemme)

Bergonzi, Giovanna and Gabriele Cateni. 1979. 'L'età del bronzo finale nella Toscana Marittima', *Istituto italiano di preistoria e protostoria; atti della riunione scientifica*, 21: 249–65

Bernardi, Manuela, Laura Cappelli, and Francesco Cuteri. 1992. 'Ceramiche a vetrina pesante e a vetrina sparsa in Toscana. Il caso degli insediamenti di Scarlino (GR) e Rocca San Silvestro (LI)', in *La ceramica invetriata tardoantica e altomedievale in Italia*, ed. by Lidia Paroli (Florence: All'Insegna del Giglio), pp. 295–302

Bernardini, Chiara. 2009. 'Il sito etrusco', in *Dieci anni di ricerche a Castel di Pietra. Edizione degli scavi 1997-2007*, ed. by Carlo Citter (Florence: All'Insegna del Giglio), pp. 81–98

Bernocchi, Mario. 1974–1986. *Le monete della Repubblica fiorentina*, I–V (Florence: Olschki)

Berti, Graziella. 1993. 'Pisa: Dalle importazioni islamiche alle produzioni locali di ceramiche con rivestimenti vetrificati (seconda metà X–prima metà XVII secolo)', in *Pisa: Piazza Dante. Uno spaccato della storia pisana: la campagna di scavo 1991*, ed. by Stefano Bruni (Pisa: Cassa di Risparmio di Pisa), pp. 119–46

——. 1997. *Pisa. Le "Maioliche Arcaiche." Secc. XIII–XV. (Museo Nazionale di San Matteo)* (Florence: All'Insegno del Giglio)

——. 2003. 'Pisa città mediterranea. La testimonianza delle ceramiche importate ed esportate', in *Pisa e il Mediterraneo. Uomini, merci, idee dagli Etruschi ai Medici* (Milan: Skira), pp. 169–74

——. 2005. *Pisa. Le ceramiche ingobbiate "graffite a stecca." Secc. XV–XVII (Museo Nazionale di San Matteo)* (Florence: All'Insegna del Giglio)

Berti, Graziella and Giovanna Bianchi. 2007. *Piombino. La chiesa di Sant'Antimo sopra i canali. Ceramiche e architetture per la lettura archeologica di un abitato medievale e del suo porto* (Florence: All'Insegna del Giglio)

Berti, Graziella, Laura Cappelli, and Giulio Ciampoltrini. 1992. 'Ceramiche a vetrina pesante e a vetrina sparsa a Lucca e in alcuni insediamenti del territorio', in *La ceramica invetriata tardoantica e altomedievale in Italia*, ed. by Lidia Paroli (Florence: All'Insegna del Giglio), pp. 279–94

Berti, Graziella, Laura Cappelli, and Riccardo Francovich. 1986. 'La maiolica arcaica in Toscana', in *La cermica del mediterrano occidentale. Atti del convegno, Siena-Faenza, Ottobre 1984* (Florence: All'Insegna del Giglio), pp. 483–511

Berti, Graziella and Sauro Gelichi. 1995. 'Le "anforette" pisane: Note su un contenitore in ceramic tardo-medievale', *Archeologia Medievale*, 22: 191–240

Berti, Graziella, Sauro Gelichi, and Tiziano Mannoni. 1997. 'Trasformazioni tecnologiche nelle prime produzioni italiane con rivestimenti vetrificati (secc. XII–XIII)', in *La céramique médiévale en Méditerranée (Actes du VIe Congrès de l'AIECM2 – Aix-en-Provence 13–18 novembre 1995)*, ed. by Gabrielle Démians d'Archimbaud and Maurice Picon (Aix-en-Provence: Narration Éditions Aubenas d'Ardeche), pp. 383–403

Berti, Graziella and Marcella Giorgio. 2011. *Ceramiche con coperture verificate usate come "bacini." Importazioni a Pisa e in altri centri della Toscana tra fine X e XIII secolo* (Florence: All'Insegna del Giglio)

Berti, Graziella, and Simonetta Menchelli. 1998. 'Pisa, Ceramiche da cucina, da dispensa, da trasporto dei secoli X–XV', *Archeologia Medievale*, 25: 307–33

Berti, Graziella, Catia Renzi Rizzo, and Marco Tangheroni. 2004. *Il mare, la terra, il ferro: Ricerche su Pisa medievale (secoli VII–XIII)* (Ospedaletto, Pisa: Pacini)

Berti, Graziella and Ezio Tongiorgi. 1985. *Ceramiche importate dalla Spagna nell'area pisana dal 12. al 15. Secolo* (Florence: All'Insegna del Giglio)

Berti, Graziella and Paola Torre. 1983. *Arte islamica in Italia: I bacini delle chiese pisane: 26 maggio–25 settembre 1983* (Rome: Palazzo Brancaccio)

Biagini, Marco. 1998. 'Reperti metallici (Me)', in *Filattiera-Sorano: L'insediamento di età romana e tardo antica. Scavi 1986–1995*, ed. by Enrico Giannichedda (Florence: All'Insegna del Giglio), pp. 173–83

Bianchi Bandinelli, Ranuccio. 1976. *Dal diario di un borghese* (Rome: Editori Riuniti)

Bianchi, Giovanna. 1996. 'Trasmissione dei saperi tecnici e analisi dei procedimenti costruttivi di età medievale'. *Archeologia dell'Architettura*, 1: 53–64

——. 2003a. 'Archeologia dell'Architettura e forme di potere tra XI e XV secolo nella Toscana sud-occidentale: il caso di Campiglia Marittima (LI)' (Unpubl. PhD thesis, University of Siena)

———. 2003b. 'Archeologia dell'Architettura nei castelli della Toscana sud-occidentale (Val di Cornia-Bassa Val di Cecina secc. IX–XII)', in *III Congresso nazionale di archeologia medievale: Castello di Salerno, Complesso di Santa Sofia, Salerno, 2–5 ottobre 2003*, ed. by Rosa Fiorillo and Paolo Peduto (Florence: All'Insegna del Giglio), pp. 567–75

———. 2003c. *Campiglia: Un castello e il suo territorio* (Florence: All'Insegna del Giglio)

———. 2003d. 'Costruire un castello, costruire un monastero. Committenze e maestranze nell'alta Maremma tra X ed XI secolo attraverso l'archeologia dell'architettura', in *Monasteri e Castelli tra X e XII secolo. Il caso di S. Michele alla Verruca e le altre ricerche storico-archeologiche nella Tuscia occidentale*, ed. by Riccardo Francovich and Sauro Gelichi (Florence: All'Insegna del Giglio), pp. 143–58

———. 2004. *Castello di Donoratico: I risultati delle prime campagne di scavo, 2000–2002* (Florence: All'Insegna del Giglio)

———. ed. 2008. *Guida all'archeologia medievale della provincia di Livorno* (Livorno: Provincia di Livorno)

———. 2010. 'Dominare e gestire un territorio. Ascesa e sviluppo delle "signore forti" nella Maremma toscana centrosettentrionale', *Archeologia Medievale*, 37: 93–104

———. 2012. 'Building, Inhabiting and "Perceiving" Private Houses in Early Medieval Italy', *Arqueología de la Arquitectura*, 9 (January – December 2012): 195–212

Bianchi, Giovanna, Enrica Boldrini, and Daniele De Luca. 1994. 'Indagine archeologica a Rocchette Pannocchieschi (GR). Rapporto preliminare', *Archeologia Medievale*, 21: 251–68

Bianchi, Giovanna, Jacopo Bruttini, and Luisa Dallai. 2011. 'Sfruttamento e ciclo produttivo dell'allume e dell'argento nel territorio delle Colline Metallifere grossetane', in *Risorse naturali e attività produttive: Ferento a confronto con alre realtà, 27–28 aprile 2010. Atti del II Convegno di studi in ricordo di Gabriella Maetzke*, ed. by Elisabetta De Minicis and Carlo Pavolini (Viterbo: Università degli studi della Tuscia), pp. 249–82

Bianchi, Giovanna, Giuseppe Fichera, and Maria Francesca Paris. 2009. 'Rappresentazione ed esercizio dei poteri signorili di XII secolo nella Toscana meridionale attraverso le evidenze archeologiche', in *V Congresso Nazionale di Archeologia Medievale*, ed. by Giuliano Volpe and Pasquale Favia (Florence: All'Insegna del Giglio), pp. 412–16

Bianchi, Giovanna and Francesca Grassi. 2013. 'Sistemi di stoccaggio nelle campagne Italiane (secc. VII–XIII): l'evidenza archeologica dal caso di Rocca degli Alberti in Toscana', in *Horrea, Barns and Silos. Storage and Incomes in Early Medieval Europe*, ed. by Alfonso Vigil-Escalera Guirado, Giovanna Bianchi, and Juan Antonio Quirós Castillo (Bilbao: Universidad del País Vasco), pp. 77–102

Bianchi, Giovanna and Richard Hodges, eds. 2018. *Origins of a New Economic Union (7th–12th Centuries): Preliminary Results of the nEU-Med Project; October 2015–March 2017* (Florence: All'Insegna del Giglio)

———. eds. 2020. *The nEU-Med project: Vetricella, an Early Medieval Royal Property on Tuscany's Mediterranean* (Florence: All'Insegna del Giglio)

Bianchi, S. 1996. 'Tegami in ceramica grezza', in *Studi sul territorio di Populonia: in memoria di Antonio Minto*, ed. by G. Capecchi and A. Romualdi (Florence: All'Insegna del Giglio), pp. 460–75

Biancifiori, Elisa, Carmen Columba Carraro, Livia Gabbrielli, Chiara Mottolese, Veronica Re, Donata Sarracino, and Maria Taloni. 2010. 'Lo scavo delle pendici sud-orientali del Poggio del Telegrafo (PdT): L'avvio della romanizzazione di Populonia', in *Materiali per Populonia*, IX, ed. by Giorgio Baratti and Fabio Fabiani (Pisa: ETS) pp. 26–60

Bierbrauer, Volker. 1994. 'Archeologia e storia dei Goti dal I al IV secolo', in *I Goti, Catalogo Mostra Milano, 28 gennaio–8 maggio 1994* (Milan: Electa Lombardia)

Bietti Sestieri, Anna Maria 1985. 'Ripostiglio di Bronzi da Campese, Isola del Giglio', in *Civiltà degli Etruschi*, ed. by Mauro Cristofani (Florence: Regione toscana), p. 42

Bignamini, Ilaria and Clare Hornsby. 2010. *Digging and Dealing in Eighteenth-Century Rome* (New Haven: Yale University Press)

Biondi, Angelo. 2002. 'Il lungo feudalesimo di un territorio di confine', in *Sorano: Storia di una comunità*, ed. by Zeffiro Ciuffoletti (Florence: Centro editoriale toscano), pp. 81–181

Blake, Hugo. 2011. 'Professionalizzazione e frammentazione: Hugo Blake ricorda l'archeologia medievale nel lungo decennio 1969–81', *Post-Classical Archaeologies*, 1: 452–80

Bloch, Herbert. 1993. 'The Inscription of the Bronze Doors of Monte Cassino: A Contribution of Classical Archaeology to Medieval Studies', *Studies in the History of Art*, 43: 446–62

Bocci, P. 1961. 'Marsiliana', *Enciclopedia dell'arte antica, classica e orientale* (Rome: Istituto della enciclopedia italiana)

———. 1978. *Roselle. Gli scavi e la mostra* (Pisa: Pacini)

Boessneck, J. 1969. 'Osteological Differences between Sheep (*Ovis aries* Linné) and Goat (*Capra hircus* Linné)', in *Science in Archaeology*, ed. by Don R. Brothwell and E. S. Higgs, 2nd edn (London: Thames and Hudson), pp. 331–58

Bojani, Gian Carlo, ed. 1992. *Ceramica fra Marche e Umbria dal Medioevo al Rinascimento* (Faenza: Publialfa)

Boldrini, Enrica and Francesca Grassi. 1997. 'Ceramiche grezze e depurate tra XII e XIII secolo a Rocca san Silvestro: dati preliminari', in *I Congresso nazionale di archeologia medievale: Auditorium del Centro Studi della Cassa di Risparmio di Pisa (ex Benedettine) Pisa, 29–31 maggio 1997*, ed. by Sauro Gelichi (Florence: All'Insegna del Giglio), pp. 352–58

———. 2000. 'I reperti ceramici', in *Archeologia a Montemassi: Un castello fra storia e storia dell'arte*, ed. by Silvia Guideri, Roberto Parenti, and Francesco Barbagli (Florence: All'Insegna del Giglio), pp. 191–206

Boldrini, Enrica, Francesca Grassi, and Alessandra Molinari. 1997. 'La circolazione ed il consumo di ceramiche fini rivestite nell'area tirrenica tra XII e XIII secolo: il caso di Rocca San Silvestro', *Archaeologia Medievale*, 24: 101–27

Boldrini, Enrica and others 2003. 'I reperti ceramici', in *Campiglia: un castello e il suo territorio*, ed. by Giovanna Bianchi (Florence: All'Insegna del Giglio), pp. 275–361

Bonelli, Conenna L. 1980. 'Cenni sulle comunità del contado senese dopo la conquista medicea', in *I Medici e lo Stato Senese*, ed. by Leonardo Rombai (Rome: De Luca), pp. 225–37

Bonghi Jovino, Maria. 2005. 'Città e territorio. Veio, Caere, Tarquinia, Vulci: appunti e riconsiderazioni', in *Dinamiche di sviluppo delle città nell'Etruria meridionale: Veio, Caere, Tarquinia, Vulci: atti del XXIII Convegno di studi etruschi ed italici: Roma, Veio, Cerveteri/Pyrgi, Tarquinia, Tuscania, Vulci, Viterbo, 1–6 ottobre 2001*, ed. by Giulio Paoletti (Pisa: Istituti editoriali e poligrafici internazionali)

Bonomi Ponzi, Laura, and Otto von Hessen. 1997. 'Catalogo', in *Umbria Longobarda. La necropoli di Nocera Umbra nel centenario della scoperta*, ed. by Lidia Paroli (Rome: Edizioni De Luca), pp. 177–99

Boschi, Enzo and others 1997. *Catalogo dei forti terremoti in Italia dal 461 a.C. al 1990* (Rome: Istituto Nazionale di Geofisica)

Boschian, Giovanni, Alessandro Bossio, Barbara Dall'Antonia, and Renzo Mazzanti. 2006. 'Il Quaternario della Toscana Costiera', *Studi Costieri*, 12: 77–187

Botarelli, Lucia, ed. 2005. *Carta archeologica della Provincia di Siena*, VII: *Radicofani* (Siena: Nuova Immagine)

Bourdin, Stéphane. 2012. *Les peuples de l'Italie préromaine: Identités, territoires et relations inter-ethniques en Italie centrale et septentrionale (VIIIe-Ier s. av. J.-C.)* (Rome: École française de Rome)

Bowes, Kimberly and others 2017. 'Peasant Agricultural Strategies in Southern Tuscany: Convertible Agriculture and the Importance of Pasture', in *The Economic Integration of Roman Italy: Rural Communities in a Globalizing World*, ed. by Tymon C. A. de Haas and Gijs W. Tol (Leiden: Brill), pp. 170–99

Bowes, Kimberly Diane, Karen Francis, and Richard Hodges. 2006. *Between Text and Territory: Survey and Excavations in the Terra of San Vincenzo al Volturno* (London: British School at Rome)

Briano, Arianna. 2020. *La ceramica a vetrina sparsa nella Toscana altomedievale. Produzione, cronologia e distribuzione* (Florence: All'Insegna del Giglio)

Brogiolo, Gian Pietro. 1996. 'Prospettive per l'archeologia dell'architettura', *Archeologia dell'Architettura*, 1: 11–16

———. 1997. 'Dall'analisi stratigrafica degli elevati all'archeologia dell'Architettura', *Archeologia dell'Architettura*, 2: 181–84

———. 1999. *S. Giulia di Brescia. Gli scavi dal 1980 al 1992. Reperti preromani, romani e alto medievali* (Florence: All'Insegna del Giglio)

———. 2001. *Archeologia a Monte Barro*, II: *Gli scavi 1990–97 e le ricerche al S. Martino di Lecco* (Lecco: Stefanoni)

———. 2002. 'L'Archeologia dell'Architettura in Italia nell'ultimo quinquennio (1997–2001)', *Arqueología de la Arquitectura*, 1: 16–26

———. 2011. *Le origini della città medievale* (Mantova: S.A.P.)

Brogiolo, Gian Pietro, Andrea Zonca, and Luca Zigrino. 1988. *Archeologia dell'edilizia storica: Documenti e metodi* (Como: New Press)

Bronson, Richard C., and Giovanni Uggeri. 1970. 'Isola del Giglio, Giannutri, Monte Argentario, Laguna di Orbetello (notizia preliminare dei rinvenimenti del 1968)', *Studi Etruschi*, 38: 201–14

Brothwell, Don R., and Eric S. Higgs, eds. 1969. *Science in Archaeology*, 2nd edn (London: Thames and Hudson)

Brown, Frank Edward. 1951. *Cosa I. History and Topography* (Rome: American Academy in Rome)

———. 1967. 'Scavi a Cosa/Ansedonia 1965–66', *Bollettino d'Arte*, 52: 37

———. 1980. *Cosa: The Making of a Roman Town* (Ann Arbor: University of Michigan Press)

———. 1984. 'The Northwest Gate of Cosa and its Environs (1972–1976)', in *Studi di Antichita in onore di G. Maetzke*, III, ed. by Maria Grazia Marzi Costagli and Luisa Tamagno Perna (Rome: L'Erma di Bretschneider), pp. 493–98

Bruni, Stefano, ed. 1993. *Pisa: Piazza Dante. Uno spaccato della storia pisana: la campagna di scavo 1991* (Pisa: Cassa di Risparmio di Pisa)

Bruni, Stefano, Elisabetta Abela, and Graziella Berti. 2000. *Ricerche di archeologia medievale a Pisa*, 1: *Piazza dei Cavalieri, la campagna di scavo 1993* (Florence: All'Insegna del Giglio)

Bruno, Vincent J. and Russell T. Scott. 1993. 'Cosa IV. The Houses', *Memoirs of the American Academy in Rome* 38.

Bruttini, Jacopo. 2007. 'Il castello di Cugnano (Monterotondo M.mo, Gr)', *Notiziario della Soprintendenza Archeologica della Toscana*, 2: 493–98

———. 2008. 'Ecclesia infra castellum de Montemasso constructa: la chiesa di S. Maria, S. Andrea e S. Genziano a Montemassi', in *Chiese e insediamenti nei secoli di formazione dei paesaggi medievali della Toscana (V–X secolo): atti del seminario, San Giovanni d'Asso-Montisi, 10–11 novembre 2006*, ed. by Stefano Campana (Florence: All'Insegna del Giglio), pp. 221–34

——. 2013. *Archeologia Urbana a Firenze. Lo scavo della terza corte di Palazzo Vecchio (indagini 1997–2006)* (Florence: All'Insegna del Giglio)

Bruttini, Jacopo and Francesca Grassi. 2010. 'Il castello di Cugnano (Monterotondo M.mo, GR)', *Notiziario della Soprintendenza Archeologica della Toscana*, 6: 419–23

Buonincontri, Mauro Paolo, Alessandra Pecci, Giuseppe Di Pasquale, Paula Ricci, and Carmine Lubritto. 2017. 'Multiproxy Approach to the Study of Medieval Food Habits in Tuscany (Central Italy)', *Archaeological and Anthropological Sciences*, 9.4: 653–67

Buttrey, Theodore V. 1980. 'Cosa: The Coins', *Memoirs of the American Academy in Rome*, 34: 11–153

——. 2003. 'The Greek and Roman Coins', in *Cosa V: An Intermittent Town, Excavations 1991–1997*, ed. by Elizabeth Fentress (Ann Arbor: University of Michigan), pp. 250–59

Cagnana, Aurora. 1994. 'Considerazione sulle strutture abitative liguri tra VI e XIII secolo', in *Edilizia residenziale tra V e VIII secolo: 4. Seminario sul tardoantico e l'altomedioevo in Italia centrosettentrionale, Monte Barro-Galbiate (Lecco) 2–4 settembre 1993*, ed. by Gian Pietro Brogiolo (Mantua: Società Archeologica Padana), pp. 169–77

——. 2000. *Archeologia dei materiali da costruzione* (Mantua: SAP)

Calamandrei, Duccio, Andrea Camilli, Fernanda Cavari, Silvia Pallecchi, Alessandra Pecci, Elena Santoro, Carmine Sanchirico, Giulia Tofani, and Andrea Zifferero. 2011. 'Etruschi nelle terre del principe', *Archeo*, 26: 54–71

Calastri, Claudio. 2007. 'Acquedotti romani della Valle d'Oro (Cosa-Ansedonia, Gr)', *Ocnus*, 15: 45–56

Cambi, Franco. 1986. 'L'archeologia di uno spazio geografico: il progetto topografico *Ager Cosanus*-valle dell'Albegna', *Archeologia Medievale*, 13: 527–44

——. 1989. 'Carte Diacroniche degli Insediamenti: alcuni esempi', in *La cartografia Archeologica. Problemi e Prospettive: Atti Del Convegno Internazionale, Pisa, 21–22 marzo 1988*, ed. by M. Pascquinucci and S. Menchelli (Pisa: Amministrazione provinciale di Pisa), pp. 217–38

——. ed. 2012. *Il ruolo degli oppida e la difesa del territorio in Etruria: Casi di studio e prospettiva di ricerca* (Trento: Tangram Edizioni Scientifiche)

Cambi, Franco, Fernanda Cavari, and Cynthia Mascione. 2009. *Materiali da costruzione e produzione del ferro: Studi sull'economia populoniese fra periodo etrusco e romanizzazione* (Bari: Edipuglia)

Cambi, Franco and Mariagrazia Celuzza. 1985. 'La centuriazione, la viabilità e gli insediamenti', in *La romanizzazione dell'Etruria: Il territorio di Vulci*, ed. by Andrea Carandini (Florence: Regione Toscana; Milan: Electa), pp. 104–06

Cambi, Franco, and Elizabeth Fentress. 1988. 'Il progetto topografico Ager Cosanus–Valle dell'Albegna', in *Structures de l'habitat et occupation du sol dans les pays méditerranéens: les méthodes et l'apport de l'Archéologie extensive. Atti del convegno, l'École française de Rome, Paris 1984* (Rome: École française de Rome), pp. 165–79

Cambi, Franco, and Elizabeth Fentress. 1989. 'Villas to Castles: First Millennium AD Demography in the Albegna Valley', in *The Birth of Europe: Archaeology and Social Development in the First Millennium AD*, ed. by K. Randsborg (Rome: L'Erma di Bretschneider), pp. 74–86

Cambi, Franco and Nicola Terrenato. 1994. *Introduzione all'archeologia dei paesaggi* (Rome: Nuova Italia scientifica)

Camilli, Andrea, and M. Letizia Gualandi, eds. 2005. *Materiali per Populonia*, IV (Florence: All'Insegna del Giglio)

Cambi, Franco and others 1994. 'Etruria, Tuscia, Toscana: la formazione dei paesaggi altomedievali', in *La storia dell'alto Medioevo italiano (VI–X secolo) alla luce dell'archeologia: Convegno internazionale (Siena, 2–6 dicembre 1992*, ed. by Riccardo Francovich and Ghislaine Noyé (Florence: All'Insegna del Giglio), pp. 183–215

Camilli, Andrea and others. 2008. 'Manciano (Gr). Marsiliana d'Albegna: Nuovi dati dall'abitato e dal suburbio', *Notiziario della Soprintendenza per i Beni Archeologici della Toscana*, 4: 352–76

Cammarosano, Paolo. 1979. 'Le campagne senesi dalla fine del secolo XII agli inizi del trecento: Dinamica interna e forme del dominio cittadino', in *Contadini e proprietari nella Toscana moderna: atti del Convegno di studi in onore di Giorgio Giorgetti*, ed. by Giovanni Cherubini (Florence: Olschki), pp. 158–222

Cammarosano, Paolo, and Vincenzo Passeri. 1984. *Città, borghi e castelli dell'area senese-grossetana* (Siena: Amministrazione Provinciale di Siena, Assessorato Istruzione e Cultura)

——. 1985. 'Repertorio', in *I castelli del senese. Strutture fortificate dell'area senese-grossetana*, ed. by Anna Della Valle (Milan: Electa), p. 28

——. 2006. *I castelli del senese: strutture fortificate dell'area senese-grossetana* (Siena: Nuova immagine)

Campana, Stefano, ed. 2001. *Carta archeologica della Provincia di Siena*, V: *Murlo* (Siena: Nuova imagine)

——. 2004. 'Ricognizione archeologica nel territorio comunale di Montalcino: campagne 1999–2001. Progetto Carta Archeologica della Provincia di Siena', in *Ilcinesia. Nuove ricerche per la storia di Montalcino e del suo territorio*, ed. by Alfio Cortonesi and Alba Pagani (Rome: Vecchiarelli Editore), pp. 37–64

——. ed. 2008. *Chiese e insediamenti nei secoli di formazione dei paesaggi medievali della Toscana (V–X secolo): Atti del seminario, San Giovanni d'Asso-Montisi, 10–11 novembre 2006* (Florence: All'Insegna del Giglio)

——. 2009. 'Archaeological Site Detection and Mapping: Some Thoughts on Differing Scales of Detail and Archaeological "non-visibility"', in *Seeing the Unseen: Geophysics and Landscape Archaeology*, ed. by Stefano Campana and Salvatore Piro (London: Taylor and Francis), pp. 5–26

Campana, Stefano, Cristina Felici, Riccardo Francovich, and L. Marasco, eds. 2005. 'Progetto Pava: indagini territoriali, diagnostica, prima campagna di scavo', *Archeologia Medievale*, 32: 97–112

——. 2008. 'Progetto Pava. Resoconto di cinque anni di indagini', in *Chiese e insediamenti nei secoli di formazione dei paesaggi medievali della Toscana (V–X secolo): Atti del seminario, San Giovanni d'Asso-Montisi, 10–11 novembre 2006*, ed. by Stefano Campana (Florence: All'Insegna del Giglio)

Campana, Stefano, Cristina Felici, and L. Marasco. 2005. 'Risultati della prima campagna di scavo archeologico sul sito di Pava (San Giovanni d'Asso, SI)', in *Archeologia dei paesaggi Medievali: avanzamento di progetto anni 2000–2004*, ed. by Riccardo Francovich and Marco Valenti (Florence: All'Insegna del Giglio), pp. 92–94

Campana, Stefano, and Riccardo Francovich. 2001. *Carta archeologica della Provincia di Siena*, v: *Murlo* (Siena: Amministrazione Provinciale di Siena Regione)

Campana, Stefano, and Riccardo Francovich, eds. 2006. *Laser scanner e GPS: paesaggi archeologici e tecnologie digitali*, 1: *I workshop, Grosseto, 4 marzo 2005* (Florence: All'Insegna del Giglio)

Campana, Stefano, Riccardo Francovich, and Emanuele Vaccaro, eds. 2005. 'Il popolamento tardoromano e altomedievale nella bassa valle dell'Ombrone. Progetto Carta Archeologica della Provincia di Grosseto', *Archeologia Medievale*, 32: 461–80

Campana, Stefano, and Salvatore Piro, eds. 2009. *Seeing the Unseen: Geophysics and Landscape Archaeology* (London: Taylor and Francis)

Campana, Stefano and others. 2009. 'Scavi archeologici sulla pieve di S. Pietro in Pava (San Giovanni d'Asso, SI)', in *V Congresso Nazionale di Archeologia Medievale*, ed. by Giuliano Volpe and Pasquale Favia (Florence: All'Insegna del Giglio), pp. 449–54

Camporeale, Giovanni. 1985. *L'Etruria mineraria* (Tuscany: Regione Toscana)

——. 1991. 'L'ethnos dei Falisci secondo gli scrittori antichi', *Archeologia Classica*, 43: 209–21

——. ed. 1997. *L'abitato etrusco dell'Accesa. Il quartiere B* (Rome: L'Erma di Bretschneider)

——. 2000. 'I tipi tombali dell'Accesa (Massa Marittima). Dal villanoviano all'arcaismo', in *L'architettura funeraria a Populonia tra IX e VI secolo a.C.*, ed. by Andrea Zifferero (Florence: All'Insegna del Giglio), pp. 123–36

Camporeale, Giovanni and S. Giuntoli. 2000. *Il Parco Archeologico dell'Accesa a Massa Marittima* (Grosetto: Follonica)

Cantini, Federico. 2003. *Il castello di Montarrenti. Lo scavo archeologico (1982–1987). Per la storia della formazione del villaggio medievale in Toscana (secc. VII–XV)* (Florence: All'Insegna del Giglio)

——. *Archeologia urbana a Siena: L'area dell'Ospedale di Santa Maria della Scala prima dell'Ospedale, altomedioevo* (Florence: All'Insegna del Giglio)

——. 2008. 'La chiesa e il borgo di San Genesio: Primi risultati dello scavo di una grande pieve della Toscana altomedievale (campagne di scavo 2001–2007)', in *Chiese e insediamenti nei secoli di formazione dei paesaggi medievali della Toscana (V–X secolo): Atti del seminario, San Giovanni d'Asso-Montisi, 10–11 novembre 2006*, ed. by Stefano Campana (Florence: All'Insegna del Giglio), pp. 65–94

——. 2010. 'Ritmi e forme della grande espansione economica dei secoli XI–XIII nei contesti ceramici della Toscana settentrionale', *Archeologia Medievale*, 37: 113–28

——. 2011. 'Dall'economia complessa al complesso di economie (Tuscia V–X secolo)', *Post-Classical Archaeologies*, 1: 159–94

Cantini, Federico, and Francesca Grassi. 2012. 'Produzione, circolazione e consumo della ceramica in Toscana tra la fine del X ed il XIII secolo', in *IX Congresso Internazionale AIECM2, Venezia, 23–28 novembre 2009*, ed. by Sauro Gelichi (Florence: All'Insegna del Giglio), pp. 129–37

Cantini, Federico, Carlotta Cianferoni, Riccardo Francovich, and Emiliano Scampoli, eds. 2007. *Firenze prima degli Uffizi: lo scavo di via dei Castellani: Contributi per un'archeologia urbana fra tardo antico ed età moderna* (Florence: All'Insegna del Giglio)

Capecchi, G. and A. Romualdi, eds. 1996. 'Il santuario e l'abitato sull'acropoli di Populonia. I materiali (campagne di scavo 1980–1982)', in *Studi sul territorio di Populonia: In memoria di Antonio Minto* (Florence: All'Insegna del Giglio), pp. 343–576

Capelli, Claudio and Chiara Maria Lebole. 1999. 'Il materiale da trasporto in Calabria tra alto e basso Medioevo', in *Contenitori da trasporto e da magazzino tra tardo antico e basso medioevo: Atti [del] XXX Convegno internazionale della ceramica: Albisola, 16-17-18 maggio 1997* (Albisola: Centro ligure per la storia della ceramica), pp. 67–78

Carancini, G. L. 1979. 'I ripostigli del Bronzo finale', in *Atti della XXI Riunione scientifica: Il bronzo finale in Italia: Firenze, 21–23 ottobre 1977*, ed. by Ferrante Rittatore Vonwiller (Florence: Istituto italiano di preistoria e protostoria), pp. 631–41

Carandini, Andrea, ed. 1985a. *Settefinestre: una villa schiavistica nell'Etruria romana* (Modena: Panini)

——. ed. 1985b. *La romanizzazione dell'Etruria: il territorio di Vulci* (Florence: Regione Toscana; Milan: Electa)

Carandini, Andrea, Franco Cambi, Mariagrazia Celuzza, and Elizabeth Fentress. 2002. *Paesaggi d'Etruria: Valle dell'Albegna, Valle d'Oro, Valle del Chiarone, Valle del Tafone: progetto di ricerca italo-britannico seguito allo scavo di Settefinestre* (Rome: Edizioni di storia e letteratura)

Carandini, Andrea and Salvatore Settis. 1979. *Schiavi e Padroni nell'Etruria Romana* (Bari: De Donato)

Cardarelli, Romualdo. 1924–1925. 'Confini fra Magliano e Marsiliana; fra Manciano e Montauto Scerpenna Stachilagi; fra Tricosto e Ansedonia; fra Orbetello e Marsiliana; fra Port'Ercole e Monte Argentario (28 febbraio 1508–2 marzo 1510)', *Bollettino della Società Storica Maremmana*, fasc. 1–2: 131–42; 155–86; 205–22; 3–36; 75–128; 147–213

Cardosa, Massimo. 2005. 'Paesaggi nel territorio di Vulci dalla tarda protostoria alla romanizzazione', in *Dinamiche di sviluppo delle città nell'Etruria meridionale: Veio, Caere, Tarquinia, Vulci: Atti del XXIII Convegno di studi etruschi ed italici: Roma, Veio, Cerveteri/Pyrgi, Tarquinia, Tuscania, Vulci, Viterbo, 1–6 ottobre 2001*, ed. by Orazio Paoletti (Pisa: Istituti editoriali e poligrafici internazionali), pp. 532–57

——. ed. 2019. *Le antiche 'mura etrusche' di Orbetello* (Arcidosso: Effigi)

Carta Topografica della Provincia Inferiore Senese [1772–1774] (Venice: n. pub)

Cartledge, Judith, Gillian Clark, and Valerie Higgins. 1992. 'The Animal Bones from Otranto: A Preliminary Assessment of the Stock Economy', in *Excavations at Otranto, II: The Finds*, ed. by Francesco D'Andria and David Whitehouse (Galatina: Congedo Editore), pp. 317–35

Carocci, Sandro. 2010. 'Archeologia e mondi rurali dopo il Mille. Uno sguardo dalle fonti scritte', *Archeologia Medievale*, 37: 259–66

Cascino, Roberta, Helga Di Giuseppe, and Helen L. Patterson. 2012. *Veii, the Historical Topography of the Ancient City: A Restudy of John Ward-Perkins's Survey* Archaeological Monographs of the British School at Rome, 19 (London: The British School at Rome)

Casi, Carlo. 2000. 'Paesaggi lagunari della costa vulcente tra preistoria e protostoria'. *Preistoria e protostoria in Etruria: Atti del quarto incontro di studi, Manciano, Montalto di Castro, Valentano 12/14 Settembre 1997: l'Etruria tra Italia, Europa e mondo mediterraneo: ricerche e scavi*, ed. by Nuccia Negroni Catacchio (Milan: Centro studi di preistoria e archeologia), pp. 301–14

Casi, Carlo, and Mariagrazia Celuzza. 2000. 'Pescia Romana', in *Vulci e il suo territorio nelle collezioni del Museo Archeologico e d'Arte della Maremma*, ed. by Mariagrazia Celuzza (Milan: Bocca), pp. 60–64

Casocavallo, Beatrice. 2002. 'Materiali ceramici dal pozzo 3 in via Lunga a Tarquinia', in *Le ceramiche di Roma e del Lazio in età medievale e moderna, IV: Atti del Convegno di studi, Viterbo, 22–23 maggio 1998*, ed. by Elisabetta De Minicis and Gabriella Maetzke (Rome: Kappa), pp. 294–303

Cassano, S. M. 1978. 'Torrionaccio (Viterbo). Scavo di un abitato protostorico', *Notizie degli scavi di antichità*, 32: 159–269

Castagnoli, Ferdinando. 1956. 'La centuriazione di Cosa', *Memoirs of the American Academy in Rome*, 24: 147–55

Castiglioncello = The Marie Mazzone Center for the Arts and Humanitites Srl, Insegnamento di Archeologia Medievale, University of Siena, and Soprintendenza per i Beni Archeologici per la Toscana. 'Castiglioncello del Trinoro. Ipotesi In progress. Periodizzazione' <http://archeologiamedievale.unisi.it/trinoro/ipotesi-progress/periodizzazione> [Accessed December 21, 2012]

Ceccarelli Lemut, Maria Luisa. 1985. 'Scarlino: le vicende medievali fino al 1399', in *Scarlino I, Storia e territorio*, ed. by Riccardo Francovich (Florence: All'Insegna del Giglio), pp. 19–74

——. 1991. 'Cronotassi dei vescovi di Volterra dalle origini all'inizio del XIII secolo', in *Pisa e la Toscana occidentale nel medioevo: a Cinzio Violante nei suoi 70 anni*, I (Pisa: GISEM), pp. 23–57

——. 1995. 'Nobiltà territoriale e comune: I conti della Gherardesca e la città di Pisa, secoli XI–XIII.', in *Progetti e dinamiche nella società comunale italiana*, ed. by Renato Bordone and Giuseppe Sergi ([Italy]: GISEM, 1995), pp. 23–100

——. 1999. 'La signoria territoriale di castello e il suo sviluppo nell'area maremmana. Alcuni esempi tra archeologia e storia', in *La signoria rurale in Italia nel Medioevo: Ati del II Convegno di Studi, Pisa 1998*, ed. by Cinzio Violante and Maria Luisa Ceccarelli Lamut (Pisa: ETS), pp. 217–31

——. 2004. 'I porti minori della Toscana nel medioevo', in *La Repubblica di Noli e l'importanza dei porti minori del Mediterraneo nel Medioevo*, ed. by Francesca Bandini and Mauro Darchi (Florence: All'Insegna del Giglio, 2004), pp. 49–67

——. 2014. *Il porto di Piombino: Tra storia e sviluppo* (Ospedaletto: Pacini, 2014)

Celuzza, Mariagrazia. 1985. 'Un insediamento di contadini: La fattoria di Giardino', in *La romanizzazione dell'Etruria: Il territorio di Vulci*, ed. by Andrea Carandini (Florence: Regione Toscana)

——. 1987. 'Guida alla visita dell'antica Cattedrale di San Lorenzo a Roselle', *Rivista Diocesana*, 7: 542–43

——. ed. 2000. *Vulci e il suo territorio nelle collezioni del Museo Archeologico e d'Arte della Maremma* (Milan: Bocca)

——. ed. 2002 [1993]. *Guida alla Maremma antica: Da Vulci a Populonia, dal Monte Argentario al Monte Amiata* (Siena: Nuova Immagine)

——. 2002. '1. La Romanizzazione', in *Paesaggi d'Etruria: Valle dell'Albegna, Valle d'Oro, Valle del Chiarone, Valle del Tafone: Progetto di ricerca italo-britannico seguito allo scavo di Settefinestre* ed. by Andrea Carandini and others (Rome: Edizioni di storia e letteratura), pp. 104–23, 135–37

——. 2015. 'Ancora su Rutilio Namaziano e l'archeologia delle coste tirreniche', in *Diana Umbronensis a Scoglietto*, ed. by A. Sebastiani, E. Chirico, M. Colombini, and M. Cygielman (Oxford: Archeopress), pp. 367–74

——. ed. 2017. *Museo archeologico e d'arte della Maremma, Museo d'arte sacra della diocesi di Grosseto* (Arcidosso: Effigi)

——. 2019. 'Ripercorrendo la Valle dell'Albegna: nuovi dati e conferme', in *Una lezione di archeologia globale: studi in onore di Daniele Manacorda*, ed. by Mirco Modolo (Bari: Edipuglia), pp. 239–44

Celuzza, Mariagrazia and Cecilia Luzzetti, eds. 2013. *Valle d'Oro: parco Archeologico e Paesaggistico – Studio di fattibilità* (Arcidosso: Effigi)

Celuzza, Mariagrazia and E. Regoli. 1982. 'La Valle dell'oro nel territorio di Cosa. Ager Cosanus e Ager Veientanus a confronto', *Dialoghi di Archeologia*, n.s. 1: 31–61

——. 1985. 'Insediamenti della Valle d'Oro e il fondo di Settenestre', in *La romanizzazione dell'Etruria: il territorio di Vulci*, ed. by Andrea Carandini (Florence: Regione Toscana), pp. 48–59

Celuzza, Mariagrazia and C. Zona. 2002. 'La valle d'Oro e l'entroterra di Orbetello', in *Paesaggi d'Etruria: Valle dell'Albegna, Valle d'Oro, Valle del Chiarone, Valle del Tafone: progetto di ricerca italo-britannico seguito allo scavo di Settefinestre* ed. by Andrea Carandini and others (Rome: Edizioni di storia e letteratura), pp, 247–48

Cenni, F., ed. 2007. *Carta archeologica della Provincia di Siena*, VIII: *Buonconvento* (Siena: Nuova Immagine)

Ceppatelli, Dario. 2008. 'I reperti metallici', in *Miranduolo in alta val di Merse (Chiusdino-SI). Archeologia su un sito di potere del Medioevo toscano*, ed. by Marco Valenti (Florence: All'Insegna del Giglio), pp. 418–30

Cerasuolo, Orlando. 2009, 'Quattordici anni di ricerche archeologiche nella fortezza tardo-etrusca di Rofalco', in *Atti della giornata di studi in memoria di Mauro Incitti*, ed. by Luciano Frazzoni (Acquapendente: Tipolitografia Ambrosini Gianfranco), pp. 23–36

Cerasuolo, Orlando and Luca Pulcinelli. 2010. *La fortezza di Rofalco. Vita quotidiana degli ultimi etruschi* (Acquapendente: Ambrosini)

Cerasuolo, Orlando and Luca Pulcinelli. 2013. 'Nuovi dati sulle mura di Piazza d'Armi', in *Mura di legno, mura di terra, mura di pietra: Fortificazioni nel Mediterraneo antico. Atti del Convegno, Roma 2012*, ed. by Gilda Bartoloni and Laura Maria Michetti (Rome: Quasar), pp. 176–83

Cerri, Laura. 2002. 'Prospezioni geofisiche a Populonia', in *Materiali per Populonia*, ed. by Franco Cambi and Daniele Manacorda (Florence: All'Insegna del Giglio), pp. 65–70

——. 2007. 'La prospezione magnetica', in *Montegrotto Terme – via Neroniana. Indagine archeologica 2006*, ed. by Paola Zanovello and Patrizia Basso, *Quaderni di archeologia del Veneto*, 23: 22

——. 2009. 'La prospezione geofisica', in *Hephaestia 2000–2006, Atti del seminario – Siena Certosa di Pontignano, 28–29 Maggio 2007. Paestum-Atene*, ed. by Emanuele Greco and Emanuele Papi (Paestum: Pandemos), pp. 181–86

——. 2009. 'La prospezione magnetica: l'abitato antico', in *Sidi Ali Ben Ahmend*, I, ed. by Emanuele Papi (Rome: Quasar), pp. 31–50

——. 2019. 'Archeologia, geofisica e geomorfologia: dati integrati per la ricostruzione del paesaggio dell'antico abitato di Pitinum Pisaurense (Macerata Feltria-PU)', in *Una lezione di archeologia globale. Studi in onore di Daniele Manacorda*, ed. by Mirco Modolo, Silvia Pallecchi, Giuliano Volpe, and Enrico Zanini (Bari: Edipuglia), pp. 245–52

Cerri Laura and Luca Passalacqua, 2000. 'Prospezioni geofisiche sul sito della villa romana di Cottanello', in *La villa romana di Cottanello*, ed. by Mara Sternini (Bari: Edipuglia), pp. 191–98

Cerri Laura and V. Lani. 2017. 'Pesaro. San Martino: Indagini archeologiche presso il lucus pisaurensis', in *Atti del Convegno dalla Val d'Elsa al Contro*, ed. by Giacomo Baldini and Pierluigi Giroldini (Florence: All'Insegna del Giglio), pp. 436–38

Cherubini, Giovanni. 1974. *Signori, contadini, borghesi. Ricerche sulla società italiana del basso medioevo* (Florence: La nuova Italia)

——. ed. 1979a. *Contadini e proprietari nella Toscana moderna: Atti del Convegno di studi in onore di Giorgio Giorgetti* (Florence: Olschki)

——. 2009. 'Le élites economiche e politiche tra campagna e città', in *La costruzione del dominio cittadino sulle campagne. Italia centro-settentrionale, secoli XII–XIV: Atti del Convegno di Siena, 2004*, ed. by Roberta Mucciarelli, Gabriella Piccinni, and Giuliano Pinto (Siena: Protagon), pp. 589–600

Cheyette, Fredric L. 2008. 'The Disappearance of the Ancient Landscape and the Climatic Anomaly of the Early Middle Ages: A Question to be Pursued', *Early Medieval Europe*, 16.2: 127–65

Chirico, Elena. 2018. 'Casale Tricosto (Capalbio, GR): da *mansio* romana a chiesa nell'antico *ager Cosanus*', *The Journal of Fasti Online*, 421 <http://www.fastionline.org/docs/FOLDER-it-2018-421.pdf>

Chirico, Elena and Alessandro Sebastiani. 2010. 'L'occupazione tardoantica del promontorio dello Scoglietto ad Alberese (GR)', *Archeologia Medievale*, 37: 331 44

Chiovelli, Renzo. 2007. *Tecniche costruttive murarie medievali. La Tuscia* (Rome: L'Erma di Bretschneider)

Christie, Neil, ed. 1991. *Three South Etrurian Churches: Santa Cornelia, Santa Rufina and San Liberato* (London: British School at Rome)

Ciacci, Andrea, Paola Rendini, and Andrea Zifferero, eds. 2007. *Archeologia della vite e del vino in Etruria: Atti del convegno internazionale di studi, Scansano, Teatro Castagnoli, 9–10 settembre 2005* (Siena: Ci.Vin)

Ciacci, Andrea, Paola Rendini, and Andrea Zifferero, eds. 2012. *Archeologia della vite e del vino in Toscana e nel Lazio. Dalle tecniche dell'indagine archeologica alle prospettive della biologia molecolare* (Florence: All'Insegna del Giglio)

Ciacci, Gaspero. 1935. *Gli Aldobrandeschi nella storia e nella "Divina Commedia."* (Rome: Biblioteca d'arte editrice)

Ciampoltrini, Giulio. 1985. 'Talamone e l'area costiera', in *La romanizzazione dell'Etruria: Il territorio di Vulci*, ed. by Andrea Carandini (Florence: Regione Toscana), pp. 115–18

——. 1991. 'Orbetello (GR): scavi in località La Parrina', *Studi e Materiali*, 6: 260–69

——. 1993a. 'Un contesto tombale del Bronzo Finale nel Museo Comunale di Orbetello', *Bollettino di Paletnologia Italiana*, 84: 491–502

——. 1993b. 'L'insediamento del Bronzo Finale alla Puntata di Fonteblanda', in *Preistoria e protostoria in Etruria: La cultura di Rinaldone, ricerche e scavi: atti del primo incontro di studi, Saturnia (Manciano)-Farnese 17–19 maggio 1991*, ed. by Nuccia Negroni Catacchio (Milan: Centro studi sulla preistoria e archeologia), pp. 387–89

——. 1995. 'Considerazioni sull'insediamento del Bronzo Finale alla Puntata di Fonteblanda (Orbetello, GR)', in *Preistoria e Protostoria in Etruria: Tipologia delle necropoli e rituali di deposizione. Ricerche e scavi*, ed. by Nuccia Negroni Catacchio (Milan: Centro studi di preistoria e archeologia), pp. 103–05

——. 1999. 'La Puntata di Fonteblanda. Un insediamento del Bronzo Finale', in *Ferrante Rittatore Vonwiller e la Maremma, 1936–1976: Paesaggi naturali, umani, archeologici: Atti del Convegno, comune di Ischia di Castro 4–5 aprile 1998*, ed. by R. Peroni and L. Rittatore Vonwiller (Florence: All'Insegna del Giglio), pp. 66–77

——. 2002. 'La necropoli ellenistica di Orbetello. Cronache archeologiche del XIX secolo', *Rassegna di Archeologia*, 19: 45–80

——. 2003. 'L'insediamento arcaico di Fonteblanda e l'urbanistica 'ippodamea' fra Orvieto e Vulci', in *Tra Orvieto e Vulci: Atti del 10. Convegno internazionale di studi sulla storia e l'archeologia dell'Etruria*, ed. by Giuseppe M. Della Fina (Rome: Quasar), pp. 279–99

——. 2006. *Glarea stratae: vie etrusche e romane della piana di Lucca* (Florence: Alinea)

——. 2009. 'L'insediamento costiero fra Chiarone e Albegna nell'età del ferro. Nuovi dati', in *Etruria e Italia preromana. Studi in onore di Giovannagelo Camporeale*, ed. by Stefano Bruni (Pisa: Fabrizio Serra), pp. 233–37

——. 2011a. *La città di San Frediano. Lucca fra VI e VII secolo: un itinerario archeologico* (Bientina: I Segni dell'Auser)

——. 2011b. 'Talamone', in *Bibliografia topografica della colonizzazione Greca in Italia e nelle isole Tirreniche. 20, Siti: Sutera-Toppo Daguzzo*, ed. by Giuseppe Nenci (Pisa: Scuola Normale Superiore), pp. 24–40

Ciampoltrini, Giulio and Marco Firmati. 2002. 'The Blacksmith of Fonteblanda. Artisan and Trading Activity in the northern Tyrrhenian in the Sixth Century BC'. *Etruscan Studies*, 9:1, 29–36 <https://scholarworks.umass.edu/etruscan_studies/vol9/iss1/4/>

Ciampoltrini, Giulio and Orazio Paoletti. 1995. 'L'insediamento costiero in Etruria nell'VIII sec. a.C.: il "caso" del territorio fra Chiarone e Albegna', *Studi Etruschi*, 60: 47–67

Ciampoltrini, Giulio and Paola Rendini. 1988. 'L'Agro Cosano fra tarda antichità e alto Medioevo: segnalazioni e contributi', *Archeologia Medievale*, 15: 519–34

——. 1990. 'L'insediamento tardo-antico nella villa marittima di Torre Tagliata (Orbetello, Grosseto). Scavi 1988–1989', *Archeologia Medievale*, 17: 625–32

——. 1992. 'Porti e traffici nel Tirreno settentrionale fra IV e III secolo a.C. Contributi da Telamone e dall'Isola del Giglio', *Annali della Scuola Normale Superiore di Pisa*, 22.4: 985–1004

——. 2004a. 'Landing Places and Trade in the Ager Cosanus and at Giglio Island from the Mid to the Late Imperial Age', in *Close Encounters: Sea- and Riverborne Trade, Ports and Hinterlands, Ship Construction and Navigation in Antiquity, the Middle Ages and in Modern Times*, ed. by Marinella Pasquinucci and Timm Weski (Oxford: Archaeopress), pp. 85–92

——. 2004b. 'Il Sistema portuale dell'*ager Cosanus* e delle isole del Giglio e di Giannutri', in *Le strutture dei porti e degli approdi antichi*, ed. by Anna Gallina Zevi and Rita Turchetti (Rubbetino), pp. 127–50

——. 2007. 'Vie e porti del vino nella Valle dell'Albegna in età etrusca', in *Archeologia della vite e del vino in Etruria: Atti del convegno internazionale di studi, Scansano, Teatro Castagnoli, 9–10 settembre 2005*, ed. by Andrea Ciacci, Paola Rendini, and Andrea Ziffero (Siena: Ci.Vin), pp. 390–401

Cicali, Cristina. 1996. 'Le monete', in *Poggio Imperiale a Poggibonsi: dal villaggio di capanne al castello di pietra, I, Diagnostica archeologica e campagne di scavo 1991–1994*, ed. by Marco Valenti (Florence: All'Insegna del Giglio), pp. 314–26

——. 2005. 'Le monete del castello minerario di Rocca S. Silvestro', *Bollettino di Numismatica*, 44/45: 81–272

——. 2008. 'I reperti monetali di Miranduolo. Prime indicazioni sulle tipologie e sugli aspetti circolatori', in *Miranduolo in Alta Val di Merse (Chiusdino, SI)*, ed. by Marco Valenti (Florence: All'Insegna del Giglio), pp. 403–14

Cimarri, Valentina 2009. 'La Rocca e la "Domus Guicciardi." Strutture del paesaggio tra XII e XIV secolo', in *Rocca Ricciarda, dai Guidi ai Ricasoli. Storia e archeologia di un castrum medievale nel Pratomagno aretino*, ed. by Guido Vannini (Florence: Società editrice fiorentina), pp. 71–87

Cina, Alberto. 2001. *GPS: Principi modalità e tecniche di posizionamento* (Turin: CELID)

Cioni, Elisabetta. 2015. *Per la storia dell'iconografia di San Galgano: Gli affreschi di Ventura Salimbeni nella chiesa di Santa Maria degli Angeli detta del 'Santuccio' a Siena* (Lugano: Agorà)

Cirelli, Enrico. 2002. 'Produzione locale e dinamiche commerciali a Leopoli-Cencelle', in *Le ceramiche di Roma e del Lazio in età medievale e moderna*, IV: *Atti del Convegno di studi, Viterbo, 22–23 maggio 1998*, ed. by Elisabetta De Minicis and Gabriella Maetzke (Rome: Kappa), pp. 266–93

——. 2009. 'Anfore globulari a Classe nell'alto medioevo', in *V Congresso Nazionale di Archeologia Medievale*, ed. by Giuliano Volpe and Pasquale Favia (Florence: All'Insegna del Giglio), pp. 563–68

Cirelli, Enrico, and Michelle Hobart. 2003. 'The Medieval Pottery', in *Cosa V: An Intermittent Town, Excavations 1991–1997*, ed. by Elizabeth Fentress (Ann Arbor: University of Michigan), pp. 320–52

Cirier, Aude, 2002. 'La fine dei conti Aldobrandeschi: il crollo di un mito (secc. XIII–XV)', in *Gli Aldobrandeschi: La grande famiglia feudale della Maremma toscano*, ed. by Mario Ascheri and Lucio Niccolai (Santa Fiora: Lions Club International), pp. 179–80

Citter, Carlo. 1995. 'Il rapporto fra Bizantini, Germani e Romani nella Maremma toscana attraverso lo studio della dinamica del popolamento – il caso rosellano', in *Acculturazione e mutamenti: Prospettive nell'archeologia medievale del Mediterraneo*, ed. by Enrica Boldrini and Riccardo Francovich (Florence: All'Insegna del Giglio), pp. 201–22

——. ed. 1996a. *Grosseto, Roselle e il Prile. Note per la storia di una città e del territorio circostante* (Mantua: Padus)

——. 1996b. *L'edilizia storia di tre castelli medievali. Batignano, Istia d'Ombrone, Montepescali* (Grosseto: Portici)

——. 1996c. 'Ricognizione archeologica al castello di Cotone', *Bollettino della Società Storica Maremmana*, 68/69: 91–102

——. 1997. 'I corredi funebri nella Toscana longobarda nel quadro delle vicende storico-archeologiche del popolamento', in *L'Italia centro-settentrionale in età longobarda*, ed. by Lidia Paroli (Florence: All'Insegna del Giglio), pp. 185–211

——. 2001. 'Castel di Pietra e Selvena: due castelli medievali a confronto', in *Scavi medievali in Italia. II Conferenza Nazionale di Archeologia Medievale*, ed. by Stella Patitucci Uggeri (Rome: Herder), pp. 261–66

——. ed. 2005a. *Lo scavo della chiesa di S. Pietro a Grosseto. Nuovi dati sull'origine e lo sviluppo di una città medievale* (Florence: All'Insegna del Giglio)

——. 2005b. 'Castel di Pietra (Gavorrano-GR)', in *Archeologia dei paesaggi Medievali: avanzaento di progetto anni 2000–2004*, ed. by Riccardo Francovich and Marco Valenti (Florence: All'Insegna del Giglio), pp. 103–12

——. 2006. 'Gerarchie sociali ed edifici di culto: Il territorio rosellano fra Longobardi e Carolingi', in *IV Congresso Nazionale di Archeologia Medievale. Abbazia di San Galgano (Chiusdino, SI), 26–20 settembre 2006*, ed. by Riccardo Francovich and Marco Valenti (Florence: All'Insegna del Giglio), pp. 360–63

——. ed. 2007a. *Archeologia urbana a Grosseto*, II: *Edizione degli scavi urbani 1998–2005: Origine e sviluppo di una città medievale nella "Toscana delle città deboli": Le ricerche 1997–2005* (Florence: All'Insegna del Giglio)

——. 2007b. 'Gli edifici religiosi tardoantichi e altomedievali nelle diocesi di Roselle e Sovana: il dato archeologico e in problemi in agenda', *Archeologia Medievale*, 34: 239–45

——. 2009a. 'L'Italia centrale tirrenica in età carolingia, spunti di riflessione alla luce del dibattito attuale', in *V Congresso Nazionale di Archeologia Medievale*, ed. by Giuliano Volpe and Pasquale Favia (Florence: All'Insegna del Giglio), pp. 302–05

——. 2009b. *Dieci anni di ricerche a Castel di Pietra. Edizione degli scavi 1997–2007* (Florence: All'Insegna del Giglio)

——. 2009c. 'Le trasformazioni dell'assetto topografico nei castelli della Toscana meridionale fra la peste nera e i Medici: alcuni casi a confronto' (unpubl. conference paper, University of Pisa)

Citter, Carlo and Antonia Arnoldus-Huyzendveld. 2007. *Archeologia urbana a Grosseto*, I: *La città nel contesto geografico della bassa valle dell'Ombrone: Origine e sviluppo di una città medievale nella "Toscana delle città deboli": Le ricerche 1997–2005* (Florence: All'Insegna del Giglio)

——. 2011. *Uso del suolo e sfruttamento delle risorse nella pianura grossetana nel Medioevo: Verso una storia del parcellario e del paesaggio agrario* (Rome: Artemide)

Citter, Carlo and others. 2002a. 'La Roccaccia di Selvena (Castell'Azzara-Grosseto): Relazione preliminare della campagna 2001', *Archeologia Medievale*, 29: 169–88

——. 2002b. 'Le grandi fasi dell'incastellamento Selvena e gli altri castelli dell'Amiata grossetano a confronto', in *Gli Aldobrandeschi: La grande famiglia feudale della Maremma toscano*, ed. by Mario Ascheri and Lucio Niccolai (Santa Fiora: Lions Club International)

Citter, Carlo, Lidia Paroli, Christophe Pellecuer, and Jean-Michel Péne. 1996. 'Commerci nel Mediterraneo occidentale nell'Alto Medioevo', in *Early Medieval Towns in the Western Mediterranean*, ed. by Gian Pietro Brogiolo (Mantua: SAP), pp. 121–42

Citter, Carlo, Hermann Salvadori, and Chiara Valdambrini. 2010. 'La città in campagna (secoli X–XII): Il caso di Siena e la Maremma', *Archeologia Medievale*, 37: 105–12

Citter, Carlo and Emanuele Vaccaro. 2005. 'Medieval Castles and Urbanism in the Light of Archaeology: The Case of Southern Tuscany', in *Papers in Italian Archaeology*, VI: *Communities and Settlements from the Neolithic to the Early Medieval Period*, ed. by Peter Attema, Albert Nijboer, and Andrea Ziffero (Oxford: Archaeopress), pp. 924–29

Clark, Anthony. 1996. *Seeing Beneath the Soil. Prospecting Methods in Archaeology* (London: Taylor & Francis)

Clark, Gillian. 1987. 'Stock Economies in Medieval Italy: A Critical Review of the Archaeozoological Evidence', *Archeologia Medievale*, 14: 7–26

——. 1989a. 'The Food Refuse of an Affluent Urban Household in the Late Fourteenth Century: Faunal and Botanical Remains from the Palazzo Vitelleschi, Tarquinia (Viterbo)', *Papers of the British School at Rome*, 57: 201–320

——. 1989b. 'A Group of Animal Bones from Cerveteri', *Studi Etruschi*, 50.3: 253–69

——. 2000. 'The Bare Bones Speak: The Potential and Problems of Archaeozoology for Reconstruction of Medieval Daily Life', in *History of Medieval Life and the Sciences*, ed. by G. Jaritz (Vienna: Verlag der Österreichischen Akademie der Wissenschaften), pp. 63–82

——. 2003. 'The Mammal Bone Finds from Montarrenti', in *Il Castello di Montarrenti: Lo scavo archeologico, 1982–1987: Per la storia della formazione del villaggio medievale in Toscana, secc. VII–XV*, ed. by Federico Cantini (Florence: All'Insegna del Giglio), pp. 181–212

Cocozza, Tommaso, M. Bertini, R. Signorini, and L. Pilato. 1968. *Carta geologica d'Italia alla scala 1:100.000. Orbetello, foglio 135* (Rome: Servizio Geologico d'Italia)

Collavini, Simone M. 1998. *Honorabilis domus et spetiosissimus comitatus: Gli Aldobrandeschi da "conti" a "principi territoriali": (secoli IX–XIII)* (Pisa: ETS)

——. 2002. 'I conti Aldobrandeschi nel contesto storico generale e locale', in *Gli Aldobrandeschi: La grande famiglia feudale della Maremma toscano*, ed. by Mario Ascheri and Lucio Niccolai (Santa Fiora: Lions Club International), pp. 21–36

——. 2007. 'Spazi Politici e irraggiamento sociale delle *elites* laiche intermedie (Italia centrale secc. VIII–X)', in *Les élites et leur espace. Mobilité, royammount, domination (du VIe au XIe siecle)*, Haut Moyen Âge, 5 (Turnhout: Brepols), pp. 319–40

——. 2013. 'Luoghi e contenitori di stoccaggio dei Cereali in Toscana (VIII–XII secolo): le evidenze delle fonti scritte', in *Horrea, Barns and Silos. Storage and Incomes in Early Medieval Europe*, ed. by Alfonso Vigil-Escalera Guirado, Giovanna Bianchi, and Juan Antonio Quirós (Bilbao: Universidad del País Vasco), pp. 57–76

Colmayer, M. F. and S. Rafanelli. 2000. 'Poggio Buco', in *Vulci e il suo territorio nelle collezioni del Museo Archeologico e d'Arte della Maremma*, ed. by Mariagrazia Celuzza (Milan: Bocca), pp. 72–83

Colonna, Giovanni. 1976. *Civiltà del Lazio primitivo* (Rome: Multigrafica Editrice)

——. 1977. 'La civiltà di Vulci nelle valli del Fiora e dell'Albegna prima del IV sec. a.C', in *La civiltà arcaica di Vulci e la sua espansione* (Florence: Olschki), pp. 189–214

Conti, Giovanni, Giovanni Alinari, Fausto Berti, Mario Luccarelli, Mario Ravanelli, Carmen Ravanelli Guidotti, and Romualdo Luzi. 1990. *Zaffera et similia nelle maioliche Italiane* (Viterbo: FAVL Edizioni Artistiche Viterbo)

Costambeys, M. 2009. 'Settlement, Taxation and the Condition of the Peasantry in Post Roman Central Italy', *Journal of the Agrarian Change*, 9: 92–119

Cora, Galeazzo. 1973. *Storia della Maiolica di Firenze e del Contado. Secoli XIV e XV* (Florence: Sansoni)

Corpus Nummorum Italicorum 1912 = *Corpus Nummorum Italicorum*, III, *Liguria, Isola di Corsica* (Rome: Tipografia della R. Accademia dei Lincei)

Corpus Nummorum Italicorum 1929 = *Corpus Nummorum Italicorum*, XI, *Toscana (zecche minori)* (Rome: Tipografia della R. Accademia dei Lincei)

Corpus Nummorum Italicorum 1933 = *Corpus Nummorum Italicorum*, XIV, *Umbria Lazio (zecche minori)* (Rome: Tipografia della R. Accademia dei Lincei)

Corsi, Cristina, Boźdar Slapsak, and Frank Vermeulen. 2013. *Good Practice in Archaeological Diagnostics. Non-destructive Approaches to Complex Archaeological Sites* (Switzerland: Springer International Publishing)

Corsi, L. and Marco Firmati. 1997. 'Il relitto di Capo Enfola all'Elba', in *Memorie sommerse: Archeologia subacquea in Toscana*, ed. by Paola Rendini and Gabriella Poggesi (Pitigliano: Editrice Laurum), pp. 148–56

Cortese, Maria Elena. 2010. 'Appunti per una storia delle campagne italiane nei secoli centrali del Medioevo alla luce di un dialogo tra fonti scritte e fonti materiali', *Archeologia Medievale*, 37: 267–76

Corti, Irene. 2008/2009. 'Edilizia civile e religiosa: Modi di progettare e costruire nel territorio a sud di Grosseto nei secoli centrali del Medioevo' (Scuola di Dottorato e Ricerca Riccardo Francovich, University of Siena)

Coscarella, Adele, ed. 2004. *Archeologia a San Niceto. Aspetti della vita quotidiana nella fortezza tra XII e XV secolo* Documenti di archeologia, 33 (Mantua: SAP)

Costa Tirrenica dall'Argentario a Corneto nel Lazio

Crader, Diana C. 2003. 'Animal Remains from Late Medieval Capalbiaccio: A Preliminary Assessment of the Stock Economy', in *Zooarchaeology: Papers to Honor Elizabeth S. Wing*, ed. by F. Wayne King and Charlotte M. Porter (Gainesville: Florida Museum of Natural History), pp. 161–72

Crader, Diana C. and M. J. Rowe. Forthcoming. 'Cracking the Shell: The Use of Tortoises at Late Medieval Capalbiaccio'

Creighton, Oliver H. 2002. *Castles and Landscapes* (London: Continuum)

Cristofani, Mauro. 1977. 'Problemi poleografici dell'agro cosano e caletrano', in *La civiltà arcaica di Vulci e la sua espansione* (Florence: Olschki), pp. 237–57

——. ed. 1981. *Gli Etruschi in Maremma* (Milan: Silvana)

Cristofani, Mauro and M. Michelucci. 1981. 'La valle dell'Albegna', in *Gli Etruschi in Maremma*, ed. by Mauro Cristofani (Milan: Silvana), pp. 97–113

Cucini, Costanza. 1985. 'Topografia del territorio delle valli del Pecora e dell'Alma', in *Scarlino I, Storia e Territorio*, ed. by Riccardo Francovich (Florence), pp. 147–320

——. 1989. 'L'insediamento altomedievale del podere Aione (Follonica, Gr)', *Archeologia Medievale*, 16: 499–512

——. ed. 1989. *Radicofani. Storia e Archeologia di un Comune senese* (Rome: Multigrafica Editrice)

Cucini Tizzoni, Costanza and Marco Tizzoni. 2001. 'Studio degli scarti metallurgici', in *Archeologia a Monte Barro*, II: *Gli scavi 1990-97 e le ricerche al S. Martino di Lecco*, ed. by Gian Pietro Brogiolo (Lecco: Stefanoni), pp. 273–79

Cuomo di Caprio, Ninina. 2007. *Ceramica in archeologia 2. Antiche tecniche di lavorazione e moderni metodi di indagine* (Rome: L'Erma di Bretschneider)

Curri, Claudio B. 1978. 'Vetulonia, I', in *Forma Italiae, Regio VII* (Rome: De Luca)

Curti, F. and D. Tami. 1996. 'La ceramica acroma comune', in *Studi sul territorio di Populonia: In memoria di Antonio Minto*, ed. by G. Capecchi and A. Romualdi (Florence: All'Insegna del Giglio), pp. 414–42

Cuteri, Francesco. 1992. 'Suvereto (LI)', in *La ceramica invetriata tardoantica e altomedievale in Italia*, ed. by Lidia Paroli (Florence: All'Insegna del Giglio), p. 303

Cygielman Mario, Elena Chirico, M. Colombini, and Alessandro Sebastiani, eds. 2010. 'Dinamiche insediative nel territorio della foce dell'Ombrone. Nuovi dati dagli scavi presso l'area templare dello Scoglietto', *Notiziario della Soprintendenza per i Beni Archeologici della Toscana*, 5: 35–92

Cygielman, Mario, Emanuele Vaccaro, Giuliana Agricoli, and Mariaelena Ghisleni. 2009. 'Vocabolo San Martino (GR)', *Notiziario della Soprintendenza per i Beni Archeologici della Toscana*, 4: 259–77

Dabas Michel, Henri Delétang, Alain Ferdière, Cecil Jung, and W. Haio Zimmermann. 2006. *La Prospection. Collection Archeologiques* (Paris: Errance)

Dadà, Massimo. 2005. 'Reperti metallici e di uso militare', in *L'aratro e il calamo. Benedettini e cistercensi sul Monte Pisano. Dieci anni di archeologia a San Michele alla Verruca*, ed. by Sauro Gelichi and Antonio Alberti (Pisa: San Giuliano Terme), pp. 361–82

——. 2007. 'Ceramica medievale e moderna dall'Acropoli di Populonia (saggio XX)', in *Materiali per Populonia*, VI, ed. by Lucia Botarelli, Marta Coccoluto, and M. Cristina Mileti (Pisa: Edizioni ETS), pp. 169–87

Dallai, Luisa, and Roberto Farinelli. 1998. 'Castel di Pietra e l'alta valle del Bruna. Indagini storiche e topografiche per la redazione di una carta archeologica', *Archeologia Medievale*, 25: 51–55

De Giorgi, Andrea. 2015. 'Scavi di Cosa: la Stagione 2014', *Notiziario Soprintendenza per i Beni Archeologici della Toscana*, 11: 521–26

——. 2016. 'Orbetello (GR). Orbetello (GR). Cosa, Ansedonia: lo scavo del 2015', *Notiziario della Soprintendenza per i Beni Archeologici della Toscana*, 10 (2015): 521–25

——. 2018. 'Sustainable Practices? A Story from Roman Cosa (Central Italy)', *Journal of Mediterranean Archaeology*, 31.1: 3–26

———2019. *Cosa and the Colonial Landscape of Republican Italy (Third and Second Centuries BCE)* (Ann Arbor: University of Michigan Press) De Greys, Agostino. [n.d.] *Paesaggio Agrario e Forestrale nello Stato dei Presìdi* ([n.pub]: [n.p.])

——. 2020 'Orbetello (GR). Ansedonia. Scavi a Cosa: il complesso termale', in *Notiziario della Soprintendenza per i Beni Archeologici della Toscana*, pp. 529–32

De Grossi Mazzorin, J. 1987. 'Populonia: reperti faunistici dall'acropoli', in *L'alimentazione nel mondo antico: Gli etruschi*, ed. by G. Barbieri (Rome: Istituto Poligrafico e Zecca dello Stato), pp. 89–93

De Luca, Daniele. 2000. 'Le armi', in *Archeologia a Montemassi: Un castello fra storia e storia dell'arte*, ed. by Silvia Guideri, Roberto Parenti, and Francesco Barbagli (Florence: All'Insegna del Giglio), pp. 216–21

——. 2003. 'Le armi da tiro nella rocca di Campiglia Marittima. Frecce per arco e dardi per balestra', in *Campiglia: Un castello e il suo territorio*, ed. by Giovanna Bianchi (Florence: All'Insegna del Giglio), pp. 397–413

De Luca, Daniele and Roberto Farinelli. 2002. 'Un approccio storico-archeologico alle armi da tiro nella Toscana Meridionale', *Archeologia Medievale*, 29: 455–88

De Luca, Ilaria. 2006. 'Ritrovamenti dei secoli IX–X dai Fori di Cesare e di Nerva', in *Roma: Lo scavo dei Fori Imperiali 1995–2000: i contesti ceramici* (Rome: École française de Rome), pp. 93–108

De Marchi, Paola Marina. 1999. 'Reperti Metallici e Miscellanea', in *S. Giulia di Brescia. Gli scavi dal 1980 al 1992. Reperti preromani, romani e alto medievali*, ed. by Gian Pietro Brogiolo (Florence: All'Insegna del Giglio), pp. 315–31

——. 2001. 'Manufatti in metallo, osso, pietre preziose', in *Archeologia a Monte Barro, II: Gli scavi 1990–97 e le ricerche al S. Martino di Lecco*, ed. by Gian Pietro Brogiolo (Lecco: Stefanoni), pp. 153–66

De Minicis, Elisabetta, ed. 1994. *Le ceramiche di Roma e del Lazio in età medievale e moderna*, I (Rome: Kappa)

——. ed. 1995. *Le ceramiche di Roma e del Lazio in età medievale e moderna*, II (Rome: Kappa)

——. ed. 1998. *Le ceramiche di Roma e del Lazio in età medievale e moderna*, III (Rome: Kappa)

De Minicis, Elisabetta and Gabriella Maetzke, eds. 2002. *Le ceramiche di Roma e del Lazio in età medievale e moderna, IV: Atti del Convegno di studi, Viterbo, 22–23 maggio 1998* (Rome: Kappa)

De Rossi, G. 1968. *La via Aurelia da Roma a Forum Aureli* (Rome: De Luca)

De Santis, Paola and Roberta Giuliani. 1998. 'I corredi funerari', in *San Giusto. La villa, le ecclesiae*, ed. by Giuliano Volpe (Bari: Edipuglia), pp. 221–32

De Vingo, Paolo. 2001. 'Miscellanea (oggetti in osso, fusaiole, pesi, gettoni da gioco, accessori di abbigliamento in legno', in *Archeologia urbana a Savona: Scavi e ricerche nel complesso monumentale del Priamar, II: Palazzo della Loggia, scavi 1969–1989*, ed. by Carlo Varaldo (Savona: Marco Sabatelli), pp. 454–74

De Vitis, Silvia. 1991. 'I vetri', in *Archeologia medievale a Lugo. Aspetti del quotidiano nei ritrovamenti della Rocca*, ed. by Sauro Gelichi (Florence: All'Insegna del Giglio), pp. 181–92

De Vos, Mariette. 2000. *Rus Africum: Terra, acqua, olio nell'Africa settentrionale: Scavo e ricognizione nei dintorni di Dougga (Alto Tell Tunisino)* (Trento: Università degli studi di Trento)

Degasperi, Angelica. 2003. 'La moneta nel medio Valdarno inferiore. Osservazioni sulla circolazione monetaria tra Lucca e Pistoia fra alto e basso medioevo', *Archeologia Medievale*, 30: 557–75

Del Chiaro, Mario Aldo. 1976. *Etruscan Ghiaccio Forte* (Santa Barbara: University of California, Santa Barbara)

Del Rosso, R. 1898. *La bonifica del lago di Orbetello* (Pitigliano: Paggi)

Della Monaca, Gualtiero, and others. 1996. *Fortezze e Torri costiere dell'Argentario, Giglio e Giannutri* (Pitiglaino)

Delogu, Paolo. 2007. 'Rome in the Ninth Century: The Economic System', in *Post-Roman Towns, Trade, and Settlement in Europe and Byzantium*, I, ed. by Joachim Henning (Berlin: De Gruyter), pp. 105–22

Delogu, Paolo and Sara Sorda. 2002. *La moneta in ambiente rurale nell'Italia tardomedievale. Atti dell'incontro di studio, Roma 21–22 settembre 2000* (Rome: Istituto italiano di Numismatica)

Delpino, F. 1981. 'Aspetti e problemi della prima età del ferro nell'Etruria Settentrionale marittima', in *L'Etruria mineraria. Atti del XII Convegno di Studi Etruschi e Italici (Firenze-Populonia-Piombino, 16–20 giugno 1979)* (Florence: Olschki), pp. 267–98

Demians d'Archimbaud, Gabrielle. 1980. *Les Fouilles de Rougiers (Var). Contribution à l'archéologie de l'habitat rural médiéval en pays méditerranée* (Paris: Valbonne)

Dennis, George. 1883. *The Cities and Cemeteries of Etruria* (London: Murray)

Detti, F. 1998. *La Valle d'Albegna. Formazione ed Evoluzione dei Paesaggi Storici* (Pitigliano: Laurum)

Di Gennaro, F. 1986. *Forme di insediamento fra Tevere e Fiora dal bronzo finale al principio dell'età del ferro* (Florence: Olschki)

Di Paola, Giorgia. 2018. 'Populonia e il suo territorio: Strategie difensive e risorse' (unpubl. report)

Dolfini, A. 2005. 'La fase di transizione Bronzo-Ferro nel territorio di Vulci: Elementi di continuità e discontinuità nella cultura materiale', in *Dinamiche di sviluppo delle città nell'Etruria meridionale: Veio, Caere, Tarquinia, Vulci: Atti del XXIII Convegno di studi etruschi ed italici: Roma, Veio, Cerveteri/Pyrgi, Tarquinia, Tuscania, Vulci, Viterbo, 1–6 ottobre 2001*, ed. by Orazio Paoletti (Pisa: Istituti editoriali e poligrafici internazionali), pp. 509–15

Donati, Luigi. 1994. *La Casa dell'Impluvium: architettura etrusca a Roselle* (Rome: L'Erma di Bretschneider)

——. 2012. 'Sulla capanna che ha preceduto la Casa dell'Impluvium di Roselle', *Notiziario della Soprintendenza per i Beni Archeologici della Toscana*, 8, suppl. 1: 67–72

Donati, Luigi and Luca Cappuccini. 2008. *Aristocrazie Agricoltura Commercio. Etruschi a Santa Teresa di Gavorrano. Catalogo della mostra archeologica* (Viterbo: Colordesoli Editrice)

Donati, Luigi and Maurizio Michelucci. 1981. *La Collezione Ciacci nel Museo archeologico di Grosseto* (Rome: De Luca)

Donati, Luigi and E. Pacciani. 1989. *Le tombe da Saturnia nel Museo archeologico di Firenze* (Florence: Olschki)

Dowding, Janka. 2006–2007. 'The Elusive Etruscans: The Quest for the Origins of the Etruscan Civilization', *Hirundo* 5: 31–56 <https://secureweb.mcgill.ca/classics/sites/mcgill.ca.classics/files/2006-7-04.pdf>

D'Ulizia, Alessandra. 2005. 'L'Archeologia dell'Architettura in Italia. Sintesi e bilancio degli studi', *Archeologia dell'Architettura*, 10: 9–43

Dyer, Chris. 1997. 'Peasants and Coins: The Uses of Money in the Middle Ages', *British Numismatic Journal*, 31: 31–47

Dyson, Stephen L. 1976. 'Cosa: The Utilitarian Pottery', *Memoirs of the American Academy in Rome*, 33: 3–175

——. 1978a. 'Report on the Wesleyan Archaeological Program at Cosa, Italy' (unpubl. manuscript on file at Wesleyan University, Middletown, Connecticut)

——. 1978b. 'Settlement Patterns in the Ager Cosanus: The Wesleyan University Survey, 1974–1976', *Journal of Field Archaeology*, 5: 251–68

——. 1979. 'Medieval Excavation at Capalbiaccio and Site Survey of Albegna Valley, Cosa, Italy' (unpubl. research grant report on file at the National Endowment for the Humanities, Washington, DC)

——. 1981a. 'Settlement Reconstruction in the Ager Cosanus and the Albegna Valley: Wesleyan University Research, 1974–1979', in *Archaeology and Italian Society*, ed. by Graeme Barker and Richard Hodges (Oxford: BAR), pp. 269–74

——. 1981b. 'Survey Archaeology: Reconstructing the Roman Countryside', *Archaeology*, 34: 31–37

——. 1984. 'Castle and Countryside: Capalbiaccio and the Changing Settlement History of the *Ager Cosanus*', in *Archaeological Approaches to Medieval Europe*, ed. by Kathleen Biddick, Studies in Medieval Culture, 18 (Kalamazoo: Medieval Institute Publications), pp. 263–78

——. 1990. 'Reconstructing the Landscape of Rural Italy', in *Earth Patterns: Essays in Landscape Archaeology*, ed. by William M. Kelso and Rachel Most (Charlottesville: University Press of Virginia), pp. 245–53

——. 1992. *Community and Society in Roman Italy* (Baltimore: Johns Hopkins University Press)

——. 2002. 'The Excavations at Le Colonne and the Villa Culture of the Ager Cosanus', *Memoirs of the American Academy in Rome*, 47: 209–28

——. 2003. *The Roman Countryside* (London: Bristol Classical Press)

——. 2005. 'Successes and Failures at Cosa (Roman and American)', *Journal of Roman Archaeology* 18: 621–23

Enei, Flavio. 1993. *Cerveteri: ricognizioni archeologiche nel territorio di una città etrusca* (Rome: Gruppo archeologico romano)

——. ed. 2013. *Santa Severa tra leggenda e realtà storica. Pyrgi e il castello di Santa Severe alla luce delle recenti scoperte (Scavi 2003–2009)* (Grotte di Castro: Ceccarelli Editrice)

Ente Maremma. 1966. *La Riforma Fondiaria in Maremma* (Rome: Vallerini)

Ermeti, Anna Lia, Daniele Sacco, and Siegfried Vona. 2008. 'Il Castello di Monte Copiolo nel Montefeltro (Marche, PU). Le prime sei campagne di scavo (2002–2007), Una sintesi', *Archeologia Medievale*, 35: 151–73

Facchin, Giulia and Matteo Milletti, eds. 2011. *Materiali per Populonia*, x (Pisa: Edizioni ETS)

Falcetti, Carlo. 2001. 'Le perle in pasta vitrea e vetro', in *S. Antonio, un insediamento fortificato nella Liguria bizantina*, ed. by Tiziano Mannoni and Giovanni Murialdo (Florence: All'Insegna del Giglio), pp. 517–20

Farinelli, Roberto. 2000. 'I castelli nei territori diocesani di Populonia-Massa e Roselle-Grosseto (secc. X–XV)', in *Castelli: storia e archeologia del potere nella Toscana medievale*, ed. by Riccardo Francovich, Maria Ginatempo, and Andrea Augenti (Florence: All'Insegna del Giglio), pp. 141–203

——. 2003. 'Centri di fondazione comunale nella Toscana meridionale (secc. XIII–prima metà XIV). Primi risultati delle ricerche nella provincia di Grosseto', in *III Congresso nazionale di archeologia medievale: Castello di Salerno, Complesso di Santa Sofia, Salerno, 2–5 ottobre 2003*, ed. by Rosa Fiorillo and Paolo Peduto (Florence: All'Insegna del Giglio), pp. 314–19

——. 2007. *I castelli nella Toscana delle città deboli: Dinamiche del popolamento e del potere rurale nella Toscana meridionale, secoli VII–XIV* (Florence: All'Insegna del Giglio)

——. 2009. *Grosseto e il suo territorio. Paesaggio agrario e risorse naturali*, I: *Le campagne medievali del districtus Grosseti (secc. IX–p. m. XIV)* (Grosseto: Effigi)

Farinelli, Roberto, Michela Corti, Luigi Marchese, and José Carlos Sánchez Pardo. 2008. 'Chiese e popolamento nella Tuscia dell'alto Medioevo. Un approccio quantitativo alla documentazione diplomatica altomedievale del monastero di S. Salvatore al Monte Amiata', in *Chiese e insediamenti nei secoli di formazione dei paesaggi medievali della Toscana (V–X secolo): Atti del seminario, San Giovanni d'Asso-Montisi, 10–11 novembre 2006*, ed. by Stefano Campana (Florence: All'Insegna del Giglio), pp. 297–336

Farinelli, Roberto and A. Giorgi. 2000. 'Fenomeni di accentramento insediativo nella Toscana meridionale tra XII e XIII secolo: Il "secondo incastellamento" in area senese', in *Castelli: Storia e archeologia del potere nella Toscana medievale*, ed. by Riccardo Francovich, Maria Ginatempo, and Andrea Augenti (Florence: All'Insegna del Giglio), p. 239

Farinelli, Roberto and Michele Pellegrini. 2009. 'Casseri e fortezze senesi a Grosseto e in altri centri della Toscana meridionale (secc. XIII–XIV)', in *Castelli e fortezze nelle città italiane e nei centri minori italiani (secoli XIII–XV)*, ed. by Francesco Panero and Giuliano Pinto (Cherasco: CISIM), pp. 161–95

Farinelli, Roberto, Emanuele Vaccaro, and Hermann Salvadori. 2008. 'Le chiese nel villaggio: La formazione dell'abitato medievale di Poggio Cavolo (Gr)', in *Chiese e insediamenti nei secoli di formazione dei paesaggi medievali della Toscana (V–X secolo): Atti del seminario, San Giovanni d'Asso-Montisi, 10–11 novembre 2006*, ed. by Stefano Campana (Florence: All'Insegna del Giglio), pp. 169–97

Farinetti, Emeri. 2004. 'Indagini topografiche & Indagini geo-archeologiche e geomorfologiche', in *Ephaestia: Prospezioni nell'area della città. Relazione della seconda missione (29 luglio–14 agosto 2003)*, ed. by Emanuele Papi (Athens: Scuola Archeologica di Atene), pp. 1088–99

Farinetti, Emeri and S. Laurenza. 2005. 'Rethinking Landscape Archaeology Theory and Spatial Analyses Techniques in GIS', in *The Reconstruction of Archaeological Landscapes through Digital Technologies: Proceedings of the 2nd Italy-United States Workshop, Rome, Italy, November 3–5, 2003, Berkeley, USA, May 2005*, ed. by Maurizio Forte (Oxford: Archaeopress), pp. 127–38

Farnese 1985 = *Farnese: ceramiche d'uso domestico dai butti del centro storico: secoli 14.–18.: Farnese, Museo comunale, settembre 1988*, ed. by Gruppo Archeologico del Mediovaldarno (Florence: All'Insegna del Giglio)

Farnese 1991 = *Farnese: Testimonianze archeologiche di vita quotidiana dai butti del centro storico*, ed. by Gruppo Archeologico del Mediovaldarno (Florence: All'Insegna del Giglio)

Favia, L. 1992. 'Reperti metallici', in 'Le campagne di scavo al Castello di Zuccola in Cividale del Friuli'. *Archeologia Medievale*, 19: 263–74

Felici, Cristina, ed. 2004. *Carta archeologica della Provincia di Siena*, VI: *Pienza* (Siena: Nuova Immagine)

Fentress, Elizabeth. 2002. 'Saturnia. La città', in *Paesaggi d'Etruria: Valle dell'Albegna, Valle d'Oro, Valle del Chiarone, Valle del Tafone: Progetto di ricerca italo-britannico seguito allo scavo di Settefinestre*, ed. by Andrea Carandini, Franco Cambi, Mariagrazia Celuzza, and Elizabeth Fentress (Rome: Edizioni di storia e letteratura), pp. 123–24

——. ed. 2003. *Cosa V: An Intermittent Town, Excavations 1991–1997* (Ann Arbor: University of Michigan)

——. 2009. 'Peopling the Countryside: Roman Demography in the Albegna Valley and Jerba', in *Quantifying the Roman Economy*, ed. by A. Bowman and A. Wilson (Oxford: Oxford University Press), pp. 127–62

Fentress, Elizabeth, Theresa Clay, Michelle Hobart, and Matilda Webb. 1991. 'Late Cosa I: The Arx and the Tower Near the Eastern Height: The Pottery', *Papers of the British School in Rome*, 59: 214–25

Fentress, Elizabeth, Sergio Fontana, R. Bruce Hitchner, and Philip Perkins. 2004. 'Accounting for ARS: Fineware and Sites in Sicily and Africa', in *Side-by-Side Survey: Comparative Regional Studies in the Mediterranean world*, ed. by Susan E. Alcock and John F. Cherry (Oxford: Oxbow Books), pp. 147–62

Fentress, Elizabeth and Katherine Gruspier. 2003. 'The Early Medieval Settlement', in *Cosa V: An Intermittent Town, Excavations 1991–1997*, ed. by Elizabeth Fentress (Ann Arbor: University of Michigan), pp. 92–119

Fentress, Elizabeth and Philip Perkins. 1988. 'Counting African Red Slip Ware', in *L'Africa Romana 5. Atti del V convegno di studio Sassari, 11–13 dicembre 1987*, ed. by Attilio Mastino (Sassari: Edizioni Gallizzi), pp. 205–14

Fentress, Elizabeth and Christopher Wickham. 2001. 'La valle dell'Albegna fra i secoli VII e XIV', in *Siena e Maremma nel Medioevo*, ed. by Mario Ascheri (Siena: Betti), 59–82

Ferlito, Gianfelice. 1994. 'Svelato il mistero degli scacchi di Venafro' <https://www.cci-italia.it/venaf.htm>

Ferrandes, A. 2006. 'Produzioni stampigliate e figurate in area etrusco-laziale tra fine IV e III secolo a.C. Nuove riflessioni alla luce di vecchi contesti', *Archeologia Classica*, 57: 115–73

Fichera, Giuseppe. 2005. 'Tecniche costruttive ed evidenze materiali in trachite nel comune di Roccastrada (GR). Secoli X–XIII', *Archeologia dell'Architettura*, 10: 191–200

——. 2005/2006. 'Archeologia dell'Architettura degli insediamenti fortificati della provincia di Grosseto. Progettazione edilizia ed ambiente tecnico nel *comitatus* degli Aldobrandeschi' (Dott., Scuola di Dottorato e Ricerca Riccardo Francovich, University of Siena)

Finetti, Angelo. 1993. *Terni. Le monete nel medioevo e la zecca del 1797* (Perugia: Volumnia)

——. 1997. *La zecca e le monete di Perugia nel Medioevo e nel Rinascimento* (Perugia: Volumnia)

——. 1999. '*Boni* e *mali Piczoli*: Moneta piccola locale e forestiera in Italia centrale (XIII–XV secolo)', in *Moneta locale, moneta straniera: Italia ed Europa XI–XV secolo*, ed. by Lucia Travaini (Milan: Società Numismatica Italiana), pp. 67–85

Fiorani, D. 1996. *Tecniche costruttive murarie medievali. Il Lazio meridionale* (Rome: L'Erma di Bretschneider)

Fiorillo, Rosa and Paolo Peduto. 2003. *III Congresso nazionale di archeologia medievale: Castello di Salerno, Complesso di Santa Sofia, Salerno, 2–5 ottobre 2003* (Florence: All'Insegna del Giglio)

Firmati, Marco. 2001. 'Età ellenistica. L'abitato fortificato di Ghiaccioforte', in *Scansano. Guida al territorio. Museo della vite e del vino. Museo Archeologico*, ed. by Marco Firmati (Siena: Nuova immagine), pp. 96–121

——. 2002. 'New Data from the Fortified Settlement of Ghiaccioforte in the Albegna Valley', *Etruscan Studies*, 9: 63–75

——. 2007. 'I Comprensori indagati nel 2005: la valle dell'Albegna (GR)', in *Archeologia della vite e del vino in Toscana e nel Lazio. Dalle tecniche dell'indagine archeologica alle prospettive della biologia molecolare*, ed. by Andrea Ciacci, Paola Rendini, and Andrea Zifferero (Florence: All'Insegna del Giglio), pp. 217–24

——. 2008. 'Scansano (GR). Necropoli arcaica di Poggio Marcuccio (VI–inizi V secolo a.C.): restauro del corredo della Tomba 4', *Notiziario della Soprintendenza per i Beni Archeologici della Toscana*, 4: 523–26

——. 2011. 'La necropoli di Poggio Marcuccio a Scansano', in *La valle del vino etrusco. Archeologia della valle dell'Albegna in età arcaica*, ed. by Marco Firmati, Paola Rendini, and Andrea Zifferero (Grosseto: Effigi), pp. 63–71

Firmati, Marco and Paola Rendini. 2002. *Museo archeologico Scansano* (Siena: Nuova immagine)

Firmati, Marco, Paola Rendini, and Andrea Zifferero. 2011. *La valle del vino etrusco. Archeologia della valle dell'Albegna in età arcaica* (Grosseto: Effigi)

Flandrin, Jean-Louis, Danièle Alexandre-Bidon, and Massimo Montanari. 1997. *Storia dell'alimentazione* (Rome: Laterza)

Forte, Maurizio, ed. 2003. *The Reconstruction of Archaeological Landscapes through Digital Technologies: Proceedings of the 1st Italy-United States Workshop, Boston, Massachusetts, USA, November 1–3, 2001* (Oxford: Archaeopress)

Fortina, Consuelo and Isabella Memmi Turbanti. 2003. 'Caratterizzazione mineralogico-petrografica di alcuni impasti ceramici provenienti dalla Rocca di Campiglia', in *Campiglia: un castello e il suo territorio*, ed. by Giovanna Bianchi (Florence: All'Insegna del Giglio), pp. 337–40

Fossati, Angelo and Giovanni Murialdo. 2001. 'Reperti metallici provenienti dai livelli medievali e moderni', in *S. Antonio, un insediamento fortificato nella Liguria bizantina*, ed. by Tiziano Mannoni and Giovanni Murialdo (Florence: All'Insegna del Giglio), pp. 719–23

Fossier, Robert. 2002. *Il lavoro nel medioevo* (Turin: Einaudi)

Fourquin, G. 1971. *Histoire économique de l'Occident médiéval* (Paris: Armand Colin)

Francovich, Riccardo. 1973. 'Forme e vicende degli insediamenti nella campagna Toscana dei secoli XIII–XV', *Quaderni storici*, 8.24: 877–904

——. 1982. *La ceramica medievale a Siena e nella Toscana meridionale (secc. XIV–XV), materiali per una tipologia* (Florence: All'Insegna del Giglio)

——. 1985. *Scarlino I, Storia e Territorio* (Florence: All'Insegna del Giglio)

——. 1991. *Rocca San Silvestro* (Rome: De Luca)

——. 1999. 'L'archeologia in Toscana fra alto e basso medioevo: una rassegna bibliografica', *Archivio Storico Italiano*, 579.1: 131–76

——. ed. 2000. 'La Roccaccia di Selvena. Rapporto preliminare degli scavi e della ricognizione archeologica 1999'. In *II Congresso nazionale di archeologia medievale: [proceedings], Musei civici, Chiesa di Santa Giulia, Brescia, 28 settembre–1 ottobre 2000*, ed. by Gian Pietro Brogiolo (Florence: All'Insegna del Giglio), pp. 183–88

——. 2004. 'Villaggi dell'Altomedioevo: invisibilità sociale e labilità archeologica', in *L'Insediamento Altomedievale nelle Campagne Toscane. Paesaggi. Popolamento e Villaggi tra VI e X secoli*, ed. by Marco Valenti (Florence: All'Insegna del Giglio), pp. ix–xxii

Francovich, Riccardo, Andrea Augenti, Roberto Farinelli, and M. E. Cortese. 1997. 'Verso un atlante dei castelli della Toscana: primi risultati', in *I Congresso nazionale di archeologia medievale: Auditorium del Centro Studi della Cassa di Risparmio di Pisa (ex Benedettine) Pisa, 29–31 maggio 1997*, ed. by Sauro Gelichi (Florence: All'Insegna del Giglio), pp. 97–101

Francovich, Riccardo and Giovanna Bianchi. 2006. 'Capanne e muri in pietra. Donoratico nell'altomedioevo', in *Il Medioevo nella provincia di Livorno. I risultati delle recenti indagini*, ed. by Chiara Marcucci and Carolina Megale (Ospedaletto: Pacini), pp. 105–16

Francovich, Riccardo, Giovanna Bianchi, Carlo Citter, and Roberto Farinelli. 1997. 'Progetto Selvena. Dati di scavo, analisi degli elevati e fonti scritte: prime acquisizioni', in *La nascita dei castelli nell'Italia medievale. Il caso di Poggibonsi e le altre esperienze dell'Italia Centrosettentrionale, Atti del Convegno di Studi, Poggibonsi 1997*, ed. by Riccardo Francovich and Marco Valenti (Siena: Poggibonsi), pp. 151–70

Francovich, Riccardo and Giovanni Cherubini. 1983. 'Insediamenti nella campagna Toscana, XIII–XV', *Quaderni Storici*, 31: 898

Francovich, Riccardo and Carlo Citter. 2002. 'Le grandi fasi dell'incastellamento. Selvena e gli altri castelli dell'Amiata grossetano a confronto', in *Gli Aldobrandeschi: La grande famiglia feudale della Maremma toscano*, ed. by Mario Ascheri and Lucio Niccolai (Santa Fiora: Lions Club International), pp. 37–46

Francovich, Riccardo and Sauro Gelichi, eds. 1980a. *Archeologia e storia di un monumento mediceo. Gli scavi nel 'cassero' senese nella Fortezza di Grosseto* (Bari: De Donato)

——. 1980b. 'Per una storia delle produzioni e del consumo della ceramica bassomedievale a Siena e nella Toscana meridionale', in *La céramique médiévale en Méditerranée occidentale, Xe–Xve s.,Valbonne, 11–14 septembre 1978* (Paris: CNRS), pp. 137–53

Francovich, Riccardo, Maria Ginatempo, and Andrea Augenti. 2000. *Castelli: Storia e archeologia del potere nella Toscana medievale* (Florence: All'Insegna del Giglio)

Francovich, Riccardo and Richard Hodges. 2003. *Villa to Village: The transformation of the Roman countryside in Italy, c. 400–1000* (London: Duckworth)

Francovich, Riccardo and Ghislaine Noyé. 1994. *La storia dell'alto Medioevo italiano (VI–X secolo) alla luce dell'archeologia: Convegno internazionale (Siena, 2–6 dicembre 1992)* (Florence: All'Insegna del Giglio)

Francovich, Riccardo and Roberto Parenti, eds. 1988. *Archeologia e restauro dei monumenti* (Florence: All'Insegna del Giglio)

Francovich, Riccardo, A. Pellicano, and M. Pasquinucci. 2001. *La Carta Archeologica fra ricerca e pianificazione territoriale* (Florence: All'Insegna del Giglio)

Francovich, Riccardo and Carlo Tronti. 2003. 'Lo scavo del castello di Montefiesole (Pontassieve, FI)', in *III Congresso nazionale di archeologia medievale: Castello di Salerno, Complesso di Santa Sofia, Salerno, 2–5 ottobre 2003*, ed. by Rosa Fiorillo and Paolo Peduto (Florence: All'Insegna del Giglio), pp. 299–302

Francovich, Riccardo and Marco Valenti, eds. 1997. *La nascita dei castelli nell'Italia medievale. Il caso di Poggibonsi e le altre esperienze dell'Italia Centrosettentrionale* (Poggibonsi: Atti del Convegno di Studi)

——. eds. 2005. *Archeologia dei paesaggi Medievali: Avanzamento di progetto anni 2000–2004* (Florence: All'Insegna del Giglio)

——. eds. 2006. *IV Congresso Nazionale di Archeologia Medievale. Abbazia di San Galgano (Chiusdino, SI), 26–20 settembre 2006* (Florence: All'Insegna del Giglio)

——. eds. 2007. *Poggio Imperiale a Poggibonsi. Il territorio, lo scavo, il parco* (Milan: Silvana)

Frazzoni, L., ed. 2012. *Carta archeologica del Comune di Farnese* (Bolsena: Città di Bolsena)

Frazzoni, L. and G. Vatta. 1994. 'Ceramiche medievali dall'insediamento di Sorgenti della Nova (VT)', in *Le ceramiche di Roma e del Lazio in età medievale e moderna I*, ed. by Elisabetta De Minicis (Rome: Kappa), pp. 75–85

Fronza, V. 2006. 'Strumenti e materiali per un atlante dell'edilizia altomedievale in materiale deperibile', in *IV Congresso Nazionale di Archeologia Medievale. Abbazia di San Galgano (Chiusdino, SI), 26–20 settembre 2006*, ed. by Riccardo Francovich and Marco Valenti (Florence: All'Insegna del Giglio), pp. 539–45

——. 2008. 'Tecniche costruttive in legno e in terra, in Miranduolo in alta Val di Merse (Chiusdino-SI)', in *Archeologia su un sito di potere del Medioevo toscano*, ed. by Marco Valenti (Borgo San Lorenzo: All'Insegna del Giglio), pp. 245–81

——. 2011. 'Edilizia in materiali deperibili nell'alto medioevo italiano: metodologie e casi di studio per un'agenda della ricerca', *Post Classical Archaeologies*, 1: 95–138

Fumi, Luigi, ed. 1884. *Codice diplomatico della città d'Orvieto. Documenti e regesti dal secolo XI al XV e la Carta del Popolo, Codice statutario del comune di Orvieto* (Florence: Presso G.P. Vieussseux)

Gabbrielli, Fabio. 1990. *Romanico aretino, L'architettura protoromanica e romanica religiosa nella diocesi medievale di Arezzo* (Florence: Salimbeni)

——. 1995. 'All'alba del nuovo millennio: la ripresa dell'architettura religiosa tra X e XI secolo', in *L'architettura religiosa in Toscana: Il Medioevo*, ed. by G. Cantelli (Florence: Banca Toscana), pp. 9–55

——. 2005. 'Toscana. Chiese rurali: Il quadro storico architettonico', in *Alle origini del romanico: Monasteri, edifici religiosi, committenza tra storia e archeologia*, ed. by Renata Salvarani, Giancarlo Andenna, and Gian Pietro Brogiolo (Brescia: Marietti), pp. 277–88

——. 2008a. 'La cappella di Sant'Antimo e le tecniche murarie nelle chiese altomedievali rurali della Toscana (sec. VII–inizi sec. XI)', in *Chiese e insediamenti nei secoli di formazione dei paesaggi medievali della Toscana (V–X secolo): Atti del seminario, San Giovanni d'Asso-Montisi, 10–11 novembre 2006*, ed. by Stefano Campana (Florence: All'Insegna del Giglio), pp. 337–68

——. 2008b. 'Toscana. Chiese rurali: Il quadro storico architettonico', in *Alle origini del romanico, monasteri, edifici religiosi, committenza tra storia e archeologia*, ed. by Renata Salvarani, Giancarlo Andenna, and Gian Pietro Brogiolo (Brescia: Marietti), pp. 70–285

Gabucci, Ada. 2005. *Informatica applicata all'archeologia* (Rome: Carocci)

Gaggio Dario. 2018. *Shaping of Tuscany: Landscape and Society between Tradition and Modernity* (Cambridge: Cambridge University Press)

Gallichi, A. 1935. 'Confini antichi tra Magliano e Marsiliana', *Studi Etruschi*, 9: 428–35

Gambacorta, Federico. 2009. 'La circolazione monetaria nella Tuscia tra Medioevo e Rinascimento. Nuovi dati dai materiali provenienti dagli scavi di Corneto-Tarquinia', *Rivista italiana di Numismatica*, 110: 129–66

Gambogi, Pamela. 2000. 'Altorilievo frontonale', in *Gli Etruschi*, ed. by Mario Torelli (Milan: Bompiani), p. 632

Gamurrini, G. F. 1888. 'Talamone. Ruderi antichi ed oggetti scoperti sul poggio di Talamonaccio', in *Notizie degli Scavi di Antichità* (Rome: Accademia Nazionale dei Lincei)

Gasparri, Stefano, ed. 2008. *774: Ipotesi su una transizione. Atti del seminario di Poggibonsi, 16–18 febbraio 2006*, Seminari del Centro interuniversitario per la storia e l'archeologia dell'alto medioevo, 1 (Turnhout: Brepols)

Gelichi, Sauro, ed. 1991. *Archeologia medievale a Lugo. Aspetti del quotidiano nei ritrovamenti della Rocca* (Florence: All'Insegna del Giglio)

——. 1997a. *Introduzione all'archeologia medievale* (Rome: La Nuova Italia Scientifica)

——. 1997b. *I Congresso nazionale di archeologia medievale: Auditorium del Centro Studi della Cassa di Risparmio di Pisa (ex Benedettine) Pisa, 29–31 maggio 1997* (Florence: All'Insegna del Giglio)

——. 2007. 'Gestione e significato sociale della produzione, della circolazione e dei consumi della ceramica nell'Italia altomedievale', in *Archeologia e società tra tardo antico e alto medioevo*, ed. by Gian Pietro Brogiolo and Alexandra Chavarría Arnau (Mantua: SAP), pp. 47–69

——. 2008. 'The Eels of Venice. The Long Eighth Century of the Emporia of the Northern Region along the Adriatic Coast', in *774: Ipotesi su una transizione. Atti del seminario di Poggibonsi, 16–18 febbraio 2006*, ed. by Stefano Gasparri, Seminari del Centro interuniversitario per la storia e l'archeologia dell'alto medioevo, 1 (Turnhout: Brepols), pp. 81–117

Gelichi, Sauro and Antonio Alberti. 2005. *L'aratro e il calamo. Benedettini e cistercensi sul Monte Pisano. Dieci anni di archeologia a San Michele alla Verruca* (Pisa: San Giuliano Terme)

Gelichi, Sauro and Claudio Negrelli, eds. 2007. *La circolazione delle ceramiche nell'Adriatico tra tarda antichità e altomedioevo* (Mantua: SAP)

——. 2008. 'Anfore e commerci nell'alto Adriatico tra VIII e IX secolo', *Mélanges de l'École française de Rome. Moyen Âge*, 120: 307–26

Gelichi, Sauro and Richard Hodges, eds. 2012. *From One Sea to Another. Trading Places in the European and Mediterranean Early Middle Ages*, Seminari del Centro interuniversitario per la storia e l'archeologia dell'alto medioevo, 3 (Turnhout: Brepols)

Giannichedda, Enrico. 1997. 'Storia della cultura materiale', in *Archeologia postmedievale: L'esperienza europea e l'Italia, Convegno internazionale di studi, Sassari, 17–20 ottobre 1994* (Florence: All'Insegna del Giglio), pp. 117–32

——. 1998a. *Filattiera-Sorano: L'insediamento di età romana e tardo antica. Scavi 1986–1995* (Florence: All'Insegna del Giglio)

——. 1998b. 'I vetri (Ve)', in *Filattiera-Sorano: L'insediamento di età romana e tardo antica. Scavi 1986–1995*, ed. by Enrico Giannichedda (Florence: All'Insegna del Giglio), pp. 168–72

Giorgetti, G. 1961. *Le armi antiche: Dal 1000 D.C. al 1800 in tre volumi* (San Marino: Associazione Amatori Armi Antiche)

Giovannini, Fabio. 1998. 'Funzioni delle forme ceramiche e modelli alimentari medievali', in *Le ceramiche di Roma e del Lazio in età medievale e moderna*, III, ed. by Elisabetta De Minicis (Rome: Kappa) pp. 15–22

Giuntoli, Stefano. 2009. 'Le tombe a circolo dell'Accesa. Riflessioni sui caratteri strutturali di un tipo tombale dell'Orientalizzante vetuloniese', in *Etruria e Italia preromana: Studi in onore di Giovannangelo Camporeale*, ed. by Luciano Agostiniani and Stefano Bruni (Pisa: Serra), pp. 441–53

Ghisleni, Mariaelena. 2009. 'Il sito di Santa Marta nel contesto delle dinamiche insediative di età romana, tardoantica e medievale della media valle dell'Ombrone (Cinigiano, GR)', in *V Congresso Nazionale di Archeologia Medievale*, ed. by Giuliano Volpe and Pasquale Favia (Florence: All'Insegna del Giglio), pp. 243–47

——. 2010. 'Carta Archeologica della Provincia di Grosseto: Comune di Cinigiano. Dinamiche insediative e di potere tra V e XI secolo nella bassa val d'Orcia e nella media valle dell'Ombrone' (Dott. Diss., University of Siena)

Ghisleni, Mariaelena and B. Frezza. 2005. *La cultura materiale di Poggio Cavolo: Le ceramiche da ricognizione*, in *Il popolamento tardoromano e altomedievale nella bassa valle dell'Ombrone. Progetto Carta Archeologica della Provincia di Grosseto*, ed. by Stefano Campana, Riccardo Francovich, and Emanuele Vaccaro, *Archeologia Medievale*, 32: 476–79

Ghisleni, Mariaelena, Emanuele Vaccaro, and Kimberly Bowes. 2011. 'Excavating the Roman Peasant I: Excavations at Pievina', *Papers of the British School at Rome*, 79: 95–145

Giannotti, Stefano. 2005. 'Reperti particolari', in *L'aratro e il calamo. Benedettini e Cistercensi sul Monte Pisano. Dieci anni di archeologia a San Michele alla Verruca*, ed. by Sauro Gelichi and Antonio Alberti (Pisa: Felici Editore), pp. 383–96

Giardino, C. 1995. *Il Mediterraneo Occidentale tra XIV e VIII secolo a.C. Cerchie minerarie e metallurgiche* (Oxford: Archaeopress)

Giardino, Claudio. 1998. *I metalli nel mondo antico. Introduzione all'archeometallurgia* (Rome: Laterza)

Gillings, Mark, D. J. Mattingly, and Jan van Dalen. 2000. *Geographical Information Systems and Landscape Archaeology* (Oxford: Oxbow)

Ginatempo, Maria. 1988. *Crisi di un territorio: Demografia del dominio senese nel XVI secolo* (Florence: Olschki)

Giorgi, A. 1994. 'Aspetti del popolamento del contado di Siena tra l'inizio del Duecento ed i primi decenni del Trecento', in *Demografia e società nell'Italia medievale: Secoli IX–XIV*, ed. by Rinaldo Comba and Irma Naso (Cuneo: Società per gli studi storici, archeologici ed artistici della provincia di Cuneo), pp. 253–91

Giorgi, Ignazio. 1878. *Il regesto del monastero di S. Anastasio ad Aquas Salvias* (Rome: Società Romana di Storia Patria)

Giovannini, F. 1998. 'Funzioni delle forme ceramiche e modelli alimentari medievali', in *Le ceramiche di Roma e del Lazio in età medievale e moderna*, III, ed. by Elisabetta De Minicis (Rome: Kappa), pp. 15–22

Glaudel, Lydie. 2002. 'Note preliminari sulla ceramica del sito di Cencelle: l'esempio del settore III F', in *Le ceramiche di Roma e del Lazio in età medievale e moderna*, IV: *Atti del Convegno di studi, Viterbo, 22–23 maggio 1998*, ed. by Elisabetta De Minicis and Gabriella Maetzke (Rome: Kappa), pp. 256–65

Goodson, Caroline. J. 2010. *The Rome of Pope Paschal I: Papal Power, Urban Renovation, Church Building and Relic Translation, 817–24* (Cambridge: Cambridge University Press)

Grant, A. 1975. 'The Use of Tooth Wear as a Guide to the Age of Domestic Animals: A Brief Explanation'. in *Excavations at Portchester Castle*, I: *Roman*, ed. by Barry Cunliffe (London: Thames and Hudson), pp. 437–50

Grassi, Francesca. 1999. 'Le ceramiche invetriate da cucina dal XIII alla fine del XIV secolo nella oiscana meridionale', *Archeologia Medievale*, 26: 429–35

——. 2006. 'La ceramica tra VIII e X secolo nella Toscana meridionale: le tipologie, le funzioni, l'alimentazione', in *IV Congresso Nazionale di Archeologia Medievale. Abbazia di San Galgano (Chiusdino, SI), 26–20 settembre 2006*, ed. by Riccardo Francovich and Marco Valenti (Florence: All'Insegna del Giglio), pp. 461–67

——. 2010. *La Ceramica, l'Alimentazione, l'Artigianato e le vie di Commercio tra VIII e XIV Secolo: Il Caso della Toscana Meridionale* (Oxford: Archaeopress)

——. ed. 2013. *L'insediamento medievale nelle colline metallifere (Toscana, Italia). Il sito minerario di Rocchette Pannocchieschi dall'VIII al XIV secolo*, BAR International Series, 2532 (Oxford: BAR)

Grassi, Francesca, and Silvia Liguori. 2004. 'Per un preliminare catalogo dei reperti ceramici: i contesti di ante X–XI secolo', in *Castello di Donoratico: I risultati delle prime campagne di scavo, 2000–200*, ed. by Giovanna Bianchi (Florence: All'Insegna del Giglio), pp. 115–38

Grey, Cam. 2011. *Constructing Communities in the Late Roman Countryside* (Cambridge: Cambridge University Press)

Grierson, Philip. 1991. *Coins of Medieval Europe* (London: Seaby)

Grierson, Philip and Mark Blackburn. 1986. *Medieval European Coinage*, I: *The Early Middle Ages 5th–10th centuries* (Cambridge: Cambridge University Press)

Grierson, Philip and Lucia Travaini. 1998. *Medieval European Coinage*, XIV: *Italy (III) (South Italy, Sicily, Sardinia* (Cambridge: Cambridge University Press)

Guaitini, Grazietta. 1981. *Ceramiche medioevali dell'Umbria* (Florence: Guaraldi)

Guarducci, Anna, ed. 2000. *Orbetello e i Presidios, Atti del convegno, Orbetello* (Florence: Centro editoriale toscano)

Guideri, Silvia. 2000a. 'Analisi preliminari sui resti di lavorazione siderurgica rinvenuti all'interno delle fortificazioni sommitali', in *Archeologia a Montemassi: Un castello fra storia e storia dell'arte*, ed. by Silvia Guideri, Roberto Parenti, and Francesco Barbagli (Florence: All'Insegna del Giglio), pp. 223–26

——. 2000b. 'Il popolamento medievale attraverso un'indagine di superficie', in *Archeologia a Montemassi: Un castello fra storia e storia dell'arte*, ed. by Silvia Guideri, Roberto Parenti, and Francesco Barbagli (Florence: All'Insegna del Giglio), pp. 11–37

Guideri, Silvia, Roberto Parenti, and Francesco Barbagli. 2000. *Archeologia a Montemassi: Un castello fra storia e storia dell'arte* (Florence: All'Insegna del Giglio)

Guidi, Pietro, ed. 1932. *Rationes decimarum Italiae nel secoli XIII e XIV. Tuscia*, I: *La decima degli anni 1274–1280* (Vatican City: Biblioteca apostolica Vaticana)

Guidi, Salvatico Guido. 1941. *Appunti storici sulla Famiglia dei conti Guidi del Casentino e di Volterra* (Volterra: Tipografia Cavalier Carnieri)

Güll, Paolo, Domenico Fronti, Giuseppe Romagnoli, and Francesca Wick. 2001. 'Viterbo, indagini archeologiche 1997–1999: nuovi dati per la topografia urbana e la cultura materiale', *Archeologia Medievale*, 28: 275–94

Halstead, P., P. Collins, and V. Isaakidou. 2002. 'Sorting the Sheep from the Goats: Morphological Distinctions between the Mandibles and Mandibular Teeth of Adult *Ovis* and *Capra*', *Journal of Archaeological Science*, 29.5: 545–53

Harris, William V. 1971. *Rome in Etruria and Umbria* (Oxford: Clarendon Press)

——. ed. 2005. *Rethinking the Mediterranean* (Oxford: Oxford University Press)

Hayes, John Walker. 1992. *Excavations at Saraçhane in Istanbul: The Pottery* (Princeton: Princeton University Press)

Haynes, Sybille. 2000. *Etruscan Civilization: A Cultural History* (Los Angeles: J. Paul Getty Trust)

Heers, Jacques. 1992. *Transizione al mondo moderno (1300–1520)* (Milan: Jaca)

Heinzelmann, M., H. Becker, K. Eder, and M. Stephani. 1997. 'Vorbericht zu einer geophysikalischen Prospektionskampagne in Ostia Antica', *Mitteilungen des Deutschen Archäologischen Instituts, Roemische Abteilung*, 104: 537–48

Herlihy, David. 1977. *The Black Death and the Transformation of the West* (Cambridge, MA: Harvard University Press)

Herring, Edward and Kathryn Lomas. 2000. *The Emergence of State Identities in Italy in the First Millennium BC* (London: University of London)

Hildebrand, M. 1955. 'Skeletal Differences between Deer, Sheep, and Goats', *California Fish and Game*, 41.4: 327–46

Hirschland Ramage, N. 1970. 'Studies in Early Etruscan Bucchero', *Papers of the British School at Rome*, 28: 1–61

Hobart, Michelle. 1991. 'La Maiolica Arcaica di Cosa (Orbetello)', in *Dalla maiolica arcaica alla maiolica del primo Rinascimento: Atti XXIV Convegno internazionale della ceramica, Albisola, 24–26 maggio 1991* (Albisola: Centro ligure per la storia della ceramica.), pp. 71–89

——. 1992. 'La ceramica Invetriata', in *La ceramica invetriata tardoantica e altomedievale in Italia*, ed. by Lidia Paroli (Florence: All'Insegna del Giglio), pp. 304–09

——. 1995. 'Cosa-Ansedonia (Orbetello) in età medievale: Da una città romana ad un insediamento medievale sparso', *Archeologia Medievale*, 22: 569–83

——. 2003 'Ansedonia: The Settlement of the Twelfth through the Fourteenth Centuries', in *Cosa V: An Intermittent Town, Excavations 1991–1997*, ed. by Elizabeth Fentress (Ann Arbor: University of Michigan), pp. 120–37

——. 2009. 'Rivisitare gli scavi. Il castello di Tricosto presso Capalbiaccio (GR). Fonti e cultura materiale', in *V Congresso Nazionale di Archeologia Medievale*, ed. by Giuliano Volpe and Pasquale Favia (Florence: All'Insegna del Giglio)

——. 2010. 'Merchants, Monks and Medieval Sardinian Architecture', in *Studies in the Archaeology of the Medieval Mediterranean*, ed. by J. G. Schryver (Leiden: Brill), pp. 93–114

Hobart, Michelle, Stefano Campana, John Mitchell, and Richard Hodges, and others 2012. 'Monasteri contesi nella Tuscia Longobarda: il caso di San Pietro d'Asso, Montalcino (Siena)', *Archeologia Medievale* 39: 175–213

Hobart, Michelle, Laura Cerri, Emanule Mariotti, Irene Corti, Valeria Acconcia, Emanuele Vaccaro, Chiara Valdambrini, and Hermann Salvadori. 2009. 'Capalbiaccio (GR) nel tempo: dalla preistoria all'età moderna. Le indagini archeologiche dagli anni '70 al nuovo progetto di ricerca', *Archeologia Medievale*, 36: 81–125

Hobart, Michelle, Laura Cerri, Emanuele Mariotti, Irene Corti, Valeria Acconcia, Emanuele Vaccaro, and Hermann Salvadori. 2010. 'Castello di Tricosto (GR)', *The Journal of Fasti Online*, 197

Hodder, Ian and Clive Orton. 1976. *Spatial Analysis in Archaeology* (Cambridge: Cambridge University Press)

Hodges, Richard. 2000. *Visions of Rome: Thomas Ashby, Archaeologist* (London: British School at Rome)

——. 2008. 'AD 774 and After: The Archaeology of Charlemagne's Age in Italy', in *774: Ipotesi su una transizione. Atti del seminario di Poggibonsi, 16–18 febbraio 2006*, Seminari del Centro interuniversitario per la storia e l'archeologia dell'alto medioevo, 1 (Turnhout: Brepols), pp. 161–71

——. 2010a. 'AD 536: The Year Merlin (Supposedly) Died', in *Climate Crises in Human History*, ed. by A. Bruce Mainwaring, Robert Giegengack, and Claudio Vita-Finzi (Philadelphia: Diane Publishing), pp. 73–84

——. 2010b. 'Ripensando San Vincenzo al Volturno', *Archeologia Medievale*, 37: 497–512

——. 2012. *Dark Age Economics: A New Audit* (London: Bristol Classic Press)

——. 2014. 'Medieval Archaeology and Civic Society: Celebrating 40 Years of *Acheologia Medievale*', *Acheologia Medievale*, 2014 special number: 205–11

Hodges, Richard, Chris Wickham, and Graeme Barker. 1995. 'The Evolution of Hilltop Villages (AD 600–1500)', in *A Mediterranean Valley: Landscape Archaeology and the Annales History in the Biferno Valley*, ed. by G. Barker (London: Leicester University Press), pp. 254–85

Hodges, Richard, S. Leppard, and John Mitchell. 2011. *San Vincenzo Maggiore and its Workshops* (London: British School at Rome)

Holdaway, Simon, Patricia Fanning, and Justin Shiner. 2005. 'Absence of Evidence or Evidence of Absence? Understanding the Chronology of Indigenous Occupation of Western New South Wales. Australia', *Archaeology in Oceania*: 33–49

Hook, J. 1977. 'Fortifications and the End of the Sienese State', *History*, 62: 372–87

Horden, Peregrine and Nicholas Purcell. 2000. *The Corrupting Sea. A Study of Mediterranean History* (Oxford: Wiley Blackwell)

Hubert, Étienne. 2000. 'L'incastellamento dans le Latium : Remarques à propos de fouilles récents', *Annales. Histoire, Sciences Sociales*, 55.3: 583–99

Iaia, Cristiano and Alessandro Mandolesi. 1993. 'Topografia dell'insediamento dell'VIII sec. A.C. in Etruria Meridionale', *Journal of Ancient Topography*, 3: 17–48

Isaacs, A. K. 1979. 'Le campagne senesi fra quattrocento e cinquecento: regime fondiario e governo signorile', in *Contadini e proprietari nella Toscana moderna. Atti del Convegno in memoria di Giorgio Giorgetti*, ed. by Giovanni Cherubini (Florence: Olschki), pp. 377–403

Izzet, Vedia. 2007. *The Archaeology of Etruscan Society* (Cambridge: Cambridge University Press)

Johnson Matthew. 2002. *Behind the Castle Gate: From the Middle Ages to the Renaissance* (London: Routledge)

Judson, Sheldon and Anne Kahane. 1963. 'Underground Drainageways in Southern Etruria', *Papers of the British School at Rome*, 31: 74–99

Kehr, P. F. 1908. *Regesta Pontificum Romanorum. Italia Pontificia sive Repertorium privilegiorum et litterarum a Romanis pontificibus ante anno MCXCVIII Italiae ecclesiis, civitatibus singulisque personis concessorum, 3: Etruria* (Berolini: Weidmann)

King, A. 1999. 'Diet in the Roman World: A Regional Inter-site Comparison of the Mammal Bones', *Journal of Roman Archaeology*, 12: 35–64

Kurze, Wilhelm, 1989. 'I momenti principali della storia di S. Salvatoare al Monte Amiata', in *L'Amiata nel medioevo*, ed. by Mario Ascheri (Rome: Viella), pp. 38–48

——. 2008. *Scritti di storia Toscana: Assetti territoriali, diocesi, monasteri dai Longobardi all'età comunale* (Pistoia: Società Pistoiese di Storia Patria)

Kurze, Wilhelm, and Carlo Citter. 1995. 'La Toscana', in *Città e castelli, champagne el territorio di frontier (secoli VI–VII)*, ed. by Gian Pietro Brogiolo (Mantua: Società Archeologica Padana), pp. 159–81

La Carrubba, Vincenza. 2003. 'Il dizionario Geogradico Fisico Storico della Toscana di Emanuele Repetti', *Trame nello spazio. Quaderni di geografia storica e quantitativa*, 1: 59–69

La Carrubba, Vincenza and Giancarlo Macchi. 2005. 'L'informatizzazione del Dizionario Geografico Fisico Storico della Toscana di Emanuele Repetti', in *Archeologia dei paesaggi medievali: Relazione progetto (2000–2004)*, ed. by Riccardo Francovich and Marco Valenti (Florence: All'Insegna del Giglio), pp. 487–503

La Salvia, Vasco. 2005. 'Appendice', in Francesca Zagari, *Il metallo nel medioevo. Tecniche Strutture Manufatti* (Rome: Palombi 2005), pp. 92–94

Lawrence, A. W. 1964. 'Early Medieval Fortifications near Rome', *Papers of the British School at Rome* n.s. 19: 89–122

Leighton, Robert. 2004. *Tarquinia: An Etruscan City* (London: Duckworth)

Le Goff Jacques. 1964. *La civilisation de l'Occident médiéval* (Paris: Arthoud)

——. 2003. *Alla ricerca del Medioevo* (Bari: Laterza)

Leo Imperiale, Marco. 2004. 'Otranto, cantiere Mitello: Un centro produttivo nel Mediterraneo bizantino', in *La ceramica altomedievale in Italia*, ed. by Stella Patitucci Uggeri (Florence: All'Insegna del Giglio), pp. 327–42

Levi, Doro. 1927. 'Escursione archeologica nell'Agro Cosano', *Studi Etruschi*, 1: 477–85

Libro d'Oro = *Libro d'Oro e registro degli Statuti della città di Orbetello del 1414, con conferme e aggiunte (anni 1573–1797), Serie 11ª, Statuti e Miscellanea (anni 1557–1865), f. 598/B* (Orbetello: Archivio Storico del Comune di Orbetello)

Liguori, Silvia. 2004. 'Ceramica depurata', in *Castello di Donoratico: i risultati delle prime campagne di scavo, 2000–2002*, ed. by Giovanna Bianchi (Florence: All'Insegna del Giglio), pp. 122–28

——. 2007. 'Le ceramiche della volta absidale con rivestimenti vetrificati', in *Piombino. La chiesa di Sant'Antimo sopra i canali. Ceramiche e architetture per la lettura archeologica di un abitato medievale e del suo porto*, ed. by Graziella Berti and Giovanna Bianchi (Florence: All'Insegna del Giglio), pp. 159–298

Lisini, A. 1932. 'La contessa palatina Margherita Aldobrandeschi e il suo matrimonio con il conte Guido di Monforte', *Bullettino Senese di Storia Patria*, 34: 335–36

Lanconelli, Angela. 1998. 'Oltre i confini di Siena: le fortificazioni pontificie nella terra del Patrimonio', in *Fortilizi e campi di battaglia nel Medioevo intorno a Siena. Atti del convegno di studi, Siena, 25–26 ottobre 1996*, ed. by Mario Marrocchi (Siena: Nuova Immagine), pp. 321–26

Lotti, Bernardo. 1891. *Rilevamenti geologici delle tavolette di Orbetello, Talamone e Grosseto*, Geologia della Toscana, 13 (Rome: Tipografia Nazionale)

Luna, Arianna. 1999. 'Nuove acquisizioni sulla maiolica arcaica senese: i dati dal pozzo di "butto" della Civetta (Siena)', *Archeologia Medievale*, 26: 411–27

——. 2002. 'Le ceramiche della volta', in *C'era una Volta. La ceramica medievale nel convento del Carmine*, ed. by Riccardo Francovich and Marco Valenti (Siena: Santa Maria della Scala), pp. 38–45

Luttazi, A. 1995. 'Le ceramiche dello scavo di S. Ilario "ad bivium" tra tardoantico e medioevo', in *Le ceramiche di Roma e del Lazio in età medievale e moderna*, II, ed. by Elisabetta De Minicis (Rome: Kappa), pp. 221–40

Luttrell, Anthony. 2001. 'The Medieval Ager Cosanus', in *Siena e Maremma nel Medioevo*, ed. by Mario Ascheri (Siena: Betti)

Luzi, Romualdo. 1990. 'La Zaffera a Viterbo e nella Tuscia', in *Zaffera et similia nelle maioliche Italiane* ed. by Conti and others (Viterbo: FAVL Edizioni Artistiche Viterbo), pp. 183–245

——. 1994. 'I luoghi della ceramica nel viterbese', in *Le ceramiche di Roma e del Lazio in età medievale e moderna*, I, ed. by Elisabetta De Minicis (Rome: Kappa), pp. 66–71

Macchi, Jánica G. 2006. 'La struttura della maglia dei castelli medievali nell'Italia centrale: paralleli tra modelli di stanziamento umano', *Archeologia Medievale*, 33: 7–18

Maetzke, Guglielmo. 1956. 'Magliano in Toscana. Tombe etrusche in località Poggio Bacchino', *Notizie degli Scavi di antichità*: 6–18

Maggiani, Adriano. 1999. 'Nuovi etnici e toponimi etruschi', in *Incontro di studi in memoria di Massimo Pallottino* (Pisa: Instituti editoriali e poligrafici internazionali), pp. 47–64

——. 2008. 'Oppida e castella. La difesa del territorio', in *La città murata in Etruria: Atti del XXV convegno di studi etruschi ed italici, Chianciano Terme, Sarteano, Chiusi, 30 marzo–3 aprile 2005* (Pisa: Serra)

Manacorda, Daniele. 1978. 'The Ager Cosanus and the Production of the Amphorae of Sestius: New Evidence and a Reassessment', *Journal of Roman Studies*, 68: 122–31

——. 1980. 'L'ager cosanus tra tarda repubblica e impero: forme di produzione e assetto della proprietà', *Memoirs of the American Academy in Rome*, 36: 173–84

——. 1981. 'Produzione agricola, produzione ceramica e proprietari nell'ager Cosanus nel I sec. A.C.', in *Società romana e produzione schiavistica*, II: *Merci mercati e scambi nel Mediterraneo*, ed. by A. Giardina and A. Schiavone (Bari: Laterza), pp. 3–54

Manacorda, Daniele. 1982. *Archeologia urbana a Roma: il progetto della Crypta Balbi* (Florence: All'Insegna del Giglio)

Manganelli, Mario and Elvio Pacchiani, eds. 2002. *Città e territorio in Etruria. Per una definizione di città nell'etruria settentrionale. Colle Val d'Elsa (12–13 marzo 1999)* (Siena: Grafiche Boccacci)

Mannoni, Tiziano. 1976. 'L'analisi delle tecniche murarie in Liguria', in *Atti del Colloquio internazionale di archeologia medievale, Palermo-Erice, 20–22 settembre 1974* (Palermo: Università di Palermo), pp. 291–302

——. 1976a. 'Una rifondazione dell'archeologia postclassica. La storia della cultura materiale', *Archeologia Medievale*, 3: 7–24

——. 1984. 'Metodi di datazione dell'edilizia storica', *Archeologia Medievale*, 11: 396–403

——. 1988. 'Archeologia della produzione', in *Archeologia e restauro dei monumenti*, ed. by Riccardo Francovich and Roberto Parenti (Florence: All'Insegna del Giglio), pp. 403–20

——. 1997. 'Il problema complesso delle murature storiche in pietra, I: Cultura materiale e crono tipologia', *Archeologia dell'Architettura*, 2: 15–24

Mannoni, Tiziano and Giovanni Murialdo. 2001. *S. Antonio, un insediamento fortificato nella Liguria bizantina* (Florence: All'Insegna del Giglio)

Mansuelli, G. 1985. 'L'organizzazione del territorio e la città', in *Civiltà degli Etruschi*, ed. by Mauro Cristofani (Florence: Regione toscana), p. 42

Manzoni, Marcello. 1968. *Dizionario di geologia* (Bologna: Zanichelli)

Marasco, Lorenzo. 2002–2003. 'Il castello di Scarlino tra VII e XIII secolo. Elaborazione e analisi dello scavo archeologico' (Laurea diss., University of Siena)

Marazzi, Federico. 1994. 'Le "città nuove" pontificie e l'insediamento laziale nel IX secolo', in *La Storia dell'Alto Medioevo italiano (VI–X secolo) alla luce dell'archeologia*, ed. by Riccardo Francovich and Ghislaine Noyè (Florence: All'Insegno del Giglio), pp. 251–98

Marchetti, Maria Isabella. 1998. 'Maiolica arcaica dai settori I e II di Cencelle', in *Le ceramiche di Roma e del Lazio in età medievale e moderna*, III, ed. by Elisabetta De Minicis (Rome: Kappa), pp. 103–08

Mariotti, Emanuele. 2009. 'Il rilievo topografico del terreno', in *Hephaestia 2000–2006. Ricerche e scavi della Scuola Archeologica Italiana di Atene in collaborazione con il Dipartimento di Archeologia e Storia delle Arti dell'Università di Siena*, ed. by Emanuele Greco and Emanuele Papi (Paestum (Salerno): Pandemos), pp. 171–79

Mariotti, Emanuele, L. Botarelli, G. Carpentiero, Laura Cerri, D. D'Aco, F. Martorella, and Emanuele Papi. 2002. 'Hephaestia: ricerche e scavi nell'area della città, 2005', *Annali della scuola di Atene* 80: 309–15

Marrochi, M. 1998. *Fortilizi e Campi di Battaglia nel medioeve attorno a Siena, Atti del convegno di studi, Siena 25–26 ott. 1996* (Siena: Santa Maria della Scala)

Mascagni, Aurora. 2006–2007. 'La cultura material da un'abitazione del castello minerario di Cugnano: l'area 6000' (Laurea diss., University of Siena)

Massari, Alessandra and Giulia Sordi. 1995. 'Monte Tellere (Pitigliano, GR). Rinvenimento di un probabile insediamento dell'età del bronzo', in *Preistoria e Protostoria in Etruria: Tipologia delle necropoli e rituali di deposizione. Ricerche e scavi*, ed. by Nuccia Negroni Catacchio (Milan: Centro studi di preistoria e archeologia), pp. 257–58

Materazzi, Filippo and Marco Pacifici. 2021. 'Novità dall'area urbana di Veio. Telerilevamento multispettrale da drone e indici di vegetazione: Nuovi strumenti per l'identificazione dei crop-mark dall'area di Campetti', *Scienze dall'Antichità*, 26.1: 95–117

Matzke, Michael. 1993. 'Vom Ottolinus zum Grossus: Münzprägung in der Toscana vom 10. Bis zum 13. Jahrhundert', *Schweizerische Numismatische Rundschau*, 72: 135–99

——. 1995. 'Daiberto e la prima crociata', in *Nel IX centenario della metropoli ecclesiastica di Pisa. Atti del convegno di studi (7–8 maggio 1992)* (Pisa: Pacini), pp. 95–129

Mazza, Guido. 1983. *La ceramica medievale di Viterbo e dell'alto Lazio* (Viterbo: Edizioni Libri d'arte)

Mazzanti, R. 1983. 'Il punto sul Quaternario della fascia costiera e dell'Arcipelago di Toscana meridionale', *Bolletino della Società Geologica Italiana*, 102: 419–556

Mazzini, Ilaria, Pere Anadon, Maurizio Barbieri, Francesca Castorina, L. Ferreli, Elsa Gliozzi, Marco Mola, and E. Vittori. 1999. 'Late Quaternary Sea-level Changes along the Tyrrhenian Coast near Orbetello (Tuscany, Central Italy): Palaeoenvironmental Reconstruction Using Ostracods', *Marine Micropaleontology*, 37: 289–311

Mazzolai, Aldo. 1960. *Roselle e il suo territorio* (Grosseto: STEM)

——. 1984. *Grosseto il museo archeologico della Maremma* (Grosseto: Comune di Grosseto)

Mazzucato, Otto. 1975. *Ceramiche medioevali e rinascimentali dall'Etruria meridionale* (Rome: Editrice Artistica)

——. 1982. *Indagine su una forma. La ciotola romana del primo quattrocento* (Rome: Consiglio Nazionale delle Ricerche)

McCann, Anna Marguerite. 1979. 'The Harbor and Fishery Remains at Cosa, Italy', *Journal of Field Archaeology*, 6: 391–411

——. 1987. *The Roman Port and Fishery of Cosa: A Center of Ancient Trade* (Princeton, NJ: Princeton University Press)

McCormick, Michael. 2001. *Origins of the European Economy: Communications and Commerce, AD 300–900* (Cambridge: Cambridge University Press)

——. 2002. 'New Light in the Dark Ages. How the Trade Slave Fueled the Carolingian Economy', *Past and Present*, 177: 18–54

Menchelli, Simonetta. 1993. 'Vasellame privo di rivestimento per usi vari. Forme chiuse (MAC)', in *Pisa: Piazza Dante. Uno spaccato della storia pisana: la campagna di scavo 1991*, ed. by Stefano Bruni (Pisa: Cassa di Risparmio di Pisa), pp. 473–524

Menchelli, Simonetta and Catia Renzi Rizzo. 2000. 'Ceramica priva di rivestimento: forme chiuse', in *Ricerche di archeologia medievale a Pisa, I: Piazza dei Cavalieri, la campagna di scavo 1993*, ed. by Stefano Bruni, Elisabetta Abela, and Graziella Berti (Florence: All'Insegna del Giglio), pp. 123–62

Meneghini, Roberto and Riccardo Santangeli Valenzani. 2004. 'Edilizia Residenziale', in *Roma nell'altomedioevo: Topografia e urbanistica della città dal V al X secolo*, ed. by Roberto Meneghini and Riccardo Santangeli Valenzani (Rome: Libreria dello Stato, Istituto poligrafico e Zecca dello Stato), pp. 31–51

Mendera, Marja. 2000. 'I vetri', in *Archeologia a Montemassi: Un castello fra storia e storia dell'arte*, ed. by Silvia Guideri, Roberto Parenti and Francesco Barbagli (Florence: All'Insegna del Giglio), pp. 207–10

——. 2003. 'Il material vitreo', in *Campiglia: Un castello e il suo territorio*, ed. by Giovanna Bianchi (Florence: All'Insegna del Giglio), pp. 362–81

Mendera, Marja and Silvia Cini. 1990. 'Vetri', in *Archeologia urbana a Roma: Il progetto Crypta Balbi, 5, L'esedra della Crypta Balbi nel Medioevo (XI–XV secolo)*, ed. by Lucia Saguì and Lidia Paroli (Florence: All'Insegna del Giglio), pp. 493–512

Merciai, Giuseppe. 1910. *Mutamenti avvenuti nella configurazione del litorale fra Pisa e Orbetello dal Pliocene in poi* (Pisa: Succ. FF. Nistri)

——. 1929. 'Sulle condizioni fisiche del litorale etrusco tra Livorno e Civitavecchia', *Studi Etruschi*, 3: 347–58

Michelucci, Maurizio. 1977. 'Per una cronologia delle urne chiusine. Riesame di alcuni contesti di scavo', in *Caratteri dell'ellenismo nelle urne etrusche: Atti dell'incontro di studi, Università di Siena, 28–30 aprile 1976* (Florence: Centro Di), pp. 93–102

——. 1981. 'Magliano', in *Gli Etruschi in Maremma*, ed. by Mauro Cristofani (Milan: Silvana), pp. 102–06

——. 1982. *Saturnia, ricerche nell'area urbana e nella necropoli del Puntone* (Pitigliano: Comune di Pitigliano)

——. 1983. 'Marsiliana', *Studi Etruschi*, 51: 449–53

——. 1984. 'Caletra, Kalousion, Heba. Indagini sugli insediamenti etruschi nella bassa valle dell'Albegna', in *Studi di antichità in onore di Guglielmo Maetzke*, II (Rome: L'Erma di Bretschneider), pp. 337–92

——. 1985a. 'Doganella-Kalousion', in *La romanizzazione dell'Etruria: Il territorio di Vulci*, ed. by Andrea Carandini (Florence: Regione Toscana), pp. 110–14

——. 1985b. 'Armi e attrezzi agricoli. I ripostigli di Talamone', in *La romanizzazione dell'Etruria: Il territorio di Vulci*, ed. by Andrea Carandini (Florence: Regione Toscana; Milan: Electa), pp. 44–47

——. 1991. 'Contributo alla ricostruzione del popolamento dell'Ager Caletranus in età arcaica. La necropoli di S. Donato di Orbetello', *Studi Etruschi*, 57: 11–52

——. 2008. 'La cinta muraria e la distruzione dell'abitato etrusco di Doganella', in *La città murata in Etruria: Atti del XXV convegno di studi etruschi ed italici, Chianciano Terme, Sarteano, Chiusi, 30 marzo–3 aprile 2005: in memoria di Massimo Pallottino*, ed. by Orazio Paoletti and Maria Chiara Bettini (Pisa: Serra), pp. 91–105

Michetti, Maria Laura. 2017. 'Osservazioni sull'architettura etrusca tra la fine del IV e il III secolo a.C., tra edilizia pubblica e committenza privata', in *L'architettura greca in Occidente nel III sec. A.C.*, ed. by Luigi M. Caliò and Jacques Des Courtils (Rome: Quasar), pp. 301–21

Milanese, Marco. 1997. *La ceramica postmedievale in Toscana. Documenti archeologici su produzione e consumo* (Florence: All'Insegna del Giglio)

Milanese, Marco and Monica Baldassarri, eds. 2004. *Il castello e l'uliveto. Insediamento e trasformazioni del paesaggio dalle indagini archeologiche di Massa in Valdinievole* (Massa e Cozzile: Comune di Massa e Cozzile)

Miller, Martin. 2013. 'Heba (Magliano)'. *Brill's New Pauly Online*, ed. by Hubert Cancik and Helmuth Schneider <https://referenceworks.brillonline.com/entries/brill-s-new-pauly/heba-magliano-e504530>

Minto, Antonio. 1925. 'Saturnia etrusca e romana. Le recenti scoperte archeologiche', *Monumenti Antichi*, 30: 585–705

—— . 1935. 'Per la topografia di Heba etrusca nel territorio di Magliano in Toscana', *Studi Etruschi*, 9: 11–59

Minto, Antonio and Tomaso Corsini. 1921. *Marsiliana d'Albegna: Le scoperte archeologiche del Principe Don Tommaso Corsini* (Florence: Fratelli Alinari)

Modolo, Mirco, Silvia Pallecchi, Giuliano Volpe, and Enrico Zanini, eds. 2019. *Una lezione di archeologia globale: studi in onore di Daniele Manacorda* (Bari: Edipuglia)

Molinari, Alessandra. 1990. 'Le ceramiche rivestite bassomedievali', in *Archeologia urbana a Roma: Il progetto Crypta Balbi, 5, L'esedra della Crypta Balbi nel Medioevo (XI–XV secolo)*, ed. by Lucia Saguì and Lidia Paroli (Florence: All'Insegna del Giglio), pp. 357–484

—— . 2003. 'La ceramica medievale in Italia ed il suo possibile utilizzo per lo studio della storia economica', *Archeologia Medievale*, 30: 519–28

—— . 2010. 'Siti rurali e poteri signorili nel Lazio (secoli X–XIII)', *Archeologia Medievale*, 37: 129–42

Molinos, Manuel and Andrea Zifferero. 1998. *Political and Cultural Frontiers*, BAR International Series, 717 (Oxford: BAR)

—— . 2002. *I primi popoli d' Europa. Proposte e riflessioni sulle origini della civiltà nell'Europa mediterranea* (Florence: All'Insegna del Giglio)

Montanari, Massimo. 1997. 'Strutture di produzione e sistemi alimentari nell'alto Medioevo', in *Storia dell'alimentazione*, ed. by Jean-Louis Flandrin, Danièle Alexandre-Bidon, and Massimo Montanari (Rome: Laterza), pp. 217–25

Moore, Valeri A. 1984. 'Florentine "Zaffera a Rilievo" Maiolica: A New Look at the Oriental Influence', *Archeologia Medievale*, 11: 477–500

Morel, Jean Paul. 1981. *Céramique Campanienne, les Formes* (Rome: École française de Rome)

Morgan, J. 2011. 'Absence of Evidence or Evidence of Absence? Mobility, Status and Housing in Early Greece' (unpubl. paper presented at the Greek Archaeology Group Seminar Series, School of Archaeology, Oxford)

Mori, Attilio. 1932. 'Ricerche sui laghi dell'Orbetellano e del Capalbiese', *Bollettino della Società Geologica Italiana*, 51: 7–22, 39–52

Muntoni, Francesco. 1972. *Le monete dei papi e degli stati pontifici*, I (Rome: Santamaria)

Murialdo, Giovanni. 2001a. 'Gli elementi da parure in osso o corno e gli amuleti', in *S. Antonio, un insediamento fortificato nella Liguria bizantina*, ed. by Tiziano Mannoni and Giovanni Murialdo (Florence: All'Insegna del Giglio), pp. 521–23

—— . 2001b. 'I pettini ad elementi multipli', in *S. Antonio, un insediamento fortificato nella Liguria bizantina*, ed. by Tiziano Mannoni and Giovanni Murialdo (Florence: All'Insegna del Giglio), pp. 525–29

Murray Threipland, Leslie and Mario Torelli. 1970. 'A Semi-subterranean Etruscan Building in the Casale Pian Roseto (Veii) Area', *Papers of the British School at Rome*, 38: 62–121

Nagle, D. Brendan. 1976. 'The Etruscan Journey of Tiberius Gracchus', *Historia*, 25: 487–89

Nardini, Alessandra, ed. 2001. *Carta archeologica della Provincia di Siena*, IV: *Chiusdino* (Siena: Nuova Immagine)

Negrelli, Claudio. 2007. 'Vasellame e contenitori da trasporto tra tarda antichità ed altomedioevo: L'Emilia Romagna e l'area medio-adriatica', in *La circolazione delle ceramiche nell'Adriatico tra tarda antichità e altomedioevo*, ed. by Sauro Gelichi and Claudio Negrelli (Mantua: SAP), pp. 297–330

Negroni Catacchio, Nuccia. 1979. 'Ritrovamenti dell'età del bronzo sul colle di Talamonaccio (Orbetello-Grosseto)', *Rivista di Scienze preistoriche*, 34.1/2: 255–62

—— . ed. 1995. *Preistoria e Protostoria in Etruria: Tipologia delle necropoli e rituali di deposizione. Ricerche e scavi* (Milan: Centro studi di preistoria e archeologia)

—— . 2005. 'L'abitato di Sovana alla luce delle recenti scoperte: Gli scavi dell'Università degli studi di Milano nell'area della cattedrale', in *Dinamiche di sviluppo delle città nell'Etruria meridionale: Veio, Caere, Tarquinia, Vulci: Atti del XXIII Convegno di studi etruschi ed italici: Roma, Veio, Cerveteri/Pyrgi, Tarquinia, Tuscania, Vulci, Viterbo, 1–6 ottobre 2001*, ed. by Orazio Paoletti (Pisa: Istituti editoriali e poligrafici internazionali), pp. 567–84

Nicosia, Francesco and Gabriella Poggesi, eds. 1998. *Roselle. Guida al parco archeologico* (Siena: Nuova immagine)

Norman, Diana, ed. 1995. *Siena, Florence and Padua: Art, Society and Religion 1280–1400* (New Haven: Yale University Press)

Nucciotti, Michele. 2005. 'Le pietre del potere. Per una storia archeologica dei quadri politico-istituzionali dell'Amiata occidentale nel medioevo (secoli X–XIV)' (Dott. Diss, Università degli Studi)

———. 2006. 'L'Amiata nel medioevo (secoli VIII–XIV): Modi, tempi e luoghi della formazione di un paesaggio storico', in *Il parco minerario dell'Amiata. Il territorio e la sua storia*, ed. by Zefiro Ciuffolotti (Archidosso: Effigi), pp. 161–99

———. 2010. 'Paesaggi dell'Impero nella Toscana del X secolo. Il *palatium* di Arcidosso: Senso storico di un tipo edilizio europero', *Archeologia Medievale*, 37: 513–27

———. 2015. 'Il palazzo comitale ducale di Santa Fiora (sec. XII–XVIII): Archeologia, ruolo storico e architettura', in *Gli Sforza di Santa Fiora. Feudalità e brigantaggio, Arcidosso (Gr)*, ed. by M. Mambrini (Archidosso: Effigi), pp. 203–18

Nucciotti, Michele and Guido Vannini 2002, 'Santa Fiora: strutture materiali di una capitale rurale nella Toscana meridionale nel medioevo', in *Gli Aldobrandeschi. La grande famiglia feudale della Maremma toscana*, ed. by Mario Ascheri and L. Niccolai (Arcidosso: Consulta cultura), pp. 111–49

Olcese, Gloria. 1993. *Le ceramiche comuni di Albintimilium. Indagine archeologica e archeometrica sui materiali dell'area del Cardine* (Florence: All'Insegna del Giglio)

Orton, Clive, Paul Tyers, and Alan Vince. 1993. *Pottery in Archaeology* (Cambridge: Cambridge University Press)

Pacciarelli, Marco. 1991a. 'Ricerche topografiche a Vulci: dati e problemi relativi all'origine delle città medio tirreniche', *Studi Etruschi*, 56: 11–48

———. 1991b. 'Territorio Insediamento, comunità in Etruria meridionale agli esordi del processo di urbanizzazione', *Scienze delle Antichità*, 5: 163–208

———. 1999. 'Le origini di Vulci e il suo entroterra', in *Atti del Convegno Ferrante Rittatore Vonwiller e la Maremma, 1936–1976, Ischia di Castro, 4–5 aprile 1998* (Florence: All'Insegna del Giglio), pp. 55–67

———. 2000. *Dal villaggio alla città. La svolta proto-urbana del 1000 a.C. nell'Italia tirrenica* (Florence: All'Insegna del Giglio)

Pallecchi, P. 2009. 'La "panchina" dell'antico bacino estrattivo dei Buche delle fate: Considerazioni sui caratteri composizionali e tessiturali e sul suo utilizzo nella costruzione dell'acropoli e delle necropoli di Populonia', in *Materiali da costruzione e produzione del ferro: Studi sull'economia populoniese fra periodo etrusco e romanizzazione*, ed. by Franco Cambi, Fernando Cavari, and Cynthia Mascione (Bari: Edipuglia), pp. 65–70

Pallecchi, Silvia. 2011. 'I tombe a circolo sul Poggio di Macchiabuia', in *La valle del vino etrusco. Archeologia della valle dell'Albegna in età arcaica*, ed. by Marco Firmati, Paola Rendini, and Andrea Zifferero (Grosseto: Effigi), pp. 87–93

Pallottino, Massimo. 1937 'Nomi etruschi di città', in *Scritti in onore B. Nogara* (Rome: L'Erma di Bretschneider)

———. 1982. *Etruscologia* (Milan: Editore Ulrico Hoepli)

Pallottino, Massimo and Örjan Wikander. 1986. *Architettura etrusca nel Viterbese: Ricerche svedesi a San Giovenale e Acquarossa, 1956–1986* (Rome: De Luca)

Pancrazi, Orlanda, Mariella Montagna Pasquinucci, and Paolo E. Arias. 1971. 'Sovana (Grosseto). Scavi effettuati dal 1962 al 1964', *Notizie degli Scavi di antichitá*, Series 8: 25, 55–194

Panero, Francesco and Giuliano Pinto. 2009. *Castelli e fortezze nella citta e nei centri minori Italiani (secoli XIII–XV)* (Cherasco: Centro internazionale di studi sugli insediamenti medievali)

Panichi, Siria and Dario Ceppatelli. 2007. 'Metalli', in *Poggio Imperiale a Poggibonsi. Il territorio, lo scavo, il parco*, ed. by Riccardo Francovich and Marco Valenti (Milan: Silvana), pp. 241–53

Paoletti, Orazio, ed. 2005. *Dinamiche di sviluppo delle città nell'Etruria meridionale: Veio, Caere, Tarquinia, Vulci: Atti del XXIII Convegno di studi etruschi ed italici: Roma, Veio, Cerveteri/Pyrgi, Tarquinia, Tuscania, Vulci, Viterbo, 1–6 ottobre 2001* (Pisa: Istituti editoriali e poligrafici internazionali)

Paolucci, Giulio. 1992. 'Ceramica invetriata da Chiusi a Chianciano Terme', in *La ceramica invetriata tardoantica e altomedievale in Italia*, ed. by Lidia Paroli (Florence: All'Insegna del Giglio), pp. 314–18

Papi, Emanuele. 1985. 'La ceramica comune', in *Settefinestre: Una villa schiavistica nell'Etruria romana*, ed. by Andrea Carandini (Modena: Panini), pp. 93–106

Papi, Emanuele, Laura Cerri, and Luca Passalacqua. 2004. 'Prospezioni geofisiche e rilievi nell'area del Plateau', in *Archeologia del territorio*, ed. by Mariette de Vos (Trento: Università degli studi di Trento, Dipartimento di scienze filologiche e storiche), pp. 207–36

Parenti, Roberto. 1986. 'Le tecniche di documentazione per la lettura stratigrafica dell'elevato', in *Archeologia e restauro dei monumenti*, ed. by Riccardo Francovich and Roberto Parenti (Florence: All'Insegna del Giglio), pp. 280–304

———. 1992a. 'Fonti materiali e lettura stratigrafica di un centro urbano: i risultati di una sperimentazione non tradizionale', *Archeologia Medievale*, 19: 7–62

———. 1992b. 'Torri e case-torri senesi: i risultati delle prime ricognizioni di superficie', in *Case e torri medievali, Atti del II Convegno di Studi 'La città e le case.' Tessuti urbani, domus e case-torri nell'Italia Comunale (secc. XI–XV). Cittàdella Pieve, 11–12 dicembre*, ed. by Elisabetta De Minicis and Enrico Guidoni (Rome: Kappa), pp. 76–88

Paribeni, Emanuele, ed. 2001. *Gli Etruschi nella Valle dell'Alma* (Pisa: Koinè Multimedia)

Paris, Maria Francesca. 2005. 'Archeologia dell'architettura in pietra e forme di potere nel territorio di Castagneto Carducci (LI). Secoli XII–XIII', *Archeologia dell'Architettura*, 10: 175–90

Paroli, Lidia. 1985. 'Ceramica a vetrina pesante (Forum Ware). Ceramica a vetrina pesante a macchia (Sparse glazed)', in *Archeologia urbana a Roma: Il progetto della Crypta Balbi*, III: *Il giardino del Conservatorio di S. Caterina della Rosa*, ed. by Daniele Manacorda (Florence: All'Insegna del Giglio), pp. 206–24

——. 1990. 'Ceramica a vetrina pesante e medievale', in *Archeologia urbana a Roma: Il progetto Crypta Balbi*, V: *L'esedra della Crypta Balbi nel Medioevo (XI–XV secolo)*, ed. by Lucia Saguí and Lidia Paroli (Florence: All'Insegna del Giglio), pp. 314–56

——. ed. 1992a. *La ceramica invetriata tardoantica e altomedievale in Italia* (Florence: All'Insegna del Giglio)

——. 1992b. 'Ceramica invetriata a macchia dagli scavi del Pionta-Arezzo', in *La ceramica invetriata tardoantica e altomedievale in Italia*, ed. by Lidia Paroli (Florence: All'Insegna del Giglio), pp. 310–13

Pasqui, Ubaldo, ed. 1899–1937. *Documenti per la storia della città di Arezzo nel Medioevo*, 3 vols (Florence: R. deputazione di storia patri)

Pasquinelli, Gianna. 1987. *La ceramica di Volterra nel medioevo (secc. XIII–XV)* (Florence: All'Insegna del Giglio)

Patterson, Helen. 1991. 'Early Medieval and Medieval Pottery', in *Three South Etrurian Churches: Santa Cornelia, Santa Rufina and San Liberato*, ed. by Neil Christie (London: British School at Rome), pp. 120–36

Patterson, Helen. 2010. 'Rural Settlement and Economy in the Middle Tiber Valley: AD 300–1000'. *Archeologia Medievale*, 37: 143–62

Peacock, David P. S. 1982. *Pottery in the Roman World: An Ethnoarchaeological Approach* (London: Longman)

Pecci, Alessandra. 2004. 'Analisi funzionale della ceramica attraverso lo studio dei residui organici', *Archeologia Medievale*, 31: 527–34

——. 2009. 'Analisi funzionale della ceramica e alimentazione medievale', *Archeologia Medievale*, 36: 21–42

Pellegrini, Enrico. 1989. *La necropoli di Poggio Buco: Nuovi dati per lo studio di un centro dell'Etruria interna nei periodi orientalizzante ed arcaico* (Florence: Olschki)

——. 1999. *Insediamenti preistorici e città etrusche nella media valle del fiume Fiora: Guida al Museo Civico Archeologico di Pitigliano* (Pitigliano: Laurum Editrice)

Perkins, Philip. 1991. 'Cities, Cemeteries and Rural Settlement of the Albegna Valley and the Ager Cosanus in the Orientalizing and Archaic Periods', in *Papers of the Fourth Conference of Italian Archaeology*, I: *The Archaeology of Power*, ed. by Edward Herring, Ruth Whitehouse, and John Wilkins (London: Accordia Research Centre), pp. 138–43

——. 1998. 'Etruscan Pottery from the Albegna Valley/Ager Cosanus Survey', *Internet Archaeology*, 4 <https://intarch.ac.uk/journal/issue4/perkins_toc.html>

——. 1999. *Etruscan Settlement, Society and Material Culture in Central Coastal Etruria* (Oxford: Archaeopress)

——. 2002. 'L'epoca etrusca. 1. L'insediamento orientalizzante e arcaico, II: L'insediamento dal V secolo alla conquista romana', in *Paesaggi d'Etruria: Valle dell'Albegna, Valle d'Oro, Valle del Chiarone, Valle del Tafone: Progetto di ricerca italo-britannico seguito allo scavo di Settefinestre*, ed. by Andrea Carandini, Franco Cambi, Mariagrazia Celuzza, and Elizabeth Fentress (Rome: Edizioni di storia e letteratura), pp. 69–89

——. 2005. 'Who lived in the Etruscan Albegna Valley?' in *Papers in Italian Archaeology*, VI: *Communities and Settlements from the Neolithic to the Early Medieval Period*, ed. by Peter Attema, Albert Nijboer, and Andrea Zifferero (Oxford: Archaeopress), pp. 109–17

——. 2010. 'The Cultural and Political Landscape of the *Ager Caletranus*, North-West of Vulci', in *L'Étrurie et l'Ombrie avant Rome. Cité et territoire*, ed. by P. Fontaine (Brussels: Belgisch Historisch Instituut te Rome), pp. 103–22

——. 2014. 'Processes of Urban Development in Northern and Central Etruria in the Orientalizing and Archaic periods', in *Papers on Italian Urbanism in the First Millennium B.C.*, ed. by Elizabeth C. Robinson (Portsmouth, RI: Journal of Roman Archaeology), pp. 62–80

Perkins, Philip and L. Attolini. 1992. 'An Etruscan Farm at Podere Tartuchino', *Papers of the British School at Rome*, 60: 71–134

Perkins, Philip and Lucy Walker. 1990. 'Survey of an Etruscan City at Doganella in the Albegna Valley', *Papers of the British School at Rome*, 58: 2–143

——. 2002. '3. Il popolamento e l'utilizzazione del suolo', in *Paesaggi d'Etruria: Valle dell'Albegna, Valle d'Oro, Valle del Chiarone, Valle del Tafone: Progetto di ricerca italo-britannico seguito allo scavo di Settefinestre*, ed. by Andrea Carandini, Franco Cambi, Mariagrazia Celuzza, and Elizabeth Fentress (Rome: Edizioni di storia e letteratura), pp. 90–95

Pianta del circondario di Orbetello 1864 = *Pianta del circondario di Orbetello con le indicazioni delle opere eseguite dalla R. amministrazione del bonificamento* (Grosseto: Archivio di Stato di Grosseto)

Piccinni, Gabriella, ed. 1992. 'Gli anni della crisi: La politica agraria del Comune di Siena e la diffusione della mezzadria', in *Il contratto di mezzadria nella Toscana medievale*, III: *Contado di Siena, 1349–1518*, ed. by Gabriella Piccinini (Florence: Olschki), pp. 11–154

Pinto, Giuliano. 1982. *La Toscana nel tardo Medioevo. Ambiente, economia rurale, società* (Florence: Sansoni)

——. 1990. 'L'agricoltura delle aree mezzadrili', in *Le Italie del tardo medioevo*, ed. by Sergio Gensini (Pisa: Pacini), pp. 433–48

Piponnier, Françoise. 1984. 'Objets fabriques autres que monnaies et céramiques', in *Brucato, Histoire et archéologie d'un habitat médiéval en Sicile*, v.2, ed. by Jean-Maric Pesez (Rome: École française de Rome), pp. 497–614

——. 1997. 'Dal fuoco alla tavola: Archeologia dell'attrezzatura alimentare alla fine del Medioevo', in *Storia dell'alimentazione*, ed. by Jean-Louis Flandrin, Danièle Alexandre-Bidon, and Massimo Montanari (Rome: Laterza), pp. 408–16

Pirillo, Paolo 2002. 'Modelli di popolamento tra signorie territoriali e dominio fiorentino: Continuità e mutamenti', *Fortuna e declina di una società feudale valdarnese: il Poggio della Regina*, ed. by Guido Vannini (Florence: Società Editrice Fiorentina), pp. 173–87

Piro, Salvatore. 2005. 'Integrazione di metodi geofisici ad alta risoluzione per l'indagine nei siti archeologici: il caso di Piazza d'Armi-Veio', in *Dinamiche di sviluppo delle città nell'Etruria meridionale: Veio, Caere, Tarquinia, Vulci: Atti del XXIII Convegno di studi etruschi ed italici: Roma, Veio, Cerveteri/Pyrgi, Tarquinia, Tuscania, Vulci, Viterbo, 1–6 ottobre 2001*, ed. by Orazio Paoletti (Pisa: Istituti editoriali e poligrafici internazionali), pp. 125–34

Piuzzi, Fabio. 2003. 'Osservazioni sui reperti di metallo. Attività artigianali legate alla fusione di metalli (fase D.2)', in *Progetto Castello della Motta di Savorgnano: Ricerche di archeologia medievale nel nord-est italiano*, ed. by Fabio Piuzzi (Florence: All'Insegna del Giglio), pp. 169–81

Piuzzi, Fabio, S. Di Meo, S. Cossio, G. Marchese, F. Putano, C. Brancati, M. Mazzei, and M. Vignola. 2003. 'La sequenza periodizzata delle fasi identificate (anni 1997–1998–1999–2001–2002)', in *Progetto Castello della Motta di Savorgnano: ricerche di archeologia medievale nel nord-est italiano*, ed. by Fabio Piuzzi (Florence: All'Insegna del Giglio), pp. 31–135

Piuzzi, Fabio, Alessandra Biasi, and R. Costantin. 1994. 'Scharfenberg – Soffumbergo: Un castello tedesco nel Friuli medievale', *Quaderni Guarneriani: Collana Cataloghi e Monografie del Museo del Territorio* (Pasian di Prato, Udine: ETC)

Potter, Timothy W. 1975. 'Recenti ricerche in Etruria meridionale: Problemi della transizione dal tardo antico all'alto medioevo', *Archeologia Medievale*, 2: 215–36

——. 1979. *The Changing Landscape of South Etruria* (New York: St Martin's Press)

Potter, Timothy W., David Whitehouse, and Hugo Blake. 1978. *Papers in Italian Archaeology I: The Lancaster Seminar: Recent Research in Prehistoric, Classical and Medieval Archaeology* (Oxford: BAR)

Prandi, Lucia and Gabriella Silvestrini. 2004. 'Un contesto di ceramica altomedievale da Cencelle', in *La ceramica altomedievale in Italia*, ed. by Stella Patitucci Uggeri (Florence: All'Insegna del Giglio), pp. 177–88

Pucciarelli, Duccio and Fabio Redi. 1997. 'Montecastrese (LU). Rapporto Preliminare 1996', *Archeologia Medievale*, 24: 225–44

Py, François and Michel Py. 1974. 'Les amphores étrusques de Gaule méridionale', *Mélanges de l'École française de Rome*, 86: 141–254

Quirós Castillo, Juan Antonio. 1999. *El incastellamento en el territorio de la ciudad de Luca (Toscana): Poder y territorio entre la Alta Edad Media y el siglo XII* (Oxford: Archaeopress)

Rasmussen, T. B. 1979. *Bucchero Pottery from Southern Etruria* (Cambridge: Cambridge University Press)

Raspi Serra, Joselita and Franco Picchetto. 1980. 'Contributi alla conoscenza della cultura materiale nella Tuscia. Un recupero di maioliche provenienti da Celleno', *Faenza*, 66: 275–95

Rathbone, Dominic. 1981. 'The Development of Agriculture in the "Ager Cosanus" during the Roman Republic: Problems of Evidence and Interpretation', *Journal of Roman Studies*, 71: 10–23

Raveggi, Paolo. 1933. 'Orbetello antica e moderna', *Maremma*, 8: 26–96

Redon, Odile. 1975. 'Le contado de Sienne 1263–1270, une frontière médiévale', *Mélanges de l'Ecole françaises de Rome. Moyen âge, temps modernes* 87: 105–39

——. 1989. 'La divisione dei poteri dell'Amiata del Duecento', in *L'Amiata nel medioevo*, ed. by Mario Ascheri (Rome: Viella), pp. 183–95

——. 1999 [1994]. *Lo spazio di una città. Siena e la Toscana meridionale (secoli XIII.– XIV.)* (Siena: Nuova Immagine)

Regoli, Edina. 1985. 'Il contesto geografico e la situazione prima della conquista. La situazione dopo la conquista', in *La romanizzazione dell'Etruria: Il territorio di Vulci*, ed. by Andrea Carandini (Florence: Regione Toscana; Milan: Electa), pp. 48–52

——. 2002. 'Dalla villa schiavistica al latifondo (III–IV secolo)', in *Paesaggi d'Etruria: Valle dell'Albegna, Valle d'Oro, Valle del Chiarone, Valle del Tafone: Progetto di ricerca italo-britannico seguito allo scavo di Settefinestre*, ed. by Andrea Carandini, Mariagrazia Celuzza, Elizabeth Fentress, and Ida Attolini (Rome: Edizioni di storia e letteratura), pp. 218–27

Reitz, Elizabeth Jean and Elizabeth S. Wing. 2008. *Zooarchaeology*, 2nd edn (Cambridge: Cambridge University Press)

Remie Constable, Olivia. 2007. 'Chess and Courtly Culture in Medieval Castile: The "Libro de ajedrez" of Alfonso X, el Sabio', *Speculum*, 82.2: 301–47

Rendeli, Marco. 1993. *Città aperte: Ambiente e paesaggio rurale organizzato nell'Etruria meridionale costiera durante l'età orientalizzante e arcaica* (Rome: Gruppo editoriale internazionale)

——. 2002. 'Sviluppo del rapporto tra centro e territorio in Etruria nel VII e VI secolo A. C.', in *Città e territorioin Etruria. Per una definizione di città nell'etruria settentrionale. Colle Val d'Elsa (12–13 marzo 1999)*, ed. by Mario Manganelli and Elvio Pacchiani (Siena: Grafiche Boccacci), pp. 41–76

Rendini, Paola. 1985. 'Ghiaccioforte', in *La romanizzazione dell'Etruria: Il territorio di Vulci*, ed. by Andrea Carandini (Florence: Regione Toscana)

——. 1998. 'L'Urbanistica di Saturnia', in *Città e monumenti dell'Italia antica*, VII, ed. by Lorenzo Quilici and Stefania Quilici Gigli (Rome: L'Erma di Bretschneider), pp. 97–118

——. 2003. 'Stipi votivi e culti nella valle dell'Albegna in età ellenistica', in *Archeologia a Magliano in Toscana: Atti dell'incontro di Archeologia Magliano in Toscana, 9 agosto 2003*, ed. by Paola Rendini and Marco Firmati (Siena: Nuova Immagine), pp. 13–26

——. ed. 2009. *Le vie del sacro. Culti e depositi votivi nella valle dell'Albegna* (Siena: Nuova Immagine)

——. 2011. 'La necropoli di Cancellone 1 a Magliano in Toscana', in *La valle del vino etrusco. Archeologia della valle dell'Albegna in età arcaica*, ed. by Marco Firmati, Paola Rendini, and Andrea Zifferero (Grosseto: Effigi), pp. 76–81

Rendini, Paola and Marco Firmati. 2003. *Archeologia a Magliano in Toscana* (Siena: Nuova Immagine)

——. 2005. 'Ghiaccio Forte: Un oppidum nella Valle dell'Albegna', in *Dinamiche di sviluppo delle città nell'Etruria meridionale: Veio, Caere, Tarquinia, Vulci: Atti del XXIII Convegno di studi etruschi ed italici: Roma, Veio, Cerveteri/Pyrgi, Tarquinia, Tuscania, Vulci, Viterbo, 1–6 ottobre 2001*, ed. by Orazio Paoletti (Pisa: Istituti editoriali e poligrafici internazionali), pp. 373–85

——. 2008. 'Ghiaccio Forte: Un oppidum nella valle dell'Albegna', in *La città murata in Etruria, Atti del XXV Convegno di Studi Etruschi ed Italici (Chiusi, 2005)*, ed. by Orazio Paoletti (Pisa: Fabrizio Serra Editore), pp. 373–87

Repetti, Emanuele. 1833–1845. *Dizionario geografico, fisico e storico della Toscana* (Florence: Presso l'autore e editore) <http://www.cortedeirossi.it/libro/libri/repetti.htm>

Retzleff, C. 1967. *Kulturgeographische Wandlungen in der Maremma* (Kiel: Selbstverlag des geographischen Instituts der Universitiit Kiel)

Reynolds, Paul. 2004. 'The Medieval Amphorae', in *Byzantine Butrint. Excavations and Surveys 1994–1999*, ed. by Richard Hodges, William Bowden, and Kosta Lako (Oxford: Oxbow), pp. 270–77

Ricci, Marco. 1990. 'Ceramica acroma depurata, II: Brocche, catini, orcioli ed altre forme minori', in *Archeologia urbana a Roma: il progetto Crypta Balbi*, V: *L'esedra della Crypta Balbi nel Medioevo (XI–XV secolo)*, ed. by Lucia Saguí and Lidia Paroli (Florence: All'Insegna del Giglio), pp. 288–308

——. 1990b. 'Ceramica dipinta in rosso', in *Archeologia urbana a Roma: Il progetto Crypta Balbi*, V: *L'esedra della Crypta Balbi nel Medioevo (XI–XV secolo)*, ed. by Lucia Saguí and Lidia Paroli (Florence: All'Insegna del Giglio), pp. 308–12

——. 1998. 'Appunti per una storia della produzione e del consumo della ceramica da cucina a Roma e nel medioevo', in *Le ceramiche di Roma e del Lazio in età medievale e moderna*, III, ed. by Elisabetta De Minis (Rome: Kappa), pp. 34–42

——. 2001. 'Accessori da toilette (tardo VI–VII secolo)', in *Roma dall'antichità al medioevo. Archeologia e storia nel Museo Nazionale romano Crypta Balbi*, ed. by Maria Stella Arena (Milan: Electa), pp. 402–08

——. 2001b. 'Armi', in *Roma dall'antichità al medioevo. Archeologia e storia nel Museo Nazionale romano Crypta Balbi*, ed. by Maria Stella Arena (Milan: Electa), pp. 395–402, 549–50

——. 2001c. 'Arnesi da lavoro', in *Roma dall'antichità al medioevo. Archeologia e storia nel Museo Nazionale romano Crypta Balbi*, ed. by Maria Stella Arena (Milan: Electa), pp. 345–49

——. 2001d. 'Elementi di bardatura del cavallo ed equipaggiamento del cavaliere', in *Roma dall'antichità al medioevo. Archeologia e storia nel Museo Nazionale romano Crypta Balbi*, ed. by Maria Stella Arena (Milan: Electa), pp. 388–94

——. 2001e. 'Elementi in osso per rivestimento di cassette in legno. Crypta Balbi. VIII–IX secolo', in *Roma dall'antichità al medioevo. Archeologia e storia nel Museo Nazionale romano Crypta Balbi*, ed. by Maria Stella Arena (Milan: Electa), p. 543

Ricci, Marco and Valeria Bartoloni. 1995. 'Produzioni ceramiche da un contesto dei secoli XI–XII a Tarquinia', in *Le ceramiche di Roma e del Lazio in età medievale e moderna*, II, ed. by Elisabetta De Minicis (Rome: Kappa), pp. 100–06

Ricci, Marco and L. Portoghesi. 1972. 'Tuscania nella storia della ceramica', in *Atti, V Convegno internazionale della ceramica, Albisola, 31 maggio–4 giugno 1972* (Albisola: Centro ligure per la storia della ceramica), pp. 211–34

Rizzitelli, Claudia. 1999. 'Roselle', in *Archeologia urbana in Toscana: La città altomedievale*, ed. by Elisabetta Abela (Mantova: S.A.P), p. 111

Rizzo, Giorgio and Micaela Vitale. 2001. 'Palatino, Vigna Barberini', in *Roma dall'antichità al medioevo. Archeologia e storia nel Museo Nazionale romano Crypta Balbi*, ed. by Maria Stella Arena and others (Milan: Electa), pp. 231–37

Robinson, James. 2004. *The Lewis Chessmen* (London: British Museum)

Rombai, Leonardo. 1980. 'Il paesaggio agrario nella pianura grossetana dalla restaurazione forense all'annessione al Regno', in *Agricoltura e società nella Maremma grossetana dell'800: Giornate di studio per il centenario ricasoliano (Grosseto, 9–11 maggio 1980)*, ed. by Giovanni Spadolini (Florence: Olschki), 103–62

Rombai, Leonardo. 2002. 'Storia del territorio e paesaggi storici: il caso della Toscana', *Storia e futuro*, 1: 1–20

Rombai, Leonardo, Gabriele Ciampi, and Maurizio De Vita. 1979. *Cartografia storica dei Presidios in Maremma (secoli XVI–XVIII)* (Siena: Consorzio universitario della Toscana meridionale)

Rombai, Leonardo, Mauro Pinzani, and Simone Squarzanti, eds. 1997. *Geografia storica dell'Europa* (Florence: Centro editoriale toscano)

Romei, Diletta. 1990. 'Ceramica acroma depurata, I: Anfore, coperchi, piedistalli', in *Archeologia urbana a Roma: Il progetto Crypta Balbi, V: L'esedra della Crypta Balbi nel Medioevo (XI–XV secolo)*, ed. by Lucia Saguí and Lidia Paroli (Florence: All'Insegna del Giglio), pp. 264–87

——. 1994. 'Apputi sulla circolazione della maiolica arcaica a Tuscania', in *Le ceramiche di Roma e del Lazio in età medievale e moderna*, I, ed. by Elisabetta De Minicis (Rome: Kappa), pp. 86–100

——. 1998. 'La ceramica medievale proveniente dal castello di Scorano (Capena, Roma)', in *Le ceramiche di Roma e del Lazio in età medievale e moderna*, III, ed. by Elisabetta De Minicis (Rome: Kappa), pp. 124–38

——. 2004. 'Produzione e circolazione dei manufatti ceramici a Roma nell'altomedioevo', in *Roma dall'antichità al medioevo*, II: *Contesti tardoantichi e altomedievali*, ed. by Lidia Paroli and Laura Venditelli (Milan: Electa), pp. 278–311

Roncaglia, Giovanni. 1986. 'La ceramica grezza medievale in un insediamento del contado senese', *Archeologia Medievale*, 13: 267–76

Roselaar Saskia. 2011. 'Colonies and Processes of Integration in the Roman Republic', *Mélanges de l'École française de Rome – Antiquité*, 123.2: 527–55

Rossetti, Gabriella. 1981. 'Gli Aldobrandeschi', in *I ceti dirigenti in Toscana nell'età precomunale. Atti del I Convegno, Firenze, 2 dicembre 1978* (Pisa: Pacini), pp. 151–65

——. 2001. 'Le tradizioni normative in Europa: facciamo il punto', in *Legislazione e prassi istituzionale nell'Europa medievale. Tradizioni normative, ordinamenti, circolazione mercantile (secoli XI–XV)*, ed. by G. Rossetti (Naples: Liguori), pp. 31–63

——. 1985. 'I reperti numismatici di S. Silvestro e il problema della datazione dei "quattrini pisani"', *Archeologia Medievale*, 12: 379–87

——. 1996. 'Le monete del castello di Scarlino. Materiali per lo studio della circolazione monetaria nella Toscana meridionale', *Annali dell'Istituto italiano di numismatica*, 43: 225–54

Rovelli, Alessia. 2000. 'La circolazione monetaria in Sabina e nel Lazio settentrionale nel Medio Evo', in *Une région frontalière au Moyen Âge: Les vallées du Turano et du Salto entre Sabine et Abruzzes*, ed. by Étienne Hubert (Rome: École française de Rome), pp. 407–22

——. 2003. 'The Medieval Coins', in *Cosa V: An Intermittent Town, Excavations 1991–1997*, ed. by Elizabeth Fentress (Ann Arbor: University of Michigan), pp. 260–65

——. 2008. '774. The Mints of the Kingdom of Italy: A Survey', in *774: Ipotesi su una transizione. Atti del seminario di Poggibonsi, 16–18 febbraio 2006*, ed. by Stefano Gasparri, Seminari del Centro interuniversitario per la storia e l'archeologia dell'alto medioevo, 1 (Turnhout: Brepols), pp. 119–40, rev. and repr. in Rovelli, Alessia, *Coinage and Coin Use in Medieval Italy* (Farnham: Ashgate)

——. 2009a. 'Coins and Trade in Early Medieval Italy', *Early Medieval Europe*, 17.1: 45–76

——. 2009b. '*Patrimonium Beati Petri*. Emissione e circolazione monetaria nel Lazio settentrionale (XI–XIV secolo)', *Annali dell'Istituto italiano di Numismatica* 55: 169–92, trans. in English in Rovelli, Alessia, *Coinage and Coin Use in Medieval Italy* (Farnham: Ashgate)

——. 2009c. 'Émission monétaire et administration dans le royaume d'Italie. À propos des analyses des deniers carolingiens du Cabinet des Médailles', *Revue Numismatique*, 165: 187–201

——. 2010. 'Nuove zecche e circolazione monetaria tra X e XIII secolo: Esempio del Lazio e della Toscana', *Archeologia Medievale*, 37: 163–70

——. 2012a. 'Gold, Silver and Bronze: An Analysis of Monetary Circulation along the Italian Coasts', in *From One Sea to Another: Trade Centres in the European and Mediterranean Early Middle Ages*, ed. by Sauro Gelichi and Richard Hodges, Seminari del Centro interuniversitario per la storia e l'archeologia dell'alto medioevo, 3 (Turnhout: Brepols), pp. 267–95

——. 2012b. *Coinage and Coin Use in Medieval Italy* (Farnham: Ashgate)

Saccocci, Andrea. 2001–2002. 'Il ripostiglio dell'area 'Galli Tassi' di Lucca e la cronologia delle emissioni pavesi e lucchesi di X secolo', *Bollettino di Numismatica*, 36/39: 167–204

——. 2004. 'Il ripostiglio di monete', in *Archeologia a Pieve a Nievole, dalla basilica sita loco Neure alla pieve romanica*, ed. by Giulio Ciampoltrini and Enrico Pieri (Pisa: Edizioni ETS), pp. 71–81

Sagan, Carl. 1997. *The Demon-Haunted World: Science as a Candle in the Dark* (New York: Ballantine Books)

Saguí, Lucia and Lidia Paroli, eds. 1990. *Archeologia urbana a Roma: Il progetto Crypta Balbi, V: L'esedra della Crypta Balbi nel Medioevo (XI–XV secolo)* (Florence: All'Insegna del Giglio)

Saguì, Lucia, Marco Ricci, and Diletta Romei. 2001. 'La cultura materiale a Roma tra VIII e X secolo: I depositi nell'esedra della Crypta Balbi', in *Roma dall'antichità al medioevo. Archeologia e storia nel Museo nazionale romano Crypta Balbi*, ed. by Maria Stella Arena, Paolo Delogu, Lidia Paroli, Marco Ricci, Lucia Saguì, and Laura Venditelli (Milan: Electa), pp. 498–528

Salmon, Edward Togo. 1970. *Roman Colonization Under the Republic* (Ithaca: Cornell University Press)

Salvadori, Frank. 2011. 'Zooarcheologia e controllo delle risorse economiche locali nel medioevo', *Post Classical Archaeologies*, 1: 195–244

Salvadori, Hermann, Emanuele Vaccaro, Marianella Ghisleni, and Elena Chirico. 2006. 'Il villaggio medievale di Poggio Cavolo: Prima indagine sul pianoro sommitale', in *IV Congresso Nazionale di Archeologia Medievale. Abbazia di San Galgano (Chiusdino, SI), 26-20 settembre 2006*, ed. by Riccardo Francovich and Marco Valenti (Florence: All'Insegna del Giglio), pp. 269–74

Salvadori, Hermann and Chiara Valdambrini. 2009. 'Produzione e circolazione della ceramica medievale a Sassoforte (Roccastrada-GR): Considerazioni preliminari', in *V Congresso Nazionale di Archeologia Medievale* (Florence: All'Insegna del Giglio), pp. 580–85

Salvini, Laura, Chiara Valdambrini, Alessandra Pecci, Carlo Citter, and Gianluca Giorgi. 2004. 'Medieval Vessels from Grosseto and Castel di Pietra: Organic Residues and Functions' (poster presented at the International Symposium on Mass Spectometry, Bari)

Sannibale, Maurizio. 1998. *Le armi della collezione Gorga al Museo Nazionale Romano* (Rome: L'Erma di Bretschneider)

Santangelo, Maria. 1954. *L'Antiquarium di Orbetello: Con brevi note su alcuni centri archeologici* (Rome: Officina dell'Azienda beneventana)

Satolli, Alberto. 1981. 'Fortune e sfortune della ceramica medievale orvietana', in *Ceramiche medioevali dell'Umbria: Assisi, Orvieto, Todi* (Florence: Nuova Guaraldi), pp. 34–78

——. ed. 1983–1985. *La ceramica orvietana del Medioevo*, 2 vols (Florence: Centro Di)

——. 1995. *Tradizione ceramica a Orvieto* (Orvieto: Comune di Orvieto)

Scalini, Mario. 2003. 'Corazzine e bacinetti dalla rocca di Campiglia', in *Campiglia: Un castello e il suo territorio*, ed. by Giovanna Bianchi (Florence: All'Insegna del Giglio), pp. 382–96

Scapaticci Perfetti, Maria Gabriella. 2000. 'Le origini di Monte Romano. Indagine di scavo sul "Poggio della Rotonda"', *Archeologia Medievale*, 27: 219–27

Schmiedt, Giulio, ed. 1972. *Il livello antico del Mar Tirreno: testimonianze dei resti archeologici* (Florence: Olschki)

Schneider, Fedor. 1907. *Regestum Volaterranum* (Rome: Loescher)

——. 1911. *Regestum Senense* (Rome: Loescher)

Sconci, Maria Selene. 2001. *Oltre il frammento: Forme e decori della maiolica medievale orvietana: il recupero della Collezione Del Pelo Pardi* (Rome: De Luca)

Scott, Russell T. 1981. 'A New Inscription of the Emperor Maximinus at Cosa', *Chiron*, 11: 309–14

Scott, Russell T., Andrea De Giorgi, Sophie Crawford-Brown, Anne Glennie, and Alison Smith. 2015. 'Cosa Excavations: The 2013 Report', *Orizzonti, Rassegna di Archeologia*, 16: 11–22

Sebastiani, Alessandro, Elena Chirico, Matteo Colobini, and Mario Cygielman. 2015. *Diana Umbronensis a Scoglietto. Santuario, Territorio e Cultura materiale (200 a.C – 55 d.C.)* (Oxford: Archaeopress)

Serdon, Valérie. 2005. *Armes di diable. Arcs et arbalètes au moyen Âge* (Rennes: Presses Universitaires de Rennes)

Sereni, Anna. 1995. 'Contenitori, suppellettile domestica, spazi funzionali: spunti di riflessione attraverso la documentazione scritta altomedievale', in *Le ceramiche di Roma e del Lazio in età medievale e moderna*, II, ed. by Elisabetta De Minicis (Rome: Kappa), pp. 270–79

Setti, B. 1995. 'Nuovi dati sul popolamento dell'alta valle dell'Albegna (GR)', in *Preistoria e Protostoria in Etruria: Tipologia delle necropoli e rituali di deposizione. Ricerche e scavi*, ed. by Nuccia Negroni Catacchio (Milan: Centro studi di preistoria e archeologia), pp. 253–354

Sfligiotti, Patrizia. 1990. 'Manufatti in metalli, osso, terracotta, pietra' in *Archeologia urbana a Roma: Il progetto Crypta Balbi, 5, L'esedra della Crypta Balbi nel Medioevo (XI–XV secolo)*, ed. by Lucia Saguì and Lidia Paroli (Florence: All'Insegna del Giglio), pp. 513–52

Signorini, Rodolfo. 1967. *Note illustrative della carta geologica d'Italia alla scala 1:100.000. Orbetello, foglio 135* (Rome: Servizio Geologico d'Italia)

Silver, I. A. 1969. 'The Ageing of Domestic Animals', in *Science in Archaeology*, ed. by Don R. Brothwell and Eric S. Higgs, 2nd edn (London: Thames and Hudson), pp. 283–302

Simpson, C. J. 2003. 'Roman Minor Objects, 1990–1997', in *Cosa V: An Intermittent Town, Excavations 1991–1997*, ed. by Elizabeth Fentress (Ann Arbor: University of Michigan), pp. 223–49

Sogliani, Francesca. 1991. 'I reperti minori e le monete', in *Archeologia medievale a Lugo. Aspetti del quotidiano nei ritrovamenti della Rocca*, ed. by Sauro Gelichi (Florence: All'Insegna del Giglio), pp. 193–207
——. 1995. *Utensili, armi ed ornamenti di età medievale da Montale e Gorzano* (Modena: Panini)
Sordini, B. 2000. *Il porto della "gente vana": Lo scalo di Talamone tra il secolo XIII e XV* (Siena: Protagon Editori Toscani)
Spufford, Peter. 1988. *Money and its Use in Medieval Europe* (Cambridge: Cambridge University Press)
Stahl, Alan M. 1988. 'A Hoard of Medieval Pennies from Arezzo'. *Rivista italiana di Numismatica*, 90: 483–93
——. 2000. 'The Orte Hoard of Tuscan Grossi', in *XII. Internationaler Numismatischer Kongress, Berlin, 1997. Acten = Proceedings – Actes*, ed. by Bernd Kluge and Bernhard Weisser (Berlin: Staatliche Museen zu Berlin), pp. 1085–90
Stek, Tesse D. and Jeremia Pelgrom, eds. 2014. *Roman Republican Colonization: New Perspectives from Archaeology and Ancient History*. Papers of the Royal Netherlands Institute in Rome (Rome: Palombi Editori)
Steingräber, Stephan. 2001. 'The Process of Urbanization of Etruscan Settlements from the Late Villanovan to the Late Archaic Period (End of the Eighth to the Beginning of the Fifth Century B.C.): Presentation of a Project and Preliminary Results', *Etruscan Studies* 8.1 <https://scholarworks.umass.edu/cgi/viewcontent.cgi?article=1000&context=etruscan_studies>
Stiaffini, Daniela. 2005. 'Reperti vitrei', in *L'aratro e il calamo. Benedettini e cistercensi sul Monte Pisano. Dieci anni di archeologia a San Michele alla Verruca*, ed. by Sauro Gelichi and Antonio Alberti (Pisa: San Giuliano Terme), pp. 397–404
Sorbo, Antonio. 2020. *Gli scacchi di Venafro. Ipotesi interpretativa e storia degli scacchi più antichi d'Europa* (Cerro al Volturno: Volturnia Editori)
Summers, G. and F. Summers. 2006. 'Aspects of Urban Design at the Iron Age City on the Kerkenes Dag as Revealed by Geophysical Survey'. *Anatolia Antiqua*, 14: 71–88
Tabacco, Giovanni. 1989. 'La Toscana Meridionale nel medioevo', in *L'Amiata nel medioevo*, ed. by Mario Ascheri (Rome: Viella), pp. 1–18
Talocchini, Anna. 1966. 'Saturnia', *Enciclopedia dell'arte antica, classica e orientale*, pp. 78–79
——. 1986. *Il Ghiaccio Forte* (Scansano: Comune di Scansano)
Tamburini, P. 2000. 'Vulci e il suo territorio', in *Vulci e il suo territorio nelle collezioni del Museo Archeologico e d'Arte della Maremma*, ed. by Mariagrazia Celuzza (Milan), pp. 17–45
Tangheroni, Marco. 1996. *Commercio e navigazione nel Medioevo* (Bari: Laterza)
——. ed. 2003. *Pisa e il Mediterraneo. Uomini, merci, idee dagli Etruschi ai Medici* (Milan: Skira)
Tarquini, Simone, Ilaria Isola, Massimiliano Favalli, Francesco Mazzarini, M. Bisson, M. T. Pareschi, and Enzo Boschi. 2007. 'TINITALY/01: A New Triangular Irregular Network of Italy', *Annals of Geophysics*, 50: 407–25
Tarquini, Simone, S. Vinci, M. Favalli, F. Doumaz, A. Fornaciai, and L. Nannipieri. 2012. 'Release of a 10-m-Resolution DEM for the Italian Territory: Comparison with Global-coverage DEMs and Anaglyph-mode Exploration via the Web', *Computers & Geosciences*, 38: 168–70
Terlizzi, Sergio, ed. 1950. *Documenti delle relazioni tra Carlo I d'Angiò e la Toscana* (Florence: Olschki)
Terrenato, Nicola. 2000. 'The Visibility of Sites and the Interpretation of Field Survey Results: Towards an Analysis of Incomplete Distributions', in *Extracting Meaning from Plough Soil Assemblages*, ed. by Riccardo Francovich, Helen Patterson, and G. Barker (Oxford: Oxbow Books), pp. 60–71
——. 2005. 'The Deceptive Archetype. Roman Colonialism and Post-colonial Thought', in *Ancient Colonizations: Analogy, Similarity, and Difference*, ed. by Henry Hurst and Sara Owen (London: Duckworth), pp. 59–72
——. 2012. 'The Essential Countryside: The Roman World', in *Classical Archaeology*, ed. by Susan E. Alcock and Robin Osborne (Hoboken, NJ: John Wiley & Sons), pp. 139–61
Tofani, Giulia and Andrea Zifferero. 2011. 'Vino e rituali funebri nei corredi del Poggio di Macchiabuia', in *La valle del vino etrusco. Archeologia della valle dell'Albegna in età arcaica*, ed. by Marco Firmati, Paola Rendini, and Andrea Zifferero (Grosseto: Effigi), pp. 94–102
Toniolo, Alessandra. 2007. 'Anfore dall'area lagunare', in *La circolazione delle ceramiche nell'Adriatico tra tarda antichità e altomedioevo*, ed. by Sauro Gelichi and Claudio Negrelli (Mantua: SAP), pp. 91–106
Torelli, Mario. 1984. *La Storia degli Etruschi* (Rome: Laterza)
——. ed. 1992. *Atlante dei siti archeologici della Toscana* (Rome: L'Erma di Bretschneider)
——. 1999. *Essays in the Cultural Formation of Roman Italy* (Oxford: Clarendon Press)
——. 2002. 'Appunti sulla genesi della città nell'Etruria centro settentrionale', in *Città e territorio in Etruria. Per una definizione di città nell'Etruria settentrionale. Colle Val d'Elsa (12–13 marzo 1999)*, ed. by Mario Manganelli and Elvio Pacchiani (Siena: Grafiche Boccacci), pp. 21–40
Toubert, Pierre. 1973. *Les structures du Latium médiéval: Le Latium méridional et la Sabine du IXe siècle à la fin du XIIe siècle* (Rome: École française de Rome)
——. 2003. 'La frontiera del medievista', in *Un incontro senese in onore di Pierre Toubert*, ed. by Mario Ascheri (Rome: Viella)

Tozzi, Carla. 2000. 'Oggetti metallici e non metallici', in *Ricerche di archeologia medievale a Pisa*, I: *Piazza dei Cavalieri, la campagna di scavo 1993*, ed. by Stefano Bruni, Elisabetta Abela, and Graziella Berti (Florence: All'Insegna del Giglio), pp. 235–39

Transano, Vincent Antone. 1974. 'The Rural Noble Family of Southern Tuscany (800–1350)' (unpubl. PhD thesis, University of California, Davis)

Travaini, Lucia. 1992. 'Monete medievali in area romana: Nuovi e vecchi materiali', *Rivista italiana di Numismatica*, 94: 169–73

——. 2000. 'Aree monetarie e organizzazione delle zecche nella Toscana dei secoli XII–XIII', in *L'attività creditizia nella Toscana comunale, Atti del Convegno di studi, Pistoia-Colle di Val d'Elsa, 26–27 settembre 1998*, ed. by Antonella Duccini and Giampaolo Francescono (Pistoia: Società pistoiese di storia patria), pp. 25–42

——. ed. 2011a. *Le zecche italiane fino all'Unità* (Rome: Istituto poligrafico e zecca dello Stato)

——. 2011b. 'Cortona', in *Le zecche italiane fino all'Unità*, ed. by Lucia Travaini (Rome: Istituto poligrafico e zecca dello Stato), pp. 624–27

Tremlett, Sophie and Catherine M. Coutts. 2001. 'Artifacts in Iron', in *San Vincenzo al Volturno*, III: *The Finds from the 1980–1986 Excavations*, ed. by John Mitchell and Inge Lyse Hansen, with Catherine M. Coutts (Spoleto: Centro italiano di studi sull'alto Medioevo), pp. 312–79

Trifone, B. 1908. 'Le carte del monastero di S.Paolo di Roma dal secolo XI al XV', *Archivio della Società Romana di Storia Patria*, 31: 267–313

Uboldi, Marina. 1999. 'I vetri', in *S. Giulia di Brescia. Gli scavi dal 1980 al 1992. Reperti preromani, romani e alto medievali*, ed. by Gian Pietro Brogiolo (Florence: All'Insegna del Giglio), pp. 271–307

——. 2001. 'I vetri', in *Archeologia a Monte Barro*, II: *Gli scavi 1990–97 e le ricerche al S. Martino di Lecco*, ed. by Gian Pietro Brogiolo (Lecco: Stefanoni), pp. 153–66

Uggeri, G. 1979. 'Il popolamento del territorio cosano nell'antichità', in *Aspetti e problemi di storia dello Stato dei presidi in Maremma*, ed. by Roberto Ferretti (Grosseto: Società storica maremmana), pp. 37–53

Ughelli, F. 1717–1722. *Italia Sacra sive de episcopis Italiane et insularum adjacentium, rebusque ab hiis preclare gestis, deducta serie ad nostram usque aetatem. Opus singolare provinciis XX disinctum, in quo Ecclesiarum origines, Urbium conditiones, Principum donationes, recondita monumenta in lucem proferuntur*, ed. by N. Coleti (Venice: n. pub.)

Urlacher, Jean-Pierre, Françoise Passard, and Sophie Manfredi-Gizard. 1998. *La nécropole mérovingienne de la grande Oye à Doubs. VIe-VIIe siècles après J.-C.* (Saint-Germain-en-Laye: Association française d'archéologie mérovingienne)

Vacano, Otto Wilhelm von, Andrea Crivellari, and Paola Castellini. 1985. *Gli Etruschi a Talamone: La baia di Talamone della preistoria ai giorni nostri* (Bologna: Cappelli)

Vacano, Otto Wilhelm von and Bettina von Freytag. 1982. 'Il frontone di Talamone e il mito dei "Sette a Tebe"', in *Talamone: il mito dei sette a Tebe* (Florence: Il David), pp. 179–287

Vaccaro, Emanuele. 2005a. '3 Dinamiche insediative; 4 I manufatti ceramici di Podere Serratone: metodi di analisi dei materiali da superficie per lo studio della cultura materiale di un abitato di pianura', in *Il popolamento tardoromano e altomedievale nella bassa valle dell'Ombrone, Progetto Carta Archeologica della Provincia di Grosseto*, ed. by Stefano Campana, Riccardo Francovich, and Emanuele Vaccaro, *Archeologia Medievale*, 32: 463–76

——. 2005b. 'Popolamento rurale tra fine V inizi X nella Maremma grossetana: indagini di superfice tra Valle dell'Ama e la valle dell'Osa', *Il popolamento tardoromano e altomedievale nella bassa valle dell'Ombrone, Progetto Carta Archeologica della Provincia di Grosseto*, ed. by Stefano Campana, Riccardo Francovich, and Emanuele Vaccaro, *Archeologia Medievale*, 32: 179–92

——. 2005c. 'Il popolamento rurale tra fine V e inizi X nella Maremma grossetana: Indagini di superficie tra la valle dell'Alma e la valle dell'Osa', in *Dopo la fine delle ville: Le campagne dal VI al IX secolo*, ed. by Gian Pietro Brogiolo and others (Mantua: Padus), pp. 179–92

——. 2007. 'Processi di trasformazione insediativa, gestione del territorio e circolazione ceramica nella Maremma costiera tra IV e XI secolo d.C' (Dott. diss., University of Siena)

——. 2008. 'An Overview of Rural Settlement in Four River Basins in the Province of Grosseto on the Coast of Tuscany (200 B.C.–A.D. 600)', *Journal of Roman Archaeology*, 21: 225–47

——. 2009. 'Cultura materiale e circolazione di merci: riflessioni su un contesto ceramico di X secolo d.C. da Capalbiaccio-Tricosto', in *Capalbiaccio (GR) nel tempo: Dalla preistoria all'età moderna. Le indagini archeologiche dagli anni '70 al nuovo progetto di ricerca*, ed. by Michelle Hobart and others, *Archeologia Medievale*, 36: 93–104

——. 2011. *Sites and Pots: Settlement and Economy in Southern Tuscany (AD 300–900)* (Oxford: Archaeopress)

——. 2013. 'Patterning Late Roman Ceramic Exchange in southern Tuscany (Italy): The Coastal and Inland Evidence, i.e. Centrality vs. Marginality', in *LRCW 4. Late Roman Coarse Wares, Cooking Wares and Amphorae in the Mediterranean: Archaeology and Archaeometry*, ed. by Aristotelis Mentzos, Natalia Poulou-Papadimitriou, and Vassilis Kilikoglou (Oxford: Archaeopress), pp. 11–26

——. 2018. 'Long-Distance Ceramic Connections. *Portus Scabris* (Portiglioni-GR), Coastal Tuscany and the Tyrrhenian Sea', in *Origins of a New Economic Union (7th 12th Centuries): Preliminary Results of the nEU-Med Project; October 2015–March 2017*, ed. by Giovanna Bianchi and Richard Hodges (Florence: All'Insegna del Giglio), pp. 81–100

Vaccaro, Emanuele, Mariaelena Ghisleni, and Stefano Campana. 2009. 'The Site of Aiali from the Late Republican Period to Middle Ages in the Light of Surface Pottery Analysis', in *Seeing the Unseen: Geophysics and Landscape Archaeology*, ed. by Stefano Campana and Salvatore Piro (London: Taylor and Francis), pp. 303–24

Vaccaro, Emanuele and Hermann Salvadori. 2006. 'Prime analisi sui reperti ceramici e numismatici di X secolo dal villaggio medievale di Poggio Cavolo (GR)', in *IV Congresso Nazionale di Archeologia Medievale. Abbazia di San Galgano (Chiusdino, SI), 26–20 settembre 2006*, ed. by Riccardo Francovich and Marco Valenti (Florence: All'Insegna del Giglio), pp. 480–84

Valdambrini, Chiara. 2005. 'Il materiale ceramico proveniente dallo scavo della chiesa di S.Pietro a Grosseto. Osservazioni preliminari', in *Lo scavo della chiesa di S.Pietro a Grosseto. Nuovi dati sull'origine e lo sviluppo di una città medievale*, ed. by Carlo Citter (Florence: All'Insegna del Giglio), pp. 33–47

——. 2006. 'Ceramiche depurate e semidepurate prive di rivestimento dagli scavi urbani di Grosseto: considerazioni preliminari', in *IV Congresso Nazionale di Archeologia Medievale. Abbazia di San Galgano (Chiusdino, SI), 26–20 settembre 2006*, ed. by Riccardo Francovich and Marco Valenti (Florence: All'Insegna del Giglio), pp. 474–79

——. 2010. 'Archeologia e archeometria in tre castelli nella provincia di Grosseto: le ceramiche di Sassoforte (Roccastrada-GR), Poggio Cavolo (GR), Castel di Pietra (Gavorrano-GR) e Grosseto, cronotipologie e analisi funzionali (secoli X–XIV). Le ceramiche grezze, depurate e semidepurate: tipologia, quantificazione e analisi archeometriche sui residui organici assorbiti' (Dott. diss., University of Siena)

Valente, Franco. 2009. 'Gli scacchi di Venafro. Storie ordinarie di ordinarie bugie archeologiche'. <https://www.francovalente.it/2009/08/15/gli-scacchi-di-venafro-storie-ordinarie-di-ordinarie-bugie-archeologiche>

Valenti, Marco. 1995. *Carta archeologica della provincia di Siena. II: Chianti senese*, I (Siena: Nuova Immagine)

——. ed. 1996. *Poggio Imperiale a Poggibonsi: dal villaggio di capanne al castello di pietra* (Florence: All'Insegna del Giglio)

——. ed. 1999. *Carta archeologica della Provincia di Siena, III: La Valdelsa (Colle Valdelsa, Poggibonsi)* (Siena: Nuova Immagine)

——. 2004. *L'Insediamento Altomedievale nelle Campagne Toscane. Paesaggi. Popolamento e Villaggi tra VI e X secoli* (Florence: All'Insegna del Giglio)

——. 2006. 'Architecture and Infrastructure in the Early Medieval Village: The Case of Tuscany', in *Technology in Transition (300–650) Late Antique*, ed. by Luke Lavan, Enrico Zanini, and A. C. Sarantis, Late Antique Archaeology, 4 (Leiden: Brill), pp. 451–88

——. ed. 2008. *Miranduolo in alta val di Merse (Chiusdino-SI). Archeologia su un sito di potere del Medioevo toscano* (Florence: All'Insegna del Giglio)

Vallat, J. P. 1992. 'Cadastre, fiscalité, et paysage: exemples en Italie et au Proche Orient dans l'Antiquité', in *Archeologia del paesaggio*, ed. by Manuela Bernardi (Florence: All'Insegna del Giglio), pp. 483–509

Vander Poppen, Robert E. 2008. 'Rural Change and Continuity in Etruria: A Study of Village Communities from the 7th Century B.C. to the 1st Century A.D.' (unpubl. Ph.D. diss., University of North Carolina, Chapel Hill)

Vanni, Franca M. 1997. *Arezzo, San Donato, le monete. Le monete della zecca aretina del Museo statale d'Arte medievale e moderna di Arezzo* (Florence: Nuova Grafica Fiorentina)

Vanni, Franca M. 2005. *Una zecca ritrovata: Cortona* (Cortona: Calosci)

——. 2011. 'Lucca', in *Le zecche italiane fino all'Unità*, ed. by Lucia Travaini (Rome: Istituto poligrafico e zecca dello Stato), pp. 785–809

Vannini, Angela. 1985. *I reperti posteriori alla vita della villa*, in *Settefinestre 3, La villa e i suoi reperti* (Modena: Pannini)

Vannini, Guido, ed. 1985. *L'antico palazzo dei vescovi a Pistoia*, II: *I documenti archeologici* (Florence: All'Insegna del Giglio)

——. 2002. 'Il castello dei Guidi a Poggio della Regina e la Curia del Castiglione. Archeologia di una società feudale appenninica', in Guido Vannini, *Fortuna e declino di una società feudale valdarnese: il Poggio della Regina* (Florence: Società Editrice Fiorentina), pp. 1–56

——. ed. 2009. *Rocca Ricciarda, dai Guidi ai Ricasoli. Storia e archeologia di un castrum medievale nel Pratomagno aretino* (Florence: Società Editrice Fiorentina)

Vannini, Guido and C. Molducci. 2009. 'I castelli dei Guidi fra Romagna e Toscana: I casi di Modigliana e Romena; un progetto di archeologia territoriale', in *La lunga storia di una stirpe comitale. I conti Guidi tra Romagna e Toscana*, ed. by F. Canaccini (Florence: Olschki), pp. 177–210

Varaldo, Carlo, ed. 1997. 'La graffita arcaica tirrenica', in *La céramique médiévale en Méditerranée, Actes du Ve Colloque (13–18 novembre 1985)* (Aix-en-Provence: Narration éditions), pp. 439–51

———. ed. 2001. *Archeologia urbana a Savona: Scavi e ricerche nel complesso monumentale del Priamar*. II: *Palazzo della Loggia, scavi 1969–1989* (Savona: Marco Sabatelli)

Venerosi Pesciolini, G. 1925. 'L'acqua potabile a Capalbio nel secolo XV', *Maremma*, 2: 53–59

Viara, Gian Giacomo. 2001. 'Manufatti in metallo', in *Archeologia urbana a Savona: Scavi e ricerche nel complesso monumentale del Priamar*, II: *Palazzo della Loggia, scavi 1969–1989*, ed. by Carlo Varaldo (Savona: Marco Sabatelli), pp. 445–52

Vigil-Escalera Guirado, Alfonso, Giovanna Bianchi, and Juan Antonio Quirós Castillo, eds. 2013. *Horrea, Barns and Silos. Storage and Incomes in Early Medieval Europe* (Bilbao: Universidad del País Vasco)

Vignola, Marco. 2003. 'Armi e armamento difensivo', in *Progetto Castello della Motta di Savorgnano: ricerche di archeologia medievale nel nord-est italiano*, ed. by Fabio Piuzzi (Florence: All'Insegna del Giglio), pp. 182–99

Villa, Luca. 1994. 'Le anfore tra tardoantico e medioevo', in *Ad Mensam. Manufatti d'uso da contesti archeologici fra tarda antichità e medioevo*, ed. by Silvia Lusuardi Siena (Udine: Del Bianco), pp. 335–431

Vitali, D., F. Laubenheimer, L. Benquet, E. Cottafava, and C. Calastri. 2005. 'Le fornaci di Albinia (GR) e la produzione di anfore nella bassa valle dell'Albegna', in *Materiali per Populonia*, IV, ed. by Andrea Camilli and M. Letizia Gualandi (Florence: All'Insegna del Giglio), pp. 259–79

Vitolo, G. 2000. *Il Medioevo. I caratteri originali di un'età di transizione* (Florence: Sansoni)

Von Hessen, Otto. 1997. 'Testimonianze archeologiche longobarde nel ducato di Spoleto', in *Umbria Longobarda. La necropoli di Nocera Umbra nel centenario della scoperta*, ed. by Lidia Paroli (Rome: Edizioni De Luca), pp. 131–34

Vivarelli Colonna, F. 1937. *Venticinque anni di lavoro nelle mie terre di Maremma: 1910–1935. Atti della Reale Accademia dei Georgofili 15* (Florence: Ricci)

Volpe, Giuliano, and Pasquale Favia, eds. 2009. *V Congresso Nazionale di Archeologia Medievale* (Florence: All'Insegna del Giglio)

Vroom, Joanita. 2005. *Byzantine to Modern Pottery in the Aegean: 7th to 20th Century: An Introduction and Field Guide* (Utrecht: Parnassus)

———. 2008. 'Dishing up History. Early Medieval Ceramic Finds from the Triconch Palace in Butrint', *Mélanges de l'École française de Rome. Moyen Âge*, 120/122: 291–305

Walker, Lucy. 2002. 'L'epoca etrusca. 3. Il popolamento e l'utilizzazione del suolo', in *Paesaggi d'Etruria: Valle dell'Albegna, Valle d'Oro, Valle del Chiarone, Valle del Tafone: Progetto di ricerca italo-britannico seguito allo scavo di Settefinestre*, ed. by Andrea Carandini, Franco Cambi, Mariagrazia Celuzza, and Elizabeth Fentress (Rome: Edizioni di storia e letteratura), pp. 90–95

Ward-Perkins, Bryan. 1997. 'Continuists, Catastrophists, and the Towns of Post-Roman Northern Italy', *Papers of the British School at Rome*, 65: 157–76

———. 2005. *The Fall of Rome and the End of Civilization* (Oxford: Oxford University Press)

Ward-Perkins, John. 1955. 'Notes on the South Etruria and the Ager Veientanus', *Papers of the British School at Rome*, 23: 44–72

Ward-Perkins, John, David Andrews, Sheila Gibson, David Whitehouse, and Bryan Ward-Perkins. 1972. 'Excavation and Survey at Tuscania, 1972: A Preliminary Report', *Papers of the British School at Rome*, 40: 196–238

Ward-Perkins, John, Jeremy Johns, Bryan Ward-Perkins, William Lamarque, and Martin Beddoe. 1973. 'Excavations at Tuscania, 1973: Report on the Finds from Six Selected Pits', *Papers of the British School at Rome*, 41: 45–154

Watt, John A. 1965. *The Theory of Papal Monarchy in the Thirteenth Century: The Contribution of Canonists* (New York: Fordham University Press)

———. 1999. 'The Papacy', in *The New Cambridge Medieval History*, V: *(c. 1198–1300)*, ed. by David Abulafia (Cambridge: Cambridge University Press), pp. 107–63

Whitehouse, David. 1970. 'Excavations at Satriana: A Deserted Medieval Settlement in Basilicata', *Papers of the British School at Rome*, 38: 188–219

———. 1980. 'The Medieval Pottery from Santa Cornelia', *Papers of the British School at Rome*, 48: 125–56

———. 1982. 'Medieval Pottery from South Etruria', in *Papers in Italian Archaeology*, III: *Studies in Architecture, Painting, and Ceramics*, ed. by David Andrews, John Osborne, and David Whitehouse (Oxford: Archaeopress), pp. 299–344

Wickham, Christopher. 1985. *Il problema dell'incastellamento nell'Italia central* (Florence: All'Insegno del Giglio)

———. 1989. *Early Medieval Italy. Central Power and Local Societies 400–1000* (Ann Arbor: University of Michigan Press)

———. 1994, *Land and Power. Studies in Italian and European Social History, 400–1200* (London: The British School at Rome)

———. 1995. 'Property Ownership and Signorial Power in Twelfth-century Tuscany', in *Property and Power in the Early Middle Ages*, ed. by Wendy Davies (Cambridge: Cambridge University Press), pp. 221–44

———. 1996. 'La Signoria rurale in Toscana', in *Strutture e Trasformazioni della signoria rurale nei secoli X–XIII*, ed. by Gerhard Dilcher and Cinzio Violante (Bologna: Il mulino), pp. 343–409

———. 2001. 'Medieval Studies and the British School at Rome', *Papers of the British School at Rome*, 69: 35–48

——. 2005. *Framing the Early Middle Ages. Europe and the Mediterranean, 400–800* (Oxford: Oxford University Press)
——. 2008. 'Rethinking the Structure of the Early Medieval Economy', in *The Long Morning of Medieval Europe*, ed. by J. R. Davis and M. McCormick (Aldershot: Scolar Press), pp. 19–31
——. 'Archeologia e mondi rurali: Quadri di insediamento e sviluppo economico', *Archeologia Medievale*, 37: 277–84
Wickham, Christopher and Elizabeth Fentress. 2002. 'Il Medioevo', in *Paesaggi d'Etruria: Valle dell'Albegna, Valle d'Oro, Valle del Chiarone, Valle del Tafone: Progetto di ricerca italo-britannico seguito allo scavo di Settefinestre*, ed. by Andrea Carandini, Franco Cambi, Mariagrazia Celuzza, and Elizabeth Fentress (Rome: Edizioni di storia e letteratura), pp. 259–83
Wilson, Andrew I. 2004. 'Tuscan Landscapes: Surveying the Albegna Valley', *Journal of Roman Archaeology*, 17.2: 569–76
Wing, Elizabeth S. and Antoinette B. Brown. 1979. *Paleonutrition* (New York: Academic Press)
Zagari, Francesca. 2003. 'Cencelle: Produzioni metalliche', in *Fonti archeologiche e iconografiche per la storia e la cultura degli insediamenti nell'alto medioevo, Atti delle giornate di studio Milano-Vercelli, 21–22 marzo 2002*, ed. by Silvia Lusuardi Siena (Milan: Litografia Solari), pp. 25–30
Zagari, Francesca. 2005. *Il metallo nel medioevo. Tecniche Strutture Manufatti* (Rome: Palombi & Partner)
Zagli, A. 2007. *Breve storia di Grosseto* (Pisa: Pacini)
Zifferero, Andrea. 1990. 'Città e campagna in Etruria meridionale: Indagine nell'entroterra di Caere', in *Caere e il suo territorio: Da Agylla a Centumcellae*, ed. by Antonio Maffei and Francesco Nastasi (Rome: Libreria dello Stato, Istituto poligrafico e Zecca dello Stato), pp. 60–70
——. 1995. 'Economia, divinità e frontiera. Sul ruolo di alcuni santuari di confine in Etruria meridionale', *Ostraka*, 4: 333–50
——. 1998. 'I santuari come indicatori di frontiera nell'Italia tirrenica preromana', in *Papers from the EAA Third Annual Meeting at Ravenna 1997, A. Pre- and Protohistory*, ed. by Mark Pearce and Maurizio Tosi (Oxford: Archaeopress), pp. 223–32
——. 2002. 'The Geography of the Ritual Landscape in Complex Societies', in *New Developments in Italian Landscape Archaeology. Theory and Methodology of Field Survey, Land Evaluation and Landscape Perception. Pottery Production and Distribution. Proceedings of a Three-Day Conference Held at the University of Groningen, April 13–15, 2000*, ed. by Peter Attema, Gert. J. Burgers, and Ester van Joolen (Oxford: Archaeopress), pp. 246–65
——. 2000. *L'architettura funeraria a Populonia tra IX e VI secolo a.C.* (Florence: All'Insegna del Giglio)
——. 2006. 'Circoli di pietre, tumuli e culto funerario', *Mélanges de l'École française de Rome*, 118: 177–213
——. 2009. 'Marsiliana d'Albegna (Manciano; GR): Cento anni di ricerche archeologiche', in *Materiali per Populonia*, VIII, ed. by Francesco Ghizzani, Marcìa Italie, and Carolina Megale (Pisa: Edizioni ETS), pp. 223–46
——. ed. 2016. *Marsiliana d'Albegna. Dagli etruschi a Tommaso Corsini* (Monteriggioni: Ara Edizioni)
——. 2017. "Le attività artigianali nel territorio vulcente: la valle dell'Albegna e Marsiliana', in *Gli artigiani e la città: Officine e aree produttive tra VII e III sec. a.C. nell'Italia centrale tirrnica*, ed. by M. Cristina Biella, Roberta Cascino, Antonio F. Ferrandes, and Martina Revello Larmi (Rome: Quasar), pp. 311–29
——. 2019. 'Ripercorrendo la Valle dell'Albegna: Orbetello, Marsiliana, Oinaréa, Kamarte', in *Una lezione di archeologia globale: Studi in onore di Daniele Manacorda*, ed. by Mirco Modolo, Silvia Pallecchi, Giuliano Volpe, and Enrico Zanini (Bari: Edipuglia), pp. 293–300
Zifferero, Andrea, Caterina De Angelis, and Marco Pacifici. 2019. 'Osservazioni sulle origini di Marsiliana d'Albegna (Manciano, GR) e nuove ricerche nell'area suburbana', *Bollettino di archeologia on line*, 10.1/2
Zifferero, Andrea, M. Milletti, Caterina De Angelis, and Marco Pacifici. 2016. 'Progetto Marsiliana d'Albegna (Manciano, GR): Nuovi dati sulla formazione del centro etrusco dai saggi di scavo sul Poggio del Castello', in *Ornarsi per comunicare con gli uomini e con i Dei. Gli oggetti di ornamento come status symbol, amuleti, richiesta di protezione. Ricerche e scavi*, ed. by Nuccia Negroni Catacchio. Preistoria e Protostoria Etrusca (Milan: Centro Studi di Preistoria e Archeologia), pp. 797–809
Zifferero, Andrea and others 2011a. 'Marsiliana d'Albegna: nuovi dati dall'area suburbana', in *Materiali per Populonia*, x, ed. by Giulia Facchini and Matteo Milletti (Pisa: Edizioni ETS), pp. 289–320
Zifferero, Andrea and others 2011b. 'Circoli con camera ipogea e "caditoia" a Marsiliana d'Albegna: Prime ipotesi di ricostruzione', in *Materiali per Populonia*, x, ed. by Giulia Facchini and Matteo Milletti (Pisa: Edizioni ETS), pp. 321–58
Zifferero, Andrea and others 2016. 'Progetto Marsiliana d'Albegna (Manciano, GR): Nuovi dati sulla formazione del centro etrusco e saggi di scavo sul Poggio del Castello', in *Ornarsi per comunicare con gli uomini e con gli dei. Gli oggetti di ornamento come status symbol, amuleti, richiesta di protezione. Ricerche e scavi, Atti del XII Incontro di Studi di Preistoria e Protostoria in Etruria (Valentano, Pitigliano, Manciano 2014)*, ed. by Nuccia Negroni Catacchio (Milan), pp. 797–812
Zifferero, Andrea, G. Pieragnoli, C. Sanchirico, and G. Tofani. 2009. 'Un sito artigianale con anfore fra trasporto Py3B a Marsiliana d'Albegna (Manciano; GR)', *Officina di Etruscologia*, 1: 101–208
Zingarelli, Nicola, Miro Dogliotti, and Luigi Rosiello. 1997. *Lo Zingarelli: Vocabolario della lingua italiana* (Bologna: Zanichelli)

Author Biographies

Michelle Hobart is a medieval archeologist and architectural historian who focuses on the southern Mediterranean and Italy. She has been a professor of the humanities at The Cooper Union in New York City since 2003. Hobart co-directs the Impero Project near Siena with the Universities of Buffalo and Siena. In 2017, she edited and authored the *Companion of Sardinian History (500–1500)*. Previously, Hobart was the medievalist and author on the Cosa V excavation of the American Academy of Rome.

Stephen L. Dyson is emeritus professor of classics at the University of Buffalo and past president of the Archeological Institute of America. He started the excavation of Capalbiaccio in 1976 and has published extensively on Roman history and culture, and archeology.

Alessia Rovelli is a professor of Numismatics at the University of Tuscia-Viterbo. She specializes in late antique and medieval coins in Italy and Europe.

Valeria Acconcia is an Etruscologist and Classicist employed by the Italian Ministry of Culture with extensive experience in the field. She has published on Central Italy and Tuscany.

Emanuele Mariotti is an archeologist and surveyor focusing on Siena, Pisa, and Florence. His most recent work has included directing the internationally recognized excavation of the Etruscan sanctuary at San Casciano dei Bagni, Siena.

Emanuele Vaccaro is an Associate Professor of Classical Archaeology at the University of Trento. A specialist in early medieval pottery, his research focuses on Trentino Alto-Adige, Tuscany, and Sicily.

Chiara Valdambrini is an archeologist specializing in medieval pottery and curatorial studies. She is the director of the Santa Maria della Scala museum in Siena and the scientific director of the Museum of Archeology and Art of the Maremma in Grosseto.

Hermann Salvadori is an archeologist and a surveyor working on medieval and post-medieval Tuscany. He studied at the University in Siena and has excavated and published extensively on the provinces of Siena and Arezzo.

Laura Cerri is a freelance archeologist with significant experience of working in Italy and the wider Mediterranean. In her work, she promotes non-invasive diagnostic techniques such as geophysical prospecting and preventative archeology.

Irene Corti is a buildings archaeologist with particular expertise in the medieval period. She has most recently been involved in the excavations at Cosa and Campiglia Marittima (Siena).

Diane Crader is a zooarcheologist and associate professor emeritus of the University of Southern Maine. Her research specializes in faunal archeology and revelations around diet.

Elisa Rubegni is an small finds archaeologist and has excavated extensively in Tuscany. She is currently the scientific coordinator for the Asciano museums in Siena.

Index

abbeys *see* monasteries
acorn missile, 204, 219
Acquarossa, 282
aerial photography, 23, 25, 29, 57, 65–67, 130, 147, 275, 278, 287, 317
ager Caletranus, 276, 280, 285–86
ager Cosanus, 24, 26, 33–35, 43, 46, 54, 74, 94–95, 98–99, 141–42, 149, 152, 273, 276, 281, 286, 291, 301, 313–19
ager Hebanus, 276
   see also Heba
Albegna Valley, 24–26, 45, 49, 50–53, 90, 94–100, 201, 251, 274, 276, 278, 280–85, 287, 301, 306, 310–11, 314–15
Aldobrandeschi family, 24, 30, 69, 72–74, 163–64, 170, 219, 225, 251, 289–90, 292–93, 295, 301–07, 311
Alma Valley, 65, 146, 156, 160
animal remains, 28, 31, 35, 38, 92, 158, 206, 217, 231–43, 250, 312
Ansedonia, 18, 28, 33, 43, 45, 47, 53, 74–75, 90, 135, 141–42, 165, 170–72, 176–77, 189, 191, 201, 223, 225, 231, 278, 290, 295, 302–03, 306–07, 313, 315
   see also Cosa
Aquas Salvias, 141, 152, 302
aqueducts *see* water management
Archaic Period, 97–99, 277, 283
Arcidosso, 251, 304
Ardengheschi family, 290, 304, 306
Arezzo, 91, 223, 225–27, 247, 266, 310
armour, 91, 203, 206, 217–19, 222
arrowheads, 206, 216–19, 221
Avignon, 230, 235, 305

bells, 206–07, 216–17
bishops and bishoprics, 74, 142, 225, 301
Berardeschi family, 290
Binetti, 94
Black Death, 24, 249, 261, 267, 307
Bronze Age, 23, 27, 89–90, 93, 96, 102–04, 273, 277, 284, 309
Bruna Valley, 131, 148, 150, 154
Buonconvento, 29
Byzantine, 34, 74, 201, 310, 311

Caere, 96, 99, 277
Camerelle di Chiusi, 155
Campiglia Marittima, 28, 120, 135, 139, 150–53, 161, 165, 169, 176, 182, 221, 290
canals, 48–50, 51–55, 248, 301
   see also water management
Carolingian era, 74, 121, 125, 224, 290, 302–04, 313–14
Carthage, 283–84, 286
Casa Andreoni, 120–21, 130, 134, 150–51, 155, 161
Casa Marotti, 257, 259, 261, 269
Casa San Pietro, 45–46
Casetta delle Forane, 95
Castel di Pietra, 120, 152–53, 169, 221, 247, 251–52, 255, 259, 261–62, 264–65, 268, 269, 273, 278
Castelfranco di Paganico, 249
Castell'Azzara, 163, 250, 252
Castiglioncello del Trinoro, 261
Castiglion della Pescaia, 50
Catasto Leopoldino, 247, 252–53, 255–57, 260–64, 269, 301
Cencelle, 126
ceramics *see* pottery
Ceri, 99
Cerveteri, 240, 242
chamber tombs, 65, 97, 278
Charlemagne, 74, 145, 301–03
Chartres, 224
chess, 37, 91, 203, 205, 219–20
Chiarone, River, 44, 51, 54, 95–96, 99
Chiusi, 139, 155
churches:
   San Donato, 94
   San Floriano, 46, 47, 50–51, 52, 54
   San Genesio, 126, 141, 150
   San Giovenale, 240, 282
   San Martino de Plano, 120–21, 148, 155, 162
   San Pietro ad Asso, 29, 139, 223
   Santa Fiora, 250, 304–05
   Santo Stefano, 46, 73, 281, 303
Ciana, 46
Cistercian order, 74, 302, 304
Classical Archaeology, 33, 34, 273
Classical period, 26, 55, 98, 201, 259, 261, 311

coins, 31, 37–38, 87, 91, 223–27, 229, 305, 307, 319
Colonnette, 46
Corneto, 225, 301, 303
Cornia, River, 123
Corsica, 145, 250
Cosa, 23–43, 46–48, 54, 74–75, 94–95, 99–100, 115, 119, 120, 131, 135, 141–42, 147–48, 151–53, 165–66, 169–70, 172, 189, 191, 203, 220, 223, 226, 231, 274–78, 281–82, 284–87, 295, 302, 310, 311, 313–17, 319, 320
see also Ansedonia
Crypta Balbi, 125, 143, 166, 190
Cugnano, 120, 156–57, 165, 247

Digital Elevation Model (DEM), 18, 24, 27, 29, 56–57, 59, 60–62, 65, 67, 232, 293
Digital Terrain Model (DTM), 24, 61, 70, 94, 119, 164, 172–74, 224, 232, 274
Doganella, 95–99, 106, 108, 110, 112, 274, 276, 281–87
Donoratico, 75, 120, 126, 135, 139, 150–53, 156, 161, 165, 169, 170, 188, 221, 247
dromos, 65

Egypt, 145
emphyteusis, 74
Etruscans, 23, 25, 27–29, 31, 34, 38, 43, 49, 54, 57, 59, 60, 89, 90, 92–101, 103–05, 115, 130, 201, 225, 231–34, 240–43, 246, 273–87, 309, 312–15, 319–20
excavations, 17–19, 23–31, 33–35, 37–39, 43, 51, 57, 69, 76, 87–89, 91, 93–95, 97, 100, 119, 121, 126, 129–30, 134, 138, 141–42, 146–47, 151–52, 163, 165, 171–72, 176, 186, 201–04, 208, 212, 219, 223–25, 232, 234, 236, 239, 240, 247, 249, 252–53, 255, 261, 267, 269, 273, 276, 278, 280, 282, 284, 292, 301, 302, 307, 309, 313, 315, 318–20

Feniglia, 44, 48–49, 53, 54, 96, 274, 302, 303
Fiora Valley, 93, 96, 99, 250, 274
fish farming, fisheries, 23, 46–49, 51–54, 274, 301, 303
Florence, 30, 91, 160, 223, 225, 229, 250, 252, 266, 280, 289, 303, 306, 310
Follonica, 141, 250
Fontanile della Strega, 257
Fontanile Secco, 46
Fonte Picchio, 256–57, 261–62, 269
Fonteblanda, 50, 93, 98, 280, 282, 285
Forum of Nerva, 125, 129, 131, 163
Fosso dei Molini, 45–46
France, 35, 145, 220

Gavorrano, 65, 169, 250, 252
Genoa, 176, 225–26, 230, 303
Gherardesca family, 29
Ghiaccioforte, 49, 95, 98–99, 282, 285
Ghibellines and Guelphs, 298, 305
Giardino:
    family, 269
    locality, 46, 95
    villa, 27, 35
Geographic Information System (GIS), 50, 60, 87, 253, 309
Greece, 277
Grosseto, 23, 26, 31, 47, 50, 54–55, 70, 74, 90, 119–20, 127, 129, 130, 134–35, 139, 142, 147, 152, 155, 165–66, 169–70, 176, 188, 201, 247–53, 255, 269–70, 289–90, 301, 303–04, 306–07
ground-penetrating readings, 87
Guidi family, 292, 305
Guido of Orso Orsini, 307

Hannibal, 26
Heba, 99, 278, 281, 310
Henry IV of Franconia, 223
herringbone masonry, 72–73
Hildebrand VII, 74, 163
historiography, 27, 249, 280, 283, 289
Holocene, 23
Holy Land, the, 224
hypothetical reconstruction, 18, 43, 54–55, 61, 71, 73, 81, 290, 309

I Poggetti, 94
Il Cristo, 96
Il Grilletto, 96
Ildebrandino VII, 163
Ildebrandino VIII, 304–05
Ildebrandino XI, 306
incastellamento, 23, 26–27, 247–48, 290, 293, 314
Iron Age, 35, 38, 90, 93–94, 96–98, 101–04, 277, 309, 320
Islamic world, 171
Isola del Giglio-Campese, 93

James I, 226–27
jewellery, 280

keys, 203, 206, 214–16, 221, 227–28, 230
kilns, 23, 90, 120, 122, 132, 147, 149, 152, 154, 162, 204, 269, 285
knives, 210–11

La Parrina, 95, 108, 112
La Torba, 96
La Tradita, 93
Lago dell'Accesa, 65, 108, 112, 282
lagoons, 43-44, 45-54, 274
lakes, 46, 52, 55
    Acquato, 46, 54
    Burano, 45, 47-48, 50-52, 54, 278
    Orbetello, 53
    San Floriano, 46, 50, 52, 54
    Scuro, 46, 52-54
    Uccellina, 46
    see also lagoons
land reclamation, 43, 47, 311
Latium, 27, 30, 35, 69, 90-91, 108, 121, 125-28, 130-32, 134-35, 139-44, 148-52, 154, 157, 159, 160, 163-70, 172-75, 196, 198, 224-26, 257, 264, 269, 301, 314
Le Mans, 224
Le Puy, 224
Liguria, 91, 141, 171, 176, 199, 200, 201, 311
Livorno, 70, 247
Livy, 98, 240
Lombard period, 74, 121, 219, 224, 290, 301-02
Lombard League, 304
Louis II, 74, 301
Lucca, 30, 74, 91, 126, 141, 150-51, 163, 223-26, 280, 290, 301, 303, 310
Luni, 281, 310, 311

Maghreb, 171
Magliano, 95, 97-99, 163, 282, 313
magnetometry, 27-29, 57, 61, 67, 273, 277, 282, 309
Manciano, 250, 313
Mandrioli, 93
Mandrioncino della Sotriscia, 95
Marche, 224
Maremma, 23, 27-28, 30, 43, 47, 53, 54, 64, 74-75, 126, 134, 170, 201, 210, 219, 221, 247, 248-51, 264-65, 267, 269-70, 273, 281, 285-86, 289, 290, 302-03, 306-07, 310-11, 314-15
maritime trade, 141, 152
Marsiliana, 45, 49, 93, 95, 97-99, 274, 276-78, 280, 282-84, 286-87, 302, 313
Marxism, 26, 33
masonry, 29-30, 46, 60, 63, 65, 69, 71, 73, 75, 76, 78, 81-82, 84, 252, 278, 293-95, 298, 300, 304, 317, 319
Massa Marittima, 23, 65, 247-48, 250-51, 290, 301
Medici, 50, 142, 290
medieval archaeology, 26, 27, 33-34, 247, 311
Melgueil, 224

Middle Ages, 26-27, 34-35, 38, 60, 69, 73-75, 90-91, 120-21, 130, 132, 138, 147, 173, 212, 223, 235, 248-50, 255, 259, 269, 277-89, 312-15, 320
Miranduolo, 205, 261, 290
modern era, 54, 210, 248-49, 251-52, 265, 267, 269
monasteries:
    Sant'Anastasio ad Aquas Salvias, 141, 149, 152
    Santi Vincenzo and Anastasio alle Tre Fontane, 71, 73-74, 141, 302, 306, 314
    San Salvatore sull'Amiata, 301-02, 304, 306
Montarrenti, 120, 127, 129, 135, 147, 155-56, 169-70, 176, 200
Monte Amiata, 251, 253, 269, 301, 304
    see also monasteries
Monte Argentario, 44-46, 48-49, 93, 274, 302-03
Monte Cassino, 302-03
Monte Nebbiello, 46, 94-95
Monte S. Angelo, 93
Montefiesole, 141
Montemassi, 120, 147, 162, 221, 261, 268-69, 311
Montepescali, 252, 262, 265-66, 269
Monterotondo, 250
Monteti, 44, 46, 93-94, 281, 302
museum archaeology, 39

Napoleonic era, 50
Nassa canal, 49
National Etruscan Museum, Tarquinia, 225
necropolis, necropolises, 65, 95-98, 280, 285,
Neolithic, 47, 208, 309
North Africa, 91, 163, 171, 200-01, 285, 311

Ombrone Valley, 126, 130, 141, 147-48, 150-52
Orbetello, 31, 44, 46-48, 50, 53-54, 73-74, 93, 95-100, 274, 281-82, 285-86, 302-03, 313-14, 315
Orientalizing period, 97, 104, 273, 277-78
Orsini of Pitigliano, 73, 255
Orvieto, 171, 173, 189, 191, 196-98, 201, 225, 241, 264, 289, 298, 304, 306-07, 314
Osa Valley, 129, 142, 150, 152, 160
Otto I and II, 130, 152
Ottonian period, 91, 119, 121, 125, 129, 131, 138, 147, 223-24, 292

Paestum, 25, 284
Paganico, 18, 249, 251-52, 304
Pannocchieschi family, 292
    see also Rochette Pannocchieschi
Papal States, 74, 314
Parco dell'Accesa, 65

Patrimonium Sancti/Beati Petri, 74, 223, 225, 301–04, 306
Pava, 29
Pecora Valley, 151, 155, 269
Peloponnese, 34
Pereta, 250
Pescia Fiorentina, 95
Pescia Romana, 45, 96
Pisa, 18, 30, 90–91, 119, 126, 134–35, 141, 146, 148, 150–51, 159, 163–64, 166, 169, 170–73, 176, 188, 191–96, 201, 223, 225, 228, 247–48, 250–51, 264, 269, 290, 292–93, 303, 307, 310, 314
Pistoia, 151
Pitigliano, 73, 96, 103, 250, 255, 304, 306–07
Piombino, 50, 75, 191, 290
Pliny, 94, 98, 240
Podere Aione, 120, 141–42, 153
Podere Serratone, 120–23, 129–32, 134–35, 148, 150, 154, 159, 162
Poggettone, 120, 150,
Poggibonsi, 139, 170, 176–77
Poggio Buco, 96, 103
Poggio Cavolo, 90–91, 119–23, 125–27, 129–61, 165, 170, 176, 223, 261, 281
Poggio del Castello, 93
Poggio della Regina, 261, 266
Poggio Malabarba, 95
Poggio Marcuccio, 65, 278
Poggio Tondo, 65
Poggio Torretta, 95
Poggio Tristo, 95
Poggione, 94, 281
Poitiers, 224
Polverosa, 94
Pope Eugene III, 304
Pope Gregory VII 74, 163
Pope John XXII, 225, 228
Pope Urban VI, 225, 230
Populonia, 74, 113, 115–16, 120, 141, 150–51, 153, 162, 240, 242, 251, 273, 286, 301
Porcareccia del Conicchio, 95
Porto Ercole, 46, 281
Porto Santo Stefano, 46, 75
pottery:
  acroma depurata, 121, 122–26, 129–32, 134, 139–40, 143–50, 153–55, 162
  acroma selezionata, 121–24, 130–32, 134, 143–46, 148, 162
  African, 310
  Albintimilium, 115
  amphorae, 23, 25, 33, 90–91, 95, 97–101, 111–12, 122, 125–26, 131–38, 140, 142–43, 145–47, 149, 152, 155–56, 165, 173, 201, 284–85, 310
  analysis of, 23, 26–29, 37–38, 87, 89–92, 95, 121, 126, 131, 138, 142, 152, 163, 175, 200, 223–24, 231, 252, 256, 258, 261, 269, 273, 301, 309, 311, 319
  Attic black figure, 95, 101, 104, 113
  black glaze, 100, 101, 113
  Bronze Age, 101, 103, 277
  Bucchero, 101, 104
  coarse ware, 99, 107, 109, 111, 113, 116, 164, 168, 175
  contextual, 71,
  Corinthian, 95, 101, 104
  Etruscan, 57, 89–90, 94–95, 104–05, 107, 273, 277, 279
  Etrusco-Corinthian, 101, 104
  fabrics, 100–01, 121, 154, 157–61, 186, 188
  fine, 99
  Forum ware, 130, 139, 140–42, 144, 152–53
  glazed, 90, 127, 163–64, 166, 171, 190–91
  graffita arcaica, 91, 171, 173, 176, 199, 201
  Iron Age, 101, 102, 277
  lead glaze, *invetriata*, 91, 165, 166, 173, 189, 190–91, 196, 199, 201
  lustreware, 175, 200
  maiolica arcaica, archaic majolica, 91, 172–76, 189–93, 195–96, 198, 200–01, 252, 269
  medieval, 31, 38, 89–90, 119–20, 126, 130, 132, 140, 143, 146–49, 163, 166–67, 191, 201, 236, 291, 309, 318
  olla acquaria, 125, 132–33, 139, 142–45, 149
  pithoi, 95, 97, 109–10
  Pre-Etruscan, 90
  production, 89, 95, 99, 112–14, 119, 121, 131, 140, 144, 146–49, 151, 153–54, 163–66, 170, 173, 175, 181, 187, 189–90, 193–95, 198, 200–04, 251–52, 284, 310
  red-painted, 12, 126, 152, 166
  Roman, 57, 90, 93, 95, 97, 105, 114–15, 147, 153, 223, 273, 286
  trade, 128, 130, 137, 139, 141, 148, 150, 152, 154, 163–64, 166, 171, 173, 175, 293
  slip ware, 252, 310
  sparse glaze, 90–91, 119, 129, 131, 139, 140–42, 144–46, 150–53, 160, 162–63, 165–66
  Tuscan, 174
  unglazed, 90, 164, 168, 170
  utilitarian, 33, 94, 277
  vetrina pesante, 130, 138–41, 142, 144, 153
  zaffera a rilievo, 91, 173, 176, 200–01
Pratomagno, 266

prehistoric period, 23, 28, 34, 43, 47, 51, 89–90, 92, 231, 256, 262, 282
Punta Fortezza, 120, 140, 142, 152–53, 160

Radicata Valley, 94–95, 99, 276, 278
Ranieri di Bartolomeo, 304
Renaissance, 43, 91, 249, 252, 311, 312
roads, 18, 23–24, 29, 46, 55, 57, 59–60, 62–63, 65, 67, 142, 239, 247, 251, 257, 262, 265, 269, 277, 280, 284, 286, 293–95, 301, 303, 309, 312, 314–15
Rocca Ricciarda, 261, 266
Rocca San Silvestro, 120, 139, 152, 165–66, 169, 176, 201, 221, 251
Roccaccia di Selvena, 252, 262
Roccalbegna, 251
Rocchette Pannocchieschi, 150–51, 153, 162, 251, 261,
Roman rural archaeology and history in Etruria, 17–18, 23–28, 33–35, 43, 51, 251, 269, 281, 301, 309–11, 315
see also ager Caletranus; ager Cosanus; ager Hebanus
Roman towns in Etruria, 282, 283, 286, 287, 309
see also Cosa; Porto Ercole; Saturnia
Romanization of Etruria, 23, 25, 99, 100, 281, 282, 284–86, 312–15
Rome, 23–27, 30, 69, 71, 90, 119, 121, 125–28, 130, 132, 139–42, 144, 149–50, 152, 157, 160, 163–64, 170, 190, 196, 200–01, 207, 217, 220, 225–26, 281, 284, 289–90, 292, 301–07, 310–12, 314, 319
Romitorio, 95
Roselle, 74, 98, 108, 110, 120, 130, 142, 150, 251, 276, 280–81, 285–86, 301, 309–10

Saint Paul Outside the Walls, 302
Salaiolo, 256, 258–59, 261, 263, 269
Sardinia, 141, 172, 220
Sasso di Furbara, 99
Sassofortino, 265
Saturnia, 95–96, 99–100, 113, 276, 310
Savona, 176, 199, 200
Scansano, 65, 250–52, 278
Scarlino, 65, 120, 129, 142, 147, 150–53, 165–66, 176, 226, 247, 250, 268–69, 293
Scoglietto, 150, 221, 310
Scopetelli, 95
Scorano, 90, 125, 170
Selvena, 25–52, 261–62, 264–65, 269
Semproniano, 163, 250–51
Settefinestre, 18, 24, 26, 51, 94, 115–16, 219, 273, 281, 286–87, 301, 309
Sicily, 91, 140–41, 171, 219, 220, 223, 226–27

Siena, 23, 25–27, 29, 30, 33, 53, 75, 97, 126, 139, 155, 164, 171, 173, 176, 188, 191, 194, 195–96, 201, 225, 247–52, 256–57, 261, 265, 267, 269, 282, 289–90, 298, 301, 303–04, 306–07, 311, 319
Sorano, 250–51
Sovana, 74, 96, 113, 250, 251, 282, 301, 305–07
Spacco della Regina, 48
Spain, 141, 171, 175–76, 200, 220
spindles, 91, 139, 140, 144, 162, 203, 205–06, 208–09, 221–22
Suvereto, 120, 152–53
swamps, 24, 43, 47, 50–51, 54, 314

Tagliata Canal, 48, 51, 54, 274
Talamonaccio, 47, 50, 93, 95–96, 98–100
Talamone, 46, 49–50, 93, 95–96, 98–100, 163, 250–51, 274, 303, 306
Tarquinia, 96, 98, 125–26, 132, 225–26, 235, 237, 240, 242, 274, 277, 283–84
terra rossa, 38, 45, 87, 89, 234, 240
thermal imaging, 27, 57, 59, 61, 63, 65, 67
thermal springs, 46
thimbles, 204, 206, 208, 210, 221
Tombolo della Feniglia, 96
Torre Argentiera, 72–73, 93
Torre Palazzi, 256–57
Torre Capo d'Uomo, 93
Torrettina, 94
Total Station, 37, 60–61
transhumance, 235
Tunisia, 141, 310
Tuscania, 189, 196, 235, 237, 242, 301
Tyrrhenian Sea, 35, 44–45, 91, 93, 100, 141, 152, 171–72, 201, 223, 225–27, 286, 290, 311

Uccellina Park, 44–47
Umbria, 166, 196, 207, 224–26, 264, 269
UNESCO, 312

Val Berretta, 65
Valence, 224
Valencia, 176, 200
Valle dell'Alma, 65, 142, 152, 160
Valle d'Oro, 18, 25–26, 30, 35, 45, 55, 90, 94–96, 98, 119, 154–55, 273–74, 276–78, 280, 284, 286–87, 306, 309
Veii, 34, 96, 99, 315, 317
Verrucano, 44–46
Vetulonia, 64–65, 273, 278
Via Aurelia, 24, 47, 50, 54, 99, 139, 142, 147, 262, 269, 306, 309, 312, 314–15

Via Cassia, 301, 307, 309
Via Clodia, 309
Via Emilia, 306
Villanovian culture, 23, 89
Viterbo, 90–91, 132, 171, 173, 176, 189, 191, 196–97, 200–01, 223, 225, 227, 230, 289, 307
Volterra, 191, 195, 201, 225, 264, 290, 292, 309
Vulci, 47, 65, 94–99, 274, 276–78, 281–86, 313

water management, 28, 43–48, 53, 81, 84, 89, 132, 287–98, 300
World War II, 25–26, 31, 34, 37, 43, 59, 64–65, 278

MediTo: ARCHAEOLOGICAL AND HISTORICAL LANDSCAPES OF MEDITERRANEAN CENTRAL ITALY

All volumes in this series are evaluated by an Editorial Board, strictly on academic grounds, based on reports prepared by referees who have been commissioned by virtue of their specialism in the appropriate field. The Board ensures that the screening is done independently and without conflicts of interest. The definitive texts supplied by authors are also subject to review by the Board before being approved for publication. Further, the volumes are copyedited to conform to the publisher's stylebook and to the best international academic standards in the field.

Titles in Series

Archaeological Landscapes of Roman Etruria: Research and Field Papers, ed. by Alessandro Sebastiani and Carolina Megale (2021)

In Preparation

Archaeological Landscapes of Late Antique and Early Medieval Tuscia: Research and Field Papers, ed. by Riccardo Rao and Alessandro Sebastiani